EUROPEAN UNION GOVERNANCE AND POLICY-MAKING

European Union Governance and Policy-Making

A Canadian Perspective

Second Edition

Edited by Amy Verdun, Achim Hurrelmann, and Emmanuel Brunet-Jailly

UNIVERSITY OF TORONTO PRESS
Toronto Buffalo London

© University of Toronto Press 2023
Toronto Buffalo London
utorontopress.com
Printed and bound by CPI Group (UK) Ltd, Croydon, CR0 4YY

ISBN 978-1-4875-4285-6 (cloth)   ISBN 978-1-4875-4287-0 (EPUB)
ISBN 978-1-4875-4286-3 (paper)   ISBN 978-1-4875-4288-7 (PDF)

All rights reserved. The use of any part of this publication reproduced, transmitted in any form or by any means, electronic, mechanical, photocopying, recording, or otherwise, or stored in a retrieval system, without prior written consent of the publisher – or in the case of photocopying, a licence from Access Copyright, the Canadian Copyright Licensing Agency – is an infringement of the copyright law.

___

Library and Archives Canada Cataloguing in Publication

Title: European Union governance and policy making : a Canadian perspective / edited by Amy Verdun, Achim Hurrelmann, and Emmanuel Brunet-Jailly.
Names: Verdun, Amy, 1968– editor. | Hurrelmann, Achim, editor. | Brunet-Jailly, Emmanuel, 1961– editor.
Description: Second edition. | Includes bibliographical references and index.
Identifiers: Canadiana (print) 20230188397 | Canadiana (ebook) 20230188400 | ISBN 9781487542856 (cloth) | ISBN 9781487542863 (paper) | ISBN 9781487542887 (PDF) | ISBN 9781487542870 (EPUB)
Subjects: LCSH: European Union – Textbooks. | LCSH: European Union countries – Politics and government – Textbooks. | LCGFT: Textbooks.
Classification: LCC JN30 .E9722 2023 | DDC 341.242/2 – dc23

___

Cover design: Val Cooke
Cover image: vladm/Shutterstock.com

We welcome comments and suggestions regarding any aspect of our publications – please feel free to contact us at news@utorontopress.com or visit us at utorontopress.com.

Every effort has been made to contact copyright holders; in the event of an error or omission, please notify the publisher.

We wish to acknowledge the land on which the University of Toronto Press operates. This land is the traditional territory of the Wendat, the Anishnaabeg, the Haudenosaunee, the Métis, and the Mississaugas of the Credit First Nation.

University of Toronto Press acknowledges the financial support of the Government of Canada and the Ontario Arts Council, an agency of the Government of Ontario, for its publishing activities.

ONTARIO ARTS COUNCIL
CONSEIL DES ARTS DE L'ONTARIO
an Ontario government agency
un organisme du gouvernement de l'Ontario

This book is dedicated to the late Donna Wood

Contents

List of Tables, Boxes, Figures, and Maps   xv

Acknowledgments   xxi

Abbreviations   xxiii

Contributors   xxxi

1 Introduction   1
   EMMANUEL BRUNET-JAILLY, ACHIM HURRELMANN, AND AMY VERDUN
   The Purpose of This Book   4
   The EU as a Peace Project: One Overarching Insight and Three Themes of Debate   7
      Theme 1: Economic Cooperation in a Mixed Economy   9
      Theme 2: More than an International Organization, Less than a State   12
      Theme 3: From Economic to Democratic Legitimation?   14
   Structure of the Book   19

Part One: Integration and Governance

2 A Short History of the European Union   25
CONSTANTIN CHIRA-PASCANUT
  European Integration: A Historical Overview   26
    The First Moves: The European Coal and Steel Community (1951), the European Economic Community (1957), and the European Atomic Energy Community (1957)   26
    The 1960s: A Decade of Mixed Results   32
    The 1970s: Facing Economic and Financial Crisis   34
    The 1980s and the 1990s: European Integration Relaunched   34
    The EU at the Beginning of the New Century   37
    The EU after 2010: Coping with Crisis   39
  Why/How Does a Historical Analysis Matter for Understanding the EU Today?   40

3 The Political Institutions of the European Union   45
FINN LAURSEN, ACHIM HURRELMANN, AND AMY VERDUN
  The European Council   47
  The European Commission   49
  The Council of the EU   53
  The European Parliament   57
  The Interplay of Institutions in EU Policy-Making   64
  Debate: Efficiency, Solidarity, and Leadership   65

4 Legal Integration and the Court of Justice of the European Union   73
MARTHA O'BRIEN AND ESZTER BODNÁR
  Primary Law: The Treaties   74
  Secondary Law: Acts of the EU Institutions   75
  Fundamental Principles of EU Law   77
  The Court of Justice of the European Union: Overview   80
  The CJEU as a Constitutional Court for the European Union   83
    Enforcing EU Law in the Member States   83
    Reviewing EU Secondary Legislation   84
    Protecting Fundamental Rights   86
  Debate: Incremental Legal Integration, Direct Effect, and Supremacy   87

5 Policy-Making and Governance in the European Union's Multilevel System   93
   INGEBORG TÖMMEL
      The Fundamental Constraints on EU Policy-Making   95
      The Evolution of EU Policy-Making and Governance   99
      Consolidating EU Multilevel Governance   107
      Debate: Is EU Governance Effective?   110

6 Theories of European Integration and Governance   115
   AMY VERDUN
      Federalism, Neofunctionalism, and Intergovernmentalism   117
         Federalism   117
         Neofunctionalism   118
         Intergovernmentalism   120
      Multilevel Governance, Governance, Europeanization, and Institutionalism   122
      Theories of Democracy, Legitimacy, and the EU as a Global Player   125
      Debate: Why Use Theories in European Integration Studies?   128

Part Two: Policies

7 Economic and Monetary Integration: Single Market and EMU   137
   PAUL SCHURE AND AMY VERDUN
      From the Common Market to the Single Market   139
      Creating Europe's Single Currency   144
      The First 10 Years of EMU   147
      From Financial Crisis to Sovereign Debt Crisis   149
      Crises Responses: New Institutions for the Single Currency   150
      Banking Union and Capital Markets Union   153
      Debate: Fiscal Federalism, the Perennial Vicious Circle, and Current Challenges   156

8 Migration, Citizenship, and Security 165
OLIVER SCHMIDTKE
   Justice, Freedom, and Security: From Humble Beginnings to a Key EU Policy Field 167
      Migration and Asylum 169
      Justice, Fundamental Rights, and Citizenship 173
      Borders and Security 175
   Debate: Governing Migration and Borders: The Refugee Crisis and Its Impact On the EU 178

9 Foreign, Security, and Defence Policies 187
FRÉDÉRIC MÉRAND AND ANTOINE RAYROUX
   A Short History of EU Foreign Policy 188
   A Hybrid Foreign Policy System 195
   Debates in EU Foreign Policy 200

10 Common Agricultural Policy 209
CRINA VIJU-MILJUSEVIC
   Common Agricultural Policy: History, Instruments, and Reforms 210
      History 210
      CAP Instruments and Their Outcomes 211
      CAP Reforms 213
   Debates: Distributing the Budget, Farm Support, and Decentralization 221

11 Regional Policy 231
EMMANUEL BRUNET-JAILLY
   The Origins and Development of the EU's Regional Policy 232
      From 6 to 12: The European Regional Development Fund (1967–1988) 234
      The Institutionalization of Cohesion Policy (1988–1993) 237
      From 12 to 15: The Maastricht Treaty (1993–1999) 239
      From 15 to 25: Making Enlargement a Success (2000–2006) 239
      At 27 Members: The World's Largest Development Program (2007–2013) 241
      The Way Forward: Cohesion Policy in an EU of 28 Member States (2014–2020) 243

The 2021–2027 Budget: Cohesion or Investment Policy? 244
Debate: Does the Cohesion Policy Work and What Is the Role of Governance in Its Success? 246

12 European External Trade Policy 255
VALERIE J. D'ERMAN
The Evolution of EU Trade Policy 256
EC Common Commercial Policy 257
Trade Policy and the Single Market 259
The Lisbon Treaty and Europe 2020 260
From Negotiation to Ratification 263
The EU and the World 266
Debate: Issues with EU Trade Policies 270

13 Enlargement 277
CHARLES C. PENTLAND
The First Three Enlargements 278
The UK, Ireland, and Denmark 279
The Southern Enlargement 281
The EFTA Enlargement 282
The EU Looks Eastward 283
Managing Enlargement: From Improvisation to Governance 286
Intergovernmental Institutions and Actors 286
Supranational Institutions and Actors 288
Debates: Assessing Enlargement 289
The 1970s to 1990s 290
The "Big Bang" and After 290
Türkiye 292
The Western Balkans, Moldova, and Ukraine 293

14 European Neighbourhood Policy 303
ASSEM DANDASHLY AND GABRIELA CHIRA
History and Origins of the ENP 305
The Development of the ENP since 2004 306
The Eastern and the Southern Neighbourhood (until 2010) 309
Post-2010 Developments in the ENP 310
Types of Agreements and Associations 312
Debate: How Successful Has the ENP Been? 314

Part Three: Challenges

15 Democracy in the European Union   327
  ACHIM HURRELMANN
  Democratic Life in the EU   329
    European Parliament   329
    National Democratic Processes   333
    Procedures for Civil Society Participation   337
    EU Democracy and the Citizens   339
  Debate: Is There a Democratic Deficit in EU Politics?   342

16 Unity in Diversity: Combating Inequalities in the European Union   349
  HEATHER MACRAE
  The Evolution of Equality and Non-discrimination Measures   350
  The Limitations to the EU's Approach   356
  Current Controversies and Debates   362
    Financial Crisis and Austerity   363
    The Rule of Law   364
    The Global Pandemic: COVID-19   364
    The EU's Responses   365

17 European Green Deal and Energy Security   371
  MICHÈLE KNODT, JULIA JÄNISCH, AND G. CORNELIS VAN KOOTEN
  History of EU Climate and Energy Policy   372
    EU Energy Policy   373
    EU Climate Policy   376
    An Integrated EU Climate Change Policy   379
  Debate: (Un)Fit for 55? The EU's Challenging 2030 and 2050 Targets in Times of War   382

18 Geopolitics of the European Union   393
  JOAN DEBARDELEBEN
  The EU: An "Accidental" Geopolitical Actor?   395
  Regional Geopolitical Challenges: The EU's Eastern and Southern Neighbourhood   399
    Conflict and Instability in Eastern Europe   399
    The Middle East and the Arab Spring   400

Global Geopolitical Challenges: The EU's Geopolitical Role Outside
of Europe   402
   The EU's Strategic Partnerships   402
   International Terrorism and Cybersecurity   405
Debate: Relations with Russia and the Ukraine War   407

19 Conclusion   413
   EMMANUEL BRUNET-JAILLY, ACHIM HURRELMANN, AND AMY VERDUN
   Theme 1: Is the EU Still Committed to Its Original Ambition of
Building a Mixed Economic System That Is Neither State Controlled
nor Left to an Unconstrained Market?   415
   Theme 2: Does the EU Remain a Political System That Is Neither an
International Organization nor a Fully-Fledged Federal State?   419
   Theme 3: How Can the EU Build Its Legitimacy in the European
Population?   421

Appendix: Research Resources   425

Chronology   431

Glossary   449

Index   469

Tables, Boxes, Figures, and Maps

Tables

1.1　The concept of a mixed economy　9
1.2　The EU between international organization and state　15
2.1　The three pillars of the EU established in the 1992 Maastricht Treaty (later dismantled by the Lisbon Treaty)　36
3.1　The most important political institutions of the EU　47
3.2　EP election turnout (%)　59
3.3　Seats in the European Parliament per member state as of February 1, 2020 (total 705 seats)　61
4.1　Development of EU primary law　75
4.2　Main competences of the Court of Justice of the European Union　88
5.1　The MFF 2021–7 (without Recovery and Resilience Facility)　97
5.2　Comparison of the political systems of the EU and Canada　100
5.3　Phases of EU policy-making and associated governance modes　106
5.4　Comparison of policies and governance modes of the EU and Canada　107
6.1　A schematic simple taxonomy of theories used in European integration studies and their focus on different actors and mechanisms　129
7.1　Institutions for policy coordination and financial support since the 2010 sovereign debt crisis　152
8.1　Member states of the Schengen Area　167

8.2   Policy areas in the AFSJ   169
9.1   Ongoing CSDP operations in 2021   192
10.1 Reforms of the CAP   214
11.1 Cohesion policy funding, 2021–2027 (current prices in million € and % of total)   244
13.1 Stages of accession progress chart: Current applicants (to August 2022)   294
14.1 ENP official agreements   307
15.1 Referendums in member states on EU issues   336
16.1 Legislative measures to address discrimination   357
17.1 Development of the EU's climate and energy targets   376
18.1 Selected EU partners for trade in goods, as % of extra-EU trade   403

Boxes

1.1   Canada's relationship with the EU   5
1.2   The reverse development of border formalities in Canada and the EU   11
2.1   The European Coal and Steel Community (ECSC)   30
2.2   Empty Chair Crisis   33
2.3   Comparison with Canada   41
3.1   Key roles of the European Council   48
3.2   Budget of the EU institutions   51
3.3   Key roles of the Commission   52
3.4   Council configurations   54
3.5   Cyprus flexing its muscles   56
3.6   Main tasks of the presidency of the Council   57
3.7   Key roles of the Council   58
3.8   Key roles of the European Parliament   62
3.9   Comparison with Canada   67
4.1   Example of a regulation   76
4.2   Example of a directive   77
4.3   Structure of EU courts   81
4.4   Budget for the Court of Justice   82
4.5   The CJEU compared to the Supreme Court of Canada   85
5.1   Decision making on the Multiannual Financial Framework (MFF)   98

6.1	Federalism in Canada and the EU	118
7.1	Stages of economic integration	139
7.2	The Canadian single market	143
7.3	Convergence criteria for EMU membership	146
7.4	EU budget and economic affairs	150
8.1	Schengen Area	166
8.2	Article 3(2) TEU	168
8.3	Key elements of an emerging EU citizenship regime	174
8.4	Key tasks of Frontex	176
8.5	Budget for the AFSJ	178
8.6	Dublin Regulation (in force since 1997)	179
8.7	Canada–EU comparison	181
9.1	Comparison with Canada	196
9.2	Budget for foreign, security, and defence policy	202
10.1	Common Fisheries Policy	217
10.2	CAP budget	221
10.3	Effects of the CAP in Hungary and Northern Ireland	224
10.4	Canada's agricultural policy	226
11.1	The Commission's four general programming principles, 1988–1993	233
11.2	Definition of regional versus cohesion policy	236
11.3	Common provision regulation: How are funds allocated?	238
11.4	Objectives of cohesion policy	243
11.5	Cohesion policy: The EU's main investment policy	246
11.6	Regional policy and multilevel governance in Canada	247
12.1	Timeline of significant events in EU trade policy	260
12.2	Customs integration	265
12.3	Trade policy decision making in Canada and the EU compared	268
12.4	Budget for EU trade and development policy	269
12.5	Benefits and costs of free trade: A critical viewpoint	271
13.1	Enlargement: The basics	278
13.2	Enlargement timeline	283
13.3	Conditionality and enlargement	284
13.4	Financing enlargement	289
13.5	Explaining enlargement	291
13.6	Enlargements compared: Europe and Canada	297
13.7	Brexit	298
14.1	Members of the Union of the Mediterranean	310

14.2   ENP Action Plans and financial instruments   313
14.3   Budget for the ENP   315
15.1   Parliamentary powers in Canada, the United States, and the EU   330
15.2   The EP and the EU budget   332
15.3   The early warning mechanism   335
15.4   Transparency Register   338
15.5   Euroskepticism   341
16.1   Defining the terms   352
16.2   The Charter of Fundamental Rights   355
16.3   Canada and the EU compared   361
17.1   Emissions trading in the EU   378
17.2   EU Energy Union   380
17.3   European Green Deal (EGD)   381
17.4   Sources of electricity generation: EU versus Canada   382
17.5   Hardening of soft governance   386
18.1   Canada's Transatlantic Connections   404

Figures

1.1   *The Economist* cover, March 20, 1982   17
1.2   Support for EU membership in the citizenry, 1973–2022   18
3.1   Party groups in the 9th European Parliament (2019–2024)   61
3.2   Ordinary legislative procedure (OLP), simplified   63
7.1   Yields ("interest rates") on 10-year government bonds of select member states   147
7.2   The Banking Union and its three pillars   155
7.3   (Potential) vicious circle of European integration   158
8.1   Foreign-born population in EU member states by country of birth as of January 1, 2020   170
10.1   CAP expenditure in total EU expenditure (current prices)   222
11.1   GDP per capita in EU member states, 2021 (purchasing power index, EU=100)   240
12.1   World trade in goods and services (2020), in US $billion   267
14.1   Trade in goods between the EU and eastern ENP states (2009–2020)   317
14.2   Trade in goods between the EU and southern ENP states (2020, percentage of total imports/exports)   318

15.1 Three channels of democratic input in the EU 340
15.2 European and national identities in EU member states (2019) 344
17.1 Compliance with Commission recommendations by member state 387

Maps

1.1 EU member states (2022) 3
11.1 Investment for jobs and growth goal: Where is the money going? 245

Acknowledgments

This book has benefited from the long-term relationships that have been built over many years, catered by the EU Centres in Canada (funded by the EU) and further developed through the activities of the Canada-Europe Transatlantic Dialogue (CETD, funded by the Social Sciences and Humanities Research Council of Canada) and by the European Community Studies Association–Canada (ECSA-C). As editors, we are grateful to our contributors, who enthusiastically agreed to help produce a second edition of this textbook and who were extraordinarily responsive and willing to accommodate our many requests in a timely manner. We are also immensely thankful to students and instructors who used the first edition of the book and provided useful feedback and suggestions for improvement.

    The original idea to produce a textbook about the European Union (EU) for Canadian students came from Amy Verdun in her role as founding director of the European Studies Program at the University of Victoria (UVic) – a role she took on in 1997. UVic is located on the traditional territory of the ləkʷəŋən peoples, who we acknowledge and respect, as well as the Songhees, Esquimalt, and W̱SÁNEĆ peoples, who have historical relationships with the land that continue to this day. Amy Verdun started coordinating a team-taught interdisciplinary course on European studies in 2003, in which Emmanuel Brunet-Jailly and several of the contributors to this book were also involved. In September 2009, Amy Verdun approached the University of Toronto Press with the idea of this textbook, and the press immediately expressed interest. She invited Emmanuel Brunet-Jailly to join her as co-editor. Shortly after, the two organized a workshop in Victoria on May 2–3, 2010, where the first versions of the chapters were discussed. Revised versions of six of the papers were presented at panels of ECSA-C in Ottawa on April 26–28, 2012. In 2015, the two editors invited Achim Hurrelmann of Carleton University to join the team of editors, and he hosted a workshop at Carleton University on March 12, 2016, where all papers were presented. Carleton University is located on the traditional unceded territories of the Algonquin nation. The first edition of the textbook went to press in March 2018.

For this second edition, the editors also organized a dedicated workshop. Due to the COVID-19 pandemic, the workshop was held virtually on September 15–17, 2021, funded in part by a connection grant from the Social Sciences and Humanities Research Council (SSHRC). This financial support facilitated not only this workshop but also a number of additional features of this textbook, such as the production of videos and other supplementary resources. A complete draft of the second edition was submitted to the publisher on February 11, 2022. The invasion of Ukraine by Russia two weeks later – on February 24, 2022 – escalated the Russo-Ukrainian war that had been going on since 2014, thereby dramatically changing the geopolitical landscape in Europe. It was clear that the editors needed to ask the authors to make a number of important changes; fortunately, they were able to do so quickly.

The project has benefited immensely from the various editors at the University of Toronto Press: first Daniel Quinlan, then Michael Harrison, Mark Thompson, Mat Buntin, and for the second edition Stephen Jones, Marilyn McCormack, and Rebecca Duce. The first and second editions of the book were aided by research and technical assistance, supported by the work study program at UVic and the CETD, as well as grants from SSHRC and the EU's Erasmus+ program. The late Donna Wood, and later Ivan Dumka, assisted in the early stages of the first edition. Research and administrative assistance were provided by Morgan Bruckner, Valerie D'Erman, Ottilie Grisdale, Alexa Lewis, Dara Marcus, and Zoey Verdun for the first edition, and by Cassandra Szabo and Malcolm Thomson for the second edition. The three editors are indebted to them all.

We dedicate this second edition to the memory of Donna Wood, a contributor to the first edition, who sadly passed away on March 13, 2019. Donna's expertise both on EU and Canadian politics, and her dedication to explore comparisons and interactions between both polities, are a lasting inspiration to us all.

Amy Verdun, Achim Hurrelmann, and Emmanuel Brunet-Jailly
Victoria, BC, and Ottawa, August 2022

Abbreviations

3Ms	money, markets, and mobility
AA	Association Agreement
AECM	Agri-Environmental and Climate Measures
AFSJ	Area of Freedom, Security, and Justice
AIT	Agreement on Internal Trade
AMIF	Asylum, Migration and Integration Fund
AP	Association Partnership
ASA	Agricultural Stabilization Act
ASEAN	Association for South East Asian Nations
AUKUS	Australia, United Kingdom, and the United States
BC	British Columbia
Benelux	Belgium, the Netherlands, and Luxembourg
BIPOC	Black, Indigenous, and People of Colour
BPS	Basic Payment Scheme
BRICS	Brazil, Russia, India, China, South Africa
BRRD	Bank Recovery and Resolution Directive
CAIS	Canadian Agricultural Income Stabilization Program
CAP	Common Agricultural Policy
CCP	Common Commercial Policy
CCS	Carbon Capture and Storage
CEAS	Common European Asylum System
CEDAW	Convention on the Elimination of Discrimination Against Women

CEE	Central and Eastern Europe
CEECs	Central and Eastern European Countries
CET	Common External Tariff
CETA	Comprehensive Economic and Trade Agreement
CF	Cohesion Fund
CFP	Common Fisheries Policy
CFR	Charter of Fundamental Rights of the European Union
CFSP	Common Foreign and Security Policy
CIP	Competitive and Innovation Program
CIVCOM	Committee for Civilian Aspects of Crisis Management
CJEU	Court of the Justice of the EU
CM	Common Market
CMPD	Crisis Management and Planning Directorate
CMU	Capital Markets Union
CO_2	Carbon Dioxide
COP21	21st Conference of the Parties to the UN Framework Convention on Climate Change
CoR	Committee of the Regions
COREPER	Committee of Permanent Representatives
CORINE	Coordination of Information on the Environment
COVID-19	Coronavirus disease
CPCC	Civilian Planning and Conduct Capability
CSDP	Common Security and Defence Policy
CU	customs union
DCFTA	Deep and Comprehensive Free Trade Agreement
DG	Directorate-General
DG DEFIS	Directorate-General for Defence Industry and Space
DG DEVCO	Directorate-General for International Cooperation and Development
DG EMPL	Directorate-General for Employment
DG JUST	Directorate-General for Justice and Consumers
DG NEAR	Directorate-General for Neighbourhood and Enlargement Negotiations
DG RP	Directorate-General for Regional Policy
DG TRADE	Directorate-General for Trade
DMA	Digital Markets Act
EAC	European Affairs Committee
EAGGF	European Agricultural Guidance and Guarantee Fund

EaP	Eastern Partnership
EAP	Environmental Action Programme
EAW	European Arrest Warrant
EC	European Community
ECB	European Central Bank
ECHR	European Convention on Human Rights
ECI	European Citizens' Initiative
ECJ	European Court of Justice (now Court of Justice of the EU (CJEU))
ECOFIN	Council of Economic and Finance Ministers
ECR	European Conservatives and Reformists
ECSC	European Coal and Steel Community
ECtHR	European Court of Human Rights
ECU	European Currency Unit
EDC	European Defence Community
EDIS	European Deposit Insurance Scheme
EEA	European Economic Area
EEAS	European External Action Service
EEC	European Economic Community
EFA	European Free Alliance
EFF	European Fisheries Fund
EFSD	European Fund for Sustainable Development
EFSF	European Financial Stability Facility
EFTA	European Free Trade Association
EGD	European Green Deal
EIB	European Investment Bank
EIGE	European Institute for Gender Equality
EMFF	European Maritime and Fisheries Fund
EMS	European Monetary System
EMU	Economic and Monetary Union
ENI	European Neighbourhood Instrument
ENP	European Neighbourhood Policy
EP	European Parliament
EPA	European Partnership Agreement
EPC	European Political Cooperation
EPP	European People's Party
ERDF	European Regional Development Fund
ERM	Exchange Rate Mechanism

ESCB	European System of Central Banks
ESDP	European Security and Defence Policy
ESF	European Social Fund
ESF+	European Social Fund Plus
ESM	European Stability Mechanism
ESS	European Security Strategy
ETS	Emissions Trading System
EU	European Union
EUAM	European Union Advisory Mission
EUBAM	European Union Border Assistance Mission
EUCAP	European Union Capacity Building Mission
EUFOR	European Union Force
EUGS	European Union Global Strategy
EULEX	European Union Rule of Law Mission
EUMC	European Union Military Committee/European Monitoring Centre on Racism and Xenophobia
EUMM	European Union Monitoring Mission
EUMS	European Union Military Staff
EUNAVFOR	European Union Naval Force
EUPOL COPPS	European Union Police and Rule of Law Mission Coordinating Office for Palestinian Police
Euratom	European Atomic Energy Community
EUR-LEX	Official website of European Union law
EURODAC	European Dactyloscopy
Europol	European Police Office
EUTM	European Union Training Mission
FAO	Food and Agriculture Organization
FDI	foreign direct investment
FEMIP	Facility for Euro-Mediterranean Investment and Partnership
FIFG	Financial Instrument of Fisheries
FP7	7th Research Framework Program
FRA	European Union Agency for Fundamental Rights
Frontex	European Border and Coast Guard Agency (formerly European Agency for the Management of Operational Cooperation at the External Borders of the Member States of the European Union)
FTA	Free Trade Agreement

GAC	General Affairs Council
GAL	green-alternative-libertarian
GAMM	Global Approach to Migration and Mobility
GATT	General Agreements on Tariffs and Trade
GCM	United Nations Global Compact for Migration
GDP	gross domestic product
GHG	greenhouse gases
GI	geographical indication
GNI	gross national income
H_2	Hydrogen
HA	High Authority
HR	High Representative
ICAO	International Civil Aviation Organization
ID	Identity and Democracy
IJG	Investment for jobs and growth
IMF	International Monetary Fund
IMP	Integrated Mediterranean Programs
IOM	International Organization for Migration
IP	Intellectual Property
IPA	Instrument for Pre-Accession Assistance
IPCC	Intergovernmental Panel on Climate Change
IR	international relations
ISDS	investor state dispute settlement
JCPOA	Joint Comprehensive Plan of Action
JHA	Justice and Home Affairs
JTF	Just Transition Fund
JTM	Just Transition Mechanism
LGBTQ+	lesbian, gay, bisexual, transgender, queer/questioning plus other identities
MENA	Middle East and North Africa
MEP	Member of the European Parliament
Mercosur	Argentina, Brazil, Paraguay, and Uruguay
MFF	Multiannual Financial Framework
NA	non-affiliated members
NAFO	North Atlantic Fisheries Organization
NAFTA	North American Free Trade Agreement
NATO	North Atlantic Treaty Organization

NDICI	Neighbourhood, Development and International Cooperation Instrument
NECP	National Energy and Climate Plan
NIP	Neighbourhood Investment Platform
OECD	Organisation for Economic Co-operation and Development
OLP	Ordinary Legislative Procedure
OMC	Open Method of Coordination
PCA	Partnership and Cooperation Agreement
PEPP	Pandemic Emergency Purchase Programme
PESCO	Permanent Structured Cooperation
PSC	Political and Security Committee
PSPP	Public Sector Asset Purchase Programme
QMV	qualified majority voting
RED	Race Equality Directive (Directive 2000/43/EC)
RP	regional policy
RRF	Recovery and Resilience Facility
SAA	Stabilization and Association Agreement
SCC	Supreme Court of Canada
S&D	Progressive Alliance of Socialists and Democrats in the European Parliament
SEA	Single European Act
SFP	Single Farm Payment
SGP	Stability and Growth Pact
SOER	State and Outlook of the European Environment
SPA	Strategic Partnership Agreement
SRF	Single Resolution Fund
SRM	Single Resolution Mechanism
SSM	Single Supervisory Mechanism
TAC	Total Allowable Catches
TAIEX	Technical Assistance & Information Exchange
TAN	traditional-authoritarian-national
TCA	Trade and Cooperation Agreement
TCN	third-country national
TEC	Treaty Establishing the European Community
TEEC	Treaty Establishing the European Economic Community
TEU	Treaty on European Union
TFEU	Treaty on the Functioning of the European Union

TREVI	Terrorisme, Radicalisme, Extrémisme et Violence Internationale
TTIP	Transatlantic Trade and Investment Partnership
UfM	Union for the Mediterranean
UK	United Kingdom
UN	United Nations
UNESCO	United Nations Educational, Scientific and Cultural Organization
UNFCCC	United Nations Framework Convention on Climate Change
US	United States
USSR	Union of Soviet Socialist Republics
WGSA	Western Grain Stabilization Act
WTO	World Trade Organization

Contributors

Eszter Bodnár, lecturer, Faculty of Law, University of Victoria; associate professor, Faculty of Law, ELTE Eötvös Loránd University, Hungary.

Emmanuel Brunet-Jailly, professor of public policy and Jean Monnet Chair in innovative governance, and director of the Jean Monnet Centre at the University of Victoria.

Gabriela Chira, PhD, works at the European Research Executive Agency. Former postdoctoral fellow at the University of Victoria.

Constantin Chira-Pascanut, privacy and data protection lawyer at the European Data Protection Supervisor, holds a PhD in history from the University of Victoria.

Assem Dandashly, assistant professor of political science at Maastricht University (Netherlands).

Joan DeBardeleben, chancellor's professor in the Institute of European, Russian and Eurasian Studies at Carleton University, Jean Monnet Chair in EU relations with Russia and the eastern neighbourhood, co-director of the Centre for European Studies at Carleton University.

Valerie D'Erman, PhD, instructor in the Department of Political Science and in the European Studies Program, University of Victoria.

Achim Hurrelmann, professor of political science at Carleton University, and co-director of the Centre for European Studies at Carleton University.

Julia Jänisch, PhD student, University of Münster, Germany, and visiting PhD student, University of Victoria.

Michèle Knodt, professor and Jean Monnet Chair ad personam, Technical University of Darmstadt.

Finn Laursen, honorary professor in international politics at the University of Southern Denmark, Jean Monnet Chair ad personam.

Heather MacRae, associate professor of political science at York University.

Frédéric Mérand, professor of political science at the Université de Montréal, director of the Centre d'études et de recherches internationales (CÉRIUM), and co-director of the Union Centre of Excellence Université de Montréal-McGill University.

Martha O'Brien, professor emerita of law at the University of Victoria.

Charles Pentland, professor emeritus in political science at Queen's University.

Antoine Rayroux, PhD, works as a civil servant in Quebec's Ministry of Economy and Innovation. Previously, he specialized in Canada–EU relations in the areas of foreign policy, public diplomacy, science and technology co-operation, both as a consultant and academic. In addition, he is a visiting researcher at CÉRIUM, the Université de Montréal's centre for international studies.

Oliver Schmidtke, professor of political science and director of the Centre for Global Studies at the University of Victoria, Jean Monnet Chair in European history and politics.

Paul Schure, associate professor of economics at the University of Victoria.

Ingeborg Tömmel, professor emerita in international politics at the University of Osnabrück (Germany), Jean Monnet Chair in European politics.

G. Cornelis van Kooten, professor of economics and Canada Research Chair at the University of Victoria.

Amy Verdun, full professor of political science at the University of Victoria. She has been teaching European integration since 1992.

Crina Viju-Miljusevic, associate professor in the Institute of European, Russian and Eurasian Studies at Carleton University.

1

Introduction

Emmanuel Brunet-Jailly, Achim Hurrelmann, and Amy Verdun

READER'S GUIDE

This chapter introduces the textbook; it explains key milestones in the development of the European Union (EU), defines important terms and concepts of EU studies, and discusses the challenges that the EU currently faces. It clarifies that some aspects of the EU's development have been highly successful, whereas others are increasingly contested. The chapter also sets out the rationale and structure of the book and introduces three main themes that are related to the EU's institutional structure, its policy portfolio, and its political legitimation. These are taken up in the individual chapters.

INTRODUCTION

In 2022, the European Union was suddenly confronted by a major change in its geopolitical outlook. The Russian invasion of Ukraine on February 24, 2022, resulted in major economic challenges – such as rising energy costs, which spilled over into higher levels of inflation – and raised questions about the role of the EU as a global actor in an increasingly uncertain international environment. These were sudden changes that offered the EU an opportunity to show itself to be "united in diversity" – the official motto of the EU. Maintaining unity is particularly challenging when the outlook is dire.

The EU had been remarkably successful in meeting this challenge over many decades. In 2012, it was awarded the Nobel Peace Prize for contributing to "the advancement of peace and reconciliation, democracy and human rights in Europe" and helping "to transform most of Europe from a continent of war to a continent of peace" (Nobel Prize 2012). The prize recognized that, since the 1950s, EU member states have collaborated to overcome historical disputes and avoid wars among them, whereas the preceding centuries had been plagued by violent conflicts and destruction. The EU set up common institutions with substantial powers to make binding decisions. It created common policies, which have helped to abolish barriers to economic exchange and increase mobility among the member states. This process of establishing common institutions and policies, bringing European states closer together, is called European integration.

Over the course of more than seven decades, European integration has fundamentally transformed the political and legal systems, economies, and societies of Europe. Originally initiated by six Western European countries (Belgium, France, Italy, Luxembourg, the Netherlands, and West Germany), it has followed two main trajectories. The first is called **widening**, meaning the successive addition of more member states. The number of member states reached 28 in 2013, but it was reduced to 27 in 2020 when the United Kingdom (UK) withdrew from the EU (Map 1.1). The second trajectory is called **deepening**, meaning that more and more powers have been shifted from the member states to the EU level. The EU now influences virtually all areas of policy-making, though its powers are more far-reaching in some areas (such as economic policy and trade) than in others (such as social policy or defence).

European integration has produced many beneficial political developments. These include the establishment of an integrated Single Market with around 450 million inhabitants, in which most internal economic barriers have been abolished. The Single Market has contributed to the economic prosperity of the member states. It provides many tangible benefits for Europeans, such as the ability to purchase goods and services from other member states without the imposition of customs duties. Another perk is the right to take a job in another member state without applying for a work permit. Many young EU citizens have benefited from travelling, living, or studying in another member state, which they can do as if it were their own. These achievements explain in part why so many European states have sought to

Map 1.1. EU member states (2022)

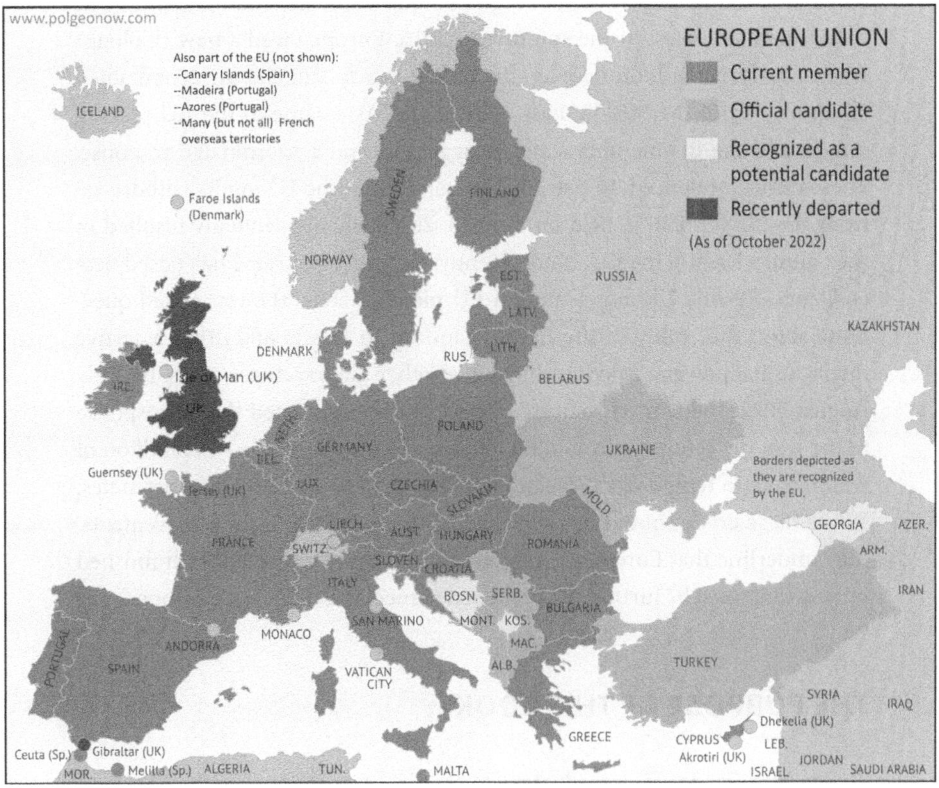

Source: Map by Evan Centanni at polgeonow.com, from blank map https://commons.wikimedia.org/wiki/File:EU_map_brown.svg (y) by Ssolbergj (https://en.wikipedia.org/wiki/User_talk:Ssolbergj). License: CC BY-SA (https://creativecommons.org/licenses/by-sa/3.0/deed.en)

join the EU and why there continues to be a queue of further applicants that seek to become members. European integration has also facilitated the peaceful reunification of the European continent after the **Cold War** – a period in the second part of the twentieth century during which Europe had been split into a Western and an Eastern bloc. By admitting post-communist states of Central and Eastern Europe as EU members, the EU has aided these states in transitioning from non-democratic one-party systems toward (in most cases) relatively well-functioning democracies.

The EU has nevertheless also been affected by major political crises. In 2008, the global financial crisis wreaked havoc on the European continent. In the years that followed, numerous member states experienced banking failures, sovereign debt crises, and severe economic recessions, leading to unemployment figures that went as high as a quarter of the adult population in some member states. In the summer of 2015, Europe faced a new challenge when nearly 1.5 million people – including nearly 120,000 unaccompanied children – from the Middle East, Africa, and Asia came to the EU seeking refuge, and the EU member states struggled to find a coordinated response. These crises influenced, in part, the referendum in the UK on its withdrawal from the EU ("Brexit"), held on June 23, 2016, which eventually resulted in the country leaving the EU. Most recently, the war in Ukraine has posed new challenges. While Ukraine is not an EU member state, the war raised questions about the ability of the EU to stand up to Russia and other assertive international powers. And it resulted in another major refugee crisis. By early August 2022, the United Nations' refugee agency estimated that in response to the war, the refugee tally had hit almost 6.5 million people – 2.4 million of whom were in temporary protection programs in various EU member states. While these crises should not overshadow the EU's long-term achievements, they underline that European integration is, in many respects, an unfinished project that must be further strengthened to meet the challenges Europe faces.

THE PURPOSE OF THIS BOOK

This book provides an introduction to the EU; it explains how the EU came about, how its institutions work, and which major policies it has established. It also takes stock of some of the most notable successes and failures of European integration, including the ones just mentioned. This book is written for readers who have not previously studied European integration. More specifically, it is directed at those studying the EU who are not themselves European (or based in Europe). More often than not, existing EU textbooks, though outstanding in their content, assume a considerable amount of prior knowledge from their readers. European students may have this knowledge, as they can learn a lot about the EU simply from being exposed to it in the media or during their high school years, but this is not true for readers who have, for a host of reasons, had less exposure to the EU.

Besides wanting to provide a textbook that did not assume too much background knowledge, nor offer too much detail, the editors and authors of this book were keen to produce a book that compares the EU to an existing federation. We chose to focus on Canada for a number of reasons. One of the most important ones is that Canada is a very decentralized federation, and Canadians are committed to such a decentralized federation. A second reason is that it is useful to have a practical case in mind, especially because there is more than one federal model. In fact, the EU is often treated as a *sui generis* polity, as if no comparisons were possible. Instead, we attempt to draw explicit links between the EU institutions, policies, and issues discussed and the situation in Canada. We also discuss various aspects of the bilateral relationship between the EU and Canada (see Box 1.1). These references to Canada are provided in specific text boxes in each chapter; readers who are less interested in the Canadian comparison can simply skip those boxes and still fully understand the chapters' main messages.

> **BOX 1.1: CANADA'S RELATIONSHIP WITH THE EU**
> Canada's relationship with Europe was initially dominated by its links to individual EU member states – especially France and the UK– as well as Canadian membership in the North Atlantic Treaty Organization, the Western defence alliance. However, relationships with the EU institutions became more important in the 1970s, when the Canadian government sought to diversify its economic relations to reduce dependence on the United States (US), and the integrated European trade bloc was an obvious partner. The 1976 Framework Agreement between Canada and the EU was the first international agreement the EU concluded with another industrialized state.
>
> In the decades that followed, Canada maintained an interest in further deepening economic relations with the EU. The EU was initially reluctant, due to a preference for multi-country trade agreements, but eventually agreed to negotiations on an ambitious Comprehensive Economic and Trade Agreement (CETA), signed in October 2016. CETA is still awaiting full ratification in the EU, which requires the approval of all national and in some cases regional parliaments. Canada has also been designated as one of 10 "strategic partners" of the EU (the others are Brazil, China, India, Japan, Mexico, Russia, South Africa, South Korea, and the United States).

We have organized the text around three themes, which are laid out in this chapter. All themes derive from one overarching insight that colours the book in its entirety: As stressed by the Nobel Prize committee, the EU aims to be a *peace project*. It was created on the ashes of World War II with the goal of not having another war. Achieving peace among its member states was a goal that was achieved through a strategy of locking the member states into ever closer economic and political interaction, as well as setting up mechanisms to regulate economic exchange, thus creating strong common interests and establishing procedures to resolve conflicts peacefully. Building on this fundamental insight, our three organizing themes point to ongoing political and scholarly debates about the development of European integration.

- The *first theme* relates to the EU as a policy-maker and deals with the socioeconomic model underlying European integration. When the design of what is now the EU[1] was created, numerous policies were inspired by the idea that the European way would be a mixed system (not communist and not uncontrolled capitalist), regulated with a view to social inclusion and market correction. Later the EU moved toward more market-oriented policy-making, which meant that its underlying socioeconomic ideas became less immediately obvious. EU policy has been faced with more explicit choices of what model the EU is to become. What are the tasks of the EU relative to its member states? How should the EU and its member states deal with new tasks, such as climate change? How much regulation should occur at the EU level? How much should be left to lower levels or the market?
- The *second theme* relates to EU institutions. The deepening of European integration has turned the EU into an entity that is much more powerful than any other international organization, and that in some ways appears almost like a federal state – in particular in its consistent output of legislation that is binding on member states. This development is unparalleled elsewhere in the world. There have been attempts to deepen integration across the globe (for instance in North America or in Asia), but none of these has managed to achieve the depth and scope of integration that the EU has achieved in the past seven decades. There are other dimensions, however, in which the EU clearly falls short of being a fully fledged state in the international system. The EU, in other words, is more than an international organization but less than a state. Recent crises have brought to the fore the question of what institutional system the EU should develop into. What are the next steps in integration that the EU needs to make to cement its goals?

- The *third theme* addresses the politics of European integration – in other words, political controversies about the EU and its development. Over the last 30 years, the EU's legitimacy has become increasingly contested. Many of these debates derive from a tension between economic integration and national identities. The EU was built on the assumption that deeper integration will generate riches that ensure the legitimacy of the emergent multinational organization. This approach to integration has been successful to some extent in building support among citizens, policy-makers, and elites. At the same time, already from the outset, identification with the nation state resulted in calls to keep decision making at the level of the state – rather than transferring sovereignty to the EU level. These calls have grown louder in recent years, fuelled by the fact that the costs and benefits of integration have not been shared evenly among EU member states and their citizens. As the EU deepened, there has also been a desire to increase citizen access to the democratic process. How can the EU deal with increasing contestation about its institutions and policies? Is this contestation a challenge to European integration, or can it provide an impetus for reforms that increase legitimacy?

THE EU AS A PEACE PROJECT: ONE OVERARCHING INSIGHT AND THREE THEMES OF DEBATE

As was mentioned previously, the EU was created in the early 1950s by six states: Belgium, France, Italy, Luxembourg, the Netherlands, and West Germany. Many of these countries – especially France and Germany – had been enemies in World War II, as well as in numerous earlier military conflicts. In the aftermath of World War II, they joined together to create a unique form of collaboration with the explicit purpose of not having war again. The integration process started off by putting the production of coal and steel – the sector of the economy that was essential for the production of tanks and cannons – under a joint regulatory authority, the **European Coal and Steel Community** (ECSC). This first step was symptomatic of what would become the distinct peace-building strategy underlying the European integration project. It was later expanded to other sectors of the economy. The idea was to build a community of states with strong economic cooperation, interdependence, and an emerging transnational solidarity that would not go to war with each other again. French foreign minister Robert Schuman, one of the founders of the ECSC, in the May 1950 Schuman Declaration, explained this strategy as follows: "Europe will not be made all at once, or according to a single plan. It will be built through concrete achievements which first create a de facto solidarity.… The solidarity in production thus established will make it plain that any war between France and Germany becomes not merely unthinkable, but materially impossible" (European Union n.d.). This strategy proved successful – so successful, indeed, that the history of conflict between European states and the memories of World War II have sunk deeper in the collective consciousness of European citizens. As a result, the origins of European integration as a peace project have become less obvious; yet they remain of central importance if one wants to understand the design of EU policies and institutions.

The ambition of the EU to bring about peace in Europe is also prominently reflected in the process of widening European integration. This process started in the 1970s and 1980s, when the UK, Ireland, Denmark, Greece, Portugal, and Spain became members, but it entered a new era in the 1990s and 2000s. It is important to keep in mind that when the European integration process was initiated, Europe was engulfed in the Cold War, the confrontation between the capitalist democracies of the "West" (led by the United States) and the communist one-party states of the "East" (led by the Soviet Union). The fall of the Berlin Wall in 1989 marked the end of the Cold War and triggered a major step in EU enlargement. Both states that had been formally neutral in the Cold War (Austria, Finland, and Sweden) and countries in Central and Eastern Europe that used to be part of the Soviet bloc (Bulgaria, Czech Republic, Estonia, Hungary, Latvia, Lithuania, Poland, Romania, Slovakia, and Slovenia) applied to join the EU. The former group of countries – the neutral states – were admitted to the EU in 1995; the latter eight joined in 2004 and 2007 (along with Cyprus and Malta). Croatia followed in 2013. The EU has recognized seven "candidate countries" who might join in the future. This group now includes Ukraine and Moldova, which were given that status in response to the Ukraine war. Yet EU accession takes years. The small Western Balkan nation of Montenegro might be the next country to join.

This peaceful reunification of the European continent under the EU umbrella is often considered the crowning achievement of the EU's peace-building strategy. At the same time, the widening process has created new challenges for the EU both externally and internally. The EU is being tested, for instance, in its relations with Russia, which for a few decades now has been a direct neighbour of the EU. Internal policies have also been challenged, as newer member states (such as Hungary and Poland) have displayed different interpretations of democracy and the rule of law. These developments

Table 1.1. The concept of a mixed economy

	State-controlled economy	Mixed economy	Free-market economy
Ownership of the means of production (factories, machines, capital, etc.)	State	Either mix of state and private, or private	Private
Core mechanism of economic coordination	State planning	Market, but within constraints established by state	Market (supply and demand)
Extent of state regulation of economic activities	High; focused on process (working conditions, etc.) and outcome (products, etc.)	Medium, focused on process (working conditions, etc.), not outcome	Low
Density of state programs to protect against social risks (unemployment, illness, etc.)	High	Medium to high	Low

indicate that the process of widening has made the EU much more diverse economically, politically, and socially. As a result, the EU's policy-making, institutions, and political legitimation have become more contested. Let us look at these three aspects in turn.

Theme 1: Economic Cooperation in a Mixed Economy

While the founding states of the EU were firmly anchored in the Western bloc during the Cold War, regime competition with the East made them acutely aware of the need to organize their economies in a way that produced high degrees of economic and social security for their citizens. The policies conducted in the EU framework were hence inspired by the idea of a **mixed economy**: one that is neither state controlled nor subject to unconstrained market forces (Table 1.1). Various chapters in this book illustrate the progressive construction of this mixed system through policies that implement solidarity across numerous areas of policy, from agriculture, energy, the environment, regional and social affairs, foreign and defence policy, justice, freedom and security, the Single Market and monetary policies, to external trade, enlargement, and neighbourhood policies.

Although the EU constituted an ambitious project of comprehensive economic and political integration, its main premise was the completion of a Single Market defined by its four freedoms: the free movement of goods, services, labour, and capital across all member states. Two strategies were used to achieve this objective. First, existing barriers inhibiting free movement between the member states – such as customs duties or employment rules discriminating against people from other member states – were abolished. This strategy is called **negative integration**. Second, common policies were created, insofar as it was necessary, to regulate economic transactions in the Single Market and to offset possible negative side effects. This strategy is called **positive integration**. Positive integration is essential in a mixed economy to achieve important social objectives, such as the stability of the food supply (an important issue, particularly in the early years of the EU), product safety, protection of workers, gender equality, and environmental sustainability. Since the late 1970s, these two strategies have been complemented by a third strategy, **mutual recognition**. It means that member states are expected to respect each other's regulatory systems. Mutual recognition allows for quicker economic integration than if one has to harmonize each and every law throughout the EU.

As an entity that seeks to shape and correct the operation of the market, as demanded by the mixed economy model, the EU possesses the ability to pass EU-wide legislation. It also has its own budget, funded by contributions from the member states. This budget is small, amounting to only about 1 per cent of the total value of the EU economy (gross national income of all member states). By comparison, public spending in the member states ranges from about 25 to 55 per cent of the value of their economy. Given the small size of its budget, the EU does not engage extensively in redistributive policies. These are measures that consist of the transfer of funds benefiting specific groups of the population. Two EU policies are the exception, since they have a redistributive character: (1) the EU's Common Agricultural Policy, which supports farmers, and (2) its regional or cohesion policy, which provides public investment to support regions or people doing poorly economically. In addition, the EU has, in response to the COVID-19 pandemic, developed a temporary instrument to support member states with loans and grants.

Apart from these areas characterized by significant EU spending, most of the EU's activities focus on regulation – that is, the establishment of standards for how economic and social actors may or may not behave. The EU is, in fact, best known for its regulatory capacity. It has been a leading actor, globally, for setting standards in numerous global arenas, including health and safety in the workplace, banking regulation, and environmental protection. From 2020 onward, the EU has been keen to focus on green and digital transitions, but also to further improve the Single Market for services, renewable and natural gases, and hydrogen. It also aims to improve energy efficiency and work toward climate goals. Regulatory policies can also apply to external relations. For instance, in response to Russia's invasion of Ukraine, the EU passed measures that penalize Russia (sanctions) and support Ukraine (for instance, by temporarily liberalizing trade). In this way it has sought to provide leadership on the war at the EU level on behalf of the EU and its member states.

While the first four decades of European integration (1950s–1980s) were characterized by building the Single Market, a major qualitative shift in European integration occurred in the 1990s. After the Single Market was declared to be largely "completed," the EU began to expand – and deepen – its competences into additional policy fields. In the economic realm, it set up a single currency, the euro. It further developed a common foreign and defence policy as well as common policies on home affairs, migration, and border control. The latter included the establishment of the so-called Schengen Area for borderless travel between EU member states (Box 1.2). These developments led to deeper integration, but they also helped sow the seeds of what has become a multi-speed Europe. Not all member states were willing to participate in all of the new initiatives. As a result, some member states negotiated selective **opt-outs**. For instance, Denmark has opted out of the euro and the EU's common defence policy, but it does form part of the Schengen Area. This process, where not all member states are equally involved in all EU policies and institutions, is referred to as *differentiation*.

BOX 1.2: THE REVERSE DEVELOPMENT OF BORDER FORMALITIES IN CANADA AND THE EU

The majority of EU member states (the exceptions being Bulgaria, Cyprus, Ireland, and Romania) as well as some non-member states (Iceland, Liechtenstein, Norway, and Switzerland) have joined the Schengen Area. Members of the Schengen Area have abandoned border controls among them; visitors from outside the EU have to abide by common visa rules. By contrast, following the terrorist attacks of September 11, 2001, in the United States, the Canada–US border became ever more difficult to cross. Since 2009, both Canadian and US citizens have been required to show a (biometric) passport (or an "enhanced" driver's licence to cross at land or sea borders); previously, a regular driver's licence sufficed to cross the border. Before the change in law, few Canadians or US citizens held passports to travel to each other's country.

Theme 2: More than an International Organization, Less than a State

While our first theme focuses on the EU as a system of policy-making, our second theme examines the EU as a system of political institutions. The unique nature of the EU is that it is an entity that is more than an **international organization** but less than a state (even a federal one). The EU has legal personality under international law. Its legal bases are its *founding treaties*. These are treaties that are negotiated and ratified by the member states. They form a sort of "constitution." The first three treaties were concluded in the 1950s (Treaty of Paris, 1951, Treaties of Rome, 1957); these have been elaborated on further and revised in the subsequent decades. Yet these international treaties have set up a political system that differs from conventional international organizations in many ways.

The first major difference is the extensive scope of EU powers. Most international organizations deal with a relatively narrow circumscribed range of issues. The EU, by contrast, has an encompassing range of policy responsibilities that is comparable to those of a state. In the exercise of these responsibilities, it is engaged in continuous EU-level lawmaking. As a result, the EU has adopted so much legislation in the past seven decades that it keeps the national parliaments of the member states busy for much of their sitting time. (It is the task of national parliaments to discuss the implications of EU legislation for their national law.) The treaties, the laws passed at the EU level, and legal decisions by the Court of Justice of the EU (CJEU) are commonly referred to as the *acquis communautaire*.

The second major difference between the EU and a conventional international organization lies in the legal quality of this law. Most international law is only binding in state-to-state relations but does not have automatic effects on the citizens. By contrast, the CJEU has ruled that EU law has direct effect, meaning that it may directly create rights and obligations for the citizens. Thus, most forms of EU law are binding on the member states and their citizens. In addition, EU law also enjoys supremacy over national law, which implies that in case of conflict the national law has to give way.

The third major difference concerns processes of decision making in the EU. Most international organizations are **intergovernmental** in character. In other words, decisions are controlled by the governments of the member states and usually require the unanimous approval of all of them. The EU also has certain elements of these intergovernmental features. The member states remain the "masters of the treaties," which means that all changes to the EU treaties must be approved and ratified by each of them. At least four times a year, member state leaders meet in the European Council to define the overall political direction and priorities of the EU. These decisions are usually taken by consensus. Ministers from member state governments meet in the Council of the EU (or Council for short), which is one of the EU's two legislative bodies. Through the Council, member states have far-reaching control over EU legislation. However, the Council may make its decisions using a qualified majority voting rule, which means that individual member states can be overruled – a first deviation from normal intergovernmental standards.

Qualified majority voting is not the only difference between the EU and conventional international organizations. The EU also stands out because of the significant importance of its **supranational** institutions. These are designed to give voice to the collective European interest, rather than to the interest of its member states. One supranational institution is the European Parliament (EP), which is directly elected by the EU citizens every five years. Originally not more than a consultative institution, the EP is now on par with the Council of the EU as a co-legislator. The vast majority of legislative proposals requires the approval of both these bodies to become law. Another supranational institution is the European Commission, the EU's main executive and administrative actor that oversees the implementation of EU law but, importantly, also has the power to initiate legislative proposals. Those working at the Commission all vow to serve the interests of the EU as a whole, *not* the interests of the member states to which they belong. The Court of Justice of the EU works in a similar way. Although judges and advocates-general are nominated by member states, when they assume office they support the EU as a whole, upholding the treaties to be precise. In so doing, they will not seek to be an advocate of any particular member state.

Considering the roles of all these institutions, we can see that the EU has many state-like characteristics. These features can be clearly observed if we compare the EU to states that are organized as a federation – that is, those composed of various regional subunits (such as the provinces in Canada) with their own institutions and responsibilities. Much as in federal states, the EU has a tripartite division of powers, with an executive (Commission), a bicameral legislature (Council of the EU representing the member states, European Parliament representing the citizens), and a judiciary (Court of Justice of the EU). It has policy competences in almost all areas of policy-making, even though in some fields its competence is either minimal or shared with its member states. All citizens of EU member states also possess EU citizenship, which provides them with some rights and duties much as citizens of a **nation state**. The EU is also represented internationally; it has become a member in some international organizations and is represented abroad through the European External Action Service (EEAS) – the EU's diplomatic service (similar to national embassies or consulates).

There are, however, important differences between the EU and a classic nation state. First, the EU lacks certain critical powers of statehood, most importantly the power of raising its own revenue through taxation and the power to implement and enforce its own decisions. The EU depends on its member states to finance the EU's operations and implement the vast majority of its laws. The EU lacks institutions that interact on a regular basis directly with the citizens, let alone exercise a state-like monopoly of force. Second, the EU is unable to define its own powers; it can only exercise powers explicitly conferred to it by the member states, thereby missing a crucial component of state **sovereignty**. While large-scale transfers of competence from the national to the European level have occurred, member states have explicitly withheld decision-making powers – or have insisted on a national veto – in policy fields that they consider particularly important to their own sovereignty, such as taxation or foreign and defence policy. Third, the legitimacy of the EU in the eyes of its citizens can be seen as more precarious than that of established federal states, because the citizens' EU-related identity and sense of belonging remain weak. In most federations the majority of citizens identify first and foremost with federal-level citizenship, or – as in Canada – attachment to federal and provincial/regional level is approximately equal. In the EU, the great majority of citizens identify more with the "national" citizenship (feeling "French" or "German") rather than with "EU" citizenship.

Thus, the EU has various elements that resemble a federal state, but it falls short of having all the characteristics of one (Table 1.2). The chapters in this book lay out the implications of this peculiar status of the EU – as being "in between" a conventional international organization and a federal state – and discuss how it influences the operation of EU institutions and the making of EU policy in different fields of activity.

Theme 3: From Economic to Democratic Legitimation?

The third theme of the book approaches the EU with a view to political debate and contestation. The key question here is how, and with what

Table 1.2. The EU between international organization and state

	Typical international organization	EU	Typical state
Policy responsibilities	Task specific, or limited range of tasks, powers controlled by member states	Encompassing a range of tasks, but EU powers controlled by member states, often shared with them	Encompassing a range of tasks, can determine its own powers
Powers of common/ central institutions	Limited (member state control)	Substantial (mix of supranational and intergovernmental decision making)	High (in federations: divided between central government and subunits)
Legislation	Operates based on founding treaties; no legislative role	Legislative actor, law binding on member states	Legislative actor
Policy implementation	Dependent on member state agencies	Largely dependent on member state agencies (limited front-line implementation powers plus oversight role)	Implements its own legislation
Sources of finances	Member state contributions	Primarily member state contributions (no taxation power) but some income from tariffs	Primarily taxation
Identification of citizens	Weak	Weak to medium	Strong

success, the EU attempts to generate support for its institutions and policies. As discussed above, the EU construction emerged from a postwar assumption that economic legitimacy is paramount, which was behind the EU's original mixed economy model. Since the early days, the EU has focused on market integration and the increase of welfare and well-being of all member states and their citizens. This economic focus implied that other ways of legitimating politics – especially through mechanisms of democratic participation and accountability – were for a long time not considered particularly important. However, concerns about democratic legitimacy have moved to centre stage since the early 1990s, when the EU's deepening and widening triggered unprecedented public debate about the benefits and costs of European integration. These debates also witnessed the emergence of explicitly "Euroskeptic" political positions that often reject European integration or parts of the European project (for instance, free movement of people between member states) or voice harsh criticism of it.

Despite the greater importance of democratic concerns, economic performance remains essential for the EU's legitimation. It represents what political scientists call *output legitimacy* – that is, legitimacy that derives from a polity's performance in safeguarding and improving its citizens' well-being. In this domain, the EU has been successful, as it has been able to regulate, and to some extent offset, a fast-moving trend toward globalization whereby marketization expands across the globe. The EU has been a leader in finding responses to financial market integration and globalization. It has been a frontrunner in regulation in areas such as climate change, sustainability, energy efficiency, setting product standards, or competition policy (anti-monopoly legislation). This approach to integration has, by and large, helped build support from EU citizens, policy-makers, and elites.

Throughout its existence, the EU has been confronted with challenges to its output legitimacy in areas where it was seen as underperforming. The EU's current difficulties in promoting inclusive economic growth that also benefits lower-skilled workers might come to mind, as do its difficulties in responding to the large number of refugees wishing to enter EU territory. Hiccups in the progress of European integration are by no means new. For instance, during the mid-1960s the French government for a while refused to participate in meetings in Brussels over integration disagreements (the so-called Empty Chair Crisis), and during the 1970s and 1980s there was talk of "eurosclerosis" (a stalemate in European integration). Many members of the public thought at this time that European integration was close to being finished.

To illustrate the mood of the day, *The Economist*, an influential British weekly magazine, put a tombstone on the front cover of an issue that took stock of advances in European integration since the 1950s (Figure 1.1). The Latin inscription quotes a line from Roman historian Tacitus (c. 56 BCE–c. 120 CE), who wrote that Emperor Galba was universally seen as being "fit to rule, had he never ruled." It hence expresses the frequent criticism of the European Economic Community, as the EU was then called, as an entity that looks attractive in theory but does not work well in practice. *The Economist* reflected a negative public sentiment at the time: The early 1980s were characterized by sluggish growth and high unemployment across Europe. Very few good things could be traced back to the European integration project. However, the EU has been able to recover from such crises – the late 1980s and early 1990s were in fact one of its most successful periods. This history

Figure 1.1. *The Economist* cover, March 20, 1982

Source: The Economist Group Limited, London

should serve as a warning to over-eager commentators who see the EU's current challenges as an indication of its upcoming demise.

Calls for the EU to legitimate itself in democratic terms have never been entirely absent in the history of European integration. They explain, for instance, why the European Parliament was created. However, democracy concerns – which represent what political scientists call *input legitimacy*, deriving from the participation of the citizens – were considered secondary to economic legitimation until the early 1990s. The main reason for this was the lack of widespread public interest in European integration. However, in light of the deepening and widening of European integration that has taken place during the past 30 years, more citizens are voicing their concerns about the political process in the EU.

To address this criticism on its democratic credentials, the EU has increased the power of the European Parliament, turning it from a consultative assembly into a fully co-equal legislator, on par with the Council of the EU. Further democratization measures have expanded the role of national parliaments in the EU and created a European Citizens' Initiative that allows

Figure 1.2. Support for EU membership in the citizenry, 1973–2022
Question: "Generally speaking, do you think that [your country's] membership of the European Union is…?"

Sources: Standard Eurobarometer, 1973–2011; Parlemeter (European Parliament Eurobarometer), 2012–2022

citizens to suggest draft legislation on a certain issue to the European Commission. Yet these changes have not alleviated concerns about the democratic quality of the EU. There have been a fair number of referendums about EU-related issues in the member states, usually organized by national governments in response to public pressure, and some of them have resulted in a rejection of further European integration.

A notable example of such a referendum was the Brexit referendum held in the United Kingdom on June 23, 2016, in which voters were asked if they wanted the UK to leave or remain in the EU. Most of the leading political parties were in favour of remaining. In the end, a small majority voted to leave. Although the process that led to the final decision was rocky, the result was that eventually the UK did leave at the end of January 2020. This process illustrates the importance of citizens' perceptions of European integration.

Public opinion research shows that the EU has not been equally popular among its citizens over time; it has experienced ebbs and flows in popularity. Looking at some of the statistics about support for the EU collected by the Eurobarometer over the past decades, we see that a majority of EU citizens have consistently supported their country's EU membership. After 1991, there was a clear drop in support for membership; however, there seems to be an upward trend in support in recent years (Figure 1.2). Although this graph may give a good bird's eye perspective of support for European integration, the picture changes significantly if one compares it by looking at country-by-country support, different demographic groups, or specific issue areas.

At the time of writing (summer 2022), the EU faces difficulties in giving citizens a sense of democratic participation and empowerment. In mature advanced liberal democracies, citizens often feel connected to the discussions about how to trade off regulation versus market freedom; transferring funds to a central pool and redistribution; or the political direction of the executive. EU citizens feel disconnected to how the EU makes such decisions and how they can influence them. The emergence of more pointed questions about what the EU is doing, questions about its direction, active national party political discussions about EU politics, or even outright vocal opposition to the EU, is referred to as *politicization* of the EU. It may be a trigger for further democratization, but it may also lead to a stagnation of the integration process.

STRUCTURE OF THE BOOK

This book is subdivided into three parts. The first part, "Integration and Governance," looks at the European integration process as well as its political and legal structure. It starts with Chapter 2 by Constantin Chira-Pascanut, who provides an overview of the history of the EU since World War II. Chapter 3, by Finn Laursen, Achim Hurrelmann, and Amy Verdun, discusses how the EU works as a political system, focusing on major executive and legislative institutions and processes. Chapter 4, by Martha O'Brien and Eszter Bodnár, sheds light on legal integration – the EU's legal instruments, the role of law in the integration process, and the powers of the Court of Justice of the EU. In Chapter 5, Ingeborg Tömmel provides an overview of governance and policy-making in the EU's multilevel system. She compares various types of EU policy to each other and also to what is typical in the member states. Chapter 6 by Amy Verdun, the final chapter in this part, focuses on the theories of European integration. It introduces the leading integration theories and more general political science theories that have become more frequently used in European integration studies.

The second part, "Policies," encompasses eight chapters that concentrate on a selected area of policy-making. They each discuss the development of the policy in question from the EU's origins to the present. Chapter 7, by

Paul Schure and Amy Verdun, offers an overview of the economic integration process, from the Single Market through the single currency to the recent developments in dealing with the financial crisis and the COVID-19 pandemic. Oliver Schmidtke, in Chapter 8, presents the policy development on matters of migration, citizenship, and security, including challenges relating to migration and refugee flows, terrorist attacks, and COVID-19 border closures. In Chapter 9, Frédéric Mérand and Antoine Rayroux offer an account of the way in which foreign, security, and defence policies have advanced from the early days till the present time. Crina Viju-Miljusevic, in Chapter 10, examines the EU's Common Agricultural Policy, one of the earliest EU policies that has in recent years undergone far-reaching reforms. Emmanuel Brunet-Jailly offers an account of regional policy since the early days in Chapter 11. He describes a policy set to alleviate the social impact of economic convergence, which has become one of the world's most ambitious investment policies. Chapter 12, by Valerie D'Erman, recounts EU trade policy, one of the earliest truly supranational policies. She also discusses the Comprehensive Economic Trade Agreement between Canada and the EU. Chapter 13, by Charles Pentland, offers an overview of the process of EU enlargement and the challenges that accompanied each enlargement; it also examines Brexit as the only case of a member state leaving the EU. The last policy chapter covers the European Neighbourhood Policy. In Chapter 14, Assem Dandashly and Gabriela Chira set out how the EU developed policies toward countries in the East and the South that are not EU members, and what policies the EU uses to deal with them.

The third part, "Challenges," starts off with Chapter 15 by Achim Hurrelmann, which examines various aspects of democracy in the EU. Dealing with the EU's recent attempts to create more democratic legitimacy, it also discusses the increasing politicization of European integration and the growth of Euroskepticism. Heather MacRae, in Chapter 16, provides an overview of social challenges. She explains the various mechanisms for governing social issues and raises the question of whether some groups of the population have profited from European integration more than others. In Chapter 17, Michèle Knodt, Julia Jänisch, and G. Cornelis van Kooten review the EU's ambition of becoming the first climate-neutral continent through a set of policies called the European Green Deal. Chapter 18, by Joan DeBardeleben, discusses the geopolitics of the EU. This chapter assesses the role of the EU in the world and examines a few of the large geopolitical issues the EU has been faced with over the past decades, including controversies about its relationship with

Russia. The final chapter by the three editors of this text returns to the three themes of the book and reassesses their importance in light of the analysis in the individual chapters.

NOTE

1 The EU as well as some of its key institutions have changed their names in the course of the European integration process. To keep matters simple, this chapter consistently uses current terminology, even when referring to a time period in which another term was in use. Subsequent chapters provide more details on the changes in terminology over time.

REFERENCES AND FURTHER READING

Bache, I., S. Bulmer, S. George, O. Parker, and C. Burns. 2020. *Politics in the European Union*, 5th ed. Oxford: Oxford University Press.

Brunet-Jailly, E., ed. 2007. *Borderlands: Comparing Border Security in North America and Europe*. Ottawa: University of Ottawa Press.

Cini, M., and N. Pérez-Solórzano Borragán, eds. 2022. *European Union Politics*, 7th ed. Oxford: Oxford University Press.

Croci, O., and A. Verdun, eds. 2006. *The Transatlantic Divide: Foreign and Security Policies in the Atlantic Alliance from Kosovo to Iraq*. Manchester: Manchester University Press.

Della Posta, P., M. Uvalic, and A. Verdun, eds. 2009. *Globalization, Development and Integration: A European Perspective*. Basingstoke, UK: Palgrave Macmillan.

Dinan, D. 2014. *Europe Recast: A History of the European Union*, 2nd ed. Boulder, CO: Lynne Rienner.

Environics Institute. 2019. "Canada: Pulling Together or Drifting Apart?" https://www.environicsinstitute.org/docs/default-source/project-documents/confederation-of-tomorrow-2019-survey---report-1/confederation-of-tomorrow-survey-2019---report-1-pulling-together-or-drifting-apart---final-report.pdf?sfvrsn=9abc2e3e_2.

European Union. n.d. "Schuman Declaration May 1950." https://european-union.europa.eu/principles-countries-history/history-eu/1945-59/schuman-declaration-may-1950_en.

Hosli, M., A. Kreppel, B. Plechanavová, and A. Verdun, eds. 2015. *Decision-Making in the EU before and after the Lisbon Treaty*. London: Routledge.

Hurrelmann, A. 2019. "Legitimacy and European Union Politics." In *Oxford Research Encyclopedia of Politics*. Oxford: Oxford University Press. https://doi.org/10.1093/acrefore/9780190228637.013.1112.

Hurrelmann, A. 2021. "Canada's Two Europes: Brexit and the Prospect of Competing Transatlantic Relationships." In *Changing Perceptions of the EU at Times of Brexit*, edited by N. Chaban, A. Niemann, and J. Speyer, 116–31. London: Routledge.

Hurrelmann, A., A. Gora, and A. Wagner. 2015. "The Politicization of European Integration: More than an Elite Affair?" *Political Studies* 63 (1): 43–59. https://doi.org/10.1111/1467-9248.12090.

Hurrelmann, A., and A. Wagner. 2020. "Did the Eurozone Crisis Undermine the European Union's Legitimacy? An Analysis of Newspaper Reporting, 2009–2014." *Comparative European Politics* 18 (5): 707–25. https://doi.org/10.1057/s41295-020-00205-6.

IRPP. 2021. "Canadians Are Still Committed to Decentralized Federalism." https://policyoptions.irpp.org/magazines/septembe-2021/canadians-are-still-committed-to-decentralized-federalism.

Leruth, B., S. Gänzle, and J. Trondal, eds. 2022. *The Routledge Handbook of Differentiation in the European Union*. London: Routledge.

Leuffen, D., B. Rittberger, and F. Schimmelfennig, eds. 2022. *Integration and Differentiation in the European Union: Theory and Policies*. Cham: Springer.

McCormick, J. 2021. *Understanding the European Union: A Concise Introduction*, 8th ed. London: Bloomsbury.

Nobel Prize. 2012. The Nobel Peace Prize 2012. Press release. https://www.nobelprize.org/prizes/peace/2012/press-release.

Tömmel, I., and A. Verdun. 2009. *Innovative Governance in the European Union: The Politics of Multilevel Policy-Making in the European Union*. Boulder, CO: Lynne Rienner.

Ugland, T. 2018. *Jean Monnet and Canada: Early Travels and the Idea of European Unity*. Toronto: University of Toronto Press.

Verdun, A. 1998. "The Institutional Design of EMU: A Democratic Deficit?" *Journal of Public Policy* 18 (2): 107–32. https://doi.org/10.1017/S0143814X98000063.

Verdun, A. 2000. *European Responses to Globalization and Financial Market Integration: Perceptions of Economic and Monetary Union in Britain, France and Germany*. Basingstoke, UK: Palgrave Macmillan.

Verdun, A. 2016. "The Federal Features of the EU: Lessons from Canada." *Politics and Governance* 4 (3): 100–10. https://doi.org/10.17645/pag.v4i3.598.

Verdun, A., and G. Chira. 2011. "The Eastern Partnership: The Burial Ground of Enlargement Hopes?" *Comparative European Politics* 9 (4/5): 448–66. https://doi.org/10.1057/cep.2011.11.

Verdun, A., and O. Croci, eds. 2005. *The European Union in the Wake of Eastern Enlargement: Institutional and Policy-Making Challenges*. Manchester: Manchester University Press.

Wallace, H., M. Pollack, C. Roederer-Rynning, and A.R. Young, eds. 2020. *Policy-Making in the European Union*, 8th ed. Oxford: Oxford University Press.

Wood, D., and A. Verdun. 2011. "Canada and the European Union: A Review of the Literature from 1982 to 2010." *International Journal* 66 (1): 9–21. https://doi.org/10.1177/002070201106600102.

PART ONE

Integration and Governance

2

A Short History of the European Union

Constantin Chira-Pascanut

READER'S GUIDE

European integration is an idea that has been advocated for centuries under different guises. However, it took concrete shape in the post-1945 era. While many projects promoted idealist visions of a unified continent, the plan that laid the basis for the first European institutions was primarily motivated by pragmatic objectives: Western European states were attracted to the idea of European integration for economic and political reasons. Since its inception, European cooperation has been a work in progress. This chapter focuses on how the European Union (EU) and its predecessor organizations were constructed, highlighting also the parallels with the formation of Canada.

INTRODUCTION

What we call today the European Union is a complex construct that is the result of more than seven decades of collaboration among the European states. Even though the idea of establishing a united Europe had been explored in intellectual circles over the centuries, it was only after World War II that a project of this sort was implemented. While plans before 1950 envisaged the creation of a European federation, with a supranational government and assembly making decisions for all of Europe, the organization established after the war had little in common with this type of political structure. Indeed, as discussed in the introductory chapter, the EU is neither a fully fledged federal state, comparable to the Canadian or the US examples, nor is it an international organization, such as the United Nations (Theme 2 of this book). While it has developed some quasi-federal characteristics, it is best described as a unique entity governed by atypical institutions designed to ensure dialogue among its members and a functioning decision-making process.

The particularities of European states that are currently part of the EU were shaped over centuries. This is one of the main reasons why the construct was challenging from the beginning. Indeed, the EU has largely been a work in progress whose end goal has been reshaped during the process. There have been different understandings of what the final constitutional architecture of the EU could be – what in French is often referred to as the *finalité*. Some maintain that the establishment of a European federation is the end goal of European integration, while others prefer intergovernmental cooperation – that is, decision making by the governments of the member states – that would advance integration gradually in specific fields. To this day, it seems that integration is walking a fine line between these two ideas.

At different moments throughout its history, choices and bargains had to be made. Not having legitimacy in its own right owing to its political specificity, the EU needed to acquire competence (power to legislate in a field) progressively; and it has done so gradually over the years at the expense of the power of the member states. However, even within these fields, the competence acquired by the EU is not always exclusive but is often shared with the member states (see Chapter 5). Transferring competence to the EU level has resulted from a process of ongoing bargaining, and with mixed results. Those choices have shaped the organization that we see today. A historical analysis enhances the understanding of the EU's functioning and sheds light on some of its unique characteristics.

EUROPEAN INTEGRATION: A HISTORICAL OVERVIEW

The First Moves: The European Coal and Steel Community (1951), the European Economic Community (1957), and the European Atomic Energy Community (1957)

Throughout centuries Europeans have seen many conflicts ravage their territory. On numerous occasions tensions between European states could not be solved diplomatically and, as a result, broke out into wars. The two World Wars of the twentieth century both had their inception in Europe and saw Germany and France pitted as major enemies. It is not surprising that in this context politicians, academics, journalists, and others sought solutions to avoid future wars in Europe. Given the Franco-German rivalry and the conflicts that it had generated, ideas ventured to preserve peace in Europe had to have a Franco-German reconciliation process at their core.

As early as the nineteenth century, one of the main solutions considered in intellectual circles was the idea of a federal Europe, similar to the United States of America. This idea aimed to bind European states and ensure dialogue between Europeans. In 1849, the French writer Victor Hugo proposed in his work *Pour les États-Unis d'Europe* the creation of a United States of Europe that would enforce dialogue between Europeans, develop a European identity, and rule out war as a means to resolve conflict.

The search for solutions intensified after World War I, which showed that, as technology developed, the devastation of wars could be catastrophic. The concept of a unified Europe continued to be developed in intellectual circles during the interwar period. In the early 1920s, a Pan-European movement, gathering notable members (including Albert Einstein, Sigmund Freud, and Thomas Mann), aimed to unify European states. This intellectual effervescence did not go without effect. In 1930, the French minister Aristide Briand proposed a plan to federate Europe under the umbrella of the League of Nations.

Since none of these ideas had been brought to fruition, the search on how to bring together European states continued during and after World War II. The first prominent move after World War II, a mammoth congress in The Hague in May 1948 organized by European movements and chaired by Winston Churchill, achieved little to advance the federalist cause. Its main outcome was the establishment of a consultative assembly in May 1949, the **Council of Europe** – an international organization that continues to exist but is institutionally unrelated to the current EU (see also Chapter 4).

In the end, it was a concrete and limited idea that laid down the foundations of what would later become the EU. In the late 1940s, a French businessman, Jean Monnet, drafted a plan focusing on economic cooperation of participating states in two key sectors of the postwar Western European economy – coal and steel. This plan had very little in common with the previous federalist projects postulated in intellectual and political circles. As spelled out in the introductory chapter, Monnet's plan was to secure peace in Europe by locking European states into a system of ever more extensive economic interactions (Theme 1 of this book).

To explain Monnet's approach, one must consider his personality, experience, and worldview. A businessperson and a financier, never elected to public office, Monnet (1888–1979) was a pragmatic individual. The son of a famous French cognac producer, he gave up university studies for more concrete endeavours – learning the art of business. In 1919, at the age of 31, he was appointed deputy secretary general of the League of Nations. Four years later, he returned to his family business. Through the wholesale trade of his brandy in the United States and Canada, he had established contacts with key players in North America. According to Trygve Ugland (2011), while in Canada Monnet was impressed by the Canadian federal system and considered it a possible model for a future federation in Europe. The economic benefits as well as the optimism of such an ethnically diverse people were the main features that caught his attention.

In the following years, he became involved in financial transactions both in Washington and New York. Owing to his extensive contacts, governments called on him to conduct key missions, such as facilitating the purchase of war supplies from the United States by the United Kingdom in August 1940. After World War II, he was put in charge of preparing and implementing a plan for postwar reconstruction and modernization of the French economy. It was in this position that, in early 1950, he drafted his plan to pool French and German coal and steel production.

As somebody outside the political establishment, Monnet realized that he lacked the key political backing for his idea, without which his plan did not stand a chance of being accepted. At the beginning of May 1950, he secured the support of the French foreign minister, Robert Schuman, who was ready to take on the plan. Schuman attached a personal interest to Franco-German reconciliation. Schuman was born a German citizen but became a French citizen after the region in which he lived (Alsace-Lorraine) changed hands in 1919. Yet this personal history was not the only reason why the politician agreed to be the political backing of Monnet's idea.

In 1950 the French foreign minister was under a lot of pressure to propose a practical solution to ease the Franco-German relationship. The postwar policy toward West Germany, which offered a number of advantages to France, was going to be revised. Schuman was aware that the future Allied Conference, scheduled for May 10, 1950, was the deadline for France to come up with a constructive proposal to reconcile its relationship with Germany. In this context, Schuman welcomed Monnet's proposal because it offered a response to the political deadlock. In addition, Monnet received the backing of his influential US friends, who held key positions in the post-1945 era, namely

John J. McCloy (the US high commissioner for Germany, arguably the most influential player in Germany) and Dean Acheson (the US secretary of state).

Monnet's idea, embodied in the **Schuman Plan**, was made public by the French foreign minister on May 9, 1950. (For this reason, May 9 was later designated as "Europe Day".) The Schuman Plan subsequently became the basis for negotiations on a future treaty between the representatives of six Western European states: France, West Germany, Italy, Belgium, the Netherlands, and Luxembourg. Political, economic, and security concerns of the participant states shaped the negotiations. French representatives were concerned about their country's security as well as defending its economic interests. To a large extent France's economy depended on the availability of German coal on advantageous terms. In addition to regaining control of its coal resources, West German representatives aimed to restore Germany's status in the international arena.

The proposed institutional design was innovative and had little in common with those suggested by previous plans. It underlined the importance of establishing a High Authority, made up of independent experts, whose decisions would bind the participating states. Although the plan did not foresee any governmental involvement, at the end of the negotiations a Council of Ministers was established. The High Authority was to become the guardian of the supranational principle, while the Council of Ministers safeguarded the intergovernmental principle – that is, the interests of national governments. This unique institutional architecture, with certain adaptations, continues to characterize the EU today.

The intensification of the Cold War, with the onset of the Korean War (1950–3), provided the background against which these discussions took place. After their military alliance during World War II, tensions broke out between the United States and the Soviet Union at the end of the war. Based on an ideological rift, the two military powers emerging after World War II intensified their rivalry, building up political, economic, and military alliances that led to the establishment of two world spheres of influence: a "Western bloc" (dominated by the United States) and an "Eastern bloc" (controlled by the Soviet Union). Characterized by constant tension between the two powers and military build-ups on both sides, which developed into various regional crises of different intensities (such as the Cuban crisis in 1962, the Korean War from 1950–3, and the Vietnam War from 1955–75), the Cold War (1945–91) never developed into an open military conflict.

The first years of the Cold War, and particularly the onset of the Korean War, accelerated the conclusion of the negotiations among the six European states, under the patronage of the United States, which aimed to build a strong regional alliance in Western Europe. The Cold War contributed to a certain extent to giving a sense of shared political identity in Western Europe. As a result, the treaty establishing the European Coal and Steel Community (ECSC) was signed in Paris in 1951 (see Box 2.1). As such, participating states decided to move away from exclusive national sovereignty and relinquished some powers, which until then were exclusively national, to the newly created organization and its institutions.

> **BOX 2.1: THE EUROPEAN COAL AND STEEL COMMUNITY (ECSC)**
> The 1951 **Treaty of Paris** established the ECSC on the basis of a proposal of the French foreign minister, Robert Schuman (originally presented on May 9, 1950). The originator of the proposal was Jean Monnet. The founding member states were France, West Germany, Italy, Belgium, the Netherlands, and Luxembourg. By aiming to regulate and oversee the production of coal and steel (primary resources for wars) at the European level, and chiefly by involving West Germany and France, the organization sought to limit the possibilities to wage wars between signatories.
>   The ECSC consisted of several institutions:
>
> - The High Authority (HA, the future European Commission), representing the supranational aspect of the organization, included nine members who were supposed to be independent and not representing their countries' interests. It exercised an executive role.
> - The Council of Ministers (now the Council of the EU), representing the intergovernmental aspect of the organization, included representatives of member states' governments. Its role was to scrutinize the HA. The presidency rotated between member states.
> - The Common Assembly (now the European Parliament) included 78 representatives. Until 1979, its representatives were elected by national parliaments. Its role was to check the HA, having the power to dismiss it.
> - The Court of Justice (seven judges) oversaw the application of ECSC law and its interpretation.
>
>   The ECSC Treaty was valid for 50 years; it ceased to exist in 2002, at which time its activities were transferred to the European Economic Community.

The European integration project of the 1950s remained limited to economic cooperation on coal and steel. The failed attempt to establish a **European Defence Community (EDC)** illustrates this limited scope. Responding to US pressure to allow West German rearmament, Jean Monnet proposed the EDC, building on the model of the ECSC, with the aim of containing the rearmament of West Germany and of preventing it from becoming a member of the North Atlantic Treaty Organization (NATO). Once again, he sought political backing for his proposal, referring this time to the French premier, René Pleven. The project was designed to include the original ECSC member states. The draft treaty explicitly mentioned that the EDC was going to have a supranational character, having joint institutions and armed forces. Underlining that its objectives were exclusively defensive, the projected EDC duplicated in some respects NATO's role, stating explicitly the common defence clause. Although the EDC treaty was signed in 1952, it was eventually rejected by the French National Assembly in 1954 and it never came to fruition. Nearly four decades later, although not in the form sought in the 1950s, the idea of European defence took shape with the establishment of the EU Common Foreign and Security Policy (see Chapter 9).

With the failure to establish an EDC, European integration in the mid-1950s seemed to have reached a deadlock. Those who believed that integration in the coal and steel sectors would spill over and stimulate other economic segments to integrate saw their hopes evaporating. Moreover, it seemed that economic cooperation would not spur political cooperation. It was in this context that the foreign ministers of the six member states met in Messina (Italy) in June 1955 to discuss a program designed to revive European integration.

The Messina Conference provided a new impetus, and two new treaties were signed in Rome: a treaty establishing the **European Economic Community (EEC)** and a treaty establishing the European Atomic Energy Community (**Euratom**). The **Treaties of Rome**, signed in 1957, entered into force on January 1, 1958. In addition to the establishment of a Common Market and an atomic energy community, these treaties formalized a series of common policies, such as the Common Agricultural Policy and the Common Commercial Policy. Furthermore, these agreements opened up the possibility of extending European competence to other policy fields. As a result, in the early 1970s the community was allowed to take action in additional fields, including environmental, regional, social, and industrial policies (see Chapter 5).

The 1960s: A Decade of Mixed Results

The 1960s showed that member states and their domestic interests could seriously influence European integration. Arguably, the best examples of this development were the political moves of French president Charles de Gaulle with respect to the EEC. Despite the fact that France was one of the most important food producers in Europe, its prices were not competitive. By contrast, West Germany was a large importer of agricultural products. De Gaulle saw this situation as an opportunity to promote domestic interests and to use the EEC to strengthen the French economy. Therefore, during the negotiations on the implementation of the EEC Treaty, de Gaulle pushed for the establishment of a mechanism that would create a market for French agricultural products. At the beginning of 1962, a Common Agricultural Policy (CAP) was established. The CAP ensured not only preference for EEC agricultural products, but it also created a subsidy mechanism that encouraged production and export while protecting the EEC market from lower-priced products. As France was the main agricultural producer in the EEC, it was the one with the most to gain (see Chapter 10).

De Gaulle's bargaining continued in the years that followed, when he even threatened the whole edifice. According to the 1962 agreement, the CAP was to be revisited by the mid-1960s. At this time de Gaulle expected the community budget to subsidize further agricultural production. However, as he did not get what he expected during the negotiations, he made use of French bargaining power. Also, he felt that France would lose its influence in the EEC once **qualified majority voting (QMV)**, offering weighted votes to each member state according to its population size, was introduced. QMV would be the dominant voting mode as of January 1966, in accordance with the EEC Treaty. Until then unanimity had been the only voting mechanism used at the EEC level. Indeed, France wanted to maintain the right to use its veto power to preserve its interests.

In this context the French president started one of the most serious crises ever faced by the EEC. France withdrew its representatives from the EEC in June 1965 and paralyzed the organization for about half a year. This period, referred to as the "Empty Chair Crisis," lasted until January 1966, when the member states managed to find a satisfactory compromise for France: QMV would apply, but a member state could veto a decision if it felt that important national interests were at stake (this is known as the "Luxembourg Compromise").

Agricultural concerns were at the core of EEC negotiations in the 1960s. Once again, they played a key part in de Gaulle's decision on two occasions (1963 and 1967) to veto Britain's application to join the EEC. He feared that Britain would favour Commonwealth agricultural products and would threaten the CAP. De Gaulle's use of unilateral policy as a bargaining tool in international negotiations demonstrates that the domestic preferences of EEC member states have had a major influence in shaping European integration (see Box 2.2).

> **BOX 2.2: EMPTY CHAIR CRISIS**
> The Empty Chair Crisis had its origin in two developments at the EEC level:
>
> - In 1965, the European Commission proposed to increase its own role as well as to enhance the European Parliament's budgetary powers with a view to developing the EEC's own financial resources.
> - The third stage of the transitional period for the establishment of the Common Market (beginning in January 1966) was upcoming, which involved the application of QMV in the Council of Ministers.
>
> These developments worried de Gaulle, who feared that the CAP might be reformed against French interests if it could no longer be protected by unanimous voting. Since a compromise could not be reached, France withdrew its representative from the Council meetings on July 1, 1965, and refused to participate in the Council's work, thus paralyzing decision making at the EEC level.
>
> After half a year of stalemate, the French government agreed to resume negotiations. In January 1966, the prime minister of Luxembourg proposed a compromise: Should a member state feel that vital national interests could be adversely affected, negotiations had to continue until all parties would accept the solution. In practice, this meant that member states could invoke the concept of vital national interests to block decisions in the Council. This practice remained in place until the Single European Act, signed in 1986, amended the Rome Treaty.

The 1970s: Facing Economic and Financial Crisis

As the 1960s were drawing to a close, new objectives were set for the EEC. The summit of The Hague (1969) defined the community's primary objectives: further membership expansion (see Chapter 13) and the establishment of an Economic and Monetary Union (EMU) (see Chapter 7). The first was achieved in 1973, when the UK, Ireland, and Denmark joined (facilitated by de Gaulle's retirement in 1969). Negotiations leading to the accession of the UK contributed to the strengthening of what was previously conceived as adjustment instruments to economic integration: competition policy as well as agricultural and social funds. In 1972, the member states agreed to a European Regional Development Fund as a redistributive mechanism similar to the agricultural policy, geared specifically to the economic challenges faced by the UK (see Chapter 11). However, the outcomes of efforts to achieve EMU were more modest. The Council of Ministers appointed a committee headed by Pierre Werner (the prime minister and finance minister of Luxembourg) whose task was to draw up a plan for the establishment of EMU. The "Werner Group" completed its work in the fall of 1970 and issued a plan that aimed at establishing EMU in successive stages by 1980.

However, the worsening international environment, marked by the onset of the oil crisis, drove the EEC member states' economies into recession. As a result, the main objectives of EEC member states became the stabilization of national currencies and financial discipline. In a first stage, member states tried to counter inflation by imposing limits on how much national currencies could fluctuate against each other. As this system failed to achieve its aims, it was abandoned in 1976 and replaced in 1979 with the European Monetary System. At its heart was the exchange rate mechanism that stipulated maintaining the fluctuation margins of national currencies (maximum ±2.25 per cent for most currencies; ±6 per cent for the weaker currencies, such as the Italian lira) but introduced a new reference – the European Currency Unit (ECU), a basket of the EEC member states' currencies. In the end, all attempts in this decade to create economic and monetary unification failed, and EMU plans were eventually abandoned by the late 1970s and only re-emerged in the late 1980s (see Chapter 7).

The 1980s and the 1990s: European Integration Relaunched

The deadlock of the 1970s was followed by an unprecedented advance of European integration driven by supranational institutions and bodies such as the Commission and the European Court of Justice (now the Court of Justice of the EU). The recurring meetings of the heads of state or governments, called "summits" or "European councils," gave the first impetus for this revival. In 1984 (Fontainebleau), European leaders reached an agreement on pending financial issues such as CAP spending and the UK contribution to the EEC budget (the UK complained about not benefiting from the CAP and obtained a rebate).

The Single European Act (SEA), signed in 1986 and entered into force in 1987, represented a major reinforcement of supranational institutions. The introduction of new decision-making procedures and the expansion of QMV made it more difficult for states to veto decisions. This feature became increasingly important as the number of member states increased (Greece became a member in 1981; Spain and Portugal in 1986). In addition, this treaty extended EEC competence to new policy fields, including social policy, research, and the environment.

The SEA was the result of extensive treaty reform preparations and negotiations not only within the intergovernmental conference charged with the revision of the treaty, but also during the first years of the Delors Commission (Jacques Delors became Commission president in January 1985). Only months after Delors took office, the Delors Commission published a key document, namely a White Paper aiming to complete the Common Market by abolishing all physical, technical, and tax barriers in the community (June 1985). The SEA took on the content of this paper and provided the instruments for completing the Common Market by the end of 1992. (The language used for the Common Market in this document was the "Internal Market".)

The successful implementation of the Internal Market project made the Delors Commission, and especially its president, more prone to undertaking bold decisions that moved European integration forward. For instance, at the request of the June 1988 European Council, an expert group of mostly central bank presidents headed by Delors issued a report that proposed the establishment of EMU in three stages (between July 1, 1990, and January 1, 2002), ending with the introduction of euro banknotes and coins (the **Delors Report**, 1989). The objective of establishing EMU was incorporated into the **Maastricht Treaty** (1992).

The other objectives listed in this new treaty were to further expand EU competence, especially in Common Foreign and Security Policy (see Chapter 9) as well as **Justice and Home Affairs** (see Chapter 8) – two areas considered particularly important for member state sovereignty. Since

Table 2.1. The three pillars of the EU established in the 1992 Maastricht Treaty (later dismantled by the Lisbon Treaty)

Pillar I European Communities: ECSC, EEC, Euratom (community integration method)	Pillar II Common Foreign and Security Policy (intergovernmental cooperation)	Pillar III Justice and Home Affairs (intergovernmental cooperation)
· Common Market · Customs Union · Economic and Monetary Union · Competition · Common Agricultural Policy · Common Fisheries Policy · Structural policy · Trans-European networks · Industrial policy · Education and vocational training · Youth · Culture · Environment · Social policy · Public health · Consumer protection · Nuclear power · Energy	· Foreign policy · Coordinated position on international crises · Respect for the obligations of member states toward NATO	· Asylum, immigration, crossing of external borders · Combating drug addiction, fraud, and international crime · Judicial cooperation in civil and criminal matters · Customs cooperation · Police cooperation

the member states were unwilling to expand the established principles of EEC decision making to these areas, the result was a fundamental reform of the organization – now called the EU – which was divided into three "**pillars**" (see Table 2.1).

The creation of this system was the result of a compromise between states that wanted to give new powers to the EU and those reluctant to surrender national power in areas considered highly sensitive, such as foreign policy, security, or justice. The arrangement created an intergovernmental side of the EU, grouping on the one hand policies such as asylum, immigration, and judicial cooperation in civil and criminal matters, and on the other hand foreign and security policy. Within the new arrangement, the Commission remained the leading body in Pillar I, while in the other two pillars the foremost institution was the Council of Ministers, with the Commission, the European Parliament (EP), and the European Court of Justice (ECJ) having much more limited powers.

The next revision of the treaties, the **Treaty of Amsterdam** (1997), further consolidated the powers of the supranational institutions such as the Commission, the EP, and the ECJ. This treaty not only extended the co-decision procedure (a legislative procedure that placed the Council and the Parliament on an equal footing, now called the ordinary legislative procedure) but also made it more efficient by enabling faster decision making. Furthermore, it transferred most areas of Pillar III (such as asylum and immigration) into Pillar I and "communitarized" them (made them subject to supranational institutions) after a period of five years.

The EU at the Beginning of the New Century

The integration trend, characterized by the expansion of the EU's areas of competence, continued throughout the last decade of the twentieth century and into the beginning of the twenty-first century. At the same time, this period was marked by an unprecedented expansion of the EU. The demise of communism in Central and Eastern Europe represented not only an opportunity for the EU but, in many respects, was seen as an event that gave rise to a moral obligation to reunify Europe. The majority of Central and Eastern European states, which were part of the Soviet bloc until the late 1980s or early 1990s, applied for EU membership.

In this context, Austria, Sweden, and Finland joined the EU in 1995. The next enlargements almost doubled the number of member states (in 2004, the Czech Republic, Poland, Hungary, Slovakia, Slovenia, Estonia, Latvia, Lithuania, Malta, and Cyprus became members; and in 2007, Bulgaria and Romania joined). Given this development, all through the 1990s EU policy-makers looked for ways to adapt the institutional mechanism to allow for a functioning, expanded EU. Because the Treaty of Amsterdam failed to a large extent to address this matter, it continued to remain on the EU agenda at the beginning of the new century. In 2001, the **Treaty of Nice** clarified many details and paved the way for the accession of new member states. Also, this new treaty modification was seen as an opportunity to broaden EU competences and the powers of supranational institutions. The co-decision procedure, one of the main tools of supranational bodies, was extended to new areas at the expense of the member states' power. One of the main beneficiaries of this was the EP, which saw its powers increasing.

While the Treaty of Nice provided the framework for the functioning of an enlarged EU, it fell short in that it had not managed to simplify the EU machinery. The overcomplicated three-pillar structure was maintained together with a system of opt-outs, where some states obtained the right not to participate in certain policy areas (see Chapter 7). The ink was barely dry on the text of the Nice Treaty when EU leaders adopted a declaration on the future of the EU (Laeken Declaration, December 15, 2001) that dealt with the "Nice leftovers" with four main issues: (1) simplification of the treaties; (2) making clear the competences of the EU and member states; (3) the legal status of the Charter of Fundamental Rights, and (4) the role of national parliaments in the EU institutional architecture. As a result, the EU convened a so-called European Convention to discuss a more far-reaching reform of the EU. It crafted an agreement, officially called the Treaty Establishing a Constitution for Europe, which aimed to achieve a comprehensive treaty revision by replacing the ECSC, EEC, and Euratom treaties with a consolidated and simplified text that gave up some of the complicated constructs such as the pillars. It integrated the Charter of Fundamental Rights of the European Union within its text, making its principles of fundamental rights mandatory for EU member states, and it introduced a number of EU symbols, such as the anthem and flag.

Although all EU heads of state or governments had signed the European Constitutional Treaty on October 29, 2004, it could only enter into force after ratification by all EU member states' parliaments, which could only be done after a national parliamentary vote and in some cases a national referendum (depending on each member state's legal system). Ireland was obliged to hold a referendum, while France and the Netherlands chose to consult their citizens. As the French and Dutch people voted against the adoption of the Constitutional Treaty in May 2005, the ratification process was postponed in other countries. In the end, the Constitutional Treaty was never ratified.

After this outcome, in mid-2007 EU leaders decided to abandon the constitutional path and turn back to the more secure strategy of treaty amending. Following the subsequent negotiations, the Lisbon Treaty was drafted by incorporating many of the innovations of the Constitutional Treaty. What were some of these changes? The European Council and the European Central Bank became official EU institutions (see details in Chapters 3 and 7). The post of the high representative of the union for foreign affairs and security policy, heading the new European External Action Service, was established with the aim to give a single voice to the EU in international affairs (see Chapter 9). In an effort to address the democratic deficit (see Chapter 15) and the increasingly challenging task to balance efficient decision making and democratic accountability, the treaty provided that national parliaments would be more involved in the legislative process and introduced the European Citizens' Initiative. As discussed in Chapter 9, the Treaty of Lisbon included a provision (Article 42) that, in the spirit of NATO's mutual defence clause, was designed to ensure aid and assistance between member states, for instance in cases of major terrorist attacks.

The treaty reform also gave up the pillar system, but it preserved the intergovernmental character of the Common Foreign and Security Policy, where decisions still require unanimity. Furthermore, it expanded QMV to more policy areas, thus restraining the fields requiring unanimity. The Lisbon Treaty was signed in December 2007 and entered into force two years later when it was ratified by all member states. Once again, ratification was troublesome because Irish citizens rejected the text in a first referendum. Only after granting a number of concessions to Ireland and a second referendum was the treaty ratified by Ireland.

The EU after 2010: Coping with Crisis

The challenges faced by the EU in the first years of the twenty-first century were further amplified in the next period, in which the EU witnessed a series of crises that affected the EU politically, economically, and socially – the **euro area financial crisis**, the refugee crisis, and the Brexit crisis. The euro area financial crisis developed in the context of the global financial crisis of 2007–8 (see Chapter 7). At the end of 2009, some EU member states (Greece, Portugal, Spain, Cyprus, and Ireland) started to experience difficulties in repaying or refinancing their government debt. These problems developed into a profound financial crisis, prompting discussion of the fundamentals of the EU, including the euro, its membership, and financial arrangements. The social consequences of the crisis were also profound, with record-high unemployment in affected countries. The following years were characterized by discussions about "bailouts" for affected member states, rescue packages, financial reforms, and austerity measures. The 2019 global economic slowdown and the economic fallout of the COVID-19 pandemic have also tested the EU, which responded by providing grants and loans to its member states. The discussions about the EU's response to the economic and financial effects of the pandemic showed once again the constant tension between the EU supranational institutions and national preferences.

The same tension surfaced when the EU and its member states were faced with a refugee crisis (see Chapter 8), erupting in 2015 and fuelled primarily by the Syrian, Afghan, and Iraqi conflicts. The dissimilar approaches of member states prompted EU institutions to attempt to bridge differences between "front-line" states in the crisis (such as Greece and Italy), "destination countries" (such as Germany), and others that were strictly opposed to taking in a greater number of refugees (such as Hungary and other Eastern European countries). In this situation, the European Commission proposed to redistribute asylum seekers between member states based on mandatory quotas, but this proposal was never implemented due to member state opposition. The 2015–6 refugee crisis hence demonstrated the limits of supranationalism. (In 2022, when Ukrainian refugees arrived in the EU after Russia's attack on their country, the EU's response was quite different; see Chapter 8.)

Both the euro area financial crisis and the refugee crisis played their part in the outcome of the UK's referendum on its EU membership. The membership crisis, which followed after the referendum of June 23, 2016, that resulted in a narrow majority in favour of Brexit, put the EU supranational institutions and its member states in an unprecedented situation. The negotiations between the EU and the UK on a withdrawal agreement were contentious, and an accord was only reached in December 2020 (see Chapter 13). The UK leaving the EU was the first time a member state had done so. A provision for such an occasion was first introduced in the 2009 Lisbon Treaty.

One of the consequences of these crises has been the amplification of concerns about the EU's legitimacy (Theme 3 of this book), reflected in the reduction of public support for the EU and an increase in Euroskepticism (see Chapter 15). Addressing this challenge is one of the aims of the Conference on the Future of Europe (launched in April 2021). EU leaders have vowed to consider the citizens' opinions in shaping EU policies and institutions for the next phase of its development.

WHY/HOW DOES A HISTORICAL ANALYSIS MATTER FOR UNDERSTANDING THE EU TODAY?

While the creation of the EU has some similarities with processes of state building in federal states such as Canada (see Box 2.3), its progression and outcome are clearly unique. Understanding the specific factors that shaped the development of the EU throughout its history is key to comprehending the uniqueness of the EU today, which is neither a federation nor an international organization, and which possesses its own unique decision-making process, at times specific to particular fields of competence. All these and many other distinctive features are the result of its specific historical process, which has been briefly painted in this chapter, characterized by a constant tension and bargaining between national and supranational interests.

BOX 2.3: COMPARISON WITH CANADA
The process leading to the construction of the EU partly resembles and partly differs from that leading to the formation of Canada. One of the main differences between the EU and Canada is their respective political organization. While Canada is a federal state, the EU is a unique construct that is neither a federal state nor an international organization. The governance established at the ECSC/EEC/Euratom level was unique, while the Confederation of Canada had a typical federal institutional system from the outset.

Turning to the process through which the EU and Canada were constructed, in both cases various plans for unification were put forward. The first supranational European organization was based on economic cooperation, not political ideas of a federated Europe. Pragmatic considerations drove European states to get involved in the ECSC. Political, economic, and financial considerations convinced British colonies to attend the Charlottetown (1864), Quebec (1864), and London Conferences (1866), leading to the Confederation of Canada. External threats also played a role in both instances, namely the increasing tensions in the Cold War in the EU case and the US doctrine of Manifest Destiny in the Canadian case.

Increased economic cooperation constituted an important incentive both in the case of Western European states in the post-1945 era (for example, the establishment of a Common Market) and the colonies of British North America (for example, the idea of an intercolony railroad across Canada). As in the case of Canada, which initially included only a few of the current provinces, the first three European Communities were established between a few European states only. The current EU, with its 27 member states, is the result of successive enlargements, just as Canada saw its borders expanding progressively. An important element in this process both in the case of the EU and Canada was the high-level meetings organized at the EU level between heads of state and government (European Council meetings) and the federal–provincial meetings in Canada (the First Ministers' Conferences). Held behind closed doors, the European and Canadian meetings are aimed at addressing topical issues to help iron out differences between participants in an informal way.

> While fundamentally different when it comes to institutional organization, the EU and Canada were established through processes that have a number of similarities, such as previous unsuccessful plans, initial limited membership, and successive territorial expansion, as well as pragmatic considerations motivating provinces/states to join the project.

While history indeed provides a window into the EU's construction and features, it currently also plays a role into shaping an emerging European memory culture. When joining the EU, states brought their historical memory. For instance, with the enlargement of the EU toward Central and Eastern Europe, anti-totalitarian perspectives "entered the discourse on European memory" (Büttner and Delius 2015, 394), competing with the established Holocaust memory ("Holocaust memory versus Gulag memory"). Such memory cultures constitute important vectors in shaping the EU's identity. Memory and the way it is interpreted, commemorated, and publicly presented continues to shape the EU construct.

CONCLUSION

The first seven decades of European cooperation show that European integration was, and to a large extent still remains, a work in progress whose final shape and result is unclear, characterized by a constant struggle between advocates of a more federal EU and others who attempt to maintain as much power as possible at the member state level. The EEC/EU treaties and the way they defined the EEC/EU organization were indeed the epitome of the compromise struck at various moments of the EU's history between these two tendencies.

The completion of the Common Market, the establishment of the euro, the extension of EU competence to new fields, as well as the increase in the number of EU member states have been considered significant advances in European integration. However, the failure to establish an EU Constitution indicated that reforms pushing the EU too much into a state-like direction generate considerable opposition. The first years of the twenty-first century and the crises witnessed by the EU have shown that these tendencies and tensions continue to characterize European integration.

REVIEW QUESTIONS

1 Explain Jean Monnet's approach to European integration. How did it differ from previous proposals to bring about a United States of Europe?
2 Why were EU policies on common foreign and security policy as well as justice and home affairs initially set up as separate "pillars" of the EU?
3 In what respects was the formation of the EU similar to the formation of Canada? What were some of the differences?
4 Which crises challenged the European integration project after 2010? What consequences did these crises have for the EU?

EXERCISES

1 Select one EU member state and examine its relationship to the EU over time. What have been the costs and benefits of being a part of the EU for this country? What does this one country's experience tell you about the project of European integration?
2 Select a different example of regional integration (e.g., ASEAN, Mercosur, or the Canada-US-Mexico Agreement). What were the origins of this organization? Are there any parallels between the origins of the selected organization and the origins of the ECSC? What do the differences tell you about European integration?

NOTE

The views expressed in this chapter are the personal opinions of the author.

REFERENCES AND FURTHER READING

Büttner, S.M., and A. Delius. 2015. "World Culture in European Memory Politics? New European Memory Agents between Epistemic Framing and Political Agenda Setting." *Journal of Contemporary European Studies* 23 (3): 391–404. https://doi.org/10.1080/14782804.2015.1056116.

Caporaso, J. 2018. "Europe's Triple Crisis and the Uneven Role of Institutions: The Euro, Refugees and Brexit." *Journal of Common Market Studies* 56 (6): 1345–61. https://doi.org/10.1111/jcms.12746.

De Cesari, C. 2017. "Museums of Europe: Tangles of Memory, Borders, and Race." *Museum Anthropology* 40 (1): 18–35. https://doi.org/10.1111/muan.12128.

Dinan, D. 2014. "The Historiography of European Integration." In *Origins and Evolution of the European Union*, 2nd ed., edited by D. Dinan, 345–75. Oxford: Oxford University Press.

Gillingham, J. 1991. *Coal, Steel, and the Rebirth of Europe, 1945–1955: The Germans and French from Ruhr Conflict to Economic Community.* Cambridge: Cambridge University Press.

Gillingham, J. 2003. *European Integration, 1950–2003: Superstate or New Market Economy?* Cambridge: Cambridge University Press.

Griffiths, R.T. 1996. "The Schuman Plan Negotiations: The Economic Clauses." In *The Reconstruction of the International Economy, 1945–1960*, edited by B. Eichengreen, 435–71. Cheltenham: Edward Elgar.

Hackett, C.P., ed. 1995. *Monnet and the Americans: The Father of a United Europe and His US Supporters.* Washington: Jean Monnet Council.

Kaiser, W., B. Leucht, and M. Rasmussen, eds. 2009. *The History of the European Union: Origins of a Trans- and Supranational Polity 1950–72.* London: Routledge.

Lipgens, W., W. Loth, and A.S. Milward. 1982. *A History of European Integration 1945–1947: The Formation of the European Unity Movement.* Oxford: Clarendon Press.

Ludlow, P. 2010. "History Aplenty: But Still Too Isolated." In *Research Agendas in EU Studies: Stalking the Elephant*, edited by M. Egan, N. Nugent, and W. Paterson, 14–36. Basingstoke, UK: Palgrave Macmillan.

Milward, A.S. 1984. *The Reconstruction of Western Europe, 1945–51.* London: Methuen.

Milward, A.S. 2000. *The European Rescue of the Nation-State.* London: Routledge.

Monnet, J. 1978. *Memoirs.* Translated by R. Mayne. Garden City: Doubleday.

Poidevin, R., ed. 1986. *Histoire des débuts de la construction européenne, mars 1948–mai 1950.* Brussels: Bruylant.

Schwabe, K. 1988. *The Beginnings of the Schuman Plan: Contributions to the Symposium in Aachen.* Baden-Baden: Nomos.

Ugland, T. 2011. *Jean Monnet and Canada: Early Travels and the Idea of European Unity.* Toronto: University of Toronto Press.

Urwin, D.W. 1991. *The Community of Europe: A History of European Integration since 1945.* London: Longman.

Verovšek, P.J. 2015. "Expanding Europe through Memory: The Shifting Content of the Ever-Salient Past." *Millennium – Journal of International Studies* 43 (2): 531–50. https://doi.org/10.1177/0305829814550325.

3

The Political Institutions of the European Union

Finn Laursen, Achim Hurrelmann, and Amy Verdun

READER'S GUIDE

This chapter provides an overview of the main executive and legislative institutions of the European Union (EU): the European Council, the European Commission, the Council of the EU, and the European Parliament (EP). Executive power in the EU is exercised by the European Council, where the heads of state or government meet to set political guidelines, and by the European Commission, which prepares policy proposals, monitors the implementation of legislation, and manages the EU's day-to-day operations. Legislative power in the EU is exercised by the EP and by the Council of the EU, which together form a **bicameral legislature**. The interplay of these institutions results in a political system that is characterized by extensive checks and balances and a consensus-oriented style of decision making.

INTRODUCTION

The European Union is in many ways a unique organization. As the introductory chapter to this book spells out, the EU has for decades been characterized as being less than a federal state, but more than an international organization or regime (Theme 2 of this book; see also Wallace 1983). These features are reflected in the EU's institutions. Some of them – such as the European Council, where member state leaders come together in summit-style meetings – have similarities with traditional diplomatic forums. Others – such as the European Parliament, which brings together democratically elected representatives of the EU's citizens – have clear parallels to institutions at the state level.

The unique shape of the EU's political system derives from the ambition to create an organization in which both the specific interests of each member state and the common interests of all Europeans are represented and protected. To achieve these objectives, the EU has created an institutional system with two core characteristics. The first is a high degree of *consensus orientation*: Decisions require the involvement of multiple institutions, and usually more than simple majorities, to prevent important interests from being overruled. The second is a *multilevel structure* that incorporates member states and EU-level institutions in decision making. This structure ensures that the EU works with the member states rather than against them (see Chapter 5). There are also advisory bodies representing interest groups and subnational regions that provide feedback on legislative proposals. The existence of this multilevel structure implies that there are multiple channels through which citizens can provide democratic input into EU decisions (see Chapter 15).

This chapter describes and analyzes the main institutions that form this political system. The chapter classifies these institutions in two ways (see Table 3.1). First, we examine the functions that they exercise, drawing on the distinction between executive and legislative institutions. (Judicial institutions are covered in Chapter 4.) In any given polity (that is, any organized society or political entity), executive institutions provide political leadership for a polity and manage its day-to-day operations. At the state level, these functions are exercised by the government and the bureaucracy. In the EU, the two executive institutions are the European Council, which provides political leadership, and the European Commission, which manages the EU's daily affairs. Legislative institutions represent the population and scrutinize the executive. They are responsible for passing laws of a polity (including the budget). At the state level, this function is exercised by parliaments. In the EU, the two legislative institutions are the Council of the EU and the European Parliament. There are some instances in which the functions of EU institutions cut across the executive–legislative divide, but it is nevertheless helpful to think about them in these general terms.

Table 3.1. The most important political institutions of the EU

	Main function	Composition
European Council	Executive (political leadership)	Intergovernmental (member state leaders)
European Commission	Executive (day-to-day administration)	Supranational (EU public servants)
Council of the EU	Legislative	Intergovernmental (member state ministers)
European Parliament	Legislative	Supranational (elected parliamentarians)

The second classification we use to make sense of EU institutions focuses on their composition. Here we distinguish between intergovernmental institutions, in which the governments of the member states are represented, and supranational institutions, which represent the EU as a whole. Among the institutions covered here, the European Council and the Council of the EU are intergovernmental institutions. Politicians representing the member states meet in these intergovernmental institutions to deliberate, negotiate, and make recommendations and decisions. By contrast, the European Commission and the EP are supranational institutions. Their members can make decisions without seeking approval from the member states. They are expected to represent the collective European interest. All four of these EU institutions have some features that blur the border between intergovernmental and supranational, but the distinction is of crucial importance to understand how they work.

THE EUROPEAN COUNCIL

The **European Council** is the meeting of heads of state or government of the member states.[1] It is thus an intergovernmental institution. Although there had been occasional summit meetings before, the creation of a more regular European Council started in 1974, following a proposal by French president Valéry Giscard d'Estaing. From 1975, this informal forum met three times a year but had no formal role. Between 1996 and 2007 the number of meetings increased to a minimum of four per year. Since 2008 there have been at least six meetings per year.

The European Council became a formal institution with the 2007 **Treaty of Lisbon**, which entered into force in 2009. That treaty states "[t]he European Council shall provide the Union with the necessary impetus and shall define the general political directions and priorities thereof" (Article 15 TEU). The European Council has also been tasked with determining "the strategic interests and objectives of the Union" for its external action (Article 22(1) TEU). It does not have a legislative role, but it will sometimes discuss highly contentious legislation and attempt to agree on guidelines that can inform the subsequent work of the legislative institutions (Council of the EU and EP). It is also responsible for nominating or appointing candidates for key leadership positions in the EU, for instance the president of the European Commission or the president of the European Central Bank (see Box 3.1).

BOX 3.1: KEY ROLES OF THE EUROPEAN COUNCIL

1 Deciding on the EU's overall direction and political priorities
2 Dealing with complex or sensitive issues that cannot be resolved at lower levels of intergovernmental cooperation
3 Defining the general guidelines for the EU's Common Foreign and Security Policy, taking into account EU strategic interests and defence implications
4 Nominating and appointing candidates to certain high-profile EU-level roles, such as the presidency of the European Commission

Source: http://europa.eu/about-eu/institutions-bodies/european-council/index_en.htm

---

In exercising these tasks, the European Council is assisted by the General Secretariat of the Council, an administrative body that it shares with the Council of the EU. Meetings are prepared by the Committee of Permanent Representatives, which brings together representatives of all member states who work for their respective delegations (called permanent representations) in Brussels.

Since the entry into force of the Treaty of Lisbon, all meetings of the European Council are held in Brussels. They are chaired by a full-time president, also based in Brussels. The current president of the European Council is Charles Michel, who had his first 2.5-year term from December 1, 2019, through June 1, 2022, and was subsequently re-elected for a second 2.5-year term. He previously served as prime minister of Belgium. His role is to call European Council meetings, set the agenda, and help the heads of state or government reach agreement. There are 29 members of the European Council: the 27 heads of state or government of the EU member states, the European Council president, and the president of the European Commission. Two other EU officials also take part in the meetings: the high representative of the union for foreign affairs and security policy (when issues pertaining to that portfolio are being discussed) and the secretary general of the Council. The president of the EP is usually invited to address the European Council at the beginning but is not a member.

The European Council normally decides by consensus, meaning that decisions are taken without a formal vote, provided there are no explicit objections. However, there are decisions that require an explicit vote with unanimous agreement, for instance the allocation of EP seats to the member states. And there are decisions that only require a simple majority; apart from rules of procedure this includes decisions to convene or not to convene a convention to examine amendments to the treaty under the ordinary revision procedure (Article 48 TEU). Finally, some decisions require a qualified majority vote, especially appointments (Commission, high representative, board of the European Central Bank). Decisions are communicated to the public through Presidency Conclusions and press conferences, not only by the president but also the national "heads," as they are usually called in Brussels. If a vote takes place, only the 27 heads of state or government have a vote (neither the European Council president nor the Commission president vote in that case).

THE EUROPEAN COMMISSION

While the European Council provides big-picture political leadership for the EU, the executive institution in charge of the EU's day-to-day operations is the **European Commission**. In a nation state, it would largely be comparable with the cabinet of ministers. The Commission dates back to the High Authority established for the European Coal and Steel Community (ECSC) in 1952. The two following Communities, the European Economic Community (EEC) and the European Atomic Energy Community (Euratom), each established an executive called the Commission in 1958. In the Merger Treaty of 1965 (in force from 1967), the three executives were merged into a single Commission for the three European Communities.

The Commission consists of one commissioner per member state, so the EU-27 today has 27 commissioners (including the Commission president). However, the commissioners do not formally represent the member states. They are expected to promote the general interests of the EU and should be completely independent from their home state. They may not seek or take instructions from any government. Because of this focus on the interests of the EU as a whole, rather than individual member states, the Commission is considered a supranational body. Still, the member states feel they are represented in an indirect way by someone who knows the country well and, in any case, they have access to the core of EU executive power through "their" commissioner. Smaller member states have often seen the Commission as a safeguard against the power of the large states.

Each commissioner has a portfolio of responsibilities. These can cut across the range of administrative **directorates-general (DGs)**. DGs are administrative subunits of the Commission, staffed by public servants. Currently there are 33 DGs. The College of Commissioners, composed of the 27 commissioners, meets weekly. Decisions can be made by a simple majority but are usually by consensus. The commissioners and their cabinets (staff in their personal office) are housed in the Berlaymont building in Brussels, but most of the policy staff is spread out in Brussels over 70 different buildings, and some staff are even in Luxembourg. In total, the Commission employs around 25,000 officials (including permanent and contract employees). Although this seems a large number, the Commission's workforce is small in relation to the EU's population (447 million people), and its salaries make up only a small part of the EU budget (see Box 3.2). As a comparison, in France (which has a population of 67 million), the finance ministry alone employs 140,000 staff.

The commissioners are appointed for a term of five years, which is aligned with the term of the EP. Since the Treaty of Lisbon, the EP "elects" the Commission, which happens in a two-step process. First, the president of the European Commission is selected. This step begins with the nomination of a candidate by the European Council, who must then be approved by the EP. If the EP does not elect the proposed candidate, the European Council has a month to come up with another candidate. When nominating

> **BOX 3.2: BUDGET OF THE EU INSTITUTIONS**
>
> - In the 2021 EU budget, €10.6 billion was allocated for the administrative expenditures of the EU institutions. That is about 6.5 per cent of the total EU budget.
> - Staff salaries and benefits as well as pension payments make up roughly three-quarters of the EU's administrative spending. The rest is spent on things like buildings, equipment, and operating expenditures.
> - Spending on salaries/benefits in the 2021 budget was €2.7 billion for the Commission (approximately 25,000 staff), €370 million for the European Council and Council, which share an administration (approximately 3,000 staff), and €1.1 billion for the EP (approximately 6,500 staff).
> - In 2021, €2.2 billion was allocated for pensions paid to people who have retired from jobs in the EU institutions.
>
> Source: Definitive adoption (EU, Euratom) 2021/417 of the European Union's general budget for the financial year 2021, https://eur-lex.europa.eu/eli/budget/2021/1/oj

a candidate, the European Council is obliged to "take into account" the outcome of the most recent EP election (Article 17(7) TEU), but it is not defined what exactly that means (see Chapter 15). After the Commission president has been elected, the second step is the selection of the other 26 commissioners. These are nominated by the governments of the member states and are assigned their portfolios by the Commission president in consultation with member state governments. Following that, the EP holds hearings to vet Commission candidates. During this process, it has sometimes rejected candidates when it found them "unqualified," thus affirming its powers in respect to the formation of the new Commission. After the hearings, the entire Commission, including the Commission president and the high representative for foreign affairs and security policy, has to be approved by the EP in a single vote of consent (Article 17(7) TEU). Once the Commission is in place, the EP has the power to force the Commission to resign by passing a so-called motion of censure; this requires a majority of two-thirds of the votes cast. This has been used as a threat but so far has never been implemented. However, in 1999 the Commission, at the time presided over by Jacques Santer, voluntarily resigned, pre-empting a vote of censure in the EP.

The Commission has a mix of responsibilities. These include proposing new legislation to the Council of the EU and the EP – a role that is legislative in character, but one that governments at the state level also frequently exercise, especially in parliamentary systems. The Commission's responsibilities also include drafting the budget and implementing it, administering policies, and making specific decisions (for instance in competition policy). It also negotiates agreements with so-called third countries (countries that are not a member of the EU). Finally, the Commission represents the EU externally in economic policy matters (see Box 3.3).

BOX 3.3: KEY ROLES OF THE COMMISSION

1 Proposing legislation to the EP and the Council of the EU
2 Managing EU policies and the budget
3 Monitoring the implementation of EU law (jointly with the Court of Justice)
4 Representing the European Union on the international stage, for example by negotiating agreements between the EU and other countries

Source: http://europa.eu/about-eu/institutions-bodies/european-commission/index_en.htm

---

When the Commission prepares legislative proposals, it usually consults with experts as well as interest organizations and other stakeholders. Legislation in the form of regulations and directives require a proposal from the Commission before the Council of the EU and the EP can adopt it (see Chapter 4). This "monopoly of initiative" allows the Commission to act both as an agenda setter and as a gate keeper. It does not extend, however, to the Common Foreign and Security Policy (CFSP), as the member states also have a right of initiative in this area. In the implementation of legislation, the Commission may be charged with passing so-called "delegated acts" or "implementing acts," which specify the piece of legislation in question. In addition, the Commission cooperates with and monitors the member states, whose bureaucratic agencies are usually tasked with the front-line implementation of EU legislation. If the Commission is of the opinion that a member state is not adequately implementing EU legislation, it will reach out to the member state government in question and may, ultimately, bring the matter to the Court of Justice of the EU (see Chapter 4). Since the member states play important roles in implementation, they are, in turn, represented in the Commission's activities in this respect through specialized committees (known as comitology committees).

The original conception of the role of the Commission was one of a supranational leader that would actively articulate goals and visions, and build coalitions of political actors and interest groups by exchanging concessions, engineering consent, and building support for the system. The extent to which the Commission has been able to play this role has varied over time. Recently, this leadership role has to some extent been taken over by the European Council; leadership has thus moved from the supranational more toward the intergovernmental realm.

THE COUNCIL OF THE EU

With respect to legislation, powers in the EU are also divided between an intergovernmental and a supranational institution. The main intergovernmental institution with legislative functions is the **Council of the European Union**. It is also called the "Council of Ministers," which was its formal name before the entry into force of the Maastricht Treaty, or just "the **Council**." The Council is composed of "a representative of each Member State at the ministerial level." The purpose of this rule is to make sure that the representative can commit the member state. Since the Treaty of Lisbon, it is spelled out that the Council, "jointly with the EP, exercise[s] legislative and budgetary functions" (Article 16 TEU).

Originally each of the three Communities established in the 1950s had their own Council of Ministers. The Merger Treaty of 1965 brought these together. Today, Council meetings take place in different (currently 10) configurations, which bring together different member state ministers, depending on their portfolios (see Box 3.4). The General Affairs Council has a coordinating role. The most important Council configurations, such as the Council of Economic and Finance Ministers, the Council of Agriculture and Fisheries Ministers, and the Foreign Affairs Council, usually meet once a month. The other Council configurations meet less frequently. Despite having different configurations, the Council acts as one body in a legal sense. This means that any Council can vote on proposals that would normally be voted on in another configuration, which may speed up the legislative process. Since 1993, the Council meets in public when it legislates. This change was introduced to increase transparency.

> **BOX 3.4: COUNCIL CONFIGURATIONS**
>
> General Affairs
> Foreign Affairs
> Economic and Financial Affairs
> Justice and Home Affairs
> Employment, Social Policy, Health and Consumer Affairs
> Competitiveness (internal market, industry, research, and space)
> Transport, Telecommunications and Energy
> Agriculture and Fisheries
> Environment
> Education, Youth, Culture and Sport
>
> Source: http://www.consilium.europa.eu/en/council-eu/configurations/

Council meetings are prepared by the **Committee of Permanent Representatives (COREPER)**. It meets in two configurations: COREPER I and COREPER II. The permanent representatives (equivalent to ambassadors, but not called ambassadors because such a designation is associated with interstate diplomacy) meet in COREPER II and their deputies in COREPER I. COREPER II is responsible for General Affairs, Foreign Affairs, Justice and Home Affairs, multiannual budget negotiations, structural and cohesion funds, institutional and horizontal questions, development policy and association agreements, accession, and intergovernmental conferences. COREPER

I is responsible for the internal market and competitiveness, the environment, employment, social policy, health, consumer affairs, transport, telecommunications, energy, fisheries, agriculture, education, youth, and culture. After receiving a legislative proposal from the Commission, COREPER divides them into A and B points for the Council. For A points, agreement is expected without debate in the Council. By contrast, B points include issues where no agreement has been reached in COREPER; it will thus be up to the Council to seek an agreement.

Working groups of national experts, some permanent, some ad hoc, are an important part of the Council system. The Council has a General Secretariat, shared with the European Council, which is headed by a secretary general who can play an important role in difficult negotiations. The secretariat gives the Council a collective memory. The secretariat is housed in the Europa building in Brussels, across from the Berlaymont building, where the Commission is based.

In the Council, the use of qualified majority voting (QMV) has now become the norm as the formal decision rule, which increases the efficiency of decision making. However, formal votes are often avoided because consensus is sought beforehand. A qualified majority is defined as "at least 55 per cent of the members of the Council, comprising at least fifteen of them and representing member states comprising at least 65 per cent of the population of the Union" (Article 16(3) TEU). This double majority system protects the interests of both small and large member states and prevents either group from outvoting the other. Apart from QMV there are some decisions that can be made by a simple majority, mostly procedural. For those votes each member state has one vote. There are other decisions that require **unanimity** (see Box 3.5). They mostly concern foreign policy and defence, but also taxation issues. Abstention does not hinder unanimity. It is estimated that roughly 80 per cent of Council decisions now fall under QMV. But in reality, there are relatively few votes, as a so-called "culture of consensus" leads member state representatives to seek mutually acceptable solutions whenever possible.

The presidency of the Council rotates every six months among the member states in a pre-established order (see Box 3.6). A representative of the member state that holds the presidency chairs the Council meetings, except for the Foreign Affairs Council, which is chaired by the high representative for foreign affairs and security policy when it does not deal with trade (on the role of the high representative, see Chapter 9). The meetings are held in

> **BOX 3.5: CYPRUS FLEXING ITS MUSCLES**
> Although most political decisions are agreed to amicably in the Council, there are situations where one or two member states block the others. In foreign policy matters, all member states need to agree to take joint action. From time to time, a small group can block a decision that a large majority favours. An example was in September 2020 when the EU foreign ministers wanted to impose sanctions on Belarus in response to human rights abuses against the opposition, which was protesting peacefully against the manipulation of the presidential elections. The plan was thwarted by the Cypriot government, which refused to agree to sanctions as it was hoping for EU action against Türkiye. Although the Cypriot government did not have a strong opinion on the sanctions against Belarus, it was using its veto as leverage to put more pressure on the other member states to impose restrictive measures on Türkiye. In this way, Cyprus, with only 0.2 per cent of the EU population, was able to block a decision of the EU by using its veto. A month later, a compromise was found. EU leaders delivered a stern warning to Türkiye that it would face EU punitive measures if undersea drilling continued. Cyprus lifted its opposition to sanctions against Belarus.

Brussels except in April, June, and October, when they are in Luxembourg. The Treaty of Lisbon attempted to increase cooperation between successive presidencies by creating a "trio" presidency. Three presidencies work together in 18-month periods. The pre-established order also determines the seating arrangement at the meeting table. At one end is the president, who does not vote. On their right side is another minister from the presidency country, who can vote, followed by the other member states around the table according to the agreed order. The Commission representative sits across from the president.

The Council is primarily a legislative institution, though it has some other tasks, for instance in implementing the EU's CFSP (see Box 3.7). When the Council acts in a legislative role, the EU treaties determine which legislative

> **BOX 3.6: MAIN TASKS OF THE PRESIDENCY OF THE COUNCIL**
>
> 1. Planning and chairing meetings in the Council and its preparatory bodies. This includes efforts to drive forward the Council's work on EU legislation, ensuring cooperation among member states. To do this, the presidency tries to act as an honest and neutral broker.
> 2. Representing the Council in relations with the other EU institutions. This role includes trying to reach agreement early on legislative files through "trilogues" with the EP and the Commission.
> 3. Working closely with the president of the European Council and the high representative of the union for foreign affairs and security (including chairing the Foreign Affairs Council when it deals with trade issues).
>
> Source: http://www.consilium.europa.eu/en/council-eu/presidency-council-eu

procedure applies. Since the entry into force of the Treaty of Lisbon, the **ordinary legislative procedure (OLP)** has become the norm. Under the OLP, the Council and the EP are co-equal legislators; both can make amendments to the Commission's legislative proposal, and both must agree on a single text for a legislative proposal to become law (see more detailed discussion below). The EU can therefore be described as a bicameral legislative system. Special legislative procedures apply in areas in which particularly sensitive issues of national sovereignty are at stake (for instance, tax harmonization or police cooperation).

THE EUROPEAN PARLIAMENT

The **European Parliament (EP)** is the supranational part of the EU's bicameral legislature. Its history goes back to the "Common Assembly" created for the ECSC in 1952. An assembly was also created for each of the other two Communities, the EEC and Euratom, which came into force in 1958.

> **BOX 3.7: KEY ROLES OF THE COUNCIL**
>
> 1. Passing EU laws – jointly with the European Parliament in most policy areas
> 2. Approving the EU's budget, jointly with the European Parliament
> 3. Defining and implementing the EU's CFSP based on guidelines set by the European Council
> 4. Encouraging coordination between the broad economic and social policies of the member states
> 5. Concluding international agreements between the EU and other countries or international organizations
>
> Source: http://europa.eu/about-eu/institutions-bodies/council-eu/index_en.htm

However, it was decided in the Convention on Certain Institutions Common to the European Communities that there would be one single assembly for the three Communities. When it first met in 1958, it decided to call itself the European Parliamentary Assembly. In 1962 it changed its name to European Parliament. The EP initially only had a consultative role, but its powers have been greatly expanded in successive treaty reforms.

Direct elections to the EP were foreseen in the three founding treaties. The ECSC treaty had mentioned them as a possibility (Article 20); the EEC Treaty made them an obligation (Article 138). It was only during the Paris summit in December 1974 (in combination with the decision to create the informal European Council mentioned above) that it was decided that direct elections should be arranged in the future. The first direct elections took place in June 1979. Until then, the members of the assembly/parliament were nominated by national parliaments from among their own members. Since 1979, elections to the EP have been held every five years. Turnout in these elections has usually been lower than in national elections. Despite the gradual empowerment of the EP, many voters did not consider EP elections to be very important. Issues that citizens care about – jobs, health, education, and pensions – largely remain national responsibilities (see Chapter 15). However, the most recent EP election in 2019 saw a significant increase in turnout (see Table 3.2).

Table 3.2. EP election turnout (%)

	1979	1981	1984	1987	1989	1994	1995	1996	1999	2004	2007	2009	2013	2014	2019
Belgium	91		92		91	91			91	91		90		90	88
Denmark	48		52		46	53			50	48		60		56	66
France	61		57		49	53			47	43		41		42	50
Germany	66		57		62	60			45	43		43		48	61
Italy	86		82		81	74			70	72		65		57	55
Ireland	64		48		68	44			50	59		59		52	50
Netherlands	58		51		47	36			30	39		37		37	42
Luxembourg	89		89		87	99			87	91		91		86	84
UK	32		33		36	36			24	39		35		36	37
Greece		81	81		80	73			70	63		53		60	59
Spain				69	55	59			63	45		45		44	60
Portugal				74	51	36			40	39		37		34	31
Sweden							42		39	38		46		51	55
Austria								68	40	42		46		45	60
Finland								58	30	39		39		39	41
Cyprus										73		50		44	45
Czechia										28		28		18	29
Estonia										27		44		37	38
Hungary										39		36		28	43
Latvia										41		54		30	34
Lithuania										48		21		47	53
Malta										82		79		75	73
Slovakia										17		20		13	23
Slovenia										28		28		25	29
Poland										21		25		24	46
Bulgaria											29	39		36	33
Romania											29	28		32	51
Croatia													21	25	30
EU total	62		59		58	57			50	45		43		43	51

Source: https://www.europarl.europa.eu/election-results-2019/en/turnout

The EP presently consists of 705 members. As the most populous member state, Germany has the maximum number of 96 members of the European Parliament (MEPs). The minimum number of six MEPs goes to the member states with the smallest populations: Cyprus, Estonia, Luxembourg, and Malta. This system for the apportionment of seats – called *degressive proportionality* – leads to a relative overrepresentation of the smaller member states (see Table 3.3). Malta has one seat per 86,000 inhabitants, whereas Germany has one seat per 866,000 inhabitants. By giving the smaller countries relatively more seats, the EU ensures that different political views can be represented in all countries.

The internal organization of the EP is similar to that of national parliaments. Most significantly, MEPs form political groups – caucuses, to use the Canadian terminology – that reflect their partisan/ideological convictions rather than their nationality. After the May 2019 elections, there were seven groups in the EP (see Figure 3.1), including one far-right group (Identity and Democracy) that is fundamentally opposed to European integration. A political group must have at least 25 MEPs from at least seven member states. Political groups help form compromises between various national positions; they vote in a fairly cohesive fashion in the legislative process. The EP elects a president for two and a half years at the beginning and mid-way in its five-year term. In recent periods the two largest political groups, the European People's Party and the Progressive Alliance of Socialists and Democrats in the EP, have often alternated the presidency between themselves.

In exercising its legislative function, the EP works mostly through its 20 committees. Legislative proposals from the Commission go straight to the relevant committee, which appoints a rapporteur in charge of drafting a report. The draft reports are debated and voted on in the plenary, which most often accepts the committee's report. EP plenary and committee meetings are public. Important meetings are attended by many stakeholders who are eager to influence the EP's position. The plenary meets most often in Strasbourg, France. The committees normally meet in Brussels. Part of the secretariat is based in Luxembourg. These rather costly arrangements, which are relics from past political choices rather than reflecting budgetary or administrative rationality, are criticized by most MEPs but defended strongly by France (which has the most to lose if the meetings in Strasbourg were scrapped). Since this arrangement is mentioned in the treaty, France has a veto against moving all meetings to Brussels.

As mentioned, the EP started out as an advisory and consultative body without the power to amend or reject legislation. In 1980, the Court of

Table 3.3. Seats in the European Parliament per member state as of February 1, 2020 (total 705 seats)

Member state	# of EP seats	% of EP seats	% of EU population	Member state	# of EP seats	% of EP seats	% of EU population
Germany	96	13.6	18.6	Bulgaria	17	2.4	1.6
France	79	11.2	15.0	Denmark	14	2.0	1.3
Italy	76	10.8	13.5	Finland	14	2.0	1.2
Spain	59	8.4	10.6	Slovakia	14	2.0	1.2
Poland	52	7.4	8.5	Ireland	13	1.8	1.1
Romania	33	4.7	4.3	Croatia	12	1.7	0.9
Netherlands	29	4.1	3.9	Lithuania	11	1.6	0.6
Belgium	21	2.8	2.6	Slovenia	8	1.1	0.5
Greece	21	2.8	2.4	Latvia	8	1.1	0.4
Czechia	21	2.4	2.4	Estonia	7	1.0	0.3
Portugal	21	2.8	2.3	Cyprus	6	0.9	0.2
Sweden	21	2.8	2.3	Luxembourg	6	0.9	0.1
Hungary	21	2.8	2.2	Malta	6	0.9	0.1
Austria	19	2.7	2.0	TOTAL	705	100.0	100.0

Sources: http://europa.eu/about-eu/institutions-bodies/european-parliament/index_en.htm#goto_1; https://ec.europa.eu/eurostat/documents/2995521/11081093/3-10072020-AP-EN.pdf/d2f799bf-4412-05cc-a357-7b49b93615f1

Figure 3.1. Party groups in the 9th European Parliament (2019–2024) (Group names and strength as of June 2021)

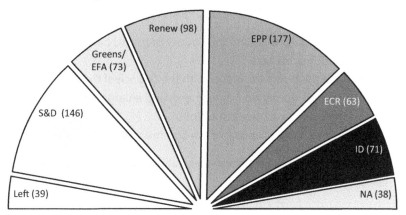

EPP: European People's Party (Christian Democrats)
S&D: Progressive Alliance of Socialists and Democrats in the European Parliament
ECR: European Conservatives and Reformists
Renew: Renew Europe
Left: The Left in the European Parliament
Greens/EFA: Greens/European Free Alliance
ID: Identity and Democracy
NA: Non-affiliated members
Source: Adapted from https://www.europarl.europa.eu/meps/en/search/table

Justice of the EU decided that the Council of the EU had to wait for the opinion from the EP where the treaties gave it the right to be consulted. The implication of this decision was that the EP could at least delay legislation, which gave the Council an interest in negotiating. The **Single European Act (SEA)** then introduced the so-called cooperation procedure, which gave the EP the power to amend some legislation; if this amendment was accepted by the Commission, the Council could only reject it by unanimity. The SEA also introduced the assent procedure (now called the consent procedure), which gave the EP the power to veto some legislation, especially association agreements and accession treaties. The next step in the empowerment of the EP was the introduction of the co-decision procedure by the Treaty of Maastricht. Subsequent treaty reforms have expanded the application of this procedure, which was named the ordinary legislative procedure in the Treaty of Lisbon. With the OLP, the EP has become a co-equal legislator on par with the Council. The Treaty of Lisbon has also given the EP the same powers as the Council in adopting the annual budget. In addition, as discussed above, the EP also has a role in appointing the Commission (see Box 3.8).

BOX 3.8: KEY ROLES OF THE EUROPEAN PARLIAMENT

1 Passing laws together with the Council of the EU based on Commission proposals
2 Adopting the budget together with the Council of the EU
3 Deciding on international agreements and enlargements
4 Scrutiny of the executive institutions
5 Appointment and dismissal of the Commission

Source: https://europa.eu/european-union/about-eu/institutions-bodies/european-parliament_en

---

Under the OLP, a proposal for legislation from the Commission goes to both the Council of the EU and EP (see Figure 3.2). Both can make amendments to the legislative proposal, and both must ultimately agree on a single text for it to become law. The OLP is designed to encourage compromise

The Political Institutions of the European Union 63

Figure 3.2. Ordinary legislative procedure (OLP), simplified

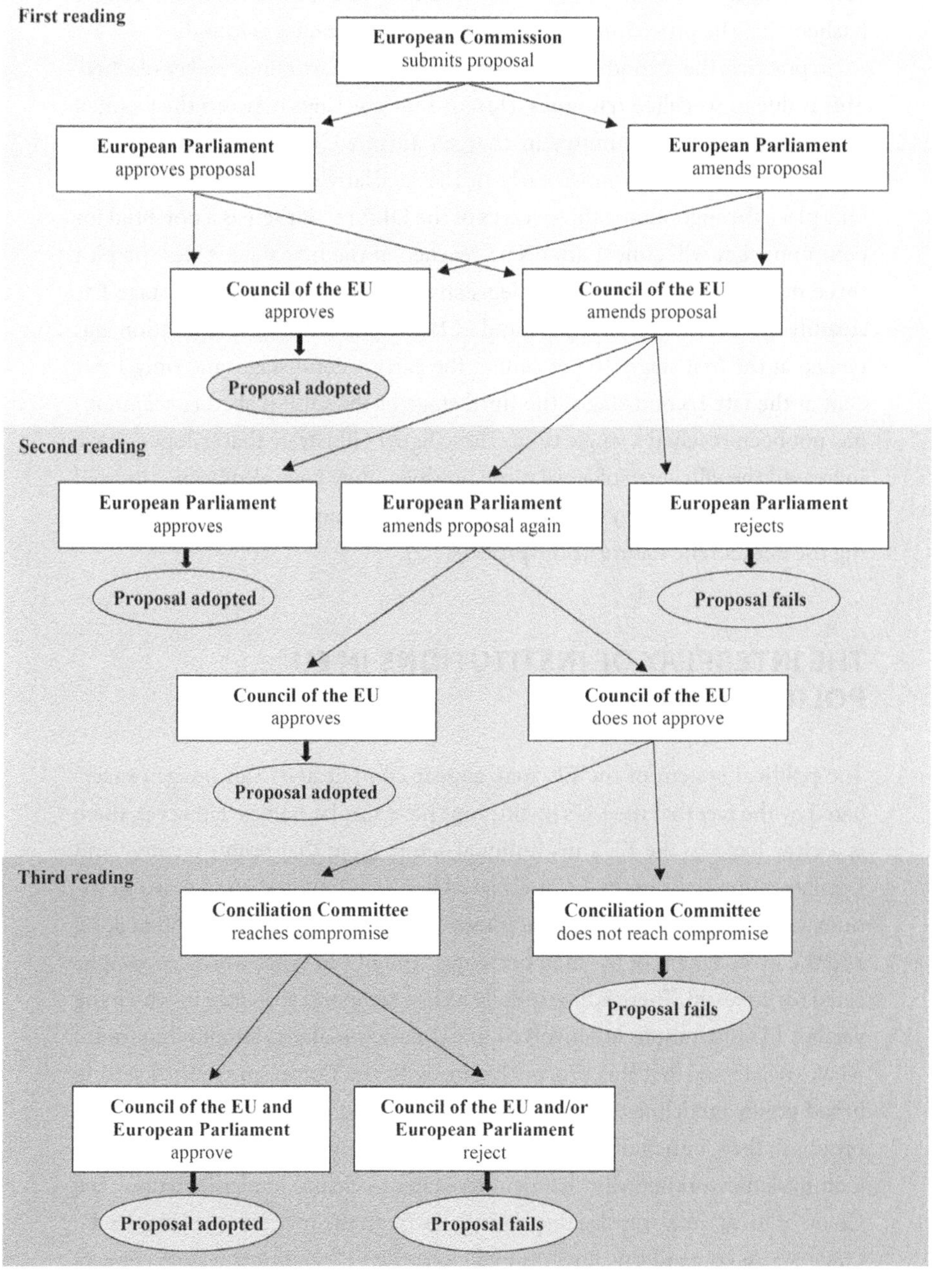

First reading

European Commission submits proposal

European Parliament approves proposal → Council of the EU approves → Proposal adopted

European Parliament amends proposal → Council of the EU amends proposal

Second reading

European Parliament approves → Proposal adopted

European Parliament amends proposal again → Council of the EU approves → Proposal adopted / Council of the EU does not approve

European Parliament rejects → Proposal fails

Third reading

Conciliation Committee reaches compromise → Council of the EU and European Parliament approve → Proposal adopted / Council of the EU and/or European Parliament reject → Proposal fails

Conciliation Committee does not reach compromise → Proposal fails

Source: Based on Article 294 TFEU

formation between the Council and the EP. This happens through three successive stages or "readings" in which mutually acceptable solutions can be hashed out. The procedure ends as soon as a compromise is found.

In practice, the second and third stage of the OLP are almost never reached. This is due to so-called **trilogues**, closed-door meetings between the Council presidency, the EP committee in charge, and the Commission that are designed to find a compromise early in the legislative process. Trilogues can take place throughout the three stages of the OLP, but if there is a potential for compromise it will almost always be reached at the first stage. Over the past three decades, the percentage of legislative files concluded at this stage has steadily increased. Between 2014 and 2019, 89 per cent of EU legislation was passed at the first stage, 10 per cent at the early second stage, and only 1 per cent at the late second stage. The third stage of the OLP (called *conciliation*) has not been reached a single time. These figures illustrate that trilogues have increased the efficiency of legislation; however, they have also been criticized for limiting transparency and broader deliberation and thus negatively affecting the democratic nature of the process.

THE INTERPLAY OF INSTITUTIONS IN EU POLICY-MAKING

The political system of the EU may appear complicated – an image exacerbated by the fact that the EU's institutions have similar names. However, there is a clear logic to the EU's institutional setup. Note that both executive and legislative functions in the EU are shared between intergovernmental and supranational institutions. This guarantees consensus-oriented decision making and the involvement of the member states. The EU, in other words, is complicated for a reason. There is also usually a clear temporal sequence in which the various EU institutions are involved in EU policy-making. Simplifying somewhat, we can say that this process begins with the European Council setting broad policy guidelines, followed by the Commission presenting a legislative proposal, the Council of the EU and the EP passing legislation, and then the Commission working with the member states to ensure implementation. The Court of Justice may resolve disputes that arise in the process (see Chapter 4). Once we understand this institutional logic, the EU's political system appears less opaque.

DEBATE: EFFICIENCY, SOLIDARITY, AND LEADERSHIP

The consensus-oriented nature of the EU's political system may slow down political decision making; sometimes it even results in stalemate. This trade-off between efficiency and the adequate representation of various interests and perspectives – including those of the member states – is as old as the European integration process itself. The founding fathers emphasized efficiency when they established the original Communities in the 1950s. The Commission was supposed to play a lead role as the engine of European integration. Jean Monnet's first proposal to the 1950 Paris Intergovernmental Conference, which negotiated the ECSC treaty, did not even have a Council. It did include a parliamentary assembly, albeit a weak one. The representatives of the Benelux countries, however, made a Council of Ministers a non-negotiable part of the initial institutional setup.

Subsequent treaties gradually increased the powers of the Council of the EU and, as we have seen, the European Council was added in 1974, first as an informal institution and later, in 2009, as a formal institution. These changes strengthened the intergovernmental institutions, arguably improving checks and balances on the supranational Commission, but weakening it at the same time. In parallel, with some time lag, the EP started to become more of a real parliament with important budgetary and legislative powers. This empowerment of the EP has been explained by pointing to the need to provide more procedural (or input) legitimacy as the functional scope of European integration increased and the role of national parliaments was reduced.

Two referendums were held in 1992 that changed the way the EU looked at including citizens and communication about the EU to the public. When the Danish citizens first rejected the Treaty of Maastricht in 1992 and the French citizens barely accepted it in a referendum, a major debate started about transparency and democracy in the EU. Several observers claimed that there was a "democratic deficit" (see Chapter 15). One approach to address this deficit was to include provisions on the role of national parliaments into the treaties. National parliaments are now tasked with overseeing the application of the principle of subsidiarity, which prescribes that decisions must be taken at the lowest level where they can be "sufficiently achieved" (Article 5 TEU). It was argued that national parliaments, being closer to the people, were necessarily more legitimate than the EP. However, increasing the powers of 27 national parliaments even more in the future will probably not increase the efficiency of decision making in the EU. In reality, the EU has many decision makers, because power is dispersed. As a result, decision making is often a cumbersome process because of many national veto points.

This insight suggests that there is still an issue of efficiency in the current institutional setup. It is a complex system, difficult to understand for EU citizens, and possibly even more difficult for citizens in third countries. However, the EU is a union of nation states with long traditions of being in charge of their own affairs. Building up strong supranational institutions therefore is a difficult process. There are forces that pull toward greater national autonomy, and at the same time forces that pull in the direction of stronger, more efficient common institutions.

The decision making in connection with the refugee crisis, which exploded in 2015, serves as an example (see Chapter 8). Southern European states, Greece and Italy in particular, were overwhelmed by the number of refugees. Many of these refugees started travelling further north, especially to Germany and Scandinavia. Some countries closed their borders to refugees. The Commission stepped in and suggested reallocation schemes, according to which all member states should take in a certain quota of refugees. Many member states opposed this quota system, especially the member states in Central and Eastern Europe. It looks as if successive enlargements have made it more difficult to have sufficient solidarity among the member states to make difficult decisions.

The lack of solidarity, according to some observers, was also an issue during the euro area debt crisis, where the EU took a very long time to agree on rescue packages for **euro area** member states in risk of bankruptcy (see Chapter 7). Richer member states worried about the conditions under which emergency financing and bailouts would take place. But the delay of decisions contributed to a worsening of the crisis, which in turn led to complaints about a lack of solidarity with the members hit hardest by that crisis, especially Greece. In the end, agreements were eventually made that in many ways have deepened integration.

It is exactly during times of crisis that the question of leadership becomes decisive. After the June 2016 UK referendum on EU membership (Brexit), the EU's leaders – European Council presidents Donald Tusk (until 2019) and Charles Michel (since 2019), Commission presidents Jean-Claude Juncker (until 2019) and Ursula von der Leyen (since 2019), but especially chief Brexit negotiator Michel Barnier – managed to keep up a united front of the remaining member states in the negotiations with the UK about a post-Brexit settlement. This unity allowed the EU to achieve most of its priorities. The conclusion can only be that efficient decision making in the EU requires a high degree of solidarity as well as efficient leadership.

CONCLUSION

The EU's political institutions have changed gradually over time. The most recent major treaty reform, the Treaty of Lisbon, introduced an elected president of the European Council. It also strengthened the role of the EP in the legislative process and in "electing" the president of the Commission. In legislation, co-decision has become the ordinary legislative procedure, indicating that it is now the procedure used most often. With the reforms of the Treaty of Lisbon, the political system of the EU has become more similar to that of a federal state, such as Canada – but key differences remain (see Box 3.9).

BOX 3.9: COMPARISON WITH CANADA

If we compare the EU and Canada, they are both polities with legislative powers on at least two levels of governance. Both are fairly decentralized systems, but the member states in the EU play a much greater political role in decision making at the central level than the provinces in Canada, especially because the Canadian provinces are not represented in a legislative chamber at the federal level. Executive leadership in the EU is more dispersed than in Canada, where the most powerful politician is the prime minister. In the EU, the president of the Commission has to share the limelight with the president of the European Council and the rotating presidency of the Council. Canada has a purer parliamentary system than the EU, although the EU has been moving slightly in that direction with the EP now "electing" the president of the Commission.

	EU	Canada
Executive leadership	The Commission is the main executive body. The president of the Commission can be compared with a prime minister in a nation state. The president of the European Council might be seen as a kind of head of state. The rotating presidency of the Council also has some executive functions. → Dispersed executive leadership	The focus is clearly on the prime minister as the leading politician and head of the federal government. → Focused executive leadership
Legislation	The EU now has a bicameral system, with both the Council of the EU and EP having legislative powers (OLP). They also have equal powers in the budgetary process. (A better comparison than Canada is the German federal system, with the directly elected Bundestag and the Bundesrat, where the 16 Land governments are represented, with the bigger Länder having more seats than the smaller ones.)	Canada does have a bicameral system (inspired by Britain), but the elected House of Commons has more powers than the appointed Senate. Bills will be considered and passed by the Senate, but only after passage by the House of Commons. The Canadian provinces are not represented in a legislative chamber at the federal level (which is rather exceptional for a federal system).
Citizen identities in the multilevel polity	Most citizens in the EU feel connected to the EU level that governs them in important ways. However, few have strong "European" identification or identify primarily as a "European citizen." Most citizens feel the closest connection to the nation state to which they belong. Many citizens feel a strong sense of connection to the regional or local level, but they expect most policies and services to come from the national government.	Many Canadians typically feel a sense of belonging to Canada. Some Indigenous Peoples do not identify at all with Canada. Most Canadians feel a sense of belonging to the provincial or territorial level. Few citizens identify first and foremost with the local level. Some citizens, in particular Indigenous Peoples, feel first and foremost a connection to their nation, based locally on their land, customs, and culture.

Source: Compiled by the authors based on various Eurobarometer surveys and the Canadian Environics Institute (https://www.environicsinstitute.org/docs/default-source/project-documents/confederation-of-tomorrow-2019-survey---report-1/confederation-of-tomorrow-survey-2019---report-1-pulling-together-or-drifting-apart---final-report.pdf?sfvrsn=9abc2e3e_2)

In the post-Lisbon situation, we can ask whether a lasting "constitutional" settlement has been reached. EU political leaders are reluctant to embark on a major treaty change because the process of obtaining approval of the revised text is cumbersome and securing treaty ratification can be fraught with challenges. However, the question of legitimacy of the current settlement remains, as the EU keeps facing challenges. Will the EU succeed in solving its problems as a group and possibly integrate deeper, or will some states not want to participate in much more than is currently the case? In the latter case, will a "hard core" of states move ahead toward "an ever-closer union among the peoples of Europe" (to use the language in Article 1 TEU) and leave the laggards behind? That would increase the already great amount of differentiation and multi-speed integration, which may make decision making even more difficult.

REVIEW QUESTIONS

1. What are the main executive and legislative institutions in the EU?
2. What is the difference between intergovernmental and supranational institutions? Who is represented by each type of institution?
3. Why are executive and legislative powers in the EU divided between one intergovernmental and one supranational institution?
4. Why is there sometimes tension in the EU's political system between efficient decision making and the protection of member state perspectives? Explain why solidarity between member states and leadership by EU personnel are essential features for resolving this tension.

EXERCISES

1. Do some research on the history of unanimous voting versus qualified majority voting in the Council. What are the strengths and weaknesses of using QMV? Draw a parallel to a familiar group setting in your own life (classroom, work setting, campus

> organization) – when should efficiency be prioritized and when should representation be prioritized?
> 2 Compare the EP to the Canadian House of Commons. What are the main similarities and differences? How does this translate to the idea of the EU being a quasi-federation?

NOTE

1 Notice the word *or*. Most countries send their prime minister (head of government; the federal chancellor in the case of Germany), but a few, especially France, send their president (head of state). The European Council should not be simply called "Council" since the latter term is reserved for the Council of the EU. The European Council should not be confused with the Council of Europe, a weaker intergovernmental organization created in 1949 that focuses on human rights (see Chapter 4). Other than having many overlapping member states, the Council of Europe has nothing to do with the EU as such.

REFERENCES AND FURTHER READING

Best, E. 2014. *EU Law-Making in Principle and Practice*. London: Routledge.
Coombes, D.L. 1970. *Politics and Bureaucracy in the European Community: A Portrait of the Commission of the E.E.C.* London: Allen & Unwin.
European Parliament. 2020. *Handbook on the Ordinary Legislative Procedure*. https://www.europarl.europa.eu/cmsdata/215107/OLP_2020_EN.pdf.
Hayes-Renshaw, F. 2017. "The Council of Ministers: Conflict, Consensus and Continuity." In *The Institutions of the European Union*, 4th ed., edited by J. Peterson and D. Hodson, 80–107. Oxford: Oxford University Press.
Hayes-Renshaw, F., and H. Wallace. 2006. *The Council of Ministers*, 3rd ed. Basingstoke, UK: Palgrave Macmillan.
Hix, S. 2008. *What's Wrong with the European Union and How to Fix It*. Cambridge: Polity Press.
Hix, S., and B.K. Høyland. 2011. *The Political System of the European Union*, 3rd ed. Basingstoke, UK: Palgrave Macmillan.
Kassim, H., J. Peterson, M.W. Bauer, S. Connolly, R. Dehousse, L. Hooghe, and A. Thompson. 2013. *The European Commission of the Twenty-First Century*. Oxford: Oxford University Press.
Laursen, F. 1996. "The Role of the Commission." In *The European Union: How Democratic Is It?*, edited by S. Andersen and K. Eliassen, 119–41. London: SAGE.
Laursen, F. 2016. *Historical Dictionary of the European Union*. Lanham, MD: Rowman and Littlefield.

Lelieveldt, H., and S. Princen. 2013. *The Politics of the European Union*. Cambridge: Cambridge University Press.

Lindberg, L., and S. Scheingold. 1970. *Europe's Would-Be Polity: Patterns of Change in the European Community*. Englewood Cliffs, NJ: Prentice-Hall.

Piris, J. 2010. *The Lisbon Treaty: A Legal and Political Analysis*. Cambridge: Cambridge University Press.

Puetter, U. 2014. *The European Council and the Council: New Intergovernmentalism and Institutional Change*. Oxford: Oxford University Press.

Rittberger, B. 2005. *Building Europe's Parliament: Democratic Representation beyond the Nation-State*. Oxford: Oxford University Press.

Roederer-Rynning, C. 2019. "Passage to Bicameralism: Lisbon's Ordinary Legislative Procedure at Ten." *Comparative European Politics* 17 (6): 957–73. https://doi.org/10.1057/s41295-018-0141-2.

Scharpf, F. 1999. *Governing in Europe: Effective and Democratic?* Oxford: Oxford University Press.

Shackleton, M. 2017. "The European Parliament." In *The Institutions of the European Union*, 4th ed., edited by D. Hodson and J. Peterson, 138–62. Oxford: Oxford University Press.

Tallberg, J. 2006. *Leadership and Negotiation in the European Union*. Cambridge: Cambridge University Press.

Teasdale, A., and T. Bainbridge. 2012. *The Penguin Companion to European Union*, 4th ed. London: Penguin Books.

Wallace, W. 1983. "Less than a Federation, More than a Regime: The Community as a Political System." In *Policy Making in the European Communities*, 2nd ed., edited by H. Wallace, W. Wallace, and C. Webb, 403–36. London: Wiley.

4

Legal Integration and the Court of Justice of the European Union

Martha O'Brien and Eszter Bodnár

READER'S GUIDE

This chapter offers an introduction to the legal foundations of the European Union (EU), the EU's legislative and judicial methods for achieving legal integration, and the role of the Court of Justice of the European Union (CJEU) in the creation of the EU's legal system. The EU is recognized as having evolved its own legal system, unique among legal systems in the world, through which the national (and subnational) laws of the member states are integrated with EU law. The body of law governing the EU and its member states and peoples is called the *acquis communautaire*. This chapter describes the sources and fundamental principles of EU law, the types of EU legislation, and the role of the CJEU in interpreting and applying EU law.

INTRODUCTION

The process of creating first a Common Market and later a union of member states and peoples is economic, political, and above all legal. It can be argued that the progressive integration that has created the EU has always depended on legal evolution, both through legislative and judicial advances as well as political impetus. The original treaties of the 1950s were broadly drafted and left many open questions as to how to attain their objectives. The creation of the EU of today depended not only on political will but also on a purposive judicial interpretation of the treaties and the legislation adopted by the institutions that could be enforced as law. Neighbouring countries in other regions of the world, such as North America, East Asia, and South America,[1] have attempted to create relationships of similar economic, political, and legal integration, but none have progressed to anything like the EU. We can therefore ask what role the types of legal instruments and fundamental judicial decisions have played in advancing legal integration. How does legal evolution affect and respond to the political and economic context and events?

PRIMARY LAW: THE TREATIES

The EU is founded on two multilateral international conventions: the **Treaty on European Union (TEU)** and the **Treaty on the Functioning of the European Union (TFEU)**. The EU is thus a creation of international law; its actions and decisions are governed by and subject to the **rule of law**. The TEU and TFEU are the current names for the founding treaties as they have been added to and amended over the years since the original Treaty of Paris was agreed in 1951 (see Table 4.1).

The treaties can be seen as the "constitutional law" of the EU, even though they are theoretically distinct from a state-like constitution. As they are the supreme law of the EU, any action by either EU institutions or member states that is inconsistent with the treaties is in principle illegal and can be declared ineffective by the EU courts. The treaties lay out the fundamental principles of EU law. TEU Article 2 expresses ideals that are commonly found in a national constitution:

> The Union is founded on the values of respect for human dignity, freedom, democracy, equality, the rule of law and respect for human rights, including the rights of persons belonging to minorities. These values are common to the member states in a society in which pluralism, non-discrimination, tolerance, justice, solidarity and equality between women and men prevail.

Another example of an important EU legal principle is found in Article 5 TEU, which establishes the "principle of conferral." This principle – meaning

Table 4.1. Development of EU primary law

Agreement name, date	Result for primary law, entry into force
Treaty of Paris, 1951	Created the European Coal and Steel Community, 1952 (lapsed 2002)
Treaty of Rome, 1957	Created the European Economic Community and the European Atomic Energy Community (Euratom), 1958
Single European Act, 1985	Amended the EEC Treaty, 1987
Treaty of Maastricht, 1992	Created the Treaty on European Union; amended the EEC Treaty, renaming it the Treaty Establishing the European Community (TEC), 1993
Treaty of Amsterdam, 1997	Amended the TEU and the TEC, 1999
Treaty of Nice, 2000	Amended the TEU and the TEC, 2003
Treaty of Lisbon, 2007	Amended the TEU; amended the TEC and renamed it the Treaty on the Functioning of the European Union (TFEU); Charter of Fundamental Rights of the European Union brought into force, 2009

that the EU cannot determine its own competences, but can only exercise powers explicitly delegated by the member states – is one of the factors that distinguishes the EU from a state (Theme 2 of this book).

The **Charter of Fundamental Rights of the EU** is also of great importance. Its legal force is equal to the treaties, and it is part of the **primary law** with the Treaty of Lisbon. However, long before the Charter was adopted, the CJEU had recognized certain general principles of EU law that protected fundamental human rights within the EU. For example, the CJEU acknowledged at an early stage of the development of EU law that the EU recognized the principle of equality and a general prohibition of discrimination.

SECONDARY LAW: ACTS OF THE EU INSTITUTIONS

One of the innovative features of the EU, which distinguishes it from other international organizations such as the World Trade Organization or the United Nations, is that the EU has its own legislative institutions, empowered to adopt legislative "acts" ("statutes" or "regulations" in Canada) that directly or indirectly constitute enforceable law in the member states. The primary legislative institutions of the EU are the Commission, the Council, and the European Parliament (see Chapter 3). The main types of legislative acts are provided for in Article 288 TFEU: regulations, directives, decisions, recommendations, and opinions.

Regulations are binding in their entirety and "directly applicable." This means that from the time they enter into force, they are automatically enforceable in the legal systems of the member states; they do not need to be transposed into national law. The national courts must apply a regulation as if it were part of the national law. Regulations are commonly used for technical changes to existing policies, such as changes to prices or quotas under the Common Agricultural Policy, but have also been used to put in place basic common rules for creating the Single Market or to impose new rules and standards in any policy area (see Box 4.1 for an example).

BOX 4.1: EXAMPLE OF A REGULATION
Regulation (EEC) No. 1612/68 on the free movement of workers within the Community, adopted by the Council in October 1968, is an example of a regulation enacting fundamental rules to create the Common Market. Article 1 of the Regulation provides as follows:

> Any national of a member state shall, irrespective of his place of residence, have the right to take up an activity as an employed person, and to pursue such activity, within the territory of another member state in accordance with the provisions laid down by law, regulation or administrative action governing the employment of nationals of that state.

Directives are commonly used to harmonize the member states' laws on a particular matter, a process also referred to as "approximation of laws." A directive sets out rules and standards that must be put in place in each member state, so that the same rules and standards apply uniformly throughout the EU. A period of time is prescribed in the directive during which the member states' legislatures must adopt the rules and standards as part of their national or subnational legal systems, a process called *transposition* of a directive into national law (see Box 4.2). Failure to transpose the directive's provisions by the deadline, or failure to do so correctly, constitutes a breach of the member state's obligations under the treaties. The Commission is responsible for ensuring that member states transpose directives and may bring an action against a member state that fails to do so before the General Court (discussed below).

> **BOX 4.2: EXAMPLE OF A DIRECTIVE**
> An example of a directive is Directive (EU) 2016/680, which protects the personal information of individuals and provides rules for processing such personal data by competent authorities for the purposes of the prevention, investigation, detection, or prosecution of criminal offences or the execution of criminal penalties, and on the free movement of such data. The directive was adopted by the Council and Parliament on April 27, 2016. The member states had until May 6, 2018, to transpose the directive into their national laws.

Decisions are a third type of binding legislative act. A decision specifies to whom it is addressed, and it is binding only on the addressees (e.g., specific member states, individuals, companies, agencies, or institutions). The EU institution having competence in a policy area, usually the Council or the Commission, may adopt a decision as provided for in the treaties (for example, in the context of competition or state aid). The Commission may have been delegated the authority to make a decision providing details of implementation of a regulation or directive that sets out only a broad framework.

Article 288 TFEU also describes two non-binding types of acts: the **recommendation** and the **opinion**. The Commission often makes recommendations to member states or to the other institutions as to how to move forward to achieve policy goals in a particular area where binding legislation is either not within the EU's competence or the necessary support in Council or Parliament for a binding legislative act cannot be achieved. Recommendations may be used in the context of "soft law" instruments, which the EU often uses to shape policy in the absence of binding EU legislation (see Chapter 5).

FUNDAMENTAL PRINCIPLES OF EU LAW

Legal integration has been a crucial part of the development of the EU. While the EU was created in the international law sphere by the founding treaties, the EU is a supranational organization with international legal personality: Its institutions are empowered to adopt legal acts that are binding on the member states and enforceable in their legal systems, mainly without any action on their side. In the last decades, the scope of EU law has become broader and the integration deeper. New member states, before joining the EU, have to undergo a multiyear harmonization process to eliminate acts and regulations in their legal system that are not in compliance with EU law.

This integration of the member states' legal systems with EU law is complemented by two fundamental principles of EU law: **direct effect** and **supremacy** of EU law. These legal principles were laid down by the CJEU in the early 1960s. At the time, the Common Market was in the process of being created, and member states were required to remove barriers in their laws to the free movement of goods, services, persons, and, to a lesser extent, capital (see Chapter 7). The Commission and Council were engaged in the early stages of the process of positive harmonization of member state laws through the adoption of regulations and directives.

The principle of direct effect holds that an EU provision that is clear, precise, and unconditional can confer legal rights on individuals that are enforceable in the courts of the member states. The free movement of goods and the right of establishment were economic rights in the EEC Treaty that the Court recognized as having direct effect, so that laws of the member states that restricted these rights were, in principle, unenforceable, even where no harmonizing legislation had been adopted. Any person could bring action against such laws in the national courts to obtain a declaration that the national law restricting a right of free movement was unenforceable. In this way, private individuals and companies joined forces with the Commission to use judgments of the Court to help construct the Single Market, even where the necessary political will did not exist.

In perhaps its best-known judgment from 1963, *NV Algemene Transport en Expeditie Onderneming van Gend & Loos v. Netherlands Inland Revenue Administration* (or *Van Gend en Loos*), the CJEU ruled in favour of a private company that alleged that an increase in the import tariff applied by the Netherlands to certain goods imported from Germany violated the EEC Treaty's guarantees of free movement of goods between member states. The Court found that the treaty prohibition on increases in tariff rates was clear, precise, and unconditional and made far-reaching statements about the nature of the EU legal system, distinguishing it from the existing conception of the enforceability of treaties in international law:

> The objective of the EEC Treaty, which is to establish a Common Market, the functioning of which is of direct concern to interested parties in the Community, implies that this Treaty is more than an agreement which merely creates mutual obligations between the contracting states....

> [T]he [European Economic] Community constitutes a new legal order of international law for the benefit of which the states have limited their sovereign rights, albeit within limited fields, and the subjects of which comprise not only member states but also their nationals. Independently of the legislation of member states, Community law therefore not only imposes obligations on individuals but is also intended to confer upon them rights which become part of their legal heritage.

In these famous words, the CJEU established the principle of direct effect, recognizing the right of the citizens of Europe to enforce their rights under EU law against laws made by their own governments and in their own courts.

Only a year after *Van Gend en Loos*, the Court laid down the principle of supremacy of EU law over inconsistent laws of the member states in the case of *Costa v. ENEL*. Mr. Costa challenged an Italian law enacted in 1962 nationalizing electricity production and distribution companies into a single state-owned company, ENEL. The government of Italy defended the law, saying that under the Italian constitution, Parliament has the power to pass a law that conflicts with its obligations under an international treaty, such as the EEC Treaty. As a matter of Italian constitutional law, the 1962 law was valid as a later enacted law, which is taken to be an implied repeal of the prior Italian law that ratified the treaty. Italy might be in breach of its obligations to the other member states as a matter of international law, but under Italian domestic law, applicable to private parties and entities such as Mr. Costa and ENEL, the 1962 law was valid and enforceable in the Italian courts. The Italian Constitutional Court held that the hierarchy of law according to Italian constitutional law applied, so the treaty obligation could not prevent the Italian legislature from passing a valid and enforceable domestic law. The Court of Justice disagreed:

> By contrast with ordinary international treaties, the EEC Treaty has created its own legal system which, on the entry into force of the Treaty, became an integral part of the legal systems of the member states, and which their courts are bound to apply....
>
> The integration into the laws of each member state of provisions which derive from the Community, and more generally the terms and the spirit of the Treaty, make it impossible for the states, as a corollary, to accord precedence to a unilateral and subsequent measure over a legal system accepted by them on the basis of reciprocity. Such a

measure cannot therefore be inconsistent with that legal system. The executive force of Community law cannot vary from one State to another in deference to subsequent domestic laws, without jeopardizing the attainment of the objectives of the Treaty....

It follows from all these observations that the law stemming from the Treaty, an independent source of law, could not, because of its special and original nature, be overridden by domestic legal provisions, however framed, without being deprived of its character as Community law and without the legal basis of the Community itself being called into question.

In making such clear statements in such forceful language about the relationship of EU law to national law, the CJEU established the doctrine of supremacy (also called primacy) of EU law. The doctrine holds that member states may not enact or enforce laws that are inconsistent with the treaty or with secondary EU law. The principles of EU law penetrate the national legal order, so that even the constitutional principles governing the national legal order of the member state concerned must give way. Supremacy is necessary to ensure that EU law is uniformly applicable throughout the EU, so that the objectives of the EU can be attained. The principle of supremacy was affirmed in Declaration 17 to the Treaty of Lisbon.

THE COURT OF JUSTICE OF THE EUROPEAN UNION: OVERVIEW

The **Court of Justice of the European Union** derives its jurisdiction directly from the treaties. From a legal perspective, it is impossible to overstate the impact that the Court has had on the evolution of the EU. The judgments of the CJEU are a source of binding EU law and form part of the *acquis communautaire*. Because of its role as the final, supreme interpreter of EU law, the CJEU controls both EU institutions and the member states.

The CJEU has forcefully used its jurisdiction, often at the behest of the Commission or a private party, to "constitutionalize" the treaties. This means that it has interpreted the treaties in an expansive way in numerous fundamental rulings, thus creating a constitutional structure and set of norms based on the rule of law and the recognition of fundamental rights of individuals. It has firmly asserted its jurisdiction to review the validity of EU acts, to control the exercise of power by the other EU institutions, to ensure the application of

EU law on the territory of the member states, and to delineate the division of competences between EU institutions and national legislatures.

The CJEU has grown immensely in size and importance; accordingly, its structure has been revised on several occasions since its creation in 1952. It was originally a single seven-judge panel for resolving disputes among the six founding member states of the European Coal and Steel Community. After the EEC came into being in 1958, the jurisdiction of the Court expanded to include almost all policy areas, and its influence over the evolution of EU law and its legal system became definitive. The Court has demonstrated that it has a distinct view of its role as ensuring that the objectives of the EU treaties are attained. It considers that it must ensure that the EU remains founded on and governed by law. In its judgments, it has emphasized the protection of free movement rights and the fundamental human rights of individuals under EU law in order to give real effect to these rights.

The number of cases the Court heard each year increased quickly, so in 1988 the Council created a second level of court, the Court of First Instance,

---

BOX 4.3: STRUCTURE OF EU COURTS

Article 19 TEU sets out the structure of the EU courts and the role of the EU judiciary to uphold the rule of law within the EU:

1 The Court of Justice of the European Union shall include the Court of Justice, the General Court and specialised courts. It shall ensure that in the interpretation and application of the Treaties the law is observed....
2 The Court of Justice shall consist of one judge from each member state. It shall be assisted by Advocates-General. The General Court shall include at least one judge per member state....

It is important to recall that the other significant European regional international court, the **European Court of Human Rights (ECtHR)** is *not* an EU institution; rather, it is governed by the Council of Europe. Created in 1959, it rules on individual or state applications alleging violations of the civil and political rights set out in the European Convention on Human Rights. The ECtHR and the CJEU are influenced by each other in the field of fundamental rights protection.

now called the General Court (see Box 4.3). The General Court originally had jurisdiction to hear appeals from decisions of the Commission in competition and state aid cases, and disputes between EU civil servants and their employer. Its jurisdiction has been broadened gradually with each amendment of the treaties, but there are still certain types of cases reserved for the Court of Justice, the highest-ranking court. In addition, the Court of Justice hears appeals from the General Court on a point of law, as well as the special categories of cases reserved to it.

As of 2022 there are 27 judges of the Court of Justice (one from each member state) and 54 judges of the General Court (two from each member state). The Court of Justice may sit in a Grand Chamber of 13 judges or smaller chambers of three to five judges; the General Court also sits in smaller chambers. Twenty-three official languages may be used at hearings. The Court of Justice also comprises 11 advocates-general whose role is to give impartial, independent, but non-binding opinions on the cases that come before the Court. The advocates-general have the same status and rank as the judges, and their opinions are valuable in understanding the factual and legal context of the dispute and the opposing arguments presented in the cases. The Court of Justice usually follows the opinion of the advocate-general in deciding a case. About 2,000 staff work for the two courts (see Box 4.4).

BOX 4.4: BUDGET FOR THE COURT OF JUSTICE
- The budget of the CJEU in 2021 was €444 million. Most of this allocation (€348 million) was for staff costs.
- The budget of the CJEU is smaller than that of the main political institutions (Commission, Parliament, Council/European Council), which employ significantly more staff.

Source: Definitive adoption (EU, Euratom) 2021/417 of the European Union's general budget for the financial year 2021, https://eur-lex.europa.eu/eli/budget/2021/1/oj

---

In the next two sections the most significant types of cases heard by the CJEU will be examined as a way of illustrating the role of the CJEU as a constitutionalizing and federalizing force in EU legal integration.

THE CJEU AS A CONSTITUTIONAL COURT FOR THE EUROPEAN UNION

Enforcing EU Law in the Member States

The CJEU ensures that the law is observed throughout the EU, thereby affirming that the EU is governed by the rule of law. This role has two primary aspects: ensuring that the member states comply with their treaty obligations and ensuring that the EU institutions carry out their roles in accordance with EU law and respect the limits of their powers as conferred by the treaties. The enforcement power of the CJEU results in *negative integration*, meaning that the judgments of the CJEU can only remove legal barriers to integration of EU law, rather than imposing positive rules and standards to advance legal integration.

The TFEU outlines two main legal actions by which the laws and actions of the member states can be challenged in the CJEU. The first, called the *infringement procedure*, is initiated by the Commission against a member state that the Commission claims has failed to fulfill its treaty obligations. In most cases, the member state is alleged to have failed to transpose correctly a directive into national law within the stipulated timeframe. Another occurrence is when an existing law may be in conflict with a treaty provision or a regulation, or a member state may have failed to implement secondary EU law in a way that ensures it is applied and respected. When these situations happen, the Commission will first advise the member state that it considers the latter has infringed the treaties, providing detailed reasons. If the response of the member state is unsatisfactory, the Commission commences an action before the Court of Justice. If the Court rules that the member state has failed to fulfill its treaty obligations, the member state must comply with the Court's ruling on how it must correct this. Since the Treaty of Maastricht came into force in 1993, the Commission has been able to go back to the Court to obtain a further judgment ordering the member state to pay a monetary penalty, sometimes totalling millions of euros, for failure to amend its law or properly implement EU policy after the first judgment of the Court that ruled the member state was not in compliance with EU law.

The *Van Gend en Loos* and *Costa* cases are examples of a second main form of legal action, the **reference for a preliminary ruling**. In these cases, a private party challenges the validity of a law of a member state on the basis that it is inconsistent with a provision of the treaty or an act of EU secondary law by commencing an action in a national court of a member state. The national court has the power and the duty, as an organ of government of a member state, to uphold the EU law and declare the inconsistent national law to be inapplicable. If the national court has any doubt as to the correct interpretation of the EU law, it may refer the question to the Court of Justice, which will give a judgment called a *preliminary ruling*. The case then goes back to the national court, which applies the preliminary ruling to decide the issues in the case. In this way, the correct interpretation of EU law as determined by the CJEU is transmitted to the national court for application within the member state. The goal is to ensure uniformity of interpretation and application of EU law throughout the Union. The courts of the other member states must also be willing to either apply the CJEU's interpretation to the domestic law of their own country, or at least refer a similar question relating to the issue of EU law to the CJEU to ensure they apply EU law correctly in their own national context.

The Commission's authority to take action against a member state for failure to carry out its treaty obligations, combined with the right of citizens to directly enforce their EU legal rights in their local courts has been referred to as a system of *dual vigilance*. The rulings of the Court in these cases have generally supported a broad and purposive interpretation of the obligations of member states and upheld the EU legal rights of individuals, particularly in relation to the fundamental freedoms. The Court's rulings as a whole are an indication to the Commission of the parameters of EU competences and objectives as set out in the treaties, so that the Commission can draft proposals that are within the EU's legal powers to intensify positive legal integration. In this way, the Court of Justice shapes and controls policy-making in all the areas in which the EU has competence.

Reviewing EU Secondary Legislation

The CJEU also has jurisdiction to ensure that the acts of the EU institutions are within their powers as conferred by the treaties. This role can be compared to that of a federal constitutional court, such as the Supreme Court of Canada (see Box 4.5), because it allows the judicial authorities at the highest level to delineate the division of powers between the member states and the EU institutions. It also guards against procedural flaws, abuse of power, or other illegalities in the actions of the institutions. An action in annulment can be brought before the CJEU by a host of actors: a member state, the European

> **BOX 4.5: THE CJEU COMPARED TO THE SUPREME COURT OF CANADA**
>
> The Supreme Court of Canada (SCC) is the final court of appeal in Canada. In this role it gives judgments that interpret and apply the Constitution that must be followed by the lower courts. Parliament and the provincial legislatures may not enact legislation that is inconsistent with the Constitution, and individuals may challenge such legislation as a violation of their constitutional rights, including their rights guaranteed in the Charter of Rights and Freedoms. The SCC is empowered to determine whether a particular legislative power belongs to the federal or provincial governments, just as the CJEU is charged with determining whether a competence is to be exercised by the EU or the member states. The principles of interpretation employed by the SCC differ from those that apply in EU law, but the balancing of federal and provincial powers and the determination of whether a federal or provincial law is consistent with broader constitutional principles is similar to the role played by the CJEU.

Parliament, the Commission, the Council, and even certain private parties can ask the CJEU to review the legality of acts of the EU institutions. If the Court concludes that any act of an EU institution is not validly adopted – whether because the act is inconsistent with the treaties, the institution did not have the competence to act, or it failed to follow the proper procedure – it will declare the act to be annulled.

A member state that has voted against a regulation or directive that has been adopted by qualified majority in the Council may challenge the validity of the act on the basis that unanimity was required, that the EU had no competence to adopt the act (for example, because the subject matter is within the exclusive power of the member states), or that a step in the legislative procedure was not correctly followed. An example of this type of case is the *Tobacco Advertising* case, decided in 2000, in which Germany challenged the legality of a directive regulating the advertising and sponsorship of tobacco products. The directive was adopted based on Article 114 TFEU, which provides for the adoption of measures for the harmonization of member state laws with the object of the establishment or functioning of the internal market. The Court held that Article 114 could not support the directive's extensive restriction of tobacco advertising and sponsorship, as it was not sufficiently connected to the internal market.

Sometimes one institution will challenge the validity of an act adopted by another institution. An early example is the *Tariff Preferences* case, decided in 1987. The Commission alleged that a regulation adopted by the Council was illegal because the treaty article on which it was based was not stated and it was adopted in a procedure that required a unanimous decision of member states, rather than qualified majority voting. The TEC (as does the TFEU) provided that all legislation had to state the legal basis (that is, the treaty article) on which it was adopted. The regulation granted special preferences for import to the European Community to products from developing countries. This is a form of international development aid. At the time, there was no provision of the treaty that clearly granted competence to the Community to provide international development aid. However, the granting of import tariff preferences is also closely concerned with the common commercial policy, where decision making required only a qualified majority in the Council. The Court ruled that the regulation was invalid because it infringed the treaty requirement to state the legal basis (usually the treaty provision) for its adoption. It also ruled that the common commercial policy included tariff preferences for development aid purposes, and that the regulation should have been adopted under that policy, by qualified majority, and was invalid for this reason as well.

Private parties can also challenge the legality of EU legislation that is addressed to them. This frequently occurs when a corporation challenges a decision of the Commission finding that the corporation has engaged in anti-competitive behaviour prohibited by EU law. An action in annulment initiated by a private party is heard by the General Court. The action in annulment allows the CJEU to ensure that the rule of law is observed not just by the member states but by the EU institutions as well. The Council, Commission, and Parliament are equally bound by the treaties, and any act they adopt that is not procedurally or substantively in accordance with their treaty powers can be nullified by the Court.

Protecting Fundamental Rights

As mentioned above, another classically constitutional role played by the Court is the protection of human rights, or fundamental rights, within the EU. The founding treaties of 1951 and 1957 did not mention human or fundamental rights, but as early as the late 1960s the CJEU began to recognize general principles of law that included protection of fundamental rights. It has affirmed on many occasions the following statement regarding the status of fundamental rights within the EU legal order:

> [A]ccording to settled case-law, fundamental rights form an integral part of the general principles of law, whose observance the Court ensures. For that purpose, the Court draws inspiration from the constitutional traditions common to the Member States and from the guidelines supplied by international treaties for the protection of human rights on which the Member States have collaborated or to which they are signatories. In that regard, the [European Convention on Human Rights] has special significance. (Joined Cases C-402 P and 415/05 P, *Yassin Abdullah Kadi and Al Barakaat International Foundation v. Council and Commission* (2008), para. 283)

In its human rights jurisprudence, the CJEU has been influenced by the highest courts of the member states and the ECtHR. The influence of the CJEU in the evolution of the EU and its legal order is evident from the fact that, after the CJEU articulated general principles of EU law, the member states agreed to revise the treaties to expressly include them. Moreover, in connection with the negotiation of the Treaty of Nice in 2000, the EU institutions reached a political agreement on a Charter of Fundamental Rights for the EU. The Charter became legally enforceable by the CJEU and member state courts with the entry into force of the Treaty of Lisbon in 2009.

Table 4.2 outlines the main competences of the Court of Justice, with references to the articles granting it those competences.

DEBATE: INCREMENTAL LEGAL INTEGRATION, DIRECT EFFECT, AND SUPREMACY

From the short description of the legal and judicial system in this chapter, one might conclude that EU legal integration has been fully achieved. However, the evolution of EU law is incremental and non-linear. There are always new cases that test existing principles and lead to further refinements. Even debates about the two most fundamental judicially created principles of EU law, direct effect and supremacy, have not completely died down. Why did member states, by and large, accept these principles, which so radically reduce

Table 4.2. Main competences of the Court of Justice of the European Union

Direct proceedings against a member state or an EU institution	Proceedings against a member state for failure to fulfill an obligation – infringement procedure (Articles 258–260 TFEU)
	Proceedings against an EU institution – action for annulment (Article 263 TFEU)
	Other direct proceedings (e.g., Articles 265, 268, 270, and 272 TFEU)
Indirect proceedings	Preliminary rulings requested by national courts (Article 267 TFEU)

their own sovereignty? How do the courts of the member states react to rulings from the CJEU? Some answers to these questions have been put forward by scholars of EU law and are offered here for debate.

The Court first enunciated these two fundamental principles in cases that were of little interest to anyone other than the private parties who initiated them. At the time, few lawyers were familiar with the Court or the nature of EU law, and the Common Market project was limited in scope and impact. By the time more sensitive cases of interest to the public came before the Court, direct effect and supremacy of EU law were well established. The Court of Justice has acted strategically and tempered its language in sensitive cases to test the acceptance of its decisions. In the exercise of its jurisdiction to give preliminary rulings, the Court has characterized its relationship with the national courts of the member states as one of cooperation. It often limits its preliminary rulings to narrow statements of the correct interpretation of the law, and then draws back to leave the final outcome of a case to the national court to decide.

From the other side, national courts may decline to make references for preliminary rulings if they believe they do not need the assistance of the Court of Justice. Rates of references from different member states vary greatly. It is also questionable whether national courts always correctly apply the preliminary rulings. The different legal and judicial traditions of the member states, particularly since the 2004 enlargement, means that uniform, simultaneous application of EU law throughout the EU is still an aspiration rather than a fact. This makes it easier for member states to continue to support EU membership while not fully implementing EU law.

It can be argued that member states had no real choice but to accept the principles of direct effect and supremacy. There is no appeal from a judgment of the Court of Justice; to overrule a judgment of the Court, one or both of the treaties must be amended. As this requires unanimity of the member states, it is a difficult task that has become ever more difficult with each enlargement of the EU. Most if not all rulings of the Court of Justice are acceptable to at least a few member states, so finding consensus to amend the treaties simply to roll back one "unacceptable" judgment is impossible.

However, this does not mean that national courts do not question the decisions of the CJEU regularly. In 2020, the German Federal Constitutional Court held in its judgment on the European Central Bank's Public Sector Asset Purchase Programme (PSPP judgment) that the CJEU exceeded its judicial mandate when it decided on a German financial regulation. Encouraged by this, the Polish Constitutional Tribunal also found a CJEU decision unconstitutional, and the Hungarian Constitutional Court also argued that it can review the judgments of the CJEU. These decisions fundamentally challenge the supremacy of EU law. In the United Kingdom, this argument went the furthest, as the campaign to have the UK withdraw from the EU was founded in part on arguments that the UK should take back its sovereignty and escape the jurisdiction of the CJEU.

A related question is whether the CJEU possesses the legal tools to sustain the rule of law principle envisioned as a basic principle in Article 2 TEU. In a few cases triggered by the recent democratic and constitutional backsliding in some member states, especially Hungary and Poland, the CJEU was able to stop the infringement of basic constitutional principles (e.g., the mandatory early retirement of judges in Hungary that violated the independence of the judiciary). However, the CJEU can only decide on concrete cases in which a member state has violated a specific provision of EU primary or secondary law. Its legal tools alone cannot comprehensively respond to the systematic degradation of the rule of law that can be observed in Hungary and Poland. For this reason, the EU has in recent years aimed to create and apply more political mechanisms in its "rule of law toolbox." These include new rule of law mechanisms that seek to foster dialogue between EU institutions and member states. In addition, the EU set up a system of rule of law conditionality when the 2021–7 Multiannual Financial Framework was negotiated; it allows the Commission to sanction financially member states whose rule of law breaches harm the EU's financial interests. Finally, steps have been taken to activate the Article 7 TEU procedure against Hungary and Poland. This provision may lead to the suspension of a member state's voting rights in the Council of the EU as a way to sanction violations of Article 2 TEU – but only if all other member states agree, which is unlikely since Hungary and Poland support each other. It remains to be seen if these political mechanisms are more effective than the CJEU's limited legal tools to respond to the deteriorating rule of law situation.

CONCLUSION

There are still many examples of imperfect integration, failures to implement EU law that are not challenged by either the Commission or private parties, and different interpretations of EU law that have not been resolved. The so-called activism of the Court has also ebbed and flowed at different periods in its 70-year history. Despite all this, it is clear that the legal integration of the EU has been far-reaching. Legal integration has promoted and solidified both political and economic integration. Its success results from the fundamental principles laid down at an early stage by the CJEU, and their reaffirmation since.

REVIEW QUESTIONS

1. What is the difference between a regulation and a directive? What is the transposition of a directive, and which EU institution(s) ensure(s) it is done correctly?
2. Where did the CJEU find a basis for recognizing fundamental rights as part of the EU legal system?
3. What is the purpose of the indirect mechanism (the reference for a preliminary ruling) for bringing cases to the CJEU? In what way does it rely on the cooperation of national courts?
4. What are the limitations of the CJEU's power to ensure that its interpretation of EU law is accepted in all member states?

EXERCISES

1. Compare and contrast the Charter of Fundamental Rights of the EU with the Canadian Charter of Rights and Freedoms.
2. Do some research on the roles and responsibilities of other supreme courts in federal countries (for example, Canada, the United States, Germany, Switzerland). What are the major differences between these supreme courts and the CJEU? Are there parallels to direct effect and supremacy of law in other supreme courts? Are there differences in monitoring and compliance of laws? What does this tell you about the level of integration in the EU?

NOTE

1 The Canada-United States-Mexico Agreement (CUSMA) entered into force on July 1, 2020. It replaced the North America Free Trade Agreement (NAFTA). Regional associations in East Asia and South America include the Association of Southeast Asian Nations (ASEAN, created in 1967) and the Common Market of the South (Mercosur, created in 1991, comprising Argentina, Brazil, Paraguay, Uruguay, and Venezuela).

REFERENCES AND FURTHER READING

Alter, K. 2003. *Establishing the Supremacy of European Law: The Making of an International Rule of Law in Europe*. Oxford: Oxford University Press.
Barnard, C., and S. Peers. 2020. *European Union Law*. Oxford: Oxford University Press.
Cichowski, R.A. 2007. *The European Court and Civil Society: Litigation, Mobilization and Governance*. Cambridge: Cambridge University Press.
Conant, L. 2013. *Justice Contained: Law and Politics in the European Union*. Ithaca, NY: Cornell University Press.
Craig, P.P., and G. De Búrca. 2020. *EU Law*, 7th ed. Oxford: Oxford University Press.
Craig, P.P., and G. De Búrca. 2021. *The Evolution of EU Law*, 3rd ed. Oxford: Oxford University Press.
Dawson, M., B. de Witte, and E. Muir. 2013. *Judicial Activism at the European Court of Justice*. Cheltenham, UK: Edward Elgar.
De Búrca, G., and J.H. Weiler. 2001. *The European Court of Justice*. Oxford: Oxford University Press.
De Mestral, A., and J. Winter. 2001. "Mobility Rights in the European Union and Canada." *McGill Law Journal* 46: 3–31.
Garrett, G. 1995. "The Politics of Legal Integration in the European Union." *International Organization* 49 (1): 171–81. https://doi.org/10.1017/S0020818300001612.
Hartley, T. 2014. *The Foundations of European Union Law*, 8th ed. Oxford: Oxford University Press.
Piris, J. 2010. *The Lisbon Treaty: A Legal and Political Analysis*. Cambridge: Cambridge University Press.
Poiares Maduro, M. 1998. *We the Court*. Portland, OR: Hart Publishing.
Schmidt, S., and D. Kelemen. 2012. *The Power of the European Court of Justice*. New York: Routledge.
Shaw, J. 2000. *Law of the European Union*, 3rd ed. Basingstoke, UK: Palgrave Macmillan.
Tsebelis, G., and G. Garrett. 2000. "Legislative Politics in the European Union." *European Union Politics* 1 (1): 9–36. https://doi.org/10.1177/1465116500001001002.
Weiler, J.H.H. 1991. "The Transformation of Europe." *Yale Law Journal* 100 (8): 2403–83. https://doi.org/10.2307/796898.

5

Policy-Making and Governance in the European Union's Multilevel System

Ingeborg Tömmel

READER'S GUIDE

This chapter highlights how European Union (EU) policy-making evolved in the course of European integration and how appropriate governance modes emerged during this process. It points to the inherent constraints that the EU as a multilevel system faces compared to federal states like Canada. Whereas federal states clearly allocate competences and tax-raising powers to the different levels of government, the EU is constrained by the member states, which retain far-reaching powers in both policy-making and financial allocations themselves. This constellation has resulted in the development of innovative modes of governance that allow for a flexible balancing of the common interests of the EU as a whole against the varying interests of the member states.

INTRODUCTION

The EU as a political system beyond the nation state has evolved through an incremental process of establishing and expanding policies. Through its policy-making, the EU aimed at steering economic and societal developments in and across its member states. To achieve these goals and to make European policies work, it has had to establish appropriate procedural avenues and build corresponding institutions.

In the 1950s, six European states founded three Communities – the European Coal and Steel Community (ECSC), the European Economic Community (EEC), and the European Atomic Energy Community (Euratom). The purpose was to jointly implement policies in a limited range of economic sectors – coal, steel, and nuclear energy – and to create a Common Market. Over the next decades, the three original Communities were merged and transformed into what is now the EU. In the process, the EU steadily expanded the scope of its policies. At present, the portfolio of European policies covers nearly all areas that typically characterize the policy spectrum of a nation state.

Despite this enormous expansion, the EU's governance tools did not expand correspondingly. The EU continues to lack the powers and competences that a state – either unitary or federal – usually has at its disposal. The fundamental reason underlying this mismatch is the fact that the member states never transferred full sovereignty to the European level. Hence the EU does not have the power to freely decide on its own competences. For both lawmaking and financial allocations, the EU is always dependent on member states' decisions and financial transfers. In response to these constraints, the EU has developed a set of unique **governance modes** that aim to ensure policy effects even in the absence of formal powers and competences.

Decision making in the EU usually involves the European and member state levels; in certain cases, it even includes regional governments within the member states. Hence, the EU has been characterized as a *multilevel system*. Policy-making in a multilevel system requires lengthy and complex processes of defining common ground and building consensus. Against this background, this chapter is structured around two basic questions. First, why is there a mismatch between the scope of EU policy-making and the governance tools available at the European level? Second, to what extent and in what ways has this mismatch shaped the evolution of EU governance?

The chapter begins by briefly sketching the fundamental constraints the EU faces in policy-making as well as some options available to compensate for these constraints. It then provides an overview of the evolution of EU policy-making and the corresponding governance modes. Then the chapter elaborates on the procedural and institutional innovations in EU governance that serve to compensate for the systemic constraints. The final section discusses the effectiveness of EU governance.

THE FUNDAMENTAL CONSTRAINTS ON EU POLICY-MAKING

The EU evolved as a political system that was superimposed on sovereign nation states to tackle common policy problems. However, the resulting multilevel system did not evolve into a fully-fledged federal state (Theme 2 of this book). Member states retained the authority to determine the EU's scope of powers, competences, and financial means. They have protected this authority through their exclusive right to make EU primary law (the treaties, see Chapter 4); their control on legislation at the European level through the Council (see Chapter 3); and their control over the EU budget through decisions on the financial transfers to the European level. Furthermore, the EU's lack of sovereignty also implies an additional constraint: The EU does not have the authority to prescribe anything to the member states beyond existing laws and regulations (for example, in cases where appropriate policy implementation is in danger).

How are EU *powers and competences* defined in the EU treaties? Since the adoption of the first treaties, member states transferred competences to the European level so that it could act for the Communities and later the EU as a whole. Initially, they did this selectively; they only transferred such powers – in the form of **exclusive competences** – that they considered absolutely necessary, particularly for the functioning of the Common Market (Article 2(1) TFEU). With ongoing integration and a functional need to integrate further policy areas, member states transferred additional powers to the European level. Yet often they did not transfer those powers fully so that they could retain some element of control for themselves. The treaties in these cases speak of **shared competences** (Article 2(2) TFEU). Finally, with integration affecting even more policy areas, the treaties envisaged various modes of policy **coordination** (Article 2(3) TFEU). In these cases formal competences remain with the member states, but they accept policy coordination by EU institutions. The procedures of coordination are defined in the treaties and may vary in their binding force (Article 5(1) TFEU). Finally, in certain policy areas the EU is also entitled "to carry out actions to support, coordinate or supplement actions of the member states" (Article 6 TFEU). In sum, the distribution of competences in the EU reflects, on the one hand, that supranational intervention, joint action, or at least policy coordination and other supportive measures are needed at the European level to tackle problems of mutual interdependence. Yet on the other hand, it also reflects member states' reluctance to definitively empower the European level in a broad set of policies. Member states thus prevent the EU from transforming into a fully-fledged federal state.

Besides the limitations on its competences, the EU is also constrained in legislation. How is lawmaking in the EU organized? As described in Chapter 3, it is a process that involves three main players: the European Commission, which proposes legal texts; the European Parliament (EP), which may amend, reject, or adopt proposals; and the Council of the EU, which also amends, rejects, or adopts proposals. It may seem that the EP and the Council are more or less on equal footing in the legislative process, but this is not the case. First, the EP is not entitled to co-legislate in all policy areas. Furthermore, the Council as the representative of national governments is, in practice, much more powerful than the EP. The Council's decisions are taken by qualified majority, and in some cases even by unanimity. Thus, a small number of states can act as "blocking minorities" and, in the case of unanimity, individual states can be veto players. The EP has a veto power as well, but only with an absolute majority of its 705 members. Because an absolute majority is difficult to achieve, the EP is often disposed to giving in when conflicts with the Council arise, especially if the alternative is no legislation at all. By contrast, in the Council, national governments that see their interests in danger do not hesitate to cast a veto and stall the legislation or to bargain until the proposal is adapted to their preferences. These voting dynamics in the Council explain why European lawmaking is often a cumbersome process, characterized by delayed and suboptimal decisions – or even non-decisions. This means that EU policy-making is severely constrained.

A further constraining factor is the EU's lack of sovereign power in budgetary matters. The EU cannot determine its revenues independently from the member states. Indeed, the EU's budget mainly consists of transfers from the member states. The size of each member state's financial transfers to the EU is expressed in terms of a certain percentage of the member state's gross national income. This system of financial transfers stands in stark contrast to both unitary or federal states, where the (central) government is sovereign in raising taxes according to its will and needs. Furthermore, budgetary transfers from the member states to the EU are not fixed once and for all; rather, they are determined by Council and EP decisions in seven-year intervals through the **Multiannual Financial Framework (MFF)**. Agreeing on the MFFs involves tough bargains among the member states, on both the overall size of the budget and the allocations

Table 5.1. The MFF 2021–7 (without Recovery and Resilience Facility)

Budget lines (policy priorities)	Financial allocations, billion euro (commitments, in 2018 prices)
Single Market, Innovation, and Digital	132.8
Cohesion, Resilience, and Values	377.8
Natural Resources and Environment	356.4
Migration and Border Management	22.7
Security and Defence	13.2
Neighbourhood and the World	98.4
European Public Administration	73.1
Total	**1,074.4**
Of which:	
Cohesion Policy	330.2
Common Agricultural Policy	336.4

Source: European Parliament (2022), "Fact sheet: Multiannual Financial Framework," https://www.europarl.europa.eu/factsheets/en/sheet/29/multiannual-financial-framework

to individual policy priorities (see Table 5.1). As compromise is difficult to achieve, the ultimate decisions are usually taken by the European Council – that is, at the highest possible level. Again, the EP can exercise influence on the decisions because it has veto powers over budgetary matters, but it often must compromise (see Box 5.1).

During the negotiations for the 2021–7 MFF, the European Council agreed on making funds available for member states in need, which includes a Recovery and Resilience Facility (RRF) in addition to the regular budget. This new instrument is intended to address the economic disruptions of the COVID-19 pandemic. The RRF has €672.5 billion at its disposal that can be used in the forms of loans and grants. From 2021 to 2025, the RRF will be able to support member states with their efforts to overcome the economic downturns and social disparities following the COVID-19 crisis. The expenses from the RRF are closely linked to the EU's policy agenda for the next five years, particularly the European Green Deal (see Chapter 17) and the digital agenda. Remarkably, for the first time in its history, member states allowed the EU to borrow money for the RRF on financial markets.

Finally, an additional limitation of EU policy-making that follows from its lack of sovereignty is that the EU does not have the authority to prescribe anything to the member states except what is laid down in primary and secondary legislation (EU treaties and laws). This situation has far-reaching

> **BOX 5.1: DECISION MAKING ON THE MULTIANNUAL FINANCIAL FRAMEWORK (MFF)**
>
> - The Commission proposes the overall ceiling of the EU budget (for at least five but usually seven years) and funding allocations to individual budget lines and policy priorities.
> - The EP may issue opinions on the Commission's proposal.
> - The Council of the EU discusses the Commission's proposal and elaborates a "negotiation box" for the European Council. This usually takes several meetings, or about one year, and exposes disagreements between member states.
> - The European Council, on the basis of the Commission and Council proposals, decides on the overall amount of the MFF and allocations to individual budget lines and policy priorities.
> - The EP discusses the European Council's proposal and proposes amendments.
> - The European Council discusses the EP's amendments and partially accepts them; it then adopts a final proposal for a regulation.
> - The EP adopts the regulation for the MFF with absolute majority. (It can also cast a veto with absolute majority; in this case the MFF is not adopted.)
> - The Council adopts the regulation for the MFF; unanimous decision is required.
>
> Source: Article 312 TFEU and Tömmel 2017

consequences. In the process of defining policy objectives and governance instruments, the EU cannot unilaterally set norms, standards, conditions, and modes of procedure, but instead must compromise with national governments. The same applies to policy implementation (putting EU policies into practice), which usually occurs through member states' administrations. Thus, the European level cannot direct national policies, but must exercise authority by using "soft" forms of influence: for example, through negotiations, persuasion, peer reviews, or naming and shaming. The member states have ample room to circumvent, evade, or simply ignore EU objectives, standards, or guidelines.

Summing up, the EU is heavily constrained in its policy-making: It is not sovereign, has limited competences to legislate, lacks budgetary powers, and lacks rights to steer policy implementation unilaterally. These constraints set the EU apart from federal states like Canada (Table 5.2). However, the EU is not powerless in the face of these constraints. The next sections show how the EU shaped new governance tools to channel policy-making and governance of the member states in the desired direction.

THE EVOLUTION OF EU POLICY-MAKING AND GOVERNANCE

EU policy-making and governance evolved in four phases. The first and the third phases focused on the expansion of policy-making while relying mainly on established and mature governance modes. By contrast, the second and fourth phases focused on developing new policies and corresponding, innovative governance modes.

The first phase started in 1952 with the foundation of the ECSC and supranational cooperation in the associated economic sectors (see Chapter 2). In the 1950s, coal and steel were important primary products for a broad range of manufacturing industries. In most of the six original member states, these sectors were state owned or run under far-reaching state control. Putting them under a supranational European umbrella was a first step toward creating a transnational, liberalized market. In 1957, the original six member states proceeded to establish the EEC as an institution to integrate their national markets. They also established Euratom to regulate another primary sector, nuclear energy, envisaged as the main energy source of the future. In addition, member states at this stage realized that the agricultural sector would not fare well in a liberalized market. Therefore, they agreed to regulate this sector as well at the European level, mainly by providing subsidies to producers (see Chapter 10). Thus, from the very beginning, the EU undertook an ambitious project of **market making** coupled with a limited set of market-correcting policies.

The dominant governance mode during this phase was hierarchical rule, with some forms of direct state intervention. In these early years of integration, political leaders were still influenced by the idea of a European

Table 5.2. Comparison of the political systems of the EU and Canada

Characteristics of political system	EU	Canada
Type of political system	Multilevel system, federation *sui generis*	Federal state
Sovereignty	National level	Federal level
Competences	Selected exclusive competences at European level; mainly shared competences; competences for policy coordination	Clear allocation to the federal and provincial levels
Finances	National level raises taxes, allocates finances to European level; limited direct revenues of the EU (so-called own resources)	Federal and provincial levels raise taxes; some transfers from federal to provincial level

Source: Compiled by author

federation, a sort of United States of Europe (see Chapter 2). Consequently, they opted for clear competence transfers to the European level. They set rules and regulations for creating a Common Market and established certain interventions to support its functioning. For example, the European level could intervene in cases of overproduction in the steel sector, falling market prices for agricultural products, or for any distortion of fair competition. Such decisions, however, were rarely taken. Where they were practised, for example in the Common Agricultural Policy, they remained highly contested. Thus, in spite of the transfer of far-reaching powers in limited areas to the European level, these hierarchical modes of governance were not necessarily effective, primarily because national governments did not support them.

By the end of the 1960s, a second phase set in. Despite major conflicts among the member states, a common understanding had emerged that the Communities should proceed on the path toward integrating more policy areas. In the following years, many such steps were discussed and projected, but implementation rarely followed. This lack of follow-through was due, among other things, to significant economic disparities between the member states. Economic crises and the first enlargement of the Communities in 1973, to include the United Kingdom, Denmark, and Ireland, sharpened these disparities. Political disagreement between member states deepened, and the room for embarking on new policies shrank. Consequently, the small number of new policies established during this phase either aimed at compensating for disparities between the member states (the regional policy, later labelled the cohesion policy; see Chapter 11) or sought to improve the Communities' competitiveness as a whole (technology policy). Furthermore, under the guise of preventing distortions of fair competition, the Communities adopted further market-correcting regulations, particularly in the areas of social and environmental policy (see Chapters 16 and 17). Finally, they introduced a European Monetary System (EMS), including fixed but adjustable exchange rates, as a first experiment on the way toward a monetary union (see Chapter 7).

Disagreement among member states during the second phase also resulted in more flexible forms of governance. A prime example is the setting of industrial norms for the Common Market. National governments could not find a consensus on the definition of appropriate norms. In the end, they defined only a few framework parameters at the European level, while devolving the definition of more specific norms to private umbrella organizations of the respective industrial sectors. Similarly, in other sectors and issue areas, if European regulations or guidelines were adopted at all, they defined only basic objectives, leaving member states much discretion. Regional policy as well as the EMS constitute prime examples of this approach. In both cases, the European level defined certain basic procedural or substantive rules, while member states designed, implemented, or adapted their policies within this framework. Thus, during this phase, EU governance was no longer conceived as a purely hierarchical endeavour, but rather as a multilevel process. That provided room for balancing the respective interests and preferences of the member states. Yet during this phase of experiments in multilevel governance, policy implementation rarely succeeded since member states often failed to observe EU norms.

In the mid-1980s, a third phase of EU policy-making began when national and particularly European political leaders forcefully advocated closer integration. After years of economic stagnation and major disagreement between the member states – aggravated by two rounds of southern enlargement (including Greece in 1981 and Spain and Portugal in 1986) – national governments rediscovered the EU as the most suited arena for improving the competitiveness of Europe's economy. Consequently, they opted for engaging in further market integration and joint policy-making. What followed was the strongest boost to the expansion and enhancement of EU policies in the history of integration. The most outstanding project of the time was the completion of the Single Market by December 31, 1992, which involved more than

300 individual regulations (see Chapter 7). In addition, policies established earlier were now more forcefully implemented – for instance, competition policy – or significantly strengthened – for instance, regional, social, and environmental policies. The latter served mainly to smooth conflicts between the member states. Indeed, poorer states claimed subsidies from regional and social policies as compensation for their weaker competitive position in the Single Market. The richer states aimed at safeguarding their higher environmental standards under such conditions. Thus, even though market-making policy was the first and foremost priority, some policy activity also focused on **market correction**.

After these successes, the next logical step was to embark on even more ambitious policy projects. The aim was to further bolster the functioning of the Single Market and, to a lesser degree, compensate for market failures. Consequently, member states agreed to create an Economic and Monetary Union (EMU) and envisaged to establish a single currency by the end of the twentieth century. Furthermore, they embarked on various approaches to coordinate a broad spectrum of national policies, such as trans-European networks, energy, tourism, and education. Most importantly, they expanded the policy spectrum at the European level to areas that were hitherto the *domaine réservée* of the member states: a Common Foreign and Security Policy (CFSP) and selected areas of Justice and Home Affairs (JHA) (see Chapters 8 and 9). Thus, within a period of 10 years the Communities, now renamed the European Union, embraced a broad spectrum of additional policies.

European governance during this phase evolved in several directions. Policies based on strong consensus between member states used hierarchical rule in the form of legislation. Member states even accepted to adopt most of these laws through qualified majority voting (QMV) instead of unanimity, thus waiving their veto power. The increased use of QMV applied in particular to the "completion" of the Single Market. Regarding other policy areas, member states had more conflicting views and preferences. In these cases, they opted for intergovernmental joint action or coordination. The Maastricht Treaty (in force since 1993) set general rules for coordinating national policies under European objectives for the CFSP, JHA, and EMU (see Chapters 7, 8, and 9). These policies were subjected to intergovernmental control – that is, decisions and actions of the Council and the European Council. The supranational institutions (the Commission and the EP) hardly played any role in proposing legislation or action in these matters (Commission) or in deciding on corresponding proposals (EP). In the case of EMU, binding decisions regarding monetary policy were delegated to an independent supranational institution, the European Central Bank. Overall, the third phase, although characterized by the expansion of hierarchical rule, introduced two additional forms of governance: one where the member states act jointly at the European level, and another where the individual member states remain the masters of policy-making, though guided by EU-wide coordination. However, these approaches often did not work as projected, and accordingly implementation only partly succeeded.

In the mid-1990s, the massive expansion of EU policy-making came to a halt and the fourth phase set in. It was now mainly external pressures that induced further changes. The end of the Cold War and the transformation of Central and Eastern European states into market economies and democratic political systems posed an enormous challenge to the EU. The Eastern neighbours knocked vigorously at the EU's doors, aspiring to full membership (see Chapter 13). In this situation, an expansion of policy-making was no longer a pressing issue. Preparing for enlargement now prevailed, which meant stabilizing the existing policy spectrum and improving its governance modes and procedural tools. From 2008 onwards, the sovereign debt and euro crises further reinforced the trend toward procedural improvements of EU governance. The measures taken to resolve the crises gave rise to governance modes that seek to influence national policies without transferring major competences to the EU. Unsurprisingly, therefore, the fourth phase was characterized by significant improvements in the procedural dimension of EU governance, particularly in those cases where the EU lacks clearly defined competences.

Within the EU, procedures of decision making were streamlined. In addition, more binding and firmly structured procedures for the coordination of national policies were introduced. The most prominent procedure in this regard was the **open method of coordination (OMC)**. This procedure was first defined in the Employment Title of the Amsterdam Treaty (in force since 1997). In 2000, the European Council adopted the procedure as the appropriate governance mode for implementing the so-called Lisbon Strategy, followed in 2010 by the Europe 2020 Strategy. Both these strategies aimed at inducing economic and social reforms in the member states through mere policy coordination.

The EU also fostered convergence of the accession states with its own regulatory framework and policy model. For instance, it required these states to adopt the so-called *acquis communautaire*, that is, the entire body of EU law (all treaties, legislation, and court decisions; see Chapter 4). Yet the most powerful governance tool to foster approximation to EU governance consisted of strict conditionality in exchange for the benefit of membership (see Chapter 13). Conditionality in this context means that the EU sets a series of conditions referring to various kinds of economic and political reforms that the candidate states had to fulfill before accession.

In the EU, the global financial crisis turned into a sovereign debt crisis in late 2009, eventually provoking a crisis of the euro area (see Chapter 7). In this situation, the use of stricter procedural tools appeared necessary. Tighter rules and stricter surveillance mechanisms at the European level were needed to safeguard compliance by the member states with EU norms of budgetary discipline, but also to provide financial support for those in need. In this situation, the EU made use of conditionality vis-à-vis its own member states. It subjected debtor states (for example, Greece) to a harsh regime of economic and social reforms in exchange for providing them with the loans they needed to cope with the sovereign debt crisis. These reforms included liberalizations of highly regulated businesses and welfare state institutions and the privatization of public goods (railways, seaports, power companies, and so on).

During this phase, the EU also devolved certain exclusive powers back to the national level. This devolution occurred in agricultural policy and competition policy. In both cases, national authorities now received broad leeway to adapt policies to local circumstances. Thus, the EU formally "softened" certain hierarchical governance modes set up during the first phase of policy-making in favour of a multilevel governance approach.

In sum, during the fourth phase policy-making did not expand significantly at the European level. Instead, procedural innovations figured centre stage, enabling the EU to exercise influence on both member states' and accession states' policies. The EU succeeded in expanding and transforming policy-making at the national level. New governance modes emerged, such as the application of conditionality in exchange for benefits, making further competence transfers unnecessary. Finally, a multilevel governance system in agricultural and competition policy replaced the hierarchical modes of governance established earlier. Altogether, during the fourth phase EU policy-making and governance rapidly evolved in line with the multilevel structure of the European polity.

At present, it appears that a fifth phase in EU policy-making and governance may be emerging. Even though EU policies governed by hierarchical rule are not significantly expanding, we are witnessing more frequent examples of common action, initiated, guided, and supervised by the European

Commission. Again, crises have triggered these changes. First, the COVID-19 pandemic resulted in the EU playing a prominent role in safeguarding the procurement of vaccines. In addition, the RRF for the first time gave the EU the right to borrow money from financial markets. As a governance mode, the RRF makes wide use of conditionality, providing grants and loans in exchange for implementing the EU's agenda, primarily the European Green Deal and digital transformation, but also the respect for the rule of law in the member states. Second, the war in Ukraine resulted in the Commission taking the lead in defining sanctions against Russia and in procuring energy – gas and oil – from other countries. Whether these changes are temporary phenomena or will permanently transform the EU's role as a policy-maker is still an open question. In any event, the EU's governance tools beyond classical hierarchical rule have been increasingly strengthened.

Drawing conclusions on the overall evolution of EU policy-making and governance, we see a process of rapid expansion of the policy portfolio without a significant strengthening of hierarchical rule. Instead, the EU increasingly developed innovative governance approaches that compensate for the constraints the system faces (see Table 5.3). Yet the process did not simply evolve incrementally. Phases of policy expansion (1 and 3) alternated with phases of relative stagnation (2 and 4). However, the latter are characterized by path-breaking policy and governance experiments (phase 2) or far-reaching improvements of policy processes, and thus the emergence of more consolidated, mainly non-hierarchical, and more effective governance modes (phase 4). Overall, the EU's broad policy portfolio, though resembling at first sight those of states like Canada (see Table 5.4), displays a clear dominance for market-making policies, while all other policies are clearly underrepresented. Whereas the former mainly underlie hierarchical governance, the latter are increasingly directed by various forms of non-hierarchical governance modes.

Looking for explanations, we can first state that EU policy-making expanded in reaction to both internal and external challenges. The problems resulting from increasing interdependencies among EU member states, but also worldwide, and the manifold crises created functional pressures to act in common. Even the larger states in Europe could not solve such problems on their own. Yet functional pressures do not automatically induce adaptations. Instead, agency is required to transform such pressures into political action. The Commission, as the institution representing the *common interests* of the member states, continuously proposed action in ever more policy areas. It put pressure on national governments to decide on corresponding action,

Table 5.3. Phases of EU policy-making and associated governance modes

Phase	Policies established	Competences	Governance mode	Function
1 (1950–1965)	Coal and Steel	European level	Hierarchical rule	Market creation
	Common market	European level	Hierarchical rule	Market creation
	Competition policy	European level	Hierarchical rule	Market creation
	Agricultural policy	European level	Hierarchical rule	Market correction
2 (1965–1985)	Regional policy	European/national level	Framework regulation	Market creation/correction
	Social policy	European/national level	Framework regulation	Market correction
	Environmental policy	European/national level	Framework regulation	Market correction
	Technology policy	European/national level	Framework regulation	Market creation
	European Monetary System	National level	Coordination of national policies	Market creation
3 (1985–1995)	Completion Single Market	European level	Hierarchical rule	Market creation
	Economic and Monetary Union	European/national level	Hierarchical rule/framework regulation	Market creation
	Foreign and Security Policy	European/national level	Intergovernmental decision	Enhancing role EU
	Justice and Home Affairs	European/national level	Intergovernmental decision	Enhancing role EU
	Various policies (trans-European networks, energy, education etc.)	National level	Coordination of national policies	Market creation/correction
4 (from 1995 to the present)	European Employment Strategy	National level	Coordination of national policies	Market creation/correction
	Lisbon Strategy	National level	Coordination of national policies	Market creation/correction
	Europe 2020 Strategy	National level	Coordination of national policies	Market creation/correction

Source: Compiled by author

Table 5.4. Comparison of policies and governance modes of the EU and Canada

Policies and governance modes	EU	Canada
Policies at European or federal level	Broad spectrum, dominance of market-making policies	Broad spectrum, market-making, market-correcting, and foreign policy
Policies at national or provincial level	Full spectrum, including foreign policy	Mainly market-correcting policies
Governance modes at European or federal level	Limited hierarchical rule, framework regulation, intergovernmental decision, policy coordination	Hierarchical rule within federal realm of competences

Source: Compiled by author

yet the latter reacted selectively to such proposals. While member states were generally reluctant to transfer competences to the European level, they more willingly accepted transfers for market-making policies. In these areas, they accepted hierarchical rule, binding decisions, and even majority voting. For all other policy areas, they clearly aimed at retaining control for themselves. Member states accepted joint action under a European umbrella only in cases in which the Commission introduced new governance approaches, relying mainly on procedural rules instead of clear EU competences. Thus, overall, EU governance modes evolved into a multilevel structure, a system that brings together two opposite objectives of policy-making: functional pressures to act jointly at the European level, and the determination of member states to safeguard, as much as possible, national sovereignty.

CONSOLIDATING EU MULTILEVEL GOVERNANCE

In a multilevel system, modes of governance are not simply established once and forever. The EU's governance modes, as described above, evolved through a process of trial and error, of piecemeal solutions to bottlenecks and dysfunctionalities. During this process, the responsible institutions had to consider the sensitivities of the actors involved, most notably those of national governments, while at the same time trying to safeguard and improve policy effectiveness. From the range of policies that emerged in this process, three cases of overarching governance innovations stand out that allow for extensive and flexible use across many policy areas: (1) the OMC as a procedure for coordinating national policies within a European framework; (2) the "system of partnership," providing an institutional arrangement for vertically linking government levels; and (3) transnational policy networks, for horizontally linking member states' institutions. These governance innovations serve to compensate for the constraints that the EU faces in policy-making: first, the lack of competences at the European level; second, the lack of authority over the lower levels; and third, the lack of both competences and authority to harmonize policies across member states.

Turning first to the *OMC*, the procedure constitutes an interactive process between the EU and national governments for jointly formulating and evaluating policies as well as supervising policy implementation in the member states. The procedure in its ideal form is described for the employment policy in Article 148(1–5) TFEU. It consists of five stages: First, the European Council, drawing on a report from the Commission and the Council, adopts conclusions on the employment situation in the EU. Second, the Council, on a proposal of the Commission, draws up guidelines that the member states "shall take into account" (Article 148(2) TFEU) in their employment policies. Third, "in the light of the guidelines" (Article 148(3) TFEU), member states are obliged to report on their policy measures. Fourth, the Council examines the implementation of the member states' employment policies and may, on a recommendation of the Commission, make recommendations to individual states. Fifth, the Commission and the Council draw up a new report on the employment situation in the EU that will serve as the basis for the conclusions of the European Council. At this point, the cycle begins afresh. Participation in the OMC procedure is required for member states, but the procedure does not entail any binding governance tools. Yet participation in the procedure means that many informal pressures arise to comply with OMC guidelines and norms.

After first experiments with the OMC in the European employment strategy, the procedure was applied in other policy areas and domains. This includes the coordination and surveillance of national macroeconomic policies within the Stability and Growth Pact of EMU, the Lisbon Strategy, the Europe 2020 Strategy, cohesion policy, and the EU's anti-poverty program. The procedure helped to expand the role of the EU in policy areas where it does not hold any competences (e.g., anti-poverty policy), but also to improve compliance of member states in clearly regulated policy areas (e.g., EMU, cohesion policy).

The so-called *system of partnership* was first introduced in the framework of cohesion policy (Chapter 11). In this policy, the EU used to set certain basic objectives while the member states designed and implemented their policies within this framework. Yet in many instances member states did not respect the European objectives but pursued their own preferences. The reform of cohesion policy in 1989 introduced the partnership system: an institutional arrangement for sequenced negotiations among all levels of government (European, national, and regional) on the elaboration, adoption, and implementation of assistance programs for less-favoured regions. It enabled the government levels to jointly define the objectives, programs, and modes of implementation of cohesion policy. It helped to mediate systematically between EU policy objectives and those of the national and regional government levels. Altogether, the system of partnership created a vertical nexus between the formally disconnected government levels and compensated for the lack of hierarchical relationships among them. This system did not remain limited to the area of cohesion policy. It quickly spread to other policy areas where multiple government levels interact to define and implement policies, for example in EU enlargement negotiations, the neighbourhood policy, or in certain sectors of environmental policy (see Chapters 13, 14, and 17).

Transnational networks were first established in competition policy (see Chapter 7). Initially, decisions regarding the distortion of fair competition were the exclusive competence of the Commission. Yet its decisions were often not welcomed or were even thwarted by the member states. In 2003, a major reform decentralized competences in minor competition cases to the member states; each state had to establish an independent competition agency. At the same time, transnational networks were created in which delegates of these agencies cooperate under the guidance of the Commission. The members of the networks discuss problems of unfair competition, exchange experiences, and give advice to colleagues. In addition, they elaborate proposals for further EU policy initiatives or for common national-level strategies. Thanks to these networks, national actors get involved in EU competition policy while the Commission enhances its ability to transfer EU policy objectives and governance practices to member states, thus enhancing policy convergence. Overall, transnational networks in competition policy tend to reduce the resistance of national authorities to EU interference and allow for more effective diffusion and implementation of EU policy strategies.

The transnational network approach spilled over to other policy areas. It allows the EU to play a role in policy areas that to date are not, or at best partially, European endeavours. It has been used, for instance, in environmental and energy policy (see Chapter 17). Remarkably, transnational networks also serve to consolidate policy implementation in areas where the EU holds nearly exclusive competences. The most prominent case is the so-called SOLVIT network that helps member states' administrations implement Single Market rules and accommodate the manifold frictions that arise when implementing uniform rules across the EU.

In sum, these three procedural and institutional innovations compensate for the constraints the EU faces in policy-making. They consolidate a multi-level system where national governments (and in some cases regions) defend their decision-making powers while joint European action is functionally required and politically desired.

DEBATE: IS EU GOVERNANCE EFFECTIVE?

Does EU governance work effectively? In view of the multiple constraints that the EU faces in policy-making, this question is important and requires multifaceted answers. By and large, scholars agree that the rules and regulations governing the Single Market work quite well (Scharpf 1999). The nature of these rules facilitates compliance: They are directly binding on member states and private businesses, and they are reinforced by market mechanisms because they unleash competitive pressures. However, these rules may create frictions at the national level. The example of competition policy shows that, even when the EU has the power to take binding decisions, their effectiveness is not assured. In many cases, such decisions, delegated to the Commission, are either not taken or delayed. Before the introduction of the transnational networks approach, the Commission was often hesitant to apply its full powers because it felt that there was no consensus among the member states. Thus, overly centralized policies and governance processes were often ineffective until complemented by more recent multilevel approaches.

When EU governance relies on framework legislation that must be transposed into national law, its effectiveness is also not assured. Scholarly research on legislative compliance points to mixed results: National governments use various ways to evade, circumvent, or delay due transposition (see Chapter 4). The European level has certain means at its disposal to counteract sluggish transposition, but these are time consuming and costly, and therefore only selectively applied.

Where the European Council or the Council make intergovernmental decisions on their own, the effectiveness of EU governance is also questionable. For example, the Stability and Growth Pact in EMU has been partly defied by member states; in the meantime, the EU introduced new rules for all member states to safeguard compliance (see Chapter 7). Another example is the Council decision regarding the refugee crisis, which were disregarded by some member states whose governments explicitly refused to admit refugees (see Chapter 8).

Finally, the effectiveness of governance processes coordinated by the EU through the OMC is an issue of much contestation (Tömmel 2020). Some scholars argue that it is only with hierarchy, or at least a strong "shadow of hierarchy" (that is, accompanying legislation), that these modes of governance are effective. Others claim that effectiveness should not be assessed by the achievement of the concrete objectives and targets set at the European level, but rather by longer-term changes in problem perceptions and strategies of national actors and elites. Accordingly, it is not decisive whether the substantial aspects of a policy are successfully transferred to member states, but rather whether member states themselves are willing to engage in and apply the governance approaches of the European level (Tömmel 2016).

At this point, it might seem that European governance, with the exception of the Single Market, is ineffective more frequently than effective. However, such a judgment would be misplaced. Rather, we should say that the effectiveness of EU governance is not guaranteed because it depends on a host of additional factors: the problems at hand and the pressure to find solutions, the combination of governance approaches used, as well as a variety of external circumstances. The most decisive factor for the success or failure of EU governance is whether national governments and political elites acknowledge EU policy objectives as appropriate, legitimate, and beneficial to their country.

CONCLUSION

In this chapter we have seen that EU policy-making evolved through a process of expansion of the policy portfolio and diversification of governance modes. The transfer of effective governance tools to the European level did not keep up with the expansion of policies. Thus, hierarchical governance could be used only for a limited set of policies. In all other policy areas, the EU developed governance modes that seek to influence national policies by passing EU framework legislation, establishing common targets, giving member states more say in EU decision making, allowing the EU to coordinate member states' policies, or making use of conditionality. These varied governance modes result from national governments' contradictory objectives:

on the one hand, the desire to promote European integration in response to functional (economic and political) pressures; on the other hand, the reluctance to transfer the corresponding powers and financial means to the EU. The contradictions between these objectives, and the ways in which political leaders have responded to them, have resulted in innovative governance modes at the European level. Instead of transforming the EU into a more hierarchically organized polity, let alone a federal state, these governance modes have evolved in adaptation to the EU's multilevel system. Yet the many procedural and institutional innovations of EU governance have not resulted in a system that would guarantee the effectiveness of European policy-making. As a result, further reforms and innovative governance approaches are likely to occur in the future.

REVIEW QUESTIONS

1 Why is there an asymmetry between market-making and market-correcting policies in the EU?
2 What are the core characteristics of the four phases of EU policy-making and governance? What triggered the changes between them?
3 Why are certain policies decided upon jointly by intergovernmental and supranational bodies and others exclusively by the intergovernmental bodies of the EU?
4 Why did the EU establish the OMC (in employment policy and elsewhere) as well as the system of partnership (in cohesion policy) and transnational networks (in competition policy)?

EXERCISES

1 Consider the role of direct taxation in governance. What does the absence of tax collection at the European level tell us about the EU's multilevel system of governance? How does tax collection compare to the Canadian federal system?
2 Select one of the major EU policy areas (e.g., agriculture, energy, Single Market, transport) and investigate the specific system of policy-making and governance in this field. What role is there for national sovereignty? How has this policy area evolved over time?

REFERENCES AND FURTHER READING

Buonanno, L., and N. Nugent. 2020. *Policies and Policy Processes of the European Union*, 2nd ed. Basingstoke, UK: Palgrave Macmillan.

Richardson, J., ed. 2012. *Constructing a Policy-Making State? Policy Dynamics in the EU*. Oxford: Oxford University Press.

Richardson, J., and S. Mazey, eds. 2015. *European Union: Power and Policy-Making*, 4th ed. London: Routledge.

Scharpf, F.W. 1999. *Governing in Europe: Effective and Democratic?* Oxford: Oxford University Press.

Tömmel, I. 2014. *The European Union: What It Is and How It Works*. Basingstoke, UK: Palgrave Macmillan.

Tömmel, I. 2016. "The Governance of Governance: Political Steering in a Non-Hierarchical Multilevel System." *Journal of Contemporary European Research* 12 (1): 406–23.

Tömmel, I. 2017. "The Standing President of the European Council: Intergovernmental or Supranational Leadership?" *Journal of European Integration* 39 (2): 175–89.

Tömmel, I. 2020. "European Union Governance." In *Oxford Research Encyclopedia of Politics*. https://doi.org/10.1093/acrefore/9780190228637.013.1479.

Tömmel, I., and A. Verdun, eds. 2009. *Innovative Governance in the European Union: The Politics of Multilevel Policy-Making*. Boulder, CO: Lynne Rienner.

Wallace, H., M.A. Pollack, C. Roederer-Rynning, and A. Young, eds. 2020. *Policy-Making in the European Union*, 8th ed. Oxford: Oxford University Press.

6
Theories of European Integration and Governance

Amy Verdun

READER'S GUIDE

This chapter looks at European integration theories. It explains how, historically, they have helped understand the European Union's formation and operation. Various theoretical approaches are used in European integration studies to analyze policies and developments in the European Union (EU). Drawing on the three main themes of this book, this chapter covers theories that seek to explain European integration as well as theoretical debates about the EU's democratic credentials and the EU as a global actor.

INTRODUCTION

European integration theories emerged to explain why and how countries in Europe collaborated. The EU was created after World War II with the goal of not having another war. Academics initially drew on international relations (IR) theories because that field had explanations about the conditions under which sovereign states would collaborate. In 1943, David Mitrany's *A Working Peace System* developed a functional theory of integration. His student, Ernst B. Haas, would later build on it to produce his leading works on neofunctionalism in the late 1950s and early 1960s. Functionalist and neofunctionalist approaches both emphasized why and how cooperation contributed to solving member states' joint policy challenges within a mixed economic system (Theme 1 of this book). The spirit of functional cooperation within the context of the Cold War was prominent in the early years of European integration (see Chapter 2). Yet as power politics started to dominate developments in the 1960s, realist approaches, notably the work of Stanley Hoffmann (intergovernmentalism), won terrain (Verdun 2020).

Today the EU is more than an international organization but less than a federation (Theme 2 of this book). Numerous federalists, such as Jean Monnet and Altiero Spinelli, provided the inspiration for embarking on the process of European integration. Yet there was no commonly agreed on grand plan for setting up a European federation, or "a United States of Europe" (see Chapter 2). While there have been developments that make the EU a supranational entity in many aspects, it still falls short of a fully-fledged federal state, with member state sovereignty retained in core areas such as direct taxation (see Chapter 5). Over time the EU became such an advanced polity (an organized society having a particular form of government) that scholars started to look at the EU as an entity in itself, rather than explaining why member states choose to join it (which had been the original interest of integration scholars). With that change in perspective, more typical political science approaches, such as governance approaches and institutionalism, were applied to the EU.

The EU construction is built on the postwar assumption that by integrating gradually in technocratic and economic areas, the rest of integration will automatically follow (Theme 3 of this book). Indeed, early theories of European integration concentrated on technocratic issues. Over time, critics examined the integration process and concluded that the EU had become a unique political entity. Citizens wanted more say in the creation of this supranational entity – one that was increasingly both a generator of as well as a response to globalization. These insights spawned theoretical contributions about how to understand the EU from a democratic theory perspective as well as how the EU is a player within and formed by globalization.

This chapter provides an overview of different integration theories as well as institutional and governance approaches developed in EU studies. The review follows a mostly chronological approach by looking at the theoretical questions EU scholars engaged with during the various phases of the EU's development while also reflecting on the three themes of this book.

FEDERALISM, NEOFUNCTIONALISM, AND INTERGOVERNMENTALISM

Federalism

The idea to create a "United States of Europe" lay at the heart of federalist thinking about European integration, which dates back well before World War II (see Chapter 2). **Federalism** refers to the distribution of power in an organization (as a government) between a central (federal) authority and its lower-level units (e.g., states, provinces). A federal state would be opposite to a unitary state; in the latter, state authority remains with the central level. It would also be distinguished from a confederation, which is a union of sovereign states that, while together, do not constitute a new state. A federation, by contrast, is a state recognized in the international state system, whereby the constituent states are partially self-governing. The constituent states are not recognized in the international state system, and they do not automatically have the right to leave (see Box 6.1).

One of the early federalist thinkers was the Italian Altiero Spinelli, who (while imprisoned by the fascist government) wrote the *Ventotene Manifesto* in 1941 calling for European integration. In 1946, in a speech delivered in Zurich, Switzerland, British prime minister Winston Churchill called for a United States of Europe, which led to the creation of the Council of Europe in 1949 (see Chapter 2). Yet there was no agreement on whether federalism was the way forward. The approach that became more successful in the early years of integration could be characterized as neofunctionalist (see below). The federalist approach to European integration has experienced somewhat of a comeback in recent years. Scholars such as Michael Burgess have spent their whole academic career studying federalism and federal states with a view to learning from those types of political systems. He and others, such as Dan Kelemen and Joseph H. Weiler, have argued that the EU has moved away from being a pure confederation and has started to resemble some parts of the definition of a federation, effectively creating its own version of federation. The Treaty of Lisbon, which came into effect in 2009, included important aspects of deeper integration that have paved the way for some level of federation in the EU: The EU now has legal personality in the international system and it has acquired new policy-making power in various areas that are typical in federations, including foreign policy, security, defence, and monetary policy. Yet the EU does not have exclusive competence over most of these fields. Also, it does not have the

> **BOX 6.1: FEDERALISM IN CANADA AND THE EU**
>
> Canada was named a "Confederation" in 1867 when it was created. This name refers to the process whereby provinces joined; however, Canada was governed as a federation. The constituent states do not have legal status in the international system. The EU was proposed in 1950 with the Schuman Declaration, which suggested pooling the markets for coal and steel and led to the European Coal and Steel Community (ECSC) in 1951. From that point on the EU has expanded in both its membership as well as the scope of policy that it is involved with. The EU maintains some policy areas at the level of member states (e.g., tax policy, primary and secondary education, health policy), while other areas are predominantly EU-level policies (trade policy, monetary policy). The Canadian federation also started with fewer provinces and eventually expanded with respect to its members as well as the policies dealt with at the federal level. In the Canadian system, most sectors fall under federal jurisdiction, such as foreign affairs, security, and monetary policy. Other sectors, such as property, civil rights, labour relations, health care, and education fall under provincial jurisdiction (even though the welfare system was, in part, built on payments from the federal government to the provinces). Some sectors are joint, such as taxation and unemployment (in that latter sector activation policy is provincial, whereas unemployment insurance is a federal responsibility; see Verdun 2016).

power to rule on the extent of its own competence on an issue, and its member states are still legal states in the international state system. These developments have made the EU move beyond a confederation, but not quite as far as becoming a federation, which is a reason why the EU has often been referred to as a *sui generis* (one of a kind) political system. Former Commission president Jacques Delors characterized the EU as an "unidentified political object."

Neofunctionalism

One of the first influential studies of the European integration process was by Ernst B. Haas. His book *The Uniting of Europe* (Haas 1958) focused on the

ECSC. Inspired by liberal IR scholar David Mitrany's functional approach, Haas referred to his own work as **neofunctionalism**. Other scholars, such as Leon N. Lindberg, also adopted this approach. They focused on the *process* of integration – one in which political actors would shift their loyalties to the supranational level and thereby create a new political community at that level. The main mechanisms to develop this new community are technocratic decision making, incremental change, and learning among elites. Haas and Lindberg saw the process of integration as an incremental one, with the concept of **spillover** at its core. Spillover means that once a particular sector becomes integrated, there would be a need to integrate other connected sectors (functional spillover); for example, the integration of the coal and steel sectors would necessitate integration of the transport sector. European integration would occur as countries go through this process. Countries would witness a gradual but automatic transfer of economic to political integration, whereby political loyalty would be transferred from the national to the supranational level. The important actors in this process would be elites – mostly peak associations (interest groups) and supranational authorities – while member states would gradually lose exclusive control over the integration process they had initiated.

Neofunctionalism was able to explain the process for a few years, but by the mid-1960s Stanley Hoffmann, a scholar of French politics, put forward his intergovernmentalist critique. Hoffmann (1966) responded to a change in the developments on the ground. The French president, General Charles de Gaulle, was less supportive of European integration, and during the "Empty Chair Crisis" (1965–6) boycotted meetings of the Council of the EU for more than six months. Hoffmann argued that one should be open to conceptualizing "spill-back" due to the re-emergence of nationalism and the continuity of national identity. By 1968, when the second edition of *The Uniting of Europe* was published, Ernst B. Haas included a prologue in which he agreed with Hoffmann that there was a difference between **high politics** and **low politics**, with the former being the policies that were central to state sovereignty (defence, foreign policy), whereas he still believed that more technocratic policies (economic policies) would fit the predictions of neofunctionalist theory. In the 1970s, other neofunctionalist scholars, such as Philippe Schmitter, a student of Haas, further developed neofunctionalism so that one can conceptually accept that neofunctionalism could also incorporate "spill-back" (reversal of integration) or "spill-around" (intergovernmental cooperation outside of the EU framework). However, by 1975 even

Haas himself declared that his theory was unable to explain the process of integration.

Subsequently, neofunctionalism was not much referred to by scholars, especially as the integration process seemed to stall in the 1970s. However, by the late 1980s the integration process had picked up speed again, and neofunctionalism experienced a bit of a revival (Mutimer 1989; Tranholm-Mikkelsen 1991). Before long, volumes reanalyzed and expanded on neofunctionalism, taking on board new insights based on the developments in the 1990s (Sandholtz and Stone-Sweet 2012) and in the 2000s (Hooghe and Marks 2009). Scholars recognized that it may not be able to explain all of the integration process (a **grand theory**), but that it served well as a **mid-range theory**. Mid-range theories seek to integrate empirical insights with more modest theoretical understandings. Grand theory, as had been advanced by scholars such as the sociologist C. Wright Mills in the 1960s, would aim at a higher level of understanding about the nature of the political system but would not concern itself too much with the details of the empirics. By differentiating between mid-range and grand theories, the scholarship of European integration sought to differentiate between producing elegant, overarching theories that explained the entirety of European integration and producing those that were better suited at explaining empirical evidence via a more specified theoretical approach. In recent years, present-day neofunctionalists have used the approach as a mid-range theory, their claim being that the approach is helpful in shedding light on aspects of European integration such as the euro crisis or the migration crisis (Niemann and Ioannou 2015; Schimmelfennig 2018; Nicoli 2020).

Intergovernmentalism

Hoffmann's **intergovernmental** critique of the 1960s drew on realist IR theory, since it focused on nation states' power and was triggered by the renewed rise in nationalism in various West European member states. Rather than concentrating on the mechanisms that neofunctionalists identified, it offered an alternative: a state-centric analysis of the integration process. The main actors in intergovernmentalism are states (national governments). In this view states would be unlikely to give up sovereignty in favour of deeper integration. When integration occurs, there would not be any automaticity assumed, but cooperation could result only if it is in the interests of the member states. Thus, intergovernmentalism assumed cooperation would occur from time to time and on a case-by-case basis. This approach does not see any leadership role for supranational actors, as neofunctionalism had. Instead, according to intergovernmentalists, actors such as the European Commission, European Parliament, or the Court of Justice of the EU operate as agents of the member states, who are tasked with brokering deals based on the instructions and guidance given by the member states. Intergovernmentalists look at European integration initiatives as a form of cooperation for which there are costs and benefits, which states weigh before deciding if an initiative is in their interests.

In the 1990s, when the integration process picked up steam again, scholars such as Alan Milward and Andrew Moravcsik continued in the tradition of this school of thought. Both emphasized the crucial role of the nation state in the integration process. Moravcsik (1998) developed his theory by adopting elements of liberal IR theory to examine the domestic reasons that could explain national interests. This approach attracted a lot of attention, as it was an approach with clear theoretical foundations and precise testable hypotheses. The approach was attractive in its simplicity and worked well in some arenas, notably when applied to Council decisions. Moravcsik's theory consists of three components. First there is a liberal theory of national state preferences. This means that state preferences are shaped by societal interests at the domestic level (demand side) and that the addition of those preferences is what makes up the state preference. The second component is interstate bargaining. States are now seen as unitary actors. The larger states, with greater influence and bargaining power, have more say in this process. The final component is institutional delegation, whereby EU institutions function to improve the efficiency of interstate bargaining. In this view, supranational institutions such as the Commission are not seen as actors that independently influence and advance the integration process, but rather as agents of the member states. Nation states create supranational institutions as a way to commit each other to their agreements, for instance by creating mechanisms in which the Commission and the Court of Justice ensure that all states adequately transpose and implement EU directives.

Recently, scholars such as Bickerton, Hodson, and Puetter (2015) have emphasized how the integration process since the 2008 financial crisis has led to the paradoxical situation whereby EU activity has increased but the constitutional features of the EU have stayed roughly the same. They call this form of integration without increased supranationalism "new intergovernmentalism." Their argument is that neofunctionalism is unable to explain why integration has fallen short in terms of institutional change. They argue that this phenomenon is part of a distinct phase in integration that occurs because of national preferences and a decline in the permissive consensus toward more European institutional integration that was present in earlier periods.

Although the approach is intuitive and helps explain some of the developments that characterized the 2010s, it is not without criticism. Frank Schimmelfennig (2015) argues that the EU in its entirety has not necessarily become more intergovernmental. He points to the growth of new supranational institutional structures that were created because of the financial crisis. Examples are the strengthening of existing institutions such as the European Central Bank and the creation of new institutional structures such as the Banking Union and the Capital Markets Union (see Chapter 7). In fact, studies of the role of the European Commission since the sovereign debt crisis suggest that the Commission has obtained a larger role in macroeconomic governance, even in steering the member states (Bauer and Becker 2014; Savage and Verdun 2015; Becker et al. 2016). What scholars have noticed in recent years, however, is the increasing influence of certain national leaders, such as the German chancellor, which seems in line with a more intergovernmental interpretation. In a similar vein, the developments around the EU's response to the COVID-19 pandemic can be attributed to renewed Franco-German intergovernmental leadership in the integration process (Krotz and Schramm 2021; Schild 2020; see also Chapter 7).

MULTILEVEL GOVERNANCE, GOVERNANCE, EUROPEANIZATION, AND INSTITUTIONALISM

The revival of European integration efforts in the 1990s led to the development of several new theoretical approaches that looked at novel ways to understand the EU. Simon Hix (1994) pointed out that the approaches derived from IR were suitable for studying the phenomenon of European integration, but he argued that approaches from comparative politics would be better suited for studying the internal politics of the EU. These approaches examine the EU as its own "polity." With the growth of the scope of European integration, scholars were also examining how the EU compares to other political systems.

The multilevel governance approach superseded the IR-based assumptions of earlier theories that sought to understand why states collaborate in the international system. Liesbet Hooghe and Gary Marks (2002) formulated their multilevel governance approach, concentrating on the activities that occurred in the EU at various levels: the EU level, the national level, and the substate level (provincial or regional level). An important innovation in their approach was to focus not only on the EU and the nation state level, but also on the substate levels. Their studies of regional policy showed how regional actors were able to move integration forward, sometimes even circumventing national state actors. This approach, and other governance approaches more generally, were able to show that the central claim of liberal intergovernmentalism – namely that state preferences are determined in national settings and that the nation state government is the advocate for national interests – does not work in every policy arena. Policy studies showed that different modes of governance could influence the process of integration. For instance, in a collection of case studies, Tömmel and Verdun (2009) identify four different, innovative modes of governance that are used in the EU: hierarchy, negotiation, competition, and cooperation. Each mode has a different influence on the integration process, and sometimes these modes are even used together (see Chapter 5). One form of cooperation that has received much attention is the open method of coordination, which brings together both public and private actors to encourage policy coordination and mutual learning; this approach was used first and foremost in the domain of social policy, but since 2013 it has been applied in macroeconomic policy coordination within the EU through the so-called European Semester (D'Erman and Verdun 2022). More generally, governance approaches spell out how integration can occur outside of the classic domain where the national government negotiates in an intergovernmental setting to advance national interests at the EU level.

Another concept that emerged in the 1990s was **Europeanization**. At first, it was loosely used by scholars without a uniform definition – sometimes even with considerably different applications. Over time this concept has been widely understood to refer to two dimensions. The first is top-down Europeanization. When used this way, this term defines how the EU impacts the member states. It focuses on how the EU shapes institutions, processes, and policies in the member states and even in countries outside the EU (in particular accession countries and countries in the EU neighbourhood). By contrast, bottom-up Europeanization refers to how member states and other domestic actors shape the EU and its policies. Here the focus is on how the member states and other actors can "upload" their interests, experiences, and practices to the EU level. The research on Europeanization studies how the EU has changed the policies and politics of its member states as well as other states outside the EU. A third and final group of research questions in Europeanization scholarship examines how the governance of the EU as a whole impacts other regional organizations, such as the African Union or the Association of Southeast Asian Nations.

Other approaches that gained attraction in the 1990s were approaches that borrowed from the more general political science toolkit of theories and approaches. These scholars conceptualize the EU as a typical political system. Recall that the early integration theories were born from international relations with a view to understanding why separate countries might wish to cooperate or integrate. With a gradual appreciation that the EU was starting to resemble a more regular political system, even if a so-called *sui generis* one (that is, one that has specific features that are unique to this particular polity), the focus changed as to what it is that has to be theorized. Rather than wondering why separate nations were collaborating, the focus now was on the actual system and how this system was functioning the way it did and what policy outcomes could be expected given the nature of the system.

With this change in the object of study, the insights from institutionalist theories became of interest. An institutionalist approach assumes that the nature of the institutions shapes the outcome of politics and policies. In the 1990s there was a revival of **institutionalism**; this revival was labelled "new institutionalism" both to mark the difference with classical institutionalism and to signal the renewed interest in focusing on institutions against the behavioural backdrop of the earlier decades. Three main approaches of institutionalism were developed in this time: historical institutionalism; rational choice institutionalism; and sociological institutionalism. Historical institutionalism defines institutions as formal or informal procedures, routines, norms, and conventions that are embedded in the structure of a polity. It conceptualizes the relationships between institutions and individual behaviour in broad terms and adopts the concepts of "path dependence," "unintended consequences," and also the "role of ideas" to highlight some of the dynamics of the development of institutions. Rational choice institutionalism examines how institutions may lower the transaction costs of making deals (passing legislative proposals). This branch of new institutionalism sees institutions as a way to solve all kinds of collective action problems that legislatures often face. Finally, sociological institutionalism argues that many of the institutional forms and procedures of organization are not adopted because they are the most efficient way to do so, but rather they are culturally specific practices and thus must be explained as such.

Sociological institutionalism resembles the IR approach of constructivism that also became popular in EU research since the late 1990s. Though there is not really one single "constructivist approach," the umbrella term brings together various approaches that themselves draw from institutionalism and interpretive approaches and aim to be mid-range theories of integration. Constructivism identifies the world as being "socially constructed," meaning that people's norms, ideas, and identity shape how they perceive social realities and how institutions and policies – including those at the EU level – come about and bring about political outcomes (Christiansen, Jørgensen, and Wiener 2001). Scholars that fall under this rubric could range from more positivist and rational to more critical and radical ones. In recent years, feminist and environmental approaches have also gained ground, which often criticize the EU for having reproduced the political status quo. Feminists in particular have been vocal in problematizing how the EU reproduces existing power relationships (Kronsell 2005; Abels and MacRae 2016; Müller and Tömmel 2022; see also Chapter 16). More radical approaches have also focused on how the EU has reproduced modes of capital accumulation. Drawing on historical materialist and Gramscian traditions, critical political economy scholars have for decades pointed to the emphasis on the economic developments of European integration, with the politics lagging behind (Van Apeldoorn and Horn 2019). Focusing on class struggles, they see the retreat of the state and an emphasis on the market and austerity measures to deal with crisis as among the main factors that have led to the challenges the EU faces today. More recently scholars have used race and postcolonial theories to assess the integration process (Haastrup 2020; Bhambra 2022). Similarly, scholars have revisited European disintegration and integration at different levels of intensity ("differentiation"; Leruth et al. 2022; Schimmelfennig et al. 2023).

THEORIES OF DEMOCRACY, LEGITIMACY, AND THE EU AS A GLOBAL PLAYER

The purpose for which theory was used changed toward the end of the twentieth century. Rather than focusing mostly on the question of why integration happens, the subject of study became concentrated on understanding how developments occur in the EU polity. Furthermore, increasingly scholars were concerned with normative questions about how the EU ought to function and what constitutional form it might need to take. A body of literature emerged that concentrated on questions around the democratic nature of the EU. It considered the EU as a polity – a form of organized society with a political organization rather than merely a collection of nation states. A wide range of studies were dedicated to analyzing the EU's democratic credentials (see Chapter 15). Some of these were more *normative* in orientation, asking the question what the EU ought to look like. Others were more *positive*, focusing on explaining why the EU looked the way it did without necessarily judging whether the EU is "good" or "bad" or how it must change to improve. From these studies, it became clear that although it was attractive to think that the democratic deficit would disappear if only the EU looked more like a regular parliamentary democracy, such a change cannot easily be made in a polity such as the EU. These studies pointed out that precisely because the EU was not a fully-fledged federal state, and given that its citizens did not fully identify with the EU, it was not (yet) possible to reproduce the standard political features of a parliamentary democracy at the EU level. It would take away from the legitimate authority of the lower levels – namely the member states. Citizens felt better represented at the member state level than at the EU level. Thus, to increase the democratic credentials of the EU, the emphasis turned to increasing the role of participation in the EU and finding gradual increases in the power of the European Parliament. To increase participation meant finding ways to have citizens connect to the EU. But it also meant encouraging interest groups, experts, and national, transnational, and European civil society groups to have access to and participate in the various stages of policy-making in the EU. This approach was often referred to as *participatory democracy*. Various scholars emphasized the importance of deliberation and having various groups be able to give their views on draft policies and legislative proposals. Finally, the concern was that the EU did not have a single **demos** – a "people" with a shared identity or values that could be represented in one single body (see Chapter 15). Even though the concept of a European citizenship emerged with the Treaty of Maastricht, it did not right away build the identity needed for all to share a common identity.

Closely related to the concept of democratic deficit is the concept of legitimacy. To what extent is the EU producing legitimate inputs or outputs? Input legitimacy means that the European peoples find the political system legitimate because they accept the process whereby the elected parliamentary and government officials have been selected, even if the outcome of their decisions is not what they would have liked. Output legitimacy, by contrast, means that people find a political system legitimate because they find the results it produces satisfactory. Such outputs could be increased well-being or the quality of governance, which refers to how transparent and coherent policies are and whether they adhere to the principles of good governance. Making sure there are improved opportunities for actors and stakeholders to be part of the policy-making process would also increase the likelihood that the policy output would be in line with what citizens and other stakeholders were hoping for.

Finally, as the EU became a more coherent actor, there were increasingly theories that looked at how to theorize the EU as a global actor. One might think that such a research topic would bring the theories of integration full circle: back to the realm of IR. To some extent, this is true. In 1982, Hedley Bull famously said of the EU that it was mainly a "civilian power" and not likely to become a main actor in international affairs (Bull 1982). Even today the EU still remains an awkward actor in the global system (see Chapters 9, 12, and 18). It lacks clear actorship. EU leadership is often weak compared to the leadership of nations, such as the United States or China. While the EU is a strong player in the global system in some policy areas (for instance trade, international development, human rights, and climate policies), it is notably less so in others (such as foreign policy and defence) because its member states have diverging ambitions in those areas and because the EU has intergovernmental decision making in these areas. The EU is obviously weaker if it has joint competence with the member states and is required to check with member states before it can act in the international arena.

The EU, therefore, has often been characterized as an economic giant but a political lightweight. However, with the entering into force of the Treaty of Lisbon it has the potential to become a more coherent foreign policy actor, because some of its leadership roles have become more empowered. In the past, it already capitalized on its relative strengths by using instruments such as norms that have been labelled by Joseph Nye (1990) as having "**soft power**" (persuasion) – rather than focusing on "hard power" (coercion), using military capacity, for instance.

When discussing the external component of Europeanization, scholars have examined the role of the EU as a global actor in inter-regionalism. Here the focus is not only on how the EU serves as a model for other regions of the globe but also to what extent these regional organizations across the globe are becoming "actors" in global politics and what influence they have in world order and global governance. As is discussed in more detail in Chapters 9,

12, and 18, various aspects of EU external relations must be distinguished to analyze the true impact of the EU on the global stage. Many of these regional organizations suffer from internal conflict, as does the EU. But remarkably, these organizations are increasingly prominent on the global stage, and the EU is the most coherent, advanced polity of all regional organizations.

DEBATE: WHY USE THEORIES IN EUROPEAN INTEGRATION STUDIES?

This chapter has pointed to the development of integration theories from the early days to the present time. In the first four decades, approaches based on IR theories aimed to put all of the activities in European integration under one umbrella. Both neofunctionalism and intergovernmentalism at first sought to explain the entire integration process through a single lens (grand theory). Over time it became clear that European integration was too complex and that a single theory was unable to do justice to all the developments that have occurred throughout the European integration process. By looking at a part of the puzzle, theories could be applied that focused on that specific part. Rather than having one theory for the whole process, a suitable theory was chosen that could speak to a specific aspect of integration or policy-making. Furthermore, with the turn toward considering the EU as a polity in its own right, scholars have increasingly considered more usual political science, comparative politics, and public administration approaches to studying the politics of and policy-making in the EU as well as the impact of the EU on member states.

Debates about grand theory were salient in the 1960s, 1990s, and 2000s when there were fervent grand theory debates about whether European integration could be characterized as more intergovernmental or more supranational. These fierce discussions dwindled in the 2010s, and recently some scholars have sought to rekindle these discussions (Hooghe and Marks 2019). Today the richness of theories that can be deployed reaches a level of detail fitting most researchers' study of the EU and has led to the existence of a large toolkit of theories and approaches. Table 6.1 offers a taxonomy of the theories and approaches discussed in this chapter.

The taxonomy in Table 6.1 should be used only as a heuristic device. It should be made clear that many of the approaches also place some value in other actors, mechanisms, or theoretical purposes than the ones listed in the

Table 6.1. A schematic simple taxonomy of theories used in European integration studies and their focus on different actors and mechanisms

Dominant actors and mechanisms in advancing European integration	Theoretical approach
1. Dominant actors:	
Supranational actors	Neofunctionalism, governance approaches
National actors	Intergovernmentalism, governance approaches
Regional actors	Multilevel governance
Transnational interest groups	Neofunctionalism, governance approaches
Organized stakeholders; civil society	Participatory democracy
2. Dominant mechanisms in advancing European integration:	
Spillover	Neofunctionalism
Bargaining	Intergovernmentalism
Unintended consequences and path dependence	Historical institutionalism
Uploading and downloading	Europeanization
Modes of governance	Governance approaches
Norms, ideas, and beliefs	Normative power Europe, constructivism, critical political economy, postcolonialism
Cultural adaptation and socialization	Sociological institutionalism, constructivism; feminism
Citizen engagement in the policy-making process	Participatory democracy
3. Theoretical objective:	
Explaining European integration	Neofunctionalism, intergovernmentalism
Understanding European integration	Federalism, multilevel governance, Europeanization, institutionalism, constructivism
Evaluating the normative quality of the EU	Normative power Europe, participatory democracy, constructivism, feminism, critical political economy

Source: Adapted from Verdun (2002a; 2002b)

table. Also, this chapter has not discussed every possible approach used by scholars of European integration. Thus, the taxonomy provided here is merely intended to sort the approaches and to summarize the overview presented in this chapter. What it does make clear, however, is that the locus of attention varies with each approach. When researchers seek to develop their research questions and reflect on what theoretical approaches would be best able to address their question, they may do well to consider the tradition of these approaches and what their prime actors and mechanisms as well as research objectives have been.

CONCLUSION

This chapter aimed to review the various theories that are adopted in European integration studies. Starting with the classic theories of neofunctionalism and intergovernmentalism that were dominant in the early decades, it then moved to looking at newer theories such as governance approaches, Europeanization, and institutionalism. Some of the theoretical debates centre on themes such as democracy and legitimacy in the EU or questions around the EU as a global actor. Although the time of grand theorization seems to have passed, remnants of those approaches still penetrate contemporary EU studies. Contemporary research draws much more on general scholarly literature in the field of political science, public administration, and adjacent disciplines. The purpose of theory in European integration studies is to build on the insights of the past so as to inform our current research questions. Whether the scope of the research is smaller or wider or whether it contributes to a smaller or larger part of the insight of European integration is left to the choice of individual academic researchers.

REVIEW QUESTIONS

1 In which ways can theories of federalism be helpful in explaining developments in the EU?
2 Why were neofunctionalism and intergovernmentalism the dominant approaches in the early years of European integration? Why did both of them witness a revival in the 1990s?
3 Why have approaches from political science and public administration emerged in more and more studies that cover developments in the EU?
4 How has widening, deepening, and differentiation affected European integration theories?
5 How have concerns over the EU's democratic credentials influenced the use of theory in EU studies?
6 Why did international relations theories lose their attraction when studying the EU, and why they are more frequently used again today?

7 How have feminist, climate activist, and anticolonial thinkers influenced the theorizing of European integration?

EXERCISES

1 When studying the EU comparatively, when is it appropriate to compare the EU to other federal countries, and when is it appropriate to compare the EU to other international organizations? What theoretical approaches are used in each tactic?
2 Consider the history and trajectory of the EU alongside the two major theories of European integration: neofunctionalism and liberal intergovernmentalism. What major events support and challenge each theory?

REFERENCES AND FURTHER READING

Abels, G., and H. MacRae, eds. 2016. *Gendering European Integration Theory: Engaging New Dialogues*. Leverkusen, Germany: Barbara Budrich Publishers.

Bauer, M., and S. Becker. 2014. "The Unexpected Winner of the Crisis: The European Commission's Strengthened Role in Economic Governance." *Journal of European Integration* 36 (3): 213–29. https://doi.org/10.1080/07036337.2014.885750.

Becker, S., M.W. Bauer, S. Connolly, and H. Kassim. 2016. "The Commission: Boxed in and Constrained but Still an Engine of Integration." *West European Politics* 39 (5): 1011–31. https://doi.org/10.1080/01402382.2016.1181870.

Bellamy, R., D. Castiglione, and J. Shaw, eds. 2006. *Making European Citizens: Civic Inclusion in a Transnational Context*. Basingstoke, UK: Palgrave Macmillan.

Bhambra, G.K. 2022. "A Decolonial Project for Europe." *Journal of Common Market Studies* 60 (2): 229–44. https://doi.org/10.1111/jcms.13310.

Bickerton, C.J., D. Hodson, and U. Puetter, eds. 2015. *The New Intergovernmentalism: States and Supranational Actors in the Post-Maastricht Era*. Oxford: Oxford University Press.

Börzel, T.A., and T. Risse. 2012. "From Europeanisation to Diffusion: Introduction." *West European Politics* 35 (1): 1–19. https://doi.org/10.1080/01402382.2012.631310.

Bull, H. 1982. "Civilian Power Europe: A Contradiction in Terms?" *Journal of Common Market Studies* 21 (2): 149–70.

Christiansen, T., K.E. Jørgensen, and A. Wiener. 2001. *The Social Construction of Europe*. London: SAGE.

De Gruyter, C. 2021. "Is Europe Any Good at Soft Power?" *Foreign Policy*, June 14.

D'Erman, V., and A. Verdun. 2022. "Policy Coordination in the EU from the European Semester to the COVID-19 Crisis." *Journal of Common Market Studies* 60 (1): 3–20. https://doi.org/10.1111/jcms.13276.

Ericksen, E.O., and J.E. Fossum, eds. 2000. *Democracy in the European Union: Integration through Deliberation?* London: Routledge.

Haas, E.B. 1958. *The Uniting of Europe: Political, Social, and Economical Forces, 1950–1957*. London: Stevens.

Haastrup, T. 2020. "Critical Perspectives on Africa's Relationship with the European Union." In *The Routledge Handbook of Critical European Studies*, edited by D. Bigo, T. Diez, E. Fanoulis, B. Rosamond, and Y.A. Stivachtis, 511–22. London: Routledge.

Hix, S. 1994. "The Study of the European Community: The Challenge to Comparative Politics." *West European Politics* 17 (1): 1–30. https://doi.org/10.1080/01402389408424999.

Hoffmann, S. 1966. "Obstinate or Obsolete? The Fate of the Nation-State and the Case of Western Europe." *Daedalus* 95 (3): 862–915.

Hooghe, L., and G. Marks. 2002. *Multi-Level Governance and European Integration*. Lanham, MD: Rowman and Littlefield.

Hooghe, L., and G. Marks. 2009. "A Postfunctionalist Theory of European Integration: From Permissive Consensus to Constraining Dissensus." *British Journal of Political Science* 39 (1): 1–23. https://doi.org/10.1017/S0007123408000409.

Hooghe, L., and G. Marks. 2019. "Grand Theories of European Integration in the Twenty-First Century." *Journal of European Public Policy* 26 (8): 1113–33. https://doi.org/10.1080/13501763.2019.1569711.

Hueglin, T.O., and A. Fenna. 2005. *Comparative Federalism: A Systematic Inquiry*, 2nd ed. Toronto: University of Toronto Press.

Kohler-Koch, B., and B. Rittberger. 2006. "Review Article: The 'Governance Turn' in EU Studies." *Journal of Common Market Studies* 44 (S1): 27–49. https://doi.org/10.1111/j.1468-5965.2006.00642.x.

Kronsell, A. 2005. "Gender, Power and European Integration Theory." *Journal of European Public Policy* 12 (6): 1022–40. https://doi.org/10.1080/13501760500270703.

Krotz, U., and L. Schramm. 2021. "An Old Couple in a New Setting: Franco-German Leadership in the Post-Brexit EU." *Politics and Governance* 9 (1): 48–58. https://doi.org/10.17645/pag.v9i1.3645.

Leruth, B., S. Gänzle, and J. Trondal, eds. 2022. *The Routledge Handbook of Differentiation in the European Union*. London: Routledge.

Leuffen, D., B. Rittberger, and F. Schimmelfennig. 2013. *Differentiated Integration: Explaining Variation in the European Union*. Basingstoke, UK: Palgrave Macmillan.

Long, D., and L.M. Ashworth. 1999. "Working for Peace: The Functional Approach, Functionalism and Beyond." In *New Perspectives on International Functionalism*, edited by L.M. Asworth and D. Long, 1–26. Basingstoke, UK: Palgrave Macmillan.

Manners, I. 2002. "Normative Power Europe: A Contradiction in Terms?" *Journal of Common Market Studies* 40 (2): 235–58. https://doi.org/10.1111/1468-5965.00353.

Marks, G., L. Hooghe, and K. Blank. 1996. "European Integration from the 1980s: State-Centric v. Multilevel Governance." *Journal of Common Market Studies* 34 (3): 341–78. https://doi.org/10.1111/j.1468-5965.1996.tb00577.x.

Moravcsik, A. 1998. *The Choice for Europe: Social Purpose and State Power from Messina to Maastricht*. Ithaca, NY: Cornell University Press.

Müller, H., and I. Tömmel, eds. 2022. *Women and Leadership in the European Union*. Oxford: Oxford University Press.

Nicoli, F. 2020. "Neofunctionalism Revisited: Integration Theory and Varieties of Outcomes in the Eurocrisis." *Journal of European Integration* 42 (7): 897–916. https://doi.org/10.1080/07036337.2019.1670658.

Niemann, A., and D. Ioannou. 2015. "European Economic Integration in Times of Crisis: A Case of Neofunctionalism?" *Journal of European Public Policy* 22 (2): 196–218. https://doi.org/10.1080/13501763.2014.994021.

Nye, J.S. 1990. "Soft Power." *Foreign Policy* 80: 153–71. https://doi.org/10.2307/1148580.

Pentland, C. 1973. *International Theory and European Integration*. London: Faber.

Piketty, T. 2013. *Capital in the Twenty-First Century*. Cambridge, MA: Harvard University Press.

Pollack, M.A. 2002. *The Engines of European Integration: Delegation, Agency and Agenda Setting in the European Union*. Oxford: Oxford University Press.

Rosamond, B. 2000. *Theories of European Integration*. Basingstoke, UK: Palgrave.

Sandholtz, W., and A. Stone-Sweet. 2012. "Neo-functionalism and Supranational Governance." In *The Oxford Handbook of the European Union*, edited by E. Jones, A. Menon, and S. Weatherill, 18–33. Oxford: Oxford University Press.

Savage, J.D., and A. Verdun. 2015. "Strengthening the European Commission's Budgetary and Economic Surveillance Capacity since Greece and the Euro Crisis: A Study of Five Directorates-General." *Journal of European Public Policy* 23 (1): 101–18. https://doi.org/10.1080/13501763.2015.1041417.

Schild, J. 2020. "EMU's Asymmetries and Asymmetries in German and French Influence on EMU Governance Reforms." *Journal of European Integration* 42 (3): 449–64. https://doi.org/10.1080/07036337.2020.1730351.

Schimmelfennig, F. 2015. "What's the News in 'New Intergovernmentalism'? A Critique of Bickerton, Hodson and Puetter." *Journal of Common Market Studies* 53 (4): 723–30. https://doi.org/10.1111/jcms.12234.

Schimmelfennig, F. 2018. "European Integration (Theory) in Times of Crisis: A Comparison of the Euro and Schengen Crises." *Journal of European Public Policy* 26 (7): 969–89. https://doi.org/10.1080/13501763.2017.1421252.

Schimmelfennig, F., D. Leuffen, and C.E. De Vries. 2023. "Differentiated Integration in the European Union: Institutional Effects, Public Opinion, and Alternative Flexibility Arrangements." *European Union Politics* 24 (1): 3–20. https://doi.org/10.1177/14651165221119083.

Söderbaum, F., and L. Van Langenhove. 2005. "Introduction: The EU as a Global Actor and the Role of Interregionalism." *Journal of European Integration* 27 (3): 249–62. https://doi.org/10.1080/07036330500190073.

Tömmel, I., and A. Verdun. 2009. *Innovative Governance in the European Union*. Boulder, CO: Lynne Rienner.

Van Apeldoorn, B., and L. Horn. 2019. "Critical Political Economy." In *European Integration Theory*, 3rd ed., edited by A. Wiener, T. Börzel, and T. Risse, 195–215. Oxford: Oxford University Press.

Verdun, A., ed. 2002a. *The Euro: European Integration Theory and Economic and Monetary Union*. Lanham, MD: Rowman and Littlefield.

Verdun, A. 2002b. "Why EMU Happened: A Survey of Theoretical Explanations." In *Before and Beyond EMU: View from Across the Atlantic*, edited by P. Crowley, 71–98. London: Routledge.

Verdun, A. 2015. "A Historical Institutionalist Explanation of the EU's Responses to the Euro Area Financial Crisis." *Journal of European Public Policy* 22 (2): 219–37. https://doi.org/10.1080/13501763.2014.994023.

Verdun, A. 2016. "The Federal Features of the EU: Lessons from Canada." *Politics and Governance* 4 (3): 100–10. https://doi.org/10.17645/pag.v4i3.598.

Verdun, A. 2020. "Intergovernmentalism: Old, Liberal and New." *Oxford Research Encyclopedia of Politics*. https://doi.org/10.1093/acrefore/9780190228637.013.1489.

Vollaard, H. 2014. "Explaining European Disintegration." *Journal of Common Market Studies* 52 (5): 1142–59. https://doi.org/10.1111/jcms.12132.

Wiener, A., T. Börzel, and T. Risse, eds. 2019. *European Integration Theory*, 3rd ed. Oxford: Oxford University Press.

Wood, D., and A. Verdun. 2011. "Canada and the European Union: A Review of the Literature from 1982 to 2010." *International Journal* 66 (1S): 9–21. https://doi.org/10.1177/002070201106600102.

PART TWO

Policies

7
Economic and Monetary Integration: Single Market and EMU

Paul Schure and Amy Verdun

READER'S GUIDE

Economic and monetary integration occurred with ups and downs. Developments in the 1950s, 1960s, and 1970s defined the early European Community. In the mid-1970s and early 1980s, integration appeared to have stalled. Completion of the Single Market and Economic and Monetary Union (the creation of a single currency) were the goals that restarted the integration process in the mid-1980s and early 1990s. Eastern enlargement, adding 10 new member states, was another important milestone in 2004. However, the 2007–8 global financial crisis and the 2010–12 sovereign debt crisis shook the European Union (EU) to its core. These were followed by further challenges – such as Brexit and the COVID-19 pandemic, and most recently the war in Ukraine. Changes in macroeconomic and fiscal coordination between EU member states can only be understood in relation to these major challenges.

INTRODUCTION

From the 1951 European Coal and Steel Community and the 1957 European Economic Community and European Atomic Energy Community, European integration has centred on taking steps toward deeper economic integration. The philosophy of the EU's founders (Jean Monnet and Robert Schuman, among others) was to integrate several key economic sectors of the member states (see Chapter 2). This chapter chronicles European economic integration since World War II, paying close attention to the challenges that emerged along the way and the institutions that were created to address them.

Initially, there were competing integration initiatives. Belgium, France, Italy, Luxembourg, the Netherlands, and West Germany formed the European Economic Community (EEC) in 1957. Austria, Denmark, Norway, Portugal, Sweden, Switzerland, and the United Kingdom formed the European Free Trade Association (EFTA) in 1960. The EFTA was a free trade agreement, while the EEC envisaged a much deeper form of collaboration and quickly went a step further than EFTA as it formed a **Customs Union** in July 1968 with a common set of tariffs for external trade. The EEC proved more successful; over time most of the EFTA states acceded to the EEC, which turned into what is today the EU (see Chapters 2 and 13).[1]

After the creation of the Customs Union in 1968, the next step for the EEC was to complete a **Common Market**, but that ended up being considerably more difficult than envisaged. It would eventually require another boost and a detailed plan, the Single Market Programme (1985), to complete what was then called the **Single Market** by a deadline of December 31, 1992. The next important plan was to create an **Economic and Monetary Union (EMU)**, which was ultimately achieved in 1999 with 12 of the 15 member states taking part in the third and final stage (the UK, Sweden, Denmark, and Greece did not introduce the euro in 1999, although Greece followed soon afterwards).

EMU was deeply affected by the 2010–12 **sovereign debt crisis**, a period of acute financial distress of the governments of Greece and, to a lesser extent, some other euro area member states, including Ireland and Spain. During this time, governments of these countries were unable to refinance their public debt at rates that were sustainable. In everyday language, without help, they could no longer pay the bills. To manage the crisis and prevent any future crises, new institutions were created at the EU level: the European Financial Stability Facility, the **European Stability Mechanism**, and the **Banking Union**. The COVID-19 crisis in 2020 and the invasion of Ukraine by Russia in February 2022 appear to have increased solidarity among the member states and may give an impetus to deeper integration, as we explain below.

This chapter discusses the main developments in economic integration since World War II, in particular the developments that led to the creation of the Single Market and EMU. We then assess the first 10 years of EMU and move to the sovereign debt crisis in its teenage years. In the debate section, we turn to the ongoing discussions on what the EU can do to deal with current issues, such as questions around fiscal federalism and legitimacy.

FROM THE COMMON MARKET TO THE SINGLE MARKET

Four stages ("degrees") of economic integration are often identified. In order of increased degree of integration they are a free trade area (FTA), a Customs Union, a Common Market, and finally an Economic Union (see Box 7.1). Bela Balassa (1961) was among the first to use these terms. Balassa's term "Common Market," which was standard in the 1960s and 1970s, was replaced by "Single Market" in the 1980s, while his "Economic Union" is known nowadays as "Economic and Monetary Union."

BOX 7.1: STAGES OF ECONOMIC INTEGRATION

Free Trade Agreement (FTA)	Zero tariffs between member countries and reduced non-tariff barriers
Customs Union (CU)	FTA + common trade relationships (common external tariff and trade agreements, if any) with countries outside the CU
Common Market (CM); from 1985 referred to as "Internal Market" or "Single Market"	CU + free movement of capital and labour (together with freedom of movement of goods and services, called the "four freedoms") and some policy harmonization
Economic and Monetary Union (EMU)	CM + common economic and monetary policies and institutions, with irrevocably fixed exchange rates or a single currency

Source: Adapted from Balassa (1961)

From its start in 1957, the EEC envisaged the creation of a Common Market based on the so-called *four freedoms*, namely the freedom of movement of goods, services, persons, and capital. Barriers to the free movement of goods include **tariffs** and quotas on imports, preferential treatment of local firms (through subsidies or preferential public procurement, for example), and **non-tariff barriers** that hinder cross-border trade (such as cumbersome border procedures or protectionist national product regulations).

The envisaged first steps toward the Common Market were the elimination of tariffs and quotas between member states and then the creation of a Customs Union. Next came the elimination of non-tariff barriers. The issue of differing product standards across the union was initially addressed through a *positive integration* strategy of replacing the patchwork of national standards with a common European standard. Yet such harmonization proved to be challenging. Common standards were often opposed by member states, in part because their adoption often had distributional effects: The choice of the common product standard may result in a competitive advantage of the firms in some countries over firms in other countries.

In this situation, a landmark ruling of the Court of Justice of the EU (CJEU) switched the focus to challenging barriers to trade based on appeals to the Court and *negative integration*, specifically mutual recognition of each other's product standards. In the **Cassis de Dijon** case (Case 120/78 *Rewe-Zentral AG v. Bundesmonopolverwaltung für Branntwein* [1979] ECR 649), the Court rejected a German ban on the sale of Cassis de Dijon, a French blackcurrant liqueur containing 15–20 per cent alcohol, as a "liqueur" in Germany. The German regulator had argued that Cassis did not conform to the product standard regarding liqueurs in Germany (German liqueur standards stipulated a minimum of 25 per cent alcohol on fruit liqueurs; Cassis fell short of that). The CJEU ruled that the Cassis sales ban was equivalent to a quantitative restriction and hence should be removed. This ruling established the principle of *mutual recognition*: If a product can be legally marketed in one member state, then it should normally be legally marketable in other member states as well. Mutual recognition of products, but also of the regulatory bodies of other EU countries and their regulations, made positive integration through harmonization unnecessary in many cases.

Despite the shift to mutual recognition, there were still abundant barriers to the four freedoms by the beginning of the 1980s. In January 1985, Jacques Delors, the president of the European Commission, declared that he wanted to push the main objective of the EEC. The Commission prepared a White Paper (a planning document), "Completing the Internal Market" (COM/85/0310), and the European Council of Milan in June 1985 agreed to call an intergovernmental conference to amend the EEC Treaty. The resulting treaty, the Single European Act (SEA, signed in 1986; entered into force July 1, 1987), introduced important changes to legislative procedures. For example, legislation on the Single Market would now be taken by qualified majority vote in the Council (see Chapter 3); previously individual member states could insist that the decision be taken by unanimity. In this way, the SEA gave an important impetus to the process of completing the Single Market.

An important common policy to make sure the Single Market functions well is competition policy. Much as the Competition Bureau in Canada, the Directorate-General (DG) for Competition of the European Commission aims at preventing anticompetitive behaviour of firms (such as price agreements or market-sharing agreements with other firms) or the abuse of a dominant position that a firm possibly has in a market. On occasion, it imposes hefty fines on firms found to have engaged in such practices. DG Competition also reviews proposed mergers between firms. DG Competition can block such mergers if their impact reaches across member state borders and the merged company would achieve a dominant position in certain markets. Finally, DG Competition can disallow national, provincial, or municipal governments from supporting companies through subsidies ("state aid"). All these pillars of competition policy aim to promote a "level playing field" among firms.

Through DG Competition – particularly under Commissioner Margrethe Vestager – the EU has placed itself at the forefront of a broad debate about the roles of leading multinational tech platforms, such as Apple, Amazon, Facebook, and Google, in the marketplace. The EU has focused on two issues. First, do these "Big Tech" firms and some other foreign companies pay the appropriate amount of taxes? In the case of Apple, the Commissioner alleged that the company paid insufficient taxes, which amounted to state support, and the Commission demanded that more taxes (€13 billion plus penalties) be collected (by the government of Ireland). Apple successfully challenged this decision in July 2020, and the Commission appealed that decision in fall 2020. The dispute is still before the EU courts. Second, in November 2020, the Commission launched the Digital Markets Act (DMA), a proposed new regulatory framework for Big Tech. DG Competition (rather than the national competition authorities) will be the sole authority responsible for enforcing the DMA.

At the start of the twenty-first century, it became clear that the free movement of services in the EU lagged behind that of goods. The Services Directive

(Directive 2006/123/EC) aimed at making it easier for services to be "traded" across borders. This directive was initially met with heavy criticism. Many questioned if such a directive might lead to a "race to the bottom" in social and labour provisions, which generated comments about "Polish plumbers" (a mythical Eastern European tradesperson that represented the threat of cheaper rates in more expensive Western European markets because of their presumed inferior social insurance and wage). Interestingly, the Services Directive contained no new policies that were not already mentioned in the EU treaties and reinforced by the CJEU in relevant case law. By making them explicit, however, the directive drew attention to the effect of the Single Market on the delivery and trade of services across borders. Critics were worried that temporary workers from EU member states with lower wages and less social security would undermine the so-called **European social model** (Theme 2 of this book; see also Chapter 16). They demanded that member state labour laws in the country where people work would apply to temporary workers and service providers as well. After numerous changes of the proposed directive, in part as a response to demands by the European Parliament, the Services Directive was accepted in December 2006 (for a comparison with Canada, see Box 7.2).

It is sometimes difficult for "ordinary citizens" to appreciate fully the value of the Single Market. We can illustrate this point by discussing **Brexit** – the withdrawal of the United Kingdom from the EU (see Chapter 13). While in the referendum held on June 23, 2016, 52 per cent of UK voters chose to "leave" the EU, they had no clear idea of what the relationship between the UK and the EU would be after Brexit. By the time UK prime minister Theresa May formally notified the EU in March 2017 that the UK wanted to leave, it was apparent she was aiming for a "hard Brexit": The UK would no longer be part of the Single Market and would no longer be subjected to rulings of the CJEU or participate in the free movement of labour (that is, the UK would regain full control over its migration policy).

The UK and the EU subsequently negotiated the conditions under which the UK and the rest of the EU would trade in goods and services after the UK's withdrawal. An agreement was reached at the eleventh hour, on December 30, 2020. The EU–UK Trade and Cooperation Agreement (TCA) came into effect provisionally on January 1, 2021, and officially entered into force on May 1, 2021. It includes preferential arrangements on trade in goods and services, digital trade, intellectual property, aviation, transportation, energy, fisheries,

BOX 7.2: THE CANADIAN SINGLE MARKET
The EU has a Single Market. Canada is a federal state that, since its creation in 1867, on paper has free movement of commerce across the country. However, contrary to what one might expect, Canada is not a fully integrated single market. An article in the influential weekly *The Economist* (2016) asked why oil and mining firms in the province of Alberta had heavy equipment bought in Asia shipped to Alberta through the United States. The argument was that Canada's single market is bogged down in bureaucracy (that is, there are non-tariff barriers, to speak in the language of Box 7.1).

In 2016, the Senate Committee on Banking estimated the cost of the incomplete single market in Canada at $130 billion a year. Various attempts have been made to eliminate trade barriers in Canada, most recently the Canadian Free Trade Agreement of 2017, but these did not manage to remove all the barriers to trade. There are differences in product and service regulations and in professional licensing requirements among the provinces. Alvarez, Krznar, and Tombe (2019) estimate that removing internal barriers to trade would boost Canadian GDP by as much as 4 per cent, which they claim is more than the effect of any possible international trade agreement.

In Canada, removing internal trade barriers is a political matter in which the provinces take centre stage. By contrast, in the EU, many past accomplishments toward the Single Market involved the judicial system, which pushed mutual recognition. Some provinces have continued to try to reduce barriers to trade, for example through the New West Partnership Trade Agreement between Alberta, British Columbia, Manitoba, and Saskatchewan. However, product and service regulations often remain a provincial matter, and provinces do not necessarily have to recognize regulations of other jurisdictions – an important difference with the EU. While removing trade barriers is arguably important, it is perhaps not a sufficiently salient matter for voters, and special interests may be hard to overcome.

social security coordination, cooperation in law enforcement, and some cooperation in other programs. Nevertheless, this agreement establishes a lower level of economic cooperation than the level of integration the UK was at before. In concrete terms, some of the effects have been more administrative red tape at borders, leading to long queues of truck drivers trying to enter the UK. In a comprehensive analysis of Brexit under the TCA (which separates out the effects of COVID-19), Dhingra et al. (2022) conclude their studies with the conclusion that the transition to a new equilibrium will take substantial time and that "a less-open UK will mean a poorer and less productive one by the end of the decade, with real wages expected to fall by 1.8 per cent, a loss of £470 per worker a year, and labour productivity by 1.3 per cent, as a result of the long-run changes to trade under the TCA.… We estimate that, by 2030, the UK will be 7 percentage points less open, have 1.3 per cent lower productivity, and real wages will be around 1.8 per cent lower than in the absence of Brexit."

CREATING EUROPE'S SINGLE CURRENCY

The idea to create EMU was first agreed to at the European Council Summit in 1969 in The Hague. In 1970, a committee chaired by Luxembourg's prime minister and finance minister Pierre Werner presented a possible blueprint (the **Werner Plan**). It foresaw the setting up of two supranational bodies: a Community System for the Central Banks (monetary policy) and a Centre of Decision for Economic Policy (to coordinate macroeconomic policies, including some tax policies). Though most of the recommendations were adopted, no action was taken to achieve the end goal of creating an EMU by 1980 (see Chapter 2).

EMU failed at the time because member states differed in their views on how to achieve it, especially in light of the changing international economic and monetary situation. Following the collapse of the Bretton Woods system of fixed exchange rates, currencies started to float, there was a major oil crisis and accompanying recession, and opinions on how to tackle the crisis differed wildly. EEC countries set up their own system of fixed but adjustable exchange rates, called the *snake in the tunnel*, in which five of the six original EEC countries (and some others) participated to keep their exchange rates stable. West Germany became central to this system, while France did not manage to stay in. In 1979, the system was reformed and the European Monetary System (EMS) was created in which all EEC countries participated. At the heart was the **exchange rate mechanism (ERM)**, which featured the currencies of all EEC member states except the UK. The UK's pound sterling was, however, part of the calculation of the European Currency Unit, the unit of account at the heart of the EMS (used for accounting and financial purposes – it was not a material currency). The British non-participation in the ERM underscores that the UK had an ambivalent relationship with Europe's monetary integration project from the outset.

The first four years of the ERM were characterized by several exchange rate realignments, but there were none from 1987 until the summer of 1992. In fact, by 1992 the ERM had become an important symbol of successful European integration. Informally, the German currency, the deutschmark, was the "anchor currency," and other monetary authorities often followed the decisions of the German central bank (Bundesbank). The success of the EMS helped create an environment conducive to deeper monetary integration. Another important development was the SEA, which, as discussed above, aimed at completing the Single Market and explicitly mentioned the need to relaunch EMU. In 1988, the European Council asked Commission president Jacques Delors to produce a blueprint for EMU. With the help of central bank presidents and a few other experts, he drew up a report (the Delors Report) by April 1989 that proposed a road to EMU in three stages.

The Delors Report envisaged the creation of a **European System of Central Banks (ESCB**, or Eurosystem) with a new supranational **European Central Bank (ECB)** that would work together with the national central banks. Contrary to what had been proposed in the Werner Plan, no supranational authority was foreseen on budgetary and fiscal policies. This choice to agree on monetary but not on fiscal integration is often called "asymmetrical EMU" (Verdun 1996). Instead of supranational decisions on budgetary and fiscal policies, the Delors Report suggested rules placing maximum limits on national budgetary deficits and national public debt. EMU was to create an integrated area with full freedom of movement of goods, services, capital, and labour and fixed exchange rates among the currencies of the member states that met the criteria, or, ideally, a single currency. At the June 1989 European Council meeting in Madrid, the EMU blueprint was adopted as a basis for further discussion in an intergovernmental conference that would discuss the next concrete steps and would eventually be included in the Treaty on European Union (or the Maastricht Treaty). Article 104 TEC (now Article 126 TFEU) stipulated the so-called **convergence criteria** that countries needed to meet to join EMU (see Box 7.3).

> **BOX 7.3: CONVERGENCE CRITERIA FOR EMU MEMBERSHIP**
> 1. The ratio of government deficit to gross domestic product must not exceed 3 per cent.
> 2. The ratio of government debt to gross domestic product must not exceed 60 per cent or must be consistently reducing and approaching the reference value.
> 3. A sustainable degree of price stability and an average inflation rate, observed over a period of one year before the examination, which does not exceed by more than one-and-a-half percentage points that of the three best-performing member states in terms of price stability.
> 4. A long-term nominal interest rate that does not exceed by more than two percentage points that of the three best-performing member states in terms of price stability.
> 5. The normal fluctuation margins provided for by the ERM on the EMS must have been respected without severe tensions for at least the last two years before the examination.
>
> To join the euro area, a member state must also have central bank laws in place that ensure that its national central bank is independent. Also, monetary financing of governments by central banks is not permitted.
>
> The Stability and Growth Pact was created in 1995 to ensure member states would maintain budgetary and fiscal discipline once in EMU. If they did not adhere to the same criteria (e.g., the budgetary deficit criterion of no more than 3 per cent) they could face sanctions.
>
> Source: Adapted from Article 126, Article 140 TFEU, and protocols

The first stage of EMU lasted from July 1, 1990, until January 1, 1994, after which capital markets were considered liberalized. In stage two (1994–8), the European Monetary Institute, the predecessor to the ECB, was set up in Frankfurt. Its task was to create the operational framework of its successor. The ECB mandate was to maintain price stability. Without "prejudice to that primary mandate," the ECB would also support the "general economic policies" and "objectives" of the EU (for example, full employment and balanced economic growth). Both the ECB and the national central banks were to be politically

Figure 7.1. Yields ("interest rates") on 10-year government bonds of select member states

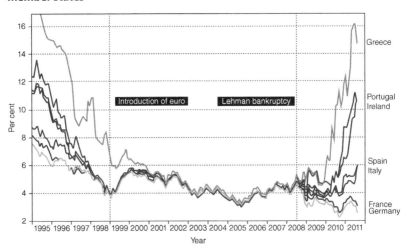

Source: *Der Spiegel*, August 15, 2011

independent. During the 1990s, it was difficult for the countries to meet the EMU convergence criteria. Public debt levels rose, and countries also found it challenging to satisfy the 3 per cent budgetary deficit criterion. Eventually, 11 member states joined the third and final stage of EMU that started with the irrevocable fixing of the exchange rates on January 1, 1999. A year later, Greece joined the third stage as well. EMU, as had been envisaged in the Maastricht Treaty, was fully completed in 12 member states when, on January 1, 2002, euro banknotes and coins were circulated in 12 member states.

THE FIRST 10 YEARS OF EMU

EMU had a number of striking initial effects. A liquid corporate bond market developed rapidly in the euro area. Before euro adoption it had been hard for firms to issue corporate bonds in their local currencies. It frequently happened that such firms borrowed in British pounds, Swiss francs, or US dollars. The cost of borrowing for firms and governments came down dramatically, especially in southern member states as well as in Finland and Ireland, where borrowing costs had traditionally been high. Investment levels went up, again particularly strongly in the south. Finally, and relatedly, long-term interest rates in the euro area revealed remarkable levels of convergence (see Figure 7.1).

The large yield differences *before* the introduction of the euro are usually interpreted as differences in inflation expectations in the bond market segments of each member state. Differences in yields *after* the introduction of the euro reflect potential differences in (1) perceived default probabilities of member state governments, as well as (2) the liquidity of local bond markets. The small differences in yields between 2000 and 2008 underscore that bond market participants initially neglected both, although they started to play an important role after 2008.

Since the start of the twenty-first century, 13 member states have joined the EU (see Chapter 13). Of these, eight have meanwhile also adopted the euro: Slovenia (2007), Cyprus and Malta (2008), Slovakia (2009), Estonia (2011), Latvia (2014), Lithuania (2015), and Croatia (2023). Some other countries that are not members of the EU also use the euro as their official currency, namely the Principality of Monaco, the Republic of San Marino, the Vatican City State, and the Principality of Andorra. Finally, there are countries, such as Kosovo and Montenegro, that use the euro as their currency even though they have not made formal agreements with the EU to do so.

In 2007–8 the world was rocked by what is now called the global financial crisis. The collapse of the US investment bank Lehman Brothers in September 2008 marked the start of the worst period of the crisis. Several other financial institutions went bankrupt, and there was an imminent danger that the entire financial system would collapse. Low interest rates and weak financial regulation led to a bloated financial sector and excessive risk taking by banks and other financial institutions. Rajan (2010) argues that these problems in the financial system themselves were a consequence of deeper underlying "fault lines," including global macroeconomic imbalances and rising income inequality in the United States. While the crisis erupted in the United States, it spread globally and hit several European countries particularly hard.

The initial perception during the global financial crisis was that EMU protected the euro area countries against the most negative effects of the crisis. Many recalled that previous crises often implied strong currency fluctuations with severe central bank intervention and capital controls as a result. Currency fluctuations were obviously no longer possible between the EMU countries, but the euro also kept up its value well vis-à-vis other currencies (for good or for bad). The euro was initially viewed to be a stable ship that made it easy for countries to navigate the crisis. However, the crisis hit the financial sectors of several countries in the Single Market (inside and outside EMU), and a need emerged to provide national support to destitute banks.

FROM FINANCIAL CRISIS TO SOVEREIGN DEBT CRISIS

Several EU governments ran higher budgetary deficits during the first years of the financial crisis. A much more important factor, however, for the public finances of several member states was that interest rates were impacted by implicit and explicit government guarantees of the banking sectors in their countries. Two years after the start of the global financial crisis it turned into a sovereign debt crisis in the euro area: interest rates on the government debt of some of the EMU countries rose to unsustainably high levels. Some other countries were deemed safe and benefited from extremely low interest rates. Interest rates on public debt started diverging in 2008 and rose to unsustainable levels in some countries (see Figure 7.1).

Although a number of countries faced challenges, the case of Greece was particularly alarming. In the fall of 2009, the newly elected Greek government announced that its budgetary deficit was much higher than previously reported. The result was a gradual spiral of downgrading Greek government bonds. It raised several questions for EMU: Would EU institutions or other member states bail out the Greek government if push came to shove? How much solidarity would the member states have with one another? What was the purpose of the EU in these difficult times?

A first consideration was the so-called "no-bailout clause" of Article 125(1) TFEU, which restricted the EU, as well as member states, from taking on the debts of Greece or any other member state. However, the clause did not prohibit member states from lending funds to another member state. Without any help, Greece would have defaulted on its public debt, an outcome that was expected to result in severe troubles inside Greece, such as social unrest, but also losses for the banks that held Greek public debt (in Greece and elsewhere in the EU). Banks had already been strained from the global financial crisis, and hence the fear was that a Greek default would trigger a second banking crisis. However, an argument levied against a bailout of the Greek government was moral hazard: A bailout would create the anticipation of future bailouts and therefore reduce the incentives for EU governments to behave in a fiscally sound manner. Furthermore, to complicate matters, it was clear that a bailout by the EU, if any, would need to be funded through a new financial commitment from the member states, given that the EU budget is only 1 per cent of gross national income (see Box 7.4).

> **BOX 7.4: EU BUDGET AND ECONOMIC AFFAIRS**
>
> The 2021 EU budget was €164.3 billion. Much of the funding was earmarked for dealing with the effects of COVID-19, the support for a sustainable recovery, and the transition toward more green and digital developments in the economy. These priorities had been formulated in the Multiannual Financial Framework, the long-term EU budget.
>
> To deal with the crisis, the Recovery and Resilience Facility was established as an additional financial instrument with €672.5 billion to spend on economic recovery from the pandemic. These funds were found by borrowing from financial markets. Together, member states have access to a total of €312.5 billion in grants and €360 billion in loans for public investment and reforms. This temporary arrangement is envisaged as a way to deal with offsetting the crisis.
>
> Source: European Union (2021); European Commission (2023)

CRISES RESPONSES: NEW INSTITUTIONS FOR THE SINGLE CURRENCY

In May 2010, Greece was no longer able to refinance its public debt and faced imminent default. The EU needed to either give up the euro, or keep it but deal with some of its design flaws through new institutions (see Table 7.1). The EU member states chose the second path. They made funds available to the Greek government through an impromptu arrangement called the Greek Loan Facility. Later, in August 2010, the euro area member states created the European Financial Stability Facility (EFSF). This temporary intergovernmental arrangement was to assist euro area member states in case any of them were unable to refinance their sovereign debt (e.g., Ireland and Portugal). The European Stability Mechanism (ESM) then replaced the EFSF. Set up as a permanent institutional structure that provides loans to member state governments, as well as equity investments for banks in need, this international organization is eventually to be incorporated into the EU treaty. The ESM has a maximum lending capacity of €500 billion, and to date it has disbursed about €300 billion. The so-called "troika" of the European Commission, the International Monetary Fund (IMF), and the ECB required that recipient countries make major administrative reforms, cut back on government spending, increase their tax base, and restructure their economies. These imposed **austerity** measures were not at all popular among the citizens of the member states that received funding through the ESM or its predecessors (see Table 7.1). ESM conditions for loans led to occasional violent protests as unemployment (especially youth unemployment) increased sharply, and the populations of the recipient countries felt government budget cuts were unreasonable. In Greece, GDP dropped by almost half as a result of the crisis. However, loans from the ESM and its predecessor institutions did ensure that Greece and other financially distressed governments could continue to access the international bond markets.

The ECB also made a key contribution to ending the crisis. ECB president Mario Draghi announced in July 2012 that the ECB would do "whatever it takes" to support the euro. Financial markets calmed down considerably in response to this reassurance. While at the start of the financial and sovereign debt crises the ECB had sometimes been criticized for being too focused on its mandate of price stability, the ECB came up with unprecedented and unconventional (non-standard) monetary policy responses. At the height of the sovereign debt crisis, through newly developed programs called "enhanced credit support" and the Securities Markets Programme, the ECB flooded financial institutions with "cheap money" in an attempt to ensure that funding remained available to businesses and households.

The COVID-19 outbreak was another major crisis for the EU. At the start of the pandemic some feared a repeat of the sovereign debt crisis if the ECB did not help out. Even though ECB president Christine Lagarde had initially signalled that the ECB might not be ready to do so, the ECB made a swift U-turn and announced a massive government bond purchase package, called the Pandemic Emergency Purchase Programme (PEPP). At first, the PEPP had a funding envelope of €750 billion, which was further expanded in June and December of that year to a total of €1,850 billion. In addition, several member states and the European Commission put forward initiatives for pandemic relief. These found broad support, as it was recognized that the COVID-19 pandemic was a crisis that impacted everyone, that no one could have anticipated it, and that demonstrating fiscal solidarity in this case could assuage potential financial market unrest. However, member states did not agree on the best way forward: Some wanted support in the form of grants without strings attached (free money); others called for support primarily through loans and argued that conditions should be put in place for all grants provided. In the end, in summer 2020, a historical settlement was made. Using the EU budget and a new temporary instrument – called **NextGenerationEU**,

Table 7.1. Institutions for policy coordination and financial support since the 2010 sovereign debt crisis

Institutions	Dates	Main content
Greek Loan Facility (formally Loan Facility Agreement between the euro member states and Greece)	May 2, 2010, Eurogroup agrees; agreement signed on May 7, 2010; entered into force May 11, 2010	Provide loans to euro area member states in need (in first instance, Greece). Commission coordinates and disburses the bilateral loans (provided by member states). IMF also contributes. Lending capacity of €80 billion (member states; later lowered to €52.9 billion); IMF contribution: €30 billion.
European Financial Stability Facility (EFSF)	Agreed to on May 9, 2010; operational August 4, 2010	Safeguards financial stability in the EU by providing financial assistance to euro area countries. No new loans since July 2013. Ireland, Portugal, and Greece benefited from the loans issued by this temporary facility.
European Semester	Agreed September 7, 2010; introduced from 2011	The European Semester is the EU's annual cycle of economic policy guidance and surveillance. Goal is to coordinate member state economic policy objectives. An abridged synopsis of the process is the European Commission adopts the "Annual Growth Survey"; the European Council provides policy orientations; member states submit their economic plans; Commission makes detailed analyses and recommendations of EU member states' economic programs; and Council adopts the country-specific recommendations.
European Stability Mechanism (ESM)	Agreed at European Council of December 16–17, 2010; inaugurated on October 8, 2012	The ESM is a permanent facility and the direct successor to the EFSF. This financial emergency loan fund provides loans to euro area countries in financial difficulty. Its own resources and credit guarantees add up to €500 billion. The IMF has guaranteed another €250 billion. Total: €750 billion.
Fiscal compact (its formal name is the Treaty on Stability, Coordination and Governance in Economic and Monetary Union)	Signed March 2, 2012; entered into force January 1, 2013	An agreement of the euro area member states and eight other EU member states. It is formally an international treaty, but there is a commitment to transfer its content into the EU treaty within five years of signing (has not yet occurred as of January 2022).
Banking Union	From 2012 to present	Stronger prudential requirements for banks, a single rulebook, a Single Supervisory Mechanism, a Single Resolution Mechanism for banks, a Single Resolution Fund, as well as a European Deposit Insurance Scheme.

(Continued)

Table 7.1. **Institutions for policy coordination and financial support since the 2010 sovereign debt crisis** *(Continued)*

Institutions	Dates	Main content
Capital Markets Union	From September 2015 to present	Enhanced capital market integration with a view to facilitating cross-border funding and investment flows, effectively creating a true Single Market for capital.
NextGenerationEU, Recovery and Resilience Facility (RRF)	Agreed to at the European Council in July 2020; formally adopted in February 2021	This temporary recovery instrument provides loans and grants to member states in need due to the COVID-19 pandemic crisis. There are grant allocations per member state. Members submit plans for approval. The EU has embedded the funds spent in the usual EU budget. Extra funds are obtained by lending from international markets. The size and scope of this funding is a historical first for the EU.

Source: Adapted and updated from online supplement of Verdun (2015)

with the **Recovery and Resilience Facility (RRF)** as its key instrument – it provided member states with a recovery plan worth €750 billion (a little more in loans than in grants). It did combine this investment package with an attempt to simultaneously address the climate crisis (see Chapter 17) through financial measures to support the Commission's European Green Deal. It also required that those seeking to benefit from this stimulus package take the opportunity to digitize their economies. The EU also coordinated a number of specific elements related to fighting the disease, such as centralized negotiations over vaccines and coordination on COVID-19 passports.

BANKING UNION AND CAPITAL MARKETS UNION

On January 1, 1993, the Second Banking Directive (Council Directive 89/646/EEC) came into effect. Its most important provisions were harmonized rules for obtaining a banking licence and bank regulation, and freedom of establishment of branches to offer banking services in EU member states other than the home member state. With the principle of mutual recognition of bank regulation in the Second Banking Directive, the feeling was that the EU had a solid foundation for a Single Market for banking services.[2] The market for banking services relied heavily on mutual recognition in the sense that banks were regulated in their home country but could offer banking services in all member states. This arrangement appeared to work well for many years during which several EU banks became multinationals and offered services in multiple EU countries.

However, during the global financial crisis, it became apparent that mutual recognition in banking regulation, meaning that the rules for banking in one country would be suitable without having to make EU-level regulations, was a recipe for easy contagion of the crisis across national borders, ironically particularly in the euro area due to the absence of exchange rate risk (Engineer et al. 2013; Schure 2013). Free capital flows in the EU resulted in a situation where small differences (or even just small *perceived* differences) between EU countries in terms of deposit insurance, bank supervision, or banking sector stability could generate large cross-border capital flows and destabilize the national banking sectors of the potential "outflow countries." The bank rescue measures that were adopted in the crisis were first of all to rescue banks, but arguably also to avoid and stem such potential destabilizing capital flows. However, these bank rescues came at a high political cost at both the national and EU levels. It became painfully clear that EMU had certain design flaws that needed to be remedied to make the project ultimately successful. The Banking Union was part of the answer: harmonized rules across the EU regarding bank supervision, deposit insurance, a safety net for banks, and a resolution mechanism for failed banks. The term "Banking Union" did not exist as such before the sovereign debt crisis. It was invented and put forward by Commission president Barroso to indicate that the euro area had insufficient integration in the area of banking and to capture various aspects of an improved financial framework for EMU.

The Banking Union proposal imposes the same rules on euro area banks as well as banks in non-EMU member states that decide to opt in. The rules aim to ensure that banks take measured risks, pay for their own losses, and face the possibility of bankruptcy with minimal damage to the economy and a minimal cost to the taxpayer. The Banking Union is incomplete as of yet and there are considerable delays and hesitations in adopting legislation toward finalizing its three pillars: the Single Supervisory Mechanism, the Single Deposit Guarantee Scheme, and the Single Resolution Mechanism (see Figure 7.2).

The June 2009 European Council recommended establishing a single rulebook for all financial institutions in the Single Market. New European supervisory authorities were created in the area of banking, securities, insurance, and occupational pensions. The European Commission also put forward plans for a Bank Recovery and Resolution Directive (BRRD). By late 2012 European member states had mobilized just under €600 billion (or 4.6 per cent of the 2012 GDP of the EU) in public funds to support their banks, and the

Figure 7.2. The Banking Union and its three pillars

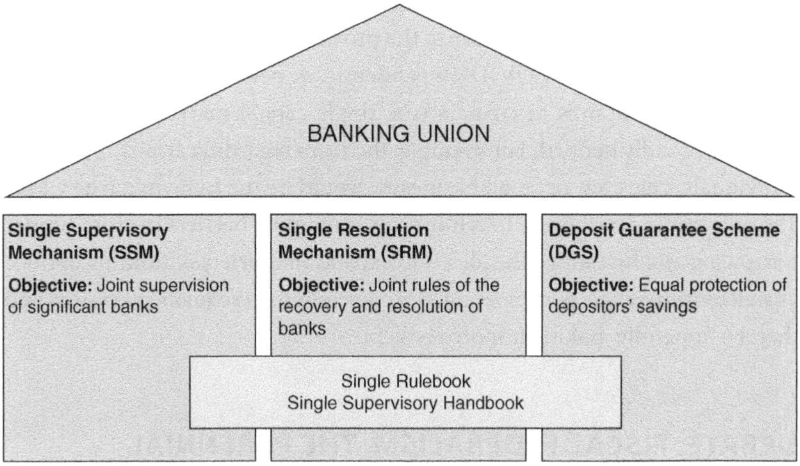

```
                        BANKING UNION

┌─────────────────────┬─────────────────────┬─────────────────────┐
│ Single Supervisory  │ Single Resolution   │ Deposit Guarantee   │
│ Mechanism (SSM)     │ Mechanism (SRM)     │ Scheme (DGS)        │
│                     │                     │                     │
│ Objective: Joint    │ Objective: Joint    │ Objective: Equal    │
│ supervision of      │ rules of the        │ protection of       │
│ significant banks   │ recovery and        │ depositors' savings │
│                     │ resolution of banks │                     │
│                     │                     │                     │
│         ┌───────────┴─────────────────────┴──┐                  │
│         │        Single Rulebook             │                  │
│         │    Single Supervisory Handbook     │                  │
│         └────────────────────────────────────┘                  │
└─────────────────────┴─────────────────────┴─────────────────────┘
```

Source: Author's design adapted from the Central Bank of Austria

DG Competition of the European Commission stated that it had approved €4.5 trillion (or 37 per cent of EU GDP) in state aid measures to financial institutions between October 2008 and 2011. The Commission proposed the BRRD to ensure that EU member states could intervene to manage local banks in distress while still trying to preserve a level playing field across the EU. Another important move toward the Banking Union was increased harmonization in terms of national deposit insurance schemes across the EU. Since 2009, EU legislation requires all EU deposit insurance schemes to guarantee deposit accounts for €100,000, while before that time there was a minimum insurance amount (of €20,000) but no maximum. The Banking Union is still a work in progress at the time of writing. For example, although standardization of the coverage amounts of national deposit guarantee schemes was a major step, an important step further would be a European deposit insurance scheme.

The **Capital Markets Union (CMU)** is another economic policy initiative launched in 2014 by Commission president Jean-Claude Juncker. EU law has prohibited all restrictions on capital movements and payments across borders since 1994. The interest rate convergence that took place before the global financial crisis (Figure 7.1) is evidence that the government bond markets are essentially fully integrated. Furthermore, a liquid corporate bond market developed rapidly after EMU was realized. This means that for governments, large businesses, and financial institutions there are essentially no barriers to the free movement of capital. However, the same is not true for small and medium-sized enterprises and consumers. Commission president Ursula von der Leyen has committed to finalize the project of the CMU during her time in office. Following the COVID-19 pandemic, a "new CMU action plan" has been launched. It aims to create a true single capital market, where *capital* has been broadly defined. For example, the rules regarding crowdfunding for individuals, charities, or small businesses would be the same in a true CMU. The overarching purpose is to remove any remaining barriers to cross-border borrowing and investing. The idea is to expand the variety of funding options as well as individuals participating, thus diversifying the financial system and thereby hopefully making it more resilient.

DEBATE: FISCAL FEDERALISM, THE PERENNIAL VICIOUS CIRCLE, AND CURRENT CHALLENGES

This chapter makes it clear that EMU had been introduced with insufficient checks and balances to deal with major financial crises. Not having these measures in place has led to a major increase in unemployment and extended periods of low, even negative, GDP growth in several countries (and a collapse of GDP in Greece). The political cost to the EU has been a severe erosion of the legitimacy of the EU because citizens equated the sovereign debt crisis with a crisis of the EU (Theme 3 of this book). EMU was originally designed as a "fair weather" arrangement, meaning that in good times EMU worked well, but it was not able to deal with crises. It is obvious that the EU still needs to increase its overall political support by the people – its democratic legitimacy (see also Chapter 15).

Following the euro area crisis, plans emerged to complete EMU. These plans could lead to much deeper integration. Some of these ideas were set out in an ambitious plan, the "Five Presidents' Report," which was considered by various national parliaments. The fundamental question about the EU it raises is whether to move in the direction of a federal state (Theme 2 of this book). Both Euro-enthusiasts and Euroskeptics have argued that the structure of a federal state is necessary because one cannot have a monetary union without deeper economic, fiscal, and thus more political integration. If this claim is true, then the choice is between either dismantling EMU (as Euroskeptics would prefer) or creating a fully-fledged federal state with expanded economic and fiscal competences. These discussions came back when the NextGenerationEU recovery plan was being discussed: How much solidarity should member states show to each other? How much money should be given to member states in need? What conditions might be put on any such loans and grants?

Seeing that there was insufficient support to make more permanent changes, the European Council agreed on a temporary arrangement. This arrangement has not answered the more fundamental question of whether deeper integration (the fiscal federalism of the Five Presidents' Report) is in fact necessary if one wants to keep the euro. Fiscal federalism is usually associated with the following key components:

1. Sharing critical functions between the different levels of government, namely the supply of public goods and services, redistribution of income, and macroeconomic stabilization
2. Identifying welfare gains for the different parts of that fiscal federation
3. Taxation at the level of government that provides the function needed – for example, economic stabilization and income redistribution could be done at the federal (supranational) level, whereas other allocation of resources could be done at lower levels
4. Using instruments of fiscal policy (tax and spend) for the purpose of redistribution at both the federal (supranational) and lower levels of government (national and subnational)

In the EU, the last two components of fiscal federalism would be controversial as there has typically been only limited solidarity among EU citizens. Whether there might be another model, some kind of "in-between Europe" that might do the trick, remains to be seen. What is clear is that EMU governance is no longer the same, and presumably is more resilient, now that the Banking Union is underway. A more deeply integrated "Labour Market Union" (to coin a new term) would also make a substantial difference, while still not turning the EU into a federal state. Indeed, what is, in our view, the essential feature of a sustainable architecture for EMU is that it incorporates "sufficiently many automatic stabilizers" (see also Schure and Della Posta 2022).

In addition to highlighting crucial issues relating to the future of economic integration, these debates also illustrate what can be described as the "perennial vicious circle" of European integration (see Figure 7.3), which is best described by providing an example. As we explained above, EMU was set up in an asymmetrical form because member states wanted to keep control of their budgetary and fiscal policies. This design contributed to an abundance

Figure 7.3. (Potential) vicious circle of European integration

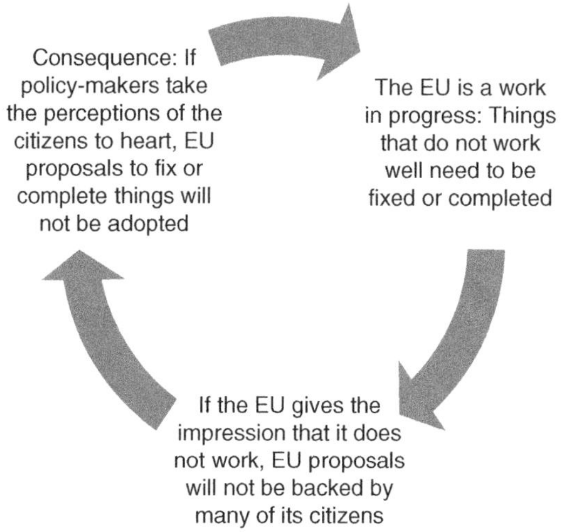

- The EU is a work in progress: Things that do not work well need to be fixed or completed
- If the EU gives the impression that it does not work, EU proposals will not be backed by many of its citizens
- Consequence: If policy-makers take the perceptions of the citizens to heart, EU proposals to fix or complete things will not be adopted

Source: Authors' own design

of cheap funding during the early years, particularly in the periphery of the EU, while clear rules on macroeconomic imbalances, good fiscal governance, and banking regulation were lacking. These imperfections contributed to the sovereign debt crisis. A logical next step was therefore to make EU-level rules to reduce the probability of a crisis as well as to manage it. However, this next step required convincing the citizens and their leaders that deeper integration was necessary. This task is difficult if, in the eyes of the citizens, the EU is in crisis because its current policies have fallen short. In this case, the EU managed to escape the vicious circle by agreeing on impressive crisis measures as well as making moves toward deeper economic integration. The case of the COVID-19 pandemic and the EU response provides another example of how the vicious circle can be broken.

As we have seen earlier, it was difficult for EU member states to decide what path to choose during the global financial crisis and sovereign debt crisis. The ECB acted as a leader when few other EU institutions felt they had the ability or legitimacy to do so. The ECB took on this role despite its permanent challenge to set monetary policy for the euro area, which consists of 20 individual member states with diverse monetary policy needs. Despite the ECB's loose monetary policy in the period following the global financial crisis, euro area inflation stayed below the ECB's inflation target of 2 per cent in most years.

The COVID-19 pandemic resulted in both supply shocks and demand shocks to the EU's macroeconomy between 2020 and 2022. Indeed, with lockdowns came disruptions in production, trade, and labour markets. Households spent less, while governments stepped up (alongside the ECB), often running substantial budget deficits to keep workers and companies afloat as companies lost business and some factories were not operating at all. Once mass COVID-19 vaccination programs had been rolled out throughout the EU, economic activity picked up again; however, some supply chains and segments of the labour market were still disrupted. With the resulting shortage of aggregate supply, the prices of various goods and services increased dramatically. The war in Ukraine that escalated on February 24, 2022, and subsequent sanctions imposed on Russia by Western countries increased supply chain disruptions further and led to substantially higher food and energy prices. In 2022 inflation in the euro area was well in excess of the ECB's inflation target. The inflation rate in Canada is also well in excess of the Bank of Canada's 2 per cent inflation target. There is substantial uncertainty regarding the consequences of the spell of high inflation that succeeded the immediate aftermath of the urgent stages of the COVID-19 pandemic.

CONCLUSION

European economic integration has had a chequered past with lots of ups and downs. Still, European economic and monetary integration has progressed immensely. Important milestones on the way to the Single Market were the Customs Union, which was completed in 1968, and the Single European Act (1986), which imposed qualified majority voting to complete the Single Market by 1992. Between these two milestones, several Court of Justice rulings furthered the process through negative integration. These rulings paved the way for a focus on mutual recognition, as the SEA also reflects.

The path to monetary integration also went through various blueprints and setbacks before the euro was introduced in 1999, initially in 11 member states and in 20 member states as of 2023. The first years of EMU were successful, but the global financial crisis and the sovereign debt crisis revealed that EMU was vulnerable and incomplete. The first years of the financial crisis were littered with bank guarantees and bank rescues, which were only possible with taxpayers' money.

As public resources reached their limit in several member states, the global financial crisis turned into a sovereign debt crisis. It was a real dilemma for EU member states whether to bail out member states in financial distress. However, with the prospect of a possible euro area collapse, member states created lending facilities for member states in distress, albeit forcing far-reaching fiscal reform on recipient countries. Other EU institutions, such as the ECB, also stepped up to act as a strong leader during this time.

The global financial crisis and the ensuing sovereign debt crisis revealed severe issues associated with the mutual recognition approach to creating a Single Market for banking and EMU: Further deepening of integration in the areas of bank regulation and financial governance was needed. Specifically, the Single Market for banking was in need of harmonization in terms of bank supervision, deposit insurance, and bank safety nets. These needs are planned to be met through the completion of the Banking Union. For EMU to function well, more supranational oversight in areas of budgetary fiscal policies appeared to be required. Some other new institutions and prospective plans have been created in response to the financial, economic, and sovereign debt crises. Still, while the EU and the member states worked on these reforms, the policies of the ECB were likely absolutely crucial for financial stability in the EU and the euro area.

The COVID-19 pandemic has changed the mood in Europe in profound ways. In 2020, the EU was able to assist member states and to show solidarity with those suffering because of the pandemic. It negotiated with pharmaceutical companies to secure a good price for member states for vaccines. On the whole, citizens were satisfied with the way the EU dealt with COVID-19 (Eurobarometer survey, July 2021). The temporary measures taken may be a precursor as to what might come. Lending money needs to be offset by having the resources to pay for loans. One possible way to pay back loans could be to impose taxes. But not all EU citizens are equally excited about the prospect of deeper economic integration. With Euroskepticism significant in several member states and the rise of populism, the challenge for the EU is to convince its citizens that it is beneficial to growth and prosperity. There are also challenges in the domain of EU democracy and legitimacy: Deeper integration requires more political integration and representation. Finally, the war in Ukraine created a sense of urgency in coming up with a European response.

REVIEW QUESTIONS

1. Why was mutual recognition a way to advance the Single Market but also at the heart of the banking crisis?
2. EMU, as introduced in 1999–2002, has had a supranational monetary authority but no supranational budgetary and fiscal authority. Which EU institution is the supranational monetary authority? What are the differences between EMU today and that of 2002? Can you explain how these differences came about?
3. What were the pros and cons of providing Greece with financial support during the sovereign debt crisis? What was the main reason that Greece ended up receiving support from the "troika"?
4. What is the NextGenerationEU, and how is it related to the Recovery and Resilience Facility and the European Semester?

EXERCISES

1. Divide students into two groups. Have one group argue the position "The EU Single Market is a form of globalization." Have the other group argue the converse: "The EU Single Market is a protective shield from the forces of globalization." Discuss together as a single group after the debate.
2. Undertake an examination of *fiscal federalism* in Canada or in another federal country. How is a province of Canada (or a US state, a German Land, etc.) protected from financial crisis as compared to Greece within the euro area post-2008?
3. Discuss in groups what the pros and cons are of having a temporary instrument that borrows large sums of money in international markets for EU spending. Who is the lender of last resort? Who is ultimately responsible? Think about the pros and cons of imposing conditionality for giving grants and loans to member states in need.

NOTES

1 In 1994, the remaining EFTA countries and the EU formed the **European Economic Area (EEA)**, which gave the EFTA countries access to the Single Market. All EFTA countries except Switzerland joined the EEA. Switzerland has bilateral agreements with the EU that effectively also give that country full access to the Single Market.
2 Together with several other important directives, that is, namely the Money Laundering Directive (91/308/EEC), the Own Funds Directive (89/299/EEC), the Solvency Ratio Directive (89/647/EEC), the Consolidated Supervision Directive (92/30/EEC), the Deposit-Guarantee Directive (94/19/EEC), the Large Exposures Directive (92/121/EEC), the Capital Adequacy Directive (93/6/EEC), and the Investment Services Directive (93/22/EEC).

REFERENCES AND FURTHER READING

Alvarez, J., I. Krznar, and T. Tombe. 2019. "Internal Trade in Canada: Case for Liberalization." IMF Working Paper 19/158, July 22, 2019.

Balassa, B. 1961. *The Theory of Economic Integration*. London: George Allen and Unwin.

Baldwin, R., and C. Wyplosz. 2015. *The Economics of European Integration*, 5th ed. London: McGraw-Hill.

Closa, C., and A. Maatsch. 2014. "In a Spirit of Solidarity? Justifying the European Financial Stability Facility (EFSF) in National Parliamentary Debates." *Journal of Common Market Studies* 52 (4): 826–42. https://doi.org/10.1111/jcms.12119.

De Grauwe, P. 2016. *Economics of Monetary Union*, 11th ed. Oxford: Oxford University Press.

Dhingra, S., E. Fry, S. Hale, and N. Jia. 2022. *The Big Brexit: An Assessment of the Scale of Change to Come from Brexit*. London: The Resolution Foundation.

Dyson, K., and K. Featherstone. 1999. *The Road to Maastricht: Negotiating Economic and Monetary Union*. Oxford: Oxford University Press.

Egan, M.P. 2015. *Single Markets: Economic Integration in Europe and in the United States*. Oxford: Oxford University Press.

Engineer, M.H., P. Schure, and M. Gillis. 2013. "A Positive Analysis of Deposit Insurance Provision: Regulatory Competition among European Union Countries." *Journal of Financial Stability* 9 (4): 530–44. https://doi.org/10.1016/j.jfs.2013.10.001.

European Commission. 2016. "State of the Union 2016: Completing the Capital Markets Union – Commission Accelerates Reform." https://ec.europa.eu/commission/presscorner/detail/en/IP_16_3001.

European Commission. 2023. "Recovery and Resilience Facility: From Plans to Payments." http://economy-finance.ec.europa.eu/eueconomyexplained/recovery-and-resilience-facility-plans-payments_en.

European Parliament. 2016. "Banking Union." Fact Sheet.

European Union. 2021. "Definitive Adoption (EU, Euratom) 2021/417 of the European Union's General Budget for the Financial Year 2021." OJ L 93, 17.3.2021, pp. 1–2286. https://eur-lex.europa.eu/legal-content/EN/TXT/?uri =celex%3A32021B0417.

Featherstone, K. 2011. "The Greek Sovereign Debt Crisis and EMU: A Failing State in a Skewed Regime." *Journal of Common Market Studies* 49 (2): 193–217. https:// doi.org/10.1111/j.1468-5965.2010.02139.x.

Heipertz, M., and A. Verdun. 2010. *Ruling Europe: The Politics of the Stability and Growth Pact*. Cambridge: Cambridge University Press.

Hodson, D. 2011. *Governing the Euro Area in Good Times and in Bad*. Oxford: Oxford University Press.

Howarth, D., and L. Quaglia. 2016. *The Political Economy of European Banking Union*. Oxford: Oxford University Press.

Juncker, J.C. 2015. *Completing Europe's Economic and Monetary Union (Five President's Report)*. Brussels: European Commission.

Katsanidou, A., and S. Otjes. 2016. "How the European Debt Crisis Reshaped National Political Space: The Case of Greece." *European Union Politics* 17 (2): 262–84. https://doi.org/10.1177/1465116515616196.

Pelkmans, J. 2013. "The Economics of Single Market Regulation." In *Mapping European Economic Integration*, edited by A. Verdun and A. Tovias, 38–56. Basingstoke, UK: Palgrave Macmillan.

Rajan, R.G. 2010. *Fault Lines: How Hidden Fractures Still Threaten the World Economy*. Princeton, NJ: Princeton University Press.

Sadeh, T., and A. Verdun. 2009. "Explaining Europe's Monetary Union: A Survey of the Literature." *International Studies Review* 11 (2): 277–301. https://doi.org /10.1111/j.1468-2486.2009.00849.x.

Schmidt, S., ed. 2008. *Mutual Recognition as a New Mode of Governance*. London: Taylor and Francis.

Schure, P. 2013. "European Financial Market Integration." In *Mapping European Economic Integration*, edited by A. Verdun and A. Tovias, 105–24. Basingstoke, UK: Palgrave Macmillan.

Schure, P., and P. Della Posta. 2022. "An Expert Survey on Fiscal Solidarity in the Euro Area." Mimeo, University of Victoria.

Sturm, J.E., U. Fritsche, M. Graff, M. Lamla, S. Lein, V. Nitsch, D. Liechti, and D. Triet. 2009, June. "The Euro and Prices: Changeover-Related Inflation and Price Convergence in the Euro Area." *European Economy, Economic Papers 381*. Brussels: European Comission.

The Economist. 2016. "Canada's Internal Trade: The Great Provincial Obstacle Course." 23 July.

Vanhercke, B., and A. Verdun. 2022. "The European Semester as Goldilocks: Macroeconomic Policy Coordination and the Recovery and Resilience Facility." *Journal of Common Market Studies* 60 (1): 204–23. https://doi.org/10.1111 /jcms.13267.

Verdun, A. 1996. "An 'Asymmetrical' Economic and Monetary Union in the EU: Perceptions of Monetary Authorities and Social Partners." *Journal of European Integration* 20 (1): 59–81. https://doi.org/10.1080/07036339608429045.

Verdun, A. 2000. *European Responses to Globalization and Financial Market Integration: Perceptions of Economic and Monetary Union in Britain, France and Germany.* Basingstoke, UK: Palgrave Macmillan.

Verdun, A. 2015. "A Historical Institutionalist Explanation of the EU's Responses to the Euro Area Financial Crisis." *Journal of European Public Policy* 22 (2): 219–37. https://doi.org/10.1080/13501763.2014.994023.

Verdun, A., and A. Tovias, eds. 2013. *Mapping European Economic Integration.* Basingstoke, UK: Palgrave Macmillan.

8

Migration, Citizenship, and Security

Oliver Schmidtke

READER'S GUIDE

The **Area of Freedom, Security and Justice (AFSJ)** – first introduced as Justice and Home Affairs in the Maastricht Treaty – covers policies related to justice, security, migration, and borders. Challenges associated with increased cross-border mobility and border security (through migration, organized crime, and terrorism) have led to a fast expansion of the policy area. The governance of migration and borders raises politically controversial issues about the politics of European integration, most prominently the tension between state sovereignty and supranational rule. The 2015–16 **refugee crisis**, the fight against terrorism, and the war in Ukraine have tested the EU's policy capacity in this area. Failing to deliver good and effective policy results contributed to the resurgence of populist–nationalist forces across the continent.

INTRODUCTION

This chapter traces the origins of the Area of Freedom, Security and Justice from its modest beginnings as part of Justice and Home Affairs (JHA) under the 1992 Maastricht Treaty to its central role in addressing migration, crime, and the threat of terrorism well into the twenty-first century. This field of European Union (EU) policy-making is relevant to each of the three themes of this textbook: The development of the AFSJ can be interpreted as an emerging policy area of the EU driven by the effects of the Single Market (Theme 1) and external shocks such as terrorist attacks and the refugee crisis. The AFSJ has posed serious challenges to and triggered some political pushback regarding the reach of EU policy-making, which challenge the viability of the EU's border and migration regime. Since the EU is not a state (Theme 2), the AFSJ has emerged as the outcome of difficult negotiations between member states that appreciate the benefits of cooperation yet seek to safeguard their sovereignty. Finally, the AFSJ has also been used as a vehicle to address the challenges the EU faces in terms of its popular legitimacy and support (Theme 3). By guarding fundamental rights and delivering EU citizenship, European integration shapes the daily lives of EU citizens.

The principle of **freedom of movement** ensures that every EU citizen has the right to move freely, to stay, and to work in another member state. It is one of the "four freedoms" guaranteed by EU law (freedom of movement of goods, people, services, and capital across borders). Yet the increasingly uninhibited cross-border mobility, first for goods and services within the Single Market, then also for people in the so-called **Schengen Area** (see Box 8.1 and Table 8.1), has created a set of new challenges. If EU citizens can move from one member state to another without being restricted by visa requirements or work permits, what should their legal status be? For instance, should EU citizens, once they reside in an EU member state of which they do not hold the national citizenship, enjoy social and political rights equivalent to citizens of that country?

BOX 8.1: SCHENGEN AREA

- The Schengen Agreement is a treaty signed in 1985 committing five member states (France, Germany, and the Benelux countries) to remove controls at their internal borders.
- The Schengen Area is currently made up of 27 countries: 23 EU member states and four non-EU states.
- Some Schengen countries have sometimes temporarily reintroduced border controls (such as after the 2015 Paris terrorist attacks, during the 2015–16 refugee crisis, and during some of the COVID-19 pandemic).

Table 8.1. Member states of the Schengen Area

EU member states part of Schengen		Non-EU member states part of Schengen	Schengen candidate countries	EU member states not part of Schengen and not a candidate
Austria	Latvia	Iceland	Bulgaria	Ireland
Belgium	Lithuania	Liechtenstein	Cyprus	
Croatia	Luxembourg	Norway	Romania	
Czech Republic	Malta	Switzerland		
Denmark	Netherlands			
Estonia	Poland			
Finland	Portugal			
France	Slovakia			
Germany	Slovenia			
Greece	Spain			
Hungary	Sweden			
Italy				

Organized crime and terrorism are no longer primarily a national phenomenon. These players operate largely on a European scale, if not a global scale. Terrorist attacks, irregular migration, and the fight against the COVID-19 pandemic are a stark reminder that key societal or political challenges transcend national borders and need to be tackled by a coordinated European response. Over the past 25 years, the EU has been trying to address the implications of cross-border mobility. The growing relevance of this policy area in the process of European integration is reflected in the swift move toward an expanding AFSJ agenda, driven by a community logic.

JUSTICE, FREEDOM, AND SECURITY: FROM HUMBLE BEGINNINGS TO A KEY EU POLICY FIELD

The AFSJ constitutes a policy field that is notably different from others due to its incremental and highly fragmented character. First, EU competences in this field started modestly. As Lavenex and Wallace (2005) put it, the policy area has traditionally been characterized by a distinct "disjointed incrementalism." Its origins lie in the anti-terrorism cooperation between member states in the 1970s under the umbrella of the TREVI agreement (TREVI stands for *"terrorisme, radicalisme, extrémisme et violence international"*). It was formally made an area of EU policy in the Maastricht Treaty that was signed in 1992 and entered into force in 1993. This treaty created policies on Justice and Home Affairs as Pillar III of the EU (see Chapter 2). Since its inception in 1992, and particularly after the 1997 Amsterdam Treaty, which renamed JHA to AFSJ, the policy area morphed quickly into a field of policy-making in which the EU developed considerable collective capacity and institutional independence.

Second, AFSJ describes a complex and somewhat disconnected field of policies that ranges from border control to cooperation in the field of law enforcement. Still, what provides a certain degree of coherence to AFSJ as a policy field is the reference to cross-border mobility as a catalyst for seeking solutions that traditionally were defined by national approaches to security, mobility, and fundamental rights. The EU describes the overall objective and rationale of this diverse policy domain in the Treaty on European Union (TEU) (see Box 8.2), alluding to freedom, security, and justice as key principles on which the EU rests and that need to be governed with a transnational approach responding to the changing nature of cross-border mobility.

> **BOX 8.2: ARTICLE 3(2) TEU**
> The Union shall offer its citizens an area of freedom, security and justice without internal frontiers, in which the free movement of persons is ensured in conjunction with appropriate measures with respect to external border controls, asylum, immigration and the prevention and combating of crime.

The issues addressed in the AFSJ reflect the ambitious agenda of the TEU to establish the EU as a political union in particular with regard to border management, migration, and judicial cooperation. Table 8.2 provides an overview of the policy fields in the AFSJ.

However, initially an intergovernmental mode of decision making was chosen. It meant that JHA legislative proposals were subject to unanimity voting in the Council of the EU and that EU institutions only had a marginal role in JHA policies. This constrained decision making increasingly became a problem in the 1990s when the EU sought to improve its status with citizens and address the practical challenges related to the aim of Schengen countries to remove border controls. Therefore, in asylum and immigration policies

Table 8.2. Policy areas in the AFSJ

Home Affairs	Justice
Immigration	Fundamental rights
Common European Asylum System	EU citizenship
Borders and visas (Schengen)	Gender equality
Organized crime and human trafficking	Fight against discrimination
Terrorism	Cross-border judicial cooperation
Police and law enforcement	

gradual "communitarization" (moving from intergovernmentalism to supranationalism) occurred. In the Amsterdam Treaty, the European Commission, the European Parliament, and most importantly the Court of Justice of the EU received a more robust role in this policy domain.

Monar (2012) describes JHA as one of the most momentous innovations of the Treaty of Maastricht. For him, this treaty was a significant "intergovernmental gate opener" for today's AFSJ, whose operational dynamic would lead to regularized institutional cooperation among member states and, as a result, the emergence of a common perception of shared policy challenges. Most notably, the 2007 Lisbon Treaty pushed for an ambitious set of policies under community authority in the AFSJ domain. With this agenda, the AFSJ has become one of the key driving forces behind what defines the EU as a political union.

Migration and Asylum

Migration has transformed European societies profoundly. This trend will likely continue, considering the far-reaching demographic changes (an aging population and a declining birth rate) these societies face. Without newcomers to these societies, these challenges are anticipated to produce labour shortages and put considerable pressure on social security systems. Without migration, countries need a birth rate of 2.1 per woman to sustain the size of the population. In Europe the average is 1.6. Many European governments have gradually provided better support for childrearing (family and social benefits, paid parental leave for both parents, and some even introduced baby bonuses), but the fertility rate has remained well below 2. Boosting regular immigration could therefore help offset these fundamental demographic challenges, but it remains a highly contested issue in many countries.

Figure 8.1. Foreign-born population in EU member states by country of birth as of January 1, 2020

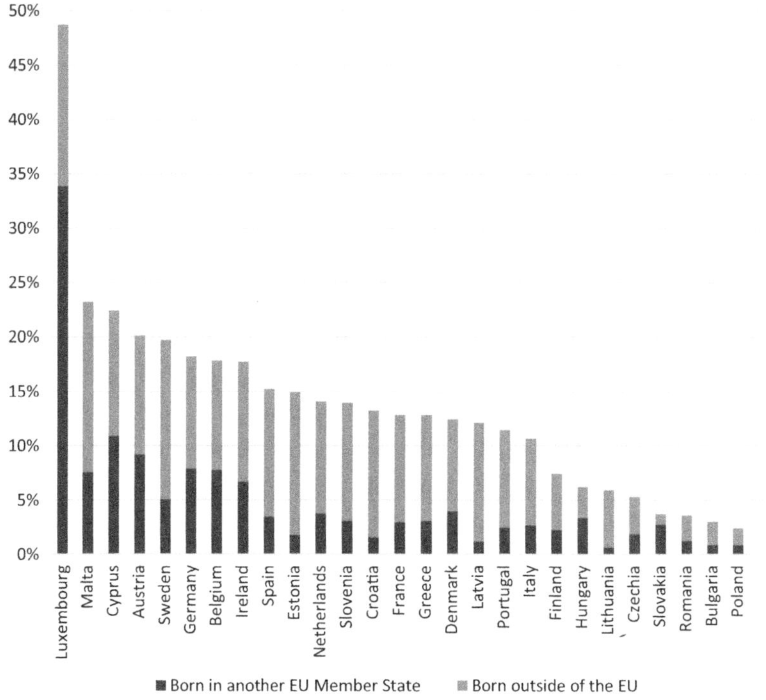

■ Born in another EU Member State   ■ Born outside of the EU

Source: European Migration Network (https://emn.ie/statistics/eu-statistics)

There are two dimensions of migration in the EU (see Figure 8.1). First, there are the challenges to the governance of borders due to the growing internal mobility within the EU. Despite widespread fears about unmanageable mass migration that most rounds of enlarging the EU provoked in public discourse, few EU citizens choose to settle in another member state. The overall proportion of EU citizens residing in a country in which they were not born makes up a small, albeit increasing, segment of EU member states. According to Eurostat (the statistical office of the EU), in 2019 only 3.3 per cent of EU citizens of working age (20–64) resided in an EU member state other than that of their citizenship (up from 2.4 per cent in 2009).

Second, Europe has persistently attracted migrants from around the world. The so-called third-country nationals (TCNs) make up a fast-growing demographic group, underlining that mobility from outside the EU constitutes a key policy challenge for the EU. In 2020, a total of 23 million non-EU citizens lived in the EU. Although these numbers are smaller than in traditional immigrant countries, such as Canada, EU member states are increasingly starting to resemble immigrant societies, with amplified cultural and religious diversity. This change in population composition has resulted in a new set of policy challenges regarding the recruitment, settlement, and long-term integration of migrants. Individual member states still determine the procedures through which migrants can settle in their country and gain access to national citizenship. However, with the AFSJ, the EU has started to pursue a coordinated European migration and asylum policy that has various components:

1 *Common framework for regular immigration*: Responding to the fact that only a relatively small number of highly skilled migrants settle in the EU as compared to North America, the EU has taken first steps toward setting the framework for regular immigration. The regulations at the EU level concern the conditions of entry and residence for certain categories of migrants, such as highly qualified workers, students, and researchers. Most notably, in 2009 the EU Blue Card Initiative introduced an EU-wide work permit for highly skilled non-EU citizens. In 2021, as part of the New Pact on Migration and Asylum (see discussion below), the EU updated its Blue Card Directive, introducing more flexible admission conditions, enhanced rights, and the possibility to move and work more easily between EU member states. This scheme of recruiting skilled labour works in parallel with national immigration laws and is designed to position the EU as an important player in the increasingly globalized labour market for highly skilled workers. The Canadian immigration regime, with its focus on recruiting skilled labour, has served as a blueprint for EU initiatives in this policy field.
2 *Supporting integration*: In the 1997 Amsterdam Treaty, the EU committed to the "fair treatment of third country nationals," targeting the long-term integration of migrants as a genuine field of EU policy-making. Between 2021 and 2027 the EU has committed €9.9 billion to this policy goal, mandating the Asylum, Migration and Integration Fund to coordinate the efficient management of immigration flows (including initiatives such as language and civic education courses and intercultural training) and to allow for fair burden sharing across the EU. The support for the societal integration of TCNs also refers to the anti-discrimination rules that were developed in the form of the Employment Equality Directive and

the Race Equality Directive in 2000 (see Chapter 16). EU policies to fight racism and xenophobia are promoted by the European Union Agency for Fundamental Rights (set up in 2007 with a mandate inherited from the European Monitoring Centre on Racism and Xenophobia), which monitors developments throughout the EU and has established legal recourse for Europe's migrant and minority population. The EU has underlined its commitment to combat racial discrimination with the launch of its EU Anti-Racism Action Plan 2020–2025.

The task of integrating migrants into society highlights the tensions between intergovernmental and supranational cooperation. As member states have jurisdiction over these matters, this dimension of the EU's migration policies is still in its infancy. While the EU set an ambitious agenda in the 2004 Hague Program with the European Council's commitment to enhancing the equal treatment of long-term residents, regardless of their place of origin, it has not yet developed the institutional capacity to follow up fully on this promise. The same holds true regarding legal immigration: Even though the principle of free movement of EU citizens is a fundamental freedom, immigration of TCNs is still handled primarily on an intergovernmental basis. Member states have been determined to hold on to this key element of state sovereignty – control of immigration and access to citizenship – a fact that has complicated the European response to the refugee crisis enormously (see more details on this point below).

3 *Asylum*: Europe has become a destination for millions of refugees and asylum seekers from around the world. In its Charter of Fundamental Rights (see also below), the EU commits to protecting those fleeing their home countries from political persecution. Introduced in 1999, the Common European Asylum System aimed to harmonize asylum processes, set standards for protecting and treating refugees, and establish a common system to enable better cooperation among member states. In an attempt to avoid asylum seekers moving from one country to another ("asylum shopping"), the EU established a single system: the **Dublin Regulation**. It stipulates that refugees need to register and claim asylum in the first EU member state they land in. However, in 2015–16, as an overwhelming number of irregular refugees arrived in the EU, typically in border EU member states in the south and east much more than those in the centre, north, or west, the Dublin Regulation was temporarily not enforced (see the section on the refugee crisis below). As part of its New Pact on

Migration and Asylum, a renewed effort to launch a European approach in this policy area, the EU proposed a new Regulation on Asylum and Migration Management in 2020 that puts more emphasis on the **principle of solidarity and sharing of responsibility fairly**. In 2022, millions of Ukrainian refugees entered the EU, and the EU and its member states provided these refugees temporary protection.

4 *Irregular migration*: Those who come to the EU without fulfilling the legal entry requirements or who overstay their visa are referred to as *irregular migrants*. This group presents a far bigger challenge in the EU than in Canada. From the 1990s onwards, Europe has become relatively easy to access for migrants. This influx of TCNs poses challenges to supranational coordination. One important initiative that the EU has developed is fighting human trafficking. In line with the EU's commitment to human rights (discussed in the next section), this initiative addresses primarily issues of sexual and labour exploitation.

5 *Cooperation with non-EU countries*: This cooperation has become a significant strategy to address global migration. Most notably, the EU recently worked through the UN system and aligned its strategy with the 2018 United Nations Global Compact for Migration (GCM). While 19 EU member states have signed the GCM and committed to cooperate internationally to facilitate safe, orderly, and regular migration under the auspices of the UN system, even this non-binding compact has underlined how divisive the issue of migration is in the EU. In addition, the EU's Global Approach to Migration and Mobility has developed the external dimension of its migration and asylum policy since 2005. It promotes cooperation in governance in the field of migration and asylum across the EU's external borders (including development cooperation). This aspect of the EU's external relations became particularly important during the years of the Arab Spring and the subsequent sociopolitical unrest it created in the EU's extended southern neighbourhood (see Chapter 14).

Justice, Fundamental Rights, and Citizenship

A critical component of the AFSJ is the legal protection that the EU is able to offer to its citizens. The status of EU citizenship was first introduced in the 1992 Maastricht Treaty. The 1997 Amsterdam Treaty gave more substance to what it means to be a citizen of the EU and declared at the same time the limitation of this legal status by asserting that the "[c]itizenship of the Union shall complement and not replace national citizenship." It is important to note that EU citizenship is a derivative of national citizenship; the EU itself does not have the authority to grant EU citizenship. Box 8.3 summarizes some of the key elements of what this status entails. A key right is political representation: EU citizens have the right to vote and stand as candidates in local and European Parliament elections regardless of where they reside in the EU. While Canada is regularly portrayed as the country with the most accomplished record of immigrant integration, its permanent residents are not able to vote in any election. Thus, for EU citizens, the EU has broken new ground in terms of decoupling some fundamental rights (such as the right to vote) from a nationally defined citizenship status.

BOX 8.3: KEY ELEMENTS OF AN EMERGING EU CITIZENSHIP REGIME

- Right to vote and stand in local government and European Parliament elections in the country of residence
- Right of petition to the European Parliament and appeal to the European Ombudsman
- Non-discrimination principle by reason of nationality
- Right to organize or support a citizens' initiative to call for new EU legislation
- Protection of fundamental civic, political, and social rights (under the Charter of Fundamental Rights of the EU)
- Right of free movement of persons

Building a "European area of justice" requires the enforceability of EU law in the EU member states. The harmonization of legal rules and procedures throughout the EU means that people as well as businesses have proper access to legal recourse. Currently the EU has two programs (Justice Program and Rights, Equality, and Citizenship) to secure an effective pan-European legal infrastructure and procedural safeguards for citizens (including initiatives such as privacy and data protection, guarantees for bioethics, and a Consumer Rights Directive).

Having had a long experience with the European Convention on Human Rights – a document originally drawn up by the Council of Europe (a body not part of the EU) in the early 1950s – the EU introduced the EU Charter of Fundamental Rights that became a legally binding component of EU law with the Lisbon Treaty entering into force in 2009. Under six titles (Dignity, Freedoms, Equality, Solidarity, Citizens' Rights, and Justice) the Charter brings together the fundamental rights protected in the EU in one single document. EU citizens have an additional legal recourse beyond national courts if they consider their fundamental rights to be violated. In practice, political advocates can use the Charter at the national and European level in their fight for human rights, gender equality, and non-discrimination.

Borders and Security

With the removal of its internal border controls, the EU's Schengen Area has faced the task of addressing the issue of border control and internal security to deal with, for instance, irregular migration, crime, and terrorism. One immediate functional requirement related to an unrestricted cross-border mobility zone was a common visa policy. Canadian passport holders, for instance, if they wish to extend their stay in the Schengen Area beyond the three months permitted for tourism, need to apply for a visa for the EU ("Schengen visa") rather than apply to individual member states. Additionally, the Schengen Information System data on non-EU visitors is shared among the authorities in the participating member states.

EU-wide information systems and an agency on the ground are tasked with the management of the EU's external borders. While the actual border control activities are carried out by member states, the central role falls to **Frontex**, the European Border and Coast Guard Agency, created in October 2016. Based in Warsaw (Poland), Frontex supports member states with the border surveillance resources of the EU's external borders (see Box 8.4). With the salience of challenges related to irregular migration, Frontex's mandate has expanded significantly, and its budget was increased to €11 billion for the 2021–7 period. The increasingly securitized and militarized EU border protection system has come under criticism when it comes to the treatment of refugees in coastal waters (see discussion below).

> **BOX 8.4: KEY TASKS OF FRONTEX**
>
> - Cooperation between member states in external border management; control and surveillance of external borders
> - Technical and operational assistance at external borders
> - Training of national border guards; carrying out risk analyses
> - Support for member states in organizing joint return operations

The EU Internal Security Strategy provides operative institutions for fighting crime, protecting borders, and policing that cover different dimensions of guarding the internal security of the EU. Headquartered in The Hague, the Netherlands, **Europol**, the European Union Agency for Law Enforcement Cooperation, plays a front-line role in coordinating Europe's fight against terrorism and cross-border crime (most importantly in the fields of illicit drugs, human trafficking, irregular migration, cybercrime, money laundering, organized crime, and terrorism). Becoming operational in 1999, Europol coordinates the sharing of intelligence among national police forces and their European collaboration. The justification for this EU organization is found in pan-EU organized crime, trafficking, and terrorism programs, which are transnational in scale and need an effective and coordinated policy response among member states.

Beyond the immediate task of fighting terrorism, the EU has embarked on the ambitious agenda to create a "European Area of Justice." At the core of this enhanced cooperation across all member states is the mutual recognition of judicial decisions – regardless of the diversity of judicial systems throughout the EU. This cooperation also extends to law enforcement. Driven by the international anti-terror efforts after the 9/11 attacks in New York and Washington in 2001, the EU launched the **European arrest warrant (EAW)** in 2004. Member states commit to surrendering to another EU member state any person on their territory if they are wanted in relation to significant crimes or to serve a prison sentence for an existing conviction. Extradition under the EAW has greatly increased: Between 2005 and 2018, 185,575 EAWs were issued, and 56,298 of these were executed. In the Schengen Area in particular, close collaboration of law enforcement agencies has led to transnational networks of police and judicial authorities.

However, the widespread recognition that a community approach to security challenges is warranted comes with a vocal public critique of how the EU balances security policies with the protection of the fundamental rights and liberties of citizens. One critical assessment of EU action points to a general conundrum that is shaping this policy field in countries around the world, including Canada. In a post-9/11 environment and faced with a series of terrorist attacks (many of which occurred on European soil), liberal democracies are confronted with a politically contested policy challenge. How should state authorities strike an appropriate balance between security and surveillance, on the one hand, and civil liberties on the other? While the EU seeks to promote a more tolerant and inclusive society as part of its AFSJ domain, it nonetheless remains a major player in fortifying its external borders, supporting a comprehensive surveillance system, and portraying migrants from outside the member states as a veritable security risk.

A further political challenge shaping this policy domain results from the tension and interplay between national and European responses to security challenges. With respect to managing migrants and refugees under the AFSJ domain, it proves to be considerably easier to find consensus among member states on EU initiatives targeted at (external) border control and policing. In contrast, the EU mandate to protect human and civil rights and to promote societal integration of non-EU nationals is regularly perceived as a more challenging infringement on sovereign prerogatives of nation states.

The EU budget reflects these concerns (see Box 8.5). The 2015–16 refugee crisis and the COVID-19 pandemic have highlighted how security and border control can compromise some of the EU's basic liberties and commitments to human rights. The inability of the EU to effectively address the suffering of the refugees on their treacherous voyage to Europe and the various measures taken to combat the COVID-19 pandemic have provoked criticism from human rights advocates. With regard to the former, the longstanding debate on "fortress Europe" reflects, among other concerns, the worry of those who consider the EU's border regime to be driven by a strong emphasis on security and militarized border control at the expense of the EU's humanitarian commitments.

The various crises the EU has faced since the 2015–16 refugee crisis have triggered a political development that challenges the EU's capacity for collective action and has emboldened critical political actors, if not sparking outright hostility to the very project of European integration (see the debate section for discussion of the rise of the populist right in Europe). The 2016 Brexit referendum and the eventual departure of the UK from the EU in 2020 are a case in point: The response to the refugee crisis and migration more broadly were key themes driving popular sentiments directed at the idea of sovereign nation states losing

> **BOX 8.5: BUDGET FOR THE AFSJ**
>
> - The EU budget for 2021 projected expenditures of €1 billion for migration, €1.3 billion for border management, €537 million for security, €93 million for rights and values, and €45 million for justice. Together, EU spending in these AFSJ fields made up around 2 per cent of the EU's overall budget.
> - The largest individual items were the Asylum, Migration and Integration Fund (€870 million), which funds measures to support legal migration, encourage the integration of TCNs, counter irregular migration, and return failed asylum applicants; the Integrated Border Management Fund (€531 million), which funds border security; and the Internal Security Fund (€174 million), which funds measures against crime and terrorism.
> - The budget also paid for EU agencies in the AFSJ, especially Frontex (€506 million) and Europol (€170 million).
>
> Source: Definitive adoption (EU, Euratom) 2021/417 of the European Union's general budget for the financial year 2021, https://eur-lex.europa.eu/eli/budget/2021/1/oj

control of their borders. Similarly, one of the central issues in the UK and EU negotiations over the terms of Brexit was the principle of freedom of movement. Thus, cross-border mobility has been at once both a driving force in nurturing a sense of Europeanness over the past decades while simultaneously being at the centre of a nationalist backlash against the scope and nature of European rule.

DEBATE: GOVERNING MIGRATION AND BORDERS: THE REFUGEE CRISIS AND ITS IMPACT ON THE EU

The 2015–16 refugee crisis and its lingering effects have clearly illustrated how politically contested and sensitive an EU-led approach to governing borders and migration can be. In the wake of the Arab Spring (see Chapter 14), Europe experienced an enormous influx of irregular migrants travelling across the Mediterranean Sea or over land through southeast Europe. Triggered further by the civil war in Syria, these numbers peaked in 2015. According to UNHCR figures, 1.3 million migrants reached the shores of Europe in 2015, and almost 4,000 migrants lost their lives – primarily during their treacherous voyage by sea. Ukrainian refugees started arriving in 2022, and the International Organization for Migration estimated that there were 2,406 deaths recorded in the Mediterranean during 2022.

As mentioned above, under the Dublin Regulation refugees need to file their asylum claim in the first EU member state they arrive in (see Box 8.6). During the 2015–16 migration crisis, in light of the sheer numbers of refugees crossing the external borders of the EU, it was temporarily abandoned. The front-line member states rapidly reached the limits of their administrative capacity when thousands of refugees arrived daily from Northern Africa. To complicate the situation further, with the reality of a borderless Europe in the Schengen Area, refugees could travel to the member state of their choice, defying the Dublin Regulation.

BOX 8.6: DUBLIN REGULATION (IN FORCE SINCE 1997)

- Establishes that the EU member state where the asylum seeker first lands is responsible for processing applications by asylum seekers.
- Its principal aim is to prevent asylum seekers from submitting applications in multiple member states.
- As part of the Dublin system, the EU has established the EURODAC Regulation, an EU-wide fingerprinting database for unauthorized entrants to the EU.
- In July 2017, the Court of Justice of the EU upheld the Dublin Regulation, declaring that it still stands regardless of the massive influx of irregular migrants in 2015.

Manifestly, the issue of external border control and asylum proved to be one that could not be tackled by individual member states and thus demanded a pan-European solution. Box 8.7 provides a comparison with border control and migration policy issues in Canada. Partly because of key elements of the project of European integration, most notably the Single Market and cross-border mobility, the EU had to address challenges that exceeded the regulative capacity of individual member states (scholars call this a "functional spillover" from the Single Market project; see Chapter 6). However, during the refugee crisis, a coherent and effective response by the EU proved to be difficult. The proposal of an EU distribution scheme for refugees across all member states was vigorously opposed by some countries, particularly in Central and Eastern Europe; Poland, Hungary, and the Czech Republic even took the issue of migrant quotas to the Court of Justice of the EU. A series of EU summits on the issue demonstrated how divided heads of state and governments were on the refugee issue. It demonstrated the sensitivity of the policy domain of borders and migration, particularly in domestic electoral politics. In the end, a series of emergency summits led to a compromise that was too limited in scope to provide a sufficient answer to the challenge. Instead, individual member states adopted their own policies that were directed primarily at border control. The principle of a borderless Europe was compromised – at least temporarily.

It is worth noting that the EU's response to the wave of Ukrainian refugees in the aftermath of the Russian invasion has followed a distinctly different script: The exodus of over 6 million refugees was met with a great degree of solidarity in many member states. For the first time, the EU activated its emergency protection system (created in 2001), facilitating Ukrainians' access to housing, health care, education, and jobs. This response included the EU's Cohesion's Action for Refugees in Europe, making emergency support available to member states that shelter refugees fleeing Ukraine. The response to the over 6 million Ukrainian refugees could pave the way toward a more robust EU migration system designed to welcome and share responsibility for refugees among member states.

The example of the refugee crisis shows that the key challenges that policies in the AFSJ face are administrative and, arguably more importantly, political in nature. In managing migration and asylum, most EU member states have fallen back on what they perceive to be in their "national interest" and have resisted the burden-sharing approach put forward by the European Commission. Essentially, most EU member states perceived the refugee crisis not as a collective but an individual member state responsibility. While the AFSJ is legally under community jurisdiction, this communitarization is still contested.

BOX 8.7: CANADA–EU COMPARISON
In order to consider the scale and nature of the policy challenges posed by governing Europe's border regime and its cross-border mobility, it is important to ponder Europe's geography. In contrast to Canada, which is protected by large oceans and a long border with one friendly neighbour to the south with similar political and economic conditions, the EU borders countries with wildly different situations. Furthermore, its external borders are subject to large-scale irregular migration and organized crime. Geographic proximity (to Eastern Europe and the African side of the Mediterranean coast) and key geopolitical developments in the region (the collapse of communism and the Arab Spring) have made EU member states far more exposed to its immediate neighbourhood (see Chapter 18). Hence, security risks related to cross-border mobility and the urgency to address them in policy terms are more pronounced in the EU than they are in Canada. From a transatlantic perspective, it is also worth noting the degree to which national borders have changed in nature as part of the European integration process. The Canada–US border used to be much more open than inner-European borders until 2001. Since then, the Canada–US border has become far more securitized while the EU has moved toward eradicating border controls inside the Schengen Area.

Another area where the Canadian and EU policy approaches differ relates to social integration of migrants and refugees: While this dimension of Canada's migration regime is strongly shaped by multiculturalism as an ethical norm and state policy, public policies in the field of cultural diversity and integration are highly diverse and politically contested in EU member states. Comprehensive integration policies directed at the long-term inclusion of newcomers are often still in their infancy in individual countries and the EU itself. Taking inspiration from Canada and other immigration countries, in November 2021 the EU Business Association advanced a proposal for a policy to welcome workers to the EU who have important skills that the EU labour market needs.

Furthermore, throughout the EU, issues such as border control, fighting terrorism, and controlling migration are prone to divisive domestic debates and mobilizing efforts of the anti-immigrant, populist right. While pursuing migration or asylum policies through the AFSJ could be interpreted as an attempt to circumvent domestic opposition against such plans, the objective to come up with an EU approach to the refugee challenge has developed into a veritable crisis for the EU. The populist backlash against refugees has sparked a re-nationalization and a great degree of skepticism with respect to the very project of European integration. In particular in some of the eastern EU member states (especially Hungary and Poland), the issue of migration has taken centre stage in popularizing anti-EU sentiments and in pushing for a nationalist agenda. The EU could have hardly been more divided than when responding to the refugee challenge. On the one end of the spectrum was the German chancellor Angela Merkel advocating a compassionate response to the suffering of the refugees and a pan-European policy response. On the other end, Hungarian prime minister Viktor Orbán opted for the fortification of borders and the categorical rejection of any collective European policy response to governing migration.

The policies subsumed under the AFSJ go to the very heart of what the EU stands for as a political union. As former European Council president Donald Tusk stated with respect to the refugee crisis: Mutual support and the readiness to stand by Greece (where the greatest number of refugees had arrived) should be seen as "a test of our Europeanness." He referred to both an effective burden sharing across the member states in the collective response to the refugee crisis as well as the political values that the EU claims to stand for in terms of its commitment to human rights and liberties. The ongoing death of refugees in the Mediterranean Sea and their agony in trying to reach the shores of Europe are difficult to reconcile with the EU's founding values of "human dignity, freedom, democracy, equality, the rule of law and respect for human rights, including the rights of persons belonging to minorities" (stipulated in Article 3 TEU).

In this political environment, the AFSJ faces enormous problems developing coherent public policies at the EU level. First, the AFSJ shows an inherent tension between some of its key policy initiatives. The drive to prop up security and external border control directed at threats emanating from irregular migration, terrorism, and organized crime is prone to come into conflict with the EU's constitutive commitment to human rights. Second, while the very nature of the open border regime gives rise to the need for EU-level governance of borders and migration issues, the AFSJ tests the resolve of member states to agree to supranational rule. Yet some of the intergovernmental cooperation in the EU over the past decade has occurred in this policy area of border security and migration. As Brexit and the resurgence of populist–nationalist politics have exemplified, there is increasing domestic pressure to "take back control" and to challenge the policy prerogative of the EU, in particular in governing migration.

CONCLUSION

The development of policies under the AFSJ was a major leap forward in bringing the JHA under community rule. In the early 1990s, a European approach to justice and security was in its infancy. Today the way in which member states address the challenge of migration, organized crime, and terrorism is almost impossible to imagine without the pivotal role that EU agencies such as Frontex or Europol play in Europe's security framework. Vitally, the creation of a Single Market and an unprecedented degree of cross-border mobility has made issues such as standardizing the EU legal framework, managing borders and migration, and fighting crime functional prerogatives of the most recent phase of European integration.

At the same time, some key policies in the AFSJ domain have led to fierce political contestation among the member states and a series of momentous setbacks in the ambitious agenda of the EU. Most significantly, far-reaching plans to implement common policies for governing migration and borders at the European level were met with strong resistance in some member states because they touch on core state powers. In a climate of a nationalist resurgence throughout Europe, the new EU initiative for a Pact on Migration and Asylum faces uncertainty and the veritable prospect of continuing to be a highly divisive issue in the politics of European integration.

REVIEW QUESTIONS

1 Why has the issue of cross-border mobility been a driving force in the expanding AFSJ policy domain?
2 What are the elements of European citizenship status and why are they important?

3 Why are many of the policies in the AFSJ domain so contested among the EU member states? Why has there been consistent resistance when it comes to bringing AFSJ policies under supranational rule?

4 In what way and why does the issue of irregular migration pose such a challenge to the EU's emergent migration and asylum policies?

EXERCISES

1 Research the specific reactions of EU member states and Schengen Area countries to the EU's 2015 proposal for a quota system for refugees. Which countries opposed the quota system, and what were their reasons? Which countries supported the proposal, and why? How do these positions for and against the quota proposal dovetail with arguments for and against the need for European integration?

2 Research the rules of the Schengen Agreement. What allowances are there for temporary reinstatement of border controls? What measures exist to monitor compliance?

REFERENCES AND FURTHER READING

Arcarazo, D.A., and A. Geddes. 2013. "The Development, Application and Implications of an EU Rule of Law in the Area of Migration Policy." *Journal of Common Market Studies* 51 (2): 179–93. https://doi.org/10.1111/j.1468 -5965.2012.02296.x.

Badell, D. 2020. "The EU, Migration and Contestation: The UN Global Compact for Migration, from Consensus to Dissensus." *Global Affairs* 6 (4–5): 347–62. https:// doi.org/10.1080/23340460.2020.1871301.

Bigo, D. 2014. "The (In)securitization Practices of the Three Universes of EU Border Control: Military/Navy, Border Guards/Police, Database Analysts." *Security Dialogue* 45 (3): 209–25. https://doi.org/10.1177/0967010614530459.

Boswell, C. 2010. "Justice and Home Affairs." In *Research Agendas in EU Studies: Stalking the Elephant*, edited by M. Egan, N. Nugent, and W. Paterson, 278–304. Basingstoke, UK: Palgrave Macmillan.

European Commission. 2020. *New Pact on Migration and Asylum*. https://ec.europa .eu/info/strategy/priorities-2019-2024/promoting-our-european-way-life/new -pact-migration-and-asylum_en.

Guild, E., C. Costello, M. Garlick, and V. Moreno-Lax. 2015. *Enhancing the Common European Asylum System and Alternatives to Dublin*. Brussels: Centre for European Policy Studies.

International Organization for Migration. 2021. "Missing Migrants Project." https://missingmigrants.iom.int/region/mediterranean.

Kaunert, C. 2018. *European Internal Security: Towards Supranational Governance in the Area of Freedom, Security and Justice*. Manchester: Manchester University Press.

Lavenex, S., and W. Wallace. 2005. "Justice and Home Affairs." In *Policy Making in the EU*, edited by H. Wallace, W. Wallace, and M. Pollack, 457–80. Oxford: Oxford University Press.

Léonard, S., and C. Kaunert. 2020. "The Securitisation of Migration in the European Union: Frontex and Its Evolving Security Practices." *Journal of Ethnic and Migration Studies* 48 (6): 1417–29. https://doi.org/10.1080/1369183X.2020.1851469.

Lock, T. 2019. "Rights and Principles in the EU Charter of Fundamental Rights." *Common Market Law Review* 56 (5): 1201–26. https://doi.org/10.54648/COLA2019100.

Maas, W. 2013. *Democratic Citizenship and the Free Movement of People*. Leiden: Martinus Nijhoff Publishers.

Marsh, S., and W. Rees. 2012. *The European Union in the Security of Europe: From Cold War to Terror War*. New York: Routledge.

Monar, J. 2012. "Justice and Home Affairs: The Treaty of Maastricht as a Decisive Intergovernmental Gate Opener." *Journal of European Integration* 34 (7): 717–34. https://doi.org/10.1080/07036337.2012.726011.

Monar, J. 2015. "Justice and Home Affairs." *Journal of Common Market Studies* 53 (S1): 128–43. https://doi.org/10.1111/jcms.12261.

Roos, C. 2018. "The Council and European Council in EU Justice and Home Affairs Politics." In *The Routledge Handbook of Justice and Home Affairs Research*, edited by A. Ripoll Servent and F. Trauner, 421–33. New York: Routledge.

Schain, M. 2009. "The State Strikes Back: Immigration Policy in the European Union." *European Journal of International Law* 20 (1): 93–109. https://doi.org/10.1093/ejil/chp001.

Schmidtke, O. 2021. "'Winning Back Control': Migration, Borders, and Visions of Political Community." *International Studies* 58 (2): 150–67. https://doi.org/10.1177/00208817211002001.

Sperling, J., and M. Webber. 2019. "The European Union: Security Governance and Collective Securitisation." *West European Politics* 42 (2): 228–60. https://doi.org/10.1080/01402382.2018.1510193.

Trauner, F., and A. Ripoll Servent. 2015. *Policy Change in the Area of Freedom, Security and Justice: How EU Institutions Matter*. New York: Routledge.

Walker, N., ed. 2004. *Europe's Area of Freedom, Security and Justice*. Oxford: Oxford University Press.

Foreign, Security, and Defence Policies

Frédéric Mérand and Antoine Rayroux

READER'S GUIDE

Issues of "high politics" – foreign affairs, diplomacy, security, and military affairs – have long been the sole preserve of member states in the European Union (EU). The emergence of a Common Foreign and Security Policy and a Common Security and Defence Policy in the late twentieth and early twenty-first centuries is a unique achievement and the result of a slow and contested process. The resulting decision-making system is a hybrid of intergovernmental and supranational institutions designed to promote consensus among member states. However, diverging interests between smaller and larger European powers, or among the latter, and the absence of a coherent strategic vision remain major hurdles for turning the EU into a fully-fledged global actor.

INTRODUCTION

In the modern international system, foreign policy, **diplomacy**, security, and defence belong to the core of sovereignty, along with the administration of justice and the issuing of currency. While the latter two have been

Europeanized and even to a large extent transferred to the EU level, the former issues remained under the sole control of member states until the 1990s. Since the enactment of a **Common Foreign and Security Policy (CFSP)** after the Treaty of Maastricht entered into force in 1993, followed by a European Security and Defence Policy (ESDP) after the Treaty of Nice entered into force in 2003, things have changed. These evolutions have pushed the reflection over the political "finality" of the EU a step further: Is the EU meant to become a federation, with its foreign policy governed by a European minister for foreign affairs and with a European army? Should the EU think of itself as a power willing to balance the United States, rival China, or protect itself against Russia? Or does it merely aim to build a large and strong economic bloc exercising soft power through trade and international norms?

As we will see in the first section of this chapter, the fact that the EU was meant as a peace project from the start influenced Europeans' early attempts at creating a common structure where hard security (the military) would be integrated supranationally. However, after this early attempt failed, the EU focused most of its common foreign policy efforts on soft foreign policy issues, in particular trade and development policies. The proliferation of regional conflicts and the unprovoked war launched by Russia in Ukraine in 2022 forced the EU to consider a much more assertive security and defence posture. Nowadays, the institutional foreign policy system of the EU still lives with this tension between supranational integration on soft issues and the preservation of national interests when it comes to hard issues related to security. This hybrid system – reflecting the character of the EU as less than a state but more than an international organization (Theme 2 of this book) – is the focus of the second section of this chapter. In the final section, we highlight some of the main debates that EU foreign policy is confronted with today. We hope to help readers make sense of why the EU is or is not able to speak with a single voice on issues as diverse as conducting diplomatic negotiations with Iran over its nuclear program; military intervention in the Balkans, Iraq, Libya, or the Sahel; or negotiating a sanctions regime against Russia.

A SHORT HISTORY OF EU FOREIGN POLICY

In the current modern world system, EU foreign policy is an anomaly for two reasons: historically, no other international organization to date has been endowed with a common foreign policy; and legally, the Westphalian international system recognizes no actor other than the nation state. How did this new and hybrid form of international actor come about?

While European integration has largely proceeded according to the economic logic of market building (Theme 1 of this book), "high politics" did come into play early. (In international relations, high politics pertain to state survival – foreign affairs, security, and defence – as opposed to "low politics," such as health, trade, or education.) Following the creation of the European Coal and Steel Community in 1951, the project of a European Defence Community (EDC) was meant to foster West European defence cooperation in the supranational framework of a European army. However, the EDC treaty failed to be ratified in 1954 (see also Chapter 2). Following this first moment of crisis in the history of European integration, high politics disappeared from the agenda for several decades, and the issue was not revived until after the Cold War ended.

The fact that the European Community nevertheless developed a key trade and development role in the following decades (see Chapter 12) created controversies concerning the international role and legal personality of the Commission. On April 26, 1977, the Court of Justice of the EU gave an opinion stating that "whenever community law has created for the institutions of the Community powers within its internal system for the purpose of attaining a specific objective, the Community has authority to enter into the international commitments necessary for the attainment of that objective even in the absence of an express provision in that connection" (Koutrakos 2015, 90). This case law allowed the Commission to gain a seat at the Food and Agriculture Organization for issues pertaining to the Common Agricultural Policy, whereas in other organizations, such as the International Civil Aviation Organization, it failed to do so.

In contrast to this movement toward narrow but supranational Community competences over development and trade, EU member states retained strict control over security issues. It was not until 1970 that a common foreign policy initiative was launched – the European Political Cooperation (EPC). Several barriers were erected to safeguard the strictly intergovernmental nature and limited role of the EPC: Diplomats and EPC working groups were authorized to discuss only the *political* aspects of security issues, and the European Commission was systematically sidelined. Despite these limitations, the EPC contributed to initiating a sense of shared European diplomatic practice through the diffusion of common norms, rules, and information among national foreign services, and thanks to the socialization among European diplomats. The voting behaviour of EU member states at the United Nations offers an oft-cited illustration of the progressive emergence of such diplomatic coordination. While they converged on a common position on only 40 per cent of UN General Assembly resolutions in the 1970s, the figure has climbed to 90 per cent in the early twenty-first century.

In the early 1990s, several events gave a new impetus to EU foreign policy: the end of the Cold War, German reunification, and the road to political union in the context of the Maastricht Treaty negotiations. The three main EU foreign policy and diplomatic powers – France, Germany, and the UK – had competing agendas: The French favoured a strong European independence, whereas the British and the Germans preferred close relations with the United States; the Germans were open to a stronger executive role for the Commission, while the British and the French were attached to the status quo. Nonetheless, all three agreed to create Pillar II of the Union, called the Common Foreign and Security Policy. The CFSP came about in a time of great optimism, characterized by the idea that the post–Cold War order marked the victory of the model of free market liberal democracies, the advent of multilateralism, and a renewed role for Europe as a global political actor. However, hopes were quickly thwarted by the erupting wars in Yugoslavia, which revealed Europe's weaknesses, and what Christopher Hill famously described as the "capabilities-expectations gap" (Hill 1993). When Bosnians and Serbs went to war against each other, the **North Atlantic Treaty Organization (NATO)** and the United States had to intervene.

The postwar settlement in Bosnia, and then the war in Kosovo in 1999, demonstrated that the EU was poorly equipped to deal with the military management of crises. The ESDP, which was created as a result of this Yugoslavian failure and the United States' increasing reluctance to act as a firefighter on the European continent, attempted to address this shortfall. The ESDP (which was subsequently renamed the **Common Security and Defence Policy**, or CSDP, when the Lisbon Treaty came into force in 2009) mostly came about as a result of UK prime minister Tony Blair's decision to drop the traditionally minimalist UK view on the CFSP and to drive the European ambition further. In 1998, Blair met with French president Jacques Chirac in Saint-Malo for a bilateral summit that established the main guiding principles of this new EU policy. France had long been a staunch advocate of a strong defence component in the CFSP – what French officials refer to as *Europe puissance*, meaning "military power Europe" – but it needed the support of the other significant military power on the continent.

Between 2003 and 2021, the EU undertook 36 civilian or military operations, from the Balkans to Indonesia, through the African Great Lakes region to Afghanistan (see Table 9.1). It is crucial to note that according to Article 43 of the Treaty on European Union (TEU), CSDP operations deal with crisis management. Possible tasks include joint disarmament operations, humanitarian and rescue tasks, military advice and assistance tasks, conflict prevention and peacekeeping tasks, and tasks of combat forces in crisis management, including peace making and post-conflict stabilization. Defence in the classical sense – repelling external aggression against the European territory – has so far remained the prerogative of NATO. Given that 23 out of 27 EU member states are members of NATO (as of 2022, after Sweden and Finland joined), it should come as no surprise that the CSDP focuses on medium- to long-term conflict prevention policies to avoid duplicating NATO's mandate and tools, which are more focused on short-term military crisis management. Even when NATO is not involved, the EU tends to focus on the lower end of the force spectrum. For example, in Mali and the Central African Republic, the EU is mostly engaged in development, capacity building, and some military training, while France and the regional G5 Sahel force do most of the fighting with insurgents.

Over the years, the EU has tried to develop a common strategic culture that would bring together traditions as varied as those of France and Estonia, or Sweden and Greece. In 2003, the first European Security Strategy was published, followed in 2016 by a Global Strategy on Foreign and Security Policy and in 2022 by a Strategic Compass for Security and Defence, in which the EU claims to "learn the language of power." These documents promote a "**comprehensive approach**" to tackling major threats in the European security environment, from terrorism to state failure: The EU claims that its added value lies in its ability to mobilize both military and civilian instruments, as well as its soft policy instruments such as economic partnerships, development cooperation, and humanitarian policy. These strategy documents provide the intellectual foundations for the **European External Action Service (EEAS)**, created in 2011 to merge the foreign, security, and defence policy functions of the EU, which were either located in different administrative services or non-existent. Under the leadership of the **high representative for foreign affairs and security policy**, who also holds the rank of vice-president of the Commission, the EEAS covers civilian and military crisis management but also standard diplomatic files, such as a national foreign ministry.

Table 9.1. Ongoing CSDP operations in 2021

Operation name and host country	Start date	Type and main objectives	Manpower (including local staff)	Number of contributing member states (plus non-member states)
ALTHEA Bosnia-Herzegovina	2004	Military: Training and capacity building of armed forces, deterrence	600	16 (plus 5 non-EU)
EUBAM Moldova and Ukraine	2005	Civilian: Support to border control, customs, and trade norms	200 (120 local)	13
EUBAM Rafah (Palestinian Territories)	2005	Civilian: Monitor Gaza Strip border crossing point	14 (7 local)	N/A
EUPOL COPPS Palestinian Territories	2006	Civilian: Support to police and law enforcement capacities	115 (45 local)	21 (plus 3 non-EU)
EUNAVFOR Somalia	2008	Military: Protection of World Food Program and AMISOM vessels, deterrence (piracy)	1200; 5 ships, 2 air assets	N/A
EULEX Kosovo	2008	Civilian: Support to rule of law institutions, delivery of rule of law	N/A	N/A
EUMM Georgia	2008	Civilian: Monitor peace agreement between Georgia, Abkhazia, and South Ossetia	200	22
EUTM Somalia	2010	Military: Training and capacity building of armed forces, strategic advice	195	11 (plus 1 non-EU)
EUCAP Nestor (Horn of Africa, based in Somalia)	2012	Civilian: Support to capacity building in maritime security (counterpiracy)	180 (40 local)	17

Mission	Year	Type and task	Size	Staff
EUCAP Sahel Niger	2012	Civilian: Support to capacity building of security forces (terrorism, organized crime)	135 (50 local)	11
EUTM Mali	2013	Military: Training and capacity building of armed forces, strategic advice	580	23 (plus 4 non-EU)
EUBAM Libya	2013	Civilian: Support to border management and security	17	N/A
EUAM Ukraine	2014	Civilian: Strategic advice for civilian security sector reform (law enforcement and rule of law)	200 (majority of which are local)	N/A
EUCAP Sahel Mali	2014	Civilian: Support to capacity building of internal security forces (police, gendarmerie, garde nationale)	100 (40 local)	13
EUNAVFOR Med (Mediterranean)	2015	Military: Identify and capture vessels of migrant traffickers, training of Libyan coastguard and navy	5 ships, 3 helicopters, 3 air assets	24
EUTM Central African Republic	2016	Military: Training and capacity building of armed forces, security sector reform	N/A	N/A
EUAM Iraq	2017	Civilian: security sector reform	N/A	N/A
EUAM RCA	2020	Civilian: security sector reform	N/A	N/A

Source: European External Action Service (EEAS), http://www.eeas.europa.eu/csdp/missions-and-operations/index_en.htm#

In the 2010s, pressure grew on the EU to adopt a more ambitious security and defence profile. The eruption of high-intensity regional conflicts (Syria, Libya) and the growing threat of militant terrorist groups (Al Qaida, Islamic State) in the neighbourhood, as well as growing military assertiveness on the part of Russia (2014 war in Ukraine), can explain the need for the EU to set more ambitious goals. The failure of the EU's "soft" instruments of conditionality in supporting democracy after the Arab Spring, the backlash against this strategy in Ukraine, and the growing indifference of the United States to European security made several capitals converge around the need to become more than a **normative power**. In 2009, the Treaty of Lisbon had adopted a new article (Article 42), which is relatively similar to NATO's mutual defence clause (Article 5 of the North Atlantic Treaty). The EU article calls for a mutual assistance commitment and states that "if a Member State is the victim of armed aggression on its territory, the other Member States shall have towards it an obligation of aid and assistance by all the means in their power, in accordance with Article 51 of the United Nations Charter. This shall not prejudice the specific character of the security and defence policy of certain Member States." The last sentence is a safeguard for the non-NATO members of the EU (Austria, Ireland, Cyprus, and Malta), which remain neutral or non-allied.

For a long time, the EU's strategic ambitions were hampered by the UK and other countries that remained wedded to the transatlantic relationship. London and Washington feared that these ambitions would lead to a decoupling of Europe from the United States and vetoed any step in that direction. In 2016, newly elected US president Donald Trump cast a shadow, however, on NATO solidarity. He refused to confirm that he would honour Article 5. Furthermore, the outcome of the 2016 Brexit referendum foreshadowed the likely exit of the UK. In a 2016 State of the Union speech reminiscent of the EDC project, European Commission president Jean-Claude Juncker even called for the establishment of an EU army with a permanent headquarters. Combined with growing geopolitical tensions, from the aggressive actions of China in the Pacific Ocean to the 2021 US withdrawal from Afghanistan, these political developments in Washington and London were a game-changer in Brussels. When, in the summer of 2021, the UK signed a special deal to collaborate with Australia and the United States (AUKUS) in the Pacific, French and numerous European diplomats were outraged.

On February 24, 2022, an even bigger game-changer upset the European security landscape in a way that will prove transformational for the next decade at least. On that day, Russian troops invaded Ukraine, a country that had tried to join NATO and considered EU membership precisely as a means to escape Russian imperialism. While NATO buttressed its eastern flank and accepted Finland and Sweden into its ranks, the EU decided, for the first time in its history, to provide a large amount of weapons to Ukraine through its own budget called the European Peace Facility. In the weeks that followed the invasion, the EU also adopted the most ambitious sanctions regime in the history of the CFSP: first against Russian assets and leaders, then oil and eventually gas. This was a watershed moment for the EU as a strategic actor, one whose consequences are difficult to ascertain at the time of writing.

One thing is certain, though: The old French discourse on "strategic autonomy" for the EU has become more widely heard in European capitals (Biscop and Howorth 2022). **Strategic autonomy** is an ambiguous concept, which means autonomous decision making, with its own capabilities, for the purpose of collective defence. Although autonomous decision making is a matter of political will, the EU continues to lack the military capabilities to provide for its own defence – that is, without the United States. That is why, in 2017, 25 member states (excluding Denmark and Malta, which decided not to join) introduced **Permanent Structured Cooperation (PESCO)** in the area of security and defence. This serves as a platform to develop joint capabilities projects with a view to attaining a full spectrum force package. The same year, the EU inaugurated its first Military Planning and Conduct Capability, a permanent headquarters for EU military operations. In 2019, the European Commission launched the European Defence Fund, a multibillion euro budget to promote defence capability–related research and development projects. In a move that would have been anathema only a few years earlier, the Commission also created a brand new Directorate General (DG) for Defence Industry and Space (DEFIS).

A permanent military headquarters for the EU? The Commission in charge of defence expenditures? The EU providing lethal military materials to a third country? Although it is too early to tell whether these initiatives will bear fruit, none of them would have been thinkable had the UK remained in the EU and had Russia not invaded Ukraine.

A HYBRID FOREIGN POLICY SYSTEM

As demonstrated at great length in this book, the EU is more than a traditional international organization but less than a federal state (Theme 2 of this book). It is a particular kind of actor whose powers ultimately depend on the member states' goodwill, and this general observation also applies to the case of EU foreign, security, and defence policies. A "European foreign policy" entails three overlapping realities: the foreign policy of individual EU member states, the external relations portfolios of what used to be known as the community pillar (Pillar I) until 2009 (mainly trade, development, and humanitarian aid), and the foreign policy of the EU as such (White 2001). The foreign policy system of the EU is the result of confrontations and compromises between these different realities and between the supranational and national levels. This context explains many of the differences between foreign policy-making in the EU and in a sovereign state such as Canada (see Box 9.1).

BOX 9.1: COMPARISON WITH CANADA
In contrast to the EU's hybrid foreign policy system, Canada has a centralized diplomacy much as other sovereign states have. The federal government enjoys a "crown prerogative" that enables it to conduct diplomatic relations unencumbered by provinces or, for that matter, genuine parliamentary oversight. This is in line with the Westphalian tradition, whereby sovereign states are the only legitimate actors in the international system; they are allowed to sign treaties, declare war, and become full members of the United Nations. As the King's representative, the governor general is the commander-in-chief of the armed forces and, although they are collectively responsible before the federal Parliament, the prime minister, the foreign minister, and the defence minister have much greater decision-making autonomy than the European Council president, the European Commission president, or the EU high representative.

Still, there are interesting parallels between the EU and Canada. While EU members were beginning to delegate a number of external competences to Brussels in the 1960s and 1970s, the Canadian federation was devolving some external competences to the provinces. This is particularly the case for Quebec, which since the late 1960s conducts its own "international relations" and has developed a kind of a "paradiplomacy" (Paquin 2010). The province has its own international relations minister and 11 delegations abroad, one of which has full diplomatic status in Paris. Quebec is a full member in La Francophonie (along with New Brunswick) and has a formally distinct status inside the Canadian delegation to the United Nations Educational, Scientific and Cultural Organization. Much as the EU does, Quebec claims that "all its internal competences are also external competences" – the so-called Gérin-Lajoie Doctrine, named after the province's education minister who stated its basic principles in 1965. This includes immigration, education, economic development, culture, health, and the environment. Other Canadian provinces also appoint agents in foreign capitals and have opened trade promotion and immigration bureaus abroad.

The powers of provinces remain residual: They cannot sign foreign treaties, cannot raise an army, and can only operate an external policy in the narrow fields of provincial responsibility. By contrast, European member states must approve treaties signed by the EU and can always decide to revoke the powers they have delegated to Brussels. An area where the EU seems to have greater power than the Canadian federal government, however, is in the enforcement of international treaties: While the European Commission can take member states to court if they fail to comply, there is little the federal government can do to force provinces to act in their area of competence, even when an international treaty was signed.

On many issues, these differences between the EU's hybrid system and Canada's federal system may not matter much. If we take development aid, trade, or the fight against climate change, the EU and its member states, just as the federal government and the provinces, must work hand in hand to shape global governance. In these areas, the EU, despite its "constitutional" limitations, is a much bigger actor than Canada when it coordinates Europe's actions and resources. This suggests that the formal division of powers does not explain everything: Remember that Canada only became a foreign policy actor, independent from the British Crown, in 1931 with the Statute of Westminster!

There are several actors in the EU foreign policy system. There are of course member states and their representatives, who sometimes consider that national interests are best defended strictly through unilateral or bilateral channels, whereas in other cases a common EU approach will be more efficient. For example, when a security crisis erupted in Mali in early 2013, France took the unilateral decision to intervene militarily to prevent a coup d'état with potentially far-reaching regional consequences; only then did the EU get involved with a military operation to train a new Malian army (operation EU Training Mission (EUTM) Mali). In Brussels, member states do not only meet at the level of the Foreign Affairs Council, which is the monthly meeting of foreign affairs, defence, and development ministers. Most of their concerns are voiced through their permanent representation, which acts as both a transmission belt for member states in Brussels and as a consensus-seeking machine. In matters of foreign and security policy, these national ambassadors meet weekly in the Political and Security Committee (PSC). In addition, national civil servants prepare PSC and Council meetings in more than 30 thematic or geographic working groups dealing with foreign affairs.

In the EU's institutional system, most foreign policy working groups and preparatory committees are spearheaded by the EEAS, which was created by the 2009 Lisbon Treaty (Spence and Batora 2015). The EEAS is the EU's diplomatic service, with headquarters in Brussels and a worldwide diplomatic presence in 140 states. It is worth noting that only two member states – France and Germany – have more embassies abroad than the EU. The EEAS was created to increase consistency in the EU foreign policy system by bringing under the same roof the Council working groups and the European Commission committees dealing with external relations. Interestingly, the EEAS works as an autonomous body, not under the control of either the Council or the Commission.

The EEAS is headed by the high representative (HR) of the union for foreign affairs and security policy, who is nominated by the European Council, that is, the member states' heads of state or government. The position of HR is probably the most telling illustration of the hybrid nature of EU foreign policy. Its portfolio is very broad: The HR acts as the EU chief diplomat in charge of overseeing certain nominations (EU special representatives) and the work of EU delegations, they represent the EU in international organizations and negotiations, chair the intergovernmental Foreign Affairs Council, coordinate the Commission's services dealing with external relations, and head a series of additional EU agencies. Needless to say, the multiplicity of tasks implies that the HR has to share their responsibilities with other key figures whose influence and autonomy in the system is significant, such as the secretary general of the EEAS or the commissioners responsible for Trade (DG TRADE), Neighbourhood and Enlargement Negotiations (DG NEAR), Development Cooperation (DG DEVCO), and Defence Industry and Space (DG DEFIS). Also, the nature of the position itself is tricky: As a Commission member, the HR is bound by the rule of collegiality while being de facto a *primus inter pares* when it comes to issues of foreign affairs; at the same time, the HR has to act as a mediator of national foreign policy views at the Foreign Affairs Council while speaking in the name of the EU at the UN or in other international forums.

Not all institutions with a foreign policy responsibility have been moved under the roof of the EEAS. Both the Commission and the member states have refused to hand over some of their foreign policy competences to the new service. At one end of the spectrum, several former Community competences such as trade and development still have their own departments and structures. In fact, the Commission has even acquired a new competence, on the defence industry, which has been given to the internal market commissioner. At the other end, working groups and structures on security and military affairs remain under the exclusive control of the Council, and hence the member states. Below the PSC level, a series of intergovernmental crisis management structures have been created to deal with CSDP operations. These include the EU Military Committee – made up of representatives of national chiefs of staff – the Committee for Civilian Aspects of Crisis Management, the EU Military Staff, the Crisis Management and Planning Directorate, and the Civilian Planning and Conduct Capability. They all support the PSC, which exercises political control and strategic direction of crisis management operations under the responsibility of the Council and the HR.

Certainly, the EU foreign policy institutional system has made progress toward greater consistency, but it has not solved the debate about which institution should ultimately be responsible for EU foreign policy. In the fields of development or partnerships with third countries, foreign policy issues work in a way similar to other EU policies. This means "open political competition" (Haroche 2009) characterized by the participation of all of the three main EU institutions (Council, Commission, Parliament), the existence of controversial debates between political parties, the involvement of interest groups and public opinion, and so on.

In contrast to this logic of open competition, decision making in the areas of diplomacy, security, and defence can be described as a "regime of closed negotiation," where the Council of the EU, deciding by unanimity, plays the central role (Haroche 2009). As spelled out in Title V of the TEU, it is up to the European Council – the meeting of heads of state or government – to decide by unanimity on the general guidelines and directions of the CFSP. On most issues, from the adoption of sanctions and arms embargoes to the launch of a CSDP mission, the Foreign Affairs Council also decides by unanimity. If a member state disagrees with a joint position or action, it may rely on the procedure of constructive abstention, which consists in not blocking a decision but not participating in its implementation either. Since the Lisbon Treaty, the CFSP/CSDP remains the only strictly intergovernmental EU policy, making security and defence the preserve of traditional diplomacy and national interests.

The description of the CFSP/CSDP decision-making machinery demonstrates that although national permanent representations and civil servants play a central role, the system also depends on a modest EU bureaucracy, in particular the 4,000 individuals working for the EEAS in Brussels and abroad. For these reasons, Jolyon Howorth (2012) argues that even the CFSP/CSDP is more than purely intergovernmental, and that it may best be described as a unique kind of "supranational intergovernmentalism," by which he means that the institutional logic of intergovernmental cooperation has come closer to the traditional culture of supranational integration and collective decision making.

DEBATES IN EU FOREIGN POLICY

Today, the EU has acquired the potential to be a significant international actor with a voice that carries beyond the continent. External action and CFSP institutions have solidified over time, and they have generated a set of rules, norms, and practices that have become internalized by civil servants, diplomats, or military officers working in Brussels. Over time, the thorny issue of EU–NATO relations, which long cast a shadow over European security and defence, has moved into the foreground. The two organizations based in Brussels now consider themselves bound by a strategic partnership, which has led to increasingly routine discussions on anything from cyberthreats to capability development. However, it would be a mistake to view this evolution as an inevitable road to success. Several important debates remain, four of which we highlight in this section.

A first debate concerns the *influence of big member states vis-à-vis smaller ones*. Leadership is a key question in foreign and defence affairs. After Brexit, France is the sole EU member that has retained a permanent seat on the UN Security Council, where Paris is merely required to inform the EU. In terms of military capabilities, France alone makes up 21 per cent of the EU's total spending, followed by Germany at 16 per cent, which is a sign of the EU's dependence on a few countries. The EU's own budget on external relations, and especially defence, remains small (see Box 9.2). France, being a strong supporter of the CSDP, usually contributes most of the troops. Germany has been more reluctant to contribute, in particular when it comes to operations that are deployed in Africa, often in former French colonies and under the pressure of French diplomacy. However, the Germans have provided a significant effort in the different EU civilian and military operations in the Balkans (such as EUFOR Althea Bosnia-Herzegovina or EULEX Kosovo). After the Russian invasion of Ukraine, Berlin also underwent the so-called *Zeitenwende* (turn of an era), which led it, followed by other EU member states, to increase its defence spending substantially.

The level of ambition of the EU's foreign and defence policy depends on the level of cooperation between large and small member states. On the one hand, it depends on whether its most powerful states – France and Germany, followed by Italy, Spain, and Poland – are willing to cooperate with one another in Brussels and to reach more than the "lowest common denominator" that the unanimity decision-making rules tend to imply. On the other hand, smaller member states have often suspected that the larger ones use the EU for their own national interests. When national interests collide, the EU is damaged, and this is often done at the expense of the smaller European states, whose diplomatic influence relies more heavily on the EU. For example, when the time came to envision a military intervention to stop Muammar Gaddafi's violent repression of protest movements in Libya in 2011, Germany's reluctance proved detrimental to a common EU operation, thus leaving France and the UK acting unilaterally with US logistical support.

A second debate concerns *whether all member states have to participate in EU actions*. In terms of decision making and implementation, a member state can always refuse to endorse a common position. Also, the Council of the EU sometimes decides on new CSDP operations before making sure that member states will actually offer sufficient contributions in human resources

> **BOX 9.2: BUDGET FOR FOREIGN, SECURITY, AND DEFENCE POLICY**
>
> - In the 2021–7 Multiannual Financial Framework, the EU budget under the heading "Global Europe" amounts to €79.5 billion for the seven-year period, roughly 7 per cent of the EU's total budget.
> - The annual budget for 2021 allocates €14.2 billion to external action and €1.2 billion to defence. Spending on external action includes cooperation with non-EU countries in the EU's neighbourhood and elsewhere, development and international cooperation, as well as rapid response actions. In the area of defence, the largest item is the European Defence Fund.
> - With a staff of around 4,000 people (including EU permanent staff, seconded national experts, and local staff in the EU delegations), the EEAS had an annual budget of €768 million in 2021, which is less than half the budget of the French or German foreign ministry.
> - Most CSDP military expenses are borne by the member states themselves and are not included in the EU's budget. This situation results from the costs-lie-where-they-fall rule, which states that every state pays for its own contribution to an operation.
>
> Source: Definitive adoption (EU, Euratom) 2021/417 of the European Union's general budget for the financial year 2021, https://eur-lex.europa.eu/eli/budget/2021/1/oj

and material capabilities. In the CSDP system, there is no permanent EU army or EU battalions, despite occasional calls from EU officials in that direction. Member states are always free to refuse to take part in an EU operation, even when they have voted in favour of it. And then, "costs lie where they fall," which means that every contributing state to an operation has to fund its own deployment. Incidentally, third countries such as Canada are able to participate in some crisis management operations, as they did in Mali

(EUCAP Sahel Mali) or Ukraine (EUAM Ukraine), because of this system of own funding.

While opt-outs and the mechanism of constructive abstention are useful to allow the EU to go forward despite the reluctance of a few member states, these provisions have created a culture of freeriding. A few member states are expected to shoulder EU foreign and defence policies while others stand on the side. This inequity diminishes the impact of the EU and creates a problem of fairness. For example, several EU military operations have experienced significant delays because of the lack of actual commitments. In Chad in 2008, it was only when Russia offered to contribute to the operation with key strategic airlift assets that the operation was able to move on.

A third debate is whether the EU should *focus on soft power or develop into a stronger military actor*. Soft power is the idea that the EU's power and global influence rely mostly on its role as a creator and promoter of global norms in areas such as the protection of human rights or the fight against climate change. There are several reasons why the EU has not developed into a fully-fledged military actor. One reason is that most EU members are also part of NATO, the military alliance that benefits from US leadership. Another reason is that some member states are either neutral (for example, Ireland) or reluctant to engage in military action (for example, Germany). For some observers, the fact that it is not perceived as a military actor helps the EU promote a normative agenda.

But for others, "the silent 'D' in CSDP" (Pomorska and Vanhoonacker 2014, 222), the generalized lack of enthusiasm for the security and military aspects of EU foreign policy, is troublesome for the future. The main reason why some worry about the lack of integration in this area is that the EU has so far proven unable to provide a satisfactory answer to the changing strategic attitude of the United States, characterized by an increasing reluctance to provide for the continent's security needs. Coupled with tensions with Moscow and Beijing, the possibility of a US retreat from the European continent has strengthened calls for the EU to invest in its strategic autonomy. But while the pooling and sharing of military resources and investments has been constantly highlighted as the solution to capability gaps and shrinking national budgets, there still seems to be a long way to go (Hagman 2013). It remains to be seen whether the momentum launched by the war in Ukraine will persist.

Finally, a fourth debate concerns the *democratic dimension of CFSP and CSDP*. There are very few checks and balances in issues of high politics (diplomacy, security, and defence). Given that a small number of member states provide the bulk of the military resources, decisions remain at the national level. Furthermore, member states differ in how much parliamentary control is involved in these policies. While some member states grant their parliaments significant say over foreign and defence policy, others entrust almost all powers to the executive. In the EU context, there is little parliamentary oversight: Although there is a foreign affairs committee where members of European Parliament can ask questions to the high representative, the European Parliament has very little scrutiny or budgetary power over the CFSP, and obviously none over the member states' national decisions on defence spending or deployment. For some observers, CSDP operations in particular suffer from a lack of democratic control (Wagner 2006). For others, foreign and defence policy will always be a sensitive area, and it would be foolhardy to instill too much democracy before the CFSP and CSDP have reached a substantial degree of maturity.

CONCLUSION

Given the challenges facing the EU at the present time, it is tempting to look at the half-empty glass when it comes to assessing the state of European foreign and diplomatic integration. The EU foreign, security, and defence policies are probably areas in which exaggerated pessimism is not appropriate. Certainly, these policies have numerous limitations, mostly when it comes to mobilizing the political energy and material resources needed to address some of the major international crises the world is faced with. That being said, these foreign and security policies have also been characterized by a remarkable set of achievements. With the notable exception of the UN Security Council, EU coordination is now routine at the UN and in several other international organizations. Also, only a decade ago no one would have believed that the EU would possess one of the largest diplomatic networks in the world. These evolutions are experiments in supranational integration not seen since the emergence of the Westphalian state system. The EU definitely deserves credit for these achievements, despite all the ambiguity and the institutional consensus-seeking machinery needed for the implementation of these policies.

Naturally, as a result of such compromise-seeking logic, the political objectives that stand out at the EU level are often the ones on which there is the highest level of consensus – promotion of human rights, conflict prevention, and development policies – while controversial issues are left behind and only show up in times of international crises. Put differently, some common norms and practices do exist amongst EU member states, but core national divergences do not seem to fade fast. At the same time, EU member states have come a long way since the end of World War II, when they were enemies in a devastating war. The mere existence of a common EU defence policy is a testament to this peace achievement.

REVIEW QUESTIONS

1 Why did it take more than 30 years before there was a successful attempt at integrating issues of "high politics" in the EU?
2 Why do supranational institutions such as the Commission or the European Parliament have so little power in issues of security and defence?
3 How might the withdrawal of the UK from the EU affect the latter's foreign and security policies?

EXERCISES

1 Take one case of a recent international crisis (possible examples include, but are not limited to, the war in Libya in 2011, the Russia–Ukraine conflict in 2014, the Syrian civil war starting in 2014). Looking at the foreign policy positions taken by France, Germany, and the United Kingdom during the selected crisis, how can you explain the weakness of the EU in addressing the crisis? Is it because of diverging national interests or something else?
2 Exercise in hypothesis: What conditions limit the possibility of an EU-level military? To make this exercise more specific, examine the structure and governance of the Canadian Armed Forces to illustrate the challenges of EU supranational authority. Is it fair to compare the CFSP to examples of national security and defence?

REFERENCES AND FURTHER READING

Adler-Nissen, R. 2014. "Symbolic Power in European Diplomacy: The Struggle between National Foreign Services and the EU's External Action Service." *Review of International Studies* 40 (4): 657–81. https://doi.org/10.1017/S0260210513000326.

Biscop, S. 2015. *Peace without Money, War without Americans: Can European Strategy Cope?* Farnham, UK: Ashgate.

Biscop, S., and J. Howorth. 2022. *Strategic Autonomy*. Oxford: Oxford University Press.

Bretherton, C., and J. Vogler. 2006. *The European Union as a Global Actor*. Abingdon, UK: Routledge.

Davis Cross, M.K. 2007. *The European Diplomatic Corps: Diplomats and International Cooperation from Westphalia to Maastricht*. Basingstoke, UK: Palgrave Macmillan.

Hagman, H.G. 2013. *European Crisis Management and Defence: The Search for Capabilities*. Adelphi Paper 353. London: The International Institute for Strategic Studies.

Haroche, P. 2009. *L'Union européenne au milieu du gué. Entre compromis internationaux et quête de démocratie*. Paris: Economica.

Hill, C. 1993. "The Capability-Expectations Gap, or Conceptualizing Europe's International Role." *Journal of Common Market Studies* 31 (3): 305–28. https://doi.org/10.1111/j.1468-5965.1993.tb00466.x.

Hofmann, S.C. 2011. *European Security in NATO's Shadow: Party Ideologies and Institution Building*. Cambridge: Cambridge University Press.

Howorth, J. 2012. "Decision Making in Security and Defence Policy: Towards Supranational Intergovernmentalism?" *Cooperation and Conflict* 47 (4): 433–53. https://doi.org/10.1177/0010836712462770.

Howorth, J. 2014. *Security and Defence Policy in the European Union*, 2nd ed. Basingstoke, UK: Palgrave Macmillan.

Jones, S.G. 2007. *The Rise of European Security Cooperation*. Cambridge: Cambridge University Press.

Keukeleire, S., and T. Delreux. 2014. *The Foreign Policy of the European Union*, 2nd ed. Basingstoke, UK: Palgrave Macmillan.

Koutrakos, P. 2015. *EU International Relations Law*, 2nd ed. Oxford: Bloomsbury.

Manners, I. 2002. "Normative Power Europe: A Contradiction in Terms?" *Journal of Common Market Studies* 40 (2): 235–58. https://doi.org/10.1111/1468-5965.00353.

Mérand, F. 2008. *European Defence Policy: Beyond the Nation State*. New York: Oxford University Press.

Paquin, S. 2010. "Federalism and Multi-Level Governance in Foreign Affairs: A Comparison of Canada and Belgium." In *Is Our House in Order? Canada's Implementation of International Law*, edited by C. Carmody, 71–96. Montreal: McGill-Queen's University Press.

Pomorska, K., and S. Vanhoonacker. 2015. "Europe as a Global Actor: The (Un)holy Trinity of Economy, Diplomacy and Security." *Journal of Common Market Studies* 53 (S1): 216–29. https://doi.org/10.1111/jcms.12272.

Spence, D., and J. Batora, eds. 2015. *The European External Action Service: European Diplomacy Post-Westphalia*. Basingstoke, UK: Palgrave Macmillan.

Wagner, W. 2006. "The Democratic Control of Military Power Europe." *Journal of European Public Policy* 13 (2): 200–16. https://doi.org/10.1080/13501760500451626.

White, B. 2001. *Understanding European Foreign Policy*. Basingstoke, UK: Palgrave Macmillan.

Wouters, J., D. Coppens, and B. De Meester. 2008. "The European Union's External Relations after the Lisbon Treaty." In *The Lisbon Treaty: EU Constitutionalism without a Constitutional Treaty?*, edited by S. Griller and J. Ziller, 143–203. Wien: Springer Verlag.

10
Common Agricultural Policy

Crina Viju-Miljusevic

READER'S GUIDE

The Common Agricultural Policy (CAP) of the European Union (EU) was one of the first European policies introduced at a time when the events of World War II and its devastating consequences were still fresh in everyone's mind. This chapter analyzes the CAP's main objectives, instruments, and outcomes. It also examines its evolution over time. The discussion focuses on core issues related to the CAP, such as pressures for reform, reasons for resistance to change, and ongoing debates.

INTRODUCTION

The main goals of creating the EU were both political (not having another war) and economic (recovering from the devastation of World War II). The means of achieving these goals were mainly economic with the view that once the EU member states were economically integrated, another war would be almost impossible. Economic integration trumped all up until the 1990s, when other non-economic issues started to gain importance for the EU political elites and citizens. Agriculture was one of the first policy areas where market integration was seen as highly important. The six founding member states of the European Economic Community (EEC) (Belgium, Luxembourg, France, Italy, Netherlands, and West Germany) considered the **Common Agricultural Policy (CAP)** a necessity to cope with food shortages stemming from the aftermath of World War II, to prevent at any cost future shortages, and to stabilize the incomes of farmers (Theme 1 of this book). The CAP was an attempt to reach these objectives by creating a common agricultural market that would facilitate the movement of goods and factors of production among European countries.

To achieve its original objectives, the CAP introduced several policy instruments, which had important domestic and international consequences and influenced the evolution of the CAP through the years. Over time, the EU has become larger, more diverse, increasingly focused on sustainable development, and competitive in a highly globalized world. Thus, the main question this chapter sets out to address is whether the objectives of the CAP have been altered according to the new domestic and international conditions. The chapter analyzes the impacts of the main agricultural policy instruments and whether the pressure for change was strong enough to result in a policy that sustains an efficient and internationally competitive sector.

COMMON AGRICULTURAL POLICY: HISTORY, INSTRUMENTS, AND REFORMS

History

The CAP is one of the oldest supranational policies of the EU (Theme 2 of this book) included in the Treaty of Rome (in legal terms, the EEC Treaty), which established the EEC in 1958. However, while the CAP's treaty foundations were established in the 1950s, the CAP only came into existence as an EEC policy in 1962. The differences in agricultural support systems between member states were an impediment to the free movement of agricultural products, and hence to the Single Market (see Chapter 7) that the EEC was seeking to establish. In light of this, the EEC Treaty (Articles 38–47) defined the main objectives of the CAP as follows:

- to increase agricultural productivity by promoting technical progress and by ensuring the rational development of agricultural production and the optimum utilization of factors of production, in particular, labour;

- thus, to ensure a fair standard of living for the agricultural community, in particular by increasing individual earnings of persons engaged in agriculture;
- to stabilize markets;
- to secure availability of supplies;
- to ensure that supplies reach consumers at reasonable prices.
(Article 39 EEC Treaty)

The Stresa conference of 1958 established the fundamental principles of the CAP, which came into force in 1962: market unity, community preference, and financial solidarity. Market unity referred to free trade within the Single Market, while community preference signified that products of European origin were to be given preference over imported products. The financial solidarity principle defined the common responsibility of EEC member states with regard to the financial consequences of the CAP; on this basis, the European Agricultural Guidance and Guarantee Fund (EAGGF) was established to provide agricultural payments. From an institutional perspective, decisions regarding the CAP were to be taken by qualified majority voting in the Council of Ministers (now the Council of the EU).

The European Parliament (EP) had no co-decision role in relation to agriculture until the entry into force of the Treaty of Lisbon. This treaty brought the CAP under the ordinary legislative procedure, meaning that the EP is now able to propose amendments and veto proposed legislation (see Chapter 3).

CAP Instruments and Their Outcomes

The CAP was focused on the development of a set of common policy instruments, including common prices. The institutional core of the CAP, as established in 1962, was a price support mechanism. Established on a yearly basis by the Council of Ministers, a target price was set for all major farm products such as grains, dairy products, beef, poultry, pork, fruits, and sugar. In the CAP system, the target price was the intended selling price on the European market and was the basis for calculating all other common prices. The threshold price (set below the target price) was a minimum entry price for products imported from third parties, while the intervention price (set below the threshold price) represented the price at which intervention agencies would purchase all farm products that would not otherwise be sold at that price. In so doing, it removed farm products from the market and kept the price up. It also led to large surpluses.

Setting a threshold price shielded European farmers from low-cost competition from non-European producers. Variable import levies were imposed on imported goods from the rest of the world. Tariffs on these fluctuated with changes in world prices. Setting an intervention price secured a minimum price floor for agricultural goods; if market prices fell below this price, intervention agencies funded from the CAP budget would purchase the goods in question to stabilize farmers' income. In addition, the CAP provided export subsidies or refunds to farmers selling their goods outside of the EEC; these support measures covered the difference between the high European prices and the lower world prices, and hence made European agricultural products internationally competitive.

Between 1962 and 1968, the CAP was considered highly successful because it achieved its main goals. The price schemes resulted in higher and more stable incomes for farmers, while European food production was substantially increased, contributing to the decline in Europe's dependence on imported food products. However, the same set of policies proved to be economically damaging and unsustainable in the long run.

Indeed, faced with stable and higher than world market prices, farmers expanded their production rapidly to such a high level that the EU ran large surpluses by the 1970s. The stockpiles of surpluses had to be purchased at intervention prices and stored by intervention agencies; the EU hence became famous for its "butter mountains" or "wine lakes." The stocks were either sold on the world markets at subsidized prices (through export subsidies), provided as aid to less developed countries, or simply destroyed. The CAP was losing support, and it seemed less legitimate to spend so much money on it when it was not producing the desired results (Theme 3 of this book).

As a result, at the beginning of the 1970s the EU became a large exporter of agricultural products. However, these subsidized exports depressed agricultural prices in the rest of the world and thus affected agricultural production outside the EU. The United States, in turn, reacted by increasing its subsidies. Such actions from other developed countries also hurt developing countries.

Other negative effects of the CAP were that European consumers had to pay higher prices for their food products while environmental damage increased due to prolonged use of chemical fertilizers and destruction of wetlands. Because support was linked to prices, larger farmers benefited the most from the system, with approximately 80 per cent of the financial support from the EAGGF going to about 20 per cent of the farmers (European Commission

1984). Furthermore, Northern European farmers benefited much more from this system than Southern European farmers, mainly because of the higher support prices for dairy products. Another negative consequence of the price mechanism was a large increase in EU budget expenditures. As world prices were depressed, the payments to farmers in the form of export subsidies and price intervention, as well as storage costs, increased significantly. Additionally, EU revenues declined due to reduced imports, which resulted in smaller tariff revenues on agricultural imports.

CAP Reforms

The reform of the CAP has proven difficult mainly because of the vested interests it created and its redistributive character. Despite being reduced in numbers, the agricultural lobby groups, specifically in countries that received the most support (such as France, Germany, Ireland, and Spain in the 1970s, 1980s, and 1990s) put strong pressure on national political elites to maintain the status quo on agriculture policy. The pressures were transferred to the EU level through the agricultural ministers in the Agricultural Council.[1] There was not much opposition from consumers and taxpayers to continue the level of agricultural spending, as the food expenditures component of their income declined while their concerns regarding food safety increased (Van Kooten 2021).

Minor reforms were implemented in the 1980s; these were mainly triggered by a large increase in costs as well as the EU accession of Greece, Spain, and Portugal in the 1980s. In 1984, milk quotas were introduced to limit production. The 1988 package brought important policy changes, such as a maximum limit on quantities that were guaranteed to receive support and setting aside agricultural land from production, early retirement, reforestation, and more extensive production methods.

However, the main pressures for reform got stronger over time. Pressure for change came from various sources (see Table 10.1). First, budget expenditures for agriculture were increasing year by year while other policy areas needed to obtain a larger part of the Community budget (regional policy, Single Market, monetary union, enlargement, and so on; see Chapters 7, 11, and 13). There were also external pressures through the multilateral trade negotiations starting with the Uruguay Round of the World Trade Organization. Finally, food safety concerns and environmental damages were becoming core issues among political elites and in public debates.

Table 10.1. Reforms of the CAP

Year	Policy	Triggers	Implemented reforms	Achievements
1984	Dairy Reform	Surpluses of products, especially butter	Introduction of quotas on dairy products	Ability to reform a small part of the CAP after years of opposition
1992	MacSharry Reforms	GATT rulings (Uruguay Round) – inclusion of agricultural negotiations	Decrease of subsidies by 35% for cereals and 15% for beef; introduction of "compensation payments" based on total cultivated area and historical yields of a product eligible for payments or total number of animals; introduction of early retirement aid, reforestation of arable land, and the set-aside system (co-financed by the Community and member states)	The CAP becomes less market distorting; the budget is kept a little more under control
1999	Agenda 2000	Preparing for future enlargement	Introduction of the two pillars of the CAP: Pillar I includes market and income support; Pillar II focuses on rural development; direct payments are given to member states based on regional priorities and the fulfillment of specific environmental criteria; compensation payments are reduced and a further decrease in subsidies by 15% for dairy, 15% for cereals, and 20% for beef is introduced	The introduction of Pillar II makes the CAP a more multifunctional policy
2003	Mid-Term Review of Agenda 2000 (Fischler Reform)	Enlargement Doha Round	Further decreases in subsidies; introduction of the Single Farm Payment (SFP) scheme and phase-out of income support; gradual transfer of payments (modulation) to Pillar II, which were saved from the reduction of direct payments from Pillar I; intervention mechanisms such as storage and export restitution are phased out and turned into safety nets	Decoupling of payments and less market interventionism
2008	Health Check		Preparing for the abolishment of milk quotas by 2015; remaining interventionist measures are phased out; the compulsory set-aside system is cancelled; financial subsidies are switched to all SFPs; increased transfer of funds to Pillar II focusing on environmental sustainability	Increased liberalization

Year	Reform	Context	Key features	Outcomes
2013	Post-2013 Reform	2008 economic crisis	Focus on organic farming and environmental stewardship; mainstream a "greening" policy by including funding for large-scale organic farming in Pillar I rather than Pillar II; devoting a small percentage of national envelopes to encourage young farmers; creation of a crisis reserve fund and a mechanism of risk prevention	Decrease of the total CAP budget; encouraging environmentally conscious farming
2021	CAP beyond 2020	Paris Agreement and UN sustainable development goals. Complexity and bureaucracy	New governance model with division of responsibilities between member states and the EU; supporting the goals of the European Green Deal through various instruments: high green ambitions, eco-schemes, rural development, climate objectives, and conditionalities; continuing support for young farmers and encouraging gender balance; increasing convergence of payments within and between EU countries	Projected achievements: greener, fairer, and more competitive

Source: European Commission (2021a), Fouilleux and Ansaloni (2019), Roederer-Rynning (2021)

Before the 1986 Uruguay Round of international trade negotiations, when agriculture was brought under the umbrella of the General Agreement on Tariffs and Trade (GATT), the sector was seen as exceptional, deserving special attention from national governments in all Western countries. However, this stance started to change in the late 1980s, first in the United States where the idea that agriculture is not that different from other economic sectors gained more and more support. The United States pushed for its so-called "zero-2000 option" in the GATT negotiations, proposing a phasing out of all agricultural subsidies that affect trade directly and indirectly, as well as getting rid of import barriers. Since then, through a series of farm bills, the United States tried to reduce programs that would incentivize farmers to produce more. Farm trade negotiations in the Uruguay Round were impacted by this switch in United States farm policy. As the United States and the EU were at the time by far the largest producers and exporters of agricultural commodities, a compromise between the two players was the only solution for successful negotiations.

As a result, the first substantial reform in the EU, the so-called MacSharry Reforms, came into effect in 1992. The MacSharry Reforms started to replace the guaranteed agricultural prices for cereals and beef with a new system of direct compensation payments to farmers that were activated if prices fell below a certain level. **Direct payments** were "decoupled" from production, meaning they were not directly related to how much a farmer produces. **Decoupled payments** implied less economic distortion than support pricing schemes or coupled payments, as they did not affect prices but the income of farmers.

In 1999, the CAP was further reformed under the Agenda 2000. These reforms came into effect because of the prospect of eastern enlargement of the EU. Production subsidies continued to be replaced by a set of direct payments, which were increasingly made conditional on food safety, animal rights, and environmental concerns. The Agenda 2000 introduced several new concepts that would define the reform process of the CAP from that point on. First, multifunctionality was introduced, which entailed that farmers should not be seen as only producers of agricultural goods, but also as important players in rural development, protection of the environment, increased safety and quality of goods, and promotion of animal welfare. Second, the Agenda 2000 introduced a second pillar of the CAP consisting of **rural development policy**, which was distinct from support payments to farmers, known as Pillar I. Pillar II includes payments for rural development, environmental protection, animal welfare, and higher food safety standards; these policies are co-funded by EU member states. Policies under Pillar II are more flexible, allowing the member states to choose their national objectives from a list provided by the EU and to implement national programs. Third, a voluntary modulation scheme was introduced that allowed member states to choose to switch up to 20 per cent of their allocation of CAP funds in Pillar I (direct support) to Pillar II (rural development). (For debates relating to the EU's Common Fisheries Policy, which is often compared to the CAP, see Box 10.1.)

> **BOX 10.1: COMMON FISHERIES POLICY**
> The Common Fisheries Policy (CFP) was established together with the CAP by Article 38 of the EEC Treaty. The main objectives of the CFP were defined by the Council in 1992 as being the conservation of fish stocks, the protection of the marine environment, the economic viability of the fleet, and respect for consumers' interests.
>
> State intervention in the fisheries sector is considered necessary because of the character of fish stocks as common goods, since the sea is a common property. Thus, without an intervention of governments in the market, overconsumption (overfishing) would be the result, with private producers and consumers ignoring the social costs.
>
> Given that not all EEC member states were interested in a CFP, the policy was not set up until 1970, and it became fully operational only in 1983. The first two regulations gave free and equal access to all EU fishers to all EU fishing grounds, with certain exceptions for sensitive coastal waters.
>
> International debates under the United Nations Convention on the Law of the Sea as to how far fishers could go established a 200-nautical mile limit that was agreed upon by the EU in 1975. The 20-year agreement achieved by the EU in 1983 introduced national zones of access of up to 12 miles and exclusive EU zones of 200 miles.
>
> In terms of market support instruments, the CFP defined quotas or total allowable catches for each member state for many fish species. Additionally, it set prices for all species of fish caught within EU waters and provided compensation for fishers who must withdraw their catch from the market. Structural measures were focused on the reduction of overcapacity and the restructuring of the fishing

industry, which would eventually make it more competitive and efficient. Conditions were set for member states to develop their fleet capacity.

Issues of overfishing have persisted for years, and thus the Commission has proposed reductions in total amounts of catch for certain species. In 1999, a new regulation was adopted encouraging fishers to only catch what they could sell. This regulation was in response to concerns about the diminishing stocks of cod and other fish. However, it was clear that the agreement was not achieving its objectives. Thus, a reform agreed in 2002 changed several characteristics of the CFP by considering the environmental sustainability of the policy. One important reform focused on regulating the number of fish that could be taken from the sea by imposing restrictions on catches of young, small fish; bans on using certain fishing techniques and gear; plus closing certain fishing areas. Public payments for modernization of national fleets were phased out, while minimum prices for fish that cannot be sold were kept in place.

In 2014, a further reform of the CFP was implemented with three important changes: a ban on the wasteful practice of discarding perfectly edible fish; a legally binding commitment to fishing at sustainable levels; and decentralized decision making, allowing member states to take measures appropriate to their fisheries.

Originally, the CFP was funded from the same fund as the CAP, the EAGGF. In 1993 a separate fund was created, the Financial Instrument of Fisheries, which was transformed into the European Fisheries Fund in 2007. With the reformed CFP of 2014, the European Maritime and Fisheries Fund was introduced with an allocated budget of €5.7 billion for the period 2014–20 and of €6.1 billion for the period 2021–7.

The CFP represented one of the important reasons for two Nordic countries, Norway and Iceland, not to become EU member states (see Chapter 13). In both countries, the fisheries sector is one of the top sectors of the economy. Despite the fact that most of their fisheries exports go to the EU, the majority of the population considers sovereignty over this sector important. Equal access,

> unlimited foreign investment in the processing industry, and the failure of the EU's CFP to limit overfishing are important contributors to the two countries' positions. Fishing was one of the most difficult sectors to negotiate in the post-Brexit EU–UK trade deal. The EU kept the right to fish in UK waters over an adjustment period (until 2026) under the condition that the UK will receive a greater share of fish caught in UK waters; post-2026, the two parties will need to renegotiate the deal on an annual basis.
>
> Overfishing was a subject of controversy between the EU and Canada as well. During the so-called "Turbot War," which started in March 1995, the Canadian government accused vessels from Spain and Portugal of overfishing turbot in international waters outside Canada's 200-mile limit. The North Atlantic Fisheries Organization established the quotas of allowable catches. The relationship between Canada and Spain (and by implication the EU) became so tense that the Canadian government even arrested the captain and crew of a Spanish vessel. Also, a Canadian ship cut the nets of one Portuguese vessel and two Spanish vessels. In response, Spain sent a warship to protect its fishers. The EU fisheries commissioner responded with severe criticism of the actions of the Canadian government. In April 1995, Spain, Canada, and the EU reached an agreement that set new quotas and tougher conservation and enforcement rules that would limit overfishing.

Another major CAP reform was the Mid-Term Review of Agenda 2000 (the Fischler Reform) that came into effect in 2003 as a result of a new round of multilateral trade negotiations (Doha Round) and the imminent enlargement of the EU to include the first eight Central and Eastern European countries (CEECs). The newest and most innovative element of this reform was the introduction of the Single Farm Payment (SFP), which replaced a vast array of direct payment schemes. Under this system, any farmer would receive an SFP regardless of whether or not the land is used to produce something; however, the EU member states were still limited by how much they could apply this decoupling. The policy was fully implemented under later reforms. This scheme was attached to cross-compliance, meaning that farmers were asked to comply with the EU's environmental, food safety, animal welfare, and occupational safety standards and keep the farmland in good agricultural and environmental condition to be eligible for the SFP. The Fischler Reform also introduced compulsory modulation – a required annual transfer of funds from Pillar I to Pillar II.

The main objective of the CAP Health Check of 2008 was the reinforcement of the Fischler Reform package. The ambition was to transform all direct payments into decoupled payments and to increase the modulation rate. Additionally, to prepare for the abolishment of milk quotas in 2015, an increase of quota sizes and a use of rural development measures for areas heavily dependent on milk production were implemented.

The core of the post-2013 reform was a "greening" of the CAP. A new green payment was introduced, representing 30 per cent of the direct payments, which rewarded farmers for respecting environmentally friendly practices. Each member state could use its own method of "greening" its farms. The 2013 CAP reform replaced the SFP with a new instrument, the Basic Payment Scheme, which offered basic income to active farmers with the goal of achieving internal convergence.

The post-2020 CAP reform enhances the "greening" measures of the CAP. The new green architecture is based on three main components. First, *enhanced conditionality* replaces previously introduced cross-compliance and greening requirements and links payments to mandatory restrictions, which include all previous greening conditions plus new ones. Second, climate and environmental *eco-schemes* are voluntary schemes for farmers financed from Pillar I direct payments. The eco-schemes represent annual payments per eligible hectare that are either paid in addition to the basic income support or fully or partly compensating farmers for the losses incurred due to implementing higher environmental and climate change commitments. Third, *agri-environmental and climate measures* under Pillar II include voluntary environmental, climate, and management commitments that target specific objectives of the CAP. They compensate farmers and other beneficiaries for costs incurred and income forgone from taking on new commitments. One of the most innovative elements of the reform is the new governance model, with more responsibility and flexibility for the member states that can propose their agricultural practices within the EU guidelines. The *national strategic plans* combine funding for income support, rural development, and market measures to contribute to the EU's

CAP-specific objectives, which are in line with the commitments of the European Green Deal (see Chapter 17).

DEBATES: DISTRIBUTING THE BUDGET, FARM SUPPORT, AND DECENTRALIZATION

Three issues are at the core of current debates in the EU regarding the CAP: (1) the distribution of the CAP budget among the member states (see Box 10.2), (2) the distribution of CAP support among different types of farms, and (3) the further decentralization of the CAP. Additionally, the use of policy instruments such as geographical indications has been brought into the debate due to the deep and comprehensive free trade agreements that the EU has been negotiating with various countries, including Canada, the United States, and South Korea.

BOX 10.2: CAP BUDGET

- As the CAP was one of the first market-correcting policies of the EU, once it was implemented it accounted for 90 per cent of the EU budget. Although the EU budget is relatively small, representing about 1 per cent of EU gross national income, the distribution of the money between EU policies/activities and among various instruments has always involved tough negotiations in the Council.
- CAP expenditures have decreased over time, with agriculture accounting for approximately half of the EU budget by 2006, falling below 40 per cent in 2013 (Figure 10.1), and reaching 30.9 per cent of the long-term budget for 2021–7.
- In the 2021 budget, €40.3 billion were allocated to spending on Pillar I of the CAP (EAGGF, which pays for income support and market measures) and €15.3 billion were allocated to Pillar II (European Agricultural Fund for Rural Development). This means that the CAP consumes about 33.5 per cent of the EU budget.

Source: Definitive adoption (EU, Euratom) 2021/417 of the European Union's general budget for the financial year 2021, https://eur-lex.europa.eu/eli/budget/2021/1/oj

Figure 10.1. CAP expenditure in total EU expenditure (current prices)

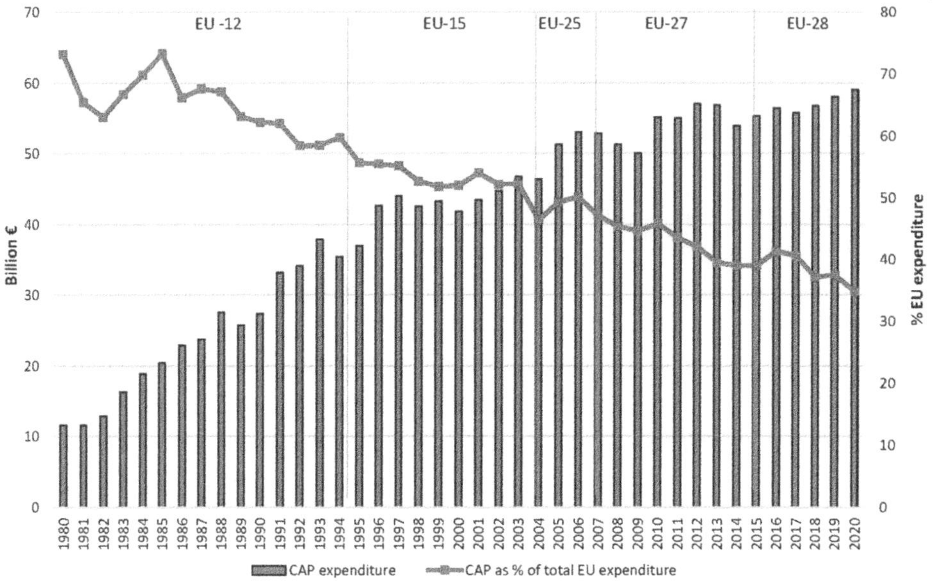

Source: European Commission, "Agriculture and Rural Development," https://ec.europa.eu
/info/sites/default/files/food-farming-fisheries/farming/documents/cap-expenditure
-graph1_en.pdf

The cost of the CAP has been a highly debated issue since the policy came into existence (see Figure 10.1). The EU member states were always divided into two groups regarding their preference on CAP spending. The large net contributors to the budget, such as Denmark, Germany, Sweden, and the UK, favoured a further reduction of CAP spending, while the large beneficiaries of agricultural payments, such as France, Ireland, and Spain, were pressuring to maintain a significant CAP budget. When joining the EU in the 2000s, Eastern European countries lobbied for direct payments that would match the EU average level, thus siding with the second group. However, accession negotiations with the CEECs in agriculture overlapped with the CAP Mid-Term Review. Accession countries had to go through a transition period of CAP direct payments and then were phased in over a period of nine years (Grant 2005). The UK withdrawal from the EU has intensified the debate, as the UK was the second-largest net contributor to the EU budget. As a result, the CAP spending negotiated as part of the

Multiannual Financial Framework for 2021–7 was decreased, with the largest cuts applied to Pillar 2.

Additionally, direct payments under CAP are higher for cattle and dairy products compared to fruits, vegetables, and oils.[2] Thus, the EU member states that specialize in the production of the former set of products (Denmark, France, Germany, Italy, Sweden) are the ones that attract the largest percentage of CAP payments. To a certain extent, the transfer of payments from Pillar I to Pillar II of CAP addresses the unbalanced distribution of payments among EU member states.

A second debate is related to the unequal distribution of CAP payments between types of farms. The enlargement of the EU from 6 to 28 countries increased diversity in terms of natural and climatic conditions, farm size and structure, and productivity – but also the importance of the agricultural sector for the respective domestic economies and the level of employment in agriculture. Indeed, 72 per cent of the farms in the new member states had a size of less than five hectares, compared to 47 per cent in the old member states (Gorton et al. 2009). For example, in 2004, when the first eight CEECs joined the EU, on average 23 per cent of the population of the new member states was employed in the agricultural sector, compared to 10 per cent in the old member states.

The EU market-based support rewards large, high-yield farms in the most favoured areas. These distributional patterns can also encourage corruption and cronyism (Box 10.3). Regardless of the method of calculation (either per hectare or per annual working unit), most payments are directed at the richer, northern areas of the EU. Thus, farms in less favoured regions and in most CEECs that have a fragmented farm sector are receiving less financial aid from the CAP. In the 2013 reform, the Commission sought to correct these imbalances and defined the goals of "internal" convergence (among farmers) and "external" convergence (among member states). The reforms included different measures, such as the replacement of payments based on historic references with a flat rate national payment, and the adjustment of direct payments in accordance with a minimum national average direct payment per hectare across all member states (European Commission 2013). The 2021 reform furthers these objectives by implementing new measures such as a redistributive income support from bigger to smaller and medium-sized farmers, additional income support to young farmers, redistributive income support for sustainability, and mandatory reduction of payments larger than specified limits.

> **BOX 10.3: EFFECTS OF THE CAP IN HUNGARY AND NORTHERN IRELAND**
> Why is the CAP controversial? Two polar-opposite cases point to the highly political nature of agriculture policy: As reported by *The New York Times* (Gebrkidan et al. 2019), in Hungary a few oligarchs and supporters of the Orbán government have benefited from millions of CAP subsidies. *Politico* (Wax 2021) reported on an EP initiative to check who benefits from CAP funds. In Northern Ireland, Brexit scholars and policy-makers pointed to EU subsidies as critical to agricultural exports to the EU: 87 per cent of their total value results from EU subsidies, hence raising the question of the post-Brexit impacts.

The third debate that takes place within the EU is related to the re-nationalization of the CAP. This debate has focused on two issues: decision making and funding. The decision-making competence is divided between the EU and the member states in certain aspects of the CAP, such as the rural development policy (Pillar II of the CAP) and the SFP, replaced in 2015 by the Basic Payment Scheme (the core of Pillar I of the CAP). In Pillar II of the CAP, the EU member states have an important role, as they are charged with choosing objectives, specifying targets, and defining measures to achieve them, while the EU's role is constrained to defining objectives, approving national plans, and co-financing. In Pillar I of the CAP, the EU member states have a more limited role, though they are charged with specifying targets for specific programs and with the implementation of cross-compliance measures. The reform of 2013 has introduced more flexibility in the application of Pillar I. The shift of funds between the pillars hence has important implications for the degree of member state influence on the CAP; however, Pillar I spending is still about three times larger than Pillar II spending. The post-2020 reform furthers the flexibility and responsibility of the member states with the introduction of a new governance model. It is the financial aspect of the CAP renationalization that is highly debated and faces major opposition from certain member states.

One of the ongoing debates at the international level is related to new policy instruments that affect the trade in food products. In the wake of CAP reforms during the 2000s that have reduced agricultural subsidies, the granting of **geographical indication (GI)** status has become an important facet of EU agricultural policy. GIs are a form of intellectual property; they require that a product with GI status may only originate from a certain place or region (for example, Champagne must be made from grapes grown in the Champagne region of France). GIs require protection from the state because they represent goods whose value is derived from *credence attributes*, those that consumers cannot identify even after the product is consumed. As agricultural policy has become more oriented toward GIs, the EU has become increasingly interested in garnering additional protection for its GIs in foreign markets. There are three contentious international issues pertaining to GIs: (1) a major global split in the mechanism used to protect this particular form of intellectual property, GIs, and trademarks; (2) the treatment of some products that have been granted GI status in the EU as generic terms in some other countries – meaning they are considered common terms and not identified with production being undertaken in a particular geographic location (for example, feta cheese in Canada); and (3) garnering foreign protection for less well known or new EU GI designations. For example, in the Canada–EU Comprehensive Economic and Trade Agreement (CETA) signed in 2016, Canada agreed to various levels of acceptance of the EU GIs for 179 foods and beers.

CONCLUSION

The CAP is one of the EU's most ambitious policies; it is as comprehensive as national agricultural policies in states such as Canada (see Box 10.4). The CAP came into existence in a period of economic turbulence when food security was one of the main goals of the EEC. It developed into a common, redistributive policy that received wide support from European citizens and political elites. The instruments that were implemented to achieve food security were initially considered legitimate regardless of the food price increases and inefficiencies that followed. In the following decades, however, the distortions of the price support system became obvious, and various intra-European and international pressures made a reform of the CAP necessary. However, the CAP proved difficult to change, mainly due to the vested interests that the price support system created.

BOX 10.4: CANADA'S AGRICULTURAL POLICY

As any other advanced economy, Canada has put in place a variety of agricultural programs that are continuously evolving. One characteristic of the Canadian agricultural policy is that it is the responsibility of both federal and provincial governments. This multilevel structure is similar to the general framework of the CAP. As Canadian provinces have the power to implement their own programs, governments at both levels must overcome the challenge of coordinating their agricultural policies. Another outcome of the dual responsibility is that some provinces offer greater assistance to their farmers than others.

The main goal of Canada's agricultural programs, as in the EU, was income stabilization for farmers, achieved by offering price or gross/net return guarantees. The two major original stabilization programs were the Agricultural Stabilization Act, which was put in place in 1958, fully funded by the Canadian federal government, and the Western Grain Stabilization Act, introduced in 1976 with the main goal of helping prairie farmers stabilize their crop incomes.

The Uruguay Round of multilateral trade negotiations in 1986 and the Free Trade Agreement signed with the United States in 1987 (superseded by the North American Free Trade Agreement of 1994, which included Mexico) pushed Canada to revisit its agricultural programs and to reduce coupled farm payments. In the 2000s, food safety and environmental sustainability became the centre of the debate related to reforms of agricultural policy. The Canadian Agricultural Income Stabilization Program (CAIS), introduced in 2003, emphasized risk management, innovation, food safety, and environmental responsibility. In 2007, the federal, provincial, and territorial governments decided to replace the CAIS with alternative business risk management programs that would follow a new market-driven vision for Canadian agriculture (labelled "Growing Forward"; see Schmitz 2008). The successor program (Growing Forward II) for the period 2013–18 aimed to generate market-based growth and manage farmers' business risk by focusing on innovation and market development. The

> latest policy framework (Canadian Agriculture Partnership) for the period 2018–23 aims to support regional-specific agricultural programs by employing a cost-shared principle, with the federal government contributing 60 per cent of the costs while provincial/territorial governments contribute the other 40 per cent. In addition to enhancing existing farmers' business risk programs, the current policy introduced new programs that emphasize innovation and sustainable growth.
>
> The Canadian agricultural policy evolved from using price-based, commodity-specific instruments to generally available farm-based instruments, which have the benefit of being less production distorting. These reforms hence go in the same general direction as the reform strategy followed by the EU. Canada still has national supply management programs for dairy, poultry, and eggs, which were implemented in the early 1970s because of depressed market conditions. The national supply management program is a policy that regulates supply through quotas for domestic production and imports. Additionally, farmers negotiate collectively the farm-gate prices for products covered by supply management.

Pressures for CAP reform have included, at various points of time, (1) oversupply of agricultural products, (2) increased budgetary expenses, (3) international trade distortions, (4) the eastern enlargement of the EU, and (5) environmental and food safety concerns. Through several different reforms in the 1990s and 2000s, the CAP has become a more efficient, less distorting, and better-targeted policy. The CAP reforms have returned some power back to the member states, first by forming a second pillar focusing on rural development, and second by proposing a new governance model in the latest reform. Compared to the agricultural policies of other Western countries (including Canada), the reformed CAP focuses not only on economic objectives but also on social and environmental goals. The Russian invasion of Ukraine has brought food security back to the centre of the debate. The crisis has exposed the EU's dependency on several imported inputs, such as energy, fertilizers, and animal feed. The emergency measures taken up to now at the European level to ensure food security include financial aid to EU farmers affected by the high cost of inputs, state aid and trade rules relaxation for agriculture and fertilizer sectors, and production of crops on land set aside for biodiversity (European Commission 2022). These measures are supported by the traditional CAP vested interests but are highly criticized by environmentalists. However, it is too early to conclude whether these measures will have negative impacts in the medium and long term on the green objectives of the new CAP.

REVIEW QUESTIONS

1 Why was the CAP introduced in the European Economic Community and why has it always played a central role in the EU?
2 Were the original objectives of the CAP achieved? Have the original objectives of the CAP changed over time? If so, how?
3 What instruments did the CAP introduce in the 1960s to achieve its objectives? What effects did they have?
4 What were the main pressures for reform of the CAP and how did they change over time? Why was the CAP resistant to reforms?
5 What are the main ongoing debates related to the CAP? Explain.
6 Compare the CAP of the EU with Canada's agricultural policy. What are the main commonalities? What are the main differences?

EXERCISES

1 Do some research on the CETA negotiations pertaining to agricultural products. What were the main areas of difficulty? How is the CAP related to some of the early Canadian objections?
2 Research the greening architecture proposed by the post-2020 CAP reform and discuss its possible impacts.
3 Discuss: What is the significance of the CAP in the context of the tension between the ideas of national security and European integration?

NOTES

1 For further information on EU decision making and the CAP, see Swinbank (1989).
2 Direct payments for beef, milk, sheep, and goats represent 73 per cent of total EU commodity-specific payments (OECD 2015).

REFERENCES AND FURTHER READING

Baldwin, R., and C. Wyplosz. 2019. The Economics of European Integration, 6th ed. Columbus, OH: McGraw-Hill Higher Education.

Burrell, A. 2009. "The CAP: Looking Back, Looking Ahead." *Journal of European Integration* 31 (3): 271–89. https://doi.org/10.1080/07036330902782113.

European Commission. 1984. Economic Effects of the Agri-monetary System. Communication to the Council. COM (84) 95 Final. http://ec.europa.eu/agriculture/cap-history/crisis-years-1980s/com84-95_en.pdf.

European Commission. 1987. The Agricultural Situation in the Community: 1986 Report. http://aei.pitt.edu/31390/1/CB4686557ENC_002.pdf.

European Commission. 2013. Overview of CAP Reform 2014–2020. Agricultural Policy Perspectives Brief No. 5. http://ec.europa.eu/agriculture/policy-perspectives/policy-briefs/05_en.pdf.

European Commission. 2020. Common Agricultural Policy: Key Graphs & Figures. https://ec.europa.eu/info/sites/default/files/food-farming-fisheries/farming/documents/cap-expenditure-graph1_en.pdf.

European Commission. 2021a. The New Common Agricultural Policy: 2023–27. https://ec.europa.eu/info/food-farming-fisheries/key-policies/common-agricultural-policy/new-cap-2023-27_en#keyareasofreform.

European Commission. 2021b. The 2021–2027 EU Budget – What's New? https://ec.europa.eu/info/strategy/eu-budget/long-term-eu-budget/2021-2027/whats-new_en.

European Commission. 2022. EU Actions to Enhance Global Food Security. https://ec.europa.eu/info/strategy/priorities-2019-2024/stronger-europe-world/eu-actions-enhance-global-food-security_en#eu-response.

Fouilleux, E., and M. Ansaloni. 2019. "The Common Agricultural Policy." In *European Union Politics*, 6th ed., edited by M. Cini and N. Pérez-Solórzano Borragán, 358–72. Oxford: Oxford University Press.

Gaisford, J.D., W.A. Kerr, and N. Perdikis. 2003. *Economic Analysis for EU Accession Negotiations: Agri-food Issues in the EU's Eastward Expansion*. Cheltenham, UK: Edward Elgar.

Gebrekidan, S., M. Apuzzo, and B. Novak. 2019. "The Money Farmers: How Oligarchs and Populists Milk the EU for Millions." *New York Times*, November 3. https://www.nytimes.com/2019/11/03/world/europe/eu-farm-subsidy-hungary.html.

Gorton, M., C. Hubbard, and L. Hubbard. 2009. "The Folly of European Union Policy Transfer: Why the Common Agricultural Policy (CAP) Does Not Fit Central and

Eastern Europe." *Regional Studies* 43 (10): 1305–17. https://doi.org/10.1080/00343400802508802.

Grant, W. 2005. "The Common Agricultural Policy: Challenges in the Wake of Eastern Enlargement." In *The European Union in the Wake of Eastern Enlargement: Institutional and Policy-Making Challenges*, edited by A. Verdun and O. Croci, 57–71. Manchester: Manchester University Press.

Josling, T. 2006. "The War on Terror: Geographic Indications as a Transatlantic Trade Conflict." *Journal of Agricultural Economics* 57 (3): 337–63. https://doi.org/10.1111/j.1477-9552.2006.00075.x.

Kerr, W.A., and J.D. Gaisford, eds. 2007. *Handbook on International Trade Policy*. Cheltenham, UK: Edward Elgar.

OECD. 2015. Agricultural Policy Monitoring and Evaluation. https://www.oecd.org/agriculture/topics/agricultural-policy-monitoring-and-evaluation.

Poon, K., and A. Weersink. 2014. "Growing Forward with Agricultural Policy: Strengths and Weaknesses of Canada's Agricultural Data Sets." *Canadian Journal of Agricultural Economics/Revue Canadienne d'Agroeconomie* 62 (2): 191–218. https://doi.org/10.1111/cjag.12023.

Roederer-Rynning, C. 2021. "The Common Agricultural Policy: The Fortress Challenged." In *Policy-Making in the European Union*, 8th ed., edited by H. Wallace, M. Pollack, C. Roederer-Rynning, and A. Young, 182–207. Oxford: Oxford University Press.

Rude, J., A. Eagle, and P. Boxall. 2015. "Agricultural Support Policy in Canada: What Are the Environmental Consequences?" *Environmental Reviews*. https://tspace.library.utoronto.ca/bitstream/1807/70016/1/er-2015-0050.pdf.

Schmitz, A. 2008. "Canadian Agricultural Programs and Policy in Transition." *Canadian Journal of Agricultural Economics* 56 (4): 371–91. https://doi.org/10.1111/j.1744-7976.2008.00136.x.

Senior Nello, S. 2013. *The European Union: Economics, Policies & History*, 3rd ed. Columbus, OH: McGraw-Hill Higher Education.

Skogstad, G., and A. Verdun, eds. 2010. *The Common Agricultural Policy: Policy Dynamics in a Changing Context*. London: Routledge.

Swinbank, A. 1989. "The Common Agricultural Policy and the Politics of European Decision Making." *Journal of Common Market Studies* 27 (4): 303–22. https://doi.org/10.1111/j.1468-5965.1989.tb00347.x.

Van Kooten, G.C. 2021. *Applied Welfare Economics, Trade, and Agricultural Policy Analysis*. Toronto: University of Toronto Press.

Wax, E. 2021. "MEPs Seek to Tackle Organ and Babis over EU Farm Funds." *Politico*, May 22. https://www.politico.eu/article/european-parliament-viktor-orban-andrej-babis-eu-farm-funds-common-agricultural-policy.

11
Regional Policy

Emmanuel Brunet-Jailly

READER'S GUIDE

Progressive economic integration and growth often primarily benefit the most competitive cities and regions. Therefore, at the outset in 1957, the European Union (EU) initiated policies to avoid such disparities and promote harmonious development. This chapter examines how such ideas evolved into current regional policy. Originally, the EU's regional policy was characterized by solidarity and partnerships among the member states, their lower-level governments (regions, cities, and other local governments), and the European Commission – multilevel governance partnerships. EU regional policy, representing about 30 per cent of the EU annual budget, transfers funds to the poorest regions. This chapter describes how the policy objectives emerged in the 1970s and were reformed in 1988, 1993, 1999, 2008, and recently. It discusses ongoing questions regarding whether the policy is a redistributive or an investment instrument of the EU.

INTRODUCTION

This chapter reviews the regional policy of the EU: its origin and development over the last 60 years. Why did the first six EU member states (Belgium, France,

Italy, Luxembourg, Netherlands, and West Germany) agree to a policy imposing forms of **solidarity** and financial redistribution across their regions from the 1950s onwards? How has this policy evolved into what it has become today? This chapter offers a review of how successive enlargements impacted regional policy. Next it discusses why, despite criticisms and doubts, the Treaty of Lisbon (post-2009) confirmed its importance, even though in 2006 the policy was refocused on investing in "smart, sustainable and inclusive growth." And finally, it looks at whether regional and cohesion policy actually works.

Against this backdrop, our goal here is to understand and assess two of the themes that organize this book. Originally, regional policy was a core component of our understanding of the European way as a mixed system (an economy that is neither state controlled nor left to an unconstrained market – Theme 1 of this book). This policy should comprise mechanisms of social inclusion and market correction, even though the EU has moved toward more market-oriented policy-making. **Regional policy** is, however, also a pan-European mechanism of redistribution and **equalization**. It is crucial for pan-EU solidarity and economic legitimacy (Theme 3 of this book). In this way it plays a fundamental role in European integration.

At their inception, EU regional programs basically provided financial support to member states for national projects. In 1988, however, the regional policy became known as **cohesion policy**. This renaming symbolized the fact that the policy was intended to bring member states together – to partner with one another. And not only states, but also European regions and cities. From the EU side, the lead actor was the European Commission, which was in the driver's seat to develop a coherent all-inclusive investment policy. Because the richest and most populated regions continued to create wealth much faster than all the other ones, critics pointed to the uneven development of the EU regions. The Lisbon Treaty nevertheless reaffirmed the EU's regional policy. Today it continues to receive over 30 per cent of the annual EU budget. This chapter explains why (see Box 11.1).

THE ORIGINS AND DEVELOPMENT OF THE EU'S REGIONAL POLICY

Regional economic development found its way into the EU right from the get-go. In the 1957 Treaty of Rome, Article 2 of the Treaty Establishing the European Economic Community (TEEC) stated that the EU (at the time called the European Economic Community)

> **BOX 11.1: THE COMMISSION'S FOUR GENERAL PROGRAMMING PRINCIPLES, 1988–1993**
>
> 1 Funds are focused on the poorest people and regions (concentration).
> 2 Funding is organized in multiannual programs of activities that require sound public policy, analysis, planning, implementation, and evaluation (programming).
> 3 Member states, their regions and other local governments, and the Commission have to work together in the implementation of the policy (partnership).
> 4 European funds can only come in addition to state funding (additionality).

shall have as its task, by establishing a common market and progressively approximating the economic policies of member states, to promote throughout the community a harmonious development of economic activities, a continuous and balanced expansion, an increase in stability, an accelerated raising of the standard of living and closer relations between the states belonging to it.

In other words, Article 2 suggested that economic integration should be harmonious, continuous, and balanced while increasing standards of living across member states. This objective pointed to policies of cohesion and solidarity. Article 3 TEEC then described a number of important intergovernmental tools of public policy: the elimination of custom duties, the Common Agricultural Policy (CAP), competition policy, the European Social Fund (ESF), and the European Investment Bank (EIB). The treaty thus provided an enhanced role for the Commission regarding EU economic and social cohesion, with three redistributive instruments: the ESF, the EIB, and the European Agricultural Guidance and Guarantee Fund (see also Chapter 10). These instruments were designed to help member states adjust to enhanced competition and economic integration, and to work out cohesion and solidarity policies based on limited forms of financial redistribution.

Initially, regional concerns were only raised in the EU context as part of **competition policy**. Indeed, the Treaty of Rome attempted to limit and regulate competition; it states that "state aids" in particular are only acceptable if they are part of market adjustments and integration. The treaty encourages economic and social cohesion across the EU. At the time, the assumption was that limiting competition would lead to a reduction of the influence of market forces on states and regional markets. Articles 92 and 93 TEEC are about competition policy. They restrict financial intervention of member states targeting mobile private sector investment to a particular location through the use of public subsidies. Hence, in line with the goals set by the Treaty of Rome, the Commission set clear guidelines to limit bidding wars between regions and states to attract foreign investors. The rationale was that financial incentives, in the form of regional or state aids, distort competition among regions across the EU.

The goal of competition policy was to limit competition and to reduce the ability of richer regions (or states) to offer larger amounts of subsidies than poorer regions (see Chapter 7). Articles 92(3)a and 92(3)c TEEC provided a basis for the limitation of state aid focusing on unemployment in regions facing industrial decline, as the Commission established aid ceilings and criteria to limit subsidies in richer regions. Although the member states that concluded the Treaty of Rome made specific references to economic and social imbalances, it was not until 1965 that the Commission adopted a communication regarding regional policy. The Directorate-General for Regional Policy (DG RP) was set up in 1968. By 1972 the member states agreed that regional policy was an essential factor in strengthening the EU.

From 6 to 12: The European Regional Development Fund (1967–1988)

The Commission came to the realization that it was nearly impossible to provide a level playing field in competition policy. First, it recognized that to gain traction such a policy should focus on areas where public authorities (governments) have some influence, such as the quality of public administration, infrastructure, telecommunications, energy policies, and also public subsidies. In this context, adequate regulation may be an important tool. Second, the Commission realized that the Treaty of Rome (Article 92, Section 3 TEEC) only provided for a small budget, one that increased marginally its influence in matters of cohesion in the EU, in particular regarding structural adjustments to the Single Market. At the time the EU budget represented 1.27 per cent of the member states' gross national income (GNI), or €97.5 billion in today's currency. Third, with the accession of Denmark, Ireland, and the United Kingdom the issue of the redistribution of EU funds in the form of EU programs became central. For instance, the UK imported many of its agricultural products from outside the EU. Therefore, it did not need the subsidies from the CAP to support its farmers. At the same time, it was facing a major transformation of its textiles and coal and steel industrial regions.

Regional policy was therefore quickly identified as offering an alternative way to provide funding to member states, complementary to the CAP (see Chapter 10). In addition to being a redistributive mechanism of equalization across EU regions, regional policy served as a form of side payment to Belgium, France, Italy, Luxembourg, the UK, and West Germany. It led to the creation of the **European Regional Development Fund (ERDF)**. Set up in 1975, it had a tri-annual budget of €1.3 billion. Its overall goal was to correct the regional imbalances that resulted from structural changes in agriculture, industry, and employment. To be eligible, member states were required to come up with 50 per cent of co-funding. The program targeted small and medium-sized enterprises and required the creation of at least 10 new jobs. It also was directed at major infrastructure developments, such as building roads and bridges, as well as investments in mountainous areas. Reviewing national practices allowed the Commission to enforce regulations in each member state and to require changes while it progressively implemented the ERDF.

The accession of Greece in 1981, and Spain and Portugal in 1986, further increased competition for EU funding. This situation affected in particular France and Italy, as those Mediterranean states had many regions that previously received ERDF support. To address this situation, the Commission agreed to test new programs, called the Integrated Mediterranean Programs (IMPs). Their goals were to alleviate multiple market-related pressures on the regions of France, Greece, and Italy while they adapted to Portuguese and Spanish competition in agriculture, fisheries, and small and medium-sized businesses. There was also funding for training youth, women, and junior executives.

Under the IMPs, regional authorities submitted proposals to the Commission through their respective member states. Representatives of the then 12 member states of the EU, with the Commission in the role of chair, assessed these proposals. The Commission was granted large administrative powers to manage the local, regional, national, and EU funds in the program. What was particularly innovative at the time was that (1) a uniform program was implemented across various locales, (2) the Commission engaged directly with local and regional authorities, and (3) it was able to work directly with a single committee of state representatives. Furthermore, (4) the Commission monitored and controlled the funding to regional and local authorities. All in all, the Commission took a stronger administrative leadership role, which led to the first partnership programs. This collaboration of different levels of governance, referred to as **multilevel governance**, was spearheaded in the administrative system of regional policy (European Union 1986).

The successful experience with the IMPs and a positive review of the ERDF gave the member states the confidence to agree that the Commission should take the lead in reorganizing regional policy. The late 1980s marked a turning point: The Single European Act reasserted the importance of "economic and social cohesion" in the EU. A new and radical idea was that the EU needed a policy that brought regional authorities, member states, and the Commission together in partnerships to work together on diverse regional strategies of development. The assumption was that broad, territorially grounded multilevel partnerships would serve rich and poor regions equally. It would allow them to rally all the forces necessary for their development. In brief, the new goal was to organize regional development work based on coordination and cooperation with member states and the Commission.

For a long time, EU institutions and policies served primarily the member states' intergovernmental agendas. However, the reorganized regional policy

---

BOX 11.2: DEFINITION OF REGIONAL VERSUS COHESION POLICY

Until 1988, EU instruments, such as the European Social Fund, the European Investment Bank, the European Agricultural Guidance and Guarantee Fund, were designed to help member states adjust to enhanced competition and economic integration – thus they provided limited forms of financial redistribution, coherence, and solidarity. After 1988, the EU's new principles (partnership and additionality) and the five geographic priorities (the objectives) provide the Commission with tools to redistribute funds and reduce economic imbalances and disparities between the regions and cities – these tools provide strong mechanisms to implement coherence in the form of the partnership frameworks across the EU.

included two important principles of management of EU funds: the partnership and additionality principles (see Box 11.2). These suggested that a project had to be co-funded by a member state and within the partnership of a member state with the Commission. The IMPs introduced a new mode of administration where member states shared decisions with – and delegated administrative powers to – the Commission. This enhanced the role of the Commission and local authorities and was the first exception to strict state control (and hence to the principle of intergovernmentalism) while asserting the EU's economic legitimacy and its mixed economic agenda.

The Institutionalization of Cohesion Policy (1988–1993)

By 1988, all of the building blocks for a reform of regional policy were in place: regional policy was formally relabelled cohesion policy and was instituted by a regulation agreed upon by member states in the Council of June 24, 1988. The Commission restructured the structural funds (ERDF and ESF), reframing the funding amounts and periods to implement four general principles of administration (see Box 11.3) and five geographic priorities (called *objectives*).

While some of the objectives focused on the poorest regions and were clearly linked to regional/territorial strategies, others were less redistributive and focused on long-term and youth unemployment and the transformation of rural areas. Importantly, though, most of the funding was placed in the objectives that related to the poorest regions. These had specific, albeit uninspiring, names.

Objective 1 regions focused on the development and structural adjustment of the regions whose development was lagging behind. These regions represented 64 per cent of the overall funding. The prime beneficiaries were Spain, Italy, Portugal, Greece, and Ireland. Selected regions in France, West Germany, and the United Kingdom, in particular Northern Ireland, were also eligible. In all, about 87 million people, or 25 per cent of the EU population, lived in these Objective 1 regions.

The unsurprising name for the next category was Objective 2 regions. This second group contained regions that had been seriously affected by industrial decline. The funding was designed to support job creation and help small and medium-sized businesses. For Objective 2 regions, the principal beneficiaries were the United Kingdom, Spain, France, and in much smaller amounts all other member states (except for Greece, Ireland, and Portugal, which already benefited from Objective 1 funding). In all, about 57 million people lived in those regions.

> **BOX 11.3: COMMON PROVISION REGULATION: HOW ARE FUNDS ALLOCATED?**
>
> A European Court of Auditors (2019) review of the allocation of cohesion policy funding to member states for 2021–7 found the following:
>
> 1. Appropriate levels of investment (regions with GDP below 75 per cent of the EU average still receive the most funds)
> 2. Targeted growth (€100 billion go to growth sectors and cities)
> 3. Accountability and results (local, regional, and national goals have to be clear and measurable – projects must be data generating)
> 4. Preconditions for funding (certain preconditions are mandatory, such as specific environmental laws)
> 5. Coordinated action (the common strategic framework provides the basis for funding coordination)
> 6. Simplification of procedures (less red tape and more measurable policy goals)
> 7. Expanded urban dimension (urban centres have earmarked funds)
> 8. Cross-border cooperation (cross-border projects are enhanced)
> 9. Consistency and coherence (regional projects have to be coherent with national reform programs that are now part of the European Semester; see Chapter 7)
> 10. Financial instruments (target small and medium-sized businesses)

The other objectives, with a smaller share of the budget, focused on combating long-term unemployment, the occupational integration of young people, adjustment to agricultural reforms, and the development of rural areas. Over the period 1988–93 the overall budget of the cohesion policy grew every year, from €6.4 billion in 1989 to €20.5 billion in 1993, which represented an expansion from 16 per cent to 31 per cent of the total annual EU budget (European Union 2008a).

The fundamental assumption was that solidarity between rich and poor regions would work to diminish economic imbalances and disparities while increasing the involvement in policy-making of regions and the EU. The

Commission became a vector of development and led many programs of cooperation. This policy led to a clear erosion of states' intergovernmental agendas. The primary breakthrough idea was the realization that there was a "geography of the EU" – the whole was greater than the sum of the parts. Furthermore, there was a pan-European rediscovery of the regions of Europe. Partners from inside and outside government and across regional, state, and EU levels started reaching out to one another and working together with a focus on regional issues. This period served as the bedrock of a new vertical partnership governance of regional policy, primarily linking the Commission, member states, and regions.

From 12 to 15: The Maastricht Treaty (1993–1999)

At Maastricht, on February 7, 1992, the member states signed the Treaty on European Union (TEU), which came into force on November 1, 1993. It bolstered cohesion policy in three ways. First, it created the Cohesion Fund, a new structural fund aimed at member states whose GNI per inhabitant was less than 90 per cent of the EU average. The Cohesion Fund was launched for a first generation of programs with a multiannual budget of €168 billion for the period 1994–9. Second, the Maastricht Treaty created a new institution called the Committee of the Regions. The Committee of the Regions was a response to growing demands from regional actors to be more involved in EU policies. As an advisory body, it reviews and expresses opinions on all legislation that impacts local and regional authorities (about 75 per cent of all new proposed legislation). Third, the Maastricht Treaty introduced the so-called **subsidiarity** principle. Defined in Article 5 TEU, this principle specifies that the EU does not take action (except in the areas that fall within its exclusive competence) unless EU-level action is more effective than action taken at the national, regional, or local level. Enshrined into the treaty, this principle compels governments across the EU to make policy closest to the citizens. The EU soon expanded. On March 30, 1994, Austria, Finland, Sweden, and Norway signed the accession treaty. All four countries held referendums; Norway's was not successful with only 47.8 per cent of the votes in favour and subsequently withdrew its candidacy (European Union 2008a).

From 15 to 25: Making Enlargement a Success (2000–2006)

The end of the 1990s is particularly interesting because of the EU's eastern expansion, with 10 former members of the Eastern bloc working toward

Figure 11.1. GDP per capita in EU member states, 2021 (purchasing power index, EU=100)

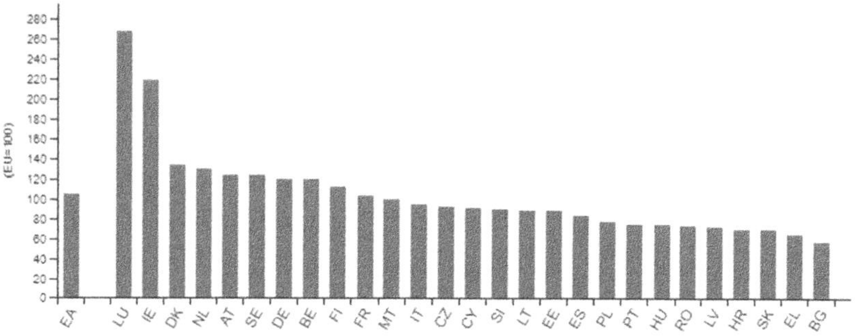

Source: Eurostat, https://ec.europa.eu/eurostat/statistics-explained/index.php?title=GDP_per_capita,_consumption_per_capita_and_price_level_indices

accession (see Chapter 13). The challenge of this new enlargement was to bring into the EU more population (170 million people, or one in three EU citizens) and 18 per cent more land mass but only 5 per cent additional GDP, as these countries were much poorer than the EU average. With a GDP below 50 per cent of the EU average, these were in fact the poorest countries, containing the least developed regions of the EU. This new situation aggravated existing regional imbalances. One of the core challenges was how to apply the Cohesion Fund to those new countries, as doing so would impact a large number of older EU member states. Without adding funds to the EU budget, eastern enlargement meant that older member states were becoming net contributors to the EU annual budget – meaning they would pay more to the EU than they would receive back from EU funds. Economic imbalances across the EU had never been greater. Even at the present time the differences are stark. In 2021, taking the EU average at 100, the gross domestic product per capita of the wealthiest country, Luxembourg, stands at 277 and the poorest, Bulgaria, at 55 (see Figure 11.1).

This situation constituted a test of solidarity and cohesion that upset some governments. To cope with this challenge, the cohesion policy for 2000–6 was increased to €213 billion (32 per cent of the EU budget), with €22 billion dedicated to the new member states. The six "concentration principles" for regional funding shifted back to three: Objective 1 still focused on regions whose development was lagging behind; Objective 2 supported regions faced with economic and social conversion; and Objective 3 focused on education, training, and employment. It is notable that the resulting program was as ambitious and as well funded as the post–World War II Marshall Plan, which demonstrates that the EU's commitment to the principle of a mixed economy was still going strong. Over the period 2000–6, 0.4 per cent of total EU GDP was invested in European regions thanks to the cohesion policy. The policy targeted 271 regions in 25 EU member states. Later evaluations of those policies document that the GDP of recipient regions grew from 66 per cent of the EU average in 2000 to 71 per cent in 2006 (European Union 2008a).

In sum, the millennium marked a new beginning for the cohesion policy. Notably, by the end of 2006 the cohesion policy linked European actors from the public, private, and non-profit sectors in aligned regional networks of policy-making that connected the local and regional levels with national and European priorities. The administration of the policies required managerial rigour and professionalism for partnership and programming, and the financial control of additionality. For this purpose, member states and regional authorities worked on single programming documents. These partnership networks were multi-partner, public–private, and non-profit, spanning various levels of government. They formed multilevel governance partnerships that designed and funded programs together, and in doing so defined local/regional priorities while working within pan-European management and evaluation standards.

At 27 Members: The World's Largest Development Program (2007–2013)

The European Council in 2006 agreed to a seven-year budget for the 2007–13 period that contributed €347 billion (3.7 per cent of annual EU GDP) to cohesion policy, a clear increase to about 35 per cent of the annual EU budget. Eighty-six per cent of these funds were dedicated to "convergence" regions (where per capita GDP was lower than 75 per cent of the EU average) – that is, where the poorest third of EU citizens lived. The three objectives for this funding period were defined as follows.

Objective 1 targeted 84 regions in 17 member states, at the time a population of 170 million people. Objective 1 included entire countries, such as Bulgaria, the Czech Republic, Estonia, Greece, Cyprus, Latvia, Lithuania, Hungary, Malta, Poland, Portugal, Romania, Slovenia, and Slovakia. The total amount of funding available was €282.8 billion for the funding period. This objective focused on economic growth, but also targeted innovation, the knowledge-based economy, and adaptability to social change as vectors of success.

Objective 2 focused on 168 regions in 19 countries, or about 314 million Europeans. All the regions of a few countries were eligible (Bulgaria, Estonia, Latvia, Lithuania, Malta, Poland, Romania, and Slovenia) and a few specific regions in the wealthiest member states also had access to Objective 2 funding (France, Germany, Italy, Spain, and – at the time – the United Kingdom). The goal was to enhance the attraction and competitiveness of those regions to business investors for the development of the infrastructure necessary for the information-communication society and the knowledge economy, and to increase job creation. Such policies invested in human capital to foster innovation and entrepreneurship and contributed funds to environmentally friendly ventures.

Objective 3 expanded on the idea of regional partnership networks by setting up the European Territorial Cooperation Policy, which encourages the formation of partnership networks across regions and across borderlands. This new objective was concerned with 13 transborder areas, or about 182 million Europeans. The funds were only available to regions that were within 150 kilometres of the border, whereas transnational cooperation and interregional cooperation included a vast grouping of regions across member states in the northern periphery, the Baltic Sea, the northwest, the North Sea, the Alpine space, Central Europe, the Atlantic coast, the southwest, the Mediterranean, the southeast, and included regions in the Caribbean, the Indian Ocean, and the Atlantic Ocean.

Clearly, these new objectives marked a fundamental priority shift, as the Commission was tying all three policy goals together. The new approach moves away from simply helping structurally backward regions toward a policy promoting competitiveness and employment while leveraging both innovative and environmentally friendly policies for the purpose of job creation – that is, the new focus is on investment-ambitious projects led by partnership networks, including the private sector. Europe 2020, the EU's 10-year growth strategy adopted in 2010, also states that the goals of the cohesion policy are "smart, sustainable and inclusive growth" (European Commission 2010).

In sum, the structure of cohesion policy agreed to in 2006 constituted a breakthrough greater than any previous reforms since the ERDF. While maintaining some solidarity, it enshrined the ideas that partnership networks should leverage EU funding to invest in smart, sustainable, and inclusive growth. Multilevel governance also faced reforms. Indeed, since 2007 the Commission has worked to bring local authorities in to develop integrated territorial approaches that link development policies to horizontal and vertical multilevel governance partnerships, with the goal of breaking through the traditional silos of policy coordination. The policy instruments took the forms of investment partnerships and contract developments, forming bottom-up partnership networks that articulated local priorities within regional, national, and European strategies across many more objectives than just equalization.

The Way Forward: Cohesion Policy in an EU of 28 Member States (2014–2020)

These new directions were confirmed in the cohesion policy program for the 2014–20 funding period, with a budget expanded to €367 billion. It included state contributions of more than €500 billion (European Union 2013b). The centrepiece focused on enhanced local–regional partnership and governance methods articulating national and European goals. The 11 policy objectives fall into three broad categories relating to innovation, sustainability, and social inclusion (see Box 11.4). The policy was designed to be data generating and results oriented while also implementing financial requirements. In addition, it allocated nearly €100 billion toward innovation and research, digital agendas, support for small and medium-sized businesses, and the low-carbon economy sectors. In sum, beyond the original goal of equalization, the policy also serves many other goals important to member states and has become a more aggressive economic development and investment instrument.

> **BOX 11.4: OBJECTIVES OF COHESION POLICY**
> There are five objectives for 2021–7:
> - A more competitive and smart Europe
> - A greener, low-carbon transition toward a zero-carbon economy
> - A more connected Europe by enhancing mobility
> - A more social and inclusive Europe
> - A Europe closer to its citizens by fostering the sustainable and integrated development of all types of territories.

Table 11.1. Cohesion policy funding, 2021-2027 (current prices in million € and % of total)

Investment for jobs and growth goal (IJG)	361,056.8	92%
Just Transition Fund	19,236,9	5%
Interreg: European territorial cooperation goal	9,041.6	2%
EU instruments	1,332.1	0%
Technical assistance	1.211,6	0%

Note: The IJG goals are funded by the ERDF, the ESF, and the Cohesion Fund as well as the new Just Transition Fund. "Interreg" is the name used in the EU for European Territorial Cooperation. The European Commission manages both the EU instruments and technical assistance.
Data source: European Union (2021)

The 2021-2027 Budget: Cohesion or Investment Policy?

Unaffected by Brexit, but concerned about the impacts of the COVID-19 pandemic, for this latest budget period the original and primary goal of the cohesion policy has given way to further expansion from its original equalization goals. This expansion sees an increased focus on coordinated investments with a greater variety of partnerships (people, economic actors, cities, and regions), a renewed focus on green policies and digital activities, and with a consequential budget (Ahner 2018; see Table 11.1 and Map 11.1). The multiannual budget of €392 billion leverages €500 billion (estimated) from economic and public sector actors and member states. In addition, "[e]ach recipient must devote at least 37% of the financing they receive under the €672.5 billion Recovery and Resilience Facility instrument to investments and reforms that support climate objectives" (European Commission 2021), while further implementing methodological and other goals. It is much less focused on compensating regions for their handicaps, and much more focused on integrated and multipronged investments in regional growth and competitiveness. Also, the regional strategies incorporate diverse local plans as well as transregional partnerships, linking governance and bureaucratic expertise (Ahner 2018, 5-6). In sum, the new cohesion policy has become an investment policy (see Box 11.5) that is competitive, smart, and green – promoting a zero-carbon economy and a connected, social, and inclusive EU that is closer to its citizens.

Regional Policy 245

Map 11.1. Investment for jobs and growth goal: Where is the money going?

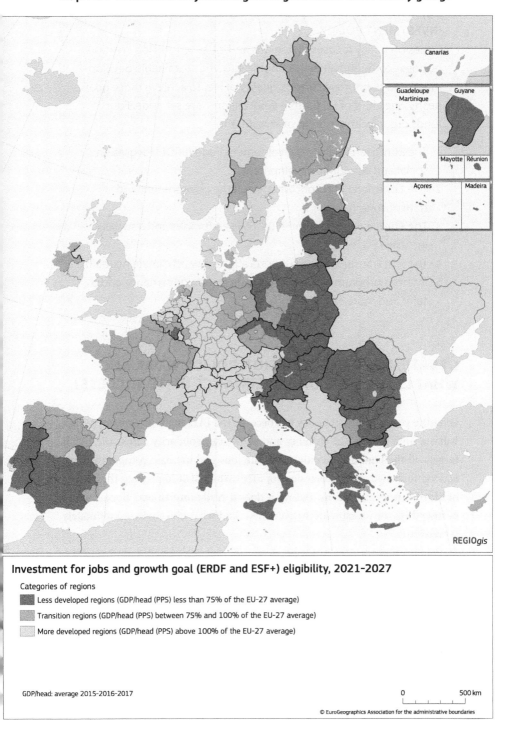

Investment for jobs and growth goal (ERDF and ESF+) eligibility, 2021-2027

Categories of regions

- Less developed regions (GDP/head (PPS) less than 75% of the EU-27 average)
- Transition regions (GDP/head (PPS) between 75% and 100% of the EU-27 average)
- More developed regions (GDP/head (PPS) above 100% of the EU-27 average)

GDP/head: average 2015-2016-2017

0   500 km

© EuroGeographics Association for the administrative boundaries

> **BOX 11.5: COHESION POLICY: THE EU'S MAIN INVESTMENT POLICY**
>
> Cohesion policy focuses on regions and cities to fund job creation, business competitiveness, economic growth, sustainable development, and to improve citizens' quality of life. To achieve those goals, nearly one-third of EU funds – €392 billion – are set aside. Four funds organize those areas of investment:
>
> 1. The European Regional Development Fund (ERDF) focuses on social and economic development.
> 2. The Cohesion Fund concentrates on the environment and transportation.
> 3. The European Social Fund Plus (ESF+) is for jobs and a socially inclusive EU.
> 4. The Just Transition Fund supports efforts toward climate neutrality.
> 5. Interreg programs foster better cooperation governance and a safer and more secure EU.

DEBATE: DOES THE COHESION POLICY WORK AND WHAT IS THE ROLE OF GOVERNANCE IN ITS SUCCESS?

Over the years, cohesion policy has become the EU's main investment policy. It has a high amount of visibility and showcases solidarity across the EU. It targets all the regions and cities to create jobs and increase competitiveness, economic growth, and green development while also improving the quality of life of European citizens. But what does it really implement? Equalization, partnerships, or investment instruments? And what objectives are ultimately served?

Policies that transfer funds between different regions are controversial – not only in the EU but also at the state level (see Box 11.6 for a discussion of Canada). In the EU, over the years the regional policy has faced a barrage of questions and criticisms from various fronts, including academics and policy-makers. There are two broad strands of criticism: First, some suggest that the methods used feed into domestic, national policies and do not address local and regional issues effectively; and second, there is much criticism regarding their expected economic and social impacts.

BOX 11.6: REGIONAL POLICY AND MULTILEVEL GOVERNANCE IN CANADA

Regional policies exist in Canada as well but are understood from fundamentally different perspectives, use a different vocabulary, and bring about debates that are distinctively Canadian. Most importantly, the issue of redistributing resources between regions is framed almost exclusively in terms of federal–provincial intergovernmental relations. Canadian provinces have been fighting for greater power since World War II, and Quebec has advocated for independence at times. Yet the federal government has maintained unity and interprovincial equalization, which means that richer provinces pay for provincial programs in poorer provinces. Another aspect that makes regional policy in Canada distinctive is that relations between the provincial and federal governments are more competitive than collaborative. At the same time, a high degree of integration of the bureaucratic elite leads to active networking practices that counterbalance these competitive trends and allow for mechanisms of accommodation, or compromise, to be worked out. This results in partnerships (so-called "collaborative federalism") that lead to economic development policies that link federal, provincial, and local governments.

A particularly important issue of multilevel governance in Canada is the role of municipalities. Historically, the relations of municipalities to provincial governments were unequal. Since the first half of the twentieth century, and despite the 1849 Baldwin Act that gave municipal governments in Ontario important autonomy, provinces across Canada progressively restricted the autonomy of municipalities. The existence of municipalities is not guaranteed under Canada's Constitution, which leaves provincial governments free to create, modify, or destroy any and all units of local government. This statutory aspect of municipalities was important because it suggested that municipal governments were subordinate to provincial authorities. Today, federal–provincial–local political processes are made up of complex systems of relations; they have led to the understanding that municipalities – especially large cities – are not entirely subordinate. Political, cultural, demographic,

> and economic factors have encouraged the formation of entrepreneurial municipal coalitions, which benefit from the support of both provincial government largesse and local groups, allowing large municipalities to gain autonomy. For instance, Toronto, the largest and richest city in the country, has its own City Act under Ontario law. Smaller municipalities, by contrast, are increasingly under provincial supervision.

The debates about the success of EU regional policy originally focused on the impact of the policy for the period 1989-99. Some studies suggest the funds had limited impact (Garcia Mila McGuire 2001; De la Fuente and Vives 1995; Rodriguez Pose and Fratesi 2002; 2004). Others find an impact, but only with a delay (Beugelsdijk and Eijffinger 2005; Ederveen et al. 2006). Also, they suggest that positive effects on the development of regions are due primarily to good regional governance and institution building. Finally, there are studies that focus on interregional linkages and suggest that these are important and should be enhanced. Dall'Erba and Le Gallo (2008), for instance, suggest that EU funds have limited impact on convergence because money targeted at peripheral regions does not spill over to neighbouring regions.

These studies posed a major challenge to the Commission's DG RP. For a long time, the DG's answers were rather weak, but from about 2008-9, the DG RP took these criticisms seriously and addressed them with the development of two macroeconomic models: HERMIN and QUEST. These models showed, for instance, that for the period 2000-6, the cumulative impact of Objective 1 funds on regional GDP, employment, and capital stock was non-questionable. QUEST showed clear GDP increases, and HERMIN showed 819,000 jobs that resulted from the cohesion policy (European Union 2013a). Also, the DG RP has started collecting and publishing numerical and qualitative indicators to measure the impact of the cohesion policy across the regions of the EU. All in all, it was able to show that regional policy accelerates growth – and that, despite persistent unequal rates of development and growth, the entire EU was better off because of its cohesion policy – for instance, infrastructure projects such as public transportation (roads, railways, airports, and seaports); environmental projects, such as improvements in access to water and wastewater treatment; as well as job creation resulting from training, education, and research and from investments in small and medium-sized businesses (European Union 2013a). Most importantly, the Commission increasingly pushed regions to manage policies of regional development across sophisticated partnership networks, also leading to improved local and regional governance. Such networks provided effective management systems for multiyear programs, broad stakeholder involvement, monitoring and evaluation, as well as effective implementation of EU legislation. In sum, the regions experienced much improved governance.

For former director general for regional policies Dr. Dirk Ahner, regional policies do not aim to make regions "equal" to reduce disparities and concurrently to bring about convergence. For Ahner (2018), there are a few troubling ideas regarding cohesion policy: (1) Assuming a correlation between cohesion and economic growth is misleading; what matters is the solidarity impact of European funds and the efficiency–equity trade-off regarding public investments in regions; (2) is cohesion policy about redistribution? For redistribution to take place a small number of member states, or regions, should pay for the policy, but the funds would be redistributed to the poorest regions. For Ahner, cohesion is not a redistributive policy because it is allocative in nature – that is, funds are selectively distributed across programs and regions. However, Ahner acknowledges that allocation of funds weighs a little more on richer rather than poorer regions. For instance, in the 2021–7 funding package, it encourages mobility infrastructure (in particular, train networks that connect all EU regions). In sum, cohesion policy has become a political as well as economic investment instrument for the EU: Its political allocative nature underscores solidarity, and its economic principle to invest in economic potentials enhances growth strategies and networked governance partnerships that benefit from strong and durable bureaucratic support above and beyond EU regions (Ahner 2018, 8–9).

Darvas, Mazza, and Midoes (2021) summarized and analyzed nearly 1,000 studies on cohesion policy to focus on unexplained economic growth in regions between 2003 and 2017. These authors found that (1) cohesion policies contribute to long-term strategies; (2) the greatest growth potentials are found in interregional partnerships (that is, partnerships bridging regions and in particular the most advanced regions); (3) greater growth correlates with lower national funding; and (4) stronger management involving national institutions benefits locally led projects.

The salience of good governance and administrative capacity continues to be extremely important, as illustrated by the principle of shared management among the EU and national and regional authorities. Today, EU member states and regional authorities should actually follow sets of rules (Common Provision Regulation #1303/2013). This provision is particularly significant with regard to the Multiannual Financial Framework and the NextGenerationEU funds that were available in 2021–2. Furthermore, it is relevant for countries such as Hungary or Poland, because it underscores the need to respect clear standards set out in articles of the TEU:

- Article 4, General principles: [F]unds shall provide support, through multiannual programmes, which complements national, regional and local intervention, to deliver the Union strategy for smart, sustainable and inclusive growth. …
- Article 5.3: The Commission shall be empowered to adopt a delegated act in accordance with Article 149 to provide for a European code of conduct on partnership (the "code of conduct") in order to support and facilitate Member States. … [The conduct includes "transparent procedure," "good practices regarding partners," "rules and memberships," and "internal procedures."]
- Article 6: Compliance with EU and national law
- Article 7: [P]romotion of equality between men and women and non-discrimination. (European Parliament 2020, 10–12)

In sum, cohesion policy is a particularly salient example of the institutionalization of innovative governance modes discussed in Chapter 5 (see also Tömmel and Verdun 2009). Indeed, the verticality of the institutional setup is reiterated in Article 4, the partnership framework, and also appears clearly in Article 6 along with the idea of hierarchical rule and coordination in Article 7.

CONCLUSION

The evidence presented in this chapter confirms that the EU's original regional policy, now called cohesion policy, has been driven by two of the three themes that organize this book. The original mixed economic system evolved toward more market-oriented policies, but it remained important to the legitimacy of the European project because it sustains forms of solidarity across the EU. It is good partnership and hierarchical governance principles that drive the smart, sustainable, and inclusive growth principles. These principles drive the bottom-up architectures of public, private, and non-profit investment and the growth objectives of the policy within the leadership framework set by the European Commission. Initially, regional policy was top down; today it is bottom up. It puts the onus on local capacity by promoting competition for EU resources while requiring a strengthening of networked governance capacities locally, including strategic planning, quality of monitoring, evaluation, as well as the human capital and funds invested. Moving from regional policy to cohesion policy has meant that this policy has become the most ambitious recurrent investment program of the EU.

REVIEW QUESTIONS

1 What is the European Regional Development Fund?
2 What is the European Cohesion Fund?
3 What country/ies triggered the need for the ERDF and then the Cohesion Fund?
4 What is multilevel governance in regional policy?
5 Is regional policy intergovernmental? Why?
6 Do you think the smart, sustainable, and inclusive growth agenda has relevance for solidarity?

EXERCISES

1 Describe how each of the following sets of actors has driven regional policy in the EU: member states, regional governments, and the EU institutions. What do the motivations of each set of actors tell us about multilevel governance in the EU?
2 Peruse the European Commission's website on regional policy. Examine the funding levels between countries and over time. Which member states are currently the main beneficiaries of regional policy funds? What variations have occurred over time?

REFERENCES AND FURTHER READING

Ahner, D. 2018. "What Do You Really Know about European Cohesion Policy?" Institute Delors. https://institutdelors.eu/wp-content/uploads/2018/01/ecp_rational_and_objectives.pdf.

Bachtler, J., and C. Mendez. 2016. *EU Cohesion Policy and European Integration: The Dynamics of EU Budget and Regional Policy Reform*. Farnham, UK: Ashgate.

Bachtler, J., and R. Michie. 1995. "A New Era in EU Regional Policy Evaluation? The Appraisal of the Structural Funds." *Regional Studies* 29 (8): 745–51. https://doi.org/10.1080/00343409512331349353.

Bachtler, J., and I. Turok, eds. 2013. *The Coherence of EU Regional Policy: Contrasting Perspectives on the Structural Funds*. Philadelphia: J. Kingsley Publishers.

Beugelsdijk, M., and S.C.W. Eijffinger. 2005. "The Effectiveness of Structural Policy in the European Union: An Empirical Analysis for the EU 15 in 1995–2001." *Journal of Common Market Studies* 43 (1): 37–51. https://doi.org/10.1111/j.0021-9886.2005.00545.x.

Dall'erba, S., and J. Le Gallo. 2008. "Regional Convergence and the Impact of European Structural Funds over 1989–1999: A Spatial Econometric Analysis." *Regional Science* 87 (2): 219–44. https://doi.org/10.1111/j.1435-5957.2008.00184.x.

Darzas, Z., J. Mazza, and C. Midoes. 2021. "European Union Cohesion Project Characteristics and Regional Economic Growth." Working Paper 02/2021. Bruegel.

De la Fuente, A., and X. Vives. 1995. "Infrastructure and Education as Instruments of Regional Policy: Evidence from Spain." *Economic Policy* 80: 13–51. https://doi.org/10.2307/1344537.

Ederveen, S., H. de Groot, and R. Nahuis. 2006. "Fertile Soil for Structural Funds? A Panel Data Analysis of the Conditional Effectiveness of European Cohesion Policy." *Kyklos* 59: 17–42. https://doi.org/10.1111/j.1467-6435.2006.00318.x.

Erlanger, S. 2018. "As Poland and Hungary Flout Democratic Values, Europe Eyes the Aid Spigot." May 1. https://www.nytimes.com/2018/05/01/world/europe/poland-hungary-european-union-money.html.

European Commission. 2010. "Europe 2020: A Strategy for Smart, Sustainable and Inclusive Growth." https://eur-lex.europa.eu/legal-content/en/TXT/?uri=CELEX%3A52010DC2020.

European Commission. 2021. "Finance and the Green Deal." https://ec.europa.eu/info/strategy/priorities-2019-2024/european-green-deal/finance-and-green-deal_en.

European Court of Auditors. 2019, March. "Rapid Case Review: Allocation of Cohesion Policy Funding to Member States for 2021–2027." https://www.eca.europa.eu/lists/ecadocuments/rcr_cohesion/rcr_cohesion_en.pdf.

European Parliament. 2018. "Regional Governance in the EU. Briefing – European Parliament." PE 628.244/October 2018. https://www.europarl.europa.eu/RegData/etudes/BRIE/2018/628244/EPRS_BRI(2018)628244_EN.pdf.

European Parliament. 2020. "Regulation no. 1303/2013 of the European Parliament and of the Council of 17 December 2013." https://eur-lex.europa.eu/legal-content/EN/TXT/PDF/?uri=CELEX:02013R1303-20201229&from=EN.

European Union. 1986. "The Integrated Mediterranean Programmes." Commission for the European Communities, Information Directorate, European File 1/86. http://aei.pitt.edu/14712/1/EUR-FILE-1-86.pdf.

European Union. 1993. *Community Structural Funds 1994–1999: Revised Regulations and Commentary*. Brussels: Office for Official Publications.
European Union. 2008a. "EU Cohesion Policy 1988–2008." *Panorama Quarterly* 26. http://ec.europa.eu/regional_policy/archive/information/panorama/index_en.cfm.
European Union. 2008b. "Regional Policy and Enlargement." *Panorama Quarterly* 27. http://ec.europa.eu/regional_policy/archive/information/panorama/index_en.cfm.
European Union. 2010. *Investing in Europe's Future*.
European Union. 2013a. "Bringing Communities Together." *Panorama Quarterly* 45. http://ec.europa.eu/regional_policy/archive/information/panorama/index_en.cfm.
European Union. 2013b. "Cohesion Policy 2014–2020." *Panorama Quarterly* 48. http://ec.europa.eu/regional_policy/archive/information/panorama/index_en.cfm.
European Union. 2021. "2021–2027: Cohesion Policy EU Budget Allocations." https://cohesiondata.ec.europa.eu/stories/s/2021-2027-EU-allocations-available-for-programming/2w8s-ci3y.
Garcia Mila, T., and T. McGuire. 2001. "Do Interregional Transfers Improve the Economic Performance of Poor Regions? The Case of Spain." *Journal of Common Market Studies* 8 (3): 281–96.
Jeffery, C. 1997. *The Regional Dimension of the European Union: Toward a Third Level in Europe*. London: Frank Cass.
McCann, P. 2015. *The Regional and Urban Policy of the European Union: Cohesion, Result-Orientation and Smart Specialization*. Cheltenham, UK: Edward Elgar.
Rodriguez Pose, A., and U. Fratesi. 2004. "Between Development and Social Policies: Impact of Structural Funds in Objective One Regions." *Regional Studies* 38 (1): 97–113. https://doi.org/10.1080/00343400310001632226.
Tömmel, I., and A. Verdun, eds. 2009. *Innovative Governance in the European Union: The Politics of Multilevel Policy-Making*. Boulder, CO: Lynne Rienner.

12

European External Trade Policy

Valerie J. D'Erman

READER'S GUIDE

This chapter discusses how the European Union (EU) handles trade with non-EU members. The Single Market not only changed how EU members trade with each other; it also affected how the EU engages in trade with countries outside the EU (so-called **third countries**). The chapter outlines how EU policy competence began in this area and how it has evolved over the years in response to both internal and international developments. Ongoing issues in the area of EU trade revolve around the respective roles and responsibilities of each EU institution, the ongoing pursuit of free trade agreements with non-EU countries, and changing norms about the role of international trade.

INTRODUCTION

Trade policy in the EU is an area where the supranational level, rather than individual EU member states, has authority over policy-making. This chapter outlines the history of how authority in this policy area came to be at the EU level of decision making. EU member states are part of a Single Market that has a single trade policy, for which the EU is responsible. When the EU begins trade negotiations with a non-EU country, the European Commission acts as the sole negotiator for the entire EU. The authority of the Commission in external trade negotiations raises questions of competences and representativeness for any student of European integration. How did trade policy come to be delegated to the EU? What role do member states have in discussions and negotiations with external trading partners? How is conflict resolved between the national and supranational levels in debates over trade policy? Are there any parallels between the EU process of trade policy-making and the process of trade policy-making in other large, decentralized countries? This chapter attends to these questions, which concern all three themes of this book: market making in and beyond the EU (Theme 1); the dynamics between EU institutions, member states, and interest groups (Theme 2); as well as the politicization of trade agreements (Theme 3).

This chapter also examines how EU trade policy affects – and is affected by – international developments. The EU is the world's largest trading bloc, accounting for approximately 20 per cent of global trade (European Parliament 2021). This economic size gives the EU a significant amount of leverage in international forums, including the **World Trade Organization (WTO)**, where the EU participates with a single voice representing all 27 EU member states. The chapter concludes with a brief discussion of the EU's efforts to conclude comprehensive free trade agreements (FTAs) with other countries around the world, among them the **Comprehensive Economic and Trade Agreement (CETA)** with Canada and a post-Brexit Trade and Cooperation Agreement with the UK.

THE EVOLUTION OF EU TRADE POLICY

Trade policy refers to how the EU manages trade in goods and services with non-EU countries. The management of trade is a way for the EU to nurture the internal development of the Single Market by creating supranational agreements with external actors. Trade policy is also a tool of economic growth for the EU, by building preferential relationships and strategic partnerships with foreign countries (see Chapter 9). Article 207 of the Treaty on the Functioning of the European Union (TFEU) defines external trade as an exclusive power of the EU. "Exclusive power" means that individual member states are not able to independently legislate on trade matters and are not permitted to negotiate their own international trade agreements outside the EU framework.

The exclusive power of the EU in trade was not conferred all at once, but rather evolved slowly in concert with the EU Single Market and other areas of EU competence in response to political dynamics from domestic actors, policy-makers, and international market forces (see Chapter 7). However, the precise boundaries of the EU's exclusive power remain contested, particularly with respect to newer areas like trade in investment or environmental and labour issues. This chapter (1) gives an overview of the history of integration in trade policy, (2) provides a description of the current steps of international treaty making, and (3) discusses the EU's role in responding to international pressures in world trade.

EC Common Commercial Policy

Trade as a community policy is emblematic of European integration arising out of the ashes of World War II. The central idea of interdependence among European countries was to make war unthinkable through member states agreeing to share sovereignty. The first steps in integration occurred in coal and steel production and atomic energy. As the integration of defence policy proved too contentious a policy area in early EU history (see Chapter 2), trade instead became a logical step in the process of making war materially unthinkable through economic interdependence.

Trade policy first began with the **Common Commercial Policy (CCP)** in Article 113 of the Treaty Establishing the European Community (TEEC), concluded in Rome in 1957. Along with its intention to build a Single Market (initially called the Common Market; see Chapter 7), the newly created European Economic Community (EEC) planned to develop a Customs Union among the then six original members. This Customs Union was established by 1968. It required the members to set common tariffs on goods arriving from non-EEC members and to develop a community trade policy. The reason was simple: Establishing the Single Market, which meant dismantling internal barriers to trade through treating internal goods and services as community goods and services, required a common policy for dealing with imports from and exports to non-EEC members. In the 1950s, commercial policy mostly attended to production and trade in industrial products (such as raw materials or manufacturing materials) through the common external tariff (CET). As the Customs Union extended to different areas (such as manufactured products and other types of goods), so did the CCP in order to match the internal process of liberalization with common external action (European Union 2000).

Before 1970, EEC members coordinated their activities with non-EEC members individually according to CET rules. An important exception to this took place with the EEC's participation as a single actor in the Kennedy Round of the General Agreement on Tariffs and Trade (GATT). The precursor to the WTO, the GATT provided a major international stage upon which the EEC began to interact in trade negotiations as a single bloc. As of January 1970, individual EEC members no longer coordinated their own activities; instead, decision making within the Council concerning the CCP was made through qualified majority voting (QMV). The Court of Justice of the EU (CJEU), then still called the European Court of Justice (see Chapter 4), extended the scope of Article 113 in 1978 by stating that the article as written should not be interpreted as an exhaustive list, and that the CCP should be extended to areas beyond traditional trade. In so doing, the CJEU enabled a more liberal interpretation of community trade policy. It could react more fluidly to changing trade situations, rather than having each new trade item become an issue of competence between the EU and member states (European Union 2000).

The CCP initially did not distinguish between trade with developed and developing countries in terms of the rules concerning general trade policy, although special considerations were given to the former colonies, territories, and countries associated with EEC members. The period of decolonization during the 1960s brought about by political developments in Africa and elsewhere, combined with the first enlargement of the EEC in 1973 to include Denmark, Ireland, and the United Kingdom, greatly increased the number of countries receiving special considerations. Over time, both the enlargement of European integration and the increase of global trading relationships have shifted the relationships with trade partners around the world.

Aside from the CET and the preferential trading arrangements extended to certain developing countries, the EEC's ability to further a common trade policy was limited by the rise of new economic protectionism in the 1970s and the slow pace of European integration. Economic stagnation and inflation during the 1970s prompted the EEC to introduce common policies such as **anti-dumping**, a tariff imposed on foreign imports that are priced below fair market value, and safeguard provisions, which allowed EEC members to temporarily restrict imports of a product to protect a specific domestic industry. What is more, European integration proceeded only slowly in the 1970s. Despite the EEC's original intent to complete the free movement of goods, services, labour, and capital in 12 years – which would have been 1969, dating from the signing of the Treaty of Rome – the 1980s arrived without a complete Single Market and with many remaining barriers to trade internally and externally.

Trade Policy and the Single Market

The Single European Act and the Maastricht Treaty made for important institutional developments in EU trade policies. These were visible in voting procedures, the role of the European Parliament (EP), and the role of the Commission. First, a central change with the EU's external trade policy in the run-up to the completion of the Single Market (aimed for the end of 1992) was the shift in voting method within the Council of the EU from mostly unanimous voting (which effectively gave each member a veto) to mostly QMV. Some parts of the CCP remained under unanimous voting – such as in the area of services – but these too were gradually made subject to QMV. Second, the Council and the Commission were now required to exchange information and consult with the EP at several stages throughout the decision-making process in trade agreements. The EP was now also able to give (or withhold) "assent" by a simple majority in some instances of EU trade decisions. Third, the role of the Commission in EU trade policy was strengthened. The EU member states began negotiating as one through the European Commission whenever the EU engaged in external trade affairs. Motivation for these changes came in part from the need to create a cohesive Single Market and in part from a gradual shift of preferences from some member states and European businesses toward export-oriented interests.

Internally, the Single Market created more trade within the EU without any significant evidence of "trade diversion," meaning negative impacts on trade with non-EU members. Externally, the EU Single Market contributed to momentum among developed nations to attend to deeper international trade liberalization. The GATT had made a great deal of progress since its establishment in 1947 in reducing tariffs and other barriers to trade. As international trade moved beyond goods alone and began to include the exchange of services, ideas, and other non-tangible goods, and as other barriers to trade (such as environmental or health safeguards) began to take more prominence, the GATT became reinstitutionalized as the WTO in 1995. The timing of the EU Single Market, as finalized in the signing of the 1992 Treaty on European Union (TEU) at Maastricht, was a significant development for international trade at large. First, the Single Market created a powerful example of how trade in tangible and non-tangible goods could be liberalized according to the rule of law. Second, the Single Market created a strong preferential trade agreement among EU members during a time of rising competition from Asian markets. These factors helped pressure other non-EU large markets to consider deeper trade liberalization worldwide.

The Lisbon Treaty and Europe 2020

The Lisbon Treaty, as noted in Chapter 4, made some sizable changes in amending the TEU and the TEEC, which is now the Treaty on the Functioning of the European Union. The consolidation of the prior three-pillar system into a single legal personality meant that the EU as a whole gained membership in the WTO right after the Treaty of Lisbon entered into force in 2009 (see Box 12.1).

BOX 12.1: TIMELINE OF SIGNIFICANT EVENTS IN EU TRADE POLICY

- 1958* Treaties of Rome
  - Common Commercial Policy (CCP), Article 113, establishing trade as a supranational competence; common external tariff (CET)
  - EEC becomes a single member of GATT, the precursor to the WTO
- 1970 Council switched to joint decision making for CCP through qualified majority voting
- 1978 European Court of Justice (now the CJEU) ruled that Article 113 was not an exhaustive list, and thus the CCP could be extended beyond areas of traditional trade
- 1987* Single European Act (aiming to complete the Single Market by the end of 1992)
- 1993* Treaty on European Union (Maastricht)
  - The EU Single Market for goods, services, people, and capital creates the need for a more elaborate CET to include services

- 1995 EC becomes a member of the WTO
- 2009* Lisbon Treaty allows EU to adopt autonomous acts on trade
  - EU becomes WTO member as a single legal personality
  - Official launch of CETA negotiations between Canada and the EU
- 2013 Launching of negotiations between the EU and the United States under TTIP (Transatlantic Trade and Investment Partnership); officially paused in 2019
- 2014 Conclusion of CETA negotiations
- 2015 Free trade agreement with South Korea comes into force
- 2016 Signing of CETA
  - Brexit referendum results in majority vote for the UK to leave the EU
- 2018 The Council of the European Union authorized opening negotiations for a comprehensive trade agreement between the EU and Australia, as well as between the EU and New Zealand
- 2019 EU signs Economic Partnership Agreement with Japan
  - EU signs a Trade Agreement and an Investment Protection Agreement with Vietnam
  - Free trade agreement with Singapore comes into force
- 2020 Conclusion of Trade and Cooperation Agreement negotiations between the EU and the UK
  - EU–China Comprehensive Agreement on Investment concludes negotiations in principle. The agreement grants EU investors a greater level of access to China's market
- 2021* EU–UK Trade and Cooperation Agreement
- 2022 United Kingdom leaves the EU

*Date refers to the year in which the agreement came into force.

The Lisbon Treaty introduced three main changes for EU trade policy: increased powers for the EU in negotiating international trade agreements, greater powers for the EP in trade policy, and QMV for almost all trade issues. First, the Lisbon Treaty created a solid legal basis for the EU as a whole to adopt autonomous acts on trade. "Autonomous" in this sense means that the EU is able to negotiate and implement trade agreements on behalf of the entire union of 27 member states. The single legal personality of the EU meant that the EU held trade authority for all areas of trade covered by the commercial aspects of the Single Market, which included trade in services, intellectual property, and **foreign direct investment (FDI)**. In some cases, trade in protected services – such as cultural, audio-visual, educational, and social services – was also included under EU trade autonomy, although with the potential to be negotiated under different internal voting rules in the Council.

Second, the increased powers of the EP under the Treaty of Lisbon meant that the EP became a full co-legislator on trade-related legislation using the ordinary legislative procedure and gained the right to give or withhold its consent on all trade agreements concluded by the EU. The EP thus is tasked with parliamentary scrutiny of all international trade activities, as the Commission must transmit all documents and report regularly to the EP during trade negotiations. As part of its budgetary powers, the EP also has a say on EU spending on trade policy.

Third, these changes mean that almost all aspects of trade policy that fall under the exclusive competence of the EU are now decided on by a qualified majority. However, in some particular areas of trade, unanimous voting is still required. As mentioned above, trade in areas that affect culturally sensitive goods or services, such as audio-visual services linked to the cultural and linguistic properties of different regions of the EU, must be subject to unanimous voting. This requirement is similar to laws in existence in Canada that concern Canadian content in national audio-visual broadcasting services, which exist in part to protect Canadian heritage and language laws. Furthermore, any trade in politically sensitive areas relating to social, educational, or health services might require unanimous voting to prevent impeding the ability of national organizations to deliver these services (European Commission 2009).

The EU regularly revisits and updates the goals of its trade policy. The Europe 2020 Strategy was introduced in 2010 by the Commission as a 10-year strategy geared toward advancing the economy of the EU with "smart, sustainable and inclusive growth." While the targets and initiatives of Europe

2020 were not focused on trade policy specifically, the broad goal of economic legitimacy directly relates to some key areas of trade policy. In particular, the Directorate-General for Trade of the European Commission identified that open trade would benefit EU growth by boosting foreign demand for goods and services, giving EU consumers access to a wider variety of goods at lower prices and allowing EU companies to use FDI to increase their competitiveness internationally and to create more jobs both at home and abroad (European Union 2011). In 2021, the EU initiated a trade policy review, geared toward supporting the existing open principles of EU trade along with setting out newer goals from the European Green Deal and the European digital strategy. This was undertaken in part to identify how trade policy could support the economic recovery from the COVID-19 pandemic, as well as in response to changing international norms concerning **multilateralism** and globalism (discussed later in this chapter). A key emphasis from this review was that the EU's commitment to open trade is necessary both for economic recovery as well as political stability (European Commission 2021). Since the launch of the WTO Doha Round in 2001, the EU has been a central actor pushing for fair trading practices in many areas, most visibly the liberalization of public procurement and fair access to raw materials. Once the Doha Round stalled in 2003 the EU adjusted its trade activities toward bilateral "second-generation" free trade areas, which are agreements that go beyond issues of tariffs and quotas to encompass trade in services (and sometimes investment), and which also touch upon questions of convergence in labour, social policies, and environmental regulations (Young 2016). In this regard, the EU's experience in designing, implementing, and constantly amending its own Single Market has given it strong international credibility for playing a dominant role in the formation of international trade rules.

From Negotiation to Ratification

The process of achieving a trade agreement between the EU and a non-EU country first begins with the decision of whether to even consider a preferential agreement with the party in question. Before starting any negotiations with a third country, the Commission holds a public consultation on the topic and conducts an assessment on the impact of any such deal on the EU and on the other country. The Commission undertakes a "scoping" exercise on the country: It begins an informal dialogue with the country in question to ascertain what the range of issues in a trade agreement might contain and whether those issues are compatible with EU trade policy. Should both the public consultation and the scoping exercise prove fruitful, the Commission then requests formal authorization from the Council to begin negotiations within the guidelines of specific negotiating directives that set out the objectives of a potential agreement. The Council then has the authority to discuss the negotiating directives and to suggest changes. Once the Council has approved and adopted the negotiating directives, the Commission is then able to proceed with negotiations.

After negotiations have closed, the final text undergoes legal scrutiny, is translated into all official languages of the EU, and is made public. The agreement will either be approved as falling under the exclusive competence of the EU or as a **mixed agreement**. The agreement is considered a mixed agreement if it exceeds the scope of the EU's exclusive powers over trade; in this case, the EU and member states share competence. Articles 3 and 216 of the TFEU specify the external competences of the EU and the areas where the EU has the exclusive authority to conclude international agreements. Should the agreement meet these criteria, the Council can give final authorization to the agreement and it can be formally signed by the EU and by the other country. The agreement must then receive EP consent. However, if there are shared competences – an example here could be the provision of some liberalized trade of health care services – the agreement is "mixed" between the levels, and all EU member states will also need to sign and ratify the agreement (EUR-Lex 2010). The first trade agreement to be approached in this manner was the EU–Singapore free trade agreement, concluded in 2014. The CJEU provided a legal opinion that, while the EU level had exclusive competence for the majority of topics in the signed agreement text, the EU level *and* the member states shared competence in the areas of portfolio investment and investor state dispute settlement.

The CETA between Canada and the EU illustrates the difference between EU trade agreements that are the exclusive competence of the EU and those that are mixed agreements. Initially the Commission assessed that CETA fell into the legal category of EU exclusive competence, and as such, signing and ratification ought to have required ratification by the EP and EU trade ministers only. However, not all member states agreed with this assessment. In September 2016, in the months following the Brexit referendum, the Commission president proposed to proceed with CETA as a mixed agreement in order to appease a general political unease with Brussels at the time (European Commission 2016b). This decision extended the process of approval and made it a more contentious process, as the new requirement of ratification by all national parliaments within the EU (as well as regional parliaments in some member states) opened up political space for local protest. This process was most visible in the Belgian region of Wallonia, which initially rejected CETA by the established signing deadline. Last-minute amendments to address protections for farmers and questions of foreign investors reversed the Wallonian opposition, and CETA was officially signed on October 30, 2016. This event provides an example of how political actors and societal interests can drive and shape the form of an EU trade agreement. CETA is now "provisionally" in force, with the Canadian side having fully ratified the agreement, but some national and regional parliaments in Europe still need to provide approval. During the summer of 2020, the government of Cyprus voted against the ratification of CETA, objecting to the lack of required geographical regulations for food products that originate from specific regions – such as the regulation of Halloumi cheese. Such examples illustrate how the "mixed" competence of CETA demonstrates the political nuances of trade dynamics within the entire EU. However, such political dynamics should not overshadow the remarkable collaboration that occurs on a day-to-day basis in implementing EU trade policy (see Box 12.2).

BOX 12.2: CUSTOMS INTEGRATION

While EU member state governments maintain tight control over trade agreements, their customs bureaucracies integrate and implement pan-EU standards. A striking example is the Union Customs Code, which came into force on May 1, 2016. For businesses, the Code provides greater transparency and clarity regarding customs rules; it strengthens procedures in a paperless environment. Easing the flow of goods into the EU and contributing to greater business competitiveness, it unifies all regulations and standards across all member states. Customs integration is also driven by 551 annual events, 26,638 officials in joint training programs, and a unified IT system.

The EU and the World

While all EU member states have individual membership in the WTO, the EU itself also holds membership. As the EU is a Single Market with a single tariff and an autonomous trade policy, the EU – through the European Commission – represents all EU member states at nearly all WTO meetings. This single representation is significant because the ability of the EU to have its own WTO membership, and speak with one voice, affords the EU greater leverage in WTO meetings and allows EU countries to further their shared interests. As the world's largest trading bloc, the EU as a whole is more competitive in international deliberations than the member states would be if they each participated independently (see Figure 12.1).

The EU has exercised its power in the WTO through pushing for stronger multilateral international trade rules. Its ability to do so comes from the size and strength of the EU market as well as the precedent the Single Market offers: In many areas of market integration, the EU provides a rare example of countries voluntarily opening up competition to each other, guided by rules and laws. However, the protracted period of the multilateral WTO Doha Round has resulted in many countries and trading blocs pursuing independent trade agreements to create areas of "preferential" free trade between two or more partners. In the twenty-first century, the EU has signed preferential trade agreements or association agreements with numerous other countries around the world, including Mexico (2000), South Africa (2000), South Korea (2012), Colombia (2012), Japan (2019), Mercosur (2019; a trade bloc comprising Argentina, Brazil, Paraguay, and Uruguay), and Vietnam (2020). At the time of writing, the EU is currently in trade discussions with both Australia and New Zealand, having launched negotiations with each country in 2018.

CETA is a notable example of an EU bilateral trade agreement. Negotiations began in 2007 and concluded in 2014, and the legal "scrubbing" of the final text took over a year after negotiations ended. CETA represents a notable achievement for both the EU and Canada, as it was the first major preferential trade agreement the EU has negotiated with a large, industrialized, developed country. It also presents an example of a "second-generation" FTA; this term refers to the evolution of FTAs from dealing with tariffs and duties only to the "new" generation of FTAs that include trade in many areas other than just goods alone. The provisions in CETA extend well beyond the removal of tariffs into liberalization of areas such as services, investment, procurement, and

Figure 12.1. World trade in goods and services (2020), in US $billion

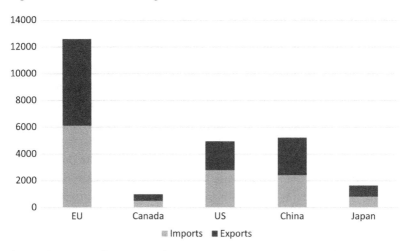

Source: Organisation for Economic Co-operation and Development (2020), data selection from indicator table for "trade in goods and services"

intellectual property. Therefore, the CETA negotiations were a very visible and political process in Canada. Some concerns raised during negotiations came from Canadian groups attached to the dairy industry, municipalities, and intellectual property proponents. The EU is Canada's second largest trading partner, so access to the EU Single Market offered powerful incentives to Canadian businesses and consumers. Because of the inclusion of "second-generation" areas of trade, some of which directly affect local municipalities and businesses, Canadian provinces participated directly in CETA negotiations – a novelty in Canada (see Box 12.3).

The EU also uses trade as a tool to support development in less-developed countries. This includes economic partnership agreements with countries in Africa, the Caribbean, and the Pacific, as well as other kinds of agreements with developing countries in Asia, Latin America, and the southern Mediterranean. The goals of these agreements are to support technical, social, and environmental issues in developing countries along with providing open access for these countries to export to the EU (without tariffs or quotas). These measures supplement development and humanitarian aid (Box 12.4). Observers of these efforts have mixed reactions on the success of the EU's efforts toward attaching trade to developmental policy.

BOX 12.3: TRADE POLICY DECISION MAKING IN CANADA AND THE EU COMPARED

How do provincial–federal dynamics in Canada compare to the dynamics between member states and the Commission in the EU in the area of international trade? Generally speaking, there are numerous parallels between the two systems. Although not a federal state, the EU has some characteristics of a federal system. These overlapping features make comparisons with other federal states interesting. Canada is a federal country that is quite decentralized. In both the EU and Canada, trade matters concerning customs, tariffs, and international agreements are the responsibility of the highest governmental level. Similar to the EU Commission having sole authority to initiate and conduct trade negotiations, the Canadian federal government in Ottawa also holds this power. In the EU, the Commission's DG of Trade is responsible; in Canada Global Affairs Canada has this role. Furthermore, the president of the EU Commission makes the final decision on international trade agreements, as is the case in Canada where the prime minister has a similar power.

However, given these similarities and despite the fact that Canada is a single country whereas the EU is a supranational polity of 27 member states, trade policy competences are actually significantly *more* centralized in the EU than in Canada. The reason is the level of integration of the EU Single Market: There are fewer barriers to goods flowing freely between EU member states than there are between Canadian provinces and territories (see Chapter 7). Thus, the EU level has more capability to negotiate trade deals as one cohesive Single Market than Canada does. Trade policy is a prominent example of how the EU itself is much more than an international organization, even though it cannot meet the definition of a full federation (Theme 2 of this book).

In the EU context, individual member states have a role in trade policy through the Council of the EU. Although the Commission represents the EU during trade negotiations, the Council must first authorize the opening of negotiations and is later responsible for signing the agreement on behalf of the EU. In Canada, the

Constitution limits the role of the provinces to merely an advisory one during international trade negotiations. However, recent trade agreements – such as CETA or the WTO Agreement on Government Procurement – have required provincial participation and consent due to the nature of issues covered under "second-generation" treaties. In fact, in 2009 the EU insisted that Canadian provinces be included in the CETA negotiation process in order to systematize a role for provinces that would both parallel internal EU trade dynamics and, ostensibly, reduce the possibility of last-minute regional protest (D'Erman 2016). Involving provinces in this way has set a precedent that has made Canadian provinces more active members in international trade negotiations. It is unclear, however, to what extent this precedent may be repeated.

BOX 12.4: BUDGET FOR EU TRADE AND DEVELOPMENT POLICY

- The costs for EU trade policy are mainly administrative in nature and are covered from the budget of the European Commission. Beyond these administrative costs, the 2021 EU budget includes only a small allocation of €18 million for "external trade relations and aid for trade."
- Non-trade-related aspects of EU development policy are supported from the Neighbourhood, Development and International Cooperation Instrument (€11.7 billion in 2021) and the budget allocation for humanitarian aid (€1.5 billion).

Source: Definitive adoption (EU, Euratom) 2021/417 of the European Union's general budget for the financial year 2021, https://eur-lex.europa.eu/eli/budget/2021/1/oj

Similar to CETA, but much larger in scope, was the attempted **Transatlantic Trade and Investment Partnership (TTIP)** between the EU and the United States. Whereas CETA was not very newsworthy in EU member states during negotiations with Canada, TTIP quickly became a much more political, controversial, and visible process. This salience is in part explained by economics – Canada is only the EU's twelfth trading partner, whereas the United States is the EU's first trading partner for exports and second partner for imports, thereby greatly raising the risks and benefits of a potential agreement. Should EU–US free trade negotiations conclude successfully, it would represent the largest free trade zone, comprising the two biggest markets, in the entire world. Talks on TTIP began in 2013, but stalled after Donald Trump was elected US president in 2016 and were officially paused in 2019. While both the COVID-19 pandemic and the war in Ukraine could stimulate a resurgence of cross-Atlantic negotiations (for example, a 2020 bilateral agreement between the EU and the United States on tariff reduction), TTIP is still likely to meet with strong public opposition from both sides.

The 2016–20 US Trump administration helped to nudge a shift in trade norms – domestically and internationally – toward more protectionist sentiments. Trump's approach included an increase in tariffs and a more cautious approach to trade negotiations. It has so far continued under President Joseph Biden, who was inaugurated in January 2021. This gradual shift in US norms has had an impact in the EU, where existing insecurities on heightened globalism and globalization had already found expression in various individual member states. Compounding this shift was the COVID-19 pandemic beginning in 2020. As countries around the world "locked down" for the purpose of containing the spread of the virus, a corresponding pause of production and supply chain shipping of goods also occurred. The reality of this period unsettled businesses and consumers alike and fuelled further public anxieties surrounding the practice of international trade. For European integration, where trade liberalization and interdependence is not just an economic practice but the core mechanism of securing postwar peace on the European continent, the challenge to the purported value of international cooperation can have potentially far-reaching implications.

DEBATE: ISSUES WITH EU TRADE POLICIES

While the EU's external trade policy provides a strong and durable example of the achievements of European integration, there remain debates over the benefits and drawbacks of free trade (see Box 12.5), as well as about the specifics of EU trade policy. This section summarizes three specific issues. First, the exclusive competence of the EU institutions in managing trade for the entire bloc has on occasion chafed with national interests. Second, the position of the EU as the most powerful trading bloc in the world brings into question what *kind* of power the EU ought to be. Third, the actual substance of recent bilateral "second-generation" FTAs has generated controversy in a number of EU member states and interest groups. These controversies have been most visible with some of the provisions (or lack thereof) in CETA and TTIP on **investor state dispute settlement (ISDS)** mechanisms, intellectual property, and public procurement.

BOX 12.5: BENEFITS AND COSTS OF FREE TRADE: A CRITICAL VIEWPOINT

Theoretically, free trade enriches all trading partners through the logic of comparative advantage. If each country specializes in what it is good at, all trade partners benefit from trading their goods with each other. However, the practical realities of mobile capital and unequal trading partners bolster the argument of national economic protectionism. Critics of free trade highlight three important considerations. First, a rising GDP from free trade does not equal an increase in the material quality of life for all citizens or a reduction in income inequality. Second, the factors of production (capital and labour) are rarely completely mobile, thwarting the opportunity to capitalize on the theoretical comparative advantage. Third, the efficiency of free trade may have negative consequences for the environment, social conditions, and sustainability of resources.

Inside the EU, the Single Market still contains some barriers to trade, particularly in the area of services. These barriers are the result of member states arguing for protectionism on the basis of cultural specificity, employment, and provision of social services. Critics of the EU's approach to trade liberalization – both internally in the Single Market and externally with other countries – argue that the EU's push for trade liberalization promotes economic efficiency and aggregate growth at the cost of local industry and natural resources.

The CCP, which governs EU trade policy, is the most prominent EU policy to have been under supranational competence from the very beginning of the EEC in the Treaty of Rome. Still, it does not mean this policy is uncontested (Meunier and Nicolaïdis 2006). Meunier (2005) states that the EU's external trade policy over time has placed a premium on efficiency in international bargaining over the impulse to protect national sovereignty. The strengthening of the EP over time has helped increase the legitimacy of the EU in many policy areas, including trade, but has not entirely removed tensions to do with delegation to supranational authority. One such example is whether CETA should be ratified as a mixed agreement or as an exclusive EU competence. The debate over competence in many ways reflects ongoing debates about the legitimacy of European integration (Theme 3 of this book). EU trade policy provides a coherent response to the economic pressures of globalization, but – as the case of Wallonia during the signing of CETA illustrates – it faces criticisms of legitimacy and regional democratic input.

The size and strength of the EU market combined with its role as the most powerful trading bloc in the world gives the EU an enormous amount of leverage in shaping the multilateral rules of international trade. How the EU chooses to exercise that leverage, however, is not always clear or consistent. Member state governments hold different views on how to wield such power through trade; for example, whether the EU should concentrate on negotiating solely its own market interest versus whether it should expend energy on shaping the entire multilateral framework. This dilemma is visible in the area of agriculture, an area of trade where the EU has been notoriously protectionist (see Chapter 10) despite its long-term commitment to using trade as a tool for economic development in less wealthy countries. This tension is also somewhat visible in the EU's surge in bilateral agreements with non-EU actors, despite the EU's advocacy of multilateralism as the primary recommended framework for international trade (although it could be argued that bilateral agreements are an indirect method of spreading multilateral norms).

Some of the newer areas of trade contained in "second-generation" agreements have been controversial for a variety of actors in European societies. ISDS mechanisms are temporary committees set up to help resolve disputes between foreign investors and states when there is a disagreement over investor rights. The draft CETA contained provisions for an ISDS system that followed precedents found in many other international agreements. However, once TTIP discussions began, many states and citizens in the EU objected strongly to the ISDS system proposed in both CETA and TTIP. The central concern has been that national rights in environmental and labour regulations have not been given enough protections with regard to foreign investors in either agreement. The resulting compromise in CETA has been to establish a permanent (rather than ad hoc) investment court with a tribunal to hear appeals. **Intellectual property** was also a contentious issue during CETA negotiations primarily because of pharmaceuticals and copyright standards. The EU demanded extended patents on prescription drugs, to match what other G8 countries (with the exception of Canada) provided for pharmaceutical research. Although this demand was met, it triggered concerns in Canada that pharmaceutical costs will jump. The EU also demanded strict copyright provisions; these demands were softened as Canada passed the Copyright Modernization Act in early 2012. **Public procurement** – the purchasing of goods and services by public entities – was a longstanding issue with CETA. The EU demanded access to Canada's full procurement market, including provinces and municipalities. As procurement is often used as a tool to support local economies, there was widespread protest among Canadian municipalities. The result in CETA's final text was that Canada's municipal market would be open to EU bids, but with certain thresholds for spending in different sectors; conversely, Canadian bids have the same level of access to the EU procurement market as EU members have themselves, reinforcing the idea that internal EU market integration is matched by external actions.

CONCLUSION

EU trade policy is one of the longest-running policy areas for which the EEC, EC, and later EU has supranational competence. Initially developed as a means to set common tariffs in accordance with the early Customs Union, it has since evolved into a far-reaching delegation of authority to the EU institutions to set the terms of external trade with non-EU actors on behalf of the Single Market. The Commission represents all 27 member states in international trade forums such as the WTO. Nevertheless, having supranational competence over trade policy has not prevented national interests from exercising their opposition on key issues, as the case of signing and ratifying CETA demonstrates. In general, the pace of external EU actions on trade has matched the internal integration of the Single Market, with the result of a great deal of autonomy being conferred on the supranational level – the strengthening of the EP is a qualification on this autonomy. Finally, the size of the Single Market and the actions of the EU internationally suggest that the EU has become a formidable trading power within the WTO and elsewhere, with the ability to create new norms and multilateral standards. Whether this form of economic power can withstand the rising and ebbing norms of protectionism remains to be seen.

REVIEW QUESTIONS

1. The Lisbon Treaty increased the authority of the European Parliament in shaping the trade policies of the EU. What is the value-added of the new role of the EP?
2. What role do international and non-EU actors have in shaping EU trade policy?
3. Why does the EU have a single voice in the World Trade Organization?
4. Why has the Comprehensive Economic and Trade Agreement between Canada and the EU been difficult to approve?
5. What are some of the areas in "second-generation" trade agreements?
6. How have changes in US presidential policies impacted EU trade policy?

EXERCISES

1. Collect information on CJEU opinions and rulings on the EU's ability to conclude free trade agreements. What legal precedence is there for EU exclusive competence? What is the substance of the arguments against that competence, and when should trade agreements be approved as "mixed agreements"?
2. The Comprehensive Economic and Trade Agreement is the EU's first free trade agreement with a wealthy, industrialized democracy. Undertake some research on other EU free trade agreements already completed. What issues of negotiation are different with CETA?

REFERENCES AND FURTHER READING

D'Erman, V. 2016. "Comparative Intergovernmental Politics: CETA Negotiations between Canada and the EU." *Politics and Governance* 4 (3): 90–9. https://doi.org/10.17645/pag.v4i3.565.

EUR-Lex. 2010. International Agreements and the EU's External Competences. Summaries of EU legislation. http://eur-lex.europa.eu/legal-content/EN/TXT/?uri=URISERV:ai0034.

European Commission. 1995. *Trade Relations between the European Union and the Developing Countries*. Luxembourg: Office for Official Publications of the European Communities.

European Commission. 2009. "Treaty of Lisbon Enters into Force: Implications for the EU's Trade Policy." http://trade.ec.europa.eu/doclib/press/index.cfm?id=493.

European Commission. 2013. "Trade Negotiations Step by Step." http://trade.ec.europa.eu/doclib/docs/2012/june/tradoc_149616.pdf.

European Commission. 2016a. "About TTIP." http://ec.europa.eu/trade/policy/in-focus/ttip/about-ttip/.

European Commission. 2016b. "European Commission Proposes Signature and Conclusion of EU-Canada Trade Deal." Press release. http://europa.eu/rapid/press-release_IP-16-2371_en.htm.

European Commission. 2021. "Trade Policy Review: An Open, Sustainable and Assertive Trade Policy." Brussels, 18.2.2021 COM (2021) 66 final.

European Parliament. 2021. "The European Union and Its Trade Partners." Fact Sheet/External Trade Relations. https://www.europarl.europa.eu/factsheets/en/sheet/160/the-european-union-and-its-trade-partners.

European Union. 2000. "Common Commercial Policy." EUR-Lex a20000-EN. http://eur-lex.europa.eu/legal-content/EN/TXT/?uri=URISERV%3Aa20000.

European Union. 2011. "Trade Policy Serving the Europe 2020 Strategy." EUR-Lex COM (2010) 612. http://eur-lex.europa.eu/legal-content/EN/TXT/?uri=URISERV:em0043.

Fafard, P., and P. Leblond. 2013. "Closing the Deal: What Role for the Provinces in the Final Stages of the CETA Negotiations?" *International Journal* 68 (4): 553–9. https://doi.org/10.1177/0020702013509319.

García, M. 2013. "From Idealism to Realism? EU Preferential Trade Agreement Policy." *Journal of Contemporary European Research* 9 (4): 521–41. https://doi.org/10.30950/jcer.v9i4.462.

Meunier, S. 2005. *Trading Voices*. Princeton, NJ: Princeton University Press.

Meunier, S. 2007. "Managing Globalisation: The EU in International Trade Negotiations." *Journal of Common Market Studies* 45 (5): 905–26. https://doi.org/10.1111/j.1468-5965.2007.00753.x.

Meunier, S., and K. Nicolaïdis. 1999. "Who Speaks for Europe? The Delegation of Trade Authority in the EU." *Journal of Common Market Studies* 37 (3): 477–510. https://doi.org/10.1111/1468-5965.00174.

Meunier, S., and K. Nicolaïdis. 2006. "The EU as a Conflicted Trade Power." *Journal of European Public Policy* 13 (6): 906–25. https://doi.org/10.1080/13501760600838623.

Organisation for Economic Co-operation and Development (OCED). 2021. "Trade in Goods and Services (Indicator)." https://doi.org/10.1787/0fe445d9-en.

Smith, M. 2001. "The EU's Commercial Policy: Between Coherence and Fragmentation." *Journal of European Public Policy* 8 (5): 787–802. https://doi.org/10.1080/13501760110083518.

Verdun, A. 2014. "Federalism in the EU and Canada." In *Understanding Federalism and Federation*, edited by A.-G. Gagnon, S. Keil, and S. Mueller, 233–43. New York: Routledge.

Young, A.R. 2016. "Not Your Parents' Trade Politics: The Transatlantic Trade and Investment Partnership Negotiations." *Review of International Political Economy* 23 (3): 345–78. https://doi.org/10.1080/09692290.2016.1150316.

Young, A.R., and J. Peterson. 2013. "'We Care about You, but …': The Politics of EU Trade Policy and Development." *Cambridge Review of International Affairs* 26 (3): 497–518. https://doi.org/10.1080/09557571.2012.734782.

13

Enlargement

Charles C. Pentland

READER'S GUIDE

Since its foundation, the European Union (EU) grew from 6 to 28 members before the United Kingdom's recent departure. It has never lacked applicants for membership. Enlargement has evolved from a series of distinct diplomatic episodes to a process integrated and consistent with EU institutions and governance. Often seen as a cumulative foreign policy success reflecting the allure of the integration project, enlargement has fundamentally changed not only the applicants but also the EU itself. Future expansion is jeopardized by major EU crises, political instability (both national and regional), and rising concerns that enlargement has been too much of a good thing.

INTRODUCTION

States, much as people, are attracted to successful groups and often seek to join them. In turn, groups of states – global organizations such as the United Nations or regional bodies such as the EU – tend to welcome others sharing their goals and offering economic, geopolitical, and other assets. It is therefore not surprising that, from the 1960s on, the early success and promise of the six-member European Economic Community (EEC; the forerunner of the EU) began to attract applicants from among its European neighbours. They were drawn to a project of regional integration – neither a traditional international organization nor a new federation – aiming to build a European zone of peace through an innovative political-economic strategy (Themes 1 and 2 of this book).

Since 1961, when the United Kingdom first applied to join the EEC, that organization and its successors have almost continuously – and often simultaneously – been eyeing prospective applicants, negotiating with candidates for admission, and accommodating new members. The map in Chapter 1 (Map 1.1) of this book shows the EU's current member states as well as those recognized as candidates for membership. But while **enlargement** is often cited as testimony to the attractions of the European project, it has rarely proceeded without controversy. A chronic concern has been whether expansion will undermine the project's capacity to achieve its economic and political aims at home and abroad. Mindful of that debate, among others, this chapter describes the organization's growth from 6 to 28 members (before Brexit) and the role of its main institutions in managing the enlargement process. It reviews discussions about the pros, cons, and consequences of expansion– both past and future.

THE FIRST THREE ENLARGEMENTS

The enlargements of 1973, the 1980s, and 1995 expanded the European integration project from 6 to 15 members. Each was a discrete episode involving a distinctive cluster of applicants in unique historical circumstances. Each was viewed as a constructive interruption of the members' linear progress toward economic integration. Each aided the growth of common norms and practices to govern anticipated future enlargements (see Box 13.1).

BOX 13.1: ENLARGEMENT: THE BASICS
Definition
For international organizations, the common sense understanding of enlargement is the admission of one or more sovereign states as new members. (In this respect, German reunification was an

unusual case; the EU territory grew when West and East Germany united, but this was not formally an EU enlargement.)

Treaty provisions: Rome and Lisbon
Article 237 of the Treaty Establishing the European Economic Community, the Treaty of Rome (1957), stated "[a]ny European state may apply to become a member of the Community." After obtaining the Commission's opinion, the Council had to decide unanimously if the application was to be accepted. The terms agreed to in the negotiations and embodied in an **accession treaty** then had to be ratified by the applicant and all member states. These have remained the core procedural guidelines, but the experience of the eastward enlargement (1993–2007) influenced the revised provisions incorporated in the Treaty of Lisbon (2009). Article 49 of the Treaty on European Union (TEU) now states that any European state that "respects the values referred to in Article 2 and is committed to promoting them may apply to become a member of the Union." (Article 2 lists civic and moral values considered fundamental to the EU and "prevailing in the societies of all member states.") The accession process described in Article 49 resembles that in the Treaty of Rome but adds the requirement of majority approval by the European Parliament and refers to "conditions of eligibility" determined by the European Council.

The UK, Ireland, and Denmark

In the 1960s the opportunity to expand the six-member EEC arose from a historic change in British thinking about Europe. The UK had stepped away from the 1955–7 negotiations that produced the EEC, continuing to favour its ties with the Commonwealth, its "special relationship" with the United States, and global trade liberalization. In 1960, it formed the **European Free Trade Association (EFTA)** with six other like-minded states as an alternative to the EEC. Within a year, however, the UK, along with two other EFTA members (Denmark and Norway) and the Republic of Ireland, had begun negotiations for admission to the EEC.

Why this dramatic shift? The EEC project was surging while the UK was languishing, and the EFTA's attractions diminished accordingly. The UK thus concluded that the future lay with the markets of continental Europe, and that access and influence required joining the EEC as a full member. Ireland, two-thirds of whose trade was with the UK, decided to follow, as did Denmark and Norway.

Accession negotiations between the UK and the EEC largely determined the fate of the other three applicants. Talks soon became bogged down over sensitive issues such as agriculture, Commonwealth trade preferences, and the budget. Underlying these issues was a fundamental divide over the nature of the European project. The British and their companions were skeptical about schemes for an "ever-closer union" among Europeans and suspicious of regional protectionism and latent rivalry with the United States. Moreover, as a great power the UK saw itself less as a supplicant than as an equal to the EEC, able to demand significant concessions at the bargaining table. Beneath the technical details of the negotiations emerged a growing French–British standoff, culminating in President de Gaulle's televised "veto" of the UK's application in January 1963.

Revived negotiations met a similar fate in 1967, but three years later new governments in London and Paris generated a change of climate. Negotiations resumed. While the issues were familiar, circumstances had changed. The EEC was thriving; it initiated a Customs Union 18 months ahead of schedule, as well as free movement of labour and agreement on the Common Agricultural Policy (CAP; see Chapters 7 and 10). The UK economy, meanwhile, remained stagnant. Negotiations underlined that the UK could no longer expect significant adjustments to EEC goals, policies, and institutions. Agreement was finally reached in 1972.

The four applicants signed accession agreements with the EEC, but only three were ratified. In Norway's referendum, intense opposition from farmers and fishers defeated the agreement. On January 1, 1973, the EEC therefore admitted three new members. Five-year transition periods were set up for them to align themselves with the tariff provisions of the Customs Union, the CAP, free movement of labour, and other EU policies, laws, and institutions.

Not only was this first enlargement prolonged and difficult, but its conclusion proved less than final. The economic crisis of the 1970s stalled much of the EEC's agenda for economic and monetary union, and the UK and Denmark witnessed growing skepticism about the European project. In 1974, the Labour Party returned to power in the UK promising a referendum on whether to remain in the EEC. With the government campaigning in favour, British voters agreed by a two-thirds majority to stay in.

The UK, however, remained an "awkward partner" (George 1994). After almost a decade of negotiations it was granted a rebate on its contributions to the EU budget in 1984. In 2016, a surge of **Euroskepticism**, especially in his own party, led Prime Minister David Cameron to put the choice of leaving or remaining in the EU to a referendum. A narrow win by the "leave" side led to bitterly fought negotiations resulting in UK withdrawal from the EU at the end of January 2020.

The Southern Enlargement

In the mid-1970s, three Southern European states applied to join what was by then called the European Community (EC). This second enlargement was, in many respects, different from the first. It saw the emergence of **conditionality** (the practice of tying membership to the fulfillment of explicit conditions), extended the use of transition periods, and confirmed that in negotiations most of the concessions would be made by the candidates.

Greece had signed an Association Agreement with the EEC in 1961, which included trade concessions, development assistance, and the prospect of eventual membership. In 1967, however, the military seized power in Athens and the EC froze most components of its relations with Greece. After the Colonels' Regime fell and relations with Brussels resumed, Greece applied for membership in July 1975 and negotiations began a year later. They were concluded in 1979, and Greece became the tenth member of the EC in 1981.

Negotiations with Portugal and Spain started later and took longer. Both countries had been under authoritarian rule since the 1930s and had limited relations with the EC; both had recent trade agreements, and Portugal was a member of the EFTA. They were less familiar than Greece with the EC, and less prepared for negotiations with it. In both countries, the collapse of an authoritarian regime was followed by two years of political instability and uncertainty.

In Portugal, a new democratic government elected in 1976 filed its application for EC membership the following March. Negotiations began in October 1978. In Spain, a difficult political transition from authoritarian rule ended with the election of a government in June 1977. An application to the EC followed swiftly and negotiations commenced in February 1979. Running almost parallel to those with Portugal, they resulted in a simultaneous accession on January 1, 1986.

All three southern candidates presented similar profiles. Economically they were underdeveloped compared to most of the EC member states, with large agricultural sectors, outdated industries, and high unemployment. Politically, they were new and fragile democracies, with deep internal divisions and untested institutions. Strategically, the Mediterranean region seemed increasingly sensitive, given its proximity to the Middle East and North Africa.

In the end, the political and strategic arguments for enlargement prevailed over the reservations of some member states. Despite their concerns about agriculture, France and Italy welcomed the "rebalancing" of the EC through the admission of states sharing their Mediterranean cultures. While sensitive to the increased financial burden, EC members welcomed democracy and stability on Europe's southern flank, along with a responsibility to legitimize and support political reform. With membership at 12, however, some were already asking whether the EC would be "wider but weaker" (Wallace 1976).

The EFTA Enlargement

Within five years of the southern enlargement, new requests for EC membership arrived – from Türkiye in 1987 and from Cyprus and Malta in 1990. These were temporarily shelved as the end of the Cold War brought a wave of new demands for admission, coming initially from four of the remaining members of the EFTA – Austria, Sweden, Finland, and Norway. The first three, geopolitically neutral but with close economic and cultural ties to the West, had remained outside the EC during the Cold War. Norway was a member of the North Atlantic Treaty Organization (NATO). Each wished to enhance its access to EC markets with a seat at the Brussels table where decisions affecting them were being made. Potential net contributors to the EC's budget, these stable democracies were a welcome change from some previous candidates.

Austria applied first, in July 1989, followed by Sweden (July 1991), Finland (March 1992), and Norway (November 1992). All four negotiations concluded in the spring of 1994. Their relative brevity reflected the fact that many barriers had already been removed through existing economic agreements between EFTA members and the EC. All four candidates then sought ratification of the accession treaty by referendum. Three succeeded while, as in 1972, Norwegian hesitation concerning fisheries, farming, and oil defeated the accession treaty. Austria, Finland, and Sweden joined what was by then the EU on January 1, 1995, bringing its membership to 15.

THE EU LOOKS EASTWARD

The EU's biggest enlargement saw it admit eight countries in Central and Eastern Europe (CEE) plus Cyprus and Malta in 2004, and two more former Soviet bloc countries in 2007, bringing its membership to 27 (see Box 13.2). Formally initiated by the Copenhagen summit of 1993, this process differed from its predecessors in at least three respects. The first was scale – there were 13 candidates. As 12 of them (all but Türkiye) negotiated entry between 1996 and 2007, the prospect of so many states – mostly small and relatively poor – entering the EU escalated the "wider but weaker" debate.

BOX 13.2: ENLARGEMENT TIMELINE

1958	Founding members: Belgium, France, Italy, Luxembourg, Netherlands, West Germany
1973	Denmark, Ireland, United Kingdom
1981	Greece
1986	Portugal, Spain
1995	Austria, Finland, Sweden
2004	Estonia, Latvia, Lithuania
	Czech Republic, Hungary, Poland, Slovakia
	Slovenia
	Cyprus, Malta
2007	Bulgaria, Romania
2013	Croatia

Second, there were concerns that if the EU was indeed reaching the upper limits of membership, its institutions might become overburdened. Increased diversity could hinder effectiveness. Third, this accession process went further than its predecessors. Each accession state had to incorporate into its legislation the full *acquis communautaire* (see Box 13.3). Doing so required it to engage in negotiations covering over 30 areas of policy ("chapters," in EU jargon). Given that most candidates perceived the EU as their only real option, Brussels held a strong hand.

The Copenhagen summit was a belated response to Europe's post–Cold War political realities. The CEE countries, newly free to chart their own course, were demanding access to Western institutions on moral and prudential grounds. The moral claim was that the West should deliver on promises it had made supporting those struggling against Soviet domination. The prudential argument was that an eastward extension of Western institutions would promote prosperity and security, the best guarantee against a reversion to anarchy or suppression.

At Copenhagen the EU laid down six conditions that applicants would have to meet before being admitted. In time, these became condensed into three **Copenhagen criteria** (see Box 13.3). The EU's capacity to integrate new members reflected some of the existing members' anxieties about the scale of this enlargement.

BOX 13.3: CONDITIONALITY AND ENLARGEMENT

Conditionality
The concept of *conditionality* refers to the obligation of applicant states to adopt the EU's legal, administrative, economic, and political standards, embodied in the *acquis communautaire* (see below) and summarized since 1993 in the Copenhagen criteria. Conditionality was first applied by the EC in the 1970s during enlargement negotiations with Greece, Portugal, and Spain. In a more structured form, it became central to the negotiations for the 1993–2007 eastward enlargement. It is the governing principle of the preparatory partnerships (European Partnership Agreements and Associate Partnerships) and Stabilization and Association Agreements.

The Copenhagen criteria
Emerging from the 1993 Copenhagen summit initiating the eastward enlargement, these criteria summarize the standards and expectations to be met by all applicants: first, stable institutions guaranteeing democracy, the rule of law, human rights, and respect for minorities; second, a functioning market economy and the capacity to cope with competition and market forces in the EU; third, the will and ability to assume the aims and obligations of EU membership as represented by the *acquis communautaire*.

> *The* acquis communautaire
> The *acquis communautaire* consists of EU treaties, legal principles, legislation, declarations and resolutions, case law, and international agreements, incorporated in over 100,000 pages of documents, which applicants must commit to adopting and applying. The *acquis* illustrates the asymmetry of accession negotiations, which require most reforms and adjustments to be made by the applicant.
>
> *Chapters*
> Chapters are categories of the *acquis* – 30 to 35 in number – corresponding to the main policy areas of the EU. Chapters provide the framework for accession negotiations. Each is opened as the applicant's preparation meets the Commission's approval. Negotiations then proceed, often involving several chapters in parallel. When the Commission is satisfied that the applicant has met EU standards in that policy field, it recommends to the Council that the chapter be closed. Some chapters are settled quickly; others can take years and may even be "frozen" for political reasons. Accession cannot proceed until all are closed.

From 1993 until late 1996, the EU received applications from the three Baltic states (Estonia, Latvia, and Lithuania), four Central European states (Poland, Hungary, the Czech Republic, and Slovakia), and three Balkan states (Slovenia, Romania, and Bulgaria). Combined with the applications received earlier from Türkiye, Cyprus, and Malta, this promised to be a large and complex agenda. Enlargement dominated EU decision making in the late 1990s and early 2000s. Two major reforms aimed at adapting EU institutions to a larger number of member states were the Treaties of Amsterdam (1997) and Nice (2000). Successive European Council summits adjusted the EU's enlargement strategy.

Türkiye, whose resentment at having been set aside was creating problems in NATO and over Cyprus, was formally accepted as a candidate with an appropriate "to do" list, although no date was set for the opening of negotiations. From 2000 onward the applicants made rapid if uneven progress in their 12 parallel accession talks. A final push led to agreement at a 2003 summit in Athens that 10 of the 12 would be admitted in May 2004. Bulgaria and Romania followed in 2007. As in previous enlargements, transition periods were negotiated, notably for phasing in CAP payments to the new members (10 years) and for restricting free movement of labour (maximum seven years). Bulgaria and Romania were subject to post-admission monitoring by the Commission concerning issues of judicial reform, corruption, and organized crime under the so-called Cooperation and Verification Mechanism.

MANAGING ENLARGEMENT: FROM IMPROVISATION TO GOVERNANCE

In the succession of enlargements described above, norms, institutions, and procedures developed as member states responded to demands for admission. By the 1990s, enlargement had become institutionally embedded as a distinct field of EU policy. In this field, the intergovernmental institutions – the European Council and Council of the EU – provide a framework in which member states, as the ultimate arbiters of enlargement, exercise power and pursue their interests, but those institutions are also actors in their own right. The supranational institutions – the Commission and European Parliament – exhibit a similar duality: Each is a political arena in which national and EU-level forces are in play, but each is also an actor whose collective positions carry weight based on technical and political legitimacy.

Intergovernmental Institutions and Actors

The role of the European Council in framing enlargement strategy, overseeing negotiations, and deciding on their outcome underlines the formally intergovernmental character of this policy area. In 1961, when the UK's application initiated the first enlargement, it was already accepted that, as Article 237 of the Treaty of Rome (EEC Treaty) indicated, the matter would be managed by the governments of the six original members and ultimately decided by consensus. Any doubts about this were removed by President de Gaulle's vetoes in 1963 and 1967.

The inauguration of the European Council as a regular (albeit initially informal) practice coincided in the mid-1970s with the southern enlargement. These summit meetings oversaw negotiations and provided a venue for the occasional high-level decision, while the Council of Ministers (now the Council of the EU) managed things between summits. In assessing and pronouncing on the state of negotiations at various stages, and in formally marking their conclusion, the European Council legitimized the process and the outcome.

The eastward enlargement showed how the summits had solidified their role in defining the strategy, managing the process, and endorsing its results. The Copenhagen summit of 1993 confirmed the decision of the then 12 member states to invite applications from the CEE countries, laid down the track along which the negotiations should proceed, and set out the standards all applicants would have to meet. Subsequent European Councils made important decisions differentiating among **candidate states** with respect to commencing accession talks and assessing their progress. Another Copenhagen summit in 2002 formalized the conclusion that 10 of the 12 candidates had met the requirements of membership. The accession treaty, signed in Athens, required ratification by the candidates and all 15 member states.

In between the meetings of the European Council, the member states manage the enlargement process at the ministerial level through the Council of the EU and at the "deputy" level through their ambassadors to the EU, who constitute the Committee of Permanent Representatives. Ministers or deputies meet to deliberate on reports or opinions from the Commission and to develop the EU's collective negotiating position.

The Lisbon Treaty created two versions of the Council in which enlargement issues may be discussed. The **General Affairs Council** is chaired by the member state holding the Council's six-month rotating presidency. While broad issues related to enlargement can be discussed there, specific issues related to negotiations over the chapters tend to surface in the more focused configurations of the Council – agriculture ministers, for example. And while the presidency can help provide continuity, it is limited by its short term of office.

The Foreign Affairs Council consists of foreign ministers or their deputies and is chaired by the high representative for foreign affairs and security policy (see Chapter 9). This helps resolve an institutional problem peculiar to enlargement: Unlike most other EU policy areas, enlargement is not managed by each member state through a dedicated governmental department. Instead, that task has usually been assumed by foreign ministries, partly because of enlargement's proximity to foreign policy, and partly because of its comprehensive content. Foreign ministers meeting as the Foreign Affairs Council with the high representative – who is also a member of the Commission – thus provide continuity and intergovernmental oversight of accession negotiations. This matters because accession negotiations are essentially a set of continuing, parallel intergovernmental meetings involving each applicant, the Commission, and all the member states.

Supranational Institutions and Actors

The Commission plays a vital part in enlargement; its findings from its extensive investigation of each applicant, embodied in a formal opinion presented to the Council, are critical in determining whether and when accession talks might begin. During negotiations, the Commission provides the Council with a continuous flow of information and evaluations. It issues annual reports on the progress of each candidate, including estimates of when some chapters should be opened for negotiations and others might be closed. Its findings provide ammunition for the member states and incentives to the applicants. Its role is thus both technical and political.

The Commission's political influence becomes more apparent if we consider the broader context in which enlargements happen. In the late 1980s, even before the collapse of the Soviet system, the Commission began to extend economic and technical assistance to the CEE states, signing Trade and Cooperation Agreements (TCAs) with them and beginning a "political dialogue." In 1992, it began to upgrade the TCAs to Association Agreements (called "Europe Agreements"), creating a political momentum toward enlargement that hesitant member states found difficult to resist. The Commission's introduction of the Copenhagen criteria in advance of the summit itself illustrated its capacity to frame the issues, set the agenda, and design the procedures for accession.

The Commission itself had to adapt to cope with the unprecedented scale of the eastward expansion. Faced with 13 applications, it could no longer rely on the traditional practice of providing data and assessments from the various Directorates-General (DGs) in a relatively uncoordinated way. To maintain its influence over enlargement policy, it would have to restructure to better manage the flow of information, oversee the process, and shape its own strategy. In 1999, it therefore created a new DG dedicated to enlargement and headed by a commissioner prepared to comment on the prospects of the negotiations and the conduct of individual applicants.

After 2004, the number of parallel accession talks shrank from 12 to a more manageable four – Bulgaria and Romania, and the early stages with Türkiye and Croatia. The Commission's re-labelled DG for Neighbourhood and Enlargement Negotiations (DG NEAR) was given responsibility for the

European Neighbourhood Policy as well. It continues to provide annual assessments of candidates' progress. It also manages the budget allocated to enlargement policy (see Box 13.4).

> **BOX 13.4: FINANCING ENLARGEMENT**
> - In the EU's Multiannual Financial Framework 2021–7, enlargement falls under the budget heading "Neighbourhood and the World." This budget heading also includes spending on the Common Foreign and Security Policy, neighbourhood policy, and humanitarian aid.
> - Spending on enlargement makes up a relatively small share of the EU budget. In the 2021 EU budget, €1.9 billion was allocated to the Instrument for Pre-Accession Assistance for six West Balkan countries plus Türkiye. This was a mere 1.1 per cent of the EU's total spending.
>
> Source: Definitive adoption (EU, Euratom) 2021/417 of the European Union's general budget for the financial year 2021, https://eur-lex.europa.eu/eli/budget/2021/1/oj

Since the Treaty of Lisbon, the European Parliament must be notified of each membership application, and the consent of an absolute majority of its members (MEPs) is required for final approval of the accession agreement, prior to its ratification by member states. In addition, the EP plays an active part in all phases of enlargement. For instance, after the Amsterdam summit it urged the European Council to negotiate with all 12 applicants at once – not just the six most advanced – and to recognize Türkiye as a candidate. After 2004, some MEPs called for a moratorium on further expansion, reflecting the **enlargement fatigue** emerging in European governments and public opinion.

DEBATES: ASSESSING ENLARGEMENT

In retrospect, enlargement may appear to have been smooth and inevitable. As we have seen, however, each expansion saw disagreements among member states, reflecting differences in their domestic politics and their national economic and strategic interests. The same was true for the applicants. The debates that ensued were sometimes specific to one enlargement, but more often they were variations on a recurrent theme: Would enlargement enhance prosperity, democracy, and security for current members, applicants, and wider Europe?

The 1970s to 1990s

Fundamental differences between the UK and France blocked the first enlargement for a decade. De Gaulle dismissed the UK as "insular and maritime"; many Britons viewed the EEC as a perfidious project for French continental domination. Although shifts in the politics of each country calmed that debate, disputes arising from UK accession continued past the 1975 referendum to the 1984 budget agreement – indeed, debates over finances and sovereignty marked the Brexit campaign launched in 2016. But membership spurred economic transformation in all three new members and helped resolve Northern Ireland border issues between the Republic of Ireland and the UK.

The southern enlargement saw French and Italian agricultural interests opposed to opening EC markets to imports from the three Mediterranean candidates, while Ireland and Italy feared the diversion of rural development aid. A shared concern for political and strategic stability helped reconcile these differences. Until the euro crisis, the economic benefits of this enlargement were clear and largely uncontested. Democracy was vibrant and security on the EU's southern flank ensured, reinforced by Spain's accession to NATO.

The EFTA enlargement of 1995 was relatively smooth, although it sparked debates in Sweden and Norway. For Finland, EU membership was crucial in overcoming the loss of its ties to the Soviet economy and transforming into a modern state. Austria, too, prospered, although in 2000 its inclusion of a far-right party in government produced a political crisis and a test for democratic values in the EU, which briefly imposed sanctions.

Up to this point, it was commonplace to celebrate enlargement as a series of foreign policy successes, demonstrating and enhancing the attractiveness of the European project. The ensuing expansion cast doubt on that optimistic view.

The "Big Bang" and After

The eastward enlargement raised concerns in France, which suspected that the CEE states would align economically with Germany and politically with the

UK. The Germans argued for enlargement on moral and strategic grounds, while the British hoped that independent-minded new members freed from Moscow's control would help resist the federalist quest for an "ever-closer union" (see Box 13.5).

> **BOX 13.5: EXPLAINING ENLARGEMENT**
>
> 1 *The EU's "vocation"*: The dynamism and ultimate success of the integration project depend on attracting more European states into the Brussels institutions. Some EU members, however, have been unprepared or reluctant when faced with opportunities for expansion.
>
> 2 *Soft power attraction*: The image of European integration as positive and inevitable attracted many applicants, including the southern candidates (for democratic and economic reasons) in the late 1970s and, more recently, the CEE states and Western Balkans. This attraction was, however, undermined by persistent challenges (migration, populism, the euro area financial crisis, and Russia's presence, leading to its full-scale invasion of Ukraine).
>
> 3 *Global change*: Gradual or sudden shifts in the international system can eliminate some options and create new opportunities. Global economic growth and trade liberalization supported the first enlargement. Decolonization reduced the alternatives available to the UK, Portugal, and Spain. The fall of the Berlin Wall removed an obstacle to Eastern Europe's engagement with the EU. But the Brussels-centred post–Cold War order is now challenged by Russia, China, and persistent Euroskepticism.
>
> 4 *External demand*: National interests drive European states to apply for membership. Broad strategic and economic calculations – the UK's historic shift in 1961, the southern three's quest for democracy and development, and the CEE states' distancing from Russia's sphere – reflect pressures from domestic interests. This liberal-institutional account portrays a demand-driven process to which the EU reacts.

> 5 *EU member states' national interests*: These can work for or against enlargement in general and the admission of certain candidates. Examples are the early French opposition to UK accession; member states' worries about security and democracy on their southern flank (Greece, Spain); German and UK support for CEE countries in the 1990s; and Greek opposition to Türkiye. This "realist" interpretation centres on calculations of power and relative advantage, as well as prospects of economic gains from expanded trade.

The dramatic expansion had three features making it difficult to assess: first, the complexity inherent in the number and variety of new members; second, the tendency of detailed economic and political debates over accession to obscure its structural and geopolitical effects; third, the difficulty of tracing these effects amid the crises that have beset Europe since 2008.

The years since the "big bang" have seen impressive economic growth in most new members, who often outperform established members (Vachudova 2014, 126–8). Eastward investment and westward labour migration have – not without controversy – transformed their economies. Democracy is robust in most new members, although questions of human rights, rule of law, and corruption persist in some, including Poland, Hungary, Romania, and Bulgaria. EU membership has given these issues prominence, generating pressure for change but also weakening Brussels' leverage. Ten of the 12 new entrants also joined NATO, adding an explicit security guarantee to that implicit in EU membership. But Russia's hostility to this dual eastward expansion, especially since 2022, has raised new tensions. While the net gains from enlargement are clear for prosperity, democracy, and security, new debates about all three have arisen in the new members and the EU at large.

Türkiye

In 1963, Türkiye signed an Association Agreement with the EEC. Its 1987 membership application was relegated to the bottom of the list as three EFTA states and then 12 others joined over the next 20 years. Finally, in

2005, negotiations began. They proceeded fitfully, hampered by disputes over the divided island of Cyprus and opposition from some EU states. Talks stalled in 2010 amid growing frustration and opposition in Türkiye, reopening in late 2013, languishing again since then. That almost 30 years have passed since Türkiye's initial application highlights the difficulty of this relationship.

Türkiye's history, location, population, modernizing economy, military strength, and NATO membership make it a weighty candidate. But EU governments worry about its record of military coups, authoritarian rule, civil rights abuses, and harsh treatment of its Kurdish minority. Barely concealed anxiety that Sunni-Muslim Türkiye would eventually become the largest EU member by population reinforces Europe's enlargement fatigue.

Cyprus remains a critical issue. In 1974, responding to an attempted coup by Greek officers, Türkiye invaded and occupied the north of the island. It created the Turkish Republic of Northern Cyprus, a state that, to this day, only Ankara recognizes. Türkiye refuses to recognize the Greek–Cypriot-led government in Nicosia as the legitimate government of all Cyprus. Notwithstanding this ongoing conflict, Cyprus joined the EU in 2004. It now wields a veto over Turkish membership.

War in Syria, and the flow of refugees via Türkiye to Europe, intensified the debate over Ankara's EU future. An agreement in March 2016 recognized a shared interest in managing the crisis (and earned Türkiye some concessions on membership), but it is legally flawed and fragile.

The Western Balkans, Moldova, and Ukraine

The EU has taken the lead in the postwar reconstruction of the Balkans. Slovenia joined in 2004. Croatia opened accession negotiations in the fall of 2005 and became the EU's twenty-eighth member in 2013. At the 2003 Thessaloniki summit, the states of the Western Balkans were granted a "European perspective": They would be invited to apply when their economies, laws, and political practices approached EU standards. The remaining six are less advanced than Slovenia and Croatia; in addition to needing fundamental political, legal, and economic reforms, several have outstanding issues relating to borders, corruption, and international recognition (Kosovo). For each, a Stabilization and Association Agreement (SAA), working toward formal recognition of its candidacy, application for membership, and eventual negotiations, is now in force (see Table 13.1). Two have begun negotiations – Montenegro (2012) and

Table 13.1. Stages of accession progress chart: Current applicants (to August 2022)

Countries	SAA and/or other preparatory agreements	Visa liberalization	Application	Candidate status granted	Negotiations opened (or preliminary dialogue)	Chapters opened	Chapters closed (provisionally)
Türkiye	Association Agreement 1963; Customs Union 1995; AP 2001, 2008	Dialogue 2013–	1987	1999	2005, but EU decides not to open 8 chapters (Cyprus issue)	16/33	1
Montenegro	EPA 2007; SAA signed 2007; in force 2010	2009	2008	2010	2012	33	3
Serbia	EPA 2008; SAA signed 2008; in force 2013	2009	2009	2012	2014	18/33	2
North Macedonia	EPA 2006; AP 2008; SAA signed 2001; in force 2004	2009	2004	2005	2021, but start of talks delayed (Bulgarian veto)		
Albania	EPA 2004; SAA signed 2006; in force 2009	2010	2009	2014	2021: Council approval of negotiation framework linked to North Macedonia talks		
Bosnia-Herzegovina	EPA 2008; SAA signed 2008; in force 2015	2010	2016	Potential candidate: "meaningful progress needed"	High-level dialogue 2012–		
Kosovo: sovereignty not recognized by 5 EU states	SAA signed 2015; in force 2016	Dialogue and roadmap 2012; Visa liberalization 2018		Potential candidate, pending progress in reforms	Kosovo-Serbia high-level dialogue 2012–		

Moldova	Association Agreement signed June 2014; in force July 1, 2016	Visa liberalization dialogue January 2011; Visa liberalization April 28, 2014	March 3, 2022	June 23, 2022
Ukraine	Association Agreement signed June 2014; in force September 1, 2017	Visa liberalization dialogue November 22, 2010; Visa liberalization June 11, 2017	February 28, 2022	June 23, 2022

AP: Association Partnership; EPA: European Partnership Agreement; SAA: Stabilization and Association Agreement

Serbia (2014) – while Bosnia-Herzegovina and Kosovo trail the pack, not yet recognized as candidates. The prize for all of Europe is the pacification and development of a notoriously troubled region increasingly prone to Russian and Chinese intervention.

Between 2014 and 2021 the EU did not indicate that it would offer a membership prospective to the countries east of the EU beyond the borders established by the "big bang" enlargement in 2004 and 2007. Those located between the EU and Russia that had been part of the Soviet Union were of particular concern. Russia wanted to keep them in its sphere of influence, while Georgia, Moldova, and Ukraine sought to move closer to the EU. They often tried to adjust their policies and practices to be in a pole position among those seeking to join the EU. Instead, the still-hesitant EU offered them participation in the European Neighbourhood Policy. Georgia, Moldova, and Ukraine therefore signed Association Agreements in 2014 that entered into force in 2016 for the first two and 2017 in the case of Ukraine.

With the outbreak of war in Ukraine in the spring of 2022, however, first Ukraine and then Moldova formally submitted applications for membership. As the war intensified, the EU elected in June 2022 to grant Moldova and Ukraine candidate status, initiating what will likely be a long process. Georgia was asked to complete further economic reforms, particularly in education, energy, and transportation. Additional concerns focused on the quality of Georgia's democracy. It remains unclear whether the EU is offering Georgia a clear membership prospective.

CONCLUSION

Welcoming new members is usually a sign of a political project's success (see Box 13.6 for a comparison with Canada). Recently, however, much of the energy that marked the EU's post–Cold War expansion has dissipated. The wider EU has certainly become more cumbersome, if not weaker, in its decisions and actions. Its impressive economic and geopolitical presence is often countered by the quarrelsome diversity of its broadened membership. Enlargement fatigue now displays two distinct components: "morning-after" regrets expressed since 2004 by some members, and deepening frustration with conditions in the Western Balkans.

BOX 13.6: ENLARGEMENTS COMPARED: EUROPE AND CANADA
Canada emerged in 1867 from negotiations among Britain's eastern North American colonies. Ontario and Quebec were the West Germany and France of this integration project, while New Brunswick, Nova Scotia, and (after 1873) Prince Edward Island resembled Benelux, a customs union of three small European states that helped to found the EEC. Both projects had external support (the UK for Canada, the US for the EEC) and perceived external threats (the US to Canada, the Soviet Union to Europe).

The accession of Manitoba in 1870 was driven by a combination of eastern Canadian interests and the demands of settlers in the Red River region. That of British Columbia in 1871 reflected similar political and economic developments and a concern about preventing northward incursions by an expansionist United States. There are some parallels with the EU's post–Cold War enlargement, although that occurred when the potential regional rival, Russia, was relatively weak and posed no apparent threat.

The disposition of the Northwest Territory (south of the sixtieth parallel) was settled by the creation of Saskatchewan and Alberta in 1905, filling the gap between Manitoba and British Columbia. These two new provinces emerged from eastern Canadian economic interests, concern about US pressures, and new facts on the ground created by immigration. This decisive act of territorial expansion by ambitious, insecure Canada contrasts with European enlargements, which sometimes lacked broad support among member states.

Newfoundland joined Canada in 1949 after a hard-fought referendum, illustrating that when they are part of an accession process, referendums introduce the uncertainties of direct democracy. Recall the two Norwegian rejections (1972, 1994) of accession agreements, but also the substantial victories in Denmark (1972) and in the UK's 1975 vote to stay in the EC. Brexit reminds us that referendums, much as the two held in Quebec (1980, 1995), may also be about secession.

Yukon became a territory in 1898. The Arctic territory of Nunavut was carved out of the Northwest Territories in 1999. These were not enlargements, but political-administrative rearrangements.

Broader European developments also pose questions about the future of EU enlargement. Europe's underperforming economy, the troubles of the euro area, its response to mass migration from the south, and the threat, chaotic negotiation, and messy aftermath of Brexit (see Box 13.7) have weakened the soft power attraction of the European project. The Brussels narrative – that integration is both progressive and inevitable – is further challenged by the rise of populist anti-EU parties in several member states (see Chapter 15). The less attractive the EU appears, the less it can demand of prospective applicants, some of whom may contemplate other options.

BOX 13.7: BREXIT

Article 50 TEU states that "any Member State may decide to withdraw from the Union in accordance with its own constitutional requirements." It must notify the European Council, which will "negotiate and conclude" arrangements for withdrawal as well as for future relations with the EU. EU laws and regulations cease to apply to the departing state from the day the withdrawal agreement enters into force or, failing that, two years from the original notification.

On January 31, 2020, the United Kingdom became the first and so far only member state to withdraw from the EU.

Timeline

2015: British prime minister David Cameron's Conservative Party is re-elected, having promised negotiations with the EU and a "leave or remain" referendum. Subsequently announcing that the talks gained the UK a "special status" in the EU, Cameron launches the referendum campaign confident of victory.

2015–16: Stoking fears of surging immigration and loss of sovereignty ("take back control"), the "Brexiteers" run a campaign appealing to rising English nationalism. The "remain" side runs a less professional, if more honest, campaign stressing longer-term costs of leaving.

June 23, 2016: Referendum sees slim (51.8 per cent) majority favouring Brexit.

> July 2016: His strategy having backfired, Cameron resigns and is replaced by Theresa May.
>
> March 29, 2017: The United Kingdom invokes Article 50, starting the two-year clock. Reduced to a minority in June, May's government struggles for over a year to devise an exit plan that is acceptable both to the EU negotiators and to quarrelling factions in her own party.
>
> November 2018: After four months of negotiations, the EU's leaders approve a British plan that would extract the UK from the Customs Union, Single Market, CAP, and other legacies of a 47-year relationship.
>
> January 2019: Ministers favouring a "quick, clean break" with the EU reject the agreement and lead a no-confidence vote in Parliament. May's government survives, but in the first three months of 2019 Parliament rejects the agreement three times, as the two-year deadline looms.
>
> July 2019: Boris Johnson succeeds May as prime minister, declaring that, deal or no deal, the UK will leave the EU on October 31, a deadline later extended to January 31, 2020.
>
> December 12, 2019: A decisive Conservative election victory clears the way for Parliament to pass the EU Withdrawal Bill on January 23, 2020.
>
> 2020: The UK formally leaves the EU on January 31. The UK and the EU take the remainder of the year to negotiate arrangements to govern their future relations. Possibilities range from "no deal" to a close commercial and regulatory framework maintaining many of the UK's former EU ties, albeit reconfigured for a future bilateral relationship. A version of the latter option prevails: The EU–UK Trade and Cooperation Agreement is signed on December 30, 2020.

Russia's actions since the autumn of 2013 have revealed flaws in the liberal assumptions underpinning the eastward expansion of Western-based institutions such as the EU. What seems a benign win-win situation when viewed from Brussels resembles a zero-sum game of *realpolitik* when viewed from Moscow. The comfortable belief that enlargement has been a triumph of EU external policy is challenged by the mixed aftermath of the 2004–7 enlargement, second thoughts throughout the EU about the wisdom of continuing expansion, and Russia's responses in Ukraine and the Balkans. Russia's wholesome invasion of Ukraine, since February 2022, has compelled the EU to rethink the geopolitical premises underlying many of its policies, not least those relating to enlargement.

REVIEW QUESTIONS

1. What trends and events in international political and economic relations influenced each round of enlargement and helped to shape its outcome?
2. Analyze the main ideas and national interests motivating the applicants and the member states in any of the rounds of enlargement discussed in this chapter.
3. What roles are typically played in the enlargement process by each of the EU institutions identified in this chapter? How have those roles evolved, and on what legal powers and political resources are they based?
4. To assess the effects of enlargement on applicant states, established members, or on the European project in general, what kind of evidence would you look for?

EXERCISES

1. Review the European Commission's Neighbourhood Policy and Enlargement website. Compare the status of current candidate countries. What progress has each candidate made toward accession and at what speed? What are the most important obstacles to accession that remain in each case? Based on these insights, where is the EU most likely to enlarge next?
2. Consider the role of conditionality in applying the EU's enlargement criteria. Do some research on the theoretical debates surrounding the EU's power as leverage on the European continent. What do these debates tell us about the EU as a source of economic, political, and normative power?

REFERENCES AND FURTHER READING

Epstein, R., and J. Wade. 2014. "Eastern Enlargement Ten Years On: Transcending the East-West Divide?" *JCMS: Journal of Common Market Studies* 52 (1): 40–56. https://doi.org/10.1111/jcms.12174.

Friis, L., and A. Jarosz-Friis. 2002. *Countdown to Copenhagen: Big Bang or Fizzle in the EU's Enlargement Process?* Copenhagen: Danish Institute of International Affairs.

George, S. 1994. *An Awkward Partner: Britain in the European Community.* Oxford: Oxford University Press.

Grabbe, H. 2014. "Six Lessons of Enlargement Ten Years On: The EU's Transformative Power in Retrospect and Prospect." *JCMS: Journal of Common Market Studies* 52 (S1): 40–56. https://doi.org/10.1111/jcms.12174.

Granell, F. 1995. "The European Union's Enlargement Negotiations with Austria, Finland, Norway and Sweden." *JCMS: Journal of Common Market Studies* 33 (1): 117–41. https://doi.org/10.1111/j.1468-5965.1995.tb00520.x.

Greer, S., and L. Laible. 2020. *The EU after Brexit.* Manchester: Manchester University Press.

Kelemen, R.D., A. Menon, and J. Slapin. 2014. "Wider and Deeper? Enlargement and the European Union." *Journal of European Public Policy* 21 (5): 647–63. https://doi.org/10.1080/13501763.2014.897745.

Kitzinger, U. 1973. *Diplomacy and Persuasion: How Britain Joined the Common Market.* London: Thames and Hudson.

Mayhew, A. 1998. *Recreating Europe: The European Union's Policy towards Central and Eastern Europe.* Cambridge: Cambridge University Press.

Mungiu-Pippidi, A. 2014. "The Transformative Power of Europe Revisited." *Journal of Democracy* 25 (1): 20–32. https://doi.org/10.1353/jod.2014.0003.

Ruge, M. 2021. "Six Principles to Guide EU Action in the Western Balkans." *IAI Commentaries*, July 21.

Tsoukalis, L. 1981. *The EC and Its Mediterranean Enlargement.* London: Allen and Unwin.

Vachudova, M.A. 2014. "EU Leverage and National Interests in the Balkans: The Puzzles of Enlargement Ten Years On." *JCMS: Journal of Common Market Studies* 52 (1): 122–38. https://doi.org/10.1111/jcms.12081.

Verdun, A., and G.E. Chira. 2011. "The Eastern Partnership: The Burial Ground of Enlargement Hopes?" *Comparative European Politics* 9 (4/5): 448–66. https://doi.org/10.1057/cep.2011.11.

Verdun, A., and O. Croci. 2005. *The European Union in the Wake of Eastern Enlargement: Institutional and Policy-Making Challenges.* Manchester: Manchester University Press.

Wallace, W. 1976. "Wider but Weaker: The Continued Enlargement of the European Community." *The World Today* 32 (3): 104–11.

Zielonka, J. 2015. *Europe Unbound: Enlarging and Reshaping the Boundaries of the European Union.* London: Routledge.

Zweerer, W., and I. van Loon. 2021. "The Limits of EU Transformational Power in the Western Balkans." *Clingendael Spectator*, June 2.

14

European Neighbourhood Policy

Assem Dandashly and Gabriela Chira

READER'S GUIDE

In the wake of its expansion to the east and south, the European Union (EU) faced complex external challenges. It acquired frontiers with countries that were less developed economically, often did not have consolidated democratic systems, and might pose security concerns. The EU has attempted to address these challenges through the European Neighbourhood Policy (ENP). The ENP provides assistance to neighbouring states and seeks to export EU values but does not promise eventual EU membership. With the increased challenges posed by various regime changes and conflicts in the east and the Arab uprisings and their aftermath in the south, the EU had to upgrade its policies and instruments within the ENP framework. This chapter discusses the origins, areas of focus, and instruments of the ENP as well as the challenges and recent developments. It reflects on the ENP as it was occurring until early 2022. The Russian invasion of Ukraine sped up having Ukraine and Moldova become candidate countries. Thus their status has changed since. However, in this chapter they are still discussed as part of the ENP.

INTRODUCTION

Based on fundamental EU principles such as a commitment to democracy, the rule of law, and respect for human rights beyond its borders, the **European Neighbourhood Policy (ENP)** was launched in 2003 and began to take shape in the years following the 2004 EU enlargement. As an external relations instrument of the EU, the main goal of the ENP is to strengthen the EU's relation with its eastern and southern neighbours at both bilateral and multilateral levels. The EU aims to influence political and economic transformations in those countries and to help them become more integrated into the EU system, without offering membership. Through the ENP, the EU seeks to guarantee its own security through trade and strong economic associations, and to establish better relations with well-governed states.

With the 2004 enlargement, the EU acquired borders with Belarus, Moldova, and Ukraine and expanded its borders with Russia. In addition, it got closer to the Middle East and North Africa (MENA) through the accession of Cyprus and Malta. The EU has sought to avoid the emergence of new dividing lines between itself and its new neighbours, but at the same time it has been unwilling to accept them as full members. Its aim, rather, has been to be surrounded by stable and well-governed states. In this way, they would help the EU secure its borders from irregular migration and terrorism and allow for productive economic exchange.

The ENP includes 16 countries:

- In the south: Algeria, Egypt, Israel, Jordan, Lebanon, Libya, Morocco, the Palestinian Authority, Syria, and Tunisia
- In the east: Armenia, Azerbaijan, Belarus, Georgia, Moldova, and Ukraine

This group of countries is very heterogeneous; it encompasses countries in which revolutions and wars have been raging. In the east, there are the longstanding tensions between Armenia and Azerbaijan and various other conflicts, which include the Russian–Georgian war in 2008, the Russian annexation of Crimea in 2014, and the full-scale Russian invasion of Ukraine in 2022. In the south, the Arab uprisings and their aftermath placed increased pressure on the EU in terms of humanitarian and development aid, security, the refugee crisis (triggered by the Syrian war), and illegal migration.

This chapter reviews the origins and rationale of the ENP as well as its development; it also examines its instruments and policy focus. The first section discusses the dilemma that led to the creation of the ENP as well as the reasons for its format (enlargement template) and for including both the eastern and southern neighbours. Next, the chapter offers a discussion of the specific EU approach to governing its relations with its eastern and southern neighbourhood. Finally, the chapter concludes with an assessment of the ENP and current debates.

HISTORY AND ORIGINS OF THE ENP

Relations between the EU and its neighbours have developed significantly over the past three decades. Following the dissolution of the Soviet Union in 1991 and the war in Yugoslavia in the mid-1990s, the EU could not turn its back on Central and Eastern Europe (see Chapters 9, 13, and 18). There were important political, economic, and social issues at stake with the collapse of communism across the region. In addition to its expansion through enlargement, the EU had to work on the geopolitical stabilization and economic revitalization of its new neighbours to curb nationalist conflict and counteract irregular migration.

In its own way, the ENP hence forms part of a strategy to consolidate geopolitical stability and to reduce the chance of war in the area. The effective resolution of security threats emerging from the neighbourhood is also important for the EU's legitimation in the eyes of its population (Theme 3 of this book). The ENP supports institutional development and capacity building in the ENP states and provides financial support. Central to this assistance is the fulfillment of democratic and human rights standards. The ENP builds on the approach developed for the eastern enlargement, whereas the Copenhagen criteria lay down explicit political and economic conditions for membership (see Chapter 13). The same idea of conditionality is also applied in the ENP, however.

With the completion of the accession negotiations with Central and Eastern European countries, discussions regarding the impact of enlargement on neighbouring states that remained outside the EU intensified. The Commission articulated a Communication on "Wider Europe" in March 2003 (COM (2003) 104), followed by a strategy paper on the ENP published in May 2004 (COM (2004) 373). In Thessaloniki, Greece, in June 2003, the EU heads of state or government endorsed the initiative with a view to developing these new policies, enabling the furthest possible form of association short of membership. The EU's focus was not only directed to the east; it also wanted to strengthen its relations with its southern neighbours and move beyond the old bilateral commercial agreements that went back to the 1960s and 1970s.

THE DEVELOPMENT OF THE ENP SINCE 2004

The European Council in Copenhagen in December 2002 committed to enhancing relations with its neighbours. The wish of the European Commission was that the EU's external border should not become a "new dividing line" (COM (2004) 373, 3). The EU aspired to become a major player working together with those states who share a land or sea border with the EU to increase their prosperity and stability. It intended to do so by building a "ring of friends," as then Commission president Romano Prodi put it. Given the difficulties facing the neighbourhood region, this action looked more like an attempt to manage a neighbouring "ring of fire." Indeed, considering the geography (see, for instance, Map 1.1 in Chapter 1) as well as the situation in which each country finds itself from a political, economic, security, and ethnic point of view, it is clear that the area has been filled with many challenges.

The objective of forging closer relations with the EU's neighbours first called for strengthening relations with Russia, as well as for enhanced relations with Ukraine, Moldova, Belarus, and the southern Mediterranean. However, Russia declined to be incorporated into the ENP and opted for developing bilateral cooperation with the EU on an allegedly more "equal" basis (see Chapter 18). In June 2004, after the "Rose Revolution" in Georgia, the ENP was further extended to the South Caucasus republics of Armenia, Azerbaijan, and Georgia. As for the states that are formal candidates for EU membership, they are not part of the ENP. Moldova and Ukraine were given candidate status following the full-scale Russian invasion of Ukraine in 2022.

The extreme variety of the countries involved in the ENP made it challenging to develop a coherent, one-size-fits-all policy. There was a need to adapt the cooperation mechanisms to the particularities of each country. The EU's main condition for cooperation was the partner countries' willingness to carry out reforms, to improve their democratic and human rights standards, to enhance trade with the EU, to advance environmental issues, as well as to increase cooperation with the EU on issues such as energy, transportation,

Table 14.1. ENP official agreements

ENP partner	Association Agreement (AA)	Preferential trade arrangements	Action plan
Southern Neighbours			
Algeria	September 2005	Yes	No
Egypt	June 2004	Yes	Yes
Israel	June 2000	Yes	Yes
Jordan	May 2002	Yes	Yes
Lebanon	April 2006	Yes	Yes
Libya	No		
Morocco	March 2000	Yes	Yes
Palestinian Authority	Interim AA July 1997	Yes	Yes
Syria	No		
Tunisia	March 1998	Yes	Yes
Eastern Neighbours			
Armenia	Partnership and Cooperation Agreement (PCA), July 1999	Not yet	Yes
Azerbaijan	Partnership and Cooperation Agreement (PCA), July 1999	Not yet	Yes
Belarus	No		
Georgia	June 2014	DCFTA	Yes
Moldova	June 2014	DCFTA	Yes
Ukraine	June 2014	DCFTA	Yes

and migration. In exchange, the EU offered financial assistance, technical help and know-how, and political support.

Although the ENP was designed to adapt to the specific situation of each country, many of the partner countries would have desired even more flexibility. Of the 16 ENP countries, 12 are currently participating fully as partners in the ENP, having concluded a bilateral agreement, usually including preferential trade arrangements – including so-called Deep and Comprehensive Free Trade Agreements (DCFTAs) – and an Action Plan (see Table 14.1). At the time of writing, no agreements have been concluded with Algeria, Belarus, Libya, and Syria.

While the ENP proposes the same policy instruments to the southern and eastern partners, it is important to distinguish the two groups of countries. Each group has had specific EU member states advocating on their behalf inside the EU. The southern partners found a loyal ally in France, whereas the eastern partners were strongly supported by the Nordic states (especially Sweden), the Baltic States, Poland, as well as the Czech Republic. Within the ENP, a differentiation emerged between the two groups because their allies lobbied for its protégés' interests, leading the ENP toward further differentiation.

Although the EU presents the ENP as a "jointly owned initiative" of the EU and the partner countries, and its implementation requires action by both parties, the ENP has been criticized as being unilaterally oriented toward the ambitions of the EU at the expense of the interests and needs of partnering countries. The ENP is explicitly based on the EU's values, as defined in Articles 2 and 3 TEU – regardless of whether these values are in line with the partnering countries' values. As the European Commission pointed out in its 2004 strategy paper on the ENP, the "level of ambition of the EU's relationships with its neighbours will take into account the extent to which [the EU's] values are effectively shared." It also outlined a clear political conditionality for the participation of neighbouring countries in the ENP that are not yet considered ready. For instance, with regard to countries of the South Caucasus, the Commission proposed that the "EU should consider the possibility of developing Action Plans … in the future on the basis of their individual merits with respect to the strengthening of democracy, the rule of law and respect for human rights" (European Commission 2004). The strategy paper also outlined a few priorities for the individual ENP Action Plans, which were designed to strengthen commitment to EU values. These included "strengthening democracy and the rule of law, the reform of the judiciary and the fight against corruption and organized crime; respect of human rights and fundamental freedoms, including freedom of media and expression, rights of minorities and children, gender equality, trade union rights and other core labour standards, and fight against the practice of torture and prevention of ill-treatment; support for the development of civil society; and co-operation with the International Criminal Court" (European Commission 2004).

Security concerns have also played a major role in the ENP. Various high-profile terrorist attacks in Paris in 2015, in Brussels, Nice, and Berlin in 2016, and in London, Barcelona, Manchester, and Paris in 2017 played a role in increasing the willingness to cooperate more closely in the political and security arena in addition to the existing cooperation in the fields of democracy promotion, economy, and trade. In the EU's analysis, economic, political, and social failures of local regimes have contributed to the increase in terrorist behaviours and attacks all over the globe (Youngs 2006). Since the launch of the European Security Strategy in 2003, the EU has emphasized that the ambition to share borders with stable and well-governed states to the east and south of the EU is also a matter of security (see Chapters 9 and 18).

THE EASTERN AND THE SOUTHERN NEIGHBOURHOOD (UNTIL 2010)

While the general objectives and principles of the ENP apply to all ENP states, the EU has developed specific initiatives for each of the two "groups" of neighbours in the east and in the south.

Relations with its *eastern neighbours* are governed through the **Eastern Partnership (EaP)**. The EaP was formally launched in Prague in May 2009; it addresses the six Eastern European partners – Armenia, Azerbaijan, Belarus, Georgia, Moldova, and Ukraine. The EaP relies on the ENP in terms of resources but creates distinct institutions within the ENP framework, and most importantly new Association Agreements (AAs). These include DCFTAs, comprehensive programs funded by the EU to improve partners' administrative capacity, "mobility and security pacts" allowing for easier travel to the EU, while at the same time stepping up efforts to combat corruption, organized crime, and illegal migration. These pacts also cover the upgrading of asylum systems to EU standards and the establishment of integrated border management structures. The long-term goal is a full visa waiver, provided that conditions for well-managed and secure mobility are in place.

Other aspects of the agreements with eastern neighbours include labour mobility (with the aim of further opening the EU labour market), enhanced energy security (support for investment in infrastructure, better regulation, energy efficiency, and early warning systems to prevent disruption of supply), as well as multilateral policy platforms for dialogue on democracy, good governance, and stability. In addition, the EaP foresees more cooperation on specific issues within the EU's Common Foreign Security Policy and Common Security Defence Policy (see Chapter 9), including the participation of partner countries in EU missions and the coordination of diplomatic activities. As we can see, while the objectives of the EaP AAs are very ambitious, they remain rather vague.

As for the *southern neighbours*, and following the launch of the ENP by a few years, relations with the EU were structured through the **Union for the Mediterranean (UfM)**. First proposed by French president Nicolas Sarkozy in 2007, the UfM was created in July 2008 as a bi-regional international organization encompassing 43 member countries. The UfM is institutionally separate from the EU but includes all EU member states and the European Commission as members (see Box 14.1); it is based in Barcelona and endowed with its own staff and resources to carry out specific projects in various domains. The main objectives of the UfM are to enhance multilateral relations, increase co-ownership of the process, and launch concrete projects visible to the citizens.

> **BOX 14.1: MEMBERS OF THE UNION OF THE MEDITERRANEAN**
> - European Union:
>   - The 27 EU member states (the United Kingdom was a member until it left the EU)
>   - The European Commission
> - Mediterranean partner countries:
>   - 15 member states: Albania, Algeria, Bosnia and Herzegovina, Egypt, Israel, Jordan, Lebanon, Mauritania, Monaco, Montenegro, Morocco, Palestinian Authority, Syria (self-suspended on June 22, 2011), Tunisia, and Türkiye
>   - Libya as an observer state
>   - The League of Arab States involved in all meetings and preparatory meetings

The UfM focuses on four priority areas: politics and security, economics and trade, sociocultural affairs, and justice and interior affairs. In addition, the UfM's Marseille summit in 2008 identified six specific projects: de-pollution of the Mediterranean, maritime and land highways, civil protection, alternative energies, higher education and research, and the Mediterranean business development initiative. Despite the political capital invested, the UfM has thus far produced limited results. The complex institutional arrangement has created obstacles, rather than easing political cooperation. Furthermore, the prioritization of economic cooperation pushed political values to the backseat. In addition, the complicated MENA regional conflicts, especially the Arab–Israeli conflict, did not make it easy for UfM to succeed in the area of political cooperation. All these issues did not allow the relations between the EU and its southern neighbours to develop beyond the already existing cooperation.

POST-2010 DEVELOPMENTS IN THE ENP

With the Lisbon Treaty, which came into force in 2009, the ENP was given official treaty status. Article 8 TEU states that "the Union shall develop a special relationship with neighbouring countries ... founded on the values of the Union." The creation of the high representative and vice-president of the Commission and the European External Action Service (EEAS), however, changed little in the design and implementation of the ENP, which still had its own budgetary line and dedicated commissioner. Important changes in the ENP resulted from external circumstances. In the southern neighbourhood, the Arab uprisings (sometimes called the Arab Spring), beginning in early 2011, led to the toppling of few regimes. In the eastern neighbourhood, Russia became more assertive; for instance, in 2013 Russia put pressure on its Eastern European neighbours to join the new Russian-dominated Eurasian Economic Union instead of signing EU Association Agreements. The situation escalated in 2013–14 in Ukraine: Following the ousting of the country's Russia-friendly president, Russia annexed Crimea and a violent conflict developed in eastern Ukraine between government forces and pro-Russian separatist groups. In February 2022, Russia launched a full-scale war on Ukraine and invaded further parts of its territory, following eight years of conflict that had included the Russian annexation of Crimea (2014) and war in Donbas between Ukraine and Russian-backed separatists.

In light of the challenges raised by both regions, the European Commission and the high representative presented a formal review of the ENP in November 2015. The ENP was redirected to focus on the most salient issues, such as security, political and economic stability, as well as development. Despite the fact that the language on democracy promotion and human rights had been toned down, the document emphasized that "the EU's own stability is built on democracy, human rights and the rule of law and we will continue to make the case for these universal values" (European Commission 2015). This new approach also informed the EU's Global Strategy (EUGS), which was launched in July 2016 (see Chapters 9 and 18).

The EU acknowledged the need for more pragmatism in its 2016 Global Strategy, which states that the security of the EU "at home entails a parallel interest in peace in our neighbouring and surrounding regions" (European Union 2016). This pragmatism implies an increased interest in dealing with problems at their source by preventing conflicts, promoting human security, and addressing the root causes of instability in the MENA and eastern neighbours. With the revised ENP and the EUGS, the EU aims to follow a more pragmatic approach, focusing on issues such as security, socioeconomic problems, infrastructure, and disaster management. By trying to promote development and human security, the EU aims to contribute to finding solutions that it considers to be at the root of the challenges posed by terrorism, illegal migration, as well as energy and climate change. There is less focus on democracy, which the EU plans to promote where the situation is more favourable, for instance in Georgia and Tunisia (until 2020). One of the main aspects highlighted in the EUGS is the clear differentiation among ENP countries; the EU expresses a willingness to be more involved in areas of common concern with countries that show more openness to cooperation.

Building on the revised ENP, the EU sought to strengthen its cooperation with both the eastern and southern neighbourhoods: A framework for the Eastern Partnership policy beyond 2020 was adopted in March 2020 in an EEAS and Commission Joint Communication. It focuses on dealing with the common challenges facing the EU and the eastern neighbours. It also focuses on measures to achieve such goals as strengthening resilience, advancing sustainable development, and placing importance on local societies (European Commission 2020).

In the southern neighbourhood, a strengthened Mediterranean partnership is a strategic priority. In February 2021 a joint communication by the EEAS and the European Commission on the renewed partnership with the southern neighbourhood was adopted. In order to achieve its goals, an "Economic and Investment Plan for Our Southern Neighbours" (European Commission 2021) was put forward.

TYPES OF AGREEMENTS AND ASSOCIATIONS

How does the ENP work in practice? Partner countries agree with the EU on an ENP Action Plan declaring their commitment to democracy, human rights, rule of law, good governance, market economy principles, and sustainable development. While following a similar template and drawing on the same toolkit (see Box 14.2), each individual agreement is different and reflects most key policy dimensions (such as democratization, trade, visas, energy links, and security), the specific realities in each of the eastern and southern neighbours, and their willingness to engage more closely with the EU.

The ENP Action Plans (called Association Agendas for the EaP countries) set out the partner country's agenda for political and economic reforms, with short- and medium-term priorities of three to five years, reflecting each country's needs and capacities as well as its interests and those of the EU. The Action Plans build on existing legal agreements with the EU – Partnership and Cooperation Agreements or Association Agreements. Implementation is monitored through committees set up by these agreements. Once a year the EEAS and the European Commission publish ENP progress reports assessing the progress made toward the objectives of the Action Plans.

BOX 14.2: ENP ACTION PLANS AND FINANCIAL INSTRUMENTS

- Action Plans
  - Main instrument of the ENP; backed by financial and technical assistance
  - List of different priorities for engagement and reforms the partner country should undertake
  - Developed for each individual partner country, defined by common consent, thus varying from country to country
  - Covers periods of three to five years
  - Focused on several priorities:
    - Commitment to shared values
    - A more effective political dialogue
    - Economic and social development policy (legislative and regulatory approximation to the Internal Market)
    - Trade and Internal Market (approximation to the Internal Market, regulatory convergence, market opening)
    - Justice and Home Affairs (border management)
    - Connecting the neighbourhood (safety and security of energy supply, transport links, the environment, information and communications technology, research and innovation)
    - People to people, programs, and agencies
  - EU offers expert advice, financial assistance programs, monitoring, and evaluations on progress achieved

- Main financing instruments
  - Neighbourhood, Development and International Cooperation Instrument, with specific programs for the eastern and southern neighbourhood, introduced in 2021 to replace the European Neighbourhood Instrument
  - Facility for Euro-Mediterranean Investment and Partnership
  - Neighbourhood Investment Facility, which became an integral part of the European Fund for Sustainable Development as the Neighbourhood Investment Platform in September 2017
- Main technical assistance instruments
  - Technical Assistance & Information Exchange
  - Twinning mechanism
  - Competitive and Innovation Program
  - 7th Research Framework Program

Following the 2011 review of the ENP, the EU introduced a new variant of conditionality, the "more-for-more principle." It states that the EU will develop stronger partnerships and offer greater incentives to countries that make more progress toward democratic reform, including free and fair elections, freedom of expression, freedom of assembly and freedom of association, judicial independence, a continued fight against corruption, and democratic control over the armed forces. Partners embarking on political reforms in these areas would be offered – in addition to the incentives available to other partners – the 3Ms: money, market, and mobility:

- Money: A greater share of EU financial support
- Market: Economic integration and development through preferential trade arrangements
- Mobility: Mobility partnerships and visa facilitation

The outcome of the ambitious 3Ms remains debatable. The money spent on the ENP (see Box 14.3) may prove insufficient to compensate for the massive injection of resources invested by other regional players (Russia, Türkiye, the Gulf monarchies, China, and so on). In addition, a certain competition over resources has emerged between the EU's eastern and southern partners and their respective mentors inside the EU.

Questions can also be raised about the other two elements of the 3Ms. With respect to markets, the opening of the EU to goods from neighbouring countries (especially from the south) has become politically more contentious in light of the economic crisis. Regarding mobility, growing fears of irregular migration considering the refugee crisis and various terrorist attacks have made the EU's pledge on visa facilitation ever more complex. In addition, the crisis in and over Ukraine has laid bare the fact that the predominantly technocratic approach represented by the DCFTAs could no longer compensate for the lack of a solid foreign and security policy framework in which the ENP is embedded (see also Chapters 9 and 18).

DEBATE: HOW SUCCESSFUL HAS THE ENP BEEN?

Assessing the success of the ENP depends on the issue area we focus on. While the outcome of democracy promotion has failed (or witnessed limited success)

> **BOX 14.3: BUDGET FOR THE ENP**
> - In the EU's 2021 annual budget, €11.7 billion was allocated to the Neighbourhood, Development and International Cooperation Instrument (NDICI). That amounts to approximately 7 per cent of the entire EU budget. The NDICI funds EU programs all over the world, not just in the neighbourhood.
> - The NDICI has a geographic pillar that focuses on specific world regions (€8.9 billion); a thematic pillar that focuses on issues such as supporting democracy, human rights, or stability and conflict prevention (€938 million); a rapid response pillar that allows the EU to respond to emerging crises (€469 million); as well as an "emerging challenges and priorities cushion" (€1.4 billion).
> - Within the regional pillar, €730 million is allocated to the eastern neighbourhood and €1.5 billion to the southern neighbourhood. These allocations amount to less than 1.5 per cent of the EU budget.
>
> Source: Definitive adoption (EU, Euratom) 2021/417 of the European Union's general budget for the financial year 2021, https://eur-lex.europa.eu/eli/budget/2021/1/oj

in most cases, in other areas, such as cooperating on matters such as border control, security, trade, and so on, the ENP has been more successful. Moreover, one can notice the differences in the levels of cooperation between the EU and its neighbours not only across the two regions (east and south) but also within the same region. Most new neighbours of the enlarged EU have clearly been attracted by the idea of economic cooperation with the EU and having access to its market. However, some ENP states, such as Ukraine and Moldova, aimed for more, hoping that faithfully applying the EU's "conditionality" might open the door to membership. Initially, these states saw their hopes shattered with the ENP. While the AAs with the eastern neighbourhood states acknowledged their "European aspirations," they carefully avoided an explicit accession prospective. However, with the full-scale Russian invasion of Ukraine, what seemed impossible became an option, as the EU accepted Ukraine and Moldova as candidate countries. For Georgia, it offered the possibility of attaining candidate status after fulfilling certain conditions. In contrast to some of the eastern neighbours, the issue of EU membership has not been a priority or a concern for the southern neighbours. In this part of the neighbourhood, the EU has not been willing to renegotiate the terms of what the ENP offers: close cooperation with the EU, but no EU accession.

Regarding trade, the results of the ENP have been relatively positive. For example, looking first at the eastern neighbourhood, Azerbaijan's exports (mainly oil and gas) to the EU increased by 918 per cent between 2004 and 2014. By comparison, Azerbaijan's exports to Russia increased by only 362 per cent in the same period. Following the full-scale Russian invasion of Ukraine and in its attempt to reduce its reliance on Russian gas, the EU signed a deal in July 2022 with Azerbaijan to double its imports of natural gas by 2027. Furthermore, the EU is the major trading partner with Azerbaijan (around 36.7 per cent of Azerbaijan's total trade in 2021). The EU is Azerbaijan's largest exporter and second-largest importer (51 per cent of Azerbaijan's exports and 16 per cent of Azerbaijan's imports). Moldova's exports to the EU more than doubled between 2004 and 2014, while the country's exports to Russia declined by 15 per cent (Gaub and Popescu 2015, 50). However, when looking at the post-2009 trade relations, aside from Moldova, we notice a declining trend in exports to the EU. Imports into ENP states from the EU have been consistent over the last decade, with a slight increase in the case of Moldova (see Figure 14.1).

Trade is also an area where improvements are substantial in the relations between the EU and its southern neighbours. The EU is the main trading partner of the MENA countries, with 60–75 per cent of their exports absorbed. Almost all states in the region have doubled and sometimes tripled the volume of their trade with the EU over the last two decades. With the exception of Syria, which has been subject to economic sanctions due to the ongoing civil war, all states have evolved in a positive direction in this regard. For example, in 2020 EU countries accounted for most of the trade activity (imports and exports) of Algeria, Morocco, and Tunisia (see Figure 14.2).

EU policies regarding conflict resolution in the neighbourhood have been limited. This does not mean that the EU has not been active or has underutilized the tools it possesses for this purpose (financial/technical aid, diplomacy and mediation, peace keeping/building missions, military missions, sanctions, and so on). However, the EU's action/inaction, and what tools it uses to fulfill its goals, depends on the margin of action it has (1) in the targeted country, (2) internationally/regionally (for instance, because of potential conflicts with other players such as Russia), and (3) within the EU (for instance, with respect to coherence of member state interests). The issue of coherence

Figure 14.1. Trade in goods between the EU and eastern ENP states (2009–2020)
(a) ENP-East countries' exports of goods from the EU (% of total exports)

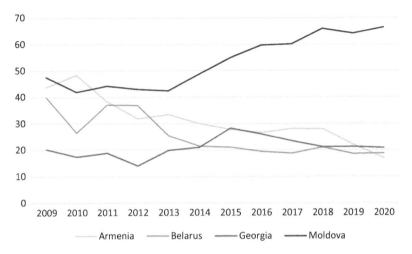

(b) ENP-East countries' imports of goods from the EU (% of total imports)

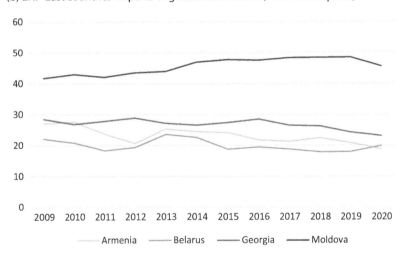

Source: Eurostat, https://ec.europa.eu/eurostat/statistics-explained/index.php?title=European_Neighbourhood_Policy_-_East_-_statistics_on_trade_in_goods_with_the_EU#The_EU_as_a_trading_partner_for_the_ENP-East_countries

Figure 14.2. Trade in goods between the EU and southern ENP states (2020, percentage of total imports/exports)

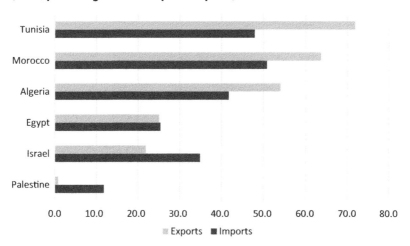

Source: Eurostat, https://ec.europa.eu/eurostat/statistics-explained/index.php?title= European_Neighbourhood_Policy_-_South_-_international_trade_in_goods_statistics

among EU member states has been problematic, for instance, in responding to the Arab uprisings, which challenged the EU's ability to be active in conflict resolution and promoting democracy and stability in the region.

Perceived security threats for the EU emerging from its neighbourhood are due both to external and internal factors. External threats are raised by other international actors, such as Russia or China. Internal threats emerge from political instability in the neighbourhood countries – their problems with terrorism, crime, religious extremism, political oppression, violations of human and civil rights, or corruption. In addition, the problems of instability, poor economic performance, climate change, etc., result in more illegal migrants from Sub-Saharan Africa and elsewhere trying to cross via the neighbouring countries to the EU. Also, terrorist attacks of the past two decades have contributed to the feeling among EU policy-makers that more cooperation is needed in the political/security arena and not only in the field of economics and trade.

In short, almost all ENP countries had to meet the EU's targets in highly conflictual political contexts, which led to the diversion of resources, destruction of capital, and a realignment of political priorities (Gaub and Popescu 2015). Not taking into consideration the difficulties and hardships that both regions are going through does not allow for meeting targets and achieving much progress at different levels. There can be no doubt that without a continuous cycle of violence, all those states would have developed further. Ending internal and external conflicts will therefore be a critical prerequisite to unlocking the potential that exists in the region. This constellation forces the EU to prioritize security at the expense of other issues, such as democracy. Furthermore, with the post–Arab uprising events, and also the full-scale Russian invasion of Ukraine, security will likely remain a key EU priority.

These challenges are reflected in scholarly debates about the ENP. Many of these debates have focused on the EU's attempts to transfer its own rules and procedures to the target states through policy conditionality, socialization, and capacity building. Through enlargement and through the ENP, the EU exports rules and institutional models, and it thus exercises what can be described as "external governance" over its partners. Schimmelfennig and Sedelmeier (2004) argue that the EU adopts an external incentive model when dealing with other countries. In the case of enlargement policy, the ultimate reward is EU membership (see Chapter 13). By contrast, under the ENP membership is not among the incentives the EU has to offer. Rather, the EU offers other rewards, such as access to the Single Market, financial support, and trade liberalization. These rewards are not as attractive as membership. This creates an asymmetric structure in which the EU has the upper hand and seems to gain more benefits from the ENP than many neighbouring countries.

The external governance framework thus helps to decode mechanisms, institutional models, and conditions of effectiveness of the ENP. It assesses the transfer and extension of the EU's internal rules and policies short of formal membership. The external governance framework also allows for an analysis of the considerable variation and lack of uniformity of this transfer of rules and institutional frameworks across countries, regions, and policy fields.

Finally, it makes it possible to place the ENP in a broader discussion of EU external relations, which include not only enlargement and policies for the EU's neighbourhood, but also external trade policies (see Chapter 12), the Common Foreign and Security Policy (see Chapter 9), and the external dimensions of EU Justice and Home Affairs policies (see Chapter 8).

Other scholars have focused on the normative power of the EU to understand the ENP. The commitment of the EU to its normative standards is reflected in the ENP's emphasis on values such as peace, democracy, human rights, good governance and transparency, economic liberalization, as well as sustainable development. Taking its own *acquis communautaire* as a starting point, the EU has sought to push its norms and standards onto its neighbours to create a ring of like-minded friends and partners that adhere to common norms. In a way, the EU uses its image as a "force for good" to push for democratic and peaceful change in its neighbourhoods. Yet many scholars have been critical of this Eurocentric approach. Scholars call for a decentring of EU foreign policy – especially with its neighbours – demanding a non-Eurocentric (decolonial) approach that takes the local context, values, and demands into consideration, instead of imposing norms that sometimes do not adhere to the beliefs and cultures of those countries.

These considerations help us understand why policy implementation in response to ENP rules is difficult if the domestic situation in targeted countries is not favourable and the local elites do not take these reforms themselves. For any change or reforms demanded by the EU to be effective, the domestic situation is the main determinant of its success. Therefore, the EU can try to empower local elites who share similar reformist ideas who can demand local institutional and democratic change.

CONCLUSION

As shown by the impact of current developments in neighbourhood countries on EU affairs, the ENP may not provide a comprehensive answer to the EU's goals and worries regarding its own and its neighbours' prosperity, stability, and security. Also, the ENP has not offered a security blanket for peace and stability, even if it may have been intended to do so. There are ongoing concerns about keeping eastern "apples" and southern "pears" in the same basket. In terms of effectiveness, there are large disparities between countries and groups of partner countries. These disparities create tensions over policy priorities and financial allocations. It is therefore virtually impossible to assess how "successful" and "effective" the ENP has been in advancing the EU's objectives.

What is certain, however, is that the ENP has constructively supported pre-existing reform processes in some participating countries. While cooperation in the areas of economics and trade as well as security has been advanced, the same does not hold in the area of democracy promotion, human rights, and civil liberties. The EU has shied away from seriously pushing for democratization due to the ongoing fear of terrorism and security threats as well as the chaos unleashed in the wake of the Arab Spring in some countries on its southern borders. This fear pushed the EU to apply a very soft approach instead of strict conditionality. As security remains the main concern for the EU, the EU continues to avoid imposing sanctions on ENP countries with problematic democratic and human rights situations. Instead, it focuses more on a soft power approach and cooperates with them on economic and security issues. ENP countries gain economic and institutional benefits when the EU maintains secure borders while also guaranteeing further cooperation on immigration, organized crime, and border control issues with each neighbouring partner country.

The ENP remains a policy in the making, but with potential for development. It was not conceived as, and it is not a launch pad for, greater expansion of the EU. This explains why the EU could not use the ENP to exercise strong conditionality for democracy, human rights, and the rule of law, as it did during the eastern enlargement in the 1990s and early 2000s. The ENP is also not formally a part of the EU's Common Foreign and Security Policy, where the focus is less on values and more on pragmatism. Instead, it encompasses elements of both. Given the various challenges in its neighbourhood that have been outlined in this chapter, it is clear that the ENP needs to become less compartmentalized, more comprehensive, and above all more consistent in its approach. It would be beneficial to avoid the vague language and the promises regarding democracy promotion while the EU's main interest lies in other areas that are more pressing, such as security, for example.

REVIEW QUESTIONS

1 Why does the EU have an interest in forging close relations with states in its neighbourhood, even when it does not want to offer these states EU membership?
2 How does the EU's conditionality exercised under the ENP differ from conditionality under its enlargement policy? What impact does this difference have on the likelihood of encouraging reform in the targeted states?
3 What are the advantages and disadvantages of governing the relationships with the 16 ENP countries based on the ENP's unitary framework?
4 While the commitment to values like democracy and rule of law is prominent in the EU's programmatic documents on the ENP, these values have in practice often been subordinated to security concerns. How can we explain this outcome?

> **EXERCISES**
>
> 1 Peruse the European Commission's ENP and enlargement website. Select a country covered under the Eastern Partnership and a country covered under the Mediterranean Initiative. Compare the Action Plan for the two countries. What issues are prominent in both countries? What issues are country specific?
> 2 Partner with another student to debate the success of the ENP. Should conditionality always be linked to eventual membership? Should the EU concentrate its efforts on economic partnership only, or is it obliged to stipulate criteria for "good governance" and democracy in the non-EU region?

REFERENCES AND FURTHER READING

Börzel, T., A. Dandashly, and T. Risse. 2015. "External Actors' Responses to the 'Arabellions': The EU in Comparative Perspective – Introduction." *Journal of European Integration* 37 (1): 1–17. https://doi.org/10.1080/07036337.2014.975986.

Börzel, T.A., and T. Risse. 2012. "From Europeanisation to Diffusion: Introduction." *West European Politics* 35 (1): 1–19. https://doi.org/10.1080/01402382.2012.631310.

Bouris, D., D. Huber, and M. Pace, eds. 2021. *Routledge Handbook of EU–Middle East Relations*. London: Routledge.

Bouris, D., and T. Schumacher, eds. 2017. *The Revised European Neighbourhood Policy: Continuity and Change in EU Foreign Policy*. Basingstoke, UK: Palgrave Macmillan.

Dandashly, A., and C. Kourtelis. 2020. "Classifying the Implementation of the EU's Normative Power in Its Southern Neighbourhood: The Role of Local Actors." *Journal of Common Market Studies* 58 (6): 1523–39. https://doi.org/10.1111/jcms.13051.

Dandashly, A., and G. Noutcheva, eds. 2022. "Whose Norms? Competing Political Models and Patterns of Diffusion in the European Neighbourhood." *Democratization* 29 (3): 138. https://doi.org/10.1080/13510347.2021.2012161.

Del Sarto, R.A., and T. Schumacher. 2005. "From EMP to ENP: What's at Stake with the European Neighbourhood Policy towards the Southern Mediterranean?" *European Foreign Affairs Review* 10 (1): 17–38. https://doi.org/10.54648/EERR2005002.

European Commission. 2003. "Wider Europe – Neighbourhood: A New Framework for Relations with Our Eastern and Southern Neighbours." COM (2003) 104 final. http://aei.pitt.edu/38141/1/com_(2003)_104.pdf.

European Commission. 2004. "European Neighbourhood Policy – Strategy Paper." COM (2004) 373 final. https://eur-lex.europa.eu/legal-content/EN/TXT/?uri =celex%3A52004DC0373.
European Commission. 2015. "Review of the European Neighbourhood Policy." JOIN (2015) 50 final. https://ec.europa.eu/neighbourhood-enlargement /document/download/6d6a2908-9d79-42ad-84ae-9122d0f863a3_en.
European Commission. 2020. "Joint Communication to the European Parliament, the Council, the European Economic and Social Committee and the Committee of the Regions: Eastern Partnership Policy beyond 2020. Reinforcing Resilience – An Eastern Partnership That Delivers for All." SWD (2020) 56 final. https:// eur-lex.europa.eu/legal-content/EN/TXT/?uri=CELEX%3A52020JC0007.
European Commission. 2021. "Joint Communication to the European Parliament, the Council, the European Economic and Social Committee and the Committee of the Regions: Renewed Partnership with the Southern Neighbourhood. A New Agenda for the Mediterranean." SWD (2021) 23 final. https://eur-lex.europa.eu /legal-content/EN/TXT/?uri=JOIN:2021:2:FIN.
European Union. 2016. "Shared Vision, Common Action: A Stronger Europe: A Global Strategy for the European Union's Foreign and Security Policy." Brussels.
Fisher Onar, N., and K. Nicolaïdis. 2013. "The Decentring Agenda: Europe as a Post-Colonial Power." *Cooperation and Conflict* 48 (2): 283–303. https://doi.org /10.1177/0010836713485384.
Freybourg, T., S. Lavenex, F. Schimmelfennig, T. Skripka, and A. Wetzel. 2009. "EU Promotion of Democratic Governance in the Neighbourhood." *Journal of European Public Policy* 16 (6): 916–34. https://doi.org/10.1080/13501760903088405.
Gaub, F., and N. Popescu. 2015. "The EU Neighbours 1995–2015: Shades of Gray." Chaillot papers. Paris: EU Institute for Security Studies.
Kelley, J. 2006. "New Wine in Old Wineskins: Promoting Political Reforms through the New European Neighbourhood Policy." *Journal of Common Market Studies* 44 (1): 29–55. https://doi.org/10.1111/j.1468-5965.2006.00613.x.
Keukeleire, S., and S. Lecocq. 2018. "Operationalising the Decentring Agenda: Analysing European Foreign Policy in a Non-European and Post-Western World." *Cooperation and Conflict* 53 (2): 277–95. https://doi.org/10.1177/0010836718766394.
Keuleers, F., D. Fonck, and S. Keukeleire. 2016. "Beyond EU Navel-Gazing: Taking Stock of EU-Centrism in the Analysis of EU Foreign Policy." *Cooperation and Conflict* 51 (3): 345–64. https://doi.org/10.1177/0010836716631777.
Lavenex, S., and F. Schimmelfennig. 2009. "EU Rules beyond EU Borders: Theorising External Governance in European Politics." *Journal of European Public Policy* 16 (6): 791–812. https://doi.org/10.1080/13501760903087696.
Schimmelfennig, F., and U. Sedelmeier. 2004. "Governance by Conditionality: EU Rule Transfer to the Candidate Countries of Central and Eastern Europe." *Journal of European Public Policy* 11 (4): 661–79. https://doi.org/10.1080/1350176042000 248089.
Schumacher, T., A. Marchetti, and T. Demmelhuber, eds. 2018. *The Routledge Handbook on the European Neighbourhood Policy*. London: Routledge.

Smith, K.E. 2005. "The Outsiders: The European Neighbourhood Policy." *International Affairs* 81 (4): 757–73. https://doi.org/10.1111/j.1468-2346.2005.00483.x.

Verdun, A., and G.E. Chira. 2008. "From Neighbourhood to Membership: Moldova's Persuasion Strategy towards the EU." *Southeast European and Black Sea Studies* 8 (4): 431–44. https://doi.org/10.1080/14683850802556418.

Whitman, R.G., and S. Wolff. 2012. *The European Neighbourhood Policy in Perspective: Context, Implementation, and Impact*. Basingstoke, UK: Palgrave Macmillan.

Youngs, R. 2006. *Europe and the Middle East: In the Shadow of September 11*. Boulder, CO: Lynne Rienner.

PART THREE

Challenges

15
Democracy in the European Union

Achim Hurrelmann

READER'S GUIDE

Critics of the European Union (EU) often argue that it suffers from a "democratic deficit." In light of this criticism, this chapter examines the EU's democratic processes and the way citizens make use of them in practice. In a first step, it takes stock of the existing mechanisms for citizen participation: European Parliament (EP) elections, elections and referendums at the national level, and procedures for civil society involvement. In a second step, it returns to the normative question of whether there is a democratic deficit in the EU. It reviews some of the main arguments often made in this debate and examines proposals for making the EU more democratic.

INTRODUCTION

When the European integration process was set in motion in the 1950s, the powers of the original European communities – the European Coal and Steel Community, European Economic Community, and European Atomic Energy Community – did not extend beyond the regulation of limited and relatively technical aspects of economic life. These predecessor institutions of today's

EU were more bureaucratic than political in nature, and hence concerns about their democratic quality were not seen as particularly pressing. This situation changed in the following decades, as more legislative powers were transferred to the EU level, and European integration began to impact an increasing number of policy fields. Although the EU has to date not witnessed a major "democracy movement" among its citizens, the architects of European integration concluded that a democratization of EU institutions was needed to safeguard political support for the integration project (Rittberger 2005). This perception led to successive rounds of reforms aimed at improving the democratic quality of EU decision making.

As a result of these reforms, the EU now possesses more mechanisms for democratic input than any other institution of regional or global governance. Many of these mechanisms have obvious similarities to state-based democracy. Yet as we shall see in this chapter, the way in which they operate – and in which politicians, parties, and citizens make use of them – reflects the peculiar non-state character of the EU (Theme 2 of this book). This peculiarity of democratic institutions and practices in the EU has given rise to debates about whether the EU is sufficiently democratic. As public controversies about European integration have become more intense (Theme 3 of this book), democracy has emerged as one of the main issues of contention. While some observers praise the EU's democratic achievements, others portray EU governance as lacking meaningful mechanisms of participation and accountability.

This debate is of more than just academic significance. For Euroskeptics, the EU's alleged **democratic deficit** has become an important rallying cry. In the United Kingdom's Brexit referendum of 2016, the depiction of the EU as an undemocratic "superstate" that takes away power from the member states' democracy was a prominent theme. The referendum result in favour of the UK's withdrawal from the EU suggests that such an argument struck a chord with many voters (see Chapter 13). Referendums in other member states have also repeatedly resulted in majorities against deeper European integration. These referendum results suggest that the democratization of the EU to date has not been sufficient to alleviate concerns about a loss of democratic quality caused by European integration.

This chapter approaches the question of democracy in the EU from two angles. The first part of the chapter looks at the existing mechanisms for democratic input in EU politics – such as elections at the European and national levels, referendums on EU issues, and other opportunities for citizen participation. It also discusses how Europeans have made use of these opportunities in practice. The second part then turns to normative debates about the EU's democratic quality. It reviews competing positions on whether there is a democratic deficit in EU politics and introduces proposals for making the EU more democratic.

DEMOCRATIC LIFE IN THE EU

Democracy means "government by the people." In the context of modern, large-scale political systems where day-to-day decisions cannot be taken by the citizens directly, it consists of institutionalized procedures that enable citizen participation in selecting political leaders, making substantive policy decisions, and holding politicians to account. Democratic states possess a considerable range of such procedures. In Canada, for instance, citizens can vote in elections at the municipal, provincial, and federal levels. In addition, they can also seek to influence politicians between elections, for instance by forming associations that lobby for specific policies. The citizens of EU member states have similar options, but for them the EU constitutes an additional political level at which they may choose to participate.

What options do citizens have to influence politics at this level? This section discusses three channels of democratic input: (1) elections to the EP; (2) national elections and referendums that shape member states' positions in EU decision making; and (3) formalized procedures for civil society input between elections. We discuss each of these channels in turn and then examine how citizens use them in practice.

European Parliament

The EP is a supranational legislature composed of 705 members from all 27 member states. Since 1979, its members have been directly elected every five years. EP elections take place at the same time in all member states, usually over a period of four days. Details of the elections differ from one member state to the next. All use a proportional representation electoral system, but they employ different variants of that system type. Furthermore, the ballot looks different in each member state; it usually lists the same parties that also dominate national politics. While most of these are associated with a European-level political party and a specific political group in the EP (see Chapter 3), this association is not always highlighted explicitly on the ballot.

EP elections are significant in EU politics for two main reasons. First, they influence the nomination of the president of the European Commission.

Article 17(7) TEU requires the European Council to "take into account" the EP elections when deciding on its nominee. The interpretation of this provision is contested. In the run up to the 2014 and 2019 EP elections, the major EU-level political parties (with the exception of Euroskeptics) each named their so-called **Spitzenkandidat** (a German term for "lead candidate") for the office of Commission president and insisted that the European Council must nominate the candidate of the largest party. However, many member state leaders disagreed with this interpretation. They argued that the European Council can nominate whomever it chooses, as long as it takes note of the election outcome. After the 2019 EP election, the latter interpretation won out. The European Council's nominee – Ursula von der Leyen – was a member of the European People's Party, the party that had won the most EP seats, but she was not her party's Spitzenkandidat. Her nomination was nevertheless approved by the EP. This dispute, which may re-emerge in future EP elections, arises in part because the EU mixes elements of parliamentary and presidential political systems in an unconventional blended system. Since there is no standard template that applies to the EU's democratic system, some of its aspects remain contested (see Box 15.1).

BOX 15.1: PARLIAMENTARY POWERS IN CANADA, THE UNITED STATES, AND THE EU

Parliaments play different roles in relation to the executive, depending on whether they operate in a parliamentary or a presidential system. In parliamentary systems, such as Canada, citizens elect the (lower house of) parliament (House of Commons), which in turn elects the head of the executive (prime minister). It is up to the parliament to nominate and approve the head of the executive, whose political survival depends on continued parliamentary support. The parliament may vote the head of the executive out of office with a simple majority. If this happens, the government falls.

By contrast, in presidential systems, such as the United States, both the parliament (Congress) and the head of the executive (president) are elected by the citizens, in separate elections. The parliament is largely restricted to legislative functions. It cannot choose, nor bring down, the head of the executive. The only exception is a process of impeachment: a special procedure reserved for crimes committed in office, which requires more parliamentary support than a simple majority.

The EU displays elements of both systems. As in a parliamentary system, the head of the EU's main executive institution – the Commission president – is not directly elected. Rather, Article 17(7) TEU establishes an explicit link between EP elections and the Commission presidency. However, while the EP must give its consent to the Commission president (as an individual) and to the College of Commissioners (as a group), it may not formally nominate the president or the individual commissioners. The Commission president is nominated by the European Council; the individual commissioners by the member states.

Once the Commission has taken office, it does not require the continuous backing of an EP majority. Therefore, the Commission, which tends to be politically heterogeneous as its members come from a range of different parties, does not need to cater its policies to a specific parliamentary majority. Rather it can seek to find majorities for its legislative proposals on a case-by-case basis. The EP can only bring down the Commission through a motion of censure – a procedure reserved for cases of gross misconduct that requires a majority of two-thirds of the votes cast (Article 234 TFEU). Overall, the EP thus operates in a way that resembles a parliament in a presidential system.

The second reason for the significance of EP elections lies in the legislative powers of the EP. While the EP originally had only a consultative role in legislation, the EU's ordinary legislative procedure (OLP) that became the norm with the Lisbon Treaty (Article 294 TFEU) requires legislative acts to be approved by both the EP and the Council of the EU. The EP also possesses co-decision powers over the EU budget (see Box 15.2). In EP committees and in the plenary, legislative proposals are carefully scrutinized and may be substantially amended or even blocked. EP political groups have emerged as powerful and remarkably cohesive legislative actors. There remain only two aspects in which the EP's legislative powers fall short of those of typical parliaments at the national level. First, the EP cannot formally initiate EU legislation; this role is left to the European Commission. Second, in a small number of policy fields the Council remains the main decision maker. These fields include areas that are considered particularly sensitive to member state sovereignty, for instance tax harmonization or security and defence policy. In these areas, the OLP is not applied. However, over the past decades, the number of such exceptions has been continuously reduced.

> **BOX 15.2: THE EP AND THE EU BUDGET**
> The EU's annual budgetary process is laid out in Article 314 TFEU. While defined as a special legislative procedure, this provision gives the EP full co-decision over the EU budget, most notably the power to amend the Commission's draft and to reject the budget if no satisfactory compromise with the Council of the EU can be found. The EP also must give its consent to the Multiannual Financial Framework (MFF), the EU's seven-year budget plan that sets the parameters for each year's budget. However, it cannot amend the MFF (Article 312 TFEU). The budgetary powers of the EP are also restricted by the fact that the EU has no taxation powers – its budget is financed largely by member state contributions – and is explicitly prohibited from running a budget deficit (Article 310 TFEU).

Given how much the influence of the EP on EU decision making has increased in recent decades, the main limitations of EP elections, as a mechanism of democratic control over EU politics, no longer rest in insufficient parliamentary powers. Rather, they stem from the way in which EP elections have been treated by political parties and voters. EP elections have traditionally been characterized as **second-order elections** (Reif and Schmitt 1980), which are interpreted by parties and voters primarily with a view to what the election means for national politics (where first-order elections are held). Parties in their EP election campaigns tend to emphasize domestic issues, assuming that voters can be mobilized more effectively by messages that refer to member state–level topics. Voters treat EP elections as less important than national elections, which has resulted in lower turnout and a greater willingness to use the election to cast a protest vote intended primarily as a signal to national governments (for instance, by voting for new or extreme parties as a sign of opposition to current policies). Both processes reinforce each other; they can be observed since the very first EP election in 1979.

The second-order character of EP elections matters for the quality of democracy at the EU level. It weakens the representative connection between members of the European Parliament (MEPs) and their voters. After all, when the second-order logic applies, MEPs win or lose their seats less because of their position on EU-level controversies, but rather as a result of domestic factors such as the popularity or unpopularity of the national government. However, the most recent EP elections may signal a turnaround. The 2019 election campaign witnessed more debates than previous campaigns about the future direction of European integration, and voter turnout increased by more than eight percentage points compared to 2014. This development was triggered in part by fears that Euroskeptic parties might make dramatic gains, which in the end did not materialize. These changes suggest that EP elections may gradually be losing their "second-order" character. This process will take time.

National Democratic Processes

The second channel of democratic input in the EU relies on democratic processes at the member state level. These include national elections but also referendums on EU affairs that have recently generated much attention. Let's examine both in turn.

National elections are relevant in the EU context because they may bring to power a government that promises to take a particular position on EU affairs, especially through its participation in the EU's intergovernmental institutions (Council of the EU and European Council). While the life and death of national governments in EU member states was traditionally only tangentially affected by EU politics, as EU-level issues played a subordinate role in national election campaigns, this pattern has slowly begun to change. Particularly in the context of the euro area financial crisis and the refugee crisis, incumbent national governments became targets of electoral punishment for their EU-level policy choices. It is important to note, however, that the EU's decision-making system greatly limits the ability of any one national government to bring about change in EU policies, especially if qualified majority voting rules are applied. As a result, changes in national governments matter for EU policy-making only to a limited extent.

National elections also influence the composition of national parliaments, which are tasked with holding their governments to account for their behaviour at the EU level. National parliaments have often been described as "losers" of European integration, as some of their legislative powers have been shifted to the EU. In response, they have sought to play a more active role in legislative processes at the supranational level. All national parliaments in the EU have established European Affairs Committees (EACs) that monitor EU legislative activities with respect to potential implications for domestic policies. In advance of key decisions in the Council or European Council, EACs consult with government ministers. In some member states they can issue binding mandates for the government's voting behaviour. Ultimately, if such mandates are not respected, parliaments may withdraw their support from the government. Nevertheless, governments usually retain a large manoeuvring room in the EU's intergovernmental procedures. One reason is that national parliaments are often unable to keep track of the EU's complicated policy processes. A second reason is that parliamentary majorities may hesitate to tie their own government to overly restrictive mandates, which would limit the government's flexibility in EU-level negotiations.

In light of these limitations of parliamentary control over national governments, an additional procedure was introduced with the Lisbon Treaty in 2009: an "early warning mechanism" that allows coalitions of national parliaments to level a direct protest against legislative initiatives at the EU level (see Box 15.3). This procedure requires the cooperation of various national parliaments, which in practice is difficult to bring about within the required timeframe.

While national elections are at best an indirect mechanism for democratic control over EU decision making, national referendums are a device to give citizens a direct voice on EU-related issues. Such referendums have been held in most member states (see Table 15.1). They are sometimes influenced by the popularity of national governments, but they usually involve spirited – though not always well-informed – debates about fundamental questions of European integration. They can hence be interpreted as important statements about the EU's legitimacy.

In the last two decades, national referendums have repeatedly resulted in the rejection of European integration initiatives. In some cases (such as

> **BOX 15.3: THE EARLY WARNING MECHANISM**
>
> Protocols No. 1 and No. 2 TFEU allow national parliaments to protest directly against legislative initiatives proposed by an EU institution (usually the Commission). Such protests must be grounded in the principle of subsidiarity, which states that the EU should only legislate on issues that cannot be addressed at a lower political level. According to the early warning procedure, the national parliaments of all member states have eight weeks to review each proposal for EU legislation. If one-third of them raise objections, the proposal must be reviewed ("yellow card"). If a majority of national parliaments protest, the proposal can immediately be voted down either by the Council or by the EP ("orange card"). However, the mechanism does not compel the EU's legislative institutions to drop the proposal in question.

the Danish referendum on the Maastricht Treaty and the Irish referendums on the Nice and Lisbon Treaties), the member state in question ended up holding a second vote on a slightly revised proposal, containing certain clarifications or opt-outs. In other cases, the rejection was more consequential. The negative vote on the proposed Treaty Establishing a Constitution for Europe in France and the Netherlands in 2005 put an end to the EU's constitutional project. Similarly, the Brexit referendum of 2016 led to the first-ever withdrawal of a member state from the EU. These cases illustrate that EU-related referendums provide a highly consequential opportunity for national electorates to leave their imprint on EU politics – an opportunity that has repeatedly been seized by Euroskeptic mobilization. However, when assessing the value of referendums as a democratic device, it is important to keep in mind that the range of issues on which referendums are held is limited. Usually, they are called in individual states to decide on questions of a constitutional nature, such as membership or treaty amendments. Referendums have never taken place simultaneously in all member states. They are not available as an avenue of democratic participation in day-to-day EU policy-making.

Table 15.1. Referendums in member states on EU issues (rejections highlighted)

Member state	Year	Subject	Yes vote	Turnout
Austria	1994	Accession to the EU	67%	82%
Croatia	2012	Accession to the EU	66%	44%
Czech Republic	2003	Accession to the EU	77%	55%
Denmark	1972	Accession to the European Communities	63%	90%
	1986	Single European Act	56%	75%
	1992	Maastricht Treaty	49%	83%
	1993	Maastricht Treaty, Edinburgh Agreement	57%	87%
	1998	Treaty of Amsterdam	55%	76%
	2000	Economic and Monetary Union	47%	88%
Estonia	2003	Accession to the EU	67%	64%
Finland	1994	Accession to the EU	57%	74%
France	1972	Accession of Denmark, Ireland, and the UK to the European Communities	68%	60%
	1992	Maastricht Treaty	51%	70%
	2005	Constitutional Treaty	45%	69%
Hungary	2003	Accession to the EU	84%	46%
	2016	Acceptance of refugee resettlement quotas	2%	44%[a]
Ireland	1972	Accession to the European Communities	83%	71%
	1987	Single European Act	70%	44%
	1992	Maastricht Treaty	69%	57%
	1998	Amsterdam Treaty	62%	56%
	2001	Nice Treaty	46%	35%
	2002	Nice Treaty	63%	50%
	2008	Lisbon Treaty	45%	53%
	2009	Lisbon Treaty	67%	58%
	2012	European Fiscal Compact	60%	51%
Latvia	2003	Accession to the EU	67%	73%
Lithuania	2003	Accession to the EU	91%	63%
Luxembourg	2005	Constitutional Treaty	57%	88%
Malta	2003	Accession to the EU	54%	91%
Netherlands	2005	Constitutional Treaty	39%	63%
	2016	Association Agreement with Ukraine	38%	32%
Poland	2003	Accession to the EU	77%	59%

(Continued)

Table 15.1. Referendums in member states on EU issues (rejections highlighted) *(Continued)*

Member state	Year	Subject	Yes vote	Turnout
Slovenia	2003	Accession to the EU	90%	60%
Slovakia	2003	Accession to the EU	92%	52%
Spain	2005	Constitutional Treaty	77%	42%
Sweden	1994	Accession to the EU	53%	83%
	2003	Economic and Monetary Union	42%	83%
UK	1975	Continued membership in European Communities	67%	64%
	2016	Continued membership in the EU	48%	72%

[a] Turnout below the required threshold

Procedures for Civil Society Participation

In addition to calling on the whole population to vote in regular elections (and occasionally referendums), democratic political systems have established procedures that are designed to allow groups of citizens to voice – and infuse into the decision-making process – their opinions on political issues about which they care particularly strongly. Such procedures for direct, policy-specific input from civil society supplement, but cannot replace, the electoral mechanism.

In the EU, procedures of this kind are widely used. Consultation mechanisms by the European Commission have the longest tradition. They aim primarily at interest associations active at the EU level. Such associations include business organizations (such as BusinessEurope), trade unions (for example, the European Trade Union Confederation); and civil society groups (such as the European Anti-Poverty Network). In addition to EU-level associations, individual corporations, national interest groups, regions of the member states, international organizations, think tanks, as well as private law firms and consultants are also active in lobbying EU institutions. The Commission follows a longstanding policy of systematically incorporating them in the policy-making process by asking them to provide information and inviting them to serve on advisory committees. From the Commission's perspective, their inclusion not only improves the quality of its legislative proposals, but also provides an avenue for civil society participation. To level the playing field for competition between various interests (such as business and consumers), the Commission provides financial assistance to less well-organized groups that supports them in setting up structures at the EU level. In recent years, the Commission has enacted measures that seek to ensure the transparency of its consultation procedures, among them a Transparency Register that lists organizations active in Brussels (see Box 15.4).

> **BOX 15.4: TRANSPARENCY REGISTER**
> The Transparency Register lists more than 12,400 organizations (as of January 2023) that interact with EU institutions to conduct lobbying and policy advice activities (https://ec.europa.eu/transparencyregister/public/homePage.do). Registration is voluntary; organizations that register must sign a code of conduct that bars unethical lobbying practices. In return, the organizations listed in the database receive invitations to all consultations the Commission initiates within their fields of interest.

In addition to the incorporation of interest associations into the policy-making process, the EU also possesses mechanisms that allow for the participation of individual, non-organized citizens. One such mechanism is the Commission's online consultations on legislative initiatives (https://ec.europa.eu/info/law/better-regulation/have-your-say_en), which invite submissions by both individuals and organizations. Another is the European Citizens' Initiative (ECI, https://europa.eu/citizens-initiative/home_en). This procedure, introduced with the Lisbon Treaty (Article 11 TEU), allows 1 million EU citizens, by signing a petition, to invite the Commission to make a specific legislative proposal. The procedural requirements for ECIs are demanding; at the time of writing only six ECIs have been successful in collecting the required number of signatures. An example is a proposal for a ban on glyphosate, a weed killer marketed under the commercial name Roundup. But even a successful collection of signatures does not compel the Commission to initiate EU-level legislation.

Procedures for the direct participation of associations and individuals in the EU are unquestionably diverse and innovative, yet they face limitations when it comes to securing an unbiased connection between the preferences of citizens and the outcome of EU decision making. Well-organized interest groups, including professional lobbyists – especially those from Northern and Western Europe – dominate the process. Their positions do not reflect the breadth of preferences that exist in society. What is more, EU institutions are selective in which civil society proposals they actually incorporate into legislation. Mechanisms of civil society participation are therefore primarily an agenda-setting device; they do not ensure democratic accountability.

EU Democracy and the Citizens

Our overview of mechanisms for democratic input in EU decision making confirms that over the past decades the EU has taken important steps toward democratization. The EU now possesses three genuine channels of democratic input, each of which provides opportunities for citizens to influence EU decisions (see Figure 15.1). We have also seen, however, that each of these channels has limitations when it comes to securing effective participation in selecting political leaders, making substantive policy decisions, and holding decision makers to account.

Some of these limitations are due to the institutional setup of the EU. It is important to understand that the EU is not a majoritarian democracy (as Canada or other Westminster systems are), in which a parliamentary majority faces few obstacles in shaping policies to its liking. Rather, the EU is a **consensus** democracy with extensive checks and balances designed to protect minorities (Lijphart 1999). This system has been adopted because the EU's population is much less homogeneous than that of most nation states. Most importantly, member states vigorously seek to protect their interests and identities in EU decision making. As a result, EU decision making usually proceeds through lengthy negotiations, involving the member states (inside and outside of the Council), the EP, and the Commission. For democratic participation, this implies that none of the three democratic channels shapes EU decision making in a direct and unmediated way. While all of them feed democratic input into EU procedures (especially the OLP), the final version

Figure 15.1. Three channels of democratic input in the EU

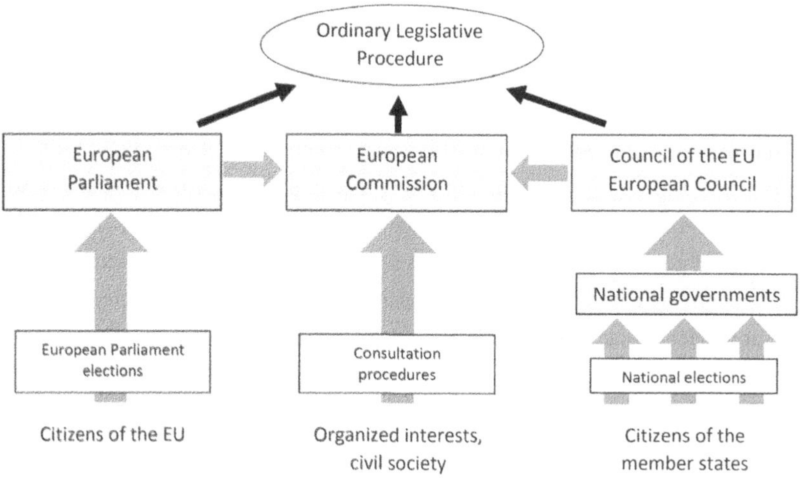

```
                    Ordinary Legislative
                        Procedure
                            ▲
          ┌─────────────────┼─────────────────┐
   European           European          Council of the EU
   Parliament   ──▶   Commission   ◀──  European Council
        ▲                 ▲                    ▲
        │                 │            National governments
        │                 │                    ▲
European Parliament   Consultation        National elections
    elections          procedures
   
  Citizens of the EU  Organized interests,   Citizens of the
                       civil society          member states
```

Source: Author's design

of most EU policy documents is ultimately agreed to in negotiations behind closed doors, such as the OLP's "trilogues" (see Chapter 3). Perhaps unavoidably, this process of building interinstitutional compromise remains opaque to outside observers.

In addition to these institutional factors, the limitations of the EU's democratic mechanisms also derive from the specific ways in which citizens, political parties, and interest groups participate in EU-level politics. These patterns of participation are shaped by the non-state character of the EU. Until about three decades ago, most observers argued that EU-level politics elicited a vague form of generalized support but very little detailed interest in the population. This constellation was described as a **permissive consensus** (Lindberg and Scheingold 1970). In this model, the European population supports the broad goals of European integration but cares little about the details, thus leaving political elites far-reaching discretion over EU policy choices. Since the early 1990s, the EU has become more explicitly politicized in the population. Issues that surround European integration have become more salient and, in some instances, controversial. This politicization has coincided with the rise of populism and Euroskepticism as political forces (see Box 15.5). Some say that the permissive consensus has been replaced by a "constraining dissensus" (Hooghe and Marks 2009), a constellation in which societal controversies about European integration have become so heated that political leaders no longer dare to push integration forward. At the same time, the extent to which EU governance has become politicized should not be exaggerated. Even after Brexit, political discussions about a member state withdrawing from the EU have not gained traction outside the UK. There are few instances in which specific EU policy issues have captured the imagination of a sizable proportion of citizens so that they clearly rally around it. In many respects, EU governance still remains an elite affair. While most citizens are well aware of the political importance of the EU, many feel they do not fully understand its unconventional, non-state political system and policy processes. Such knowledge deficits deter many citizens from participating more actively in EU democracy.

BOX 15.5: EUROSKEPTICISM

The term *Euroskepticism* is used to describe parties, social movements, and political attitudes that explicitly oppose European integration, either in principle ("hard Euroskepticism") or in its current form ("soft Euroskepticism"). Euroskeptic positions can be found both on the left (in favour of state intervention) and on the right (in favour of free markets) of the political spectrum. Liesbet Hooghe and Gary Marks (2018) argue that Euroskepticism cuts across these traditional political differences and adds a new dimension to political competition, which pits green-alternative-libertarian (GAL) positions, which tend to view transnational connections as an opportunity, against traditional-authoritarian-national (TAN) views, which perceive them as a risk. Indeed, Euroskeptic positions are usually grounded in the perception that European integration has undermined national sovereignty and identity, democracy, or established systems of social protection. Ironically, the EU's own democratic mechanisms – including EP elections – have often provided particularly prominent venues for Euroskeptics to voice their positions.

DEBATE: IS THERE A DEMOCRATIC DEFICIT IN EU POLITICS?

While these characteristics of democratic life in the EU have been analyzed comprehensively, there is no consensus on how they should be interpreted from a normative vantage point. The question here is whether the limitations of the EU's democratic mechanisms seriously undermine the quality of EU decision making. When answering this question, we should keep in mind that even consolidated state democracies, such as Canada, the United States, or the EU's own member states, can be criticized for democratic imperfections. For example, citizens do not all participate in politics, some interest groups have privileged access to power, and various decision makers are not directly accountable to the voters. Is the situation in the EU significantly worse?

One of the most prominent authors who has answered this question with a resounding "no" – and hence argues against the democratic deficit thesis – is Andrew Moravcsik (2002). He advances three main arguments. First, he claims that there is less of a need for democratic control in the EU than in typical Western states, because the EU's legislative and executive powers are more constrained, its budget and bureaucracy are smaller, and its decision-making processes include extensive checks and balances. Second, he points out that EU decision makers are not unaccountable, especially due to the existence of EP and national elections that serve as mechanisms of democratic control. Third, he argues that the main reason why citizens are not more involved in the EU is not a deficiency of the EU's democratic institutions but derives from the fact that the EU's main powers – trade liberalization, technical regulation, agricultural policy, and so on – generate little interest in the population. By contrast, most of the issues that citizens really care more about, such as social policy, law and order, or taxes, are dealt with at the member state level. Unless the EU gains powers in such areas, Moravcsik argues, it is unrealistic to expect more participation from the citizens.

Other scholars are less optimistic about the state of democracy in the EU than Moravcsik. One line of argument advanced by them focuses on the lack of meaningful political competition about EU policy and political personnel (Føllesdal and Hix 2006). As we have seen, EP elections are often not fought about EU-related issues. Because of the nomination of EU leaders by the European Council, they also do not serve as a forum in which rival European elites – a European government and a European opposition – would battle for leadership positions. The most important decisions about EU policy and personnel are, in other words, not made electorally. A second line of argument points to the impact of European integration on democracy at the national level and raises concerns about national democratic processes being hollowed out. The limited powers that national parliaments have acquired in EU decision making do not fully compensate for this loss. Taking both arguments together, Vivien Schmidt (2006) describes the system of decision making at the EU level as "policy without politics" (important decisions are made without adequate democratic debate), while national decision making increasingly turns into "politics without policy" (intensive debates are conducted, but crucial decisions are taken elsewhere).

The more pessimistic view on the state of democracy in the EU raises the question of what (if anything) can be done to make the EU more democratic. Three types of answers have been given to this question in the EU studies literature:

- The first answer claims that it is impossible to further democratize the EU, as the European population is just not ready for more EU-level democracy. The main reason is that Europe lacks a cohesive *demos*, that is, a community of citizens who identify strongly with the EU and other Europeans. Authors arguing for this no-demos-thesis point out that citizens' identification with the EU is weaker than their attachment to their nation state (see Figure 15.2). This weakness of a European demos, in these authors' view, is the main reason why democratic processes at the EU level remain impoverished. Citizens who do not feel attached to the EU are not motivated to participate in EU decision making. Furthermore, they will be unwilling to contribute resources for the benefit of other Europeans and will not accept majority decisions in which they are overruled by nationals of other member states (Greven 2000). According to the no-demos theorists, there is little that can be done about this conundrum. Since collective identities change only in the long run, there are no short-term solutions to the EU's democratic deficit.
- The second answer takes a more optimistic view; it argues that targeted institutional changes at the EU level can encourage greater citizen participation in EU politics. Simon Hix (2008) is a prominent advocate of this position. Among his proposals is the above-mentioned Spitzenkandidaten process, which, if applied more systematically, would transfer the nomination rights for the European Commission president from

Figure 15.2. European and national identities in EU member states (2019)

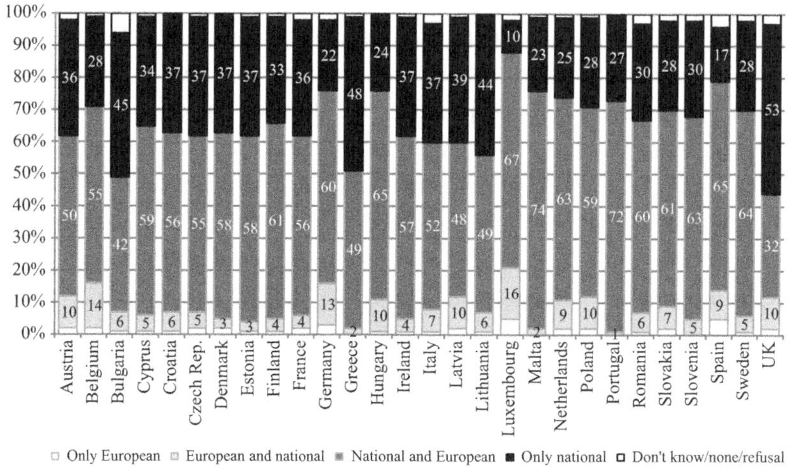

Question: "Do you see yourself as…?"
Source: Eurobarometer 91

the European Council to the largest political group in the EP. Further changes that Hix suggests include rewarding the largest EP group with a disproportionate number of committee chairs and putting all legislative proposals to a formal vote in the Council. Hix's hope is that such changes, which would infuse more majoritarianism into the EU's consensus-based system, would encourage more visible competition between different political agendas. Such competition, in turn, would make it easier for the citizens to understand what is at stake in EU decisions, encourage more active participation, and ultimately lead to a stronger European identity.

- The third answer seeks to define an intermediate position between the first two views. It rejects as unrealistic (and potentially dangerous) the hope that institutional changes can fundamentally change patterns of political engagement and collective identity, but also opposes the fatalistic pessimism of the no-demos theorists who consider EU democracy impossible in the absence of such changes. As an alternative, Kalypso Nicolaïdis (2013) proposes to conceptualize the EU as a **demoi-cracy** (*demoi* being the Greek plural of *demos*), that is, as a political system composed of multiple political communities seeking to work together without giving up their distinctiveness. The most important communities in the

EU are, of course, the national communities of the member states. As their interests must be respected, the EU's political system, according to demoi-cratic theory, must remain consensus oriented. However, the interplay of democratic channels can be made more effective and transparent. Proposed solutions include strengthening the powers of national parliaments in EU decision making, building more mechanisms of horizontal coordination between member states, which may make top-down decisions unnecessary, as well as allowing for a greater use of member state opt-outs from EU legislation. These measures would protect the concerns of national *demoi* without relying primarily on elite-based negotiations. They would, however, result in less EU-wide consistency in public policy.

The positions summarized here are rooted in different normative conceptions of democracy – for instance, different degrees of emphasis put on negative liberty (individual freedom and restraint on power holders) as opposed to positive liberty (participation in collective self-government). They also reflect different assumptions about the malleability of citizens' participation patterns and collective identities. At the same time, they all revolve around the master question of EU politics: how to balance common European interests and perspectives against the specific interests and identities of the member states and their political communities.

Since about 2010, concerns about democratic backsliding in some member states – especially Hungary and Poland – have added a new dimension to these debates. In both countries, nationalist governments have used their majorities to systematically undermine the independence of courts, the media, universities, and civil society, thus diminishing the quality of democracy and the rule of law (see Chapter 4). These measures have led to calls for the EU to intervene, for instance by suspending payments to Hungary and Poland from the EU budget. (Both countries are among the greatest beneficiaries of EU programs.) The EU's MFF for 2021–7, agreed to in December 2020, created the possibility of such sanctions. The Hungarian and Polish governments have denounced criticism of democratic backsliding as an illegitimate intervention in internal affairs. From the vantage point of democracy, however, developments in both countries raise the question of whether the EU's real democratic problem lies not in deficiencies of democratic procedures at the EU level, but in the EU's inability to ensure that all member states respect essential democratic norms.

CONCLUSION

As this chapter has shown, the EU has developed a large array of procedures that allow for the democratic input of citizens. These developments have addressed some of the concerns of those who argue that the EU suffers from a democratic deficit. However, the specific character of the EU as a polity – the non-state character of its institutions as well as the heterogeneity of its society – implies that the EU's democratic institutions and practices look different than those in most member states. When it comes to ensuring effective citizen participation in selecting EU leaders, making substantive policy decisions, and holding EU politicians to account, limitations undeniably remain. While some authors argue that the overall democratic quality of the EU is nevertheless satisfactory, these limitations will continue to fuel political criticism of the EU and scholarly debates about its democratic deficit. This political and scholarly contestation is not necessarily a bad thing, since such debates are themselves an important driving force for democratization. Concerning its democratic quality, the EU has come a long way, but there is surely room for further improvement.

REVIEW QUESTIONS

1. What are the three channels of democratic input distinguished in this chapter? How does democratic participation occur in each of these channels? What are their limitations when it comes to ensuring citizens' effective participation in selecting political leaders, making substantive policy decisions, and holding leaders to account?
2. Why does the chapter argue that the limitations of the EU's democratic mechanisms are due not only to institutional factors but also to participation practices by political parties, interest groups, and citizens? Provide examples from the material discussed in this chapter.
3. What arguments can be used to dispute the claim that the EU suffers from a democratic deficit? How convincing do you find these arguments?

4 The chapter discusses three perspectives on the potential and strategies for further democratization in the EU. Summarize the main arguments of each perspective. Which one makes the most sense to you?

EXERCISES

1 Collect information on the most recent EP election, examining factors such as voter turnout, results in various member states, as well as election campaign activities both at the European and member state level. Based on this research, list evidence for and against the claim that EP elections are losing their second-order characteristics.
2 Explore the Transparency Register. What types of organizations are listed? What information is provided about them? Which aspects of the organizations' lobbying activities are not disclosed? How would you assess the democratic value of the register?

REFERENCES AND FURTHER READING

Auel, K., O. Rozenberg, and A. Tacea. 2015. "To Scrutinise or Not to Scrutinise? Explaining Variation in EU-Related Activities in National Parliaments." *West European Politics* 38 (2): 282–304. https://doi.org/10.1080/01402382.2014.990695.

Baglioni, S., and A. Hurrelmann. 2016. "The Eurozone Crisis and Citizen Engagement in EU Affairs." *West European Politics* 39 (1): 104–24. https://doi.org/10.1080/01402382.2015.1081507.

De Vries, C. 2018. *Euroscepticism and the Future of European Integration*. Oxford: Oxford University Press.

Føllesdal, A., and S. Hix. 2006. "Why There Is a Democratic Deficit in the EU: A Response to Majone and Moravcsik." *Journal of Common Market Studies* 44 (3): 533–62. https://doi.org/10.1111/j.1468-5965.2006.00650.x.

Franklin, M., and S.B. Hobolt. 2015. "European Elections and the European Voter." In *European Union: Power and Policy-Making*, 4th ed., edited by J. Richardson and S. Mazey, 399–418. London: Routledge.

Greenwood, J. 2017. *Interest Representation in the European Union*, 4th ed. Basingstoke, UK: Palgrave Macmillan.

Greven, M.T. 2000. "Can the European Union Finally Become a Democracy?" In *Democracy beyond the State: The European Dilemma and the Emerging Global*

Order, edited by M.T. Greven and L.W. Pauly, 35–61. Toronto: University of Toronto Press.

Hix, S. 2008. *What's Wrong with the European Union and How to Fix It*. Cambridge: Polity Press.

Hix, S., and B. Høyland. 2013. "Empowerment of the European Parliament." *Annual Review of Political Science* 16: 171–89. https://doi.org/10.1146/annurev-polisci-032311-110735.

Hooghe, L., and G. Marks. 2009. "A Postfunctionalist Theory of European Integration: From Permissive Consensus to Constraining Dissensus." *British Journal of Political Science* 39 (1): 1–23. https://doi.org/10.1017/S0007123408000409.

Hooghe, L., and G. Marks. 2018. "Cleavage Theory Meets Europe's Crises: Lipset, Rokkan, and the Transnational Cleavage." *Journal of European Public Policy* 25 (1): 109–35. https://doi.org/10.1080/13501763.2017.1310279.

Hurrelmann, A., and J. DeBardeleben. 2019. "Demoi-cracy: A Useful Framework for Theorizing the Democratization of Multilevel Governance?" In *Configurations, Dynamics and Mechanisms of Multilevel Governance*, edited by N. Behnke, J. Broschek, and J. Sonnicksen, 293–310. Basingstoke, UK: Palgrave Macmillan.

Kelemen, R.D. 2017. "Europe's Other Democratic Deficit: National Authoritarianism in Europe's Democratic Union." *Government & Opposition* 52 (Special Issue 2): 211–38. https://doi.org/10.1017/gov.2016.41.

Kohler-Koch, B., and C. Quittkat, C. 2013. *De-mystification of Participatory Democracy: EU Governance and Civil Society*. Oxford: Oxford University Press.

Lijphart, A. 1999. *Patterns of Democracy: Government Forms and Performance in Thirty-Six Countries*. New Haven, CT: Yale University Press.

Lindberg, L., and S. Scheingold. 1970. *Europe's Would-Be Polity: Patterns of Change in the European Community*. Englewood Cliffs, NJ: Prentice-Hall.

Moravcsik, A. 2002. "In Defence of the 'Democratic Deficit': Reassessing Legitimacy in the European Union." *Journal of Common Market Studies* 40 (4): 603–24. https://doi.org/10.1111/1468-5965.00390.

Nicolaïdis, K. 2013. "European Demoicracy and Its Crisis." *Journal of Common Market Studies* 51 (2): 351–69. https://doi.org/10.1111/jcms.12006.

Reif, K., and H. Schmitt. 1980. "Nine Second-Order National Elections: A Systematic Framework for the Analysis of European Elections Results." *European Journal of Political Research* 8 (1): 3–44. https://doi.org/10.1111/j.1475-6765.1980.tb00737.x.

Rittberger, B. 2005. *Building Europe's Parliament: Democratic Representation beyond the Nation State*. Oxford: Oxford University Press.

Schmidt, V. 2006. *Democracy in Europe: The EU and National Polities*. Oxford: Oxford University Press.

16

Unity in Diversity: Combating Inequalities in the European Union

Heather MacRae

READER'S GUIDE

Over its history, the European Union (EU) has developed a comprehensive set of institutions and legislation to combat discrimination and to promote equality among its citizens. However, in practice inequalities abound. As this chapter notes, addressing these inequalities requires action from both the member states and the EU, where it is the EU's responsibility to create a common framework for action through legislation. There are, however, limits to this approach, and the chapter questions how effective these tools are, especially during times of crisis. If substantive equality is not more firmly embedded into the EU and its structures, this deficiency will undermine the overall legitimacy of the integration project.

INTRODUCTION

In the EU, equality among citizens is a fundamental value to be respected by member states and the EU institutions. The commitment to equality is entrenched in the treaties as well as secondary legislation. Article 2 of the Treaty on European Union (TEU) states:

> The Union is founded on the values of respect for human dignity, freedom, democracy, equality, the rule of law and respect for human rights, including the rights of persons belonging to minorities. These values are common to the Member States in a society in which pluralism, non-discrimination, tolerance, justice, solidarity and equality between women and men prevail.

In this chapter, I investigate the EU's commitment to equality and **non-discrimination**. I argue that the EU's approach, with its focus on legal equality, is insufficient to address the sources of inequality. The first section of the chapter shows how equality legislation and non-discrimination policies fit within the EU's overarching legislative framework. I briefly consider the origins, evolution, and institutionalization of the EU's equality and non-discrimination measures, and highlight inconsistencies in these anti-discrimination policies. The second section reflects on the limitations of the EU's approach and shows how the current strategies are flawed. The final section presents some of the main challenges and debates that position the EU's commitment to equality and non-discrimination against the powers of the member states and the responsibilities of the EU to the overall well-being of all its citizens.

The issue of equality and non-discrimination is central to all three themes presented in this book. The EU's involvement in this area has come about partly to satisfy the EU's commitment to social inclusion and free movement, which is inherent to the EU's mixed economy (Theme 1). However, the EU's unique position as neither an international organization nor a state (Theme 2) contributes to power struggles between the supranational and the national levels. The EU has plenty of formal legislation and rules to prevent discrimination, but few powers to enforce these. Finally, as outlined in Theme 3 of this book, the EU struggles to balance economic and democratic legitimacy. Economic implications of crises such as the COVID-19 pandemic and Brexit also demonstrate that the democratic legitimacy generated through more inclusive policies is often sidelined in favour of economic goals.

THE EVOLUTION OF EQUALITY AND NON-DISCRIMINATION MEASURES

There are two fundamentally different stories of (in)equality in the EU. First, there is a story of legal equality. This story is well developed and is mostly a story of successes. Scholars have declared the EU to be among the global leaders in terms of rights and the promotion of equality. A wide variety of formal measures protect individual rights from discrimination based on characteristics such as race, ethnicity, religion, sex, gender identity, age, nationality, and physical ability (see Box 16.1 for a definition of key terms). There is little question that, on paper, the EU recognizes and embraces principles of equality and that member states are legally obliged to act within this framework.

The other story is, however, less optimistic and is infused with systemic and historic inequalities and entwined with questions of identity, belonging, and (white, male) privilege. This story of substantive (in)equalities shows that individuals are often unable to exercise their right to equality in their day-to-day lives, despite legislation that promises it. Structural, material, and social inequalities limit the effectiveness of legal equality, and individuals are often unable to reach their full potential despite the formal freedom to do so. If we want to understand how the EU responds to inequalities and why the policies are not leading to a more equitable society, we must consider both stories.

The European integration project began in the 1950s, when many of the member states were still colonial powers and racial and social equality were far from foremost in the minds of the founders. However, they recognized the importance of "social progress" as integral to the peace project and acknowledged this to be a key aim of the process of integration. Importantly, they believed that social progress would be an organic consequence of economic integration. Thus, the early treaties did not contain many specific references to social equality. Moreover, the member states remained responsible for most social measures, including those we consider to be important to the contemporary welfare state, such as child benefits, old age security, and unemployment insurance, as well as broader policies to address the overall well-being of citizens such as education, social housing, and health care. From the very beginning, the EU's jurisdiction over social policy has been limited and generally includes only those areas that can be defined as necessary for the smooth functioning of the Single Market. However, activists inside and outside the institutions have fought for a gradual expansion of the EU's mandate and increased relevance of social policy to the EU's core principles. In fact, in a recent Eurobarometer survey, 48 per cent of respondents agreed that "the main priority of the European Parliament should be to fight poverty and social inequalities" (European Parliament 2020, 6).

> **BOX 16.1: DEFINING THE TERMS**
>
> Equality, equity, discrimination, and non-discrimination are concepts that we generally recognize but which can be challenging to define. In the EU, *equality* is defined as an absence of discrimination. In turn, *discrimination* is an absence of equality. It can be either direct or indirect. *Direct discrimination* occurs when a person is treated less favourably than another as a result of racial or ethnic origin, sex, gender, religion, or other characteristics. *Indirect discrimination* occurs when something perceived as neutral can put individuals of a specific group at a disadvantage relative to others. Some different treatment can be permitted if it can be justified by the circumstances. In other words, equality means that, unless there is reasonable justification, "like cases must not be treated differently, and different cases must not be treated in the same way" (McCrudden and Prechal 2009, 11). This recognition of difference in the pursuit of equality is implicit in the term *equity* versus the term *equality*. In contrast to *equality*, in which everyone is treated the same, *equity* implies that individuals and groups are given what they need to succeed. In this chapter, I tend to use equality more broadly because this is the terminology employed by the EU; however, it is with the recognition that the end goal is equity.
>
> It is important to distinguish between formal or legal equality and substantive equality. *Legal equality* is the basic principle that all individuals are equal under the law and that the law needs to be applied in the same way to cases that are the same. *Substantive equality* looks to the roots of inequality and recognizes that differences in circumstances lead to different outcomes. While the EU's recognition of direct and indirect discrimination can begin to address issues of substantive inequality, there are many barriers that continue to prevent individuals from exercising their capabilities. These must be overcome if we want to consider equality measures a success.

Moreover, 88 per cent of Europeans considered a "Social Europe" to be important to them personally. Clearly, social equity is both a European and a national issue of concern.

The EU's involvement in social policy began with Article 119 of the Treaty of Rome (now Article 157 TFEU), which required states to implement the basic principle of equal pay for equal work. Importantly, this principle was not included out of concern for women's rights or a commitment to feminist principles of equality. Rather, this commitment was included to assuage France's concern about potential social dumping through a lower paid female workforce in some states. Equal rights were not about justice between individuals or groups, but about creating a level playing field to maintain fair competition between the member states (Hoskyns 1996; Van der Vleuten 2007; MacRae 2010). However, when promises of equal pay went unfulfilled, activists in the 1960s and 1970s called on the European institutions to respond (Abels and MacRae 2021). A series of judgments by the Court of Justice of the EU (CJEU) in the 1970s led to the expansion of what was meant by "pay" and ruled that Article 119 had a direct effect on the citizens of the EU (see Chapter 4). As the definition of equal pay and equality was gradually expanded, specific rights for women were elaborated in several directives of the 1970s and early 1980s. However, all of these related directly to women's labour market participation. As Roberta Guerrina (2003, 101) notes, "women acquired equality in Europe as workers rather than citizens."

By the mid-1990s, a gradual shift in the EU's approach to non-discrimination became apparent. Until this time, the EU had generally addressed equality by encouraging women to change their relationship with the labour market. However, by the 1990s, shifting social norms acknowledged that women's equality was dependent on the behaviours of both men and women. This is reflected in policies and legislation that seek to reconcile work and employment for both sexes and was further supported by the introduction of gender mainstreaming in 1996. While reconciliation policies remained grounded in the EU's economic principles, gender mainstreaming sought to bring gender[1] awareness into all aspects of policy-making. It is an overarching strategy for the advancement of women's equality that relies on a systematic evaluation of policy processes to ensure that possible gender inequalities are identified and corrected at all stages, in all policy areas, and by all actors.

A further shift in the approach to non-discrimination arose at approximately the same time, largely in response to rising racism and anti-Semitism in the mid-1980s. In 1986, the EU issued a joint declaration on racism, xenophobia, and anti-Semitism that condemned all forms of racial, ethnic, religious, or cultural intolerance. The declaration was largely symbolic and did not confer any powers on the European institutions. Much like other aspects of social policy, the member states remained responsible for combating racism and discrimination. The European institutions could, at best, issue statements and guiding principles, but the enforcement of these fell to the member states. Other equally symbolic steps, such as the proclamation of 1997 as the "European Year Against Racism," helped to bring racism and other forms of discrimination onto the EU's agenda but continued to fall short of conferring power on the EU institutions. The creation of the European Monitoring Centre on Racism and Xenophobia in 1998 (EUMC) was promising, but its mandate was extremely narrow, allowing the organization only to provide information and raise awareness.

Near the end of the 1990s the balance of power began to shift slightly toward the EU institutions. The Amsterdam Treaty (1997) entrenched non-discrimination and equality as core values of the EU. Going beyond sex equality, the relevant treaty provision (Article 13 TEC, now Article 19 TFEU) defines discrimination as unequal treatment "based on sex, racial or ethnic origin, religion or belief, disability, age or sexual orientation."[2] The newly formalized commitment to non-discrimination was further institutionalized in a variety of bodies and agencies tasked with gathering data and carrying out research on inequalities and discrimination in the EU. Some of these, such as the European Institute for Gender Equality and the European Union Agency for Fundamental Rights, the successor to the EUMC, are directly linked to the institutions and generate information and research around a specific topic, while others remain independent and lobby the EU for change. When all these initiatives are viewed together, the EU appears to be on track to a broader, more inclusive set of tools to combat racism and discrimination and realize equality for its citizens.

The momentum of the 1990s carried into the early years of the 2000s, as two key anti-discrimination directives as well as the Charter of Fundamental Rights (see Box 16.2) were passed, signalling a broader commitment to combat discrimination. Directive 2000/43/EC, referred to as the Race Equality Directive (RED), prohibits discrimination on the grounds of racial or ethnic origin; Directive 2000/78/EC, often called the Framework Directive, extends the principle of non-discrimination in employment to age, disability, religion, and sexual orientation. Importantly, neither directive is comprehensive. The RED bans discrimination across multiple policy areas, but only based on race and ethnicity; the Framework Directive bans all forms of discrimination, but only in the field of employment. These differences, combined with the pre-existing measures to combat discrimination against women, create a hierarchy of rights and of those entitled to protection. Protections against discrimination based on racial and ethnic origin are the strongest. Gender and sex are protected in most areas, except education. At the bottom of the hierarchy are other grounds of discrimination including religion, (dis)ability, age, and sexual orientation. These are protected from discrimination only in the field of employment. As a result, there are no provisions at the EU level that would, for example, prevent a landlord from refusing to rent an apartment to a same-sex couple. However, these rights can be protected at the member state level. The EU itself, for the most part, can only protect rights that are connected to the Single Market, such as access to employment and training or to goods and services. In recent years, as the principle of free movement has become more important to the EU, there have been some attempts to address social inequalities that might be viewed as a barrier to an EU citizen's right to move throughout the Union, and in the process the EU's reach in non-discrimination policy has expanded.

BOX 16.2: THE CHARTER OF FUNDAMENTAL RIGHTS

The Charter of Fundamental Rights of the European Union was adopted by EU institutions in December 2000. It enshrines specific political, social, and economic rights for the citizens of the EU. The Charter requires the EU, its institutions, and the member states to act in accordance with the principles expressed therein. If the EU or the member states pass legislation that contravenes these principles, the courts have the power to strike the legislation down. The Charter was further codified in 2009 with its entrenchment in the Treaty of Lisbon.

A comprehensive directive to harmonize all these anti-discrimination measures, introduced in 2008, stalled in the EU institutions shortly thereafter when member states were unable to agree on the details (European Union Agency for Fundamental Rights 2019, 23). Since 2010, there has been little forward momentum on issues of equality. Even as demands for equal treatment have increased from civil society organizations such as Black Lives Matter and other rights-based organizations, the differences in the member states' commitment and approaches to equality has meant that the EU has been unable to agree on any further legislation. Its actions have all been in the form of non-binding action plans, reports, and other forms of soft law (see Table 16.1). With the formal responsibility for social policy still largely in the hands of the member states, it is perhaps not fair to blame the EU for the lack of progress in recent years.

THE LIMITATIONS TO THE EU'S APPROACH

The critiques of the EU's non-discrimination policies are multilayered and interconnected. The EU tends to focus on employment and the economic sphere, often at the expense of the social and political. In those rare instances where the institutions are able to make a case for further integration in areas beyond this, differences in member state interpretation and implementation as well as ongoing power struggles between the EU and the member states limit the scope of the legislation. Furthermore, the reliance on legal avenues leads to an adversarial and at times inaccessible approach to the enforcement of principles of non-discrimination. These factors all contribute to institutional barriers that often render the policy initiatives ineffective.

It is ironic that the EU's focus on non-discrimination in employment policy is frequently criticized. Feminists and other activists initially used the EU's role in employment policy to bypass the member states and bring equality onto the EU's agenda. These issues were institutionalized in the Commission's Gender Equality Unit, which was based in the Directorate General for Employment (DG EMPL). This institutionalization reinforced the economic goals of equality and provided a strong legal basis for action. The Gender Equality Unit also tended to act as a bridge between the economic and social (Hubert and Stratigaki 2016). However, in 2010 the unit was moved to the smaller portfolio of justice (DG JUST) as part of a new anti-discrimination directorate. This shift could have been a positive one, signalling that equality is

Table 16.1. Legislative measures to address discrimination

Year	Name	Reference	Notes
1975	Equal Pay Directive	75/117/EC	Amended and replaced in 2006
1976	Equal Treatment Directive	76/207/EC	Amended and replaced in 2002
1979	Social Security Directive	79/7/EEC	Amended and replaced in 2006
1986	Equal Treatment in Social Security Schemes	86/378/EEC	Amended in 1996 and replaced in 2006
1992	Pregnant Workers Directive	92/85/EEC	
1996	Parental Leave Directive	96/34/EC	Replaced in 2010 and 2019
1997	Directive on the Burden of Proof in Sex Discrimination	97/80/EC	
2000	Charter of Fundamental Rights		Embedded into the Lisbon Treaty 2009
2000	Equality Framework Directive	2000/78/EC	
2000	Race Equality Directive	2000/43/EC	
2002	Amending Equal Treatment Directive	2002/73/EC	Amended the 1976 Equal Treatment Directive
2004	Goods and Services Directive	2004/113/EC	
2006	Recast Directive Equal Treatment for Men and Women in Matters of Employment	2006/54/EC	Amended the early equal treatment directives
2008	"Horizontal Directive"	Only proposed – stalled in Council	Would extend principles of non-discrimination beyond employment
2010	Revised Framework on Parental Leave	2010/18/EU	Revised the replaced Directive 96/34/EC
2012	Gender Balance on Corporate Boards and in Decision Making	(EU) 2022/2381	Adopted in November 2022
2019	Directive on Work-Life Balance for Parents and Carers	2019/1158/EU	Replaced 2010/18/EU
2021	Pay Transparency Proposal	Proposed – in process. Provisional agreement reached December 2022	If passed, would require transparency in pay schemes to allow workers to recognize and prove discrimination in pay

not just a question of employment but rather a matter of fundamental justice. In practice, however, it may have weakened the unit's powers and pushed the responsibility for anti-discrimination measures back to the member states.

Both DG EMPL and DG JUST are relatively weak, as EU jurisdiction is quite limited in these areas because member states have retained a substantial amount of control (see also Chapter 5). Although the EU can set broad guidelines, member states have considerable scope over the definitions and details of any measures. For example, in Austria and Germany, a disability is defined as an impairment likely to last at least six months; in Cyprus or Sweden an impairment must be indefinite for it to be considered a disability. These definitions both conform to the EU's guidelines that a disability is a "long-term" impairment, but they have very different implications for an individual's ability to access services. Thus, member states can use national legislation to narrow or broaden the scope of the EU guidelines. In so doing the member states can shift the scope of the legislation. Over time and through legal challenges, these definitions may be modified and a common European standard can evolve. This process is often gradual. There is usually little ability for the EU to ensure that changes are reflected in the national legislation and considered in the national courts. The latter would be the first hurdle that individuals must overcome if they want to claim discrimination has occurred.

A recent case around the definition of marriage offers a good example of this conflict and the limits of the EU's powers. Marriage is defined in national-level legislation. In recent years, most EU states have legalized same-sex marriage or granted equal rights to couples in same-sex civil unions, but in a few EU states marriage is viewed as a union between a man and a woman.[3] In 2018, the CJEU ruled that even if a state does not recognize the legality of same-sex unions in its national legislation, non-discrimination measures prevent this provision from being used to limit the residency rights of the same-sex partner of a European citizen. In the 2018 *Coman* case (Case C-673/16),[4] the CJEU ruled that the term "spouse" is gender neutral and that member states (in this case, Romania) are obliged to treat all spouses equally in terms of residency rights. As such, Romania was obliged under EU law to grant residency rights to Mr. Coman's husband, who is not an EU citizen. However, as of October 2021, these rights had still not been granted. This type of issue challenges long-held social and political norms in the member states and can contribute to a power struggle between the member states and the EU, where the EU cannot force the member states to comply. This power struggle can be particularly pronounced when the issues at stake appear to move beyond the

EU's traditional scope of regulating equality in the labour market. It is one of the primary barriers to the implementation of equality measures.

The EU's rights-based and litigation-focused approach creates economic and structural barriers to the realization of equality. Only a small number of issues can be challenged in court, and even then only a small number of people will choose to challenge the state (or their employer or landlord) when they feel they have been discriminated against. Many instances of day-to-day discrimination – including harassment in public, the ways in which individuals are perceived and treated by service providers, or the criteria upon which academic performance is evaluated – are difficult to address through legislation. Statistics indicate that as much as 90 per cent of racist and discriminatory acts go unreported. The strong reliance on litigation to realize equality rights is hence a major barrier to many marginalized communities (Guth and Elfving 2018). Those individuals most likely to experience discrimination in the labour market are often non-EU citizens. They may be working without the proper labour or residency permits. It will come as no surprise that it is unlikely that someone without legal residency rights will challenge their employer in court over alleged discrimination. Even when litigation is an option, it can be difficult to find a lawyer who will argue a case based on EU law (particularly if this conflicts with national law), and there is no guarantee that the national judges will take EU law into consideration in their decisions (see Chapter 4). Clearly litigation is not the best way to ensure that discrimination does not happen; this is a structural limitation to the implementation of EU equity and equality principles.

The EU's approach to discrimination identifies several different categories, such as age, sex, religion, and ethnicity, that may form the basis of discrimination. However, these categories are themselves problematic as they render multiple and intersectional discrimination invisible. Intersectional discrimination exists when several characteristics come together and interact, leading to multiple and overlapping forms of discrimination. For example, an individual may experience discrimination as a Muslim woman that is not common to all women, or to all Muslims, but is a result of the intersection of her identity as both Muslim and female. This intersectional discrimination requires more complex analytical tools to respond to these unique experiences. However, the EU measures remain compartmentalized around specific forms of discrimination. There are measures in place to combat anti-Semitism; projects to reduce youth unemployment; legislation to increase the representation of women on corporate boards; and guidelines to address the educational needs of Roma. Each of these addresses only a single form of discrimination and fails to recognize that intersectional discrimination can lead to significant social and economic exclusion (Elman 2014).

Two recent cases decided by the CJEU in the summer of 2021 demonstrate the complexity in this policy domain. Both cases had been referred by German courts and both concerned Muslim women in employment who had been asked to remove their hijab in compliance with a neutrality provision prohibiting employees from wearing signs of religious, political, and philosophical convictions. In both cases, the CJEU ruled that the hijab ban was justified in certain instances. What is especially important is that in issuing its decision, the CJEU did not consider the possibility of indirect gender discrimination, but rather only indirect religious discrimination. The CJEU recognized that, statistically, the ban would concern almost only female Muslim workers, however it ruled that this constitutes a difference in treatment based on religion, but not based on gender (Howard 2021). Reaction to this ruling from the legal community has been mixed, but what is important in terms of the categorization of grounds for discrimination is that the CJEU continues to think in set categories and does not consider how multiple characteristics interact to create a particular form of discrimination.

The EU's newly published *Anti-Racism Action Plan 2020–2025* may be an important step in addressing structural inequalities in an intersectional manner. The document declares that "racist and discriminatory behaviours can be embedded in social, financial and political institutions, impacting on the levers of power and on policy-making" (European Commission 2020, 1–2). The document furthermore acknowledges that an intersectional approach can help to overcome multiple forms of discrimination as it "deepens understanding of structural racism, and makes responses more effective" (13). Going beyond the individual legislative approach, the action plan also looks to improve data collection, develop task forces and oversight agencies, undertake funding programs, and support networks to combat racism and discrimination in multiple policy areas, including health care, education, and housing. Moreover, the action plan commits the EU to a project of mainstreaming equality within the Commission's policy cycle in much the same way as gender was mainstreamed into policy-making nearly 20 years earlier. As with those implemented for gender equality, these measures are extensive and potentially transformative. However, if the experiences of gender mainstreaming have taught us anything, it is that mainstreaming does not work without the full support of all actors at all policy stages (Cavaghan 2017). The action plan continues to depend on member states designing and implementing their own national plans to address inequalities at the national level, again downloading the responsibility for equality and fighting discrimination to the member states.

In summary, the EU's legislative tools are limited in that the member states remain largely responsible for implementation and enforcement. In addition, the EU's approach allows primarily for non-discrimination in economic spheres. This feature represents one of the differences between the EU and Canada (see Box 16.3). As we have seen, there are few options in the EU to pursue justice except through litigation. While there is some evidence in the EU's soft law measures that could point toward a positive shift in understanding a more intersectional approach, it is likely that this will remain hampered by member state concerns. Moreover, as we explore below, in times of crisis the EU frequently prioritizes its economic goals, sidelining the political and social goals that are essential for the establishment of democratic legitimacy. In fact, without legitimacy these economic goals are unlikely to be reached.

> **BOX 16.3: CANADA AND THE EU COMPARED**
> There are similarities between Canada and the EU in terms of the ways in which they approach the task of overcoming inequalities through a legislative and legal perspective. However, while Canada still has its own inequalities to manage, overall the country has adopted strategies that are better able to bring actual equality more in line with the legal provisions. Canada has a unique history as a legally multicultural society, which is reflected in a demographic makeup that is much more diverse than that of any of the EU member states. Consequently, the Canadian government and society have been navigating questions of equality for much longer than the EU. Whereas many of the EU's measures have only been in place for a decade or two, Canada's formal recognition of its multicultural identity goes back to 1971.
>
> It is difficult to offer a detailed comparison of the realities of marginalized groups within these two polities, or even of the effectiveness of their respective anti-discrimination measures. Of course, there are far greater differences between the member

> states than there are within the provinces or regions of Canada, largely because issues of equality and non-discrimination can be the purview of the federal government. However, it is worth noting that the EU does not collect data on key indicators organized by race, religion, or ethnicity. Whereas the Canadian government has made data collection a key component in its equality policy strategies, many EU member states remain opposed to the collection of this type of information at a national level. This lack of data makes a comparison almost impossible. However, the very fact that the EU governments do not actively collect and disaggregate data based on ethnicity, religion, and so on may be interpreted as an unwillingness to acknowledge the depth of the issues.
>
> Many of the formal and legal strategies embraced by Canada and the EU rest on the same set of international conventions, such as the Convention on the Elimination of Discrimination Against Women, the Organisation for Economic Co-operation and Development, and the Council of Europe's mainstreaming strategies. In recent years, Canada and the EU have pledged to work together to advance gender equality and the empowerment of women and girls on the international stage through various joint initiatives.

CURRENT CONTROVERSIES AND DEBATES

In the past decade, several events have challenged the EU, tested its commitment to its fundamental values, and demonstrated where the institution's priorities lie. The financial crisis, the migrant and refugee crisis, Brexit, and the global COVID-19 pandemic all challenged the legitimacy of the EU and, in several member states, sparked support for right-wing movements and illiberal, populist governments. These events and the EU's responses have brought the EU's commitment to equality, non-discrimination, and fundamental values into the mainstream of media and scholarly debates. While there is some room for optimism on the future position of equality and non-discrimination in the EU, there is still much that needs to be done.

Not surprisingly, feminist and critical approaches have been most proactive in drawing the links between the crises, social justice, and the legitimacy of the EU project (see Chapter 6). Whereas mainstream approaches generally consider the crises from the perspective of the member states, feminist approaches consider the implications of policies at the micro level, demonstrating how inequalities are exacerbated through EU responses. This final section shows how a critical feminist lens can help scholars better recognize the inequalities resulting from the EU's own policy initiatives and the importance of equity in moving forward with integration.

Financial Crisis and Austerity

One of the main outcomes of the sovereign debt crisis that was most intense between 2010 and 2012 (see Chapter 7) has been an increase in austerity measures at both the EU and the national levels. As austerity became more widespread, the marginalized became even more marginalized. Feminist scholars and activists were quick to demonstrate how cutbacks to government services exacerbated inequalities. They urged the EU and member state governments to consider equality more closely during the restructuring that would inevitably follow the crisis. They argued that the crisis could potentially offer an unprecedented opportunity to embed equality concerns into the structures of the EU. However, rather than upend "long-standing **neoliberal** rules of the game," policy-makers opted to "reinscribe the standing institutional order." Rather than deepen its commitment to equality measures, in light of evidence from the financial crises, the EU "reaffirmed and fortified its collective neoliberal rationale" (Weiner and MacRae 2017, 86). As a result, "women, youth, migrants, people suffering from mental illnesses, drug addicts, the incarcerated and other minority communities ... are bearing the burden of a social process of an 'upwards' redistribution of wealth" (Kosyfologou 2018, 23).

A decade after the crisis, we can see that many of the predictions regarding increased inequalities were correct. As the EU continues to move from one crisis to the next, the lessons of the importance of maintaining an equality perspective at all times have gone unheeded, demonstrating that, at its core, the EU remains more committed to economic growth than to social justice. Importantly, the majority of Europeans believe that the EU institutions have an important role to play in reducing poverty and social inequality (see, for example, European Parliament 2020).

The Rule of Law

The immediate post-crisis era spawned a wave of support for right-wing, populist movements across the EU. In some cases, such as Poland and Hungary, right-wing governments came into power, seeking to re-establish the primacy of the member states over the EU and to reaffirm national sovereignty. In Hungary, Viktor Orbán's government has openly rejected the principles of liberal democracy, including the rule of law, minority rights, gender mainstreaming, and the separation of the judicial and legislative branches of government. His success draws on racist and exclusionary language to reinforce a homo-nationalist understanding of who belongs to – and who is excluded from – the state. In a direct rejection of the EU's position on social inclusion, more than 100 communities in Poland have declared themselves to be LGBT-free zones. The EU institutions have condemned these actions, with the European Parliament responding by declaring the whole EU an "LGBTIQ Freedom Zone." However, as is the case in many of the EU's equality initiatives, this declaration is largely symbolic and does not change the realities of discrimination and exclusion facing LGBTQ+ people in Poland.

In response to widespread concern and outrage, the EU has begun to explore options to sanction these illiberal governments. In December 2020 member states agreed to a new mechanism that makes financial payouts to the states contingent on their adherence to the rule of law. Not surprisingly, the governments in these two states denounce this as an unauthorized intervention in national affairs by the European institutions. In July 2021, the Commission formally launched infringement proceedings against Hungary and Poland in response to their stance on the protection of equality and fundamental rights of the LGBTQ+ community. The other member states have shown a strong and uncharacteristically united stance in favour of penalizing states that do not uphold the EU's values, including specifically those pertaining to the rights of the LGBTQ+ community. In a best-case scenario, this conflict could precipitate a reconsideration of the position of fundamental values as part of the integration process. A reconfirmation of these values could help to project non-discrimination and equality to the forefront and may open space for activists to encourage steps to substantive rather than legal equality.

The Global Pandemic: COVID-19

The most recent challenge to the EU's governance has been the global health crisis precipitated by the COVID-19 pandemic. While experts initially claimed that the virus was an "equal opportunity" virus, striking equally the young, old, wealthy, and poor, we now know that this is not true. Material conditions played an important part in determining an individual's risk factors, and analyses show that women, the poor, as well as Black, Indigenous, and People of Colour (BIPOC) individuals have been among the hardest hit. In England and Wales during the first six months of the pandemic, Black individuals had a three to four times higher rate of death following a COVID-19 infection than the white population; other racialized groups fared only slightly better (Office for National Statistics 2020). The gender impacts of the pandemic are also visible in connection to a decline in job security and financial safety for female workers, the intensification in the dual burden of paid and unpaid work, an elevation of violence in and outside the home, and a heightened risk exposure to the virus and associated health outcomes. A critical feminist analysis can draw attention to these inequalities, as gender, race, and class are often rendered invisible in mainstream analyses and statistics.

The EU's Responses

What is common across all these crises is the failure of mainstream academics and policy-makers to recognize the advantages of and need for an intersectional framework in their analyses. This dismissal of social equity in favour of neoliberal economic principles demonstrates "the decay of democratic and fundamental values" and challenges the integrity of the integration project (MacRae, Guerrina, and Masselot 2021, 197). If individuals do not recognize a benefit to membership, they may cease to support integration. Although it is becoming increasingly common for mainstream scholars to think about the EU in terms of crisis, for many who have lived on the margins of integration for years this terminology comes far too late. They have been in crisis for decades (Bassel and Emejulu 2017). In fact, the EU's management of multiple crises over the past decade, with its focus on austerity, has deepened this crisis for many.

Even as the institutional restructuring inherent in crisis responses has opened the possibility of developing new gender and diversity aware structures, the EU has failed to do so. It is only now, with the benefit of hindsight, that the EU is beginning to recognize how its responses exacerbated existing inequalities. It is, however, difficult to imagine that the current attention being paid to an "intersectional response," such as that outlined in the Anti-Racism Action Plan, will be taken any more seriously than those expressed in the wake of the financial crisis.

CONCLUSION

Recent crises upended the EU's usual way of operating, necessitating fast action by the member states on controversial matters. This sense of urgency has permeated much of the decision making in the past decade and has been detrimental to the project of non-discrimination. Not only do the EU's tools fail to offer substantive equality, equality may actually be undermined by aspects of the EU's own processes and policies. Many of the barriers to the realization of substantive equality in the EU are systemic. Institutional and structural barriers limit access to the equality measures that the EU has put in place. Moreover, the EU's continued narrow focus on economics and employment limits the impact of the measures. Arguably, the way out of these crises is to incorporate an intersectional approach to policy-making. It appears that the EU is beginning to acknowledge the value in this, although it remains to be seen how an intersectional approach will be institutionalized. Inaccessible, weak policy measures are insufficient to bring about substantive equality in the EU.

There are two different stories of (in)equality and (non)discrimination in the EU. The story that is most often told is the one of the EU as a success story. This fact alone is evidence of the privileges inherent in EU studies and in the EU institutions. We must make space for marginalized voices in scholarship and in formal and informal institutions. Only when their stories are both told and heard are we able to speak of democracy and legitimacy in the EU.

REVIEW QUESTIONS

1 There is a move to develop a pan-European approach to non-discrimination and equality. However, there are still huge differences among the member states. What do you think accounts for these differences? Do you believe the EU can overcome these differences?
2 How are equality and non-discrimination related to economic policies in the EU?
3 Does the EU have a legal obligation to protect minority rights in the member states? How can this be reconciled with the autonomy and sovereignty of the member states?

4 Which aspects of non-discrimination and equality policies are most developed at the EU level? Why do you think this is?

EXERCISES

1 Compare the Gender Equality Strategy 2020–5 with the Anti-Racism Action Plan 2020–5. In what ways are they similar and in what ways are they different? What does this tell us about the EU's priorities? How realistic are the goals set out in both documents?
2 Select a court case that has addressed inequalities from the CJEU's list of case law on the equality of treatment between women and men and on non-discrimination in the EU (https://op.europa.eu/en/publication-detail/-/publication/e8711e0f-767c-466e-9fae-325dd6d2544f). Review the facts of the case and the ruling of the CJEU. Do you agree with how the Court ruled? What are the implications of this ruling for the further development of equality rights in the EU?

NOTES

1 Note that at this time, the EU was interested in equality for men and women, and framed measures within this binary of male/female. The term *gender*, while broader, continued to assume this binary and the EU did not address non-binary sexual identity until much later.
2 Although measures now include rights around sexual orientation, gender identity and gender expression are not formally protected at the EU level. However, case law in both the European Convention on Human Rights and the CJEU as well as legislation in some member states may offer protection based on gender identity and gender expression. The TFEU enshrines these rights under Articles 8 and 10.
3 Marriage is defined as the union of a man and a woman in Bulgaria, Croatia, Hungary, Latvia, Lithuania, Poland, and Slovakia. Even within these there is substantial variation. Poland and Slovakia recognize contractual co-habitation (regardless of sexuality), while Hungary and Croatia recognize same-sex unions (but not marriage).
4 The non-recognition of same-sex unions is a violation of a ruling by the European Court of Human Rights.

REFERENCES AND FURTHER READING

Abels, G., and H. MacRae. 2021. "Whose Story Is It Anyway? Studying European Integration with a Gender Lens." In *The Routledge Handbook of Gender and EU Politics*, edited by G. Abels, A. Kriszán, H. MacRae, and A. van der Vleuten, 17–29. Abingdon, UK: Routledge.

Bassel, L., and A. Emejulu. 2017. "Whose Crisis Counts? Minority Women, Austerity and Activism in France and Britain." In *Gender and the Economic Crisis in Europe*, edited by J. Kantola and E. Lombardo, 185–208. London: Palgrave.

Cavaghan, R. 2017. *Making Gender Equality Happen: Knowledge, Change and Resistance in EU Gender Mainstreaming*. New York: Routledge.

Elman, A. 2014. *The European Union, Antisemitism and the Politics of Denial*. Lincoln: University of Nebraska Press.

European Commission. 2020. *EU Anti-Racism Action Plan 2020–2025*. https://commission.europa.eu/strategy-and-policy/policies/justice-and-fundamental-rights/combatting-discrimination/racism-and-xenophobia/eu-anti-racism-action-plan-2020-2025_en.

European Parliament. 2020. "Parlemeter 2020: A Glimpse of Certainty in Uncertain Times." Eurobarometer 94.2 of the European Parliament. https://www.europarl.europa.eu/at-your-service/files/be-heard/eurobarometer/2020/parlemeter-2020/en-report.pdf.

European Parliament. 2021. "Parliament Declares the European Union an LGBTIQ Freedom Zone." Press release. https://www.europarl.europa.eu/news/en/press-room/20210304IPR99219/parliament-declares-the-european-union-an-lgbtiq-freedom-zone.

European Union Agency for Fundamental Rights. 2019. "Fundamental Rights Report." http://kirp.pl/wp-content/uploads/2019/06/fra-2019-fundamental-rights-report-2019_en.pdf.

Guerrina, R. 2003. "Gender, Mainstreaming and the EU Charter of Fundamental Rights." *Policy & Society* 22 (1): 97–115. https://doi.org/10.1016/S1449-4035(03)70015-0.

Guth, J., and S. Elfving. 2018. *Gender and the Court of Justice of the European Union*. Milton, UK: Routledge.

Hepburn, E. 2020. "Social and Equality Impacts of Brexit: A Report for the Scottish Government." https://www.gov.scot/publications/social-equality-impacts-brexit/documents/.

Hoskyns, C. 1996. *Integrating Gender: Women, Law and Politics in the European Union*. London: Verso.

Howard, E. 2021. "German Headscarf Cases at the ECJ: A Glimmer of Hope?" *European Law Blog: News and Commentary on EU Law*. https://europeanlawblog.eu/2021/07/26/german-headscarf-cases-at-the-ecj-a-glimmer-of-hope/.

Hubert, A., and M. Stratigaki. 2016. "Twenty Years of EU Gender Mainstreaming: Rebirth Out of the Ashes?" *Femina politica* 25 (2): 21–36. https://doi.org/10.3224/feminapolitica.v25i2.25350.

Kosyfologou, A. 2018. *Gendered Aspects of the Austerity Regime in Greece: 2010–2017: Austerity, Gender Inequality and Feminism after the Crisis*. Berlin: Rosa-Luxembourg-Stiftung. https://www.rosalux.de/en/publication/id/39020/gendered-aspects-of-the-austerity-regime-in-greece-2010-2017.

MacRae, H. 2010. "The EU as a Gender Equal Polity: Myths and Realities." *Journal of Common Market Studies* 48 (1): 155–74. https://doi.org/10.1111/j.1468-5965.2009.02046.x.

MacRae, H., R. Guerrina, and A. Masselot. 2021. "A Crisis Is a Terrible Thing to Waste: Feminist Reflections on the EU's Crisis Responses." *International Studies (New Delhi)* 58 (2): 184–20. https://doi.org/10.1177/00208817211004026.

McCrudden, C., and S. Prechal. 2009. *The Concepts of Equality and Non-discrimination in Europe: A Practical Approach*. Brussels: European Commission, Directorate-General for Employment, Social Affairs and Equal Opportunities.

Office for National Statistics. 2020. "Updating Ethnic Contrasts in Deaths Involving the Coronavirus (COVID-19), England: 24 January 2020 to 31 March 2021." https://www.ons.gov.uk/peoplepopulationandcommunity/birthsdeathsandmarriages/deaths/articles/updatingethniccontrastsindeathsinvolvingthecoronaviruscovid19englandandwales/24january2020to31march2021.

Van der Vleuten, A. 2007. *The Price of Gender Equality: Members States and Governance in the European Union*. Aldershot, UK: Ashgate.

Weiner, E., and H. MacRae. 2017. "Opportunity and Setback? Gender Equality, Crisis and Change in the EU." In *Gender and the Economic Crisis in Europe*, edited by J. Kantola and E. Lombardo, 73–93. London: Palgrave.

17

European Green Deal and Energy Security

Michèle Knodt, Julia Jänisch, and G. Cornelis van Kooten

READER'S GUIDE

The Russian war against Ukraine poses the greatest challenge to the security of energy supply in Europe since World War II. While the European Union (EU) is desperately trying to overcome its years of dependence on fossil fuels from Russia, its aspirations remain to be a leader in the global fight against climate change. It has established ambitious plans for a European Green Deal, with the objective of making the EU carbon neutral by 2050. Based on a review of the EU's climate and energy policy, this chapter assesses the achievements of EU efforts at climate change mitigation and identifies obstacles the EU must overcome to reach its climate goals, especially in the new setting following the war against Ukraine. These goals will require significant economic restructuring, while member state interests on climate and energy policy frequently diverge. The EU may only be able to reduce its energy dependency and at the same time reach its climate ambitions if changes in its governance increase its ability to enhance the compliance of its member states.

INTRODUCTION

When Russian troops crossed the border of Ukraine on February 24, 2022, and launched the war of aggression against Ukraine, this military action was not only a turning point in geopolitical terms, but also one of the greatest energy policy challenges for the EU since World War II. In early 2022, the EU was 25 per cent dependent on Russian oil, 45 per cent on Russian coal, and up to 40 per cent on Russian gas. Drastic measures were needed to reduce this dependence in the shortest possible time – above all, an even faster transition toward renewable energies. However, the short-term measures taken in response to the Russian invasion did not always go hand in hand with the fight against climate change and the EU's claim to lead in this domain.

An ambitious climate change policy is high on the agenda of EU policy-makers. The European Commission that came into office after the 2019 European Parliament (EP) elections, led by Ursula von der Leyen, made climate change mitigation the centrepiece of its political agenda. It put forward the **European Green Deal (EGD)**, a political program aimed at establishing sustainable, affordable, and secure climate and energy policies (Bongardt and Torres 2022). Its main goal is to make the EU climate neutral by 2050. How close is the EU to reaching these objectives? What has already been achieved and which obstacles remain to be overcome for the EGD to be successful? How has the war in Ukraine complicated the picture? Will the partial offsetting of gas by coal-fired power plants endanger the EGD? How can member states be made to contribute adequately to the ambitious European targets?

To answer these questions, it is necessary to understand the specificities of climate and energy policy development and the respective competences of the EU. These will be outlined first in this chapter. The chapter then assesses how innovative and ambitious the EU has been in dealing with the challenges of energy security, climate change, and bringing about the transition toward climate-friendly energy sources. Finally, the chapter discusses obstacles that have stood in the way of greater progress, including the EU's restricted competences to force policy change on the member states.

HISTORY OF EU CLIMATE AND ENERGY POLICY

The success of the EU in implementing the EGD depends to a large extent on the competences that are delegated to the European level in the fields of energy and climate policy, but also on energy policies outside the EU. Although energy policy has always played a major role in the EU, it was only included in the primary treaties in 2009, when the Lisbon Treaty came into force. Climate change was first addressed through measures based on the EU's environmental policy competences. Starting in the 1990s, climate change targets also became increasingly important in the EU's energy policy. Energy and climate are closely connected because energy consumption is a major source of greenhouse gas (GHG) emissions, which contribute to climate change. However, EU competences in both fields differ significantly. When climate policy measures can be based on the EU's environmental competence (Article 191–192(2) TFEU), legislation is passed by majority vote in the Council of the EU, which makes it easier to come to an agreement. The resulting policy decisions are binding on the member states. By contrast, when a measure falls under the EU's competence on energy (Article 194(2) TFEU), the EU can only define European policy objectives – it is not allowed to intervene into member states' rights to determine the conditions for exploiting their energy resources, their choice between different energy sources, and the general structure of their energy supply. This section will examine EU activities in both energy and climate policy in more detail.

EU Energy Policy

The EU has pursued policies on matters of energy since the early years of European integration. Two of the three original European Communities founded in the 1950s – the European Coal and Steel Community and the European Atomic Energy Community – were related to matters of energy production, particularly to the establishment of markets for coal and oversight of nuclear energy. However, in the European Economic Community (EEC), which emerged as the most important of the three original communities, energy played virtually no role – the EEC Treaty contained no energy-specific provisions. Also, the link between energy policy and environmental concerns was initially overshadowed by other policy objectives.

Energy policy in the EU is characterized by three primary goals: (1) integrating the internal energy market to ensure liberalization and competitive prices (competitiveness), (2) energy security with regard to supply, and (3) minimizing the environmental impacts of energy consumption, which primarily entails reducing CO_2 emissions (sustainability). The three goals have received different degrees of attention in various time periods, and they have guided European action in different ways. The discussion of the goals was driven by external as well as internal developments (Knodt 2018).

Especially in the early years, European energy policy was focused on the competitiveness goal. EU policy aimed to reduce trade barriers and enhance competition in energy markets as well as the competitiveness of European industry. In 2005, the European Commission launched an inquiry into energy markets to identify barriers to competition; this inquiry was triggered by the lack of cross-border trade and high market concentration, particularly in the gas and electricity sectors. In the following years, the completion of infrastructure projects in the electricity sector to support an influx of **renewable energy** sources and efforts to ensure more diverse origins of supply across the EU became a central focus of EU energy policy (Herranz-Surrallés 2015).

The discussion on the energy security goal has been influenced by the perception of international energy threats. Energy security first became an issue in 1968 as a direct result of the Six-Day War in the Middle East, which had an impact on oil supplies. After the oil crisis of the 1970s, the Commission continuously sought to extend its energy competences, even in the absence of a formal treaty change to enhance its powers over energy matters (McGowan 2011). This increased power was achieved through (1) making use of the new environmental competences created in the Single European Act; (2) the development of the Single Market, including a market for electricity, petroleum, and natural gas; and (3) the cross-border construction of energy infrastructure, such as trans-European networks. The sharp increase in oil prices in the late 2000s again demonstrated the EU's increased vulnerability to external energy suppliers. At the time, the EU met up to 50 per cent of its energy needs via imports, especially from the Middle East and Russia. Dependence on Russia, in particular, deepened as Central and Eastern European countries joined the EU in 2004 and 2007 (see Chapter 13). At the same time, disputes over gas deliveries between Ukraine and Russia (2006 and 2009) and between Belarus and Russia (2007) challenged the security of the EU's energy supply.

The external threat posed by reliance on foreign suppliers, and especially Poland's efforts to reduce its dependency on Russian energy, led to renewed European energy policy-making. In 2007, the Commission adopted new structural rules for the gas and electricity sectors, which included unbundling of ownership as well as a system of regulatory bodies and networks to promote cross-border interconnections and other infrastructure projects. The EU identified and invested in projects of common interest in an effort to accelerate infrastructure projects necessary for meeting energy objectives and completing the internal energy market.

Nonetheless, the EU depended on energy imports to a high degree. Before the war in Ukraine, almost 40 per cent of oil imports into the EU came from Russia and Iraq, followed by Saudi Arabia and Norway. Together with Russia, Norway and Algeria account for over 70 per cent of the EU's natural gas imports, with the remainder coming from the Middle East. More than three-quarters of imported coal comes from Russia, the United States, Colombia, and Australia. The EU must compete for natural gas and coal with growing needs for these fossil fuels by countries in Asia. Although the Commission had repeatedly urged diversification of imports, dependence has increased over the years.

As a result, the Russian invasion of Ukraine has hit the EU hard, first through the sanctions imposed on energy imports in the oil and coal sectors, and second through the Russian shutdown of an oil pipeline and curtailment of gas supplies. Oil and coal can be relatively easily substituted by other supplier countries, although at much higher prices than previously. By contrast, the EU remains vulnerable to potential reductions in Russian gas exports since it is a pipeline-bound energy. The loss of Russian gas threatens the supply both for heating for the population and, more importantly, for maintaining energy-intensive industries such as steel, chemicals, and pharmaceuticals.

The **sustainability** goal entered the picture in the 1990s. Sustainability gained increasing prominence by the end of the 2000s when it was linked with concerns about climate change. The triangle of objectives was spelled out explicitly for the first time in a 1994 Green Paper of the Commission and taken up in follow-up reports on climate and energy policy. In 2007, the European Council decided to develop a sustainable integrated European climate and energy policy. The focus was to take seriously the cross-cutting nature of energy policy and link it closely to EU climate policy by focusing on emissions reduction, expansion of renewable energy, and energy efficiency (Knodt 2018).

The targets for these three main objectives of the EU were established under the slogan "20-20-20 by 2020" – a reduction of at least 20 per cent in GHGs compared to 1990, a 20 per cent share of renewables in EU energy consumption, and a reduction in primary energy use by 20 per cent compared to projected levels through energy efficiency, all by the year 2020. In 2014 and 2016, the EU defined even more ambitious targets for 2030 (see Table 17.1). To achieve agreement on these more ambitious objectives, the member states in the Council had to accommodate the opposing Visegrád states (Czech Republic, Hungary, Poland, and Slovakia), along with Bulgaria and Romania, and to agree not to translate them into "nationally binding targets" (Knodt 2018).

Table 17.1. Development of the EU's climate and energy targets

	Reduction in CO_2 emissions	Share of renewable energies	Increase in energy efficiency
2020 targets (2008)	20%	20%	20%
2030 targets (2014)	40%	27%	27%
2030 targets (2018)	40%	32%	32.5%
2030 targets (2021) "Fit for 55" proposal	61%	40%	36/39%*
2030 targets (2022) "REPowerEU"	61%	45%	40/43%

*Final energy consumption/primary energy consumption

EU Climate Policy

Climate policy in the EU has evolved from European environmental policy. The EU started to be active in the environmental policy arena in the 1970s, even before environmental policy was formally defined as an EU competency in the Single European Act of 1985. The EU adopted the first of its eight **Environmental Action Programmes (EAP)** in November 1973, following the first United Nations Conference on the Environment in Stockholm and the Club of Rome's internationally acclaimed report, "Limits to Growth." The first EAP outlined general environmental objectives and strategies, while the implementation through specific measures remained the responsibility of the member states. The EAPs of 1973–6 and 1977–81 focused primarily on controlling and combating problems caused by environmental pollution, but, from the third EAP onwards, the precautionary principle – focusing on preventative decision making when faced with environmental risks – was increasingly strengthened as the guiding principle of European environmental policy. The 1980s also saw an increase in procedural legislation leading to more institutional support for EU environmental policy. European legislation included the Environmental Impact Assessment Directive (1985), the creation of the European Commission's Directorate-General for Environment, and the establishment of the Coordination of Information on the Environment Programme. Much of the legislation focused on harmonizing the procedural and institutional basis for environmental intervention across the member states. A stronger institutionalization of EU environmental policy also took place through the establishment of the European Environment

Agency and its "State and Outlook of the European Environment" reports, published every five years.

In the mid-1980s, climate change appeared on the political agenda of the EU for the first time. In 1986, the EP recognized climate change as a cross-policy and cross-sectoral problem that required political action. In 1988, the Commission's first communication on the greenhouse gas effect followed, in which policy options for limiting climate change were developed for the first time. Together with specific targets and measures for reducing emissions, timetables were developed for the negotiation of an international climate protection agreement. The Commission also demanded that the greenhouse gas effect should be taken into account in the European Community's and member states' political decision making in relevant sectors such as energy.

In international comparison, the EU can be considered a pioneer in climate protection during this period. At the international level, the EU supported (without success) the establishment of binding national reduction targets for GHG emissions in industrialized countries during the founding negotiations of the United Nations Framework Convention on Climate Change (UNFCCC). These international efforts were flanked by an increased strengthening of climate protection within the EU at the beginning of the 1990s. Altogether, we can say that the EU attempted to "lead by example" in climate protection (Jordan and Rayner 2010).

The entry into force of the Maastricht Treaty in 1993 and, thus, the expansion of qualified majority voting to nearly all environmental and climate policy decisions broadened the range of policy instruments. Already in the fifth EAP (1993-8), climate protection was named as one of seven priority objectives of EU environmental policy, which finally anchored climate policy at the EU level. In addition, the EAP used economic and financial incentives to change the behaviour of the economy and EU citizens by informing them about environmental problems. However, the first attempts to introduce a tax on CO_2 failed in the Council of the EU in 1992 and again in 1995 because of resistance from member states, which vehemently rejected the encroachment on their sovereignty over taxes and energy matters. Despite internal European conflicts and limited progress in the introduction of climate policy instruments within the EU, the EU continued to play a central role in the international climate regime. For example, the so-called two-degree target – that global temperature should not increase by more than 2° Celsius (3.6° Fahrenheit) compared to pre-industrial times (nineteenth century) – dates back to a decision taken by the EU environment ministers in 1996 in response to the report of the Intergovernmental Panel on Climate Change. This target had a formative influence on international climate negotiations.

The new millennium marked the beginning of a new phase in environmental and climate policy. In particular, regulation increasingly gave way to market incentives. Under the 1997 Kyoto Protocol, which the EU ratified in 2005, the EU committed to reducing its CO_2 emissions by 8 per cent by 2012 compared to the reference year 1990 (van Kooten 2004). The existence of differing national contexts was acknowledged and the possibility for burden sharing between member states was introduced. The implementation of the EU's climate policy demonstrated an explicit desire to integrate policies and set longer-term sustainability goals. The sixth EAP identified combating climate change as the highest priority for environmental protection. An additional milestone was the introduction of the European **Emissions Trading System (ETS)** in 2005 (see Box 17.1).

BOX 17.1: EMISSIONS TRADING IN THE EU

The EU's ETS is a cap-and-trade system that sets a limit ("cap") on total emissions of GHGs in high-emitting industries – such as power generation and manufacturing – by creating CO_2 emission permits (CO_2 is the dominant GHG). These allow firms to buy and sell ("trade") permits and find the least costly mechanism to reduce emissions. The ETS is the largest international system for trading carbon emission allowances; it alone accounts for three-quarters of international carbon trading. The ETS is emblematic of the new era of flexible regulations in the EU. However, it has suffered from a surplus of allowances as a result of including carbon offsets (for example, from tree planting), overreporting of emissions by companies (the issued number of emission permits exceeded actual emissions), and slow growth after the 2008 global financial crisis. These caused the price of permits to drop to a level below what was necessary to incentivize firms to reduce emissions. This changed after 2018, because massive regulative interventions made the price of carbon rise continuously from less than €10 per tonne of CO_2 to more than €55 in 2021. As a result, the ETS has become more effective.

In addition to the ETS, the EU introduced the so-called Effort Sharing Regulation by which member states commit to reduce their CO_2 emissions significantly. This legislation covers emission sectors unaffected by the ETS, such as transport, buildings, agriculture, and waste. The reduction targets vary between member states, depending on their level of prosperity. Together, the ETS and the Effort Sharing Regulation are intended to achieve the EU's climate change mitigation targets.

The EU is currently operating under the eighth EAP (2021–30), which relies on six priority objectives: (1) meeting the EU's objectives to reduce GHG emissions by at least 55 per cent by 2030 from baseline 1990 emissions and becoming climate neutral by 2050; (2) becoming more adaptive, resilient, and less vulnerable to climate change; (3) developing a circular economy that leads to regenerative growth; (4) stopping all pollution; (5) protecting biodiversity; and (6) adopting more environmentally conscious behaviours with respect to production and consumption, especially in the areas of energy, industry, infrastructure, mobility, and nutrition. A central element of the eighth EAP is the EGD. In addition to these internal measures, the EU's approach to climate policy also includes its role as an international player in climate negotiations, as was the case at the twenty-first Conference of the Parties to the UNFCCC in December 2015, where the Paris Agreement was ratified. The EU was an influential leader in these negotiations, though it had to share the stage with up-and-coming players such as China (Oberthür and Groen 2017; Parker et al. 2017).

An Integrated EU Climate Change Policy

While initially pursued in parallel through the EU's climate and energy policies, the EU made an explicit move to develop a more integrated climate change policy with the establishment of the **Energy Union**, first proposed in 2015 (see Box 17.2). Jean-Claude Juncker, Commission president at the time, initiated the establishment of an Energy Union at the beginning of his term in office; its purpose was to overcome discord and blockades within European climate change policy. The Commission presented its vision of a European energy system that addresses all three objectives – competitiveness, security of supply, and sustainability.

The key challenge that the EU faces in the development of the Energy Union is the fact that, as noted earlier, the EU lacks competences to pass binding legislation on energy matters. Article 194(2) TFEU explicitly states that each

> **BOX 17.2: EU ENERGY UNION**
> In its "Framework Strategy for a Resilient Energy Union with a Forward-Looking Climate Change Strategy" (European Commission 2015), the Commission presented its vision of a European Energy Union. A comprehensive Energy Union was adopted by the European Council in 2015. The 2016 legislative package "Clean Energy for All Europeans" further specified the Energy Union. The union contains five dimensions: (1) ensuring energy security, (2) fully integrating the internal energy market, (3) improving energy efficiency, (4) reducing CO_2 emissions, and (5) promoting research, innovation, and competitiveness.

member state retains the right to decide how to exploit its energy resources and to choose between different energy sources. The positions of member states on energy matters (for example, the desired speed of phasing out coal, the acceptability of nuclear energy) differ significantly. Yet because of the restrictions on EU competences over energy, these disputes cannot be authoritatively resolved at the EU level. Rather, the Energy Union is dependent on non-hierarchical **soft governance** mechanisms that set targets and provide incentives for member state activities (see Chapter 5).

The most important instrument in this context is the Governance Regulation. Its core elements are the National Energy and Climate Plans (NECPs), which the member states are required to provide to the Commission alongside long-term strategies. Within the NECPs, member states present their national objectives, strategies, and measures. The NECPs are then evaluated by the Commission to assess whether the targets, strategies, and measures are "ambitious" enough, and whether their implementation plans are appropriate to achieve the EU's targets. Member states must respond to these recommendations and close ambition or implementation gaps within one year. Nevertheless, because of its soft governance and lack of competences, the EU cannot enforce member state planning.

An ever-stronger integration of climate and energy policy came into force in 2019 when the European Commission under Ursula von der Leyen launched the EGD, labelling it "Europe's 'man of the moon' moment" (see Box 17.3). Since then, climate protection through the EGD has become a new "signature

> **BOX 17.3: EUROPEAN GREEN DEAL (EGD)**
>
> In 2019, the newly elected Commission president Ursula von der Leyen presented the so-called EGD. The deal is part of the priorities of the Commission for the 2019–24 period and is intended to help reduce CO_2 emissions in the EU by at least 55 per cent by 2030 compared to 1990. The EGD comprises three core elements: measures to make the EU climate neutral by 2050, measures to separate economic growth from resource use, and measures to take into account regional needs in the process of achieving these goals. To achieve the latter goal, financial assistance will be provided to disadvantaged regions, particularly in the period 2021–7. The necessary economic and social change should thus be fair, cost efficient, and socially just. Other EGD priorities outlined include strengthening protected areas, supporting EU industry while rethinking consumption, decarbonizing the energy sector, curbing the use of harmful chemicals, reducing transport sector emissions by 90 per cent by 2050, and creating a more sustainable food system. Overall, the EGD includes a new growth strategy with 50 policies to help achieve the EU's climate change goals.

policy" of the EU, which envisages a carbon-neutral European economy and society by 2050 (European Commission 2019). The EGD is an expression of the need to address collaboratively climate and environment-related challenges under the sustainability goal.

To transform the EU's economy for a sustainable future, an increase in the EU's 2030 and 2050 climate ambitions was announced. In December 2020, the European Council agreed on a new EU-wide climate protection target, in addition to the already agreed on goal of climate neutrality by 2050: Instead of a 40 per cent reduction in GHGs, a reduction of 55 per cent compared to 1990 was now deemed to be achievable by 2030. In July 2021, the Commission presented further details in its legislative package "Fit for 55." The share of renewable energies is to increase from 32 per cent to at least 40 per cent by 2030. In the area of energy efficiency, an increase in the target from 32.5 to 36 per cent (final energy consumption) and 39 per cent (primary energy consumption) is proposed (see Table 17.1). These targets are to be reached through expanded emissions trading combined with new regulatory measures.

In response to the Russian war of aggression against Ukraine and to achieve the climate protection targets, the Commission presented the REPowerEU plan on May 18, 2022. In addition to short-term measures to avert the threat of gas shortages and high energy prices, the EU is pursuing four objectives: (1) accelerating the energy transition, (2) saving energy, (3) diversifying energy imports, and (4) linking these reforms to investment. However, this renewed increase in targets is not accompanied by any new governance mechanisms to ensure their achievement.

DEBATE: (UN)FIT FOR 55? THE EU'S CHALLENGING 2030 AND 2050 TARGETS IN TIMES OF WAR

Is the EU indeed "Fit for 55," especially in times of war? How realistic is it that the EU achieves the EGD and REPowerEU targets, let alone the even more ambitious demands put forward by climate activists?

Even though climate change mitigation has been on the EU's agenda for decades, much work remains to be done. For instance, the EU's electricity generation mix continues to consist predominantly of conventional energy sources, with only 38 per cent coming from renewables. Coal, oil, and natural gas account for up to 37.2 per cent; when nuclear power is also taken into account, 62 per cent of electricity in the EU is generated from non-renewable sources. Within the renewable energies, the EU counts on hydrogen, wind, solar energy, and biomass. Other renewable energy options, especially hydropower, are expected to make only minor contributions to future electricity supply because of high costs or, in the case of new hydroelectric dams, adverse environmental impacts. Compared to its ambitious targets, and also compared to Canada, this is a disappointing outcome (see Box 17.4).

BOX 17.4: SOURCES OF ELECTRICITY GENERATION: EU VERSUS CANADA

The energy makeup of Canada is characterized by a higher share of renewables than that of the EU (see the figure below). Coal plays only a small role. Alberta, Saskatchewan, and the Maritime provinces employ coal to generate electricity, but it is responsible for less than half of the electricity produced in those jurisdictions.

Other provinces rely primarily on hydroelectric power (British Columbia, Manitoba, Quebec, and Newfoundland and Labrador) or a combination of hydro and nuclear power (Ontario).

European Union

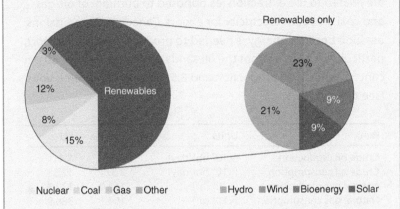

Canada

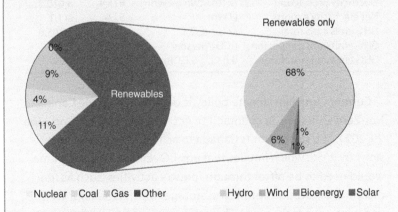

Sources: Agora Energiewende (2021); Canada Energy Regulator (2021)

Politically, Canada has some similarities with the EU. Jurisdictional power over the environment and energy resides primarily with the provinces; in the EU context it resides with member states. Canada differs in two important aspects, however: (1) Energy security is not a concern because Canada is a net exporter of oil, natural gas, coal, and electricity; and (2) Canadian GHG emissions are among the highest in the world on a per capita and per-dollar-on-GDP basis. Much of Canadian GHG emissions are related to the extraction (as opposed to burning) of oil, gas, and coal and even electricity for export. Canadian CO_2 emissions are high because energy is needed to produce energy for export, particularly crude oil from the oil sands, which account for 60 per cent of national oil production and 8.5 per cent of CO_2 emissions (see table).

Item	Units	Canada	EU
Crude oil production	($\times 10^6$ bbl/day)	4.29	1.41
Crude oil consumption	($\times 10^6$ bbl/day)	2.37	12.53
Natural gas production	($\times 10^9$ m^3)	162.0	132.3
Natural gas consumption	($\times 10^9$ m^3)	104.2	386.9
Coal production	($\times 10^6$ tonnes)	68.8	537.6
Coal production	(Mtoe)	36.6	151.4
Coal consumption	(Mtoe)	21.2	269.8
Electricity production	($\times 10^6$ MWh = TWh)	615.4	3,010.5
Net electricity exports	(TWh)	57.6	-11.1
GHG emissions total	($\times 10^6$ tCO_2)	620.5	3,705.0
GHG emissions per person	(tCO_2/person)	16.2	7.7
GHG emissions intensity	(kg CO_2/\$ GDP)	0.34	0.20

Current Canadian climate policy is determined by the Canadian Net-Zero Emissions Accountability Act, which was passed on June 29, 2021. The Act commits Canada to achieving net-zero emissions by 2050, which implies that any CO_2 emissions at that time would need to be offset through forestry activities (such as tree planting) or carbon capture and storage, which is an unproven and expensive technology. There are two problems with the plan: (1) While CO_2 emissions fell and the economy grew between 2005 and 2013, since then, despite below-expected economic growth, only limited annual emission reductions transpired; (2) the burden of emissions reduction falls on individual provinces, who do not appear to have an appetite for imposing those costs onto their citizens.

For the EU's "Fit for 55" package and the REPowerEU to achieve its 55 per cent emissions reduction target by 2030, the EU still counts on the effect of carbon taxes or carbon emission trading schemes to drive up fossil fuel prices, thereby inducing industry and private consumers to switch to alternative clean energy sources. Energy prices have risen since the end of 2021 due to various developments, which could support these efforts. Energy prices had already risen sharply before the Ukraine war due to the strong increase in demand following the COVID-19 lockdowns, the sharp rise in CO_2 prices due to speculation, among other things, as well as a restricted supply due to OPEC (the Organization of the Petroleum Exporting Countries) agreements and the reduction of fracked gas production in the United States. In addition, the EU relies on large investments in renewable energy and energy efficiency. In the latter cases, however, the member states are not yet on track to meet their ambitions: The national climate and energy plans so far include measures that would increase the share of renewables by only 33 per cent by 2030, which is 7 percentage points away from the target. In the case of energy efficiency, the measures in the national plans would not even reach the current target of 32.5 per cent (defined in 2016) – not a good starting point for moving to the even more ambitious target recently proposed by the Commission.

One important reason for this unconvincing implementation of these EU goals is the limited competence of the EU in energy policy. As we saw above, the Commission's hands are tied in all areas that affect the national energy mix. Nationally binding targets can only be adopted unanimously – a utopia given the member states' disunity in climate and energy policy. The Commission is left with only soft governance mechanisms, and it has no sanction power for the implementation of EU goals in the field of renewable energies and energy efficiency. As the member states resist giving up control over the national energy mix, the only option remaining for the EU has been to try to "harden" its soft governance mechanisms as much as possible to strengthen their ability to bring about policy change at the national level. Such attempts to harden soft governance can be observed, most importantly, in the Governance Regulation (see Box 17.5).

It is questionable whether this hardening of soft governance will be sufficient to compel member states to pass the measures needed to live up to the targets defined at the European level. A first analysis of the implementation of the Commission's recommendations on the so-called ambition gaps – in other words, insufficient levels of ambition in the NECP compared to the EU-wide targets – speaks volumes: The Commission's recommendations on

> **BOX 17.5: HARDENING OF SOFT GOVERNANCE**
>
> A hardening of soft governance can be identified in the following areas of the Governance Regulation (Knodt et al. 2020):
>
> 1. With regard to the draft NECPs, each member state is obliged to take due account of the Commission's recommendations in its integrated national energy and climate plan.
> 2. At the same time, a justification requirement is introduced: A member state must state and publish why it might fail to address the Commission's recommendations on the draft NECPs.
> 3. In the case of a renewable energy "ambition gap," Annex II of the Governance Regulation provides for an algorithm that defines the allocation of the missing percentage points to the member states. This formula compensates for the absence of missing binding national targets. However, the algorithm does not apply to the energy efficiency target. In addition, the national contributions must be supplemented by an "indicative target path" with regard to increasing the share of renewable energies. Again, such a regulation is missing for energy efficiency; it only refers to the possibility of additional European measures to close any gap between ambitions and outcomes.
> 4. The Governance Regulation also offers more opportunities for "blaming and shaming" compared to the monitoring system for the 2020 targets, as the State of the Energy Union report has to be submitted to the Parliament and the Council.
> 5. The role of the Commission is strengthened by the possibility of adopting "delegated acts" that specify certain requirements of the Governance Regulation.
> 6. However, the Governance Regulation still does not provide for sanction mechanisms. Thus, it has only slightly hardened soft monitoring and control mechanisms, especially in the area of renewable energies and to a lesser extent in the area of energy efficiency.

how to address these gaps were "largely implemented" by only a minority of member states. In the area of renewable energies, this was enough to close the ambition gap, but a gap remains in the area of energy efficiency. This finding

Figure 17.1. Compliance with Commission recommendations by member state

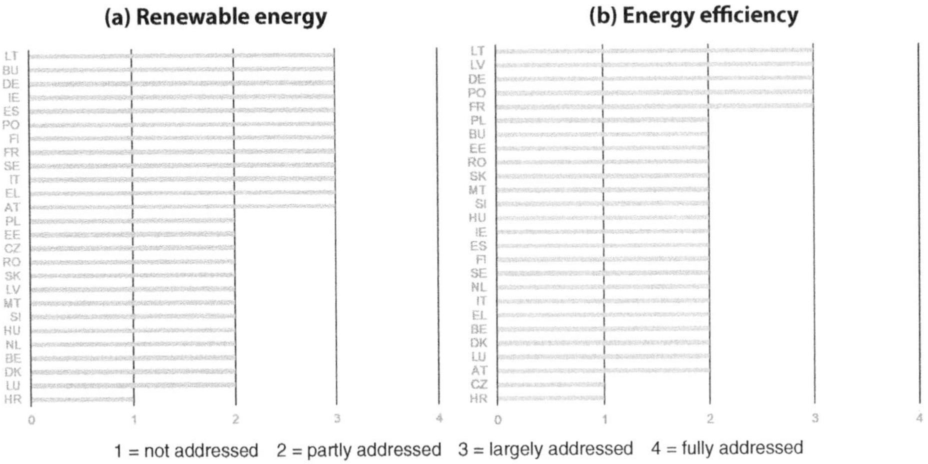

(a) Renewable energy

(b) Energy efficiency

1 = not addressed   2 = partly addressed   3 = largely addressed   4 = fully addressed

Source: Knodt et al. (2021)

suggests that the harder elements of soft governance that exist for renewable energy may indeed have made a difference (see Figure 17.1). The Commission learned from this experience and recently proposed additional measures to further harden rules that apply to energy efficiency as well.

In addition to the institutional constraints, the EGD also requires that the EU addresses challenges to physical infrastructure that currently limits the EU's ability to achieve carbon neutrality. Although renewable energy holds many promises, it presents considerable challenges and costs. Solar and wind are two excellent sources of renewable energy, but they are natural resources that face physical limitations, and there are costs associated with expanding their use (although technological advances could overcome some of these challenges). Securing energy supply will require diversifying sources of imports. Implementing these policies without further fragmenting the internal energy market will require political coordination and increased coordination of infrastructure projects to integrate new energy sources into existing electricity grids and across national borders.

In this context, the EU will have to address the topic of sector coupling of the electricity, heat, and transport sectors. The idea of coupling is to use electricity produced from renewable energy sources to produce hydrogen (H_2) that can be used to provide fuel for transportation, heating, mobility, and storage as needed. Indeed, the Commission indicates in its Hydrogen Strategy (European Commission 2020) that the aim is to produce hydrogen from wind or solar energy and use it primarily as a fuel in sectors where extensive electrification is difficult. Electrolysers with a capacity of 46 gigawatts are to be installed in the EU by 2030. As the capacity of electrolysers is currently inadequate, the EU will become dependent on hydrogen imports. Bilateral partnerships, especially in the neighbourhood of the EU, and multilateral governance will play a central role in establishing international markets for hydrogen and secure hydrogen for the European market.

Finally, it is important to note that many of the policy instruments of the EU are built on the premise that, because renewables potentially displace emission intensive electricity, the social benefits of increasing renewable energy capacity will exceed the social costs associated with phasing out non-renewable energy (van Kooten 2016). These social costs affect member states that are heavily reliant on non-renewable energy (for instance Poland) more than others that have already taken greater strides toward carbon neutrality. The EU is fully aware of these social costs and their potential to create division not only between member states but also within national societies. This is the reason why the EGD installed a Just Transition Mechanism (JTM) as a key tool to ensure that the transition toward a climate-neutral economy happens in a fair way – "leaving no one behind," as the Commission puts it (see Chapter 11). The JTM provides support to help mobilize at least €65–€75 billion over the period 2021–7 in the most affected regions to smooth the socioeconomic impact of the transition. However, the war against Ukraine and high electricity prices are now creating a completely different dimension of social division. As soon as the old gas supply contracts expire and gas suppliers are allowed to pass on the higher costs to customers, the costs for private households may increase many times over, making energy unaffordable for low-income households. It is questionable whether the JTM will be able to compensate for these price increases.

CONCLUSION

For many Europeans, especially but by no means only the younger generations, climate change is one of the most pressing problems of humankind. These EU citizens expect the EU to be a global leader in addressing this challenge. The EU has a strong track record as a climate policy-maker, whereas its achievements in the field of energy policy have been more modest. The war against Ukraine, however, confronts European citizens with a different energy challenge. The fear of unheated homes in winter and of the collapse of energy-intensive sectors of the economy make it necessary to accelerate the energy transformation. But to fight climate change at the same time, a policy approach that integrates climate and energy policy is required.

In crafting the EGD, the "Fit for 55" package, and the REPowerEU, the EU has shown awareness of this need for ambitious, integrated policy solutions. However, the EU's limited competences, especially in the field of energy, continue to post obstacles for aggressive energy transformation and climate change mitigation. While climate policy is regulated under the environmental competences allowing for majority voting in the Council and the passage of binding legislation, crucial competences on energy policy – renewables and energy efficiency – remain at the national level. An increase in the EU's supranational competences on energy issues, to make energy policy more like climate policy, would require a unanimous decision by the member states, which is something that currently seems unrealistic. In its absence, only the coordination of member state policies through soft governance remains. But this approach reaches its limits where member states have divergent ideas about how to combat climate change and achieve energy transformation. To address this shortcoming, the EU's energy policy must be further hardened. However, the first legislative package to implement the EGD still contains few signs of such hardening. Without a revision of the Governance Regulation to bring about a further hardening of EU energy governance, the 2030 and 2050 targets will be difficult to achieve.

Despite these challenges and the changes of war time, climate policy in the EU should not be seen only in a negative light; indeed, it can be viewed as one of the greatest successes of the European integration project. Although the shape and future of the EU may be uncertain, EU-level climate change policy has served to reinvigorate support for European integration and has enhanced the EU's legitimacy on the international stage (Theme 3 of this book). Although much work remains to be done, the EU has earned the reputation as a leader in combating climate change and spearheading environmental regulation. There are good reasons to believe that the EU will continue to exercise this leadership role, not only because of policy developments within the EU setting, but also through its advocacy for high standards internationally. The enormous challenges related to the Russian invasion of Ukraine and its accompanying impact are leading to an acceleration of the energy transformation and thus of climate policy, even if in the first year of the war a small part of the gas consumption in the field of electricity generation was compensated for by coal-fired power generation. This short-term regression is expected to be followed by an acceleration of the transformation toward climate neutrality as EU member states increase their efforts to reduce import dependence on fossil energies.

REVIEW QUESTIONS

1 Outline the differences between how climate policy and energy policy are governed in the EU. How far-reaching are the EU's powers in each policy area?
2 Elaborate on the differences in the energy mix of the EU and of Canada and explain possible reasons for these differences. Also outline how the energy mixes need to be changed to address climate change.
3 Discuss why the objectives of the EGD will not be easy to implement in the EU.

EXERCISES

1 Which legal tools are used to regulate climate and energy policy in the EU? What does this toolkit indicate about the depth of European integration in both fields and the potential of the EU to bring about policy change?
2 Research the position of (the governments of) various EU member states on climate change. Which member states would you characterize as leaders in the fight against climate change? Which ones emerge as laggards?

REFERENCES AND FURTHER READING

Agora Energiewende. 2021. "The European Power Sector 2020." https://static.agora-energiewende.de/fileadmin/Projekte/2021/2020_01_EU-Annual-Review_2020/A-EW_202_Report_European-Power-Sector-2020.pdf.

Bongardt, A., and Torres, F. 2022. "The European Green Deal: More Than an Exit Strategy to the Pandemic Crisis, a Building Block of a Sustainable European Economic Model." *Journal of Common Market Studies* 60 (1): 170–85. https://doi.org/10.1111/jcms.13264.

Canada Energy Regulator. 2021. "Canada's Energy Future." Data Appendices. https://apps.rec-cer.gc.ca/ftrppndc/dflt.aspx?GoCTemplateCulture.

European Commission. 2015. "A Framework Strategy for a Resilient Energy Union with a Forward-Looking Climate Change Policy." Communication from the Commission to the European Parliament, the Council, the European Economic

and Social Committee and the Committee of the Regions, COM (2015) 80 final. Brussels: European Union.
European Commission. 2019. "The European Green Deal." Communication of the Commission to the European Parliament, the European Council, the Council, the European Economic and Social Committee and the Committee of the Regions, COM (2019) 640 final. Brussels: European Union.
European Commission. 2020. "A Hydrogen Strategy for a Climate-Neutral Europe." Communication of the Commission to the European Parliament, the European Council, the Council, the European Economic and Social Committee and the Committee of the Regions, COM (2020) 301 final. Brussels: European Union.
Herranz-Surrallés, A. 2015. "An Emerging EU Energy Diplomacy? Discursive Shifts, Enduring Practices." *Journal of European Public Policy* 23 (6): 1386–405. https://doi.org/10.1080/13501763.2015.1083044.
Jordan, A., and C. Adelle, eds. 2013. *Environmental Policy in the EU: Actors, Institutions and Processes*. Abingdon, UK: Routledge.
Jordan, A., and T. Rayner. 2010. "The Evolution of Climate Policy in the European Union: A Historical Overview." In *Climate Change Policy in the European Union: Confronting the Dilemmas of Mitigation and Adaptation*, edited by A. Jordan, D. Huitema, H. van Asselt, T. Rayner, and F. Berkhout, 52–81. Cambridge: Cambridge University Press.
Knodt, M. 2018. "Energy Policy." In *Handbook of European Policies: Interpretive Approaches to the EU*, edited by H. Heinelt and S. Münch, 224–40. Basingstoke, UK: Palgrave Macmillan.
Knodt, M., R. Müller, M. Ringel, and S. Schlacke. 2021. "(Un)fit for 55? Lehren aus der Implementation der Governance-Verordnung." Ariadne Analyse, PIK Potsdam. https://ariadneprojekt.de/publikation/analyse-unfit-for-55.
Knodt, M., N. Piefer, and F. Müller, eds. 2015. *Challenges of EU External Energy Governance towards Emerging Powers*. Aldershot, UK: Ashgate.
Knodt, M., M. Ringel, and R. Müller. 2020. "'Harder' Soft Governance in the European Energy Union Policy." *Journal of Environmental Policy & Planning* 22 (4): 787–800. https://doi.org/10.1080/1523908X.2020.1781604.
McGowan, F. 2011. "Putting Energy Insecurity into Historical Context: European Responses to the Energy Crises of the 1970s and 2000s." *Geopolitics* 16 (3): 486–511. https://doi.org/10.1080/14650045.2011.520857.
Oberthür, S. 2011. "The European Union's Performance in the International Climate Change Regime." *Journal of European Integration* 33 (6): 667–82. https://doi.org/10.1080/07036337.2011.606690.
Oberthür, S., and L. Groen. 2017. "The European Union and the Paris Agreement: Leader, Mediator, or Bystander?" *WIREs Climate Change* 8 (1): 1–8. https://doi.org/10.1002/wcc.445.
Parker, C.F., C. Karlsson, and M. Hjerpe. 2017. "Assessing the European Union's Global Climate Change Leadership: From Copenhagen to the Paris Agreement." *Journal of European Integration* 39 (2): 239–52. https://doi.org/10.1080/07036337.2016.1275608.

van Kooten, G.C. 2004. *Climate Change Economics: Why International Accords Fail.* Cheltenham, UK: Edward Elgar.

van Kooten, G.C. 2016. "The Economics of Wind Power." *Annual Review of Resource Economics* 8 (1): 181–205. https://doi.org/10.1146/annurev-resource-091115-022544.

18

Geopolitics of the European Union

Joan DeBardeleben

READER'S GUIDE

This chapter considers resources the European Union (EU) has to exert international influence, as well as challenges and obstacles that limit the EU's geopolitical power. While the EU has made efforts in recent years to increase its collective presence in the international sphere, the rise of new powers and difficulties in reaching a common EU position have limited the EU's economic and political leverage. Specific issues are examined, including relations with Russia, the war in Ukraine and frozen conflicts in the post-Soviet countries, challenges emanating from the Middle East, and the growing influence of emerging powers. This chapter will give particular attention to how Russia's attack on Ukraine, beginning in February 2022, marked a turning point for the EU's approach to its geopolitical power.

INTRODUCTION

This chapter explores the nature of the global influence of the EU and the way the EU has responded to challenges in an evolving geopolitical environment. **Geopolitics** refers to the exercise of power within a particular spatial or geographic context. The EU's regional and global environment is one of flux and change; at the same time, the EU's enlargement has brought new countries into the Union, and with them, new perspectives and different priorities about **foreign policy**. Only slowly and unsurely has the EU come to realize the geopolitical implications of its actions. Russia's attack on Ukraine, which began on February 24, 2022, marked a turning point in how the EU perceives itself as a geopolitical actor and the resources that it is able to muster to defend its geopolitical interests.

Three factors are of key importance in understanding the geopolitical forces that have shaped and continue to shape the EU's understanding of itself as a regional and global force. The first involves changing circumstances in Europe itself. As discussed in Chapter 1, European integration was initiated as an effort to create a viable and stable system based on economic interdependence to assure the maintenance of peace in Europe. With the collapse of the Soviet Union in 1991, however, the geopolitical context changed radically. The bipolar structure, termed the Cold War, which was characterized by rivalry between the Union of Soviet Socialist Republics (USSR) and the West, came to an end. The Soviet collapse resulted in the emergence of a large number of newly independent countries, including the Russian Federation, which had to find their place in Europe as well as in the larger international sphere. Over time, establishing a constructive relationship with the Russian Federation has remained a particular challenge, escalating to a full-scale adversarial relationship in 2022. At the same time, the EU, through its Eastern Partnership policy (see Chapter 14), sought to develop partnerships with other post-Soviet states and achieved particular success with Ukraine, Moldova, and Georgia.

The second set of factors has to do with the altered structure of the larger global geopolitical environment in the last two decades. Countries such as China, India, and Brazil are taking on increased importance, challenging the previous structures of international relations. Along with Russia and South Africa, these are referred to as the BRICS countries. A third factor is continuing instability in the Middle East, including ongoing tensions between Israel and its Arab neighbours, continuing impacts of the so-called Arab Spring (anti-government uprisings beginning in 2011 that spread across a range of Middle Eastern countries), and the return to power of the Taliban in Afghanistan in August 2021 following the withdrawal of US and allied forces. Other developments, such as climate change, disputes over the Arctic, and worries about energy security, have also affected Europe's geopolitical position.

In areas clearly within the jurisdiction of EU institutions or where EU member states have been able to agree on priority objectives, such as trade, non-proliferation of nuclear weapons, humanitarian assistance, and climate change policy, the EU has achieved the status of a global power. By contrast, in terms of a range of other concerns, particularly relating to security, the EU's global and even regional influence has been more limited. For security, Europe's reliance on the North Atlantic Treaty Organization (NATO) and the United States continues to be strong. As discussed in Chapter 9, because many foreign policy functions are retained by the member states, the EU often lacks the capability and instruments to react effectively on its own to geopolitical challenges or to accept the geopolitical power that it potentially commands. This reality sometimes contributes to unpredictable outcomes, such as deteriorating relations with Russia and challenges in handling large refugee flows from northern Africa, the Middle East, and in 2022, Ukraine.

THE EU: AN "ACCIDENTAL" GEOPOLITICAL ACTOR?

The EU operates in a geopolitical environment, but the EU itself is not a traditional geopolitical actor. This disjunction has led the EU to overlook geopolitical implications of its actions or to underestimate geopolitical challenges at an early stage. We coin the phrase *accidental geopolitical actor* to describe the EU because, to a large extent, the Union has traditionally defined itself in terms of a set of normative objectives rather than as an international actor promoting its own geopolitical interests. The EU's normative objectives derive from its basic value commitments – for example, promoting democracy, multilateralism, rule of law, and good governance. However, over time the EU has been pressed, without having any clear strategy, to consider the geopolitical implications of its policy choices because of the expanded range of its activities, its greater geographical span, unexpected impacts of its economic influence, and the interconnectedness of social, economic, and political processes. At the same time, challenges to stability in the EU's eastern and southern neighbourhood (see Chapter 14), along with a sometimes ambivalent and fluctuating US commitment to providing leadership to the Western alliance, have instilled a greater appetite among some European leaders for the EU to forge an independent geopolitical role.

Unlike nation states that formulate foreign policy goals reflecting their own understandings of national interest and capabilities, EU decisions almost always represent a compromise between various member state positions. On the other hand, compared to most international organizations, the EU has a broader mandate as well as a stronger capacity to make decisions binding on its members in particular policy arenas (Theme 2 of this book). To discern how the EU's geopolitical position is understood in Brussels, the preferences and strategies of key member states such as France, Germany, Poland, and Spain (and until Brexit, also the United Kingdom) need to be considered. These national conceptions can differ significantly from one another on key issues such as relations with Russia, responses to refugee flows, policy in the Sahel, and reactions to US actions. Unlike the EU, most often individual member states quite readily acknowledge geopolitical (national) interests. One exception is Germany, which has been a reluctant geopolitical actor, similar to the EU itself. German elites are unsure about how assertively their country can wield its power without evoking distrust and suspicion among other countries. Given that Germany has often filled a leadership vacuum in recent years in addressing a range of European problems, this reluctance has reinforced the EU's difficulties in acknowledging its own geopolitical role.

The tools that the EU commands to influence its external environment are more limited than those that a country of similar size and economic importance would be expected to have. Already in 1993, in an influential article, Christopher Hill identified the "capability-expectations gap," referring to the distance between the EU's aspirations and the tools it has to realize these goals (Hill 1993). For example, the EU lacks a credible military capacity, and with Brexit the military capacity of the EU was reduced even further. An important 2016 EU strategy document called *Shared Vision, Common Action: A Stronger Europe* – also called the EU's **Global Strategy** (European Union 2016) – suggests that the EU's military capability should be reinforced, but there are both budgetary and political obstacles to realizing this objective. The Lisbon Treaty had laid out the basis to develop the EU's defensive and security capacity through Permanent Structured Cooperation (PESCO), which was activated in late 2017 (see also Chapter 9). However, PESCO remains a member state–driven mechanism, even if the commitments made under it are binding on countries that participate.

Nonetheless, the EU still has other important sources of power, primarily of two types: normative power and economic might. Political scientist Joseph Nye (2004) developed the concept of "soft power" to depict the manner in which non-material resources can be deployed to effectively establish international influence. Among the EU's most important soft power tools is normative power, a notion explored by Ian Manners in a seminal article in 2002. Normative power refers to the "ability to shape conceptions of 'normal'" (Manners 2002, 240) – that is, to influence ideas and opinions about appropriate norms and values governing decisions and actions. Manners argued that the EU is often able to achieve its objectives by using the "soft" powers of persuasion, example, and socialization, convincing leaders and publics in other countries that the European model is desirable, both due to the intrinsic values it represents as well as the security and prosperity that it has afforded its citizens. The values that underlie the European model in exercising normative power are concepts such as democratic governance, rule of law, and universal human rights, as well as the proclaimed superiority of a liberal competitive market economic system to promote prosperity and human welfare. These, of course, are the very values that form the legitimizing basis of the EU itself, and they have indeed gained wide adherence, ascribed to, at least rhetorically, by leaders worldwide, even when they are not honoured in practice. More recently, values such as sustainable development and limiting climate change have been taken on by the EU (see Chapter 17). The use of normative power as a resource to influence other countries, however, has some pitfalls, in that it easily opens the door to charges of hypocrisy if those values are not realized at home. It can also engender resistance if other countries resent the EU's efforts to export its values.

The EU's normative power is augmented by its economic force. Despite a decline because of Brexit (and also due to the impact of the COVID-19 pandemic), the EU had a gross domestic product (GDP) of €13.25 trillion in 2020 and a population of 447.1 million inhabitants at the start of 2021, making it one of the largest potential markets in the world as well as a source of foreign direct investment for partner countries. While the average level of GDP per capita for the EU overall is well below that of Canada and the United States, it considerably exceeds that of other potentially influential countries such as Russia, China, India, and Türkiye. Furthermore, the more affluent countries of the EU stand at the top of the World Development Index. Countries of the former Soviet bloc that have joined the EU have experienced a much clearer upward economic trajectory compared to those that have remained outside. This combination of factors has accorded the EU credibility and attractiveness as an economic model, giving the EU the capacity to generate support for free trade agreements and other forms of partnership that other countries believe will be beneficial in economic terms. The EU's economic might also allows it to use the tool of economic sanctions, when agreed to unanimously by member states, as has occurred in relation to Russia since 2014 when Russia annexed Crimea and even more assertively since February 2022 when it launched a full-scale military attack on Ukraine.

The EU's soft power tools – namely reliance on its "power of attractiveness" – generally are effective only if viewed in the medium to long term, since the underlying socialization effects and benefits of association with the EU do not take place immediately. Furthermore, the economic problems that the EU and the euro area have experienced since 2008, as well as the EU's faltering response to the migration and COVID-19 crises, have to some extent undermined the credibility of the EU economic and governance model.

An important element of the EU's geopolitical reality is the relationship of Europe to the US as well as to Canada. A key vehicle for securing this transatlantic connection has been NATO. With the collapse of the USSR in 1991 (the adversary that triggered NATO's original formation after World War II), NATO has had to find a new mandate. It turned to crisis management and disaster relief activities in conflict zones, as well as combating terrorism. With Russia's attack on Ukraine in 2022, NATO's mandate of military defence took on renewed importance. Article 5 of the NATO treaty, which states that an "armed attack against one or more of them in Europe or North America shall be considered an attack against them all," provides the foundation for a US security commitment to Europe. Ukraine is not a NATO member, so the alliance has not become a direct combatant in Russia's war on Ukraine. However, NATO members have provided military assistance and weapons to Ukraine. Furthermore, NATO itself has strengthened its military presence on the eastern flank to provide reassurance to NATO members that border Russia (Estonia, Latvia, Lithuania, and Poland – all of which are also EU members) and feel under increased threat due to Russia's evident readiness to use military force to threaten the national sovereignty of neighbours. The level of military spending of the US, as a percentage of GDP, exceeds that of any of the EU countries except Greece.

While the US has been the most important ally of the EU, areas of tension also exist. With the global balance of power shifting away from Europe to Asia, some US administrations have seemed to place a decreased priority on the transatlantic alliance in favour of positioning the US as a stronger power in relation to China and other rising powers. In addition, the tendency of the US to take unilateral action outside the framework of international organizations has been an irritant to the EU and some of its largest member states. While these differences were augmented during the time that Donald Trump was US president (2017–21), they have abated significantly since Joseph Biden became president in 2021, especially given the unity of the alliance and the commitment of the US to resisting Russian aggression in Ukraine.

Nonetheless, uncertainty remains in Europe about the reliability and durability of the US commitment to common goals, given the possible outcomes of future US presidential elections. This uncertain prospect has pushed some member states, such as France and Germany, to advocate for greater "strategic autonomy" for the EU (see Chapter 9).

REGIONAL GEOPOLITICAL CHALLENGES: THE EU'S EASTERN AND SOUTHERN NEIGHBOURHOOD

Until the collapse of the Soviet Union in 1991, the postwar geopolitical environment in which European integration was unfolding was marked by the division of Europe into two clearly defined blocs. "Eastern" and "Western" Europe stood in a competitive relationship to one another on many different dimensions. This split formed the basis of the Cold War. The Cold War defined the geopolitical challenges that the EU faced in its regional environment. Despite the competitive military build-up of the Cold War, the situation took on a certain stability and predictability that allowed the European integration project to progress. The fall of the Berlin Wall in 1989, the reunification of Germany in 1990, followed by the collapse of the USSR that marked the end of the Cold War in 1991 together represented a major geopolitical earthquake in Europe. These changes upset the terms of the postwar settlement, introducing the possibility of instability and uncertainty to the continent.

Conflict and Instability in Eastern Europe

From the 1990s and into the 2000s, the EU's policy in relation to Eastern Europe was largely premised on an enlargement logic (see Chapter 13), culminating in the addition of 10 new members in 2004, two in 2007, and one in 2013. However, using enlargement as a foreign policy tool has carried with it geopolitical implications that were not adequately foreseen. One of these is what Tom Casier (2008) calls the "insider/outsider paradox": As more countries join the EU, it becomes more costly for others to remain outside. This situation arises because the benefits of being in such a strong free trade and customs zone are largely restricted to members. Thus, through enlargement, the EU indirectly affected the economic and geopolitical calculations of its eastern neighbours, strengthening the desire for membership in countries such as Georgia, Moldova, and Ukraine. The EU's response, the EU's European Neighbourhood Policy, encouraged neighbours to adopt EU regulatory standards and to seek greater integration to achieve trade access. However, until recently the EU did so without offering the prospect of eventual membership (see Chapter 14).

These policies, intended to create a stable and secure environment for democratic and market development, also failed to address the three "frozen conflicts" that had developed in the post-Soviet space. *Frozen conflicts* refer to international disputes that have proven intractable to resolution; while the regions may appear relatively calm for some period of time, they are capable of erupting into violent conflict in the face of minimal provocation. Each of the three frozen conflicts in Europe involves countries that had emerged as newly independent states following the Soviet collapse. The first is the contested region of Nagorno-Karabakh, located geographically within Azerbaijan but claimed by Armenia due to the strong Armenian population base and for historical reasons. The second involves two secessionist regions, South Ossetia and Abkhazia, which are located in Georgia. The third case is Transnistria, a region with a significant Russian population located in the eastern part of Moldova, bordering southwestern Ukraine. The EU has, for a variety of reasons, been largely unable to contribute for sustainable solutions for these three frozen conflicts.

An even greater problem emerged when Russia annexed a part of Ukraine in 2014 and then attacked Ukraine militarily in February 2022, trying to take over large parts of that country (see Chapter 14 and below). Russia's justification for its attack on Ukraine was not explicitly related to expanding EU influence, but rather to the prospect of Ukraine's eventual NATO accession and the alleged militarization and Nazification of the country. Russia's actions spurred the EU to consider how to wield its geopolitical power more effectively to resist forces that undermine both its normative values and its immediate security interests. One such response was the EU's unanimous decision on June 23, 2022, to grant Ukraine and Moldova the official status of EU candidate states (see Chapter 13). While the process of accession for Ukraine and Moldova is expected to be a long one, the EU's decision suggests an increased willingness to take bold geopolitical action in the face of international threats to stability.

The Middle East and the Arab Spring

The geographic proximity of the Middle East gives issues in this region special importance for the EU; instability there can have dramatic consequences. As

Dandashly and Chira highlight in Chapter 14, the Arab Spring that erupted in December 2010 in Tunisia led to demonstrations and revolts throughout the Arab world. It gave rise to regime collapse or civil war in Bahrain, Egypt, Libya, Syria, Tunisia, and Yemen, opening up a Pandora's box of dilemmas in numerous countries in the region. While the EU welcomed the civil society activism and democratic impulse that underlay these changes, the resultant destabilization of existing governments introduced new sources of instability in Europe's larger neighbourhood.

One particular example is the civil war in Syria and the associated influx of hundreds of thousands of asylum seekers, which took first place as the EU's primary geopolitical concern in 2015 (see Chapter 8). This crisis demonstrates graphically how political unrest in adjacent regions can dramatically affect the political and social situation inside the EU itself. Both within particular member states and at the level of EU institutions, disagreements have raged over an appropriate response, for instance regarding the relative weight of the EU's humanitarian obligations to asylum seekers compared to concerns about the EU's absorptive capacities. On another level, the issue crystallized differing member state positions regarding whether the EU could, or should, impose obligations on its member states to share the burden of accepting refugees.

Although formally a candidate for EU accession since 1999, it seems unlikely at present that Türkiye will become a member in the foreseeable future because of tensions over an authoritarian turn in the country. Even so, Türkiye has emerged as an important geopolitical actor. While areas of tension between Türkiye and the West (including the EU) have the potential to unsettle the fragile balance of power in the Middle East, Türkiye also has the potential to play a constructive role in addressing regional conflicts. As a member of NATO, Türkiye has long been considered a linchpin of Western influence in the region, despite more recent doubts about the extent to which Türkiye and other NATO members share common interests. The initial resistance of Türkiye to applications made by Finland and Sweden for NATO membership in May 2022 indicate that Türkiye can wield its bargaining power within its alliance to achieve national political goals. For instance, Türkiye played a role in facilitating negotiations between Ukraine and Russia in summer 2022. An earlier agreement between the EU and Türkiye to address the 2016 refugee crisis was only partially successful (Terry 2021). It involved the return to Türkiye of irregular migrants arriving in Greece in exchange for various concessions from the EU. This agreement between the EU and Türkiye highlighted the difficulties the EU faces in balancing its normative concerns (related to democratic governance in Türkiye as well commitments of the EU member states under the Refugee Convention and its Protocol) with its geopolitical interests (bringing massive refugee flows to Europe under control).

A notable success in EU foreign policy in the Middle East appeared to be its effort, in cooperation with Russia and the US, to prevent Iran from developing a nuclear weapons capacity. Non-proliferation of weapons of mass destruction has been a key policy goal of the EU, and one on which all member states remain highly united. The EU's mobilization of diplomatic resources, in conjunction with key EU member states (France, Germany, and the UK), resulted in 2015 in the Joint Comprehensive Plan of Action that saw Iran agreeing to desist from developing a nuclear weapons capacity in exchange for a strict monitoring regime and the lifting of economic sanctions. However, the deal collapsed when US President Trump removed the US from the agreement in 2018; subsequent developments made clear the limits of the EU's power – the US imposed sanctions on Iran and on European companies continuing the deal with Iran. Efforts by US President Biden to restore the agreement have so far been unsuccessful. In 2022, the Iranian government has shown clear support for Russia in its moves against Ukraine, heightening the division between the West and Iran.

GLOBAL GEOPOLITICAL CHALLENGES: THE EU'S GEOPOLITICAL ROLE OUTSIDE OF EUROPE

At the same time that the broader European geopolitical environment has undergone radical change, the balance of power on the global scale has also seen significant alteration. The increasing economic and political importance of countries such as China, India, and Brazil has led the EU to focus on intensified relations with them. One of the tools that the EU has developed is the notion of strategic partnership. In addition, the EU's attention has also been devoted to pressing global problems such as terrorism, cybersecurity, refugee flows, and climate change.

The EU's Strategic Partnerships

While there are no clear criteria defined to determine which countries should be designated as **strategic partners**, those included are countries considered to be of long-term importance to the EU's objectives. Of the 10 originally

Table 18.1. Selected EU partners for trade in goods, as % of extra-EU trade

	Exports from the EU		Imports from the EU	
	2016	2021	2016	2021
US	20.8	18.3	14.5	11.0
China	9.7	10.3	20.2	22.3
United Kingdom	Part of EU	13.0	Part of EU	6.9
Switzerland	8.2	7.2	7.1	5.8
Russia	4.1	4.1	7.0	7.7
Türkiye	4.5	3.6	3.9	3.7
Japan	3.3	2.9	3.9	2.9
Norway	2.8	2.6	3.7	3.5
South Korea	2.6	2.4	2.4	2.6
India	2.2	1.9	2.3	2.2
Canada	2.0	1.7	1.7	1.1
Brazil	1.8	1.6	1.7	1.6
Mexico	1.9	1.7	1.2	1.1

Sources: European Commission, Directorate General for Trade, DG Trade statistical guide (June 2017), p. 58, https://data.europa.eu/doi/10.2781/229117; European Commission, Directorate General for Trade, DG Trade statistical guide (August 2022), p. 36, https://data.europa.eu/doi/10.2781/83367

designated strategic partners, several share a common values agenda with the EU (Canada, Japan, South Korea, and the United States); the others were newly emerging international powers referred to as the BRICS (Brazil, Russia, India, China, South Africa) along with Mexico. Since 2014, the EU has disavowed Russia as a strategic partner, and since February 2022 Russia has clearly been viewed as an adversary rather than a partner of the EU. The strategic partners of the EU are all members of the G20 – a group created in 2009 to bring together the world's strongest economies. No doubt an important motivation for identifying strategic partnerships has to do with reinforcing the EU's global economic position in the face of a changing balance of global power; also, four of the five BRICS are among the EU's 12 largest trading partners (see Table 18.1).

Strategic partnerships are also seen as a vehicle to mobilize support for key EU values such as multilateralism and to gain cooperation in addressing global or regional issues such as climate change or regional conflicts. However, the weakness of this approach became evident in March 2022 when India, China, and South Africa abstained on a UN General Assembly vote condemning Russia's military actions in Ukraine. At the same time, other strategic partners (Canada, Japan, South Korea, and the US) have stood strongly together in opposing Russian aggression. Box 18.1 takes a closer look at the strategic partnership with Canada.

BOX 18.1: CANADA'S TRANSATLANTIC CONNECTIONS
Canada is closely tied to the US by trade, geography, and history. While 75 per cent of Canada's exports went to the US in 2019, only 8 per cent went to the EU; for imports the figures were 51 per cent and 13 per cent (Government of Canada 2020; World Bank 2021). Canada's membership in NATO provides a critical link to both the US and Europe in the security sphere, but Canada's role there is often overshadowed by the greater international political weight of the US. Therefore, Canada's direct bilateral ties to the EU are an important vehicle in Canadian efforts to diversify its trade and international profile beyond its relationship with the US.

To reduce Canadian dependence on the US economy and to expand Canada's links with Europe, a Comprehensive Economic and Trade Agreement (CETA) was negotiated over several years and signed in 2014 (see Chapter 12). Alongside CETA, the EU and Canada also negotiated a Strategic Partnership Agreement that reaffirms a broad range of shared commitments, including in the areas of political values, sustainable development, anti-terrorism, non-proliferation of weapons of mass destruction, and the important role for effective multilateralism. Already Canada has supported several EU activities, including EU missions in the Palestinian Territories, Kosovo, and Ukraine, as well as providing financial support to the EU's training mission in Mali.

As noted in this chapter, the EU's strategic partnerships are viewed as important instruments for the EU to achieve its foreign policy objectives. But among those partnerships EU officials frequently emphasize the important place of Canada in this group. In a visit to Canada in 2016, the EU's high representative for foreign and security policy stated, "we really see Canada as a key partner in multilateralism, in conflict management and conflict prevention, for stabilizing the different crises we have around us," and referred to Canada as a "like-minded partner" (Delegation of the European Union to Canada 2016). In particular, Canada has traditionally shared the EU's strong commitment to multilateralism, which involves support for international law, a rule-based international order, and

> strong international institutions, most importantly the United Nations. One expression of this has been a commitment to the United Nations Framework Convention on Climate Change, a priority shared with the EU and also with the US Biden administration.

The EU's relationship with China has taken on particular importance, poses unique challenges, and has spurred a broader evaluation of global geopolitical relationships. China is now the EU's second-largest trading partner after the US; imports from China exceed exports, leaving the EU with a significant negative trade balance. Alongside strong trade ties, significant areas of tension with China have arisen, both in political and economic spheres. In December 2020 the EU and China reached an agreement in principle on an investment agreement that could give greater access in China for European investors, as well as including commitments from China in the areas of environmental and labour standards, two key normative priorities of the EU (European Commission 2020). However, progress on the agreement has stalled due to several issues: a dispute over human rights violations against the Uyghur minority in China's Xinjiang region, Chinese sanctions against Lithuania after the latter opened a representative office in Taiwan in October 2021, and finally (and most importantly) China's failure to condemn Russian aggression against Ukraine. The EU has also had significant concerns regarding China's alleged "dumping" of products at prices below their value on the export market, and so far the EU has not granted China "market economy status," which disadvantages some Chinese imports. China's Belt and Road Initiative has also evoked concern in Brussels, as China strives to increase its influence in investment-hungry countries of the EU by funding large infrastructure projects that are part of an effort to construct an integrated economic structure from China to Eurasia and Europe. These developments illustrate the EU's difficulties in balancing economic and normative concerns in its foreign policy relations with emerging powers.

International Terrorism and Cybersecurity

Since the dramatic attacks on the World Trade Center in New York City in September 2001, European capitals have also been the victims of high-profile terrorist attacks by Islamist radical groups, with significant loss of life. The most dramatic instances were attacks on Spanish commuter trains in 2004, on the Brussels airport and metro in March 2016, and on multiple locations in France in 2015 and 2016. Alongside these more widely publicized events, a larger number of smaller terrorist incidents have occurred, although the number of casualties from terrorist incidents in the EU is relatively low, in part due to increased cooperation among EU member states on anti-terrorist measures (see Chapter 8).

Following the November 2015 Paris attacks, increasing concern arose about the number of radicalized "home grown" youth involved with terrorist organizations. These incidents have fed Islamophobic sentiments across Europe; right-wing politicians have mobilized popular sentiments against asylum seekers. These events also brought increased attention in Europe's capitals to the roots of the problems. The risks generated by failed or failing states, socioeconomic dislocation, ideological radicalization, and civil wars in various African and Middle Eastern countries came more sharply into focus as geopolitical concerns of national and EU leaders. Other concerns centred on cybersecurity, with incidents emanating from both state and non-state actors. Effectively addressing cyberthreats is challenging because it is often difficult to identify the exact perpetrators or the degree of foreign state involvement. While primary responsibility for addressing cybersecurity rests with the member states, in 2013 the first EU Cybersecurity Strategy was adopted. It has been enhanced since then by various pieces of legislation, including the National Information Systems Directive and the Cybersecurity Act. A new Cybersecurity Strategy was adopted in 2020.

The arenas of counterterrorism and cybersecurity, much like the question of refugee flows, make evident the manner in which the geopolitical environment can complicate management of the EU's internal political situation and demand greater member state coordination, increasing the impetus for policy integration. And, as in the regional sphere, these examples illustrate the mixed capacity of the EU to exert effective international influence. In part, this situation arises from the intractable nature of the problems being addressed, which require cooperation with a wider variety of international partners, some of whom may not share the EU's basic value commitments. This area is also one in which the EU and its member states share competence (see Chapter 8). At the same time, effects of international crises, such as the ones in Syria and Ukraine, have also had a critical impact on domestic politics in Europe, making the EU more vulnerable to the destabilizing effects of international conflict.

DEBATE: RELATIONS WITH RUSSIA AND THE UKRAINE WAR

The relationship with Russia is among the most important, but has also been among the most difficult, foreign policy issues facing the EU. In the 1990s there was widespread hope that the new Russian Federation would pursue a path of economic and political reform that would bring it into the mainstream of European development, as understood by the EU. Indeed, in 1997 a Partnership and Cooperation Agreement between the EU and Russia came into effect and was extended on an ad hoc basis after it formally expired in 2007. Negotiations to renew the agreement failed, however, and discussions were cut off by the EU after the Russian annexation of Crimea in 2014. In 2003, four "common spaces" of cooperation were agreed to between the EU and Russia. They relate to economic cooperation; freedom, security, and justice; external security; and research, education, and culture. In 2004, the EU invited Russia to join the European Neighbourhood Policy (see Chapter 14), which it refused because it did not wish to sign on to a made-in-Brussels initiative that would put it on equal footing with other "smaller" partner countries. In June 2010, the EU and Russia announced a new initiative, the Partnership for Modernization, intended to assist the Russian government in its effort to modernize and diversify its economy. However, from the beginning Russia resisted the EU's attempt to include issues of political modernization (rule of law, human rights, democratic governance) in the shared agenda.

Over time, Russia expressed more and more irritation at the EU's efforts to export its version of European norms and values. In order to deal with underlying differences between the EU and Russia, issues of contest were increasingly redefined as technical issues in an effort to make them less politically charged and more amenable to compromise. The most serious problems between the EU and Russia, however, have stemmed from policies of the two parties in the "shared neighbourhood." This area refers to those countries that were formerly part of the USSR but are now independent states, situated close to both Russia and the enlarged EU (i.e., Armenia, Azerbaijan, Belarus, Georgia, Moldova, and Ukraine). After the EU launched the Eastern Partnership in 2009, the Russian leadership apparently concluded that if these countries moved closer to the EU, Russia's leverage would be threatened. The Russian leadership responded by reinforcing its own regional integration efforts, involving a regional customs union that became the Eurasian Economic Union in 2015. Ukraine, however, refused to join these initiatives, despite Russian pressure. Ukraine made a radical turn to the West in the face of Russian annexation of part of its territory – the Crimean peninsula – in February 2014 and in light of Russian support for separatist forces in the eastern Ukrainian provinces of Donetsk and Luhansk.

The Russian annexation of Crimea was viewed by the EU, as well as by other Western countries, as a blatant violation of Ukraine's sovereignty and of international law. When EU member states were able to agree on a package of sanctions against Russia in 2014, veteran EU observers were quite surprised; previously the EU member states had severe difficulty forging a common stance toward Russia. A freeze in relations between the EU and Russia ensued. Efforts to fashion a compromise regarding the conflict in the eastern Ukrainian regions, initiated by the German chancellor Angela Merkel and the French president, François Hollande, led to the so-called Minsk II protocol in February 2015. However, the terms of that agreement were not fulfilled either on the Russian or the Ukrainian side. Further Russian actions led to new spikes in tensions – for example, the poisoning of Sergei and Yulia Skripal in the UK (2018) and the poisoning (2020) and subsequent arrest (2021) of Russian opposition leader Alexey Navalny.

A build-up of Russian military forces near the Ukrainian border in late 2021 and early 2022 elicited warnings from Western security analysts of a possible Russian attack on Ukraine. Russia put forth stark demands that Ukraine permanently disavow a NATO membership aspiration and that it demilitarize its territory and "de-Nazify" its government, which, in fact, had been elected through democratic means and espoused a commitment to Western liberal values. Diplomatic efforts to avert a conflict failed. Then, on February 24, 2022, Russia launched an aggressive assault with the apparent intention of capturing Kyiv, the Ukrainian capital, as well as large parts of the country. While the Russian leader, Vladimir Putin, is reported to have expected a quick victory, the Ukrainian military, with the help of Western military equipment, proved surprisingly effective in pushing Russian forces back, exacting heavy losses on them. The Russian military effort subsequently refocused on eastern Ukraine; in fall 2022 the Russian government illegally proclaimed the annexation of four Ukrainian regions, parts of which were controlled by Ukrainian forces. At the time of writing, it is not clear how the war will end. There is no doubt, however, that this conflict has produced a paradigm shift in EU–Russian relations that will have a long-lasting legacy. It also has awakened the EU out of its geopolitical slumber. There is a wide recognition in Brussels, as well as in most European capitals, that geopolitical decisions cannot be avoided. Geopolitical interests must be defended, not only to safeguard European values but also to ensure European security.

Following the events of February 2022, the EU has mobilized its considerable economic power to thwart Russian elites and Russian military action. EU sanctions against Russia, coordinated with Canada, the US, and other allies, have been progressively expanded, including export and import bans, exclusion of several key Russian and Belarusian financial institutions from the SWIFT payments system, other financial sanctions, measures against particular individuals, and a commitment to wean the EU off its energy dependence on Russian oil and gas (see Chapter 17). In addition to economic tools, the EU agreed, in an unprecedented move, to mobilize €2 billion (by May 2022) to support the transfer of military equipment and other support from EU member states to Ukrainian forces.

Given the sheer size and unprecedented nature of these actions it will come as no surprise that some of them have been somewhat contentious within the EU. Weaning off Russian energy supplies creates greater difficulties for some member states than others. For example, Hungary raised objections to banning Russian oil imports and exacted specific exemptions, which also apply to other Central European countries. Despite these differences, the degree of unanimity has been impressive. The EU's decision to dramatically reduce its reliance on Russian fossil fuel imports represents a radical geopolitical as well as economic shift.

There are ample examples of these changes. In late February 2022 Germany stopped certification of a major new natural gas pipeline linking Russia and Germany (Nordstream 2); in May 2022 the European Commission proposed a plan (REPowerEU) that included reducing Russian gas imports by two-thirds by the end of 2022; and in June 2022 the EU committed to ceasing all oil imports by sea from Russia by the end of 2022 (see Chapter 17). Not only do these plans raise the prospect of energy shortages in EU countries and associated economic fallout for industry, they also represent a turn away from the logic that drove EU policy toward Russia until 2014, which saw energy interdependence as a source of stability for the relationship. Economic and energy interdependence between the EU and Russia have not, in fact, provided the hoped-for foundation for positive political relations. Overall, the EU's transformative power on the European continent, exemplified through the enlargement process, has not been effective with Russia. Accordingly, the EU has felt compelled to mobilize other forms of economic and geopolitical might.

CONCLUSION

The EU has had some notable successes in exerting its influence both regionally and globally. At the regional level, it has displayed strong unity in placing unprecedented sanctions on Russia, in using the enlargement incentive to promote good governance in the West Balkans (see Chapter 13), and in accepting Moldova and Ukraine as EU candidate states. The EU is a global actor in the field of trade and economic relations (see Chapters 7 and 12). The EU has also exerted influence in the area of climate policy (see Chapter 17) and, through the Common Security and Defence Policy, in executing civilian and crisis management missions in Africa (see Chapter 9). Nonetheless, it has not yet established itself as a real global force.

While facing considerable internal challenges, the EU's external environment also seems fraught with danger. The stability of the post–Cold War order in Europe has proven to be more fragile than anticipated, undermining the overarching goal of the European integration project – namely, to avoid war. In addition, in the face of new challenges, including an aggressive Russia, continuing instability in the Middle East, and the rising power of China and other BRICS countries, the EU has struggled to increase its capacity to act in a unified manner as a foreign policy actor. Differing member state perspectives have created difficulties in generating common positions in many arenas, highlighting the weaknesses of the EU's governance model, which falls short of a true federal state since member states retain significant autonomy in the foreign policy arena (Theme 2 of this book). The continuing importance of individual member states' leadership has been both a resource the EU has been able to harness and an obstacle in the EU's search for a clear geopolitical perspective.

REVIEW QUESTIONS

1 Is the EU a geopolitical actor? How is the EU similar or different in its geopolitical role from countries such as Canada or the United States?
2 How does the EU exercise soft power (particularly normative power) and what are the limits and benefits of this?

3 Explain the EU's geopolitical influence on immediate neighbours and then on a global level. How does the influence differ?
4 Why did the EU's efforts to develop a constructive partnership with Russia fail?

EXERCISES

1 Familiarize yourself with definitions of *geopolitics* in different theories of international relations (realism, liberalism, constructivism, and so on). Which best explains the EU's evolution to date?
2 How has the UK's exit from the EU affected the geopolitics of the EU? How has Brexit influenced the EU's self-conception and changing position as an international actor?
3 Consider different possible future scenarios for how the EU–Russia relationship might develop in the future, and identify factors that would make the various scenarios more or less likely.

REFERENCES AND FURTHER READING

Casier, T. 2008. "The New Neighbours of the European Union: The Compelling Logic of Enlargement?" In *The Boundaries of EU Enlargement: Finding a Place for Neighbours*, edited by J. DeBardeleben, 19–32. London: Palgrave Macmillan.

Cottey, A. 2020. "Astrategic Europe." *Journal of Common Market Studies* 58 (2): 276–91. https://doi.org/10.1111/jcms.12902.

DeBardeleben, J. 2020. "Crisis Response, Path Dependence, and the Joint Decision Trap: The EU's Eastern and Russia Policies after the Ukraine Crisis." *East European Politics* 36 (4): 564–85. https://doi.org/10.1080/21599165.2020.1832474.

Delegation of the European Union to Canada. 2016. "Mogherini Welcomes Close EU-Canada Cooperation." https://www.eeas.europa.eu/node/4037_en.

European Commission. 2020. "EU and China Reach Agreement in Principle on Investment." https://trade.ec.europa.eu/doclib/press/index.cfm?id=2233.

European Union. 2003. *European Security Strategy: A Secure Europe in a Better World*. http://www.consilium.europa.eu/ueDocs/cms_Data/docs/pressData/en/reports/78367.pdf.

European Union. 2016. *Shared Vision, Common Action: A Stronger Europe: A Global Strategy for the European Union's Foreign and Security Policy*. https://eeas.europa.eu/archives/docs/top_stories/pdf/eugs_review_web.pdf.

Forsberg, T., and H. Haukkala. 2016. *The European Union and Russia.* Basingstoke, UK: Palgrave Macmillan.
Geerearts, G. 2019. "The EU-China Partnership: Balancing between Divergence and Convergence." *Asia Europe Journal* 17 (3): 281–94. https://doi.org/10.1007/s10308-019-00554-2.
Government of Canada. 2020. "Canada's Merchandise Trade Performance with the EU after the Entry into Force of CETA." https://www.international.gc.ca/trade-commerce/economist-economiste/statistics-statistiques/eu-marchandise-ue.aspx?lang=eng.
Hill, C. 1993. "The Capability-Expectations Gap, or Conceptualizing Europe's International Role." *Journal of Common Market Studies* 31 (3): 305–28. https://doi.org/10.1111/j.1468-5965.1993.tb00466.x.
Howorth, J. 2019. "Autonomy and Strategy: What Should Europe Want?" Egmont Institute, Security Policy Brief No 110. http://www.jstor.org/stable/resrep21390.
Keukeleire, S., and T. Delreux. 2022. *The Foreign Policy of the European Union*, 3rd ed. Basingstoke, UK: Palgrave Macmillan.
Lavery, S., and D. Schmid. 2021. "European Integration and the New Global Disorder." *Journal of Common Market Studies* 59 (5): 1322–38. https://doi.org/10.1111/jcms.13184.
Manners, I. 2002. "Normative Power Europe: A Contradiction in Terms?" *Journal of Common Market Studies* 40 (2): 235–58. https://doi.org/10.1111/1468-5965.00353.
Menon, R., and E. Rumer. 2015. *Conflict in Ukraine: The Unwinding of the Post-Cold War Order.* Cambridge, MA: MIT Press.
Nielsen, K.L. 2013. "EU Soft Power and the Capability-Expectations Gap." *Journal of Contemporary European Research* 9 (5): 723–39. https://doi.org/10.30950/jcer.v9i5.479.
Nye, J. 2004. *Soft Power: The Means to Success in World Politics.* New York: Public Affairs.
Renard, T. 2016. "Partnerships for Effective Multilateralism." *Cambridge Review of International Affairs* 29 (1): 18–35. https://doi.org/10.1080/09557571.2015.1060691.
Smith, K.E. 2014. *European Union Foreign Policy in a Changing World*, 3rd ed. Cambridge: Polity Press.
Terry, K. 2021. "The EU-Turkey Deal, Five Years On: A Frayed and Controversial but Enduring Blueprint." Washington, DC: Migration Policy Institute. https://www.migrationpolicy.org/article/eu-turkey-deal-five-years-on.
Verdun, A. 2021. "The EU-Canada Strategic Partnership: Challenges and Opportunities." In *The European Union's Strategic Partnerships: Global Diplomacy in a Complex and Contested World*, edited by L.C. Ferreira-Pereira and M. Smith, 121–48. London: Routledge.
World Bank. 2021. "Canada Monthly Trade Data." https://wits.worldbank.org/countrysnapshot/en/can.
Wouters, J., and S. Van Kerckhoven. 2018. "A European Perspective on the G20 and the BRICS." *International Organisations Research Journal* 13 (2): 60–75. https://doi.org/10.17323/1996-7845-2018-02-04.

19
Conclusion

Emmanuel Brunet-Jailly, Achim Hurrelmann, and Amy Verdun

READER'S GUIDE

Over a period of more than 70 years, the European Union (EU) has developed into a political system that has increasingly federal features, even if it falls short of being a federation. In this concluding chapter, we review the three themes that were set out in Chapter 1: the EU's policy portfolio and attempts to regulate a mixed economy, its institutional structure in between state and international organization, and the recent challenges to its legitimacy. The chapter highlights the areas in which the Union has been challenged, particularly in the past two decades. It shows that the various crises the EU experienced since 2010, such as the financial crisis, the migration crisis, the Brexit referendum, the COVID-19 pandemic, as well as global and regional geopolitical challenges such as the Russian invasion of Ukraine, have provided the EU opportunities to respond and to adapt. None of these developments are easy to resolve, and the path ahead is far from clear.

INTRODUCTION

The primary goal of this book has been to provide an introduction to more that 70 years of history of the EU and to explain its current political system and policy-making processes. The preceding chapters have detailed the expansion of the EU's institutions, legal system, and governance, as well as the history of ideas and theories of the European integration process. The book has also discussed eight policy areas to provide a nuanced overview of the EU's day-to-day activities. Finally, we have discussed four overarching challenges to the EU: namely, the democratization of its internal processes, social justice, climate and energy policies, and the expansion of its geopolitical role. In this concluding chapter, we return briefly to what we have learned from each chapter, and reflect on future challenges of the EU.

In the introductory chapter of this book, we spelled out three themes that sum up the foundations and the logic of operation of the EU project. Theme 1 refers to the EU as a system of policy-making. It points out that the EU was created as a mixed economic system that combines market making with social inclusion and market correction, though over time it has moved toward a more market-oriented system. Theme 2 addresses the institutional structure of the EU; it emphasizes that the EU is neither an international organization nor a federal state. In some areas of policy-making, it much more closely resembles a federal setup (for instance in agricultural policy; see Chapter 10), while in others it remains much more intergovernmental (such as in defence; see Chapter 9). Theme 3 focuses on the legitimation of the EU. Traditionally, the legitimacy of the EU could be traced back to the positive economic effects of European integration. This strategy of maintaining legitimation – producing what has been labelled a *permissive consensus* – has been found wanting over the past two decades, as people voice criticism of the EU's democratic credentials. The widening and deepening of the EU – that is, respectively, the addition of more member states and the expansion of EU powers above and beyond the core areas of economic policy as well as adding more powers to the EU in the economic domain – have added to these legitimation challenges.

As the chapters in this book illustrate, the idea that economic integration alone is at the core of the EU is no longer accurate: The policy spectrum of the EU is nearly as vast as that of its constituent member states (see Chapter 5). Indeed, in some policy areas, such as agriculture, the EU acts as a pseudo-federal government (see Chapter 10). EU policies have often originated and evolved out of an iterative – and not always well-planned – process of expansion. Ironically, EU policies have often developed further during and after crises, as was recently illustrated in response to the COVID-19 pandemic, which led to the emergence of the NextGenerationEU program in 2021 (see Chapter 7). In this process, the EU has progressively become a policy instrument that

European governments turn to for the resolution of issues "bigger" than those that any one single member state could deal with in isolation. As anticipated by the original architects of European integration, the creation of EU institutions and policies has created strong interdependencies among the member states, which indeed make the prospect of war between them appear remote.

Despite these developments, there have repeatedly been controversies between the EU institutions and select member states, or between various member states. These disputes have in the past decade often dominated media headlines, for instance in debates about the 2008 euro area financial crisis (Chapter 7), the 2015 refugee crisis (Chapter 8), or in 2021 about COVID-19 vaccination supplies. Citizens do not feel connected to the EU quite as much as would be desired for a political system that has so much impact. But these instances of disagreement, and the need to grow a sense of citizen belonging, should not overshadow the achievements made by the EU in bringing the member states together, and also in addressing the aforementioned crises.

This concluding chapter draws some lessons from the preceding chapters about the EU and European integration within the context of the book's three themes. The chapter thus sums up this book's historical (Chapter 2), institutional (Chapter 3), legal (Chapter 4), policy-oriented (Chapter 5), and theoretical (Chapter 6) tour of the construction of the EU. It reviews the EU's success in building institutions, policies, and its own legitimacy. But it also returns to the challenges faced by the EU in each respect, be it in defining a common understanding of solidarity (Chapters 5 and 11) or in building consensus among the member states on issues such as neighbourhoods, health, climate and energy, as well as the place of the EU in the world (Chapters 14, 16, 17, and 18). In particular, we see ongoing challenges regarding legal and democratic principles (such as freedom of the press and rule of law; see Chapters 4 and 15). In the end, how does our team of experts assess the construction of the EU collectively across these three themes? What perspectives emerge for the EU's future development?

THEME 1: IS THE EU STILL COMMITTED TO ITS ORIGINAL AMBITION OF BUILDING A MIXED ECONOMIC SYSTEM THAT IS NEITHER STATE CONTROLLED NOR LEFT TO AN UNCONSTRAINED MARKET?

Our review of the EU's history, institutions, and law – but especially the discussion of the market and trade policies, as well as its agricultural, climate, and regional policies – suggests that the EU is possibly the world's largest *regulating polity* in existence today (Chapters 10, 11, and 17). Its institutions follow a logic of diversity that encompasses multiple forms of governance (see Chapter 5). This diversity in EU governance has been created, in large part, to accommodate the different perspectives and preferences of the member states, which points to forms of intergovernmental integration (see Chapter 6).

The most notable success of European integration has been the creation of the Single Market and the associated policies on external trade as well as monetary and financial integration. In these policy areas, supranational institutions dominate policy-making (see Chapters 7 and 12). The jurisprudence of the Court of Justice of the EU has played an important supportive role (see Chapter 4). Recent economic challenges have not undermined the Single Market. Even in the case of the financial crisis of 2008 or COVID-19 and the associated economic crisis of 2020–1, the EU's anti-crisis measures have consisted of a further strengthening of the supranational and integration agendas. In trade policy, the signing of bilateral agreements such as the Comprehensive Economic and Trade Agreement between Canada and the EU (see Chapter 12) illustrates both the dominant importance of the European Commission's supranational strategy, but also the increasing pressures from the member states and their citizens to democratize trade policy-making by allowing for more democratic consultation and engagement with both national and regional parliaments.

In addition to the abolition of trade barriers through strategies of negative integration, including the mutual recognition of national regulatory regimes, the creation of the Single Market has also entailed positive integration: the production of EU-level rules aimed at achieving a variety of social purposes, from product safety to environmental sustainability. In the process, the EU has developed a diverse and innovative regulatory toolkit. Climate policy is an example of a policy area in which the EU has pioneered new regulatory approaches (such as the emissions trading scheme), which have turned the EU into a world leader in the fight against climate change – despite the complexity of energy integration and the geopolitical dependency on Russia for oil and gas (see Chapters 17 and 18).

In contrast to regulatory policies, the EU's attempts at market correction through *redistributive policies* involving financial transfers have been more fragmented. In part because of the limited size of the EU budget, agricultural

(Chapter 10) and regional (Chapter 11) policies have remained the only major fields in which the EU applies redistributive strategies. The EU's agricultural policy achieved its original ambition of stabilizing food supplies but led to overproduction and thus was criticized for its negative impact on world markets; recent reforms have seen the emergence of a "rural development" paradigm that many observers in other countries (including Canada) view as exemplary. Regional policies, which started as a small area of intergovernmental partnerships, have evolved over a 40-year span to become an ambitious system for supporting regional development through investments in infrastructure and human capital. One could argue that it is the largest economic development policy instrument in the world. This policy showcases member state solidarity across the EU. Yet such redistribution takes place in a context in which the policy is driven by an investment strategy across the Union, rather than the more classic forms of intergovernmental redistribution, which point to member state pressures to liberalize development. In recent years, some of the mechanisms from regional policy have been transferred to climate policy – especially through the creation of the Just Transition Mechanism (see Chapter 17).

By contrast, the main fields of social policy, such as health care, pensions, unemployment insurance, and support for the poor, have remained largely the responsibility of member states, because they control implementation and provide most of the funds in this policy area (see Chapter 16). There have been social funds at the EU level, and these assist many EU citizens in improving their skills and abilities to find jobs. Furthermore, in the social domain there are also pan-European standards and systems of non-binding coordination among member states. Yet each member state has to define – and fund – its own social policy regime. The way in which this policy area is governed thus emphasizes the interconnection between EU and member state governance. In member states – or specific policy areas within them – that are traditionally characterized by a liberal model of social policy with low levels of generosity, the EU adds to the social protections enjoyed by the citizens. By contrast, in member states with policy sectors that have traditionally been characterized by high levels of social protection, the EU's mixed economy model may imply pressure toward liberalization and deregulation. These pressures are especially strong if the member state in question has adopted the euro and hence must coordinate its economic policies with the other economies of the euro area (see Chapter 7).

Such pressures for liberalization emerging from EU policy have in recent years contributed to opposition to European integration, particularly in Southern Europe and most pronounced among parts of the population that have suffered the most from the 2008–9 or 2020–1 recessions, such as the unemployed, ethnic minorities, and women who depend on social transfers. One of the main challenges for the future development of the EU is to update and further develop its mixed economy model to address the concern, felt throughout parts of the EU, that the EU is only working for the "winners of globalization" (for example, young or middle-aged, well-educated, geographically mobile professionals). This objective requires coordinated activities by EU institutions and the member states, as the EU's supranational institutions do not have all the competences to implement a European mixed economy model entirely on their own.

In addition, while most of the EU's policies remain focused on economic issues, the importance of non-economic policies in the EU policy portfolio has grown markedly since the 1990s. The most prominent of these are migration, citizenship, and security (Chapter 8), foreign and security policy (Chapter 9), but also neighbourhood relations (Chapter 14). These policies have raised issues that are very different from the traditional economic policies. They relate, for instance, to the promotion of democratic and human rights values outside of the EU's territory. In so doing, they have added a new dimension to debates about solidarity among EU member states. Transatlantic relations illustrate this development well. The EU's commitment to such relations is strong and resilient for both endogenous and exogenous reasons. Today, Canada, the EU, and the United States share a bedrock of liberal international values and norms that have fashioned their relationship since World War II and continue to inform their values today. These norms and values have guided their relationship in the face of recent and major transformations across the world. These include Russia's full-scale invasion of Ukraine in February 2022, which constituted a major shock to the European security architecture and highlighted the dangers of the EU's dependence on Russian oil and gas. Another recent geopolitical shift is the increasingly assertive international role of China. The EU views this country as both a geostrategic rival and a major trading partner. In this setting, EU and member state governance cannot be considered in isolation; member states increasingly work together, but with diverging and continually evolving understandings of solidarity.

THEME 2: DOES THE EU REMAIN A POLITICAL SYSTEM THAT IS NEITHER AN INTERNATIONAL ORGANIZATION NOR A FULLY-FLEDGED FEDERAL STATE?

There can be no doubt that the EU is the most deeply integrated regional organization anywhere in the world. And yet, the chapters in this book consistently emphasize that the EU has not become a fully-fledged federal state. Federalist ideals, shared by some of the EU's founders (see Chapters 2 and 6), have been frustrated by disagreements among the member states on the larger institutional architecture of the EU, such as the relative powers of the Commission, the Council of the EU, the European Council, and the European Parliament. These disagreements have resulted in the creation of complicated procedural mechanisms that limit the transfer of policy competences from member states to the supranational institutions. Some of them, still to this day, require a consensus-oriented style of EU policy-making in which even small coalitions of member states possess veto powers. As discussed in the institutional and governance chapters (Chapters 3, 4, and 5), EU policy-making usually resorts to formal or informal mechanisms (including the so-called trilogues) that seek to construct a broad consensus both within and among the EU's legislative institutions. In sum, for idealists, the federal project for Europe is still a work in progress.

At the same time, the EU has indeed progressed much beyond a typical international organization. For instance, in its justice, freedom, and security policies (Chapter 8) it has taken a leap forward into supranational governance, thanks to the standardization of an EU framework for managing borders and migration. Also, in the face of the multiple veto points that exist in its political system, the EU in practice often turns out to be a surprisingly successful decision maker that relies on a multitude of modes of governances, which have made it possible to push the integration process forward despite opposition. This phenomenon is discussed in detail in the governance chapter (Chapter 5), which explains that because member states have granted additional responsibilities to the EU, while simultaneously refusing to expand its policy toolkit and budget, the EU is forced to develop innovative governance mechanisms. By means of ongoing and recurrent processes of institutional innovation, including modes of governance that focus on coordinating policies and sharing best practices, it has been able to develop policies with a significant effect on European society. Such phenomena occurred in various policy arenas, as discussed for instance in the chapters on regional policy (Chapter 11) and energy policy (Chapter 17).

Despite these adaptations, the EU's peculiar character, as more than an international organization yet less than a federal state, implies challenges for the functioning of its political system. While its consensus-oriented style of policy-making has helped maintain member states' support for European integration, as neither large numbers of national elites nor citizens have a clearly articulated desire to see the EU acquire statehood, it has severely hampered the development of some EU policies. For instance, any expansion of the EU budget, which might help the EU develop policies that address the concerns of the "losers of globalization" (for instance, people who are unemployed or work in low-skilled, low-paying jobs), tends to be resisted by the richer member states (especially Germany and recently by the so-called "four frugals": Austria, Denmark, the Netherlands, and Sweden). They fear the development of a "transfer union," and although fundamentally transformed by the COVID-19 crisis, they remain in favour of an EU budget ceiling of around 1 per cent of gross national income. Similarly, since the 2015 migration crisis, some member states in Central and Eastern Europe have resisted attempts to develop an EU-wide scheme for the relocation of refugees, which would have eased pressures on border states in the Schengen Area (such as Greece and Italy) as well as states that have seen a particularly large influx of refugees (such as Germany or Sweden; see Chapter 8). Likewise, there continue to be disagreements in the areas of foreign and defence policy as well as on the geopolitical position of the EU in the world (Chapters 9, 13, and 18). The need to play a stronger role on the world stage was heightened following the wholesome invasion of Ukraine by Russia from February 2022 onwards. Indeed, the EU has grown as an actor on the global scene. Yet many argue that it is held back because enlargement has reached its limits (Chapter 13). Furthermore, despite having one of the largest diplomatic networks in the world, and even though it may speak with one voice in trade matters (Chapter 12), it does not always speak with one voice on, for instance, matters of foreign and defence or neighbourhood policies (Chapters 9 and 14). And, it has weak political legitimacy to speak on behalf of all of its citizens in these matters (Chapter 15) and thus lacks the necessary centralization in its decision-making apparatus. In these fields, the EU faces the continuous task of reforming its institutional structure to increase its ability to deal with situations of "realpolitik," such as the war in Ukraine.

The character of the EU as an "unidentified political object" (as former Commission president Jacques Delors once labelled it) also complicates the democratization of the EU. As explained in Chapter 15, democratization is an area in which considerable progress has been made, in particular by strengthening the legislative powers of the European Parliament. Nevertheless, the EU's consensus-oriented policy processes, which often take place behind closed doors, make it difficult to secure democratic accountability and to increase meaningful participation of EU citizens and representative organizations. State-based models of democracy prove difficult to apply to the EU system, but alternative ideas, such as Nicolaïdis's "demoi-cracy," thus far lack resonance in the citizenry. Furthermore, a small number of governments have very different views on the relevance of such issues, which impacts policy outcomes and discussions across member states. These considerations take us to the last theme of this book.

THEME 3: HOW CAN THE EU BUILD ITS LEGITIMACY IN THE EUROPEAN POPULATION?

In the post–World War II era, European integration was constructed with the primary goals of promoting peace and economic prosperity. The EU focused on economic integration, which was expected to solidify support for the overall integration project. Some have described this process of legitimizing the integration process by way of securing positive economic effects as focusing on "output legitimacy." As the discussion in this book shows, this strategy worked well for many years. Increased economic interdependencies in the Single Market not only greatly contributed to achieving the original goal of peace building (Chapter 7) but also helped to turn the EU into an area of prosperity that neighbouring states and their populations have been eager to join (Chapters 13 and 14).

In recent years, however, the EU's output-based legitimation strategy has faced two challenges. First, a sequence of crises linked to core EU policies raised doubts about the material benefits of EU membership. The euro area crisis pointed to a major tension between the rules of Economic and Monetary Union, which demanded austerity policies in the states most severely hit by the crisis, and the political and social realities on the ground. Protestors in the streets criticized the EU for a lack of solidarity with those who were losing their jobs and seeing their state structures crumble (Chapter 7). The

2015 refugee crisis, triggered by the entry of more than 1.2 million people into the EU territory, raised concerns about the EU's ability to control its external borders, pacify conflicts in its neighbourhood that give rise to refugee movements, and agree on a fair sharing of responsibility among member states. Many citizens felt threatened by the influx of refugees and other migrants, and some of them perceived these newcomers as a source of competition for low-skilled jobs and scarce state resources (Chapters 8 and 14). The COVID-19 pandemic and economic crisis in 2020–1 underscored the fragility of the whole EU edifice. On the one hand, it demonstrated that the EU can draw on its inherent strength when solidarity brings together all the states, as occurred when the heads of states and governments committed to borrow together as the EU and redistribute billions of euros across the EU member states in the form of loans and grants (Chapter 7). On the other hand, member states set up this system only on a temporary basis and demanded some commitment to reforms in return for benefiting from common resources. In the light of these challenges, the significant financial transfers that the EU provides hardly resonated in public discussions.

The second challenge to the EU's traditional model of economic legitimation originates from increasing demands for more democratic participation and greater transparency. The Brexit referendum in the United Kingdom, resulting in the decision to initiate the UK's withdrawal from the EU, is in many ways the clearest indication that economic legitimation alone is no longer sufficient for the EU. With good reasons, the "remain" campaign in the referendum emphasized the negative economic consequences of Brexit (Chapter 7). But the arguments of the "leave" campaign – many of them framed in terms of UK identity and national sovereignty – were ultimately more compelling for a majority of citizens participating in the referendum. Although the Brexit referendum encouraged Euroskeptic movements in other member states, once the UK actually left the EU few domestic players in other member states were keen to follow in its footsteps. In other words, Brexit showed that input legitimacy, which is grounded in the participation of the citizens, has gained importance in the EU. Yet this does not mean that the EU's output has become irrelevant. The difficulties the UK had in 2020–1 related to leaving the EU (for instance, long queues of trucks at the border and difficulties finding seasonal workers) were a reminder that output legitimacy remains important.

These considerations show that the EU faces a dual challenge of increasing both its output and input legitimacy. On the output side, it needs to find ways to address more effectively the concerns of the citizens, especially by providing tangible benefits for the aforementioned "losers of globalization." There are also a number of policy successes that the EU could exploit more systematically to build its legitimacy. One example is its successful sustainability agenda, as detailed in the chapters on regional and climate policy (Chapters 11 and 17). The distinctive patterns of multilevel governance developed in these policy areas may result in adjustments to the EU's broader institutional architecture.

On the input side, the EU requires further democratic reform (Chapters 15 and 16). The EU needs to make explicit efforts to explain the workings of the EU to its citizens, who perceive it as elitist and complicated. Many are unaware of the existing opportunities for political participation. Furthermore, a few member states' democratic backsliding also contributes to further debates and confusion. Given these difficulties, another strategy for reform would involve trying, once again, to simplify the decision-making processes. It is a challenge because the last time a major overhaul of the EU decision-making rules was attempted, with many access points for citizens, the end result was a draft constitution that was subsequently rejected by citizens in two national referendums. Thus, varied understandings of the meaning of "solidarity" remain at the core of discussions among civil society and governments across the EU: Often it is easier for them to agree on market-based and investment forms of solidarity rather than rights issues (Chapter 16). Despite the need for reforms, the exact path to get there remains unknown.

To sum up, our book contends that the EU has been a peace driven, mixed economic system, which developed more recently as a liberal market maker and an international regulator. In terms of social inclusion and market correction policies, its successes are less pronounced, which has given rise to concerns about the connection between the EU and its citizens. EU citizens do not feel as connected to the EU as most citizens of a typical federation feel connected to their federal institutions. This fact alone presents a democratic challenge that needs to be reckoned with. The EU is neither a federal state nor an international organization, but a polity that rules thanks to complex modes of multilevel governance and partnerships. Its legitimacy was originally based on peace building and economic integration. Today and in the future, new forms of legitimacy originating in the green agenda for "smart, sustainable and inclusive growth" (to quote the EU's own "Europe 2020" agenda) and greater democratic transparency and engagement will have to supplement these traditional foundations.

Since 2010 the EU has faced many crises: a sovereign debt crisis affecting many member states of the euro area; a refugee crisis with over 1.2 million people entering the Union; the UK referendum of 2016 that led to the exit of that member state from the EU; and the COVID-19 pandemic that challenges European health care systems and economies. In the meantime, relationships with the United States, Russia, and China have been fluctuating. Transatlantic relations during the US presidency of Donald Trump (2017–21) made European leaders realize the difficult reality of security dependency on the United States, the fragility of their shared North Atlantic Treaty Organization, and the delicate state of the international liberal order. Russia annexed Crimea and later launched a large-scale war against Ukraine, motivated in part by the objective to keep the country in its own sphere of influence. China's geopolitical ambition and economic affirmation became clearer thanks to the "belt and road" policy, a trillion-dollar initiative.

Despite all of these crises, the EU remains strong. European institutions are more directly involved in member state well-being than ever before, but also are much more responsible for the well-being of Europeans on a day-to-day basis. Indeed, between 2010 and the early 2020s, the EU faced both economic and humanitarian crises but also a crisis of solidarity. In response to these crises, it has strengthened both its intergovernmental and supranational ability to manage economic interdependencies, migration, and border policies. A post-Brexit trade agreement was signed with the UK, and in 2020 the remaining 27 members of the EU agreed on an ambitious program to help member states rebuild their economies after the pandemic.

As a next generation of students study the EU, within and beyond the EU's borders, the hope is that they seek to understand the inner workings of the EU as well as the role of the EU in the world. With all of its imperfections, the EU has offered a path toward closer collaboration – one that seeks to avoid war and contributes to peace, both within its borders and beyond. Furthermore, it has sought to offer an interim solution to globalization by contributing to regulation amidst a commitment to market principles. Its challenge in the years ahead will be to reorient itself to increase its legitimacy and democracy and find a way to restructure to stay effective in achieving its goals.

Appendix: Research Resources

Research on European integration can make use of a wide variety of sources. Most primary sources (such as legal or policy documents, party manifestos, statistical data) are available on the internet. There is also a large scholarly literature on EU studies, which includes book publications and journal articles. This appendix provides sources that might be useful for students who are doing research on the EU's history, institutions, legislation, current policies, or democratic life; sources for EU-related socioeconomic data; as well as listing some of the most important scholarly journals focusing on European integration.

EU HISTORY

The **Historical Archives of the EU** (HAEU) preserves and makes accessible for research the archives deposited by EU institutions according to the thirty-year rule governing access to archival material. It is housed at the European University Institute in Florence and provides access to a broad range of documents (https://www.eui.eu/en/academic-units/historical-archives-of-the-european-union). Further historical sources are available through the University of Luxembourg's **CVCE.eu database** (https://www.cvce.eu/en). Jean Monnet's papers, and other material relating to this key framer of European integration, are available at the **Jean Monnet Foundation** (https://jean-monnet.ch). The **House of European History**, a museum in Brussels, allows you to browse their galleries online (https://historia-europa.ep.eu).

EU INSTITUTIONS

The **Europa website** (http://europa.eu) is the official web portal of the EU. Offered in 24 languages, it contains basic information about the EU. It also houses the websites of the EU institutions and provides links to EU legislation and other policy documents.

Each EU institution has its own website on the Europa platform; these include the **European Commission** (https://commission.europa.eu/index_en), **Council and European Council** (http://consilium.europa.eu/en), **European Parliament** (EP; http://europarl.europa.eu/portal/en), **Court of Justice** (https://curia.europa.eu/jcms/jcms/Jo1_6308), and the **European Central Bank** (http://ecb.europa.eu/home/html/index.en.html). These websites contain information about the institutions' personnel and administrative structure, current policy processes and priorities, as well as important policy documents.

In addition, the **rotating presidency of the Council** sets up its own website, hosted by the government that holds the current presidency (for instance, the French presidency in the first half of 2022 established the website https://presidence-francaise.consilium.europa.eu/en). This website has information about Council meetings and other activities of the current presidency.

EU LAW

The texts of the EU treaties (primary law), legislation passed by the EU (secondary law), as well as case law by the Court of Justice can researched using the **EurLex database** (http://eur-lex.europa.eu). The website has a differentiated search function that makes it possible to search for specific pieces of legislation or all legislation passed in a given issue area. When working with the EU treaties, it is important to refer to the most recent, consolidated version (that is, the version that incorporates all amendments passed to date) – unless of course your research has a historical interest.

For ongoing legislative processes, the **EP's Legislative Observatory** (https://oeil.secure.europarl.europa.eu/oeil/home/home.do) is a helpful resource. Its "procedure files" trace the steps of each bill and contain documents produced in the process (such as the Commission's legislative proposal, EP Committee reports, or Council positions on the bill). The Legislative Observatory also allows for research on legislative processes that have been concluded or abandoned, going back to 1994.

EU POLICIES

The websites of the EU institutions contain a wealth of information about the diverse range of EU policies covered in this book. The **European Commission website** is particularly useful; its list of topics (https://commission.europa.eu/topics_en) is a good starting point that leads to detailed descriptions of EU policies, including official policy documents, publications for a wider audience, and press releases. For each topic, this website also links to websites of other EU institutions with information on the same topic.

An important resource for research on various policies is the EU's website on its **budget** (https://commission.europa.eu/strategy-and-policy/eu-budget_en). It includes figures on the Multiannual Financial Framework (MFF) as well as the yearly budgets. The website provides an interactive tool that allows researchers to look up various revenue categories (including contributions per member state) and expenditure items.

Another useful tool is **Agence Europe** (http://agenceurope.info/en/home.html). It is a daily newsletter that provides online full-text access to the **Bulletin Quotidien Europe** (French edition) and **Europe Daily Bulletin** (English edition). Students can use a free trial. A helpful supplement is its **Europe Documents**, which consists of analytical reviews and presentations of the rotating presidencies. It may also include full reproduction of reports. It has been in place since the early days and can be used for research about historical time periods.

SOCIAL AND ECONOMIC DATA

A number of EU websites contain useful statistical data. A good starting point is **Eurostat**, the EU's statistical agency (http://ec.europa.eu/eurostat). Its website includes publications but also a large database that allows researchers to run customized searches for data in a variety of fields, including demographics, regional development, economy and finance, trade, environment, and energy.

Some EU institutions have their own databases. The Commission's Directorate-General for Economic and Financial Affairs runs the **Annual Macro-Economic Database** (AMECO; https://ec.europa.eu/economy_finance/ameco_dashboard), which contains important indicators on gross domestic product, labour costs, trade flows between member states, and government debt and deficit. This database is the reference point for procedures relevant to Economic and Monetary Union, such as the European Semester. The European Central Bank also has its own database, called **Statistical Data Warehouse** (SDW; http://sdw.ecb.europa.eu); it contains a broad range of macroeconomic statistics, including data on interest rates and exchange rates.

In addition, a number of Commission Directorates-General (DGs) provide publications with statistical data, but not searchable databases. For instance, the DG for Trade publishes its own **trade statistics** (http://ec.europa.eu/trade/policy/countries-and-regions/statistics) and the DG for Regional and Urban Policy has its own website for data on the various **European Structural and Investment Funds** (https://cohesiondata.ec.europa.eu/).

DEMOCRATIC LIFE AND PUBLIC OPINION

The EU-level political parties, as well as the political groups in the EP, all have their own websites, which provide information on programmatic standpoints, leadership personnel, and current events. Links to the **EP political groups** are prominently posted on the EP website (https://www.europarl.europa.eu/portal/en); if a group is associated with an EU-wide political party, the group's website will provide a link.

For interest groups, civil society organizations, and lobbying firms active in Brussels, the EU's **Transparency Register** (https://ec.europa.eu/transparencyregister/public/homePage.do) is a useful resource; it lists information on more than 12,000 organizations active in Brussels.

Public opinion data on European integration are systematically collected in the **Eurobarometer** (https://europa.eu/eurobarometer/screen/home), which is based on public opinion surveys financed from the EU budget that are conducted every six months in all member states as well as current candidate countries. The surveys contain questions on items such as trust in the EU, desired policy priorities, or strength of European and national identities. Eurobarometer data allow for comparisons both between member states and over time. The Eurobarometer website provides access to written reports as well as detailed data tables.

MEDIA SOURCES

A number of major English-language news sources provide good coverage of EU politics; these include, for instance, the **Financial Times** (https://

www.ft.com), **The Economist** (https://www.economist.com/), and **The Guardian** (https://www.theguardian.com/international). There are also some specialist news sources focusing primarily on EU politics; these include the Europe edition of the weekly **Politico** (https://www.politico.eu) and **EUObserver** (https://euobserver.com) as well as the web blog **EurActiv** (https://www.euractiv.com). Students researching current events and decision-making processes in the EU are advised to follow reporting in these sources. The news channel **France24** (https://www.france24.com/en), in English, has two shows that specialize in EU politics: *Talking EUROPE* interviews EU elected and public officials, and *EUROPE Now* profiles EU member states.

SCHOLARLY SOURCES

While the above contain useful primary sources for EU-related research, it is important to relate your research to the scholarly literature in EU studies. The titles provided as "further reading" at the end of this book's individual chapters are a good starting point for researching this literature. In addition, students are advised to review articles in scholarly journals that specialize in EU politics. The most widely used journals in this category are the **Journal of Common Market Studies** (JCMS; https://onlinelibrary.wiley.com/journal/14685965), the **Journal of European Public Policy** (JEPP; https://www.tandfonline.com/toc/rjpp20/current), **European Union Politics** (EUP; https://journals.sagepub.com/home/eup), and the **Journal of European Integration** (JEI; https://www.tandfonline.com/loi/geui20).

In addition to these EU-focused journals, EU-related research is also frequently published in a number of **political science journals with a more general focus**: for instance, **Comparative European Politics** (CEP; https://www.palgrave.com/gp/journal/41295), **European Journal of Political Research** (EJPR; https://ejpr.onlinelibrary.wiley.com/journal/14756765), **West European Politics** (WEP; https://www.tandfonline.com/toc/fwep20/current), and many more. Depending on the research topic, useful scholarly literature can also be found in more **specialized journals** that focus on a specific policy field (for example, **European Journal of Migration and Law**, https://brill.com/view/journals/emil/emil-overview.xml) or a specific region (such as **South European Policy and Politics**, https://www.tandfonline.com/toc/fses20/current).

THINK TANKS

There are a number of think tanks that focus on EU politics. Their policy papers and other publications may be useful, especially when researching relatively recent political developments (scholarly journals, because of their peer-review policies, often take longer to publish articles that reflect on recent events). Major think tanks in this category include **Bruegel** (http://bruegel.org), the **Centre for European Policy Studies** (CEPS; https://www.ceps.eu), the **Centre for European Reform** (CER; https://www.cer.org.uk), the **European Trade Union Institute** (ETUI; https://www.etui.org), the **European Social Observatory** (https://www.ose.be), the **European Policy Centre** (EPC; https://www.epc.eu), **Notre Europe/Jacques Delors Institute** (https://institutdelors.eu), the **Robert Schuman Centre for Advanced Studies** at the European University Institute (https://www.eui.eu/en/academic-units/robert-schuman-centre-for-advanced-studies), and the **Centre for Economic Policy Research** (CEPR; http://CEPR.org), including its useful policy portal (http://voxeu.org) that provides policy analysis and commentary by economists.

CANADA–EU RELATIONS

There are various useful resources for those studying the EU from Canada. The EU is studied in many Canadian universities. Canadian-based scholars or those interested in being connected to a network of Canadian scholars, graduate students, and professionals who study the EU are members of the **European Community Studies Association–Canada** (ECSA-C; https://www.ecsa-c.ca). Its young researchers are further organized in the **Young Researchers Network** (YRN; https://www.ecsa-c.ca/who-we-are-yrn). Another useful source is the **Delegation of the EU to Canada** (https://eeas.europa.eu/delegations/canada_en), which is the official EU diplomatic representation in Canada. Within the Canadian government, **Global Affairs Canada** (GAC) is responsible for managing relations with the EU; GAC's website includes a broad range of information on EU–Canada relations (https://www.international.gc.ca/world-monde/international_relations-relations_internationales/eu-ue/index.aspx?lang=eng).

Chronology

1945 **May** – Germany surrenders, signifying the end of World War II in Europe.

September – World War II ends following Japan's signing of the Instrument of Surrender.

1946 **September** – British prime minister Winston Churchill gives a speech in Zurich calling for a "United States of Europe." This speech led to the creation of the Council of Europe in 1949.

1948 **January** – The General Agreement on Tariffs and Trade (GATT) comes into force.

1949 **April** – The North Atlantic Treaty is signed, creating the North Atlantic Treaty Organization (NATO).

May – The Council of Europe is established following the 1948 conference in The Hague on the future of Europe after World War II.

1950 **May** – The Schuman Plan is published, which proposes the pooling of French and German coal and steel production.

1951 **April** – The Treaty of Paris establishing the European Coal and Steel Community (ECSC) is signed.

1952 **July** – The ECSC enters into force.

1957 **March** – The Treaties of Rome are signed, establishing the European Economic Community (EEC) and the European Atomic Energy Community (Euratom).

1958 **January** – The Treaties of Rome enter into force formalizing the Common Market, the Atomic Energy Community, the Common Agricultural Policy (CAP), the Common Commercial Policy (CCP), common external tariff, as well as a series of other common policies. These treaties also made the EEC a single member of GATT and gave the Court of Justice of the European Union (CJEU) jurisdiction over all policy areas.

January – Walter Hallstein becomes president of the EEC Commission.

March – The European Parliamentary Assembly, precursor to the European Parliament (EP) and made of appointed representatives, meets for the first time.

1959 **February** – First Session of the European Court of Human Rights (ECtHR).

1960 **May** – The European Free Trade Association (EFTA) between Austria, Denmark, Norway, Portugal, Sweden, Switzerland, and the United Kingdom enters into force.

1961 **July** – Ireland submits its official accession application to the EEC.

August – Denmark and the United Kingdom submit official accession applications to the EEC.

1962 **February** – Spain submits its official accession application to the EEC.

April – The CAP enters into force.

1963 **January** – France president Charles de Gaulle "vetoes" the United Kingdom's EEC application.

1964 December – Ankara Agreement between the EEC and Türkiye signed in 1963, comes into force.

1965 June – Start of the "Empty Chair Crisis," in which French president Charles de Gaulle withdrew French representatives from the EEC over issues with the proposed EEC qualified majority voting (QMV) procedure.

1966 January – End of the "Empty Chair Crisis" following a compromise in the EEC to introduce the "Luxembourg Compromise" on QMV procedures.

1967 May – Denmark, Ireland, Norway, and the United Kingdom submit official accession applications to the EEC.

July – The Merger Treaty (signed in 1965) enters into force, merging the three European Community Executives and Council of Ministers into a single "European Communities" (EC) Commission and Council.

July – Jean Rey becomes president of the Commission of the EC.

November – French president Charles de Gaulle rejects United Kingdom's application to become a member of the EEC for the second time.

1968 July – The Customs Union of the EEC is completed.

1970 July – Franco Malfatti becomes president of the Commission of the EC.

October – The Werner Report is published, establishing a plan for the creation of Economic and Monetary Union by 1980.

October – The European Political Cooperation is launched to facilitate a common foreign policy initiative between EU member states.

1972 July – Sicco Mansholt becomes president of the Commission of the EC.

September – Norway referendum results in a rejection (54 per cent) of joining the EEC.

1973 **January** – François-Xavier Ortoli becomes president of the Commission of the EC.

January – Denmark, Ireland, and United Kingdom become members of the EEC.

November – The first Environmental Action Programme (EAP) is adopted by the EU.

1974 **December** – The European Council informally meets for the first time.

1975 **March** – The European Regional Development Fund (ERDF) is established.

June – Greece submits its official accession application to the EEC.

1976 **June** – The ministers of justice from members of the EEC form the "TREVI Group" to further cooperation in the field of law and justice.

July – Canada and the EC sign a Framework Agreement for Commercial and Economic Cooperation marking the first formal relationship between the EC and an industrialized country.

1977 **January** – Roy Jenkins becomes president of the Commission of the EC.

March – Portugal submits its official accession application to the EEC.

April – The CJEU gives the Commission legal authority to represent the EU in international organizations.

1979 **March** – The European Monetary System is created.

June – The EP holds its first direct elections.

1981 **January** – Greece becomes a member of the EC.

January – Gaston Thorn becomes president of the Commission of the EC.

1984 **April** – Dairy reform is introduced to the CAP.

June – EP elections.

1985 **January** – Jacques Delores becomes president of the Commission of the EC.

June – The Schengen Agreement is signed between Belgium, France, West Germany, Luxembourg, and the Netherlands, committing them to remove controls at their internal borders. As of 2023, the Schengen Area contains 27 members (23 EU member states and 4 non-EU states).

November – The Delors Commission publishes a White Paper that aims to complete the Common Market through the Single European Act (SEA) by the end of 1992.

1986 **January** – Portugal and Spain become members of the EC.

February – The SEA is signed, reinforcing supranational institutions, introducing new legislative procedures for the EP, expanding the use of QMV, as well as giving the EEC competence in new policy fields including social policy, research, and the environment.

1987 **April** – Türkiye submits its official accession application to the EC.

July – The SEA enters into force.

1988 **June** – Regional Policy is reformed and formally named "Cohesion Policy."

December – The Intergovernmental Panel on Climate Change is created.

1989 **April** – The Delors Report is published, proposing the establishment of Economic and Monetary Union (EMU) through three stages and ending with the introduction of euro banknotes and coins by January 1, 2002.

June – EP elections.

July – Austria submits its official accession application to the EC.

November – The Berlin Wall falls.

1990 **May** – The European Environmental Agency and the European Environment Information and Observation Network are established.

July – The first stage of EMU begins.

July – Cyprus submits its official accession application to the EC.

July – Malta submits its official accession application to the EC.

October – Germany is reunified.

1991 **July** – Sweden submits its official accession application to the EC.

December – The Soviet Union officially dissolves.

1992 **February** – The Treaty of the European Union (also called the Maastricht Treaty) is signed, formalizing the plan for establishing EMU and creating three pillars of EU organization: Pillar I European Communities (ECSC, EEC, Euratom); Pillar II Common Foreign and Security Policy (CFSP); Pillar III Justice and Home Affairs (JHA). The Maastricht Treaty also established the co-decision legislative procedure between the EP and the Council.

March – Finland submits its official accession application to the EU.

May – The MacSharry Reform Package of the CAP comes into effect.

June – Danish referendum results in a rejection (51 per cent) of the Maastricht Treaty.

November – Norway submits its official accession application to the EU.

December – The Single Market is completed.

1993 **May** – Danish referendum results in approval (57 per cent) of the Maastricht Treaty with opt-outs for participation in JHA and the euro.

June – European Council Summit in Copenhagen creates the Copenhagen Criteria, establishing three major conditions for applicant countries to become member states.

November – The Maastricht Treaty enters into force.

1994 **January** – The first stage of EMU ends and the second stage begins.

March – Hungary submits its official accession application to the EU.

March – The United Nations Framework Convention on Climate Change is signed.

April – Poland submits its official accession application to the EU.

June – EP elections.

November – Norway referendum result opposes (53 per cent) accession to the EU.

1995 **January** – Jacques Santer becomes president of the European Commission.

January – Austria, Finland, and Sweden become members of the EU.

January – The World Trade Organization (WTO) is established and incorporates the GATT.

June – Romania submits its official accession application to the EU.

June – Slovakia submits its official accession application to the EU.

July – The Europol Convention is signed, creating EU-wide coordination and sharing of intelligence among national police forces and their European collaboration.

October – Latvia submits its official accession application to the EU.

November – Estonia submits its official accession application to the EU.

December – Lithuania submits its official accession application to the EU.

December – Bulgaria submits its official accession application to the EU.

1996 **January** – Czech Republic submits its official accession application to the EU.

June – Slovenia submits its official accession application to the EU.

1997 **June** – The Stability and Growth Pact is created.

October – The EU and Russia sign a Partnership and Cooperation Agreement.

October – The Treaty of Amsterdam is signed, further consolidating the powers of EU supranational institutions including the Commission, the European Central Bank, and the European Court of Justice. This treaty also extended the co-decision legislative procedure, introduced the open method of coordination (OMC) in employment, and moved most areas of JHA (Pillar III) into the European Communities (Pillar I), renaming it the Area of Freedom, Security, and Justice (AFSJ).

1998 **December** – The second stage of EMU ends.

1999 **January** – The third stage of EMU begins.

March – Agenda 2000 reforms to the CAP are introduced.

May – The Treaty of Amsterdam enters into force.

May – The Common European Asylum System (CEAS) is created to harmonize asylum policies around the EU.

June – EP elections.

July – The Europol Convention enters into force.

July – Romano Prodi becomes president of the European Commission.

December – Türkiye is formally accepted as a candidate country for EU membership.

2000 **September** – Danish referendum results in a rejection (53 per cent) of joining EMU.

December – The Charter of Fundamental Rights of the European Union is adopted by the EU institutions.

2001 **February** – The Treaty of Nice is signed, outlining the details of accession to the EU, expanding the co-decision procedure, and giving increased competency and powers to the EU's supranational institutions.

June – Irish referendum results in a rejection (54 per cent) of the Treaty of Nice.

2002 **January** – The third stage of EMU ends with euro banknotes and coins being introduced as the physical currency of 12 member states.

May – The EU and all EU member states ratify the Kyoto Protocol.

October – Irish referendum results in an approval (63 per cent) of the Treaty of Nice.

2003 **February** – The Treaty of Nice comes into force.

February – Croatia submits its official accession application to the EU.

March – The European Commission publishes the "Wider Europe Neighbourhood: A New Framework for Relations with Our Eastern and Southern Neighbours," launching the European Neighbourhood Policy (ENP).

May – The EU and Russia agree to commit to cooperation in four "common spaces" covering areas such as economics; freedom, security, and justice; and research, education, and culture.

September – Swedish referendum results in a rejection (58 per cent) of joining EMU.

December – The European Council agrees on a "European Security Strategy," creating the European Security and Defence Policy (ESDP).

2004 **March** – North Macedonia submits official accession application to the EU.

March – Canada and the EU sign a partnership agenda outlining their common goals and values.

May – Cyprus, Czech Republic, Estonia, Latvia, Lithuania, Hungary, Malta, Poland, Slovakia, and Slovenia become members of the EU.

June – EP elections.

June – The ENP is extended to include Armenia, Azerbaijan, and Georgia.

October – The European Constitutional Treaty is signed. This treaty aimed to consolidate the EU pillars, integrate the Charter of Fundamental Rights of the European Union, and establish many EU symbols such as an anthem and a flag.

November – José Manuel Barroso becomes president of the European Commission.

2005 **January** – The European Emissions Trading System (ETS) comes into force.

May – French referendum result rejects (54 per cent) ratifying the European Constitutional Treaty.

June – Dutch referendum result rejects (62 per cent) ratifying the European Constitutional Treaty. Following this rejection, all other proposed referendums on ratification were postponed and the treaty never entered into force.

October – Negotiations on accession begin between Türkiye and the EU.

December – The EU's Global Approach to Migration and Mobility is created to promote cooperation in governance in the field of migration and asylum across the EU's external borders.

2006 **June** – The European Council agrees to a 2007–13 Financial Framework, which includes new Cohesion Policy objectives of competitiveness, employment, innovation, and environmental protection.

December – The European Institute for Gender Equality is created.

2007 **January** – Bulgaria and Romania become members of the EU.

February – The European Union Agency for Fundamental Rights (FRA) is created.

December – The Treaty of Lisbon is signed, containing many innovations of the European Constitutional Treaty, including the incorporation of the European Council and the European Central Bank as official EU institutions and abandoning the pillar system. The treaty gives an increased role to national parliaments and the EP, expands the use of co-decision (now called ordinary legislative procedure (OLP)), and incorporates the Charter of Fundamental Rights. It also gives the EU power to adopt autonomous acts on trade, further competence in AFSJ, renames the ESDP to the Common Security and Defence Policy (CSDP), and gives treaty status to the ENP.

2008 **June** – Irish referendum results in a rejection (53 per cent) of the Treaty of Lisbon.

July – The Union for the Mediterranean (UfM) is officially launched with the EU and 15 Mediterranean partner countries.

September – American investment bank Lehman Brothers files for bankruptcy. This marks the beginning of the worst period of the 2007–8 global financial crisis.

December – Montenegro submits official accession application to the EU.

December – The EU establishes its "20-20-20 by 2020" emissions targets.

2009 **May** – The EU Blue Card Initiative is introduced as an EU-wide work permit for highly skilled third-country nationals in the EU.

May – The Eastern Partnership (EaP) is formally launched with Armenia, Azerbaijan, Belarus, Georgia, Moldova, and Ukraine.

June – EP elections.

July – Iceland submits its official accession application to the EU.

October – Negotiations begin for a Comprehensive Economic and Trade Agreement (CETA) between Canada and the EU.

October – Irish referendum results in an approval (67 per cent) of the Treaty of Lisbon.

November – Albania submits its official accession application to the EU.

December – Serbia submits its official accession application to the EU.

December – The Lisbon Treaty enters into force.

December – Greece reveals it has a government debt of €300 billion. This period marks the start of the euro area financial crisis, as several member states start to witness difficulties in repaying or refinancing government debt.

2010 **May** – The Greek government announces that it faces imminent default.

May – The Greek Loan Facility enters into force.

June – The EU and Russia agree to a "Partnership for Modernization" initiative.

August – The European Financial Stability Facility (EFSF) is created.

November – José Manuel Barroso receives a second term as president of the European Commission.

December – The Jasmine Revolution in Tunisia sparks the Arab Spring.

December – The European Stability Mechanism (ESM), the permanent replacement to the EFSF, is created.

2011 **January** – The European External Action Service (EEAS) is created, merging foreign, security, and defence policy functions of the EU into one overarching EU institution.

January – The European Semester, an annual cycle of economic policy guidance and surveillance within the EU, begins.

2012 **March** – The Fiscal Compact is signed.

June – European Council opens accession negotiations with Montenegro.

October – The ESM comes into effect.

December – The Banking Union is created.

December – The EU wins the Nobel Peace Prize.

2013 **January** – The Fiscal Compact enters into force.

June – Negotiations for the Transatlantic Trade and Investment Partnership (TTIP) between the US and the EU begin.

July – Croatia becomes a member of the EU.

July – The Dublin III Regulation (commonly known as the "Dublin Agreement") enters into force, requiring refugees to register and claim asylum in the first EU member state they land in.

December – "Post-2013" reforms are introduced to increase environmental sustainability of the CAP.

December – The Icelandic government places EU accession negotiations on hold.

2014 **January** – The European Council opens accession negotiations with Serbia.

February – Conflict between Russia and Ukraine erupts following the ouster of Ukraine's president Viktor Yanukovych.

May – EP elections.

August – CETA negotiations conclude.

November – Jean-Claude Juncker becomes president of the European Commission.

2015 **February** – The EU publishes the "Framework Strategy for a Resilient Energy Union with a Forward-Looking Climate Change Strategy," establishing the EU Energy Union.

March – The foreign affairs minister for Iceland confirms to the EU that Icelandic accession negotiations with the EU will not continue.

June – "The Five Presidents' Report: Completing Europe's Economic and Monetary Union" is published.

September – The Capital Markets Union is created.

November – Terrorist attack in Paris prompts several Schengen Area member states to temporarily reimpose national border controls.

December – Over 900,000 migrants arrive in Europe over the course of the year. This marks the beginning of the 2015–16 migrant crisis, prompting internal disagreement in the EU over border controls and a temporary pause on Dublin Agreement enforcement.

December – The UN Paris Agreement on climate change (commonly referred to as the Paris Agreement) is signed.

2016　**February** – Bosnia and Herzegovina submits its official accession application to the EU.

March – Terrorist attack in Brussels.

March – The EU and Türkiye agree to the "EU-Turkey Statement & Action Plan" in which Türkiye accepted the return of irregular migrants from Greece in exchange for economic and political benefits from the EU.

April – Dutch referendum results in a rejection (62 per cent) of an EU–Ukraine Association Agreement.

June – United Kingdom referendum on EU membership ("Brexit") results in majority (51.8 per cent) favouring to leave the EU.

July – The EU's Global Strategy is launched.

October – CETA is signed.

October – Canada and the EU sign a Strategic Partnership Agreement (SPA).

October – The Paris Agreement is ratified by the EU.

October – Frontex, the European Border and Coast Guard Agency, is created.

December – TTIP negotiations are "ended without conclusion."

2017　**March** – UK prime minister Theresa May invokes Article 50 of TEU, signalling the beginning of the formal Brexit process.

April – The Canada–EU SPA enters into force provisionally.

June – The EU's Military Planning and Conduct Capability is created, establishing a permanent headquarters for EU military operations.

June – The European Commission launches the European Defence Fund, a multibillion-euro budget to promote defence capability–related research and development projects.

September – CETA begins provisional application.

December – 25 member states (all but the UK, Denmark, and Malta) introduce the Permanent Structured Cooperation (PESCO), increasing joint capability and cooperation in security and defence.

2018   **October** – The EU signs a Trade Agreement and an Investment Protection Agreement with Singapore.

June – The General Affairs Council of the EU declares that negotiations between Türkiye and the EU on membership are "effectively frozen."

December – The Governance Regulation (Regulation 2019/1999) enters into force, requiring member states to draft National Energy and Climate Plans.

2019   **May** – EP elections.

April – TTIP negotiations are paused indefinitely.

December – Ursula von der Leyen becomes president of the European Commission.

December – The European Green Deal (EGD) is created.

2020   **January** – United Kingdom Parliament passes the EU Withdrawal Bill, signalling the official end to UK membership in the EU.

January – The first cases of COVID-19 in the EU are diagnosed in France. This marks the beginning of the COVID-19 pandemic crisis in the EU.

March – European Council opens accession negotiations with Albania and North Macedonia.

March – The Pandemic Emergency Purchase Programme is announced.

September – The Pact on Migration and Asylum is adopted by the EU, putting a larger emphasis on sharing and solidarity in migration and asylum policies.

September – The EU's "Anti-Racism Action Policy (2020–2025)" is published.

October – EU member states adopt a European Council recommendation on a coordinated restriction of the Schengen Agreement in response to the COVID-19 pandemic crisis.

December – NextGenerationEU and the Recovery and Resilience Facility (RRF), the EU's COVID-19 recovery instruments, are created.

December – The EU–UK Trade and Cooperation Agreement is signed, marking the first significant step in post-Brexit EU–UK relations.

December – EU member states create a new mechanism in which financial payouts to member states are contingent on their adherence to the rule of law (Regulation 9980/20).

December – The EU's 2020 Climate & Energy Package is signed.

2021   **January** – The 2021–7 Multiannual Financial Framework (MFF) enters into force.

January – The EU–UK Trade and Cooperation Agreement comes into effect provisionally.

February – The Commission and EEAS adopt a joint communication on a "Renewed Partnership with the Southern Neighbourhood," including a new "Investment Plan for the Southern Neighbours."

February – European Commission publishes its 2021 trade policy review, outlining the next 10 years of EU trade policy.

February – NextGenerationEU and the RRF enter into force.

April – The Conference on the Future of Europe is launched.

May – The EU–UK Trade and Cooperation Agreement enters into force.

July – The EU "Fit for 55" legislative package is proposed.

July – The Commission formally launches infringement proceedings against Hungary and Poland for their challenges to the EU's principle of equality and fundamental rights of the LGBTQ+ community.

December – The "Post-2020" reform package of the CAP is agreed upon. This package will cover the 2023–7 period.

Glossary

accession treaty   A treaty whereby a new state accepts to become a member state of the EU. The treaty is concluded between the accession state and all current EU member states.

acquis communautaire   A French term that refers to the cumulative body of EU law presently in force, consisting of all treaties, legislation, court decisions, and international agreements.

anti-dumping   A set of measures that, in the context of the EU, can be taken by the European Commission under its Common Commercial Policy (CCP) to respond to non-EU companies that export a product to the EU at prices lower than the normal value of the product. These measures usually take the form of a duty.

Area of Freedom, Security and Justice (AFSJ)   The label the EU has given to its policies related to justice, security, migration, and borders.

austerity   An approach to a state's budgetary policy that aims to reduce budget deficits through aggressive cuts to public spending.

Banking Union   A set of policies developed in the context of Economic and Monetary Union (EMU) that places responsibility for supervision, resolution, and funding of banks and bank failures at the EU level. It applies to banks of euro area member states and to non-euro area banks if their member state has opted in.

bicameral legislature   A legislative body that has two chambers or houses. In the EU, the European Parliament and the Council of the EU can be described as forming a bicameral legislature.

Brexit Abbreviation for "British exit"; the term refers to the United Kingdom's withdrawal from the EU on January 31, 2020 (implementing the result of a popular referendum held on June 23, 2016).

candidate state A European country that has been formally recognized by the EU as a candidate for EU membership. Candidate states must pass far-reaching reforms to domestic legislation before they can be admitted to the EU.

Capital Markets Union (CMU) A plan launched by the European Commission in 2016 to increase the integration of capital markets in the EU.

Cassis de Dijon A landmark ruling by the Court of Justice of the EU in 1979 that established the principle of mutual recognition: If a product is legally marketed in one member state, the product should normally be considered legal in other member states as well.

Charter of Fundamental Rights of the European Union Legal document that defines the rights and freedoms of EU citizens and residents. The Charter was proclaimed in 2000 and formally became part of the EU's primary law in 2009 with the entry into force of the Treaty of Lisbon.

cohesion policy The formal name of the EU's regional policy that seeks to address regional economic disparities and to promote smart, sustainable, and inclusive growth through targeted investments in physical infrastructure and human capital.

Cold War A state of geopolitical tension between countries that were part of the Western alliance (United States, Canada, Western Europe, and other NATO allies) and the Eastern alliance (Soviet Union and the Warsaw Pact countries) between 1947 and 1991.

Committee of Permanent Representatives (COREPER) An institution composed of representatives of the member states permanently located in Brussels. COREPER is charged with managing intergovernmental relations between the member states and preparing meetings of the Council of the EU.

Common Agricultural Policy (CAP) A set of EU policies to stabilize the food supply, guarantee the economic viability of farming through agricultural subsidies (direct payments to farmers), and promote rural development in the EU.

Common Commercial Policy (CCP) The EU's policy on trade with non-EU countries; it encompasses managing the EU's common external tariffs, concluding trade agreements with non-EU states, and employing commercial instruments in the context of the EU's existing trade agreements.

Common Foreign and Security Policy (CFSP)   The EU's policy framework for dealing with issues of foreign, security, and defence policy. The CFSP encompasses the EU's Common Security and Defence Policy (CSDP). The CFSP is governed through rules that are more intergovernmental in character than regular EU policies.

Common Market   A term used in the 1950s, 1960s, 1970s, and early 1980s that has since been replaced by the term "Single Market."

Common Security and Defence Policy (CSDP)   The EU's policy framework for defence policy issues, including civilian and military intervention in international crises (see also "Common Foreign and Security Policy").

competition policy   A set of policies to secure free competition between companies in the EU's Single Market, *inter alia* by reviewing mergers and acquisitions, sanctioning the establishment of cartels or the abuse of a dominant market position, and limiting state aid to companies.

comprehensive approach   Term used by the EU to describe the character of its crisis management operations under the Common Security and Defence Policy (CSDP); the comprehensive approach is characterized by a mix of military and civilian instruments.

Comprehensive Economic and Trade Agreement (CETA)   An economic agreement between Canada and the EU (provisionally applied as of 2017) covering tariff barriers, government procurement, investment protection, intellectual property, and regulatory cooperation.

conditionality   The requirement of legal, administrative, economic, and political reforms that an EU candidate state must make as a condition for membership (see also "Copenhagen Criteria").

consensus   A constellation in which all decision makers support a certain decision or action, or at least do not object to it.

convergence criteria   A set of criteria (first defined in the Maastricht Treaty) that EU member states must meet to join Economic and Monetary Union (EMU). These include upper limits for budgetary deficits, public debt, inflation rates, long-term interest rates, and participation for at least the last two years in the exchange rate mechanism.

coordination   A form of non-binding intergovernmental policy-making; it consists of setting common policy targets and peer-reviewing member state policies without binding EU legislative measures.

Copenhagen criteria   A set of conditions that candidate states must meet before their accession to the EU. These include stable political institutions that guarantee democracy, the rule of law, human rights, and minority protection; a functioning market economy that can cope with competitive pressures in the EU's Single Market; and adoption and effective implementation of the *acquis communautaire.*

Council See "Council of the European Union."

Council of Europe A regional organization, separate from the EU, that seeks to promote human rights, democracy, and the rule of law in Europe. It was set up in 1949 and currently has 47 member states. Canada was granted official observer status in 1996.

Council of the European Union One of the EU's core legislative institutions; the Council of the EU (or Council for short) is an intergovernmental institution that brings together ministers from each member state, meeting in various formations (depending on the policies discussed). The Council presidency rotates between member states on a half-yearly basis. Formerly referred to as the Council of Ministers.

Court of Justice of the European Union (CJEU) The EU's judicial institution; the CJEU is tasked with interpreting EU law to make sure it is applied in the same way in all EU countries and with settling legal disputes between national governments and EU institutions.

crisis management In the context of the EU's Common Security and Defence Policy, a military or civilian intervention in an international crisis or emergency, such as peace making or post-conflict stabilization.

Customs Union An area of free trade with a common external tariff (common import duties).

decision A type of EU secondary law; a decision is a flexible legislative instrument that is binding to specific addressees.

decoupled payment In the context of the Common Agricultural Policy (CAP), an agricultural subsidy to farmers that is not tied to production.

deepening of European integration A term used to describe the growth of EU powers either through transferring policy competences from the member states or through increasingly supranational forms of decision making.

Delors Report A proposal by European Commission president Jacques Delors in 1989 that formed the basis for the establishment of Economic and Monetary Union (EMU).

democratic deficit A prominent theme in academic and political discourse. This term captures a list of reasons why the EU is insufficiently democratic.

demoi-cracy A model of democracy that takes the diversity of the EU's political community – the existence of various national *demoi* (peoples) – as a starting point and seeks to develop consensus-oriented political institutions that protect the integrity of these *demoi*.

demos The Greek work for people; in discussions about democracy in the EU, it is used for a political community of citizens united by a shared identity. Plural: *demoi*.

diplomacy The profession, activity, or skill of maintaining international relations, typically by a political entity's representatives abroad.

direct effect A core principle of EU law established by the Court of Justice of the EU. Direct effect means that EU law can create rights and obligations for citizens (not just for the member states) that are enforceable in court.

direct payments Subsidies paid to farmers under the EU's Common Agricultural Policy (CAP). Direct payments constitute the first pillar of the CAP; the second pillar is the rural development policy.

directive A type of EU secondary law; a directive establishes binding objectives that the member states are obliged to transpose into domestic legislation. Directives are commonly used to harmonize the laws of the member states on a particular matter, so that the same rules and standards apply uniformly throughout the EU.

directorate-general (DG) An administrative unit in the European Commission responsible for a specific task or policy area.

Dublin Regulation A piece of EU legislation in the area of asylum policy; it stipulates that refugees need to register and claim asylum in the first EU member state they land in.

Eastern Partnership (EaP) Initiative in the context of the European Neighbourhood Policy (ENP) aimed at six states in the EU's eastern neighbourhood (Armenia, Azerbaijan, Belarus, Georgia, Moldova, and Ukraine).

Economic and Monetary Union (EMU) Arrangements that form the legal and policy foundation of the EU's single currency, the euro. EMU consists of a supranational monetary policy for member states that are part of the euro area, set by the European Central Bank, as well as mechanisms to coordinate the member states' economic and budgetary policies.

Emissions Trading System (ETS) A cornerstone of the EU's policy to combat climate change; the ETS is a cap-and-trade system applied to high-emission industries that disburses a limited (and shrinking) number of emissions permits that can be traded between companies.

Energy Union A 2015 EU initiative launched to move toward achieving energy security, liberalizing energy markets, improving energy efficiency, and reducing emissions.

enlargement In the EU context, the accession of new states to the EU.

enlargement fatigue Sentiments in public opinion in existing EU member states that are characterized by increasing opposition toward further enlargement.

Environmental Action Programme (EAP) A document defining the future orientation of EU policy in the environmental field and suggesting specific proposals that the Commission intends to put forward over the coming years. The duration of EAPs ranges from 3 to 10 years.

equalization In regional policy, a term used to describe programs that redistribute funds from richer to poorer regions.

Euratom European Atomic Energy Community, one of the three original European communities. Euratom was established in the Treaties of Rome in 1957; it aims to create and develop the peaceful use of atomic energy in Europe. It is legally distinct from the EU but has the same members.

euro area The countries using the euro as their currency.

euro area financial crisis Also referred to as the "sovereign debt crisis" or "euro area crisis," a crisis between 2010 and 2016 in which various euro area member states (Greece, Ireland, Portugal, Spain, and Cyprus) were unable to refinance their government debt or to bail out their financial sector. To assist these countries, other euro area member states and the International Monetary Fund (IMF) provided financial support and in return demanded national reforms, monitored by a "troika" of three institutions (the European Central Bank, European Commission, and IMF).

European Arrest Warrant (EAW) A mechanism under the EU's Area of Freedom, Security and Justice that commits member states to surrender citizens to other EU member states if they are wanted in relation to significant crimes or to serve a prison sentence for an existing conviction.

European Central Bank (ECB) An independent central bank, and EU institution, that sets monetary policy for the euro area.

European Coal and Steel Community (ECSC) The first European Community, created by six Western European states (West Germany, France, Italy, Netherlands, Belgium, and Luxembourg) through the Treaty of Paris in 1951; the ECSC subjected the member states' coal and steel production to a supranational regulatory regime.

European Commission   The main executive body of the EU that also possesses the monopoly of legislative initiative in most policy areas. The Commission is a supranational body composed of one commissioner per member state, each with a portfolio of responsibilities, tasked with promoting the general interests of the union.

European Council   The summit meeting of heads of state or government of the member states, tasked with defining the general political directions and priorities of the EU. The European Council is headed by a president serving a two-and-a-half-year term.

European Court of Human Rights (ECtHR)   An international court set up in 1959, which rules on individual or state applications alleging violations of the civil and political rights set out in the European Convention on Human Rights (ECHR). The ECtHR is not an EU institution; rather it is governed by the Council of Europe.

European Defence Community (EDC)   Proposed by Jean Monnet and launched in 1951 by the French head of government René Pleven, this proposed community was meant to allow for the rearmament of West Germany in a supranational framework (as opposed to having that country join NATO). The EDC would have had the same member states as the ECSC. The proposal to establish the EDC failed as it was not ratified in the French Parliament.

European Economic Area (EEA)   The Single Market of the EU member states and three of the four EFTA countries (Iceland, Liechtenstein, and Norway). The agreement ensures that non-EU countries can be part of the EU Single Market; they have to adopt all EU laws but have exemptions in the area of agriculture and fisheries (see also "Single Market").

European Economic Community (EEC)   One of the three original European Communities. It was established in 1957 through the Treaties of Rome by the same states that had established the European Coal and Steel Community. It aimed to promote economic integration between member states, mainly through the establishment of a Common Market and a Customs Union. The EEC was later renamed the European Community (EC). In 2009 it formally became absorbed into the EU by the Treaty of Lisbon.

European External Action Service (EEAS)   Foreign affairs department of the EU. Led by the high representative of the union for foreign affairs and security policy, the EEAS is staffed both by EU officials and by national diplomats temporarily seconded from the member states.

European Free Trade Association (EFTA) A free trade agreement formed in the 1960s by European states that did not want to join the European Economic Community. Most states have since joined the EU, but the EFTA remains a separate institution with four member states (Iceland, Liechtenstein, Norway, and Switzerland).

European Green Deal (EGD) A framework for EU climate and energy policies that aims to turn Europe into a carbon-neutral continent by 2050. First presented in December 2019, the EGD encompasses a large number of measures to reduce CO_2 emissions and to support the transition to more sustainable economic practices.

European Neighbourhood Policy (ENP) An EU policy that aims to improve the EU's relations with countries in its eastern and southern neighbourhood; the ENP is based on bilateral agreements on closer economic and political cooperation but does not provide the participating states an explicit membership perspective.

European Parliament (EP) One of the core legislative institutions of the EU; the EP is composed of 705 elected members of the European Parliament (MEPs); its primary roles include passing laws together with the Council of the EU, adopting the budget with the Council of the EU, deciding on international agreements and enlargements, scrutinizing the executive institutions, and approving the nominations for the members of the European Commission.

European Regional Development Fund (ERDF) One of the structural funds set up in the context of the EU's regional policy to support regional economic development.

European Social Fund (ESF) One of the structural funds set up in the context of the EU's regional and social policy to support employment and labour mobility; education, skills, and lifelong working; social inclusion; as well as efficient public administration.

European social model A vaguely defined set of values and institutions that are said to define a European approach to social policy, characterized by a higher degree of solidarity and more generous social programs than in North America.

European Stability Mechanism (ESM) An intergovernmental institution set up by euro area member states in the context of the euro area financial crisis to provide loans to euro area member states that experience sovereign debt crises.

European System of Central Banks (ESCB) The institutional framework for monetary policy in Economic and Monetary Union; it consists of the European Central Bank working together with the national central banks of the member states.

Europeanization A concept in EU studies that describes how the EU impacts the member states. It can refer to a top-down process in which research focuses on how the EU shapes institutions, processes, and policies in the member states, or to a bottom-up process in which research examines how member states and other domestic actors shape the EU and its policies.

Europol The European Police Office, headquartered in The Hague (Netherlands). It plays a front-line role in coordinating the EU member states' fight against terrorism and cross-border crime. It also collaborates with non-EU states and international organizations.

Euroskepticism A political opinion, manifested in parties and social movements, that explicitly criticizes or opposes the European integration project, often because of concerns about the dilution of national sovereignty and identity.

Exchange Rate Mechanism (ERM) A system of fixed but adjustable exchange rates that started in 1979. Today it ties to the euro currencies of participating non-euro member states who agree to keep their exchange rates stable. These countries are Bulgaria, Croatia, and Denmark.

Exclusive competence When the EU has exclusive competence over a policy area, this means that only the EU can set policy and the member states have given up the right to make their own rules in this area.

federalism A political system composed of multiple political levels (usually a federal level and multiple regional subunits), each of which possesses its own legislative, executive, and judicial institutions. The decision-making competences of each level are defined in a constitution, which cannot be unilaterally amended by any one level. Federalism can also refer to the theory or advocacy of reaching a federal political system.

foreign direct investment (FDI) An international investment whereby a resident entity in one economy seeks to obtain a lasting interest in an enterprise resident in another economy.

foreign policy The strategies chosen by a country or political entity to safeguard its interests and to achieve its goals in its regional or global environment.

freedom of movement (of people) The right of EU citizens to travel between EU member states without restrictions or barriers and to take up employment or establish a company in another member state. Freedom of movement is one of the core principles of the EU's Single Market.

Frontex The European Border and Coast Guard Agency, which provides support to national authorities in monitoring and controlling the EU's external borders.

General Affairs Council (GAC) The configuration of the Council of the EU that discusses overarching concerns not restricted to any specific policy area; member states are usually represented by their foreign minister or European affairs minister in this Council configuration.

geographical indication (GI) A form of intellectual property used in the Common Agricultural Policy (CAP) and in EU trade agreements; a GI requires that a product with GI status may only originate from a certain place or region (for example, Champagne must be made from grapes grown in the Champagne region of France).

geopolitics A framework for the analysis of power in international relations that takes into account spatial or geographic contexts.

Global Strategy A document presented by the EU in July 2016 to define the principles and objectives of the Common Foreign and Security Policy (CFSP).

governance mode The specific configuration of strategies and tools that the EU uses to reach policy objectives; these might include the exercise of authority, where permitted by the treaties; financial transfers, where the EU has the necessary resources; as well as non-hierarchical approaches such as information sharing or coordination among member states.

grand theory A theory that aims at a higher level of understanding about the nature of the political system but does not concern itself too much with the details of the empirics. Advanced by scholars such as the sociologist C. Wright Mills in the 1960s (see also "mid-range theory").

high politics Political issues that relate to the exercise of power and are deemed to be politically central to national sovereignty, including the politics of foreign and military affairs.

high representative for foreign affairs and security policy EU official tasked with coordinating the Common Foreign and Security Policy (CFSP). The high representative leads the European External Action Service (EEAS) and serves as a vice-president of the European Commission.

institutionalism A group of theories in the social sciences that focus on the emergence, operation, and effects of political institutions (that is, formal and informal rule systems). Three important strands of this theory are rational choice, historical, and sociological institutionalism.

intellectual property A work or invention that is the result of creativity, such as a design, to which one has rights and for which one may apply for a copyright, trademark, or patent.

intergovernmental/intergovernmentalism In EU decision making, processes whereby member states, as opposed to supranational institutions, play the most important role in determining policy outcomes. An intergovernmental theory of European integration is one that privileges the role of states in describing and explaining the integration process.

international organization A system of legal rules established by states to govern their interactions and cross-border policy challenges.

investor state dispute settlement (ISDS) A component in bilateral trade agreements concluded by the EU; it establishes a system through which individual companies can sue countries for alleged discriminatory practices.

Justice and Home Affairs (JHA) The former label used for the EU's policies related to justice, security, migration, and borders. The name was introduced when the policy area became Pillar III of the EU in the Maastricht Treaty; it was replaced by the name "Area of Freedom, Security, and Justice (AFSJ)" in the Treaty of Lisbon.

low politics A term used for policies that are relatively technical in nature and do not normally elicit great public interest (such as product regulation).

Maastricht Treaty A major reform of EU primary law that came into effect in November 1993. The Maastricht Treaty formally established the European Union, alongside the previously existing European Communities (European Coal and Steel Community, European Community, Euratom). It first established the EU's Common Foreign and Security Policy and EU policies in the area of Justice and Home Affairs. It also created the institutional foundations for Economic and Monetary Union.

market correction Broad term to describe policies aimed at limiting or compensating for the operation of free markets in the EU.

market making Broad term to describe policies aimed at expanding free market principles across the EU.

mid-range theory A theory that seeks to integrate empirical insights with modest theoretical understanding (see also "grand theory").

mixed agreement   An EU trade agreement that exceeds the scope of the EU's exclusive competence over trade agreements; in case of a mixed agreement, each member state needs to separately ratify the agreement in addition to the EU.

mixed economy   An economic system that is neither state controlled nor entirely left to the operation of market principles. A mixed economy is defined by markets that are subject to government intervention and regulation.

Multiannual Financial Framework (MFF)   The EU's seven-year budget plan that sets the parameters for each year's budget. Decisions concerning the MFF are characterized by tough bargains among member states and between intergovernmental and supranational institutions in the EU.

multilateralism   International cooperation of multiple countries to address or solve a given issue.

multilevel governance   A theoretical framework for research on the EU that focuses on the interactions between the EU level, the national level, and the substate level.

mutual recognition   A principle in EU law that requires member states to respect each other's regulatory policies. Applied to the trade in goods, the principle states that member states must normally allow goods that are legally sold in another member state to also be sold in their own territory.

nation state   A system of legislative, executive, and judiciary institutions for a specific territory and population; states are defined as possessing sovereignty in defining their own competences and regulating internal affairs.

negative integration   A form of integration that involves the removal of barriers to integration between the member states (see also "positive integration").

neofunctionalism   A theory of regional integration that emphasizes how integration processes can develop their own dynamics (most importantly through processes of spillover between policy areas) and hence spiral out of the control of the member states.

neoliberalism   A term used to describe an ideology and set of policies that embrace free market capitalism and call for the reduction of market-correcting policies, domestically and in international trade agreements.

NextGenerationEU   A package of measures agreed to by EU member states in 2020 to support the member states' economic recovery from the negative effects of the COVID-19 pandemic. The package made available a total of €750 billion in loans and grants in addition to the EU's regular budget; the largest component was the Recovery and Resilience Facility (RRF).

non-discrimination A core principle of European integration, stating that citizens of the member states must be treated in the same way regardless of their nationality. The principle has also been applied to other relevant differences, such as gender or age.

non-tariff barriers Barriers to trade that do not originate in tariffs; the most important non-tariff barriers in the EU today result from the regulation of products (for example, technical standards) or production processes (such as environmental or workplace safety rules).

normative power Concept used to describe international influence exercised by the EU through its commitment to political values and principles, such as democracy, human rights, and peaceful conflict resolution.

North Atlantic Treaty Organization (NATO) A defence alliance of 30 countries, including the United States, Canada, and 21 member states of the EU (all except Austria, Cyprus, Finland, Ireland, Malta, and Sweden). Finland and Sweden applied for NATO membership in 2022.

open method of coordination (OMC) A mechanism developed in the area of social and employment policy to coordinate member state policies. The procedure entails a four-step process, where the EU level defines policy guidelines and targets while member states formulate and implement their policies within this framework.

opinion A decision by the Court of Justice of the EU on the legality of a proposed agreement between the EU and a third country. EU institutions such as the European Parliament may request an opinion before the proposed international agreement enters into force.

opt-out A clause in the EU treaties or in EU legislation that allows member states to refrain from participation in certain political actions.

ordinary legislative procedure (OLP) The normal procedure for most legislation of the EU, in which the European Parliament acts on an equal footing with the Council. The OLP was built on the co-decision procedure introduced by the Maastricht Treaty. It requires that legislation proposed by the Commission can be amended, and must be approved, by both the Council and the EP.

Permanent Structured Cooperation (PESCO) An initiative within the Common Security and Defence Policy (CSDP) that allows groups of member states to pursue capacity-building initiatives without requiring the participation of all member states. PESCO was initially launched in

December 2017; currently there are more than 50 individual PESCO projects.

permissive consensus   A term introduced first by academics Lindberg and Scheingold in 1970 that described the European integration process as passively approved by public opinion or at least not actively disapproved.

Pillars of the EU   A system of organizing the EU, established in the Maastricht Treaty and abolished in the Treaty of Lisbon, that distinguished (I) the European Communities (European Coal and Steel Community, European Community, Euratom), (II) the Common Foreign and Security Policy, and (III) Justice and Home Affairs. Pillars II and III were based on intergovernmental cooperation, whereas Pillar I was based on the community integration method.

populism   A political ideology or style of discourse that interprets politics as a conflict between the people (defined as virtuous) and the political elite (defined as corrupt). In the EU context, Euroskeptic positions often – but not always – make use of populist arguments.

positive integration   The creation of binding EU-level rules (normally in the form of legislation) that replace previously existing member state law with a view to deeper integration (see also "negative integration").

primary law   In EU law, the name given to legal acts of the highest order. The EU's primary law is constituted by the EU treaties. Primary law is comparable to constitutional law at the state level.

public procurement   The process by which public entities (such as governments) purchase work, goods, and services from companies.

qualified majority voting (QMV)   A mode of decision making in the Council of the EU; QMV requires that at least 55 per cent of the member states, representing at least 65 per cent of the EU population, support a proposal for it to pass and become law. QMV is the standard decision rule of the Council under the ordinary legislative procedure.

recommendation   In EU law, a non-binding legislative act. The Commission often makes recommendations to the member states or other institutions as to how to move forward to achieve goals in a particular area where binding legislation is either not within the EU's competence or the necessary support in the Council or Parliament for a binding legislative act cannot be achieved.

Recovery and Resilience Facility (RRF)   A temporary fund agreed to by EU member states in 2020 as part of the NextGenerationEU package to support the member states' economic recovery from the negative effects of the COVID-19 pandemic. The RRF is an addition to the regular EU budget. It makes available €672.5 billion (€312.5 billion in grants and €360 billion in loans), financed by joint borrowing of EU member states on financial markets.

reference for a preliminary ruling A procedure exercised before the Court of Justice of the European Union (CJEU). Under this procedure, national courts are required to request a decision from the CJEU whenever a case before them rests on an undecided question of EU law. The reference for a preliminary ruling therefore offers a means to guarantee legal certainty by uniform application of EU law.

refugee crisis A crisis that occurred in Europe in 2015–16 (after building up over many years) when more than 1 million refugees and other undocumented migrants arrived in EU member states, mostly fleeing war and terror in Syria and other countries. This influx was considered a crisis in part because of the sheer number of people, the casualties and hardship related to their journey, as well as the difficulties the EU had in finding the appropriate policy response.

regional policy See "cohesion policy."

regulation A type of EU secondary law. A regulation is a legal act that is immediately enforceable simultaneously in all member states (meaning that it does not first need to be transposed into national law). A regulation is binding in its entirety for all natural and legal persons in the EU.

renewable energy Power generated from resources that can naturally be replenished. Examples are energy from sunlight, wind, tides, geothermal heat, and biomass.

rule of law The idea that every person, including rulers, are subject to legal principles that can be enforced by independent courts. In some EU member states, especially Poland and Hungary, concerns have recently been raised about governments undermining the rule of law.

rural development policy One of two pillars of the Common Agricultural Policy (CAP); focuses on economic, environmental, and social development in rural areas. The other pillar includes direct payments to farmers.

Schengen Area The territory of member states that are signatories to the Schengen Agreement. At the time of writing, the area encompasses 23 EU member states and 4 non-EU states. Member states of the Schengen Area have abolished internal border controls (between each other), though such controls may be temporarily reintroduced in emergency situations.

Schuman Plan An official statement made on May 9, 1950, by the French foreign minister Robert Schuman proposing to pool French and West German coal and steel production.

second-order election An influential characterization of European Parliament (EP) elections that points out that many voters approach these elections primarily as a relatively non-consequential opportunity to express an opinion about member state politics. According to this view, the second-order character of EP elections explains why turnout may be low and the campaign dominated by national issues.

shared competence A policy area where the EU has the power to set policy but the member states are allowed to supplement EU policy with their own rules. Most EU policy competences are shared competences.

Single European Act (SEA) A major reform of EU primary law that came into effect in 1987. The Single European Act expanded qualified majority voting in the Council, thus making it easier to pass legislation. The main objective of the SEA was to complete the Single Market by December 1992.

Single Market An area of free movement of goods, services, persons, and capital between the EU member states. Also referred to as the "internal market" or (formerly) the "Common Market." All EU member states are part of the Single Market. Three of the four EFTA countries also form part of it through their membership in the EEA. Switzerland has not joined the EEA but has made bilateral agreements so it can also be part of the Single Market.

soft governance A term used to describe modes of EU governance that seek to encourage member states to change domestic policies. Soft governance tends to be used in areas in which the EU does not have the competence to pass binding legislation.

soft power A form of power in the international sphere that derives not from military resources but from economic, cultural, and other non-material factors that may appeal and attract, such as ideas, discourse, and example setting.

solidarity In the context of European integration, the willingness of EU member states and their citizens to share resources for joint European programs or to support the weakest member states or parts of the population.

sovereign debt crisis See "euro area financial crisis."

sovereignty   In international relations, national sovereignty refers to the principle of supreme power or authority of the state. In concrete terms it means that states have the right to define their own competences and to determine their internal affairs without outside interference.

spillover   In the theory of neofunctionalism, the term is used to describe a situation in which regional integration in one policy sector creates pressures to integrate in another connected sector.

Spitzenkandidat   German term for "lead candidate"; used for candidates for the office of European Commission president who were nominated by European political parties in advance of the 2014 and 2019 European Parliament elections.

strategic autonomy   In discussions about the Common Foreign and Security Policy (CFSP), a term used to describe the objective of achieving greater independence of the EU from other world powers, especially the United States.

strategic partner   In EU external relations, a vaguely defined status accorded by the EU to countries with whom it would like to build particularly close relations. The EU's current strategic partners are Brazil, Canada, China, India, Japan, Mexico, South Africa, South Korea, and the United States.

subsidiarity   A principle for the allocation of powers in multilevel systems stating that political problems should be addressed at the lowest level where their resolution is possible. The subsidiarity principle appears explicitly in Article 5(3) TEU.

supranational/supranationalism   In EU decision making, processes that are controlled by institutions that represent the EU as a whole, rather than the member states, and are designed to express the common European interest.

supremacy (also called primacy)   A core principle of EU law stating that EU law takes precedent over the law of the member states. The principle was established by the Court of Justice of the EU and is affirmed in Declaration 17 of the Lisbon Treaty.

sustainability   The ability to use a resource within a given territory without damaging future resources or the environment's ability to reproduce that resource.

tariffs   A tax on imports or exports.

third country   In EU terminology, any country that is not an EU member state.

Transatlantic Trade and Investment Partnership (TTIP)   Proposed trade agreement between the EU and the United States. Negotiations started in July 2013 and stalled in 2016.

Treaties of Rome   The treaties that established the European Economic Community and the European Atomic Energy Community (Euratom); signed in 1957, came into effect in 1958.

Treaty of Amsterdam   The treaty that further consolidated the powers of EU supranational institutions, extended co-decision legislative procedure, introduced open method of coordination (OMC) in employment, brought the Schengen Agreement into EU primary law, and allowed more supranational decision making on Justice and Home Affairs (JHA), which was renamed Area of Freedom, Security and Justice (AFSJ). This treaty was signed in 1997 and came into force in 1999.

Treaty of Lisbon   The most recent major reform of EU primary law. It came into effect in December 2009. The Treaty of Lisbon gave the EU a unified legal personality by abolishing the previous pillar structure. It contained major institutional reforms, such as the creation of the president of the European Council. It also contained reforms that strengthened the European Parliament and other democratic mechanisms.

Treaty of Nice   The treaty that further outlined the details of accession to the EU, expanded the co-decision procedure, and gave increased competency and powers to the EU's supranational institutions. It was signed in 2001 and came into effect in 2003.

Treaty of Paris   The treaty that established the European Coal and Steel Community. It was signed in 1951, came into effect in 1952, and expired in 2002.

Treaty on European Union (TEU)   One of two main treaties that make up EU primary law; the TEU defines the EU's objectives, governing principles, and institutions; it also defines EU powers and decision-making procedures in the Common Foreign and Security Policy (CFSP).

Treaty on the Functioning of the European Union (TFEU)   One of two main treaties that make up EU primary law; the TFEU defines EU powers and decision-making procedures in most policy areas; it also includes detailed provisions on institutions.

trilogue   A system of informal consultations between the European Commission, the European Parliament, and the Council of the EU that takes place in the context of the ordinary legislative procedure (OLP). The goal of the trilogue is to produce a compromise on a specific piece of EU legislation, if possible, without going through all three stages of the OLP.

unanimity A form of decision making that requires explicit support by all decision makers (such as member states in the Council of the EU).

Union for the Mediterranean (UfM) International organization involving all EU member states, the European Commission, and 15 Mediterranean countries, including states addressed by the European Neighbourhood Policy (ENP) in the EU's southern neighbourhood.

Werner Plan An early blueprint for Economic and Monetary Union proposed by a committee chaired by Luxembourg's prime minister and finance minister, Pierre Werner, in 1970.

widening of European integration A term used to describe the geographical expansion of the EU through the addition of new member states.

World Trade Organization (WTO) An international organization that oversees global trade in goods and services.

Index

3Ms (money, markets, and mobility), 314

accession treaty, 62, 239, 449
   ratification of, 279, 282, 287
acquis communautaire
   accession state adoption of, 103–4, 283, 451
   concept of, 12, 80, 285, 449
   conditionality and, 284, 319
Afghanistan, 39, 191, 194, 394
Agenda 2000: 214, 216–17
   Mid-Term Review of, 219
   reforms, 438
agricultural policy, 342
   Canada's, 226–7
   devolution of powers in, 104, 414
   EEC negotiations, 33
   geographical indication status, 225
   governance of, 104, 106, 415–17
   intervention prices in, 212, 216
   reforms, 213–14, 220–1, 227, 238
   subsidies in, 99–100, 212–13, 224–5
   See also Common Agricultural Policy
Agricultural Stabilization Act, 226
anti-dumping, 258, 449
Arab Spring, 194, 400–1, 442

EU neighbourhood relations, 173, 180, 311, 320, 394
   migrants from, 178–9
Area of Freedom, Security and Justice (AFSJ), 449, 454
   budget, 177–8
   challenges of, 173–4, 180, 182–3
   origins of, 165–8, 438, 459, 466
   as policy field, 167–9, 171–4, 177, 441
association agreements (AAs), 266, 281
   decision making on, 54, 62, 288
   Eastern Partnership (EaP), 309, 311, 316
   European Neighbourhood Policy (ENP), 307, 312
   with Türkiye, 292, 294
   with Ukraine, 295–6, 307, 336, 444
association partnerships (APs), 294–5
Association of Southeast Asian Nations (ASEAN), 91n1, 124
asylum, 309, 406
   as EU pillar, 36–7
   member state management of, 181–2
   policies, 168–9, 171–3, 440
   seekers, regulations for, 40, 172–3, 178–9, 401

asylum (*Cont'd*)
  See also Dublin Regulation; Pact on Migration and Asylum
Asylum, Migration and Integration Fund (AMIF), 171, 178
austerity, 39, 125, 150–1, 363, 421, 449
Australia, 194, 261, 266, 375
Austria, 437
  accession to EU, 8, 37, 239, 282–3, 336, 435
  EP elections, 59, 61, 290
  integration initiatives, 138, 432
  NATO non-membership, 194, 461
  population identities in, 170, 344, 358, 420
  in Schengen Area, 167

bailouts, euro area financial crisis, 39, 66, 14
Banking Union, 449
  creation of, 122, 138, 443
  managing sovereign debt crisis, 138, 152–4
  three pillars of, 155
  as work in progress, 154–5, 157, 160
Bank Recovery and Resolution Directive (BRRD), 154–5
Barnier, Michel, 67
Basic Payment Scheme (BPS), 220, 224
Belgium, 49, 265, 454
  creation of EU, 2, 7, 29–30, 138, 210, 283
  election turnout, 59
  European Parliament seats, 61
  population identities, 170, 344
  regional policy, 231, 235
  Schengen Agreement, 167, 435
Benelux, 65, 166, 297
bicameral legislature. *See* legislatures
Blair, Tony, 190
Blue Card Initiative, 171, 441
bond markets, 147–8, 151, 155
borderless travel, 11, 166, 179
  temporary limits on, 180, 444
  See also Schengen Area

border regime, 290, 387
  budget, 97, 177–8
  Canadian versus EU, 41, 181
  CDSP operations and, 192–3
  EU challenges to, 166–70, 178, 182, 293, 422
  expansion of, 296, 304
  external, 36, 172–3, 175–83, 440
  mobility (*see* cross-border mobility)
  policies, 168, 172–5, 179–83, 242, 419
  refugee crisis (*see* refugees)
  security issues and, 306–9, 315, 320–1, 398–400
  trade, 140–2, 144, 153–6, 374
  US-Canada, 11–12, 181
  See also Area of Freedom, Security and Justice; borderless travel; Frontex
Bosnia-Herzegovina, 190–2, 201, 294–6, 310, 444
Brazil, 5, 394, 402–3, 416, 465
  See also BRICS countries; Mercosur
Brexit, 2, 183, 201, 450
  crises influencing, 3–4, 39–40, 177–8, 362
  debates from, 278, 290, 341, 422
  EU-UK negotiation of, 66–7, 142–5, 299
  geopolitics and, 396–7
  impacts on EU, 278, 298, 328
  referendum voting, 4, 18, 194, 261, 335, 444
  timeline of, 298–9
  trade relations after, 219, 224, 256, 264, 424, 446
  See also Trade and Cooperation Agreement (EU-UK)
BRICS countries (Brazil, Russia, India, China, South Africa), 394, 403, 410
British Columbia, 143, 297, 383
budget, EU, 62, 160, 218, 345, 427
  agricultural policy, 32, 35, 212–15, 221–2, 227
  for EU institutions, 50–1, 82, 157, 177–8

Index   471

member state funding of, 10, 96–9,
  222, 240, 281–2
process for, 68, 332
proposals to enhance, 33, 151–3, 195,
  240–4, 419–20, 460–2
Recovery and Resilience Facility (*see*
  Recovery and Resilience Facility)
regional policy, 232–5, 238–9, 280,
  311, 314–15
responsibility for, 46, 52–4, 58, 95,
  289, 456
small, 10, 149, 201, 342, 417
trade, 269
See also Multiannual Financial
  Framework
Bulgaria, 11
  accession to EU, 8, 37, 282–8, 292,
    437, 440
  European Parliament elections, 59, 61
  North Macedonia versus, 294, 447
  population identities, 170, 344, 367n3
  poverty funding for, 240–2
  Schengen candidacy, 167
  sustainability goal in, 375
Bull, Hedley, 127
Burgess, Michael, 117

Canada, 273, 397, 450
  agricultural policy, 226–7
  Confederation of, 41–2, 117–18
  as decentralized federation, 5, 13–14,
    26–8
  EU agreements with, 434, 439, 444, 152
  EU enlargement versus enlargement
    in, 297
  executive leadership, 67–8
  foreign policy and diplomacy, 196–7,
    203, 225
  governance modes, 106–7, 330–1
  inflation in, 159
  judicial system, 84–5
  legislative system, 68, 75, 361–2
  migration and borders, 171–4,
    178–81, 461

political system, 40–2, 60, 67–8,
  99–100, 452
power generation versus EU, 382–4
regional policy, 247, 417, 461
relationship with EU, 5, 175, 219–21,
  266–7, 404
relationship with US, 11, 91n1, 330–1,
  404, 418, 465
single market in, 141–3
Supreme Court of, 84–5
trade policy, 256, 261–70, 398, 416
Canada-United States-Mexico
  Agreement (CUSMA), 91n1, 226
Canadian Agricultural Income
  Stabilization Program (CAIS), 226–7
Canadian Free Trade Agreement, 142
candidate states, 104, 287, 400, 410, 450–1
Capital Markets Union (CMU), 122,
  155–6, 443, 450
carbon capture and storage, 384
Cassis de Dijon case, 140, 450
Central African Republic, 191, 193
Central and Eastern Europe (CEE)
  demise of communism in, 37, 284, 374
  enlargement toward, 42, 219–20,
    283–4, 290–2
Central and Eastern European
  countries (CEECs), 288
  EU membership negotiations, 37,
    103, 222–3, 287, 305
  post-communist, 3, 8, 37, 103, 305
  refugee crisis, 66, 180, 420
Charter of Fundamental Rights of the
  European Union, 450
  adoption and integration of, 38, 75,
    87, 438, 440–2
  rights enshrined in, 172, 174–5,
    354–7
Charter of Rights and Freedoms
  (Canada), 85
China
  Belt and Road Initiative, 405, 424
  as EU strategic partner, 5, 314, 402–5,
    416, 465

China (*Cont'd*)
  geopolitics with, 194, 291, 296, 318, 394, 397–8
  leadership in, 127, 188, 382, 410, 418
  trade with, 261, 267, 403–5
  See also BRICS countries
Chirac, Jacques, 190
Churchill, Winston, 27, 117, 431
citizenship, 169
  country of residence versus, 166, 170
  identification of national versus EU, 14, 126, 173–4
  migrants and member state, 171–2
  rights involved in, 166
class dynamics, critiques of, 125, 365
climate change, 197, 311, 443, 446
  Canadian policies on, 383–4
  emissions (*see* greenhouse gas emissions)
  EU leadership on, 10–11, 16, 127, 203, 388–90, 416–17
  geopolitical concerns and, 394–5, 402–5, 410
  international efforts on, 435, 437, 444
  policies and programs for, 372–3, 375–82
  RRF instruments and, 153, 244, 456
  steps taken to address, 215, 220, 246, 380, 385–6, 453
coal production, 235
  Canada versus EU, 382–4
  EU policies on, 7, 106, 257, 380, 389
  geopolitics and, 372, 375
  Monnet/Schuman plans for, 27–31, 431, 463
  spillover from integration, 119
  See also European Coal and Steel Community; steel production
Cohesion Fund, 54, 239–40, 244, 246
  Action for Refugees in Europe, 181
cohesion policy, 440, 450
  budget for, 97, 238, 240–4
  goals and evaluation of, 232, 240–4, 246–51
  as redistributive, 10, 235–8, 239, 249
  regional versus, 232, 236, 435
  system of partnership, 108–9
Cold War, 41, 394
  Eastern bloc countries, 3, 8–9, 29, 37, 239, 450
  European enlargement after, 3, 189, 282–3, 296–7, 397–9
  foreign policy after, 190, 284, 291, 410
  postwar cooperation, 103, 116
  Western bloc countries, 3, 8–9, 29–30, 450
Committee for Civilian Aspects of Crisis Management, 199
Committee of Permanent Representatives (COREPER), 48, 54–5, 287, 450
Committee of the Regions, 239
Common Agricultural Policy (CAP), 97, 286, 450, 458
  Agenda 2000 (*see* Agenda 2000)
  budget and payments, 221–3, 452–3
  Canadian agricultural policy versus, 226–7
  concerns with, 33–5, 212–13, 220–4, 227–8
  Dairy reform, 214, 434
  Fischler reform, 214, 219–20
  "greening" measures of, 215, 220
  Health Check, 214, 220
  MacSharry reforms, 214, 216, 436
  objectives, 32, 189, 210–12, 225, 463
  post-2013 reform, 220, 223–4, 443
  post-2020 reform, 220, 223–4, 447
  as redistributive, 10, 76, 100, 221–5, 212, 227
  regional policies versus, 235, 280, 299
  treaty formalization of, 31, 36, 217–18, 233, 432
Common Assembly. *See* European Parliament
Common Commercial Policy
  decision making on, 86, 449–50
  treaty formalization of, 31, 257, 260, 432
Common European Asylum System (CEAS), 169, 172, 438

common external tariff (CET), 139, 257–61, 432, 450–2
Common Fisheries Policy, 36, 217–19
Common Foreign and Security Policy (CFSP), 289, 451, 465
　decision making on, 200, 204
　establishment of, 31, 102, 187–90, 458–9
　EU versus member state competence in, 48, 52, 102, 319, 459, 466
　implementation of, 57, 102
　neighbourhood policy and, 195, 319–21
　pillar system and, 35–6, 39, 190, 436, 462
Common Market, 88, 106, 451
　establishment of, 31, 33, 94–5, 138, 432, 455
　four freedoms of, 140
　legislation creating, 76, 78, 100–1, 233
　SEA completion of, 35–6, 41–2, 435
　to Single Market, 138–9, 257, 464
　See also Single Market
Common Provision Regulation, 238, 249–50
Common Security and Defence Policy (CSDP), 410, 461
　comprehensive approach, 191, 451–2
　emergence of, 190, 440–1
　EU integration and, 201–4, 309
　operations of, 191–3, 199–204
communitarization, 37, 169, 182
competences, 42, 117–18, 167
　constraints on EU, 75, 96–9, 103–4, 389, 462
　delegation of external, 196–7, 199, 257–8, 372–3
　division of, 77, 81, 85–8, 106–8, 156
　energy and climate policy, 372–4, 379–80, 385
　EU policy expansion and deepening, 11, 31, 35–8, 84, 435–6, 452
　exclusive, 95, 100, 109, 239, 264, 457
　member state versus EU, 14, 26, 94–5, 189, 460
　mixed, 264–5, 272, 460
　shared, 13–14, 95, 127, 224, 406, 464
　supranational, 260, 272–3, 389, 418–19
　trade, 239, 257–60, 262–4, 268–71
competition
　distortion of fair, 100–1, 109, 212
　fair, 353
　increasing global, 260, 314, 374, 422
　logic of open, 199–200, 266
　mode of governance, 9, 106, 123, 251
　political, 341–2, 344
　regulation of, 233–7, 338
competition policy, 451
　competence in, 77, 81, 106, 110, 141
　decision making on, 36, 52, 110
　devolution of, 104
　EU leadership on, 16, 233, 284
　strengthening of, 34, 102, 155, 374
　transnational networks in, 109–10
　See also Directorate-General for Competition of the European Commission
Competitive and Innovation Program, 313
comprehensive approach, 191, 451
Comprehensive Economic and Trade Agreement (CETA), 256, 416, 451
　concerns with, 269–73, 445
　as mixed trade agreement, 264–7, 272
　negotiations, 5, 225, 261, 404, 441–4
　provincial participation in, 266–9
conditionality, 194, 451
　application of, 89, 104–5, 111
　enhanced, 220
　enlargement and, 281, 284
　neighbourhood policy, 305, 308, 314–15, 319–21
consensus-oriented decision making, 89, 177, 451
　cases with lack of, 65, 89, 101, 110, 122
　in Council of the EU, 12–13, 49, 55, 198, 286
　debates over use of, 344–5

consensus-oriented decision
making (Cont'd)
in EU Commission, 50
in EU political system, 46, 64–5, 198, 204–5, 339, 419–21
permissive, 340–1, 414, 461
qualified majority voting versus, 55, 102
See also demoi-cracy
Constitution, EU, 440
failure to establish, 38, 42, 335–7, 423
founding treaties as, 12, 72, 80
constructivism, 125, 129
Convention on the Elimination of Discrimination Against Women (CEDAW), 362
convergence criteria, 145–7, 451
cooperation, 189, 460
bilateral, 306
borders and defence, 199–202, 315, 402–3, 440
development, 191, 199, 239
European territorial, 242, 244, 246
focus on economic, 7, 27, 31, 41, 144, 439
institutional-member state, 53, 56–7, 88, 406
intergovernmental, 26, 48, 120–1, 166–8, 334, 462
judicial, 36, 168–9, 434
mode of governance, 123
neighbourhood/regional, 202, 236–8, 242, 306–9, 315–16
police and security, 36, 57, 175–6, 183, 318
political, 31, 124, 310, 318, 456
procedure, 62
supranational, 99, 109, 172–3, 200
See also Neighbourhood, Development and International Cooperation Instrument; open method of coordination; Partnership and Cooperation Agreements; Trade and Cooperation Agreements
coordination. *See* policy coordination

Coordination of Information on the Environment Programme, 376
Copenhagen summit, 283, 287, 306, 436
criteria, 284, 288, 305, 451–2
Costa v. ENEL, 79–80, 83
Council of Europe, 362, 455
establishment of, 27, 70n1, 117, 431
focus on human rights, 70n1, 82, 87, 175, 452
See also European Court of Human Rights
Council of the European Union, 70n1, 121, 196, 439–40
climate and energy policy, 373–5, 379–82, 389
Common Agricultural Policy, 211, 221
configurations and roles of, 53–8, 279, 287, 298, 332–5, 458
decision-making challenges, 85–6, 89, 110–11, 199–202, 419
on Economic and Monetary Union, 144–5, 154, 157
enlargement, 279, 285–9, 294, 436, 442–3
establishment of, 58, 65, 433–4, 441–2, 466
intergovernmentalism of, 53, 62–4, 102–3, 168, 286, 452
legislative role of, 62–4, 68, 75–8, 97–8, 446, 449
open method of coordination, 102–3, 108, 152–3
presidency of, 56–7, 66–8, 330–1, 452, 466
qualified majority voting in, 85–6, 95–7, 141, 258–60, 389, 462–4
regional and trade policy, 237, 241, 258–64, 268, 436
Council of Ministers. *See* Council of the European Union
Court of First Instance. *See* General Court
Court of Justice of the EU (CJEU), 77, 367, 426, 434
acquis communautaire and, 12, 80
budget, 82

direct effect and supremacy, 12, 78–80, 88–90, 353, 453, 465
EU integration and, 34–6, 62, 73–4, 82–4, 416
fundamental rights protection, 82, 86–7, 353, 358–60, 367n2
law enforcement, 13, 30, 52–3, 83–4, 86
member states versus, 78–80, 83–4, 87–9, 121, 450
procedures, 83–5, 88–9, 461–3
roles of, 64, 80–1, 83–8, 432, 438, 452
rulings, 62, 159, 169, 179–80, 358–60, 450
secondary legislation review, 80, 83–6, 89
structure and growth of, 81–2, 432
Supreme Court of Canada versus, 85
trade law, 140–2, 189, 258–60, 264
COVID-19 pandemic, 122, 270, 385, 397–8
border controls, 166–7, 177
inequalities and risk of, 10, 365
member state integration, 138, 156, 158–60, 416, 422–4
member state support amid, 10, 39, 150–1, 156–7, 263, 350, 420
NextGenerationEU program (*see* NextGenerationEU program)
Pandemic Emergency Purchase Programme (PEPP), 151, 446
Recovery and Resilience Facility (RRF), 97, 105, 150, 153, 244, 446, 460–2
vaccinations, 105, 153, 160, 415
crime, 331
cross-border, 36, 175–6, 318, 457
cyber-, 176
fighting, 168, 176–8, 183, 454
organized (*see* organized crime)
See also terrorism
Crimea, 443
Russian annexation of, 304, 311, 397, 407–8, 424
crisis management, 191–2, 203, 398, 410, 451–2

Crisis Management and Planning Directorate, 199
critical political economy, 125, 129
Croatia, 443
accession to EU, 8, 167, 283, 288, 293, 439
adoption of euro, 148, 456
European Parliament elections, 59, 61, 336
population identities in, 344, 367n3
cross-border mobility, 178
implications of, 166–8, 180, 183
visa policy, 175
currency, 187
corporate bonds in local, 147
euro (*see* euro; euro area)
fluctuations, 148
single, 11, 102, 139, 453
stabilization of national, 34, 144–5
Customs Union, 280, 407, 452
accession process and, 294
formation of and extraction from, 297, 299, 433
as pillar of EU, 36, 273
stage of integration, 138–40, 159, 257
Cyprus, 241, 439
accession to EU, 8, 37, 148, 282–5, 304, 436
European Parliament elections, 59–61
financial crisis, 39, 454
NATO non-membership, 194, 461
population identities in, 170, 344, 358
Schengen candidacy, 11, 167
Türkiye-EU conflict, 285, 292–4
use of veto, 56, 265
Czech Republic, 241, 344
accession to EU, 8, 37, 283–5, 437, 439
climate and energy targets, 375
European Parliament elections, 59, 61
neighbourhood policies for, 307
referendums in, 336
refugee crisis, 180
Schengen Area member state, 167

decision making, 25–6, 285, 357, 457
  autonomous, 195
  in Canada, 196, 267
  consensus (*see* consensus-oriented decision making)
  democratic, 328–9, 332, 335–9, 342–4, 366
  efficiency, issues with, 38, 55, 64–7, 121, 198
  EU mixed, multilevel structure, 15, 40, 46, 94–8, 110, 419–20
  intergovernmental, 12–13, 127, 168, 343, 459
  member state versus EU, 7, 67, 111, 218, 224
  paralyzed, 33
  qualified majority voting (*see* qualified majority voting)
  streamlining, 36–7, 103, 200, 345, 423
  supranational, 259, 332, 389, 452, 465
  technocratic, 119
  unanimity (*see* unanimity)
  withholding powers of, 14, 35–6, 69
decisions (legislative acts), 77, 449, 452
decoupled payments, 216, 220, 452
deep and comprehensive free trade agreements, 221, 307, 309, 315
deepening, 233, 452
  of integration, 41, 94, 137–8, 189, 257–8, 327
  policy competences, 11, 31, 35–8, 84, 435–6
  widening versus, 2, 6–11, 15–17, 414, 467
de Gaulle, Charles, 34, 119
  against British accession, 33–4, 280, 286, 290, 432–3
  CAP negotiations, 32–3
  See also Empty Chair Crisis
Delors, Jacques, 35, 118, 140, 421, 430
Delors Report, 35, 145, 435, 452
democracy
  concerns about neighbourhood, 290–2, 296, 304, 308–12, 318–21

  consensus, 339
  decision making (*see* decision making)
  definition of, 329
  EU advancement of, 2, 194, 204, 282–4, 452
  normative versus positive, 126, 345, 395, 461
  parliamentary, 126, 297, 339
  participatory, 126, 129
  quality of, 333, 345
  treaty reinforcement of, 74, 182, 315, 350, 451
  varying interpretations of, 8–9, 126, 315
democratic deficit, 38, 328, 364, 452
  concerns about, 65, 126, 341–3, 346
democratic participation
  challenges with legitimacy, 19, 126, 160, 424
  channels for, 337, 339
  demands for, 366, 422
  public debate on, 15–17, 65, 129–30
demoi-cracy, 344–5, 421, 453
demos, 126, 453
  theory of no-, 343–4
Denmark, 456
  accession to EU, 8, 34, 100, 235, 258, 433–4
  differentiation, 11, 138, 167, 195, 420, 445
  European Parliament elections, 59, 61, 297
  integration participation, 138, 222–3, 279–80, 283, 432
  population identities in, 170, 344
  referendums in, 336
differentiation, member state, 11, 69, 125, 307, 312
digital agenda
  budget for, 97, 150, 243
  EU focus on, 10, 142, 244, 263
  RRF expenses, 97, 105
Digital Markets Act, 141

diplomacy, 204, 453
  Canada's centralized, 196–7
  coordination of, 189–90, 204, 309, 402, 420
  forums for, 46, 200, 316–17
  sovereignty and, 187–8, 196
  tensions with, 26–7, 188–9, 201–2, 408
  See also European External Action Service
direct effect, 12, 78–80, 88–9, 353, 453
directives (legislative acts), 75, 78, 264, 453
  adoption requirements, 52, 76–7, 121
  challenging, 83, 85–6
  examples, 77, 141–2, 153–4, 171–2, 353–7
Directorate-General for Competition, 141, 155
Directorate-General for Defence Industry and Space, 195, 199
Directorate-General for Employment, 356, 358
Directorate-General for Justice, 356, 358
Directorate-General for Neighbourhood and Enlargement Negotiations, 199, 288
Directorate-General for Regional and Urban Policy, 234, 248, 428
Directorate-General for Trade, 199, 268, 428
direct payments, 222–3, 229n2, 450, 453, 463
  decoupled versus, 214, 216, 220
  Single Farm Payment replacement, 214, 219
discrimination, 459
  barriers to addressing, 357–9, 361–6
  direct, 351–2
  efforts to reduce, 10, 169, 171, 354–7, 446
  gender, 351–2, 354–5, 358–60, 367n2
  indirect, 351–2, 360

intersectional, 359–60
  LGBTQ+, 364, 447
  non- (*see* non-discrimination)
  racial, 172, 354–5, 359–60, 364
  treaty prohibition of, 74–5, 174–5, 250, 350
Dublin Regulation, 172, 179, 453

Eastern Partnership (EaP), 320–1
  agreements for, 309–10, 312–17, 439, 456
  countries in, 296, 307, 400, 441, 453
  Russia and, 311, 394, 400, 407
economic integration, 351
  enlargement and, 278, 314
  four stages of, 139–40
  historical focus on, 27–8, 138, 209, 421–3, 455
  legal integration and, 90
  mutual recognition and, 10
  national identities versus, 7
  redistribution and, 34, 236–7
  treaty reinforcement of, 233
  "vicious circle" of, 157–60
Economic and Monetary Union (EMU), 36, 428, 443
  budget for, 213
  critiques of, 154, 156–7, 280, 336, 421
  effects of, 147–9
  establishment of, 34–5, 102–3, 137–9, 459, 467
  financial crisis and, 155–7, 159–60
  membership criteria, 145–6, 451–3
  policy coordination via, 108–10, 152, 449, 457
  three-stage launch of, 106, 144–7, 433–6
Economist, The, 122, 429
  Euroskepticism in, 16–17
Effort Sharing Regulation, 379
Emissions Trading System (ETS), 377–9, 416, 440, 453
Employment Equality Directive, 171
Empty Chair Crisis, 16, 32–3, 119, 433

energy efficiency
　challenges with, 386-7, 389
　EU goals of, 10, 309, 375-8
　EU leadership on, 16, 386-7
　investments in, 385
energy policy
　challenges with EU, 385, 389-90, 414
　climate policies and, 373-7, 456
　competition policy and, 234
　goals of, 373-4, 386, 445
　renewable (*see* renewable energy)
　Russian invasion of Ukraine, 372, 374
　transnational network approach in, 109
Energy Union, 379-80, 386, 443, 454
enlargement
　to Central and Eastern Europe, 42, 219-20, 283-4, 290-2
　conditionality and, 89, 104-5, 111, 281, 284
　economic integration, 278, 314
　post-Cold War, 3, 189, 282-3, 296-7, 397-9
　southern, 281-4, 290
enlargement fatigue, 289, 293, 296, 454
Environmental Action Programmes (EAPs), 376, 434, 454
environmental policy
　climate policy from, 373, 376
　market correction and, 101, 106
　strengthening, 102, 376-7
　transnational network approach in, 109
equality
　austerity measures and, 363-5
　barriers to, 352, 355-9, 362-6
　Canada's navigation of, 361-2
　definition of, 352
　equity versus, 351-3, 363
　EU strengthening of, 173-4, 350-1, 354-7
　feminist analyses of, 353, 356, 363-5
　gender (*see* gender equality; gender mainstreaming)
　labour market, 353, 359
　lack of income, 148, 271, 353
　legal, 350-2, 358, 364
　legislative reinforcement of, 74-5, 182, 250, 349-50, 354
　LGBTQ+, 358, 364, 447
　social, 352-3, 355-6, 360-4
　structural, 351, 359-60, 362-3, 365-6
　substantive, 351-2, 364, 366
　See also discrimination
equalization, 232, 235, 243-4, 454
Estonia, 191, 336, 398
　accession to EU, 8, 37, 283-5, 437, 439
　convergence funding, 241-2
　euro and Schengen Area adoption, 148, 167
　European Parliament elections in, 59-61
　population identities in, 170, 344
Eurasian Economic Union, 311, 407-8
Euratom, 41, 459, 465
　establishment of, 31, 49-50, 58, 75, 432
　EU integration and, 137-8, 327-8
　as EU pillar, 36, 436, 462
　purpose of, 94, 99, 373, 454
　replacement of, 38
euro, 453
　introduction of, 11, 35, 42, 148, 435, 439
　non-EU member use of, 148, 449
　opting out of, 11, 138, 436
euro area, 66, 120, 333, 398, 421, 454
　financial crisis, 39-40, 103-4, 148-54, 290-1, 454
　inflation in, 146, 148, 158-9
　joining the, 146-7, 417, 449
　temporary assistance in, 150-3, 155-60, 456
　See also Economic and Monetary Union
European Affairs Committee (EAC), 334
European Agricultural Guidance and Guarantee Fund (EAGGF), 211-13, 218, 221, 233, 236
European arrest warrant, 176, 454
European Atomic Energy Community (*see* Euratom)

Index 479

European Border and Coast Guard
 Agency (*see* Frontex)
European Central Bank (ECB), 89, 457
 establishment of, 38, 145–7, 440, 453–4
 financial crisis and, 150–1, 158–60,
 454
 governance and competences of,
 48–9, 103, 122, 428, 438
 See also European System of Central
 Banks
European Citizens' Initiative, 17–18,
 38, 338
European Coal and Steel Community
 (ECSC), 75, 373, 454
 deepening integration via, 94, 137–8,
 189, 327, 455
 establishment of, 7, 30, 49, 118,
 431, 466
 governance of, 81, 106, 459, 462
 See also Treaty of Paris
European Commission, 169, 455
 accession and enlargement roles,
 285–8, 305–6
 action in annulment, 84–6
 budgetary roles, 50–3, 82, 96–7,
 269, 332
 climate change and energy policy,
 372–9, 385–8, 409
 commissioner election and roles in,
 50–2, 330–1
 Common Agricultural Policy, 223
 Court of Justice of the EU and,
 78–80, 83–6, 89–90
 creation and structure of, 49–52,
 454–5
 defence and foreign policy, 169,
 189–91, 196–9, 445
 democratic representation and, 18,
 52–3, 121, 337–9, 356, 360
 as driver of integration, 34–5, 65, 78
 dual vigilance, 84
 economic policy, 151–5, 218, 454
 as EU pillar, 36–7
 European Green Deal, 153, 372, 381

European Neighbourhood Policy,
 308–14, 439, 446, 466
European Parliament and, 55–7,
 60–4, 456, 466
 executive roles, 13, 46–53, 68, 104–10,
 140–1, 419
 general programming principles, 233,
 236–7, 250
 infringement procedure, 83, 88,
 364, 447
 legislative powers of, 13, 33, 51–6,
 75–81, 462
 motion of censure, 51–2, 331
 Multiannual Financial Framework,
 89, 96–8, 332
 president selection, 48–52, 66–7,
 329–31, 343–4, 432–43
 in refugee crisis, 40, 66, 180, 182
 regional/cohesion policy, 232–9,
 242–3, 248–50
 Single Market and trade policy, 155–6,
 189, 262–9, 273, 416, 446
 as supranational institution, 47, 50–3,
 65, 102, 121–2, 286, 438
 See also High Authority
European Communities (EC), 373, 459
 establishment and growth of, 41, 257,
 336–7, 454–5
 EU pillars and, 36, 436, 438, 462, 466
 governance of, 50, 58, 433–5
 southern enlargement, 281–4, 290
 trade with, 86, 189, 261, 273, 373, 434
European Constitutional Treaty, 38,
 336–7, 440
European Convention on Human
 Rights, 82, 87, 175, 367n2, 455
European Council. *See* Council of the
 European Union
European Court of Human Rights
 (ECtHR), 367n4, 432
 governance of, 81, 87, 455
European Court of Justice. *See* Court of
 Justice of the EU
European Currency Unit, 34, 145

480 Index

European Defence Community (EDC), 194
  proposal of, 31, 189, 455
European deposit insurance schemes, 152, 154–5, 160
European Economic Area, 162n1, 455
European Economic Community (EEC), 260, 297, 327, 455
  budget, 35
  critiques of, 16, 33, 290, 373
  deepening integration via, 41–2, 94, 137–41, 233, 257–8
  enlargement, 278–81, 286, 292, 432–4
  establishment of, 30–2, 75, 79–81, 432, 465
  governance of, 38, 41, 49–50, 58, 272–3
  member state interests versus, 32–4, 79, 144–5, 217, 280–1
  objectives and competences of, 34–6, 78–80, 99, 210–12, 225, 435
  See also Empty Chair Crisis; Treaty Establishing the European Economic Community
European External Action Service (EEAS), 202, 311, 446, 458
  Competences of, 191, 198–201, 312, 314, 442
  international representation via, 14, 38, 455
European Financial Stability Facility (EFSF), 138, 150, 152, 442
European Fisheries Fund, 218
European Free Trade Association (EFTA), 162n1, 292, 456
  enlargement, 281–2, 290
  formation of, 138, 279–80, 432, 455–6
European Green Deal (EGD), 456
  Common Agricultural Policy reforms for, 215, 220–1
  elements of, 372, 380, 381, 379
  launching of, 379, 445
  Recovery and Resilience Facility support, 97, 105, 153

  steps to meet, 263, 387–9
European Institute for Gender Equality, 354, 440
European Investment Bank (EIB), 233, 236
Europeanization, 127–30, 187–8, 457
  top-down versus bottom-up, 123–4
European Monetary System (EMS), 146
  introduction of EMU, 34, 101, 106, 144–5, 434
European Monitoring Centre on Racism and Xenophobia, 172, 354
European Neighbourhood Policy (ENP), 456
  Action Plans, 307–8, 312–14, 444
  budget, 311, 315
  design and revision of, 288–9, 307–12, 441
  Eastern Partnership (see Eastern Partnership)
  origins and launch of, 304–6, 439
  partner countries and, 304–8, 310, 400
  Russia versus, 304, 306, 311, 407
  system of partnership and, 107–9, 466
  Union for the Mediterranean, 309–16, 439, 441, 466
European Parliament (EP), 57–64, 121, 142, 204
  budget, 51
  citizen representation, 30, 46, 49, 60–1, 65, 332–3
  democratic processes and, 332–5, 341–4, 436, 463–4
  elections, 58–60, 174, 329–33, 434–45, 463–5
  enlargement, role in, 286, 289
  European Commission and, 50–2, 67, 96–8, 102–3
  legislative and budgetary roles, 17, 33, 47–8, 57–8, 60–4, 75, 421
  ordinary legislative process (see ordinary legislative process)
  powers of, 13, 36–7, 96, 126, 169, 279, 419

social policy and, 339, 351, 353, 363–4, 372, 376
structure of, 57–60, 432, 449, 456
as supranational institution, 13, 36, 47
trade policy and, 259, 262, 264, 272–3
European Partnership Agreements, 284, 294–5
European People's Party, 60–1, 330
European Police Office (Europol), 176, 178, 183, 437–8, 457
European Political Cooperation, 189
European Regional Development Fund (ERDF), 237, 242–6, 434
as redistributive mechanism, 34, 234–6, 456
European Security and Defence Policy (EDSP), 188, 190, 439, 441. *See also* Common Security and Defence Policy
European Security Strategy, 191, 308, 439
for cyberattacks, 406
European Semester, 123, 152, 238, 442
European Social Fund (ESF), 233, 236–7, 244, 417, 456
Plus (ESF+), 246
European social model, 142, 456
European Stability Mechanism (ESM), 138, 150–2, 442, 456
European System of Central Banks (ESCB), 35, 144–5, 457
European Union, 127
Canadian political system versus, 5–6, 40–1, 67–8, 100, 226, 247, 268
executive leadership, 13, 46–53, 68, 104–10, 342, 140–1, 419
as global actor, 1, 127–30, 410
federal states versus, 5–6, 40–1, 45, 195, 419–20
as federation, 13–15, 25–8, 67–8, 268
international organizations versus (*see* international organization)
legislative system, 68, 76, 81, 124, 329
politicization of, 19, 256, 340–1

European Union Advisory Missions (EUAMs), 193, 203
European Union Agency for Fundamental Rights, 172, 354, 440
European Union Capacity Building Missions (EUCAPs), 192–3, 203
European Union Global Strategy (EUGS), 311, 396, 444, 458
Euroskepticism, 422
British, 280–1
concept of, 341, 457
democratic legitimacy and, 156, 328
hard versus soft, 341
increasing, 15–16, 40, 160, 280, 291
political party, 330, 333, 335
populism and, 160, 182, 340, 462
exchange rate mechanism (ERM), 34, 145–6, 451, 457

federalism, 129
in Canada versus EU, 100, 107, 118, 142, 196–7
CJEU role in, 82–5
collaborative, 247
concept of, 117–18, 457
constraints on EU, 94–6, 99, 112, 126, 410
fiscal, 157
proponents of, 116
federal system, 414
Canada's enactment of, 5–6, 40–1, 226, 247, 268
democratic participation under, 329, 362, 423
EU movement toward, 156
EU similarities with, 13–15, 25–8, 67–8, 268
EU uniqueness against, 5–6, 40–1, 45, 195, 419–20
feminists, 353
critiques of EU power relations, 125, 129
on employment policy, 356
on inequalities, 363, 365

482 Index

financial crisis, 39–40, 416
　austerity and, 362–3
　capital flows amid, 153–5
　development of, 148–50, 159–60, 441
　EMU issues and, 156, 158–60
　EU impacts, 3–4, 121–2, 378, 441
　euro area (*see* euro area)
　See also sovereign debt crisis
financial transfers
　as governance mode, 9, 44, 58
　member state control through, 94–6
　redistribution through, 416, 422
Finland, 290
　accession to EU, 8, 37, 239, 282–3, 336, 436–7
　EMU impacts on, 147, 167
　European Parliament elections, 59, 61
　NATO membership, 191, 195, 401, 461
　population identities, 170, 344
fiscal compact, 152, 336, 442–3
fiscal federalism. *See* federalism
Five Presidents' Report, 156–7, 443
Foreign Affairs Council, 54–7, 198–200, 287
foreign affairs and security policy, 204, 455, 457
　actors in EU, 198–200, 410
　budget for, 202
　Canadian federal jurisdiction, 118
　decision making on, 55–6, 117, 287, 395
　enlargement, 287–90, 320, 394, 399
　EU common/hybrid, 188–90, 196–7, 433
　EU geopolitical strategies, 127, 188, 203, 394, 402–5, 407
　EU phases of, 106–7
　EU pillar of, 36
　as high politics, 119, 189
　union high representative, 38, 49–51, 57, 191, 198–9, 458
　See also Common Foreign and Security Policy
foreign direct investment (FDI), 262–3, 397, 457

France, 50, 70n1, 147, 353, 406, 445
　agricultural production, 32, 213, 222–5, 458
　Canada's relationship with 5, 196–7
　creation of EU, 2, 7, 29–30
　as EEC country, 138, 144, 210
　enlargement and, 282–3, 290, 297
　European Parliament elections, 59–61
　foreign and defence policies, 190–1, 198, 201–2, 402
　Germany and, 7–8, 27–9, 122
　intergovernmental leadership, 122, 396, 399, 454
　population identities in, 170, 344
　referendums in, 38, 335–6, 440
　regional policy, 232, 235, 237, 242, 307
　as Schengen country, 166–7, 435
　temporary refusal of integration, 16, UK versus, 290, 432
　See also Empty Chair Crisis
freedom of movement, 9–10, 76–8, 280, 350, 355
　four freedoms and, 139–40, 145, 210, 258, 464
　of people, 16, 168, 172–4, 178, 286, 458
　protection of, 81, 142, 166
free-market economies
　concept of, 9
　correction of, 459–60
　expansion of, 190, 341, 459–60
　regulation versus, 19
free trade agreements, 138–9, 142, 260–1, 264, 416
　EU pursuit of, 221, 255–6, 307, 397
　See also Canada-United States-Mexico Agreement; deep and comprehensive free trade agreements; European Free Trade Association; North American Free Trade Agreement
Frontex, 178, 183, 444
　border surveillance support, 175–6, 458

functionalism, 16
  neo- (*see* neofunctionalism)
fundamental rights, 354
  AFSJ and, 166, 169
  decoupling from citizenship, 174, 447
  EU Charter of (*see* EU Charter of Fundamental Rights)
  mandatory principles, 38, 84, 88–90, 279, 349
  neighbourhood policy and, 304, 308
  protection of, 75, 80–2, 86–7, 174–7, 364

gender equality
  EU Charter of Fundamental Rights, 175
  organizational commitment, 362
  pandemic impacts on, 365
  policy, 10, 169, 308, 353–4, 357
  young farmers, 215
gender mainstreaming, 353, 360, 364
General Affairs Council, 53–4, 287, 445, 458
General Agreement on Tariffs and Trade (GATT), 258–60, 431, 437
  CAP reforms and, 214, 216, 432
General Court (Court of First Instance), 76, 81–2, 86
geographical indication (GI), 221, 225, 458
geopolitics, 393–4, 458
Georgia, 296, 407
  CSDP operations in, 192
  Eastern Partnership, 394, 441, 453
  Neighbourhood Policy, 304–12, 315–17, 400, 439
Germany, 14, 122, 431
  agricultural production, 213, 222–3
  Berlin Wall, fall of, 8, 291, 399, 435
  CJEU cases, 78, 85, 89, 140
  ECSC member, 30, 454, 463
  EMU involvement, 145, 147
  enlargement, 283, 290–2, 399
  European Parliament elections, 59–61, 330, 465

federal system in, 68, 70n1
foreign and defence policies, 190, 198–203, 396, 402, 409
France and, 7–8, 27–9, 122, 190, 290–1, 431
population identities in, 170, 344, 358, 360
refugee crisis, 39, 66, 182, 420
regional policy, 232, 235, 237, 242
reunification, 190, 278–9, 399, 436
as Schengen country, 166–7, 435
West (*see* West Germany)
Global Approach to Migration and Mobility, 173, 440
Global Compact for Migration (United Nations), 173
globalization
  EU responses to, 16, 116, 210, 272
  labour market, 171, 270
  winners versus losers of, 418, 420, 423–4
governance modes, 94, 129, 423
  Canada versus EU, 107, 111, 247
  CAP, 220, 224, 227
  competition, 123
  cooperation, 123, 215, 246
  hardening soft, 203, 380, 385–6
  hierarchical, 99–107, 111–12, 123, 250
  negotiation, 123, 250
  multilevel, 101, 107–8, 122–3, 236, 241, 460
  non-hierarchical, 105, 109, 380, 458
  Phase 1: 99–100, 104–6
  Phase 2: 100–1, 105–6
  Phase 3: 101–3, 105–6
  Phase 4: 103–4, 105–6
  Phase 5: 104–6, 183
  soft, 380, 385–9, 464
  See also soft power
Governance Regulation, 380, 385–6, 389, 445
grand theory, 120, 128, 130, 458. *See also* mid-range theory

Greece, 35, 305, 398
 accession to EU, 8, 101, 138, 235, 434
 enlargement, 281, 283–4, 292
 European Parliament elections, 59, 61
 population identities in, 170, 344
 refugee crisis, 66, 182
 regional policy, 213, 235, 237, 241
 Schengen membership, 167, 420
 sovereign debt crisis, 39, 104, 147–51, 156, 442, 454
 Türkiye, opposition to, 292–3, 401, 444
Greek Loan Facility, 150, 152, 442
greenhouse gas emissions
 Canadian, 384
 EU, 375, 377–81
gross national income (GNI), 239, 420
 EU budget from members', 10, 96, 149, 221, 234

Haas, Ernst B. (*The Uniting of Europe*), 115–16, 118–20
Hague, The
 Europol in, 176, 457
 meetings for EU formation, 27, 34, 144, 431
hierarchy
 in law, 79, 111, 250
 mode of governance, 100–3, 107, 111, 123, 250
 of rights, 355
 "softening" of, 104–5, 107–9, 112, 458
High Authority (HA), 29–30, 49
high politics, 119, 154, 189, 204, 458
high representative for foreign affairs and security policy, 191, 196, 287, 404, 458
 appointment of, 51, 198–9, 311
 duties of, 38, 49, 56–7, 204, 455
Hill, Christopher, 190, 396
Hoffman, Stanley, 116, 119–20
Hooghe, Liesbet, 123, 341
Howorth, Jolyon, 200
humanitarian commitments, 177, 395, 401
 aid, 196, 269, 289, 304
crises, 424
CSDP operations, 191
human rights
 abuses, 56, 405
 CJEU jurisprudence on, 81, 86–7
 compromising, 177, 182–3, 292, 407
 Copenhagen criteria, 284, 451
 EU protection of, 2, 70n1, 127, 173, 203–5, 461
 neighbourhood policy, 304–8, 311, 315, 319–21, 418
 principles of, 74–5, 304, 350, 397
 See also European Convention on Human Rights; European Court of Human Rights
human trafficking, 169, 173, 176, 193
Hungary, 89
 accession to EU, 8, 37, 285, 336, 437
 CAP impacts in, 224
 democratic backsliding in, 89, 292, 345, 364, 447, 463
 energy policy, 375, 409
 enlargement, 283, 439
 European Parliament elections, 59, 61
 population identities in, 170, 344, 367n3
 refugee crisis, 40, 180, 182
 regional policy, 241, 250
 Schengen membership, 167

Identity and Democracy party, 60–1
immigration policies, 321
 anti-, 182, 298
 Canadian versus EU, 171, 174, 181, 197, 297
 framework for regular, 171–2
 movement to supranationalism, 168–9
 pillar for, 36–7
India, 397
 as EU strategic partner, 5, 394, 402–3, 416, 465
 See also BRICS countries
inflation
 attempts to counter, 34, 158, 451
 euro area's versus Canada's, 158–9

increasing, 1, 258
member countries', 146, 148
infringement procedure, 88
cases using, 83, 364, 447
institutionalism, 116, 459
historical, 124, 129
rational choice, 124
revival of, 124
sociological, 124-5, 129
institutions, EU
budgets for, 51, 82, 157, 177-8
founding treaties (*see* Treaties of Rome; Treaty of Paris)
intergovernmental (*see* intergovernmental institutions)
Lisbon Treaty changes in, 38, 48, 69, 118, 442, 455
member state cooperation with, 53, 56-7, 88, 406
powers of, 36-7, 168-9, 285, 289, 465
primary law, 75
supranational, 13, 36, 47, 102, 121-2, 286, 438
Integrated Mediterranean Programs (IMPs), 235-7
integration, European
COVID-19 and, 138, 156, 158-60, 416, 422-4
economic (*see* economic integration)
intergovernmental theories on, 116-21, 128-30
international relations theories on, 115, 119, 122, 127-8
negative, 10, 83, 140, 159, 416, 460
positive, 10, 140, 416, 462
(potential) vicious circle, 157-8
process of, 2, 10-11, 33, 39, 96, 101-2, 109
security and defence policy, 202-4, 309
skepticism of, 6-7, 16 (*see also* Euroskepticism)
stagnation of, 19, 105
widening versus deepening, 2, 6-11, 15-17, 414, 452, 467

intellectual property, 225, 262, 458-9
trade agreements on, 142, 266-7, 271, 273, 451
interest rates
EMU membership, 146, 451
financial crisis, 147-8, 155
sovereign debt crisis, 149
intergovernmental institutions, 70n1, 378
Canadian, 247
citizen participation in, 333
conferences and, 35, 54, 65, 141
EU, 53, 110, 198-9, 286-8, 452, 456
supranational versus, 47, 64, 172, 187-9, 460
intergovernmentalism, 236-7, 459
cooperation, 26, 36, 172, 183, 462
Council of Ministers and, 29, 47-8, 53-5, 450
EU deviations on, 13-15, 36, 414-17
international institutions and, 12-13, 404-5
liberal, 121, 123
member state decision making, 102, 106-7, 127, 168-9, 334, 451-2
new, 121-2
principle of, 29, 123, 233, 239
to supranationalism, 47, 169, 196, 200, 424
temporary, 150, 236
theories on EU integration, 116-21, 128-30
treaty reforms and, 35, 39, 168-9
Intergovernmental Panel on Climate Change, 378, 435
internal market, 86, 313
commissioner duties, 199
competitiveness, 54-5
establishment of, 35, 85, 139, 141
See also Common Market; Single Market
International Monetary Fund (IMF), 150-2, 454

international organization, 6, 58,
  116, 459
  EU as more than, 12–15, 26, 40–1,
    45–6, 268, 350, 419–20
  hybrid system of, 188, 195–6, 395
  intergovernmentalism of, 12, 278, 309
international relations theories
  constructivist, 125, 129
  on EU integration, 115, 119, 122, 127–8
  intergovernmentalist (*see*
    intergovernmentalism)
  neofunctionalist (*see*
    neofunctionalism)
investor state dispute settlement (ISDS),
  271–2, 459
Iraq, 39, 188, 193, 375
Ireland, 141
  accession to EU, 8, 34, 235, 336,
    432–4
  CAP reforms, 213, 222–4, 235
  debt crisis, 39, 138, 147, 150–2, 454
  enlargement, 100, 147, 358, 279–80,
    283, 290
  European Parliament elections, 59, 61
  NATO non-membership, 194, 203, 461
  Northern, 224, 237, 290
  population identities in, 170, 344
  referendums in, 38–9, 335, 439, 441
  regional policy, 235, 237
  Schengen membership, 11, 167
Israel, 304, 307, 310, 318, 394
Italy, 34, 118
  CAP reforms, 210, 223
  CJEU cases involving, 79–80
  creation of EU, 2, 7, 29–31, 454
  debt crisis, 147
  EEC membership, 138
  enlargement, 282–3, 290
  European Parliament elections, 59, 61
  foreign and defence policy, 201
  population identities in, 170, 344
  refugee crisis, 39, 66
  regional policy, 232, 235, 237, 242
  Schengen membership, 167, 420

Juncker, Jean-Claude, 66, 155, 194,
  379, 443
Justice and Home Affairs (JHA), 54, 459
  as EU pillar, 36, 168–9, 436, 438, 466
  expanded EU competence in, 35, 102,
    107, 165, 313
  See also Area of Freedom, Security
    and Justice
Just Transition
  Fund, 244, 246
  Mechanism, 388, 417

Kelemen, Dan, 118
Kosovo, 148, 190–2, 201, 293–6, 404

Latvia, 148, 283, 285
  accession to EU, 8, 37, 336, 437, 439
  European Parliament elections, 59, 61
  population identities in, 170, 344,
    367n3
  regional policy, 241–2, 398
  Schengen membership, 167
law enforcement. *See* police
League of Nations, 27–8
legitimacy of EU, 130
  building, 389, 421–4
  contestation of, 7, 9, 40, 69, 272, 420
  democratic, 15–18, 126–7, 156, 160,
    361–3
  focus on economic, 16, 158, 232, 236,
    263, 414
  input, 17, 65, 126, 422–3
  member states versus, 196, 293
  output, 16, 127, 421–2
  political, 250, 272, 286
  popular, 14, 26, 156, 166, 305, 334
legislatures
  bicameral, 13, 58, 449
  Canadian provincial, 85
  EU supranational versus member
    state, 76, 81, 124, 329
Libya, 188, 193–4, 201, 304, 307–10, 401
Lindberg, Leon N. 119, 461
Lisbon Strategy, 103, 106, 108

Lithuania, 148, 405
　accession to EU, 8, 37, 336, 437
　enlargement, 283, 285, 439
　European Parliament elections, 59, 61
　population identities in, 170, 344, 367n3
　regional policy, 241–2, 398
　Schengen membership, 167
low politics, 119, 189, 459
Luxembourg, 50, 56, 240
　Compromise, 32–4, 433
　creation of EU, 2, 7, 29–30, 138, 210, 454
　EMU creation, 144–5, 433, 467
　enlargement, 283, 336
　European Parliament elections, 59–61
　population identities in, 170, 344
　regional policy, 232, 235
　Schengen membership, 167, 435

Maastricht Treaty, 239
　EMU and, 35–6, 102, 145, 436, 451
　greater EU integration, 126, 436
　EU law development, 62, 75, 83, 377, 461
　on migration, 165–6
　pillars of, 35–6, 436, 459, 462
　referenda on, 65, 335–6, 436
　See also Treaty on European Union
Mali, 191–3, 198, 203, 404
Malta, 148
　accession to EU, 8, 37, 336, 436, 439
　enlargement, 282–3, 285, 304
　European Parliament elections, 59–61
　NATO non-membership, 194–5, 461
　population identities in, 170, 344
　regional policy, 241–2
　Schengen membership, 167
market correction, 101–2, 106–7, 459
　policy prioritization of, 6, 221
　reduction in, 99, 232, 460
market making policies, 256, 459
　prioritization of, 99, 102, 105–7, 232
Marks, Gary, 123, 341

May, Theresa, 142, 299, 444
members of European Parliament, 58–61, 96, 329, 333, 456
　defence policy oversight, 204
　See also European Parliament
member states, 3, 16, 26
　big versus small, 55, 201–2
　burden sharing among, 171, 182, 378, 422
　consensus among (see consensus-oriented decision making)
　convergence/coordination among, 39–40, 223, 345, 417, 422, 458
　cooperation, 166–7, 169, 172, 176–7
　disagreement among, 98, 100–1, 289–90, 460
　diversity among, 297, 388
　referendums in (see referendums)
　solidarity among, 57, 156–7, 180
　trade among, 78, 139–40, 210, 215, 267
　voting rights, 89
Mercosur, 91n1, 266
Merger Treaty, 50, 53, 433
Merkel, Angela, 182, 408
Michel, Charles, 49, 66
Middle East
　Arab Spring (see Arab Spring)
　EU energy supply and, 374–5
　instability in, 304, 394, 402, 406, 410
Middle East and North Africa (MENA), 282, 310–11, 316, 406
　refugees from, 4, 395
　See also Middle East
mid-range theory, 120, 125, 459. See also grand theory
migration, 177–8, 424, 449
　budget for managing, 97, 177–8
　Canada's regime for, 171, 181
　control over, 142, 171–2, 180–3, 298, 419
　crisis, 120, 179, 419–20 (see also refugee crisis)
　dimensions of, 170–3, 318
　illegal, 307, 309, 311

migration (Cont'd)
  irregular, 167, 173-80, 183, 304-5, 315
  labour, 291-2
  treaties on, 165-6, 168
  policies on, 11, 36-7, 169-73, 398, 440, 446
  See also refugees
military operations
  crisis management, 127, 190-1, 195, 451-2
  EU international, 190-4, 198, 445
  EU lack of capability over, 195, 316, 396
  external country, 281, 293
  institutional powers over, 199-200, 316, 458
  member state spending on, 201-4
  Russian-Ukrainian, 372, 397-9, 403, 408-9
  See also Common Security and Defence Policy
Milward, Alan, 121
Mitrany, David (*A Working Peace System*), 115, 119
mixed agreements, 264-7, 272, 460
mixed economy
  concept of, 9-10, 250, 459
  EU as, 6, 15, 236, 241, 350, 423
  impacts of, 116, 414, 417-18
mobility, 382
  cross-border (*see* cross-border mobility)
  efforts to increase, 2, 243, 309, 456
  internal, 170, 249
  partnerships, 314-15
  from third countries, 170-1, 440
Moldova, 192
  in Eastern Partnership, 304-9, 394, 407, 441, 453
  EU candidacy, 8, 295-6, 400, 410
  trade relations, 315-17
Monnet, Jean, 425
  European Defence Community plan, 31, 455
  federalism of, 28, 116, 138

  postwar coal and steel plan, 27-30, 65
Montenegro, 148, 310
  EU candidacy, 8, 293-5, 441-2
Moravcsik, Andrew, 121, 342
Multiannual Financial Framework (MFF), 89, 250, 427, 446
  budget allocations in, 150, 202, 222-3, 239, 244, 289
  decision making on, 96-8, 332, 345, 460
multilateralism, 190, 266, 304, 460
  Canada's, 404
  enhancing, 309-10, 388, 395
  policy, 74, 263, 273-4, 403
  trade negotiations, 213, 219, 226
multilevel governance,
  in Canada, 226, 247-8
  citizen identities in, 68
  EU as, 46, 94-5, 100
  evolution of, 104, 107, 110-12
  partnerships in, 236, 241-3, 423
  theory on, 101, 122-3, 129, 460, 465
mutual recognition, 176, 416
  concept of, 10, 460
  issues with, 154, 160
  legal directives on, 140, 143, 153, 159, 450

national energy and climate plans (NECPs), 380, 386, 445
nationalism
  Brexit, 177-8, 183, 298
  homophobic, 364
  member government, 345
  neighbourhood policy, 305
  refugee crisis, 177-8, 182
  resurgence of, 119-20, 183
  supra- (*see* supranationalism)
nation states
  citizen rights and duties, 14, 123, 177, 343
  EU versus classic, 14, 49, 68, 93-5, 339
  EU as union of, 66, 126, 395
  intergovernmentalist theory on, 120-1, 189
  sovereignty of, 177-8, 460

negative integration, 10, 83, 140, 159, 416, 460
negotiation, mode of governance, 123
Neighbourhood, Development and International Cooperation Instrument, 269, 313–14
neofunctionalism, 116–22, 128–30, 460, 464
neoliberalism, 363, 365, 460
Netherlands, the, 78, 176, 420
   Constitutional Treaty, 38, 335–6, 440
   creation of EU, 2, 7, 29–30
   EEC formation, 138, 210, 454
   European Parliament elections, 59, 61
   population identities in, 170, 344
   Schengen membership, 167, 435
networks
   diplomatic, 204, 420
   regional partnership, 241–3, 249, 435
   trans-European (*see* trans-European networks)
NextGenerationEU program, 446, 462
   cohesion policy and, 249–50, 414
   loans and grants under, 151, 153, 156–7, 460
non-discrimination, 460–1
   definition of, 351–2
   EU principle of, 74, 174–5, 250, 354–5
   policies, 350, 353–5, 358
   shifts in approaches to, 353–4, 356–7, 361–6
non-tariff barriers, 143, 461
   elimination of, 139–40
normative power, 129, 194, 319, 395–7, 400, 461
North American Free Trade Agreement (NAFTA), 91n1, 226
North Atlantic Treaty Organization (NATO), 36, 203, 431, 461
   accession to, 285, 290–2
   conflict intervention, 190–1, 195, 450
   EU relations with, 200, 395, 398
   membership of, 31, 194–5, 282, 293, 404

   non-members of, 194, 450
   Türkiye in, 285, 401
   Ukraine in, 194–5, 398, 400, 408
nuclear energy, 380
   Canadian, 383
   EU, 36, 94, 99, 373, 382–3
nuclear weapons, 395
   Iranian program, 188, 402
NV Algemene Transport en Expeditie Onderneming van Gend & Loos v. Netherlands Inland Revenue Administration (*Van Gend en Loos*), 78–9, 83

oil crisis, 34, 144, 374
open method of coordination (OMC), 111, 438, 465–6
   as decision-making procedure, 103, 107–8, 123, 461
opinions (legislative acts), 62, 75–7, 189, 264, 288, 461
   non-binding, 82
opt-outs, 11, 37, 203, 335, 345, 436, 461
Orbán, Viktor, 182, 224, 364
ordinary legislative procedure (OLP), 441
   European Parliament role in, 57, 62–4, 211, 262, 331–2
   processes of, 37, 67–8, 339–40, 461–2, 466
Organisation for Economic Co-operation and Development, 362
organized crime, 193, 321
   EU strategies for, 169, 176, 183, 308–9
   global scale of, 167, 181, 286

Pact on Migration and Asylum, 171, 173, 183, 446
Palestine, 192, 304, 307, 310, 404
Pandemic Emergency Purchase Programme (PEPP), 151, 446
pan-Europeanism, 27, 239
   policy infrastructure for, 174, 179, 182, 232
   for standards, 241, 417

Paris Agreement, 215, 379, 444
Partnership and Cooperation
   Agreements (PCAs), 307, 312
   EU-Russia, 407, 438
peace project, EU as, 6–8, 188, 351
Permanent Structured Cooperation
   (PESCO), 195, 396, 445, 461
permissive consensus. *See* consensus
pillars of the EU, 462
   Constitutional Treaty on, 38–9, 440
   Maastricht Treaty on, 36, 436
   Pillar I (European Communities),
      36–7, 196, 438, 466
   Pillar II (Common Foreign and
      Security Policy), 36, 190
   Pillar III (Justice and Home Affairs),
      36–7, 168, 438, 459, 466
   Treaty of Amsterdam on, 36–7, 438
   Treaty of Lisbon abandonment of,
      260, 440–1
Pleven, René, 31, 455
Poland, 175, 201, 447, 463
   accession to EU, 8, 37, 283–5, 336,
      437, 439
   democratic backsliding in, 89, 250,
      292, 345, 364, 367n3
   energy policy, 374–5, 388,
   European Parliament elections, 59, 61
   population identities in, 170, 344
   refugee crisis, 180, 182
   regional policy, 241–2, 307, 396, 398
   Schengen membership, 167, 435
police
   AFSJ policy areas, 168–9
   cooperation of, 36, 57, 144, 192–3
   See also Area of Freedom, Security
      and Justice; Common Security and
      Defence Policy; Europol
policy coordination, 451
   competences, 100, 107
   institutions for, 152
   open method of, 103, 123
   silos of, 243
   treaties on, 95

policy-making, EU
   constraints on, 95–7
   coordination (*see* policy
      coordination)
   market-oriented, 6, 232, 250, 414
   mixed system of (*see* mixed
      economy)
   Phase 1: 99–100, 104–6
   Phase 2: 100–1, 105–6
   Phase 3: 101–3, 105–6
   Phase 4: 103–4, 105–6
   Phase 5: 104–6, 183
Political and Security Committee
   (PSC), 198–9, 308
political systems, 122
   Canada versus EU, 40–2, 60, 67–8,
      99–100, 452
   democratic, 103, 329, 337
   EU blending of, 5, 330
   sui generis, 118, 124
polities, 128, 416
   Canada versus EU as, 67–8, 112, 361
   definition of, 46, 116, 125–6
   executive institutions in, 46, 124, 346
   legitimacy of, 16
   multilevel, 46, 94–5, 100, 104, 423
   supranational, 268
populism, 291
   Euroskepticism and, 160, 298, 462
   resurgence of, 182–3, 298, 340
   right-wing, 182, 362–4
Portugal, 219, 291
   accession to EU, 8, 35, 213, 434–5
   debt crisis, 39, 147, 150, 152, 454
   enlargement, 101, 281, 283–4
   European Free Trade Association,
      138, 432
   European Parliament elections, 59, 61
   population identities in, 170, 344
   regional policy, 235, 237, 241
   Schengen membership, 167, 435
positive integration, 10, 140, 416, 462
postcolonial theory, 125, 129
powers, EU

executive, 50, 342
institutional, 36–7, 168–9, 285, 289, 465
legislative, 12, 65–8, 85, 328, 331–4, 421
over member state policy-making, 2, 67, 95–7, 111, 218, 224
soft (*see* soft power)
tripartite division of, 13, 84
preferences, state, 396
export-oriented, 259
integration process and, 33, 39, 96, 101–2, 109
intergovernmentalist theory on, 121–3, 416
trade-related, 86, 280
primary law, EU, 426, 462
development of, 75, 95, 450, 459, 464, 466
fundamental principles of, 74–5
institutions of, 75
product standards regulation, 16, 140
Progressive Alliance of Socialists and Democrats in the European Parliament (S&D), 60–1
public debt
EMU limits on, 145, 451
inability to refinance, 138, 150
rises in, 147, 149
public procurement, 140, 263, 271, 273, 462

qualified majority voting (QMV), 102, 262, 377
Council use of, 13, 49, 55, 141, 258–60
in EEC, 32–5, 39, 433, 435
imposition of, 159, 211, 333–4, 464
member state challenging of, 31–2, 85–6, 96
requirements for, 55, 462
Quebec, 41, 196–7, 247, 297, 383

race
discrimination based on, 352, 355
lack of equality data on, 362
theoretical critiques of, 125, 365

Race Equality Directive (RED), 171–2, 354–5, 357
recession, 4, 34, 144, 418
recommendations (legislative acts), 47, 75–7, 108, 152, 385–7, 462
Recovery and Resilience Facility (RRF), 105, 460
budget, 97–8, 150, 153, 244,
establishment of, 150, 446, 462
redistribution, 19, 363, 422
in Canada, 247
cohesion policy (*see* cohesion policy)
Common Agricultural Policy (*see* Common Agricultural Policy)
EU budget and, 10
EU efforts at, 34, 232–5, 238, 416–17
federalism and, 157, 257
proposed refugee, 40
regional (*see* regional policy)
reference for a preliminary ruling, 83–4, 88, 462–3
referendums
accession, 280, 282, 290, 433, 437–8
Brexit (*see* Brexit)
Canada, 297
democratic feedback through, 328–9, 333, 335–7
EU membership, 18–19, 280–1
on treaties, 38–9, 65, 239, 423, 436, 439–41
refugee crisis, 415
border controls amid, 165–6, 177–8
EU overwhelmed with, 16, 66, 175–7, 422–4, 463
limits of supranationalism, 40, 401
Syrian, 304, 463
UK leaving EU and, 40
Ukrainian, 4, 40, 66, 173, 179–81, 315
varied responses to, 39–40, 304, 333, 463
refugees
Canada versus EU approaches to, 181
crisis of (*see* refugee crisis)
deaths of, 177, 179, 182

refugees (*Cont'd*)
  EU as destination for, 172, 293, 463
  legislation on, 172, 443, 453
  member state refusal of, 39–40, 66, 111, 180, 1822
  migration through EU, 66, 172, 315
  redistribution of, 40, 180–2, 401, 420
  right-wing backlash against, 178, 182, 362, 422
regional policy, 10
  administration of, 236
  in Canada, 247–8
  cohesion versus, 236–7, 249
  conceptualization of, 231–5
  critiques of, 246, 248–51
  equalization, 232, 235, 243–4, 454
  redistribution through, 10, 232–6, 247
  reforms, 238–9, 435–6, 450
  See also cohesion policy
regulations (legislative acts), 75–7, 102, 463
  accession harmonization of, 78, 83, 265
  EU decision making on, 10–11, 98, 100
  framework, 106–7
  legal cases on, 86, 89
  member state compliance with, 85, 95, 101, 298, 446
  See also Common Provision Regulation; Dublin Regulation; Effort Sharing Regulation; Governance Regulation
renewable energy, 10, 372–8, 382–9, 463
rights, 216, 272, 308
  abuses of, 56, 293, 352, 364, 405
  barriers to equality, 351, 358–9
  citizen obligations and, 12–14, 79
  civil, 82, 118, 177, 318
  conferral of, 78–80, 171, 343
  direct effect, 78–80, 171, 453
  EU institutional, 62, 105, 262, 457
  fundamental (*see* fundamental rights)
  human (*see* human rights)
  legal, 78, 84, 459

  LGBTQ+, 351, 358, 364, 367n3,4, 447
  member state voting, 32, 89, 117, 377
  mobility, 2, 81, 166, 168, 355
  political and social, 82, 166, 174
  property, 118
  states' sovereign, 79, 95, 99, 272, 373, 464
  women's, 351, 353, 355
  See also Charter of Fundamental Rights
Romania, 292, 358
  accession to EU, 8, 37, 283–6, 288, 437, 440
  energy policy, 375
  European Parliament elections, 59, 61
  population identities in, 170, 344
  regional policy, 241–2
  Schengen candidacy, 11, 167
Rome Treaty. *See* Treaties of Rome
rule of law, 192–3, 452, 463
  CJEU upholding of, 80–3, 86, 105
  conditionality, 89, 284, 321, 446, 451
  deterioration of, 89–91, 292, 364, 415
  ENP Action Plans and, 304, 308, 311–12, 321
  EU foundation of, 74, 182, 350, 395–7
  member state interpretations of, 8–9, 292, 345, 407
  toolbox, 89
  trade according to, 259–60
rural development policy, 213–17, 227, 417, 450, 453, 463
Russia, 11, 40, 372, 424
  eastern neighbourhood security, 304–6, 311, 316–19
  EU energy supply, 372–5, 389, 409, 418
  EU enlargement and, 291–2, 296–300
  EU versus, 8, 188, 201, 227, 397
  invasion of Ukraine, 1, 138, 194–5, 304, 397–400, 403–8
  geopolitics, 4, 394–400, 402–3, 420, 443
  sanctions against, 105, 159, 181, 403
  strategic partnerships with, 5, 203, 306, 416, 438–42

Scheingold, Stuart, 461
Schengen Area
  border control in, 166–9, 175–6, 181, 444, 446
  establishment of, 11, 435
  member states of, 167, 463
  refugees in, 179, 420
  See also borderless travel
Schimmelfennig, Frank, 122, 319
Schmitter, Philippe, 119–20
Schuman, Robert, 7, 28–30, 138
Schuman Declaration/Plan, 7–8, 29, 118, 431, 464
secondary law, EU
  CJEU review of, 84–6
  types of, 75–7
  See also decisions; directives; opinions; recommendations; regulations
second-order elections, 332–3, 464
Serbia, 190, 294–6, 441, 443
Services Directive, 141–2
shared competence, 13–14, 95, 127, 224, 406, 464
Single European Act (SEA), 75, 236, 336
  changes resulting from, 33, 62, 374
  on climate and energy policy, 374, 376
  Single Market via, 35, 141, 145, 159, 435, 464
  on trade policy, 259–60
Single Farm Payment (SFP), 214, 219–20, 224
Single Market, 111, 142, 355, 464
  AFSJ development, 166
  Banking Union, 153–4, 160
  benefits of, 2–3, 263, 266, 319, 421
  budget for, 97, 234
  Canadian versus EU, 143, 268
  Common Agricultural Policy, 210–11, 213
  competition policy, 141–2, 451
  completion of, 101–2, 106, 141, 258–60, 436
  concept of, 2
  creating common rules for, 76, 78, 110, 374
  decision making on, 141, 159–60, 451
  EU focus on, 10–11, 145, 179–80, 183, 351
  financial crisis and, 148, 153, 416
  four freedoms, 9–10, 140, 457, 464
  history of, 139, 210, 455
  Programme, 138
  trade, 210–11, 255, 259–62, 273–4
  UK leaving, 299
  See also Common Market
Single Deposit Guarantee Scheme, 154–5
Single Farm Payments, 214, 219
Single Resolution Mechanism, 152, 154–5
Single Supervisory Mechanism, 152
Slovakia, 148, 375
  accession to EU, 8, 37, 337, 437, 439
  European Parliament elections, 59, 61
  population identities in, 170, 344, 367n3
  referendums in, 283, 285
  regional policy, 241
  Schengen membership, 167, 435
Slovenia, 148
  accession to EU, 8, 37, 337, 437, 439
  European Parliament elections, 59, 61
  population identities in, 170, 344
  referendums in, 283, 285
  regional policy, 241–2, 293
  Schengen membership, 167, 435
soft law, 77, 356, 361
soft power
  attraction, 291, 298
  concept of, 396, 464
  EU use of, 127, 320–1, 396–8
  hardening soft, 203, 380, 385–7
  peer reviews, 99, 452
  persuasion, 99, 127, 397
  policy instruments, 188, 191, 194, 389
  shaming, 99, 386
  See also governance modes

494 Index

solidarity, 173, 464
   EU legitimacy and, 74, 249–50, 350, 424, 456
   policy of, 7–9, 232–7, 242, 417, 446
   practising, 138, 151, 157–60, 180, 238–40, 246
   varied understandings of, 65–7, 194, 415, 418, 421–3
Somalia, 192
South Africa, 5, 266, 394, 403, 416, 465. *See also* BRICS countries
sovereign debt crisis, 4, 122, 424
   Banking Union in (*see* Banking Union)
   development of, 104, 138, 149–51, 160, 454
   EMU impacts, 138, 151, 159
   EU legitimacy and, 156–8, 362
   measures taken since, 151–4, 160, 363, 456
   See also euro area
sovereignty, 166, 272, 465
   Brexit campaign and, 14, 290, 298, 422
   components of state, 35–6, 119–20, 187, 458, 460
   EU lack of, 95–6, 97, 100
   lack of recognition of, 294, 341, 457
   legislative procedures for, 57, 107, 332
   member state safeguarding of, 7, 94, 116, 172, 218–19
   reaffirmation of, 364, 377
   relinquishment of some state, 30, 88–9, 257
   violations of, 398, 408
Spain, 337
   accession to EU, 8, 35, 281, 432, 435
   Common Agricultural Policy, 213, 222
   debt crisis, 39, 138, 147, 454
   enlargement, 101, 283–4
   European Parliament elections, 59, 61
   geopolitical considerations, 290–2, 396
   population identities in, 170, 344
   regional policy, 201, 235, 237, 242
   Schengen membership, 167
   terrorist attacks in, 308, 406
   Turbot War, 219
"spill-back," 119–20
spillover, 119, 129, 180, 460, 465
Spinelli, Altiero (*Ventotene Manifesto*), 116, 117
Spitzenkandidat, 330, 343, 465
Stability and Growth Pact (SGP), 108, 110, 146, 438
Stabilization and Association Agreements (SAAs), 284, 293–5
state-controlled economies, 99
   mixed economies versus, 9, 232, 236, 459
steel production
   Canada versus EU, 382–4
   EU policies on, 7, 100
   geopolitics and, 235, 375
   Monnet/Schuman plans for, 27–31, 431, 463
   spillover from integration, 119, 257
   See also coal production; European Coal and Steel Community
strategic autonomy, 195, 203, 399, 465
Strategic Partnership Agreements (SPAs), 416, 444
strategic partnerships, EU, 200, 256, 402–5
subsidiarity, 65, 239, 465
supranationalism
   cooperation, 99, 109, 172–3, 200
   decision making, 259, 332, 376, 452, 465
   European Commission, 47, 50–3, 65, 102, 121–2, 286, 438
   European Parliament, 13, 36, 47
   institutional, 13, 36, 47, 102, 121–2, 286, 438
   intergovernmentalism to, 47, 169, 196, 200, 424
   refugee crisis and, 40, 401
supremacy (primacy), EU law, 12, 78–80, 88–9, 465

Supreme Court of Canada (SCC), 84–5
sustainability, 223, 243, 271, 423, 465
　environmental, 10, 16, 214, 218, 226, 416
　goal of, 373, 375–8, 378
Sweden
　accession to EU, 8, 37, 239, 336, 436–7
　Common Agricultural Policy, 222–3
　enlargement, 282–3, 290
　European Parliament elections, 59, 61
　NATO non-membership, 191, 195, 401, 461
　population identities in, 170, 344, 358
　regional policy, 138, 241, 307, 420, 432
　Schengen membership, 167, 435
Syria, 406
　neighbourhood policy, 304, 307, 310
　refugees from, 39, 179, 293, 463
　war in, 194, 304, 316, 401

Tariff Preferences case, 86
tariffs, 263, 280, 465
　common external, 138, 257–60, 273, 432, 450–2
　court cases on, 78
　elimination of, 139–40, 259, 266–9
　fluctuations in, 212, 270
　revenue from, 15, 213
taxation, 342
　carbon, 385
　corporate, 141
　national sovereignty over, 96, 100, 377
　redistribution and, 157, 160
terrorism
　AFSJ policy, 166–9, 177–8, 192–3
　border security, 11, 175, 183, 304, 444
　comprehensive approach, 191, 451
　counter-, 167, 176, 404, 406
　domestic debates about, 182
　global scale of, 166–7, 183, 402
　NATO mutual defence, 38–9, 194, 398
　neighbourhood policy, 308, 311, 315–20
　post-9/11: 11, 176, 405–6

Terrorisme, Radicalisme, Extrémisme et Violence Internationale (TREVI), 167, 434, 436
third countries, 52, 66, 203, 465
　EU partnerships with, 195, 199, 461
　trade with, 255, 263
third-country nationals (TCNs), 170–3, 178, 441
Tobacco Advertising case, 85–6
trade
　border regimes, 140–2, 144, 153–6, 374
　Brexit and, 219, 224, 256, 264, 424, 446
　Canada's policies on, 256, 261–70, 398, 416
　competences over, 239, 257–60, 262–4, 268–71
　Court of Justice of the EU rulings, 140–2, 189, 258–60, 264
　Directorate-General for, 199, 268, 428
　European Parliament policy, 259, 262, 264, 272–3
　free (*see* free trade agreements)
　member state, 78, 139–40, 210, 215, 267
　removing barriers to, 143, 374, 416
　Single Market, 210–11, 255, 259–62, 273–4
Trade and Cooperation Agreement (EU-UK), 142, 256, 261, 299, 446
Transatlantic Trade and Investment Partnership (TTIP), 466
　negotiations, 261, 269–73, 443–5
trans-European networks, 36, 102, 106–7, 176, 374
　approach, 109–10, 360
transposition, 76–7, 83, 110, 121, 453, 463
Treaties of Rome, 258, 279, 286, 466
　amendments to, 33
　European Communities' establishment, 454–5, 465
　founding of EU, 12, 31, 75, 260, 432
　social policy in, 353
　trade policies in, 210, 233–4, 257, 272

Treaty of Amsterdam, 75, 354, 438, 466
  on immigration and citizenship, 171, 173–4
  institutional powers, 36–7, 168–9, 285, 289, 465
  procedural provisions, 103, 465
  referendums on, 336
Treaty Establishing the European Community (TEC), 75, 86, 145, 354
Treaty Establishing the European Economic Community (TEEC), 286, 432
  amendments to, 75, 141, 260
  provisions of, 58, 78–80, 210–11, 217, 373
  regional development in, 232–5
  Single/Common Market, 32, 78–9, 257
Treaty on European Union (TEU), 69, 350, 444
  on Area of Freedom, Security and Justice, 165–9, 173, 182, 188, 459
  cohesion policy, 239, 250
  development of EU law, 74–5, 81, 89, 338, 466
  on diplomacy and defence, 190–1, 200
  on EU membership, 145, 279, 298
  on European Council functioning, 48–51, 53–5, 330–1
  on neighbouring countries, 308, 310–11
  principle of subsidiarity, 65, 239, 465
  on Single Market, 259–60
  See also Maastricht Treaty
Treaty on the Functioning of the European Union (TFEU), 466
  development of EU law, 74–7, 83–5, 88, 331–5
  EMU and, 145–6, 149
  energy policy, 373, 379–80
  on EU competences, 95
  on EU membership, 145–6
  on European Council functioning, 108
  on Single Market, 95
  social policy, 353–4, 367n2

  trade policy, 256, 264
Treaty of Lisbon, 80, 194, 373, 459
  on Charter of Fundamental Rights, 75, 87, 175, 355–7, 442, 450
  European Parliament and Council roles, 50–3, 56–7, 67, 211, 287–9, 466
  foreign policy changes, 127, 169, 190, 198–200, 310, 396
  institutional changes in, 38, 48, 69, 117, 442, 455
  Maastricht Treaty versus, 36, 462
  ordinary legislative procedure, 57, 62, 67, 331, 334
  provisions in, 38–40, 232, 279, 338, 465
  referendums on, 39, 334–6, 441
  signing and entry into force, 39, 260, 440–1, 466
  trade policy changes, 260, 262
Treaty of Nice, 75, 87
  critiques of, 37–8
  European Parliament powers, 37, 188, 285, 438–9, 466
  referendums on, 334–6, 439
Treaty of Paris, 466
  amendments to, 58, 74
  founding of ECSC, 12, 30, 65, 75, 431, 454
trilogues, 57, 63–4, 340, 419, 466–7
Trump, Donald, 194, 270, 398, 402, 424
Türkiye, 56, 310
  accession to EU, 282–3, 285, 288–9
  Association Agreement with, 292–4
  refugees through, 293
  tensions with, 293, 314, 401–2
  trade with, 397, 403
Tusk, Donald, 66, 182

Ukraine, 270
  challenges resulting from war in, 4, 159–60, 227, 291, 418–20
  Crimea (*see* Crimea)
  defence expenditures and, 195, 201–3, 316, 319, 398–400

Eastern Partnership, 309, 441, 453
energy and climate policy and, 372–5, 382, 385, 388–9
EU Association Agreement, 8, 295–6, 307, 316, 336, 410, 444
EU-Russian relations, 11, 105, 304–6, 311, 394–7, 406–9
EU support for, 11, 192–5, 399–401
neighbourhood policy for, 304, 309, 315, 399–400
refugees from, 40, 173, 179–81, 395
Russian invasion of, 1, 188, 194–5, 300, 400–9, 424, 443
See also Russia
unanimity, 62, 409, 467
qualified majority voting versus, 55, 96, 102, 141
voting mechanism of, 32, 39, 85, 88–9, 168, 200–2
unemployment, 118, 282, 420
financial crisis, 39, 156, 418
insurance, 351, 417
policy mitigation of, 9, 234, 238, 359
rising, 4, 16, 151
youth, 151, 238, 359
Union for the Mediterranean, 309–16, 439, 441, 467
Union of Soviet Socialist Republics (USSR), 394
collapse of, 398–9
Eurasian Economic Union, 311, 407–8
See also Russia
United Kingdom, 8, 59, 258, 310, 337
Brexit (*see* Brexit)
Canada and, 5, 41, 68, 197, 297
Common Agricultural Policy, 32–5, 222, 235
democratic participation in, 336–7, 341
EU accession, 33–5, 100, 278–83, 431–4
geopolitics, 190, 194, 201, 290–2, 402
national identities in, 344
regional funding, 235, 238, 242

sovereignty campaign, 40, 89, 422, 445
trade relations, 138, 219, 261, 403, 446
in wartime, 28, 118, 190
United Nations, 4, 215, 217
Canada in, 196–7, 403
Charter, 194
on climate change, 376–7, 382, 437, 444
EU presence in, 190, 199, 201, 204, 403
as international organization, 26, 75, 277, 405
Security Council, 201, 204
trade relations, 91n1
United Nations Framework Convention on Climate Change (UNFCCC), 377, 379, 437
United Nations Global Compact for Migration (GCM), 173
United States, 41, 216, 221, 342, 418
Canada versus, 5, 11, 143, 181, 297, 330, 404–5
in Cold War, 8, 29, 450
energy policy, 375, 385
EU modelling after, 27–8, 100, 116–18, 397, 431
financial crisis in, 148
geopolitics, 194–5, 203, 394–9, 402–3, 465
integration, 31, 270, 424
political leadership versus EU, 127, 188–90, 203, 461
trade relations, 212, 226, 261, 279–80, 416, 443

Van Gend en Loos. *See NV Algemene Transport en Expeditie Onderneming van Gend & Loos v. Netherlands Inland Revenue Administration*
von der Leyen, Ursula, 66, 156, 330, 372, 380, 381, 445

Weiler, Joseph H., 117
Werner, Pierre, 34, 144, 467
Werner Plan, 34, 144–5, 433, 467

West Germany, 144, 435, 455
    creation of EU, 2, 7, 29–32, 138, 210, 454
    enlargement, 283, 297
    regional policy, 232, 235, 237, 463
Westphalian states, 188–9, 196, 204
widening, 2, 6–11, 15–17, 414, 467
workers
    COVID-19 and, 144, 159
    highly skilled, 171, 181
    lower-skilled, 16
    mobility of, 76, 144
    permits for, 171
    protection of, 10, 353, 357, 365
    temporary/seasonal, 142, 422
    women, 353, 360, 365

World Trade Organization (WTO), 467
    Canada in, 269
    Doha Round, 263, 266
    EU participation in, 256, 260–3, 266, 273–4
    GATT as precursor to, 258–9, 437
World War II, 247, 431
    devastation after, 205, 209–10
    EU creation after, 6–8, 25–8, 115–17, 421
    geopolitics after, 257, 372, 398, 418

xenophobia, 172, 354

Yugoslavia, 190, 305

Printed and bound by CPI Group (UK) Ltd, Croydon, CR0 4YY
31/08/2025

14727219-0004